M A Y
SARTON

Selected Letters

1955–1995

BOOKS BY MAY SARTON

A Reckoning
Anger
The Magnificent Spinster
The Education of Harriet Hatfield

M A Y
SARTON

Selected Letters

1955–1995

edited and introduced by

SUSAN SHERMAN

With a Foreword by Warren Keith Wright
An Appreciation by William Drake

W. W. NORTON & COMPANY
NEW YORK · LONDON

Since this page cannot legibly accommodate all the copyright notices, page 426 constitutes
an extension of the copyright page.

For information about permission to reproduce selections from this book, write to
Permissions, W. W. Norton & Company, Inc., 500 Fifth Avenue, New York, NY 10110

The text of this book is composed in Bembo with the display set in Castellar
Composition by Tom Ernst
Manufacturing by the Haddon Craftsmen, Inc.

Library of Congress Cataloging-in-Publication Data

Sarton, May, 1912–1995
[Correspondence. Selections]
Selected letters / May Sarton edited and introduced by Susan Sherman.
p. cm.
Contents: v. 1. 1916–1954
Includes index.
ISBN 0-393-03954-4 (v.1)
1. Sarton, May, 1912– —Correspondence. 2. Women authors, American—20th century—
Correspondence. I. Sherman, Susan. II. Title.
PS3537.A832Z48 1997
811'.52—dc20

[B]   96-43614
                                                                    CIP

ISBN 0-393-05111-0 (v. 2)

W. W. Norton & Company, Inc., 500 Fifth Avenue, New York, N.Y. 10110
www.wwnorton.com

W. W. Norton & Company Ltd., Castle House, 75/76 Wells Street, London W1T 3QT

1 2 3 4 5 6 7 8 9 0

FOR
MAY SARTON
In memoriam aeternam

Not ripeness but the suffering change is all.

—"Der Abschied"
(The Farewell)

CONTENTS

EDITOR'S NOTE

One great testimony to May Sarton's prowess as a writer of letters is the sheer number that were saved; perhaps even more impressive is how many of such quality were written. In October 1992, she signed an appeal for correspondents to share those letters with me, as her editor, and more than 750 have gladly complied. My gratitude is great, for without such assistance, these two selected volumes would not display her true depth of interest and breadth of acquaintance. Other letters are drawn from some sixty libraries all over the country, large and small, as well as Sarton's personal archive, now housed at the Berg Collection in the New York Public Library.

Such abundance makes choosing what to omit a painful privilege. Some long and fruitful exchanges are represented by a single note; often, friends whom she rarely saw received the longest, most revealing responses; she maintained ties with her dispersed family by visits, and by post; and, as with any successful author, professional matters demanded attention, and admirers deserved it. All these varieties receive representation in this selection and, given the constraint of pages, in my judgment these chosen letters provide an exhilarating narrative of their own. When read consecutively it is hoped that their effect will be continuous and cumulative, a self-portrait May Sarton paints word by word. Despite the staggering amount of mail received in later years, she always strove to emulate a motto from her cherished Isak Dinesen: *"Je répond*erai*"*—"I will answer." Here is her reply to the world.

The editing of this volume follows standard procedures. In keeping with the practice of *May Sarton: Selected Letters 1916–1954,* letters are printed complete. Writing to Warren Keith Wright, 14 December 1982, Sarton objected to the omissions enforced on another author's correspondence: "I minded the salutations were cut—letters are TO some-

one, after all, & in the salutation is part of the relationship." Hers are all
retained, and her closings as well. Every effort has been made to reproduce the holographs as far as typography permits, though Sarton's typing could be erratic and her handwriting increasingly difficult. Her
idiosyncrasies—the French custom of not capitalizing nationalities
("english," "jewish"), the British spellings and punctuation, the unclosed
parentheses and closed ellipses—remain as she left them. Letters written
in French, or containing extensive passages in French—her first language—are noted as such in the text, where they are given in translation; the originals are printed in an appendix.

The annotation is offered to serve as broad a readership as possible,
which Sarton always wished to reach. But what requires explanation,
what does not? Today "common knowledge" will recognize Einstein,
the Beatles, and the Vietnam War; but what else, an editor asks, can be
taken for granted? I have attempted to identify each person and every
allusion. Anything left unexplained cannot be explained, as yet. Those
who rate such footnotes excessive can take comfort from the fact that
others find them welcome; and wherever feasible, Sarton's own words
have been used for commentary.

In general, celebrated personages (such as Sylvia Plath or William
Butler Yeats) are treated briefly, while lesser-known figures (such as
Charles Barber and Sister Maris Stella) are given more extended notice.
Though Sarton's life did encompass an international cast, the characters
here are assumed to be American, unless otherwise specified. First names
left untagged in her text can usually be found by scanning the list of
recipients that precedes the index proper.

Sarton was acutely conscious all her life of events in the news, at
home and abroad. Since it would be ponderous to explain all her comments, I have tried instead to provide enough information to make her
point clear. All Biblical citations are to the King James Version. To sim-
plify the documentation, publishers of books mentioned in passing are
not always named, unless doing so serves some point. As for keeping up
with Sarton's intensely mobile life, the Key to Addresses in the front can
pinpoint her location while writing. The goal throughout has been to
help today's reader taste what it was like to receive each letter soon after
it was written.

Upon first citation, each of May Sarton's books is given its full subtitle and the year when it appeared; at the start of each annual summary,
the Chronology supplies a listing of the books she published during this
volume's four decades. Likewise, when first cited, her poems are given
their year of first publication. Unless otherwise indicated, they are
included in *Collected Poems 1930–1993* (henceforth *Poems 1930–93*) or

the final collection, *Coming into Eighty* (1994). Fourteen unpublished poems are gathered in an appendix. As for the series of eight journals, a brief "bridge" in the text signals when each begins and ends. While an effort has been made to cross-reference Sarton's correspondence with her published writings, those who read the journals (and poems, and memoirs, and novels) in conjunction with the letters will enjoy an even richer context and experience.

As I continue with my ongoing project of a complete Life in Letters, I would ask other recipients, or descendants with correspondence in their possession, to contact me via my agent, Timothy Seldes at Russell & Volkening, 50 West 29th Street, New York, NY 10001. Every letter, note, or postcard, however seemingly slight, is of interest in this endeavor. Help me celebrate May Sarton's singular legacy.

Susan Sherman
Riverdale, New York
31 January 2001

Foreword by Warren Keith Wright

Do not be deceived. Though this looks like a culling of correspondence from a prolific author's life, legibly printed and thoroughly footnoted, the book you hold in your hands is in fact a mystery story.

In these letters—two hundred picked from thousands—the reader will meet May Sarton in every regard: at peace, at war; the hard-pressed writer, the tormented lover, at her fiercest and most fond; friend, memorialist, confidante, excoriator, always with an eye on the world at large—every role lived to the hilt. The reader will partake of her joys and learn well her griefs: it is no coincidence she always capitalized "Hell." In these missives—sometimes missiles—one will find, as is common in the second half of life, many deaths but—in keeping with Sarton's phoenix image—much rebirth.

"I am pondering the idea of a novel where just these discrepancies might be the theme," she proposed, 22 January 1975 (*The House by the Sea*), "a powerful personality being tracked down (after his death) by several biographies that give a totally different picture, using the same *facts*." She never wrote that book, but it has become the story of her afterlife. "I have suffered . . . from certain small people's behavior," she wrote Florence Day, a colleague of her father, George Sarton, 30 May 1961. Though considered in his day the founder of the history of science as a discipline, he often encountered opposition, and increasingly after his death in 1956, his achievement was belittled by some successors. "But I say to myself that mice will not affect the mountain in the long run! And it is the long run that matters. . . . [I]t often happens that the negative reaction follows quickly upon the death of a great controversial figure—Virginia Woolf is now only beginning to recover from the ebb tide of her reputation . . . since her death." Sarton was speaking of her father's place in history; but she was her father's daughter.

By 22 June 1958, she could assert to Julian Huxley that she was "getting a reputation not based on any single great success (which I have not had), but on the whole body of work," a concept that was to affect her writing, its reception, and her reaction to criticism for the rest of her career. "What I have not had," she could contend by 1 December 1970 (*Journal of a Solitude*), after disappointing notices for *Kinds of Love*, "is the respect due what is now a considerable opus." But one drawback of relying on an entire corpus for vindication is that each addition to the oeuvre can become less important in and of itself. The hope is that the greater work will carry the lesser, but the truth is that an artist is judged anew each time in the dock, and the task of establishing one's worth is never finished. If you depend upon "the long run" of posterity for justice, the jury may stay out longer than you can wait. What did she think thwarted her deserts? As readers will discover, May Sarton felt shut out by the Establishment.

Could we ask our author just who constituted that elite, she might have cited writers appointed to chairs at top-rank universities; editors of influential Book Reviews and Publishing Weeklies and their chosen reviewers; judges of legendary literary awards; and the recipients of those awards, with newsmagazine cover profiles recounting their honors, their contracts, their appearances on the best-seller lists. But such distinctions do not always permit honorees to produce more or better work; Sarton would have found the requisite socializing glib, discomfiting, even dread-inducing. (She preferred the one-on-one encounter, in depth, and shone when appearing onstage to "give tongue," invited and cherished. Often boisterous, she was also shy.) She seems never to have been considered for Consultant in Poetry to the Library of Congress, the position now called Poet Laureate. Louise Bogan, Léonie Adams, and Elizabeth Bishop had already served, and several men stayed several years; it does not seem wishful thinking that Sarton, a lifelong proselytizer for poetry, might have been tapped for office. But she knew she was by nature a solitary worker, and the call never came.

From the start Sarton received assurance that she was earning loyal readers; all her books found ready publication and in time she garnered eighteen honorary degrees. Nonetheless, it was the "big" credits and the "big" prizes that defined her sense of "never having really gotten through." "Prizes, prizes!" she quoted, only half-mockingly, to Madeleine L'Engle, 13 January 1966. Despite representation in scores of anthologies, she had been excluded from those assembled by Oscar Williams, John Ciardi, Louis Untermeyer—once a sure sign of being inducted into the canon. Sarton waited all her life but never acquired a Pulitzer, a National Book Award, a MacArthur Foundation grant. She had known the great; why couldn't others see that she was one of them? Yet had she won entry into that Establishment, how long would it have been before she wanted out again? Imagine the ways in which her life would have altered had she enjoyed, or endured, even more celebrity than was to be hers.

Yet she could claim, to Katharine White, 7 September 1961, after a needling review, "I am a realist." Her most famous heroine, Mrs. Stevens, insists that hers is only "A small, accurate talent, exploited to the limit—let us be quite clear about *that!*" But no one should mistake Hilary for her creator in that respect. Sarton knew the precise character of her gifts, and their range is astonishing. Nonetheless the posthumous career is following the classic trajectory: tributes, the last publications, a drop in interest, sales, reputation—and then, in due course, a rediscovery, when the toughest work wins out. For Sarton's foresight about her fiction was accurate and sound. "I still believe that a few of my novels will prove to have value in the end," she wrote in *Recovering*, 17 March 1979. "*Mrs. Stevens, Faithful Are the Wounds, As We Are Now,* and possibly *A Reckoning*"—with *The Small Room* as well—are fine and durable books that lay deep claims upon the intellect and the emotions. Of the autobiographical works, some titles will never fall out of favor or print: *I Knew a Phoenix, Plant Dreaming Deep, Journal of a Solitude*—that landmark *cri de coeur*—and the profiles, however partial, in *A World of Light*.

But Sarton's dearest hopes were reserved for her poems, which she often referred to as "orphans." Choose your personal favorites: "All Souls," "The Light Years," "Moving In," "The Autumn Sonnets," "The Phoenix Again"—these and many others are great and lasting examples of "the pure lyric" she prized above all. (*Coming into Eighty* provides a startling and poignant envoi.) Though poetry rarely grabs headlines, the mighty *Collected Poems 1930–1993* was in truth shamefully ignored by the press. Indignant at being denied fair treatment, she kept green the memory of bad reviews that otherwise might have died in the archives. Perhaps inevitably, in later years the only praise that seemed to count was the praise she could not get—although a little of that irony she eschewed, or even just a touch more humor, might have spared the poet much torment and her supporters much dismay on her behalf.

Yet audiences stood and cheered when she lectured and read, which she did with missionary fervor as long as she could physically manage. Book lovers bought all her backlist and spread the word to friends. Libraries re-bound their Sartons and purchased fresh ones. The academic attention she had yearned for arrived, only for her to find much of it, well, academic. The mail cascaded down in a torrent of love and beseeching that she eventually could neither cope with nor forswear.

Praise poured in, from the famous and the obscure, confirming that her work could change minds and move hearts. Maybe, as she wrote Ashley Montagu, 2 October 1977, "it's better to be loved than famous"; but she had already informed Bill Brown, 27 January [1971], "If I got the Nobel Prize tomorrow, it would not make up for the humiliations of the last thirty five years."

Then what could ever *be* "enough"? What more could this great-hearted woman do to win over the Furies that endow grants and strew laurels? Hadn't she driven herself to make, over and over, the human connection? Didn't her fifty books articulate her "vision of life"? And what exactly was that? Perhaps the only vision which an artist, as opposed to a philosopher, or a savior, has the gift to give us: what it is like to be her. Is such a "talent" mere self-absorption? Or is it not art's peculiar power to make the individual case universal?

No, no, you will not get around May Sarton by facile psychologizing. As the leading persona in her lifelong drama, she outstrips theory and leaves labels behind. Now, as you read these two hundred letters, ask yourself: What was it she searched for and never quite found? What, in the end, did she want? That is the mystery which you, the reader—the current incarnation of posterity—must solve.

Warren Keith Wright
Arbyrd, Missouri
January 2001

An Appreciation by William Drake

"May's brilliant gift was her ability to concentrate on her emotional experience and yet, while observing constantly, remove egoistic concerns so as to use it for an art both personal and impersonal (as it must be). . . . I always found that May was great in the ways that count—as an artist—understanding what her assignment was, so to speak, and letting nothing stand in the way of carrying it out."

So William Drake wrote me, on 28 January 1997. He had already proved himself an adept advocate for the worth of Sarton's oeuvre in his 1987 study *The First Wave: Women Poets in America 1915–1945*, to which the overworked adjective "unique" can be fairly applied. Any reader interested in these authors, or twentieth-century literary trends, or good poetry will find his book an exhilarating encounter with brave spirits and bold writing, not least his own.

That was why, just before the publication of *May Sarton: Selected Letters 1916–1954* in June 1997, I proposed to Mr. Drake that perhaps his estimation of her oeuvre could now, with her death, attain a fuller dimension. Here is the bulk of his response. Though written as a personal letter, it has the force and cogency of what May called "primary intensity"—where the writer comes fully focused on the task at hand, ready to share the results of long consideration. He began with an observation borne out by her extant letters to him, about the openhanded welcome she gave to intelligent appreciation of her work:

May 26, 1997

Dear Susan,

. . . When I was working with May on material for *The First Wave*, I was struck by the almost naïve way she opened herself up to examination, her letters and records and reminiscences, with instant generosity, not knowing what I might do with it all. She didn't demand veto power or even to be shown what I was writing (unlike the protective children and heirs of some of the other poets). This trust touched me very much, and it gave me a feeling of profound responsibility.

He acted upon that sense of responsibility by seeking the roots of her creativity:

When I talked with May about poets that she had loved, she dwelt at some length on Paul Valéry. As a result I looked into that source of inspiration and was able to trace some very important ideas relating to him when I wrote the essay that appeared in *That Great Sanity.* Surely [any study] of a poet, a person wholly immersed in art and literature, ought to take seriously the cultural milieu and the ideas of that poet about art and writing

—one of the guiding principles behind the editing of her posthumous legacy. A glance at the index to this collection will reveal the range of her associates and the reach of her intelligence. How better to underscore that

May had a first-rate intellect for which she has been given little credit. Her poems have a structured inner logic, that relates them, for me, to the best work in the English tradition, with echoes of Rilke as well as French poets. Like Eliot, she was a serious artist, and I know she always hoped, rather vainly it seems, to be taken as such. While she yearned for respect from the academics,

highly partisan approaches, though valuable when breaking through outworn traditions, sometimes tended to

box her in and limit the universality that she saw in herself. Everyone belongs to some category or other, but May, as I believe, held to the sense of a common and overarching humanity that transcends the bounds of social categories. Perhaps that idea seems old-fashioned in an age of competing, self-defining groups. Yet I personally believe that May belongs to no one because she hoped to belong to all.

And that leads me to a crucial point, the one everyone seems to stumble over:

the difficulty of dealing justly with such a complicated personality, so that she seems neither Jekyll nor Hyde, nor a mass of contradictions, but one unitary being, herself. This he sought to do by describing his encounters with her:

I only met May twice, in a San Francisco hotel when she was here for readings in 1985 and 1989. We talked for no more than a total of four hours or so all together, and I had perhaps a few telephone conversations after that. When I came into her room, I felt that I was immediately seized by her interest, her desire to make connection. It was very vital but not a personal thing. She never gave the impression of trying to manipulate me for any purpose. She established a field of mutual awareness, or a stage, on which she could roam and explore whatever might occur between us. [Some skeptics might find it hard] to conceive of this beyond the personal or erotic plane, but I know it was essentially what I would call a spiritual juncture. I spoke to her about the spiritual depth implicit in her work, and I sensed that she had not thought through this consciously (her spirituality strikes me as never consciously formulated but intuitively lived). She told me of her stay in a monastery in Indiana and how the nuns loved and understood her work. There is her love for Rilke and sense of affinity with him. There is Carolyn Heilbrun's perceptive comment about Sartre and belief in the Holy Spirit. May had the quality of openness and even naiveté that comes with this spirituality—which in itself is not at all incompatible with her tormented behavior, in fact, may be indissolubly a part of it. At one point she asked me wistfully, "I *am* famous, aren't I?" She was always swift and candid in her responses, never calculating or posed. She spoke of having lived longer than her parents had, and I joked, "Now you're older than they are." She looked thoughtful and quiet, then said, "Older than my own parents. I'm going to use that in a poem." And she did, I can't recall now which one. In 1989 she had changed a great deal in the four years since I had seen her, because of failing health and strength. She seemed to have shrunk, grown small and wrinkled. Her bright eyes searched me as if wondering what I saw, as if she was trying to figure out how to take herself now. She sighed, "I'm just a little old lady." Of course that's the last thing anyone would ever say about her.

So what I am building up to is this: that people for May were there for endless discovery and relating to, not to "use," but to fulfill some creative need in her greater than either herself or the other person. It was a necessity, not a choice. Another person was needed to share the spark and start the blaze, for she created out of this joining with others, not as a solitary genius. Perhaps you could say that the encounter with the greater, creative force in herself could only be realized when projected or discovered in others. But most people live in a world where more personal needs come first and where relationships remain strictly personal and wicked saints are never understood. I don't think she "used" people and then dropped them as much as she endured a never-ending process of rediscovering what she called her muse. Her creativity depended on this continual discovery, not on habit. There was no gain for her in terms of prestige, power, money, comfort, or self-importance, the usual reasons why people use others. "Muse" is just a conventional word for what was a living process for her, a spiritual compulsion that was very real. She herself was completely humble before that force, completely honest and unselfish. I can understand why many people have felt hurt by her. No one can be expected to give themselves to the goddess she served and like it, but she treated them in a sense as she herself was treated. She was also only human, after all, but to be in the grip of Love as an impersonal force is somewhat inhuman, and so she and others suffered. The volatility is almost unavoidable to one who subjects herself to such unrelenting self-scrutiny and self-use for the sake of poetry. Academic literary critics and biographers and apologists for causes can't be expected to understand such matters. May provides a revelation of much more, I suspect, than she herself was aware of or consciously intended. She has been taken to task for not listening to criticism or refining her work more, but I can understand her impatience and refusal to listen. She was not willing to risk losing the power for the sake of a more polished perfection. I'm glad she was exactly the person she was, and it will be a long time before we comprehend all that was in her. She was also unashamedly ordinary and down to earth—always the sign of a superior being who has no false pretensions. Of course she was hopelessly flawed. How else could she write so humanly? And of course because she would not be anything other than what she was impelled to be, she has had to endure cruel treatment and insult.

He ended by welcoming

your suggestion that I write some sort of appreciation . . . perhaps as a way of reconciling the apparent conflicts in May's character and behavior in the light of her art, along the lines I've expressed in this letter.

And, with characteristic grace, concluded:

— In the meantime, please don't let yourself be too disturbed by the wrong-headed things people say about May. I've always found that the most difficult people can be the most worth knowing and treasuring. . . .

Yours sincerely,
Bill
William Drake

It is not surprising that in January 1990 she called him "my good friend, my best critic."

Though he did not live to write the appreciation he envisioned, in a sense he had already done so. With blessings to his memory, I invoke the spirit of this fine scholar to encourage readers to enlarge their conception of May Sarton, writer and woman, through the letters that follow.

Susan Sherman
January 2001

CHRONOLOGY

Eléanore Marie (later May) Sarton was born on 3 May 1912 in Wondelgem, Belgium. For a brief account of the years leading up to this volume, see the Chronology in Selected Letters: 1916–1954.

It was Sarton's custom to set out on extensive lecture tours in the fall and spring of each year; I have not recorded these semiannual trips. Not all of Sarton's friends mentioned below appear in this volume.

Annually, after World War II, Sarton returned to England and Europe to visit the Limbosches, her second family, and those of her old beloved friends still alive. Despite relationships in America and the Wright Street home she shared with Judith Matlack for many years, it was in Europe that Sarton's passionate attachments had always flowered and to which she returned to water the sources of her poetry.

Rinehart was Sarton's publisher until 1961.

1954 Spends August–November in Europe; meets Janet Flanner and Leonard Woolf; sees Evelyn Pember, Basil de Sélincourt, Isabel Fry, Adrienne Rich, et al. Receives Guggenheim Foundation Fellowship in poetry. Writes seven articles for *The New Yorker.* Travels in Italy with Eugénie Dubois. Meets Cora DuBois.
1955 *Faithful Are the Wounds* (novel).
      Lyric's Tidewater prize. Honorary Phi Beta Kappa, Radcliffe. Elizabeth Bowen visits from England. Boulder and Bread Loaf Writers' Conferences. Deaths of S. S. Koteliansky and Agnes Hocking.
1956 Lamont Poetry Contest judge. Lyric Prize for "Lady with a Falcon." Teaches at Radcliffe College (until 1958). Deaths of Alice

and Haniel Long; Dorothy Wellesley, Duchess of Wellington; Rollo Walter Brown; and, on 22 March, George Sarton. Sale of the Sartons' house, 5 Channing Place, Cambridge, Massachusetts. *Faithful Are the Wounds* nominated for National Book Awards.

1957 *The Fur Person* (novella); *The Birth of a Grandfather* (novel).
Teaches "The Art of the Short Story" at the Radcliffe Seminars. Visiting lecturer at Scripps College in California. Trip to Hawaii with Cora DuBois. Meets Ellen Douglass Leyburn and Hannie Van Till. In Europe sees Elizabeth Bowen, Anthony Huxley, Sybille Bedford, et al. Judith Matlack enters analysis. Deaths of Francesca Greene and "Tom Jones" of *The Fur Person*.

1958 *In Time Like Air* (poems).
Finds Nelson house in May; signs papers in June; moves in during October, dividing time between there and Cambridge. Céline Limbosch visits Nelson. Introduces Robert Frost at Sanders Theatre, Harvard. Nominated for National Book Awards in two categories, as poet and as novelist (*The Birth of a Grandfather*). Teaches at Radcliffe. Lyric Prize for "Minting Time." Phi Beta Kappa visiting scholar. Made a fellow of the American Academy of Arts and Sciences.

1959 *I Knew a Phoenix* (memoir).
Consults analysts Volta Hall and Izette de Forest. Translates Paul Valéry with Louise Bogan for the Bollingen Foundation. First Honorary Doctor of Literature, Russell Sage. Death of Meta Budry Turian.

1960 Attends PEN Writers Congress in Brazil, where she meets Elizabeth Bishop, Alberto Moravia, and Robie Macauley. Lectures in creative writing, Wellesley College (through 1964). Danforth Visiting Lecturer, College Arts Program.

In 1961 Sarton signed with W. W. Norton, who remains her principal publisher. Earlier novels and *I Knew a Phoenix* have been reissued under their imprint.

1961 *The Small Room* (novel), *Cloud, Sun, Stone, Vine* (poems).
Meets editor Eric P. Swenson. Basil de Sélincourt visits Nelson. Death of Albert "Quig" Quigley. Johns Hopkins Poetry Festival.

1962 Finishes *The Music Box Bird* (play, intended for Eva Le Gallienne). Death of Dr. Volta Hall. 50th birthday trip around the world.

1963 *Joanna and Ulysses* (fable). Death of Margaret Foote Hawley.

1964 Wellesley College contract not renewed; takes year off to work on novel. Resident fellowship at Yaddo. Judith Matlack retires from Simmons and teaches at Douglas College. Karen O. Hodges visits Nelson.

1965 *Mrs. Stevens Hears the Mermaids Singing* (novel).
September–December, Poet in Residence, Lindenwood College, St. Charles, Missouri (also 1968). Eleanor Blair's first trip to Nelson.

1966 *A Private Mythology* (poems), *Miss Pickthorn and Mr. Hare* (fable).
Writes series of articles for *Woman's Day* and *Christian Science Monitor.* The Shipley School in Bryn Mawr cancels lectureship. Cuts hair extremely short. Since 1958 has been dividing time between Nelson and 14 Wright Street; in June, moves permanently to Nelson. Emily Clark Balch Prize for poems. Deaths of Katharine Davis, Katrine Greene, Basil de Sélincourt, "Aunt" Mary Bouton, Ellen Douglass Leyburn.

1967 *As Does New Hampshire* (poems; William L. Bauhan, Publishers).
Death of Mark de Wolfe Howe. Grant, National Foundation of the Arts and Humanities (ten thousand dollars), to fund research and writing of a series of novels.

1968 *Plant Dreaming Deep* (memoir).
Borrows donkey, Esmeralda, in June. Writes series of columns for *Family Circle* under title "Homeward." Baroness Hannie van Till visits Nelson. Perley Cole goes into nursing home; basis of *As We Are Now.* Meets Marion Hamilton.

1969 *The Poet and the Donkey* (fable).
Series for *Family Circle* ends. Bill Brown buys house in nearby Dublin, New Hampshire. Visits MacDowell Colony. Marion Hamilton visits Nelson. Turns novel series into *Kinds of Love.* Death of Jay de Sélincourt.

1970 *Kinds of Love* (novel).
Begins *Journal of a Solitude.* First correspondence with Carolyn G. Heilbrun. Meets Marynia F. Farnham. Deaths of Perley Cole and Louise Bogan.

1971 *A Grain of Mustard Seed* (poems).
Visits Bermuda and Belgium. Death of Punch, the parrot. First visit of Carolyn G. Heilbrun to Nelson. Hears of Wild Knoll, the house in York, Maine, from Mary-Leigh Smart and Beverly Hallam; visits it in April and twice in August. Judith Matlack's memory begins to fail. Litter of kittens, including Bramble and Bel-Gazou, born. Doctor of Humane Letters, New England College. Break with Marion Hamilton.

1972 *A Durable Fire* (poems).
Writer in resident, Agnes Scott College, Georgia. Nelson house goes on the market. Tamas, the Shetland sheepdog, arrives. Judith

Matlack, after an operation for a ruptured appendix, enters a nursing home. Sara Josepha Hale Award, Newport, New Hampshire. *May Sarton* (Twayne Authors Series) by Agnes Sibley published.

1973 *Journal of a Solitude* (journal), *As We Are Now* (novel).

Moves from Nelson to York. Interviewed by Barbara Walters for three shows of *Not for Women Only*. Modern Language Association seminar held on "The Art of May Sarton." Deaths of Elizabeth Bowen, Conrad Aiken, and her agent, Diarmuid Russell.

1974 *Collected Poems (1930–1973)*, *Punch's Secret* (children's book; Harper & Row).

In Europe, visits the Huxleys but sees Juliette only momentarily. Scrabble, the cat, put to sleep. The Reverend Richard Henry visits. Appears on the *Sonia Hamlin* show in Boston with John Kenneth Galbraith; Robert Cromie interview on *Book Beat*, Chicago; the *Today* show in New York.

1975 *Crucial Conversations* (novel).

Working on *A World of Light*. Juliette Huxley comes to New York but does not see Sarton. Visit to Thomas Starr King School of Ministry. Honorary Doctor of Letters, Clark University. Alexandrine Award, College of St. Catherine, St. Paul. Meets bibliographer Lenora P. Blouin and Huldah Sharpe. Deaths of Helen Howe Allen, Céline Limbosch, Julian Huxley, Rosalind Greene.

1976 *A World of Light* (memoirs), *A Walk Through the Woods* (children's book; Harper & Row).

Closing of the Wright Street house. Meets Doris Grumbach. Honorary Doctor of Letters, University of New Hampshire; Honorary Doctor of Letters, Bates College; Honorary Doctor of Humane Letters, Colby College; Honorary Doctor of Letters, Thomas Starr King School of Ministry.

1977 *The House by the Sea* (journal).

Appears on *Good Morning America*. In England, visits Juliette Huxley for the first time since 1948. Death of Anne Thorp.

1978 *A Reckoning* (novel). *Selected Poems*, ed. Serena Sue Hilsinger and Lois Brynes.

Lenora P. Blouin's *May Sarton: A Bibliography* (Scarecrow Press), first edition, is published. Attends Inter-American Women Writers Conference in Ottawa. Carolyn G. Heilbrun visits York.

1979 Filming of *World of Light* by Martha Wheelock and Marita Simpson, and *She Knew a Phoenix* by Karen Saum. Mastectomy in June. Reads at the Library of Congress. Nancy J. Hartley begins work as Sarton's secretary and eventually archivist. Deaths of Marynia F. Farnham and Katharine Taylor.

1980 *Halfway to Silence* (poems), *Recovering* (journal), *Writings on Writing* (Puckerbrush Press; essays 1957–67: "The School of Babylon," "The Design of a Novel," "The Writing of a Poem," "Revision as Creation," "On Growth and Change."
Karen Saum lives at Wild Knoll for part of the year. Honorary Doctor of Humane Letters, Nasson College. Deaths of Agnes Sibley and Muriel Rukeyser.

1981 Honorary Doctor of Humane Letters, University of Maine, Orono. Deborah Morton Award, Westbrook College, Portland, Maine. Sails on the *QE II* for Europe.

1982 *Anger* (novel). *A Winter Garland* (poems; first collaboration with William B. Ewert).
May Sarton: Woman and Poet, ed. Constance Hunting (Puckerbrush Press). Writer in Residence, Colby College. Richard D. Perkins Memorial Award, Thoreau School, Eastern Connecticut State College. Gives the Ware Lecture, "The Values We Have to Keep," Bowdoin College; Unitarian Universalist Women's Federation Award. *May Sarton: A Self Portrait,* ed. Martha Wheelock and Marita Simpson (from *World of Light* video) to honor Sarton's seventieth birthday. Meets Elizabeth Bristowe. Deaths of Judith Matlack, Eugénie Dubois, and Archibald MacLeish.

1983 Begins work on *The Magnificent Spinster.* Honorary Doctor of Letters, Bowdoin. Avon/COCOA Pioneer Woman Award. Meets Susan Sherman. Death of Mildred Quigley.

1984 *At Seventy* (journal), *Letters from Maine* (poems).
Honorary Doctor of Letters, Union College. Fund for Human Dignity Award, Plaza Hotel, New York. Attends the George Sarton Centennial in Belgium. First London poetry reading ever, at the Poetry Society in London. First meeting with her new English publisher, The Women's Press. Visits the Dordogne with Dr. Annella Brown.

1985 *The Magnificent Spinster* (novel).
Christmas tree fire. All Sarton's teeth extracted. Human Rights Award. American Book Award for *At Seventy.* Honorary Doctor of Humanities, Bucknell College. Appears on *Mister Rogers' Neighborhood* and at the Smithsonian. Death of Bramble, the cat.

1986 Edits *Letters to May by Eleanor Mabel Sarton* (Puckerbrush Press).
Pierrot, the cat, arrives. Maryann Hartman Award, University of Maine, Orono. Stroke in February; spring lecture tour canceled for the first time since 1940. Resumes lectures in the fall. Deaths of Peggy Pond Church, Baroness Hannie van Till, and Tamas, the Shetland sheepdog.

1987 *The Phoenix Again* (poems; Ewert).
Receives keys to the city of Los Angeles; April 10 declared May Sarton Day by Mayor Tom Bradley. Lifetime Achievement Award from West Hollywood Connexus Women's Center. Arrival of Grizzle, the dachshund. Asks Susan Sherman to become editor of her letters.

1988 *After the Stroke* (journal), *The Silence Now* (poems), *Honey in the Hive* (celebration of Judith Matlack; Warren Publishing).
Retires from giving lectures and readings. Attends Modern Language Association's "In Honor of May Sarton," in New Orleans. Deaths of Theodore Morrison and Theodore Amussen.

1989 *The Education of Harriet Hatfield* (novel).
Lambda Rising Award for *The Silence Now. May Sarton Revisited* (Twayne U.S. Authors Series), Elizabeth Evans. Sarton's car catches fire. Grizzle is given to another owner. Honorary Doctor of Literature, Rhode Island College. Death of Camille Mayran.

1990 New England Booksellers' Award as Outstanding New England Writer for 1990. Acutely ill; loses fifty pounds. Honorary Doctor of Literature, Centenary College (accepted by Susan Sherman). New England Booksellers' Author of the Year Award. Maine Author Award, Portland Public Library. Remains ill; Susan Sherman arrives as caregiver for three months. Deaths of Sylvie Pasche, Evelyn Ames, Lotte Jacobi, and Lola Szladits.

1991 *Sarton Selected*, ed. Bradford Dudley Daziel (anthology).
Writing in the Upward Years, film by Stephen Robitaille. *Conversations with May Sarton,* ed. Earl G. Ingersoll (University of Mississippi Press). Daylong conference held in the Sarton Reading and Reference Room, Westbrook College, Portland, Maine, in celebration of her seventy-ninth birthday. Seriously ill; begins to see holistic doctor. Nancy Hartley retires after thirteen years as secretary and archivist. Susan Sherman begins commuting regularly to Wild Knoll from New York. Deaths of Cora DuBois and Eva Le Gallienne.

1992 *Endgame* (journal); *Coming into Eighty* (special edition; Ewert).
Forward into the Past (festschrift) honoring her eightieth birthday, ed. Sherman, published by Ewert. "A Celebration for May Sarton," three-day national conference, Westbrook College. Honorary Doctor of Letters, Westport College. Two trips to London to see Juliette Huxley; small strokes. Deaths of Charles Barber, Anthony Huxley, John Summerson, and Leslie Hotson.

1993 *Encore* (journal); *May Sarton: Among the Usual Days* (portrait in unpublished letters, poems, and journals), ed. Sherman; *Collected Poems 1930–1993*.

That Great Sanity: Critical Essays on May Sarton, ed. Susan Swartzlander and Marilyn Mumford (University of Michigan Press); *A House of Gathering: Poets on May Sarton's Poetry*, ed. Marilyn Kallet (University of Tennessee Press). *May Sarton Live!* (poetry reading, 1987), Ishtar Films. Second stroke, April. World premiere of *The Music Box Bird*, produced by The Chamber Theatre of Maine. The Women's Press publishes her poetry in London for the first time in many years; *Halfway to Silence* samples her three most recent volumes of poems. Trip to London to see Juliette Huxley. Pneumonia. Filming for Ishtar project on aging and poetry.

1994 *Coming into Eighty* (poems) includes those which win her *Poetry's* Levinson Prize. *A Celebration for May Sarton*, ed. Constance Hunting (Puckerbrush Press). *From May Sarton's Well*, selected writings with photographs by Edith Royce Schade (Goodale Hill Press). Third stroke, April 2. Chairlift installed in August. University of New England films *Old Age Is a Foreign Country*. Audio Bookshelf releases four-cassette album, *May Sarton: Excerpts from a Life: Journals and Memoirs*, read by Andrea Itkin. Deaths of Bradford Dudley Daziel and Juliette Huxley.

1995 Trip to London in April. Eighteenth honorary degree from the University of New England, May. *May Sarton: Woman of Letters*, interview with David Bradt (produced by New Hampshire Public Television), filmed in May and aired in June. Sends off completed manuscript for *At Eighty-Two* (journal). Dies at 5:15 P.M., Sunday, July 16, at York Hospital.

KEY TO ADDRESSES

Beloit
> 745 Church Street, Beloit, Wisconsin. Home of the Reverend Chad Walsh and his wife, Eva.

Cambridge
> See Wright Street.

Cornwall
> Kilmarth, Par, Cornwall, England. Home of Dorothea (Waley) and Charles Singer, historians of science.

Greenings Island
> A Maine island in Somes' Bay off the coast of Mount Desert Island. Summer home of Anne Longfellow Thorp.

Le Pignon Rouge
> 16 Avenue Léquime, Rhôdes St. Genèse, Brussels, Belgium, home of Céline and Raymond Limbosch and their children.

London (JS)
> In London Sarton often stayed with her friend Jane Stockwood, who lived at various addresses over the years.

Nelson
> The eighteenth-century farmhouse in Nelson, New Hampshire, which Sarton bought in 1958 and where she lived until 1973.

Rhôdes
> See Le Pignon Rouge.

St. Charles, Missouri
> Lindenwood College.

Wright Street
> 14 Wright Street, Cambridge, Massachusetts. Home of May Sarton and Judith Matlack.

Yaddo

Writers and artists retreat in Saratoga Springs, New York.

York

Wild Knoll, the house in York, Maine, where Sarton lived from 1973 until her death.

May seemed to have a self-generating energy so that she responded with passion to all of life's complexities. But it was a passion of concern, expressed with wit and humor, and without a trace of sentimentality. That would have been abhorrent to her. And this zest for the importance of life in all its forms was so skillfully conveyed in her letters that at least, in my case, I felt elated and, often, a little drunk after receiving them.

—Bill Brown to
Susan Sherman
26 July 1997

Sentiment, authentic feeling, is what we live by. It is what makes us human. Sentimentality in life as in art kills the authentic by setting up a screen against it, the screen of the expected and the commonplace. It is therefore in life the enemy of growth and understanding and in the arts the enemy of reality and imagination.

—May Sarton,
"Against Sentimentality"
(unpublished essay)

M A Y
SARTON

Selected Letters

1 9 5 5 – 1 9 9 5

March 10th, 1955
[Wright Street]
Dear Louise,

—and here I sit ten minutes silent, hardly knowing how to begin. Because it was such a beautiful time and, in spite of all the grumbles, I am so grateful and speechless—wondering too if (as in James' "Sacred Fount") all I take from you, the stream of poetry which you induce, if that is the word, leaves you <u>empty</u> in just the proportion that I am <u>full</u>, for that would be too sad. Yet it may be so. Anyway all the way down through the moonlight beside the river I was literally attacked by so many poems that I felt like a juggler, terrified that I couldn't keep them all going long enough at least to jot down a note. When I arrived, I made a dash for the typewriter, coat still on and typed like automatic writing for half an hour. So there are about six embryonic poems on that sheet, two of which are nearly done. I enclose a new one, written on the train yesterday, and a better version of the Falcon (I still am not satisfied and may do it in a different form as time goes on. It was in cutting and condensing it that night that the less conventional stanza got lost somehow and it turned out to be the boring old four line thing.)

About the content of the poems I can do nothing, as I don't need to tell you and where passionate love belongs now in our relation is (I fully realize) <u>there</u>. But they are themselves and not requests or demands in the open air of our friendship—that said, I feel I can release all this submerged and until now so frustrated part of me in peace and you will understand. On the other side—real life or whatever—the truth seems to be that we must bear with each other (don't laugh)—I know you have much to bear with in me, and I really do sometimes in you, but I have never looked at friendship in a deep sense as easy or entirely comfortable. And oh my dear, what a rich and wonderful thing it has become all this year to think of you, to be thought <u>of</u>, and I am bitterly ashamed of having complained about letters.

Now the cleaning woman has come and I must clear out and do some laundry. There are an awful lot of "things" ahead just now and the mail brings so many letters about the book, I feel a bit swamped. I am to speak at one of the Harvard Houses next week <u>and</u> to Philly on Tuesday for that book fair (a 12-minute speech) and on Friday to New London for a day to sign books etc. All I want is to play music and write poems but that will come.

Do you know the tapestry in the Mediaeval dept. at the Met which this poem is about? The lady has the most brooding hooded face—the whole thing is a masterpiece of understatement and very troubling. There is no postcard but it is reproduced in the little booklet "Mediaeval Tapestries"— the poem is not nearly good enough, but I'll redo it after awhile better.

There is just one thing I wish to add to our old controversy re women and you. How to say it? It would be in just accord with Jung's theory that submerged parts of the subconscious which had to be repressed may come into play in the later years. I do feel that your very dread is a sign that this is a more important thing to you (not me personally, the whole <u>idea</u>) than you quite admit—it is tied up with poetry, or might be (this is my theory and you can smile)—and acting out these fears would perhaps dispel them—you always in your talking and writing put the negative aspects of love <u>first</u> which seems very strange. That is, you think of "jealousy" apparently before you think of peace or communion or the relief of coming through, of being accepted, of accepting, and the extraordinary sense of fulfillment and joy. If this is not what you have experienced, my guess would be that then it was quite clear that a woman would be better not worse for you. Time to stop—high time. I am terribly anxious now to see the prose book—another thing before I forget. It is surely true that you are a critic, yet the critic in you is the escaper—you put criticism as a legitimate screen between you and what takes more of you, is more painful, more disturbing etc. This does not mean that we who read you with such grateful attention are not the benefiters—but I am thinking of you the total human being now, and more especially the total <u>artist.</u>

I did enjoy those Prévert Songs

I did think you looked perfectly beautiful, in those unclouded moments when your face is not a mask.

That is all.

Love from
May

P.S. A "kind" friend took it upon himself to phone me yesterday to say that he had met the real Perry Miller and P.M. said "May's book is lousy, just lousy." I am so puzzled by this, darling, and tried not to worry, but all night I had terrible dreams of guilt, one that Matty [F. O. Matthiessen] had a son who was terribly hurt by the book and that Benny had written this son to tell him what a louse M.S. was to have written it. Oh dear, would all this were over and done with.

Another friend phoned just now, a very deaf woman who cannot hear a word I say, to tell me the minister at Christ Church told her I <u>hated</u> the Episcopal Church! But at least she told him to read the novel and he would change his mind. This is, I think, because I wrote a piece about "Why I Don't Go To Church" at the request of an Episcopal Minister some years ago.

I feel very exposed. That is all.

Louise Bogan: American poet (1897–1970) and poetry critic for *The New Yorker* (1931–69). Having spoken at Briarcliff Junior College in New York on 3 March, Sarton saw Bogan on 5 March.

James' "Sacred Fount": Man of letters Henry James (1843–1916). In his 1901 novel *The Sacred Fount*, a nameless observer at an English country house tries to unriddle odd interactions between the guests. In the case Sarton alludes to, marriage to a younger man (now rapidly aging) has rejuvenated an older woman, who seems to have usurped "the sacred fount" of his partner's life-force.

The Falcon: "Lady with a Falcon: Flemish tapestry, 15th century" won the Lyric Prize in 1956. See *In Time Like Air*, reprinted only in *Selected Poems of May Sarton,* ed. Serena Sue Hilsinger and Lois Brynes (1978).

our friendship . . . having complained about letters: Sarton first wrote Bogan on 21 April 1940; though they were first introduced in February 1953, their friendship did not truly begin until November 1953. For the older woman's correspondence, see *What the Woman Lived: Selected Letters of Louise Bogan 1920–1970,* ed. Ruth Limmer (1973). Her last previous letter seems 4 January 1955, soon after Sarton assured her, "When I say I love you, I am saying that I love poetry."

"things" ahead just now . . . about the book: Though Sarton was only an acquaintance, when the Harvard professor of literature F. O. Matthiessen (1902–1950) committed suicide, she was impelled to write *Faithful Are the Wounds,* published 14 March 1955. She spoke about the novel in Philadelphia and New London, Connecticut, at the Phi Beta Kappa dinner at Radcliffe College and the Signet Club in Boston.

one of the Harvard Houses: On 17 March Sarton discussed "Poet versus Novelist" at Apthorpe House on Bow Street.

play music and write poems: As a child Sarton was taken to Boston Symphony concerts at Harvard and also was exposed to her father's vast record collection; listening to music became inextricably connected with writing poetry. In later years, when unable to write, she could not bear to listen to music either.

the tapestry . . . this poem is about: "The Lady and the Unicorn: The Cluny Tapestries," an image not as well known then as today.

Jung: Visionary Swiss psychoanalyst and defector from Freud, C. G. Jung (1875–1961) informed Sarton's thinking all her life.

a woman would be better not worse: For Sarton's comments on their "old controversy," see *May Sarton: Selected Letters 1916–1954,* ed. Susan Sherman (W. W. Norton, 1997)—henceforth *Letters 1916–54.* Bogan's romantic involvements were with men; intellectually tough but susceptible to depression, she did not wish to risk hard-won equilibrium. "Jealousy" and "morbid fidelity" bedeviled her marriage to second husband, poet Raymond Holden, for years before and after their 1937 divorce. (See her 28 January 1954 letter to Sarton in *What the Woman Lived.*)

the prose book: Selected Criticism: Poetry and Prose (1955) contains sixty-nine reviews and essays; not included is Bogan's brief 27 February 1954 *New Yorker* notice about *The Land of Silence.* Her *Collected Poems 1923–53* had appeared the previous year; the publishing imprint was soon sold, and both titles remaindered.

those Prévert Songs: French screenwriter and poet Jacques Prévert (1900–77), the "voice of the wise street urchin." Sarton probably heard Joseph Kosma's popular settings, such as "Autumn Leaves."

when your face is not a mask: The image of the mask recurs throughout Bogan's poetry; *The Blue Estuaries: Poems 1923–1968* (1968; reprinted 1977) closes with "Masked Woman's Song."

the real Perry Miller: Historian (1905–63), who taught at Harvard 1931–63, best known for *The New England Mind* (1939, 1953; reissued 1961).

Benny: Critic Bernard De Voto (1897–1955), who taught at Harvard, was a Cambridge neighbor; he and Sarton had planned a freshman textbook called *Versus* (*Letters 1916–54,* pp. 324–27).

"Why I Don't Go to Church": "Those Who Stay Away," *Episcopal Church News,* 3 February 1952. The charge may stem from the funeral scene in *Faithful Are the Wounds* (part II, ch. IX).

TO EVELYN PEMBER   March 10th, 1955
[Wright Street]

Dearest Evelyn, I was naturally rather excited to have this letter and I know it is a mistake (one which you have just committed yourself) to throw down too fast a first impression—that is what I am doing about your letter and what you did with the book. But we are friends and so can take this really rather enormous risk. I will first say my very real rage when I put it down because you make such impossible demands on other writers and such very small ones on yourself. You cover yourself by saying that all you do is piffling etc. and that you never meant to write a story but a "reportage" (whatever that means, since any piece of writing needs form and focus, as you point out to me in three pages preceding this excuse.) That said, thank you—of course I am enormously interested in this first impression. I do not think you have given yourself time to take in either what the point of this book is nor what the technical problems were and how solved and for what reasons.

Let me answer a few things as they come to mind. About why Isabel and why the prologue. If you can believe it the book was even more what you think is bad about it <u>before</u>—Isabel emerged as a major character during one of the revisions. But I believe this is the right beginning though I am very aware of the dangers involved, not the least, making the reader observe a grief which he cannot feel. Isabel lets in <u>air</u> as someone said. But as for her crying, she does this to a stranger. That is the whole point. When the sister of a very reserved Bostonian friend of mine committed suicide at 24, the family gathered and for a whole week-end they all talked, never breaking down (perfect British control etc.) Only when my friend got on a train for Cal[ifornia]. did she break down and the whole thing tore through to a perfectly strange man who happened to be sitting beside her. She is an admirably controlled person. So I believe (though I may not have handled it successfully) that there is a truth in this fact—i.e. the fact that you can cry before a stranger, and not possibly otherwise.

The question of form: that is, seeing Cavan through a whole group of people was the major problem I had to face. So far you are the only reader who has not felt that it succeeded. The idea was of course that the thread was Cavan himself. It was not a perfectly simple feat to draw the reader on (as I honestly believe now I do from the very various people, all ages, nationalities and temperaments from whom I have heard) through the whole book, read mostly I hear in <u>one</u> gulp, when all the material is intellectual, with no compromise in ordinary "story" love interest or whatever. This is, I believe, something of a triumph, damn it.

The book is not about Cavan. It <u>is</u> about the lack of communication between people, the enormous unresolved subterranean emotions which <u>divide</u> us, especially about politics. I felt the truth of it when I read your irresponsible sentence about communists in England. Very well, they wear red ties and seem ludicrous. One was called Allan Nunn May and he did not wear a tie, another Pontecorvo. What made such men do what they did, the kind of loyalties involved must be taken seriously. To do otherwise may be to be British but frankly I find it superficial to a dangerous degree. You know where I stand on the hysteria here, but the answer to it is on a slightly deeper level than your remarks suggest—and that answer, I at least partially tried to suggest in the book.

The danger of so much talk was ever present in my mind and hence very drastic cutting. It was originally just twice as long. I am prepared to admit that you are right but so far no one else has said so. I do not believe that it is an "unfocussed" book. I think you never got what the focus is. Oh dear, I never should have begun this letter.

I'm just too tired to think today. The virus is back again with a vengeance—my desk a massive mess—and next week nothing but speeches, public appearances (what a horror really)—the reviews are quite terrific. I'll send you the Times, the one extremely intelligent one.

Incidentally, all you say about the intelligence of vision is quite right, especially about the poems. But there are different kinds of poems and The Phoenix [new poem] cannot be written very often. When I send you experiments do not imagine I always think them good—I am making tries. You are right about the ballad. I sort of knew this but then I saw it quite clearly after what you said, hence the value of your criticism.

About the novel—never did have pretensions to "greatness" by the way. A book such as this would have to be translated out of the moment in time in some way to achieve greatness—about the novel I am a bit recalcitrant. But you must understand what a queer exposed state I am in, with so many impressions piling in on me all at once after such a struggle to express it all. I am not quite sane and at the limit of exhaustion today.

Send this then? You know, darling, I trust how very glad I am to have your letter and probably in a month or two I shall agree with every word you say. But let me indulge in a few moments of relief and joy that to a few people at least, it does seem to communicate what I hoped. That you are not one of them is sad, but hardly fatal, and I do remind myself that you consider To the Lighthouse [Virginia Woolf, 1927] a failure!

You see, I have had such grave doubts about this that the effect of a little reassurance has almost knocked me over. Tear this letter up. I have an awful week ahead and God knows when I can write properly, but I have two new poems to send one of these days.

Meanwhile, dear love and thanks

[　]

And you will get a real answer later

Evelyn Pember: Novelist (*Coucou,* 1929) who sent Sarton manuscripts. Neighbor and friend of Leonard Woolf, she lived with Odette Norman in Rodmell, Sussex, where Sarton visited her during these years. "In Time Like Air" (1956) was written for her, as was "Moment of Truth" (December 1954); see appendix of unpublished poems.

the point of this book: Faithful Are the Wounds. Driven and isolated by his social and moral convictions, Professor Edward Cavan breaks down and kills himself. His sister, Isabel Ferrier, who has never understood his passions, comes East and encounters those who knew him best, such as departmental colleague and adversary Ivan Goldberg and lifelong friend physicist Damon Phillips, who shirked supporting Cavan in an ACLU struggle. Intense public scenes reflect the tense early 1950s and the blight of McCarthyism; but the story concludes with the strong suggestion that Cavan's death will lead to greater engagement on the part of those he left behind.

sister . . . committed suicide: Ernesta Greene. Rosalind (see 10 February 1965) and Henry "Harry" Copley Greene (d. 1951) and their four daughters had long been friends of the Sartons; Ernesta's death in June 1939 left Joy, Francesca, and Katrine, Sarton's reserved friend. On 24 January 1940 Sarton wrote "For Ernesta—Who Took Her Own Life," unpublished; see appendix.

communists in England: "It is an exciting subject—a thrilling scene—and interesting for 'us' as a revelation of what is happening in America—so difficult to understand in this country about to call itself a communist or to put an amusing red bow on one's hat—no more than that." Pember's handwriting is very hard to read; she seems to allude to Britons' taking up communism as a passing frivolous fashion.

May . . . Pontecorvo: Naturalized British physicist Bruno Pontecorvo (1913–95) defected to the Soviet Union in 1950; he reappeared in 1955 at a Moscow press conference promoting peaceful applications of nuclear power. Allan Nunn May, another physicist, spied for the USSR in Britain until exposed by Soviet defectors to the United States.

one extremely intelligent one: "Hinged on irony it swings open into tragedy. . . . Miss Sarton's method, even as that of her men and women who crave the light of day against self-inflicted darkness, is to turn to light what is shadowed, raise to the level of common ground what is half-buried underground." (William Goyen, *New York Times,* 13 March 1955)

Tear this letter up: Pember, like many correspondents, saved and returned Sarton's letters, recognizing their worth to her legacy.

[ ]: Lily of the valley hieroglyph.

TO MARIANNE MOORE   March 11th, 1955
[Wright Street]
Dear Marianne,

   Evie Ames described to me the afternoon at the poetry club and I was very jealous! Also she intimated that you had sounded as if you might have answered the phone had I had the courage to call. But I did not have it, fearing to interrrupt, being also in such a naked and exposed state about the novel. I thought you had perhaps received a copy and hated it. I did not want to exert pressure—well, all these explanations are only to say how dearly I long to see you, and may I? And won't you ever be in Boston again? Patrick, my car, purrs at your name.

   I went home full of thoughts, because of what Evie said about your method of criticism, which I had also observed in some notes on poems at Bryn Mawr. The fact is that praise is what gives impulse, rather than negative criticism—and you are wonderfully generous always in getting inside the poem and looking out from it, instead of staying outside and frowning as I am so apt to do when asked to be a critic. You teach me humility every day.

   That is all, except much love

                                                            From
                                                            May

P.S. I often think of Matty's charming introduction of you at Harvard. Also about that owl—Do you remember? The book was such an anguish, Marianne, and I am so _afraid_ now it is awful.

Marianne Moore: Poet (1887–1972) whose work is distinguished by wit and idiosyncratic metrics.

For earlier correspondence, see _Letters 1916–54_; for Evelyn Ames, 27 March 1955.

praise is what gives impulse: Sarton often cited Rilke's "For Leonie Zacharias": "Oh tell us, poet, what you do?—I praise." (See _Encore: A Journal of the Eightieth Year_ [1993], p. 17.) Moore had been lecturing at her alma mater, Bryn Mawr, and probably held student workshops.

TO ALICE JAMES   March 21st, 1955
[Wright Street]
Dear _admirable_ Alice,

My delight at your kind words about the novel aside, how glad I am that you have spoken out about the Goldberg-Levin thing and so given me a chance to explain. This is true friendship and honesty and I do love you for it.

First of all, when I first began to think of this novel I considered placing it elsewhere, but had I done so, it would have lost much of its reality for me. I compromised by laying it in Cambridge, by basing the Cavan character quite obviously on Matty, _but_ by inventing all the others out of whole cloth. Because I did this and knew I had done it, it never occurred to me until after the book came out what I was in for, in people delving about for keys to what looks like a _roman à clef._

I believe as I look back that I got the image of Goldberg, as physical presence, also his race from the face of an instructor who may no longer be at Harvard, whom I saw once at a meeting when I was teaching Gen. Ed. A. I know nothing about this man, not even his name, so that I felt entirely safe in building a character around this image which had snap-shotted itself into my subconscious. Had I intended a portrait of Harry, I hope I am perspicacious enough to have made it more like! From what I know of Harry—I do not know him well—I would say that he is a very gentle and kind person, less fiery, less absolute, and if arrogant, then arrogant in an entirely different way. But Harry has enemies of course, and they seize on this chance both to misunderstand him and to misunderstand my character.

I am glad to say that several people have seen that I love Goldberg and have extreme sympathy for him (I have often _been_ Goldberg in refusing to do political things to protect myself and my work)—_but he is not Harry._ Incidentally, Harry is one of the very few Cambridge people I have talked with in the last few years who has spoken to me without condescension of Matthiessen. One of the reasons why I felt compelled to write this book has been to see how easily and quickly people cast earth on the dead, how smug the living can be because they <u>are</u> alive.

Begun in indignation, perhaps, this novel surely has ended in love. If it is about anything it is about how we have all suffered from each other in the very real anguish of these last years. I have been dreadfully upset to have it thought that I have (under these circumstances of rigorous self-examination in the cause of <u>understanding</u>), cast a stone. Whatever you can do to dispel and squash the gossip, will be an act of true friendship. Also if you see Harry, perhaps you can convey the gist of this to him.

Just one more point. More than anything this all has brought home to me how much anti-semitism there must be about, if, if you make a professor a Jew, then he must be Harry Levin, who is also Jewish! As if all people of one race were the same person.

This has turned into a longer letter than it should be. I have until now, in some misery, held my tongue, since it is useless to "explain" oneself. A work of art must stand on its own feet.

But I am grateful to you for giving me the chance. Please tell Billy all this <u>before</u> he reads the book, and my love to you both. Yes, do let's meet soon. I go west to lecture April 13th but shall be here until then.

Yours most affectionately
May

The reviews have been wonderful, to my <u>huge</u> relief! I had a wonderful week with Elisabeth in August at her aunt's house, Corleagh, near Dublin—shall be eager to know what you think of her new novel—

Alice James: Chicago heiress Alice Runnells married Henry James's nephew William ("Billy"), a painter and art teacher. In early February 1953, when Elizabeth Bowen visited Sarton in Cambridge, Alice James hosted a party for her.

Goldberg-Levin thing: "[A]n excellent novel—finely written & well done & absorbing," Alice James had written, while wishing to discuss matters such as the character named Goldberg, "who appears to me to be Harry Levin and not quite fair to him"—Levin being a very real Harvard professor and literary critic (1912–94).

the Cavan character: Like Matthiessen, Cavan is a brilliant and respected Harvard professor of American literature, intimately involved with politics and life outside the university; but Matthiessen's motives for suicide were more personal than Cavan's. See *Rat and the Devil: Journal Letters of F. O. Matthiessen and Russell Cheney,* ed. Louis Hyde (Hamden, Connecticut: Archon Books, 1978.) At a party where those who had known Matthiessen discussed the novel, Bogan reported that "everyone thought you had done a difficult job well." (*What the Woman Lived,* 8 February 1956)

<u>*roman à clef*</u>: French, "novel with a key," in which real people appear thinly disguised, intended to be readily identifiable.

week with Elisabeth . . . her new novel: The aunt of Elizabeth Bowen (Anglo-Irish woman of letters, 1899–1973) was Edie Colley, whom they visited at Corkagh House, Clondalkin, County Dublin, inspiring "The Walled Garden at Clondalkin." See "Elizabeth Bowen," *A World of Light: Portraits and Celebrations* (1976), pp. 206–08. *A World of Love* (1955) is the shortest and most intensely lyrical of Bowen's ten novels.

TO EVELYN AMES   March 27th, Sunday [1955]
[Wright Street]
Evie darling,

How have three days gone by without my yet finding time to answer your wonderful letter? I can imagine, I think, what an act of true love it was to find the time to do this in the midst of your scattered and scattering life of the moment—but what a boon! You have so completely understood what I was trying to do—to get down under the politics to the roots in human love, and the lack of it, and so often our inability to communicate. So when you say "it is really about love", that is what I so hoped but one can never be sure that an intention is realized.

Your question about how much of this under theme was in the original conception is hard to answer: I don't really know, except that from the beginning I saw the book, and a woman's job re these matters, as essentially to get under the intellectual surface to something else.

In my notebook on it the first page has this quote from Jung: "The man whom we can with justice call <u>modern</u> is solitary. He is so of necessity and at all times. For every step towards a fuller consciousness of the present removes him further from his original <u>participation mystique</u> with the mass of man— An honest profession of modernity means voluntarily declaring bankruptcy, taking the vows of poverty and chastity in a new sense." I'm not sure I understand exactly what this means, but it seemed to say something about Cavan.

And the other thing that was much in my mind while writing this book was Traherne: "Since therefore we are born to be a burning and shining light, and whatever men learn of others, they see in the light of others' souls"—and finally four bitter lines of Yeats (for I have in the last few years hardly heard an uncondescending word here about Matthiessen):

> "We who seven years ago
> Talked of honor and of truth,
> Shriek with pleasure if we show
> The weasel's twist, the weasel's tooth."

It is quite true that the book, begun in indignation, did end in love and most clearly through the character of Isabel whom I began by treating ironically as a foil, and then came to understand and to love.

I'm glad you liked the cemetery—that and Isabel alone in the room are my favorites. I think you may well be right about the scene at the Phillipses—there, of course, I wanted the confrontation of Isabel and "the intellectuals" and in places it comes off, but not perhaps as a whole.

One big piece of news and then I'll stop maundering on—is that Victor Gollancz, the Eng. publisher wrote and said "It's a noble book and I want to publish it," but the really exciting thing is that he would do a book of poems as well. All this is still in the air, but I am seeing him on Tuesday. It all depends on whether I can be extracted from Hutchinson's who have an option.

If you can rest like a seagull in the air, with some part of you swung out over all these movings about and distracting atomizing things, then I'm sure you will feel eventually that you have a great treasure which will bear fruit when there is time again, and in this letter, you sound as if you were accomplishing this incredibly difficult feat.

I never thanked you for your earlier note and Louise's poem (I'm so glad to have it!)

Here is a little new poem you might like: ["Where Dreams Begin"]

We have just heard that a dear friend, a woman my age with four children under 15 and an impossible husband she has also mothered, is dying of cancer. The injustice of this has really thrown me. How <u>can</u> one accept? She is the most radiant being, and so dreadfully <u>needed</u> by life—

Well, darling, Italy should be full of graces once you are really off. I hope there are some still blue days, and peace and joy and poems—shall be thinking of you—

You are an angel to have found time to write that letter!

Your
May

Evelyn Ames: Evelyn "Evie" Perkins (Mrs. Amyas) Ames (1908–90), poet, memoirist, and naturalist.

chastity in a new sense: Sarton had been reading volume 7, *Two Essays on Analytical Psychology,* of *The Collected Works of C. G. Jung,* trans. R. F. C. Hull (1953).

[Thomas] *Traherne:* English metaphysical poet and clergyman (1636–74), whose writings emphasized the untutored perception of truth by children. Bowen took her epigraph for *A World of Love* from his prose *Centuries of Meditations:* "There is in us a world of Love to somewhat, though we know not what in the world that should be. . . . Do you not feel yourself drawn by the expectation and desire of some Great Thing?" When Traherne's anonymous poems were rediscovered in the early twentieth century, they were first thought the work of Henry Vaughan (English, 1621–95), from whom Sarton took the phrase *A World of Light.*

the weasel's tooth: From Part IV of "Nineteen Hundred and Nineteen," *The Tower* (1928) by William Butler Yeats (1865–1939), another of Sarton's touchstone poets.

Victor Gollancz: 1893–1967. Founder of Victor Gollancz Ltd. (which published Bowen for a time) and the well-known Left Book Club, he was highly active in social and socialist causes and did bring out *Faithful Are the Wounds* later in 1955.

Hutchinson's . . . option: Hutchinson and Hutchinson had brought out *A Shower of Summer Days* in Britain (1954); but it was 1971 before another book of Sarton's poems was distributed there.

Louise's poem: Possibly "The Catalpa Tree," *Voices* 164 (September–December 1951), not included in *Collected Poems 1923–53*.

TO EVELYN AMES   Sunday May 22d, 1955
[Wright Street]
Evie darling,

How good to hear and to see that fabulous place—is it the house at the end of the point? A kind of citadel? And the whole trip sounds like a dream in spite of all the hard work. I am so very happy that it turned out to have its own light and joy for you as I know you rather dreaded it. But it does seem, too, as if long summers there might be opening out, a real haven—and how lovely for the children!

You will laugh but I have been thinking with nothing but commiseration of Anne Lindbergh because her book is a best-seller and the small success of mine has nearly killed me so what it must be like with the inundation of correspondence she must be getting! Have you heard how she is surviving? I had not realized that it was her first book in ten years.

I still get some wonderful letters. Ada Comstock wrote eight pages of praise (and that was balm as surely she knows both Harvard and Cambridge and felt it all <u>true</u>, as against the damned Eng. dept. here who look sourly at it all) But I am trying desperately to get away from it now and onto something else. I really need the anchor of a major piece of work and hope to start in this fall. Until then I must work at lectures and odd jobs (two writers' conferences ahead and not an idea in my head!) and am hoping to crack the New Yorker with a short story, just to prove to myself that I can—and because it will make all the difference to the financial state in the next years if I can. I sent them one that I like, but of course they probably won't, and am brewing another to begin tomorrow.

The lecture trip was emptying, but rewarding as always. It is rather wonderful to tap a hunger, to make a hunger known which the people who suffer it did not even know they have. That is an awful way of expressing something I feel rather vaguely. The fact is that poetry is nonexistent in the places where I talked. And now perhaps here or there someone is finding his way into it for the first time. The letters are touching, so grateful— But at the end of the last big lecture (1500 freshmen forced to come and hating the idea) I sobbed for an hour and thought I would never get myself back <u>in</u>—one has to send some inmost psychic essence out so far to reach them at all. Then I swore "Never again," but I have forgotten it (like childbirth) and am all ready to go again now. Then Santa Fe was really a dream—I had a little bee-hive of a house all to myself, those wonderful empty mornings, looking out on mountains through the upper half of a Dutch door—and the lit-tle brown town all lit up by lilac and flowering plum and peach. I did write a few poems, too, and roughed out a story. So it did what I had hoped i.e. get me back into work.

I still feel queerly disgruntled and off-center, I don't know quite why. I suppose that when one is not embarked on a big job, then all the little threads of life pull at one more than ever and one is distracted.

I have read over the poem you gave me about your mother over and over and always with a flash of recognition and satisfaction (if that is the word) at its being so beautifully said forever. What are your summer plans? How did you find your father when you got back?

Of course you must come here or phone from the Square and I'll dash out for a few minutes, even, if there is a chance of an <u>Augenblick</u>—that is June and soon. Hurrah!

Love and blessings—I devoured every word of that wonderful letter!

Love

M

P.S. Frances Howard is getting the Golden Rose of the N[ew].E[ngland]. Poetry Society (I am <u>so</u> glad but the p.c. announcing it was pure Boston: she writes, "from Boston, for the universe" (wow!)

Anne Lindbergh . . . is a best-seller: Gift from the Sea, a short introspective study of the problems of women, became a runaway success for Anne Morrow Lindbergh (1906–2001).

Ada Comstock: Ada Louise Comstock (1876–1973) was the dean of Smith College (1912–23) and president of Radcliffe College (1923–43). Her husband, Wallace Notestein, was named Sterling Professor of English History at Yale in 1928.

crack the New Yorker: In 1954–55 Sarton published seven memoirs in *The New Yorker* (see 30 March 1956), and poetry as well, but never any fiction.

<u>*Augenblick:*</u> German for "moment, instant"—here, a visit brief as the blink of an eye. Sarton had used the term to title a poem in *The Land of Silence,* reprinted only in *As Does New Hampshire.*

Frances Howard: Boston poet Frances Minturn Howard (1905–95) wrote *Sleep Without Armor* and the prizewinning *All Keys Are Glass.* In a 27 August 1957 journal entry, Sarton writes about discussing with her how "everything that makes one a good <u>person</u> (balance, tolerance, generosity, etc) makes one a bad writer or artist—(solitude, violence, etc)." For a 1990 reunion with Howard, see *Endgame: A Journal of the Seventy-Ninth Year* (1992), pp. 41–42.

[Wright Street]
Dear Louise,

I am in a state of heat exhaustion (it was 94 <u>in</u> this house all day yesterday, at least in the upper rooms) and much too feeble-minded to
answer your wonderful letter about the Wescott week-end properly—so
here is a Siamese cat which cheered me a good deal during these last
intolerable (from a weather point of view) days. However I was driven
from sheer boredom to do a lot of cleaning out of cupboards and drawers and now everything is in apple-pie order. And luckily the lectures
only need polishing now and I can do that on the Vineyard as I shan't
need books any longer.

It is so fine to know that the Apparat (all machines are German as far
as I am concerned) is installed and what a blessing these last days. We
shall have to get one eventually, but not this year. You seem to have it
thoroughly tamed already!

The whole Wescott story is very fascinating—I used to hear about
him and Munroe Wheeler from Marion Dorn and from Muriel
Rukeyser who saw them occasionally. But there is a kind of subtle poison that destroys the galaxy of corn-fed young Westerners who come to
N.Y. and suddenly acquire total sophistication. The Glenway Wescott of
The Grandmothers [1927 novel] is very far away and deep down now
and over him there are a great many coats of lacquer. And whether it is
good for talent to have "a patron" is another factor isn't it? But I do not
mean to sound (as [E. E.] Cummings would say) like an Un-New
England non-ancestor of mine!

It is ironic, though not intentionally so, to say that Le Gallienne "is
not always actively concerned" with the theatre, and that this is a pity. I
feel that her talents are wasted partly because it is so very hard to find a
play just right for her rather special quality—but no one gave more or
(after the Civic) has been more consistently and brutally beaten up by
the critics. What is interesting is that she has put her great intelligence
and spirit to work on handling failure and making of it at least an
<u>inward</u> conquest of herself. In this light—the light of eternity—it does
not matter now whether she ever finds a play or not. And she will, I
think, be very valuable as a teacher which she is doing this summer with
a group of professional and semi-professionals. Of course I have also
come to see that failure of such a prolonged kind comes, at least in part,
from some flaw within—and whether she has ever admitted or recognized this I don't know. I sometimes imagine that as one grows older
one comes to <u>live</u> a role which as a young person one merely
"played"—and Le G. when she first starred at 22 in Liliom took on the

role of the sufferer and martyr, of the inward-looker, of the mystic—
now she is having to <u>become</u> all this in reality, and to make something
grown-up and positive out of it, a life in fact.

I had a letter from Carey McWilliams asking me to do some reviewing and an "occasional article" for the Nation, but I do not believe that
I wish to become a critic, at least not for another ten years. It would be
a fearful interruption just now. What do you think?

Oh dear, what a feeble thing I am—I've lain down twice since I
started this and eaten some grapes and a coke to revive. Address from
July 5th–15th Daggett House, Edgartown—how lovely to swim in the
ocean! Good luck in your lectures—and bless you for the great letter. By
the way, what an odd badly written book Constance O'Hara's is. But
there are fascinating glimpses of Claire Ives and also Le G. (who comes
off very well in that she saw at once that C.O.H. had to go back into the
church. She is a fearful Catholic <u>snob</u> (O. H. I mean)

Love from

May

---

lectures . . . on the Vineyard: During a two weeks' stay with her father George, Sarton finished
preparing for the Boulder Writers' Conference later that month, and Bread Loaf in August.

the Apparat: German for "apparatus, device," which Sarton here uses for "air conditioner."

Wescott . . . and Munro Wheeler: Bogan had described a bemusing New Jersey weekend at
Stone-blossom estate; see *What the Woman Lived,* 7 July 1955. Monroe Wheeler (1900–88),
author and director of the Museum of Modern Art, was the companion of poet and fiction
writer Glenway Wescott (1901–87). Long an expatriate (*Apartment in Athens,* 1945 best-
seller), he won esteem for works about his native Wisconsin. For Sarton's mixed reaction to
his published 1937–55 journals, *Continuing Passions* (1990), see *Encore,* p. 62.

Marion Dorn: Mrs. Ted McKnight Kauffer (1890–1954), artist and textile designer, became a
friend and the subject of "The Clavichord" (1948). For Muriel Rukeyser, see 27 October 1964.

Le Gallienne: London-born American actress (1899–1991), producer, director, writer, and
teacher. Daughter of English man of letters Richard Le Gallienne. Trained at the Royal
Academy of Dramatic Arts. Founder of the Civic Repertory Theatre in New York where
Sarton worked first as an apprentice, then as a member of the First Studio, and finally as
director of the Apprentice Theatre for four years before starting her own company. The critic
whom Sarton quotes has not yet been traced.

to live a role . . . in Liliom: For the young Sarton's reading notes on *Liliom,* the 1909 "legend in
seven scenes with prologue" by Hungarian playwright Ferenc Molnár (1878–1952), see *At
Fifteen: A Journal,* ed. Susan Sherman (Puckerbrush Press, 2002)—henceforth *At Fifteen.* The
leading female role of Julia (more familiar from Rodgers and Hammerstein's 1945 musical
adaptation *Carousel*) is an abused and deserted wife.

Carey McWilliams . . . the Nation: The California attorney and author became editor of the
dissenting weekly *The Nation* in 1955.

I do not . . . wish to become a critic: Sarton decided to restrict her reviewing and did not publicly judge her peers in poetry, the novel, and the memoir often. Commiserating with writer

Jean Burden (see 15 February 1964) about a bad review from another poet, she observed, "The trouble is that poets always defend themselves when they attack others—and so are both the best and the worst critics" (28 January 1964). But Sarton did write, for example, about Anne Morrow Lindbergh's diaries and letters *Hour of Gold, Hour of Lead* in *Vogue* (April 1973): "One Life: Glory and Torture."

TO ALICE AND HANIEL LONG   Sunday, Nov. 6th, 1955
[Wright Street]
Dearest Alice and Haniel,

It seems a very long time since we have communicated, and it is my fault. But I was swept on to Bread Loaf and then somehow the autumn has fled away with a little too much to do on every side. But here I am thinking of you very often though I do not write, and longing for news of you and of Haniel's novel and of the air and light out there. Has the autumn been beautiful?

We have just had a solid week of rain which is, I must confess, dampening to the spirits! It has torn all the leaves off the beautiful maple just outside my window. From my desk in autumn I look out into pale gold leaves, through dark gold curtains and it is very wonderful—

My best news is that I have finally got into a new novel. It took a whole year before I felt any little stirring of a seed, but now I am really <u>in</u> I think and I hope you will like the idea. It is called (so far) The Birth of a Grandfather and takes place in the six months between the time when the grandchild is announced as on the way and his birth six months later, the core of the book being the marriage of the grandparents and its metamorphosis in that time from a period of silent estrangement to a new kind of communion. But it is really a family novel like The Bridge, all about parents and children and grandparents, about memory and love. It is laid in Cambridge, but not in academic circles.

Unfortunately just as I was moving along happily within it, Daddy's housekeeper, our dear Julia, fell ill and has been in hospital also I have been dashing over there at seven each morning to feed his cat, feed <u>him</u>, do the shopping etc. and then back again to cook the supper. It is queer how cooking in not your own kitchen is a strain, and now living in two places makes one feel slightly frantic all the time. I get also into terrible secret rages against my father because he is so perfectly able to shut out any human thing which might upset him, and so is quite cruel without knowing it. It brings back all that my mother suffered and I get into a well of bitterness and then feel so guilty—for what is the point of that? In his way Daddy is an angel, always even tempered and cheerful and childishly humourous, always working away so hard, but being an angel is <u>not</u> being human, alas.

Well, it will seem all the more wonderful to come "home" again tomorrow when Julia gets back—she had an ear infection and we are hoping against hope that she will be able to go on with us a few more years. I have realized these weeks how much we depend on her presence and her dearness. And it seems in some ways very sad to be so depended on and yet not quite a member of the family.

It did not after all work out very well with Eleanor Bedell—an admirable person, but we were just as incompatible really as a bird and a cat! When I saw you two and heard that little bit of Haydn I felt I was coming back from exile—

Well, that is all my news in brief. Now I long for yours. I want to copy a new poem on the other side of this—["All Souls"]

Love and love from
May

Alice and Haniel Long: Author Haniel Long (b. 1888), founder of Writer's Editions, was born to missionary parents and held deeply independent religious beliefs. In 1929 he settled in Santa Fe with his wife Alice, and died three days after her in 1956; Haniel was responsible for Sarton's going there in December 1940. She wrote a portrait of the couple for *A World of Light*, and the preface for his posthumous poetry collection *My Seasons* (Boise, Idaho: Ahsahto Press, 1977). For earlier correspondence, see *Letters 1916–54*; for samples of his work, see *Journal of a Solitude* (1973; hereafter *Solitude*), p. 195, and *Endgame*, pp. 344–45.

Bread Loaf: Founded in 1926, sponsored by Middlebury College, Vermont, Bread Loaf Writers' Conference remains one of the most prestigious. Robert Frost, Richard Wilbur, Archibald MacLeish, and other notable authors have served as instructors; Sarton taught both the short story and the novel there.

The Birth of a Grandfather: Published fall 1957. In fall 1971, when Norton reissued *The Bridge of Years* (1946), Sarton quoted one of the characters: "It takes a long time, all one's life, to learn to love one person well—with enough distance, with enough humility." See *Solitude,* pp. 139–49, 201.

our dear Julia: Having worked for the Sartons many years, Julia Martin stayed on after Mabel died in 1950 and remained indispensable to George.

Eleanor Bedell: Sarton told this editor that Bedell had briefly been a lover in Santa Fe; there followed a great buildup to a later meeting which proved a disaster. "She liked to tease without resolution," Sarton said. "Our temperaments were very different." Bedell was for many years a prominent figure in the Santa Fe arts community.

TO KATHARINE WHITE   Nov. 27th, 1955
[Wright Street]
Dear Katharine,

Thank God this hideous month is nearly over—I gather it has been a devilish one for you, and for everyone I know—there must have been spots on the moon, Mars and Venus nearly colliding or some astral disturbance of major proportions! I was relieved to have your letter—I suppose because I am overtired I get terrible anxieties and one of them was that you were still cross about my careless words to your sister—but then you say it is all right. Thank goodness.

In a way, I should think Maine would be peaceful and work have a good rhythm there, but you did not sound enthusiastic. Still, I think of the great expansive view over the bay, and the dear house and you and Andy peacefully working—probably when you get this the boil will have burst and you will groan! One's images of peoples' lives are so often wrong.

I have in the back of my mind two humourous pieces for you—but I have to get a stint done on the novel before I allow any interruptions so it won't be till after Christmas that I shall start. They are two personal experiences, one a disastrous yachting trip which is rather like a Marx brothers film, (in Belgium) and the other about my adventures in buying a very old car which finally died on the third drive in the middle of a forest. You can have no idea from this brief description what horrors these two experiences contain! And whether they turn into pieces is a moot point, but we shall see.

I am reading Zen Buddhism to bolster up my fainting courage—and have almost convinced myself that by not worrying about how to live, I shall live somehow or other. Louise is back now so perhaps the Bollingen people will fork out some cash.

I still cannot get used to Benny not being there. I did not know him very well, but somehow the idea that he was over there on Berkeley St. was important. Yes—and Sherwood. It is very strange—and it happens to everyone—when at a certain point one suddenly comes to see that more of one is with the dead than with the living. I do not mean that one looks back, but there is a real shift, very much like that other major one of maturity when one becomes one's parent's parent instead of his or her child. These are the things that concern me in the novel—if only it could be worthy of the theme.

I do hope things are better for you now. I hate the atmosphere of crisis and calamity in which you have been forced to live lately—

Love and blessings
May

My father's maid is back. Glory be to God!

Katharine White: Katharine Sergeant Angell White (1893–1977), writer and longtime *New Yorker* fiction and poetry editor; for earlier correspondence, see *Letters 1916–54.* She was married to man of letters and children's writer E. B. "Andy" White (1899–1985).

a very old car: While Sarton was driving with Bill Brown in the Belgian countryside in 1949, "La Vieille Caroline" died. An account named for her was written but never published.

reading Zen Buddhism: Probably Eugen Herrigel's *Zen in the Art of Archery* (translated from the German, 1953). In "Books with a Lasting Effect" (*Rocky Mountain News*, 11 April 1962), Sarton called it "the best book I have ever read about the art of teaching and what is demanded both of student and teacher when the chips are really down."

the Bollingen: In January 1955 the Bollingen Prize for Poetry went to both Bogan and Léonie Adams. Commissioned by the Foundation at Bogan's suggestion, she and Sarton translated at least nine Valéry poems. The results were not used, but the poets were paid as they worked, and published their renderings elsewhere. See Elizabeth Frank's richly wrought biography *Louise Bogan: A Portrait* (Knopf, 1985), pp. 352–57, for insight into their working methods and their relationship during this period.

Benny . . . and Sherwood: Bernard De Voto had recently died. Robert Sherwood (1896–1955) was an author and Secretary of the Navy (1945) who wrote the script for *The Best Years of Our Lives* (1946).

TO GEORGE SARTON   March 20th, 1956
[Wright Street]
Daddy dear,

Just a little word to say that I am thinking of you especially on this first day of spring (when this reaches you I trust) and of your engagement—your marriage, as I see the many poor ones around seems such a wonderful thing, and how lucky I am to have had such parents.

Your loving little

[   ]

---

such parents: Sarton's mother, English-born Eleanor Mabel Elwes (1888–1950), was—among other roles—a distinguished clothes designer, and co-founder of the firm of Belgart, in Washington, D.C. On 21 June 1911 she married George Sarton (Belgian, 1884–1956). After they emigrated to the United States, he rose to become professor of the History of Science at Harvard, while researching and writing his many volumes on that vast subject; he was regarded as the founding father of the discipline. Their daughter's extensive correspondence with both parents is represented in *Letters 1916–54.*

On 22 March 1956, en route to Boston's Logan Airport to fly to Montreal for a lecture, George Sarton suffered a heart attack; he had the cab turn back and take him home to Channing Place, where he died.

TO KATHARINE WHITE   March 30th, 1956
[Wright Street]
Dear Katharine,

It is a relief to sit down and think of you—as I look at the immense pile of letters about Daddy, so many from people I do not know myself. I am so very happy that the New Yorker pieces did come out—as well as the note about him in "Talk of the Town." Both gave him very great pleasure—he even had fan mail about "In My Father's House"! And I am so glad I wrote them in time. By one of those blessed coincidences March 21st, the day before he died, was the anniversary of his engagement, and I had sent flowers and a letter, so that I did say one last time how much I loved him and how wonderful it was to have such parents. Thank God for that!

I had just arrived in Dallas to lecture and flew back at once, just as I arrived. It has all been strange and unreal—not the least that I have just heard that the Channing Place house where he lived is already <u>sold</u>. I put it on the market thinking it would take six months and this is really a shock—it means I shall have to break up the dear place by Aug. 1st and all the work you can imagine. I guess that piece I hoped to do will never get written—

He did have a triumphant life and the death we all hope for, while he was still undiminished and happy in his work—he had just sent to press a further huge volume on Hellenistic science and culture.

I am so buried under the immediate material problems that I have not really realized what has happened—it is so queer to be the only survivor of a family. It makes friends all the more precious—bless you for writing—

Devotedly,

May

---

pile of letters: Among hundreds of condolences from all over the world, Sarton copied this 30 March passage into her journal: while Margaret McLean had not known George Sarton, it did strike her that the "death of the parents is, to the child, a kind of second birth, or perhaps a continuation of the first one; a further severance of the close physical bonds; a further release—even propulsion—into freedom and its aloneness."

the New Yorker pieces: Between 9 January and 11 September 1954, six memoirs appeared there, recalling Sarton's earliest years: "In My Father's House," "O My America," "Wondelgem, the House in the Country," "I Knew a Phoenix in My Youth," "A Wild Green Place," and "Titi." Revised and sometimes retitled, they formed the foundation for *I Knew a Phoenix: Sketches for an Autobiography* (1959). A seventh, "Marc the Vigneron," 8 January 1955, was held over for *A World of Light.*

a further huge volume: The first of nine projected volumes of George Sarton's history of all the sciences to 1900 had been published in 1952, covering ancient science through the Golden Age of Greece. The second volume, dealing with Hellenistic science and culture in the three centuries before Christ, had just been delivered to Harvard University Press; at the time of his death he was assembling the illustrations.

TO DOROTHY STIMSON   April 15th [1956]
[Wright Street]
Dear Miss Stimson,

It was so dear of you to write, as well as making the long trip up to come. It meant a great deal to me to have you there—you seemed in coming so far to be the visible symbol of how far his light threw its beams. And you can imagine now the avalanche of letters that pour in from all over the world. I do feel mostly the triumph of this life, so round and whole, and so fulfilled, even to that wonderful way of going out on the full tide.

I am in a kind of limbo of Things now, selling the house and breaking up all that <u>life</u>. It's hard to know what has happened really—that will come later—and perhaps too the poems I hope to write for and about my father.

Meanwhile, may I say again how deeply touched I was by your presence at the funeral. I am so glad you felt it was right. I wanted that triumphant music at the end—

Yours cordially and gratefully
<u>May Sarton</u>

———

Dorothy Stimson: A historian of science herself, she edited a book of essays and prefaces from *Isis* (1912–52), the journal founded by George Sarton and devoted to the history of science; during a 29 December 1955 ceremony she presented him with the first Sarton Medal for his lifetime contributions to the discipline. She had driven through a blizzard, probably from Stonington, Connecticut, to attend the funeral. She was the sister of Henry Stimson, U.S. Secretary of War, 1940–45.

poems . . . for my father: Sarton wrote "A Celebration for George Sarton" at Christmas 1956 and, in 1957, "My Father's Death." *In Time Like Air* (1958) was dedicated to him in memoriam, as *The Land of Silence* (1953) had been to Eleanor Mabel Sarton.

triumphant music at the end: Bach, Beethoven, and Brahms were part of a service that ended with a Bach prelude in G and his chorale "What tongue can tell Thy greatness, Lord." "[T]he last entry in his diary [was] 'Lovely Day,' " Sarton wrote Eleanor Blair on 13 May 1956, "and I have been haunted by Dylan Thomas's line 'After The First Death There is no Other,' " which concludes his 1946 poem "A Refusal to Mourn the Death by Fire, of a Child in London."

TO WILLIAM JAMES, JR.   April 30th, 1957
[Wright Street]
Oh Billy,

I feel so grieved and distressed at having put you through that moment's dismay and anguish in the Post Office! I have just come back from Honolulu, where there is no decent newspaper, and have seen no one, so I did not know. There Mrs. Dillingham and Mrs. Alfred Castle spoke feelingly of Alice's ordeal, but we did not know that it was over. I am writing to Mrs. Castle today.

And I have been thinking since yesterday of you and Alice and your life together, and remembering Homer: "For there is nothing more potent or better than this: when a man and a woman, sharing the same ideas about life, keep house together. It is a thing which causes pain to their enemies and pleasure to their friends, but only they themselves know what it really means." One fears to tread—even angels might!—

on the inwardness of such a marriage as yours, but at least on the threshold one can pause and bow one's head. My dear, how cruel to be so cut in two, you who were one.

But I think also of what Alice and you together meant in the life of Cambridge. I who am un-social marvelled at all you gave, opening your beautiful house and your beautiful selves and making them a place where so many meetings of all kinds took place, meetings of ideas, and minds, and hearts, and friends. In energy, in love, it was an expensive gift—expensive, I can imagine, to your own work. But it was a very great one and its loss is quite immeasurable.

I am off to Ireland to Bowen's on Sunday, home in August. It would be good next fall to come and see you and talk of Alice with you—

Bless you, dear treasured Billy

with my love and deep sympathy
May

Forgive my typing—my hand is <u>too illegible!</u>

———

off to Ireland: For this less enjoyable return visit to Bowen's Court, see *A World of Light*, pp. 208–09.

TO JUDITH MATLACK   June 6th, Thursday [1957]
[London (JS)]
Darling one,

I was so happy to have your letter of the 3rd and to know the flowers were there to welcome you home. K.T. wrote me about Francesca and I must say it was much more of a shock than I somehow expected—I suppose one is never really prepared, however much one may think one is. I went through that day (yesterday) in a sort of queer daze, and finally had to lie down, as if all the blood were draining away from my heart, but then I revived and managed to write to Rosalind, and Katrine and a word to K.T. to thank her. I am awfully grateful that you did send flowers, darling—that was very sweet of you and they do sound just right. Let me know what I owe you—whenever I think of Bunny the tears come, I really don't know why—but I suppose it is the absolute <u>wall</u> that comes down forever, the person who was so there, so absolutely and forever <u>not</u>-there.

But your letter was the first ray of hope I have had since I left home, so very sadly and bitterly, and I cannot tell you how relieved I felt as I read it in a taxi on the way to see Marjorie Wells (I caught the postman on the way out)—and now there is just a few minutes before I have to go out to dinner with Jane to Sybille Bedford's. I do know, my dear heart, how awfully difficult it all is, but I have felt in a kind of despair because there seemed no solution, nowhere to go, nothing to be done. Now in these last days all on my own, and before your letter came I have been thinking how wonderful it would be if we could get back somehow to a normal reasonable and loving life together—and perhaps we can. It seems to me that we have so much that it would be just plain tragic if we could not maintain what we have, even though a part of me is not yours. But that part never was, really, and you did not want it, really.

It is awful to have to write this so fast, but tomorrow I go to Amersham all day to see the Hanbury-Sparrows, and Sat. fly to Belgium, so it's my last chance for some days. You will understand and forgive what may be said clumsily. I am so relieved to be able to write a letter from my heart.

This has been a hard week because a letter of Cora's made me terribly angry—I keep thinking of those awful black rages mother suffered about Daddy, the waste of it and C. is so like Daddy! I think that her vision of life is in essence different from mine and the difference is what makes the attraction between us magnetic and nourishing. But I think that you and I have much the same vision of life and that is what makes our life peaceful at its best and nourishing in a different way. There is no point in trying to change Cora, any more than I can change fundamentally. But perhaps we can learn little by little to enjoy what we can give each other instead of merely suffering and raging! These are not very conclusive remarks, I fear.

I think Ruth can be very helpful, but she is sometimes irritating, I know—and one has to be patient. But she is a real friend in a way that perhaps Sigrid cannot be, because she is so "outside." By the way, have you seen Edith at all?

I sent you today a little book called A Hare About the House that I hope you will like—and also I sent off a package addressed to me (and with the Fosters' address as well in case you are away) with my very expensive black silk dress in it and a sweater I shall not need from now on. Could you unpack these and hang them up when they arrive? Thank you also, darling for all the mail—two fat envelopes arrived with various things in them.

Darling, your hand must be a terrible nuisance—I wish I could wish away these next two weeks—but when the cast is off you must be very careful for a while. Cora, by the way, wrote me very feelingly about it. This is the sort of thing she can "take in," but I have more and more the understanding that she will not admit inward agonies of a non-physical nature because perhaps to do so would upset her too much. This is what I have to accept.

Well, I'll write more—from Belgium. I am longing for peaceful time, to think, to be, to write poems. This whole time in England has been good, but under it I must say, a very troubled mind and heart.

Perhaps now we can write a bit more open-heartedly and that will be a great help.

With very dear love, my treasure
M—

Judith Matlack: 1898–1982. Her Quaker father, Charles Matlack of Philadelphia, inherited a fortune but, lacking business acumen, lost it all. During Judith's first year at Smith College, Mrs. Matlack's anxiety over her husband's financial innocence led to a mental breakdown; she "spent the last 30 years of her life in an asylum," Sarton explained to friend of the work Jane Leonard, 21 July 1976. "[W]hen Judy was 19 she faced working her way through college and lost her mother to madness…a very hard time…from then on she earned her living."

A committed Quaker, Matlack in 1957 was an instructor of English at Simmons College, admired and loved by her students, discreet, erudite, shy. She and Sarton met in 1945 as paying guests at Edith Ricketson's in Santa Fe; Matlack, on sabbatical, was 47, Sarton 35. Their relationship quickly shifted from passion to domesticity, evolving over time until Sarton equated Matlack with "the earth under my feet," while seeking elsewhere the muses necessary for creation.

While still in New Mexico, Sarton wrote a booklet of eleven poems for Matlack, *The Singing Tree* (unpublished), followed by "A Light Left On" in 1952 and others later.

K. T.: For former teacher Katharine Taylor, see 5 May 1966.

Francesca ("Bunny"), one of the three remaining Greene daughters, had died of cancer at 51.

Marjorie . . . Jane . . . Sybille: Marjorie Craig Wells was H. G. Wells's former daughter-in-law, a staunch support to Sarton's difficult friend S. S. "Kot" Koteliansky (1880–1995; see *Letters 1916–54*). As he lay dying, he asked Wells to read and reread Sarton's letters to him.

For years, when visiting London, Sarton stayed with Jane Stockwood (staffer on *Harper's Bazaar*, reviewer for *Queens*) and her friend Annie Duveen Caldwell.

For author Sybille Bedford, see 10 January 1977.

Amersham: Amélie and Alan Hanbury-Sparrow were German English friends living in Buckinghamshire. Sarton was godmother first to their daughter, Gisele, killed by a robot-bomb, then to the twins the couple later adopted.

Cora's: Cora DuBois (1904–91) worked under Franz Boas and Ruth Benedict, becoming the Zemurray Professor of Anthropology at Harvard and an authority on Southeast Asia. She wrote the two-volume anthropological classic *The People of Alor: A Social-Psychological Study of an East Indian Island* (1944; reissued 1961). Her relationship with Sarton was closest from 1955 to 1960; they met intermittently for years thereafter.

Ruth . . . Sigrid . . . Edith: Ruth Harnden was an Irish-American author and editor. Sigrid Edge, professor of library science, and Edith Hellman, distinguished professor of Spanish at Simmons College, along with five other Simmons instructors, including Matlack, made up an informal group called "The Fish," which met several times annually for dinner and conversation.

A Hare About the House: By Cecil S. Webb, author of *The Odyssey of an Animal Collector* (London, 1954).

TO JUDITH MATLACK   June 18th, 1957
[Le Pignon Rouge]
Darling,

We are having a heat wave and there is a soft haze over everything. I have much to tell you and am writing this at 8:30 A.M. before making a desperate attempt to crash into poetry. I think what has kept me from it has been partly at least a real state of confusion in approaching our whole problem in the wrong way for <u>me</u>. This came to me in the middle of the night last night—and perhaps came out of things Eugénie has said (she is such a beneficent person in somewhat the way Louise [Bogan] is only less detached—Louise has given up being "inside" and remains wisely "outside" but E. is both "inside" and "outside", a far more saintly way of being, to my view. There is no way for me except through love. I may have been trying to write you a hard factual letter, in an effort to get things clarified between us once and for all. But now I see this is like forcing a plant, and a most extraordinary thing happened this morning which made me see it even more clearly. From a book dropped out that dear note you wrote me on April 26th after our cruel discussion—in which you quote Frost about home, and end by saying "Sometimes it seems to me the wonder is we have had <u>so many</u> unselfconsciously congenial hours together, as we honestly have had, since this overpowering chapter in both our lives began."

Isn't this what we must stand on as a foundation? We must learn to love each other better, not cease to love each other. Something has to go, something that has been false, something <u>over</u>-sensitive and selfbound I think in both of us. I have allowed myself to become confused by guilt but that is not real guilt (E. keeps telling me "the whole thing is to accept oneself, and then to be oneself as fully as one can"). I have been over-protective of you, and this is not good love, mature and honest. It does not do justice to our true relationship. You have allowed what we have <u>not</u> to cloud what we <u>have</u>, and that is poor love too. One can lose everything by wanting the impossible. What we have is <u>good</u>, not <u>perfect</u>. But that is life itself. I think there is a danger in too much outsideness and reason—i.e. one can stand <u>outside</u> and emphasize that the whole situation is a mess. One can get into a spiral of refusal and denial of what <u>is</u> and has to be accepted. But to us who are within our own relationship, it should be possible to believe that it is not a mess, because we refuse to allow it to be, and because we build on a firm foundation of mutual tenderness, trust, and respect. We can look at the impossible circumstances and say, this is something we can handle because there is real love and we are mature people.

It would be so wonderful to be able to come back and move about freely in my life, to be able to go to Cora when the spirit moves me, without guilt, and to share with you freely and gently all the dear things we do share. We all have to handle "division" of one sort or another, not only you and not only I do. Darling, look for a moment at the positive side of all this and try to take your stand there. I think you must see that unless there were real love I would during those two years have ceased to feel so tenderly toward you, might even have come to resent you, might have taken out my dividedness on you. But I didn't. The love may have been clumsy but it was always there. Just as my love for Cora (so different) is always there and will not be denied. You could not live in the climate I live in (where so much of the conflict is constantly translated into work) but some of the reasons why you love me are just because I am this sort of person. I bring you a taste of life you would not have without me. On the other hand I could not live in the climate in which you live, but it is just because you <u>do</u> live in it, that I love you and together we create a whole.

What I would hope is that when I come back we simply live as best we can (there will be ups and downs inevitably) and take it for granted that we are each doing the <u>best we can, and not discuss it very much.</u> Just try <u>to be</u> what we are to each other. Accepting each other's needs as much as we can. Isn't this au fond what we both deeply want? What stands in the way (in me as much as in you) is a bad kind of self-absorption. I need to see Cora for a week alone when I first get back, but if I can do that, then we (you and I) can have a real and lovely holiday together and I shall <u>not</u> be wanting to be somewhere else: trust the long years when we have been happy and believe that I am happy with you.

Do not let yourself think, May gets everything she wants and I get the small end. This is again one of those surface "reasoned" judgements. What I get is division within, which may be, in its way, just as hard to handle as <u>jealousy.</u> Let us be compassionate for each other's problem. That is true love—

Well, that is all. I shall wait for your answer.

I had a most beautiful evening with Jacqueline at her farm which is a perfect <u>dream</u>—a real farm and set out in those wonderful open fields around Waterloo (do you remember?)—she has converted the court at the back into a ravishing garden. You sit out there watching pigeons on the red roof.

I go over to E[ugénie]'s Thursday (address 12 Longue Haie, Linkebeek, Brabant) but shall take Aunty Lino to Ghent for two nights the 26th and 27th. On the 4th of July E. and I set out for Vouvray for a few days.

I feel much more peaceful since I have come to these conclusions— as I hope you may do, darling. And now to work!

Yours ever,

M

Eugénie: Sarton met Eugénie Dubois (Belgian, c. 1896–1982) through the Limbosch family (see note below on "Jacqueline"). Their mutual love for Jean Dominique (see 29 June 1958)—Dubois belonged to the Belgian poet's circle of friends "Les Fidèles"—brought them close. Dubois, an astrologer by avocation, had taught in an experimental school in England, run by Sarton's idiosyncratic friend Isabel Fry; see *May Sarton: Among the Usual Days,* ed. Susan Sherman (W.W. Norton, 1993), pp. 183–84—henceforth *Among the Usual Days.* At the time of this letter Dubois was a teacher in a school run by her sister; more sophisticated than Céline Limbosch, for the rest of her life she remained Sarton's intimate friend.

Frost about home: Probably Robert Frost's "The Death of the Hired Man," *North of Boston* (1914). Husband Warren tells wife Mary: " 'Home is the place where, when you have to go there, / They have to take you in.' "

<u>not discuss it very much</u>: "It is one of the modern problems," Sarton wrote her friend Esther Rohr on 28 September 1957. "Often the analytic approach conceals superficiality, I think: for one can <u>see</u> things and explain them and still not live them. Sometimes it seems too pat, since human relations are so delicate and various and no two alike."

au fond: French: at bottom, basically, fundamentally.

Jacqueline: She, Jacques, Claire, and Nicole were the children of Raymond and Céline Dangotte Limbosch, "Aunty Lino." Raymond was a poet; for Céline, see the essay bearing her name in *A World of Light*; for Jacqueline in particular, see 16 August 1981. The Limbosches' home, Le Pignon Rouge, was on the avenue Léquime, in Rhôdes St. Genèse, on the outskirts of Brussels, Belgium.

Yours ever: Immediately after meeting in 1945, Matlack and Sarton started living together in Matlack's apartment on Oxford Street, Cambridge, later moving to Wright Street. By 9 January 1958, Sarton was writing to Evelyn Ames: "Judy suddenly this morning re-opened the question of our possible separation, which I must confess, threw me, as things have seemed much better in our life together this autumn. I cannot believe that she would be happier if we did separate, and I'm sure I would not. Ten years is a big investment. But I do see that she suffers from my going off on my own—and the decision to separate will be made by her if she has to do it." While maintaining a foothold with Matlack at Wright Street, Sarton started living in the house at Nelson on a part-time basis in October 1958, moving in for good in June 1966; but the bond between them lasted the rest of their lives.

TO KATHARINE DAVIS   Sunday, Sept. 29th [1957]
[Wright Street]
Dear Katharine,

I do not know where to begin to answer your rich letter, but I was delighted with every word and have now copied out into my journal (which is mostly composed of other men's flowers!)what you say so beautifully about old age and the courage it needs—and the morning star!

I must speak a word about Yeats who is the reverse of most poets in that he did not begin to write his great poetry until he was over 45 and wrote some of his very best in his seventies—in some ways I am sorry that you have begun at the beginning of the great tome—the best poems only begin with the Green Helmet although there are beautiful single lyrics, of course, all the way through. He is a very curious poet also because, having no religion, he really had to construct for himself a System, a construction from a philosophical point of view—and this system was built partly from occult sources (his wife was a medium) and finds its expression in a very curious prose work called "A Vision." I don't really give a hoot about that because the great poems communicate whether one knows about it or not. It is just interesting. I think the weakness in the later Wordsworth comes partly from a real weakness of intellect. The pantheistic view worked for the young man, but really didn't nourish his intellect. Yet he wanted to write "philosophical" poems! Also, a difference is, that Yeats, for better or worse, loved Maud Gonne in vain for fifty years so the romantic vein which usually dies with youth, was sustained in him into his real maturity. And there is the other unusual fact, that being Irish at the time when modern Ireland was in the making, he really took part in the revolution, helped found the Abbey Theatre, and was a Senator. With all his occultism he was steeped in the <u>facts</u> of life.

I agree with you, by the way, about Marianne Moore. You know, of course, that what she writes is Syllabic Verse defined by Babette Deutsch as follows: "The determining feature of syllabic verse is neither stress nor quantity but the number of syllables in a line. This practice is acceptable for poets writing in a language such as French, when word accent is negligible. The poet using a heavily stressed language such as English may be betrayed into awkwardness.

"Among 20th cent. poets, the one notable for writing in syllabic verse is Marianne Moore. Indeed, many of her lines, unlike those of her great predecessors (Pope, Milton) must be counted on the fingers if a metrical pattern is to be perceived in them. Her long poem on the jerboa illustrates her practice. It is composed of stanzas of six lines in which the syllables number 5, 5, 6, 22, 10, 7 as here:

> By fifths and sevenths,
> In leaps of two lengths,
>   like the uneven notes
>   of the Bedouin flute, it stops its gleaning
>   on little wheel-castors, and makes fern seed
>   footprints with kangaroo speed."

My own feeling is that this is no good in English verse, so I agree with you. One just misses the <u>music</u> and the stress too much. She lives because 1) she is an exquisite eccentric who has been "taken up" by great critics like T.S. Eliot and 2) because she does have a most extraordinary power of observation of minute and significant detail. Of course she is a moralist too!

To go back to your letter, after this long digression, I was most interested in what your minister said. To Hell with Dogma, say I, being a Unitarian (if anything!) and prayer is the thing.

The forma [sic] must be filled with the spirit of each communicant in his own way and according to his own understanding. They are like metaphors. The essential truth is seen <u>through</u> them.

The time has flown by and now it is time I began to get our lunch. This grippe has made me very depressed, and also I feel always somehow bereft and naked after a book comes out [*The Birth of a Grandfather*]—something gone forever, and I am always too aware of the failure involved. There is such a fatal gap between the original vision and what ever gets down on paper!

I am slowly gathering myself together for the winter ahead—October 15th I go South for a week of lectures at Johns Hopkins amongst others—and early in Nov. the Radcliffe Seminars start. I hope to feel more zestful about it all soon.

And forgive this feeble letter. Anyway it brings dear love. Did I tell you that we have a new (not very wonderful) white and tiger kitten, who was brought to us starving? We cannot quite accept her yet because of Tom Jones ["The Fur Person"], but she is slowly entering our hearts. How is poor Mittens?

Please tell Helen I feel like a heel not to have answered her two letters and think of you both very tenderly—

Love from
May

Katharine Davis: A retired teacher of English, Davis (1878–1966) was a friend of the work who lived in Glen Falls, New York, with her companion, Helen Chitty (d. 1962); at this time Davis and Sarton had met only once. When this editor asked why she wrote so much to someone she did not really like, Sarton responded that Davis's critical faculties "challenged me as a poet," and "She was an arch-conservative [politically] and I rose to the bait." For a late dream about Davis, see *Encore*, pp. 29–30.

other men's flowers!): These "journals" were less diaries than writer's workbooks. Quotations from reading or correspondents mingle with lines for poems, exercises for teaching, names for characters, notes for lectures. Reminiscences mix with financial reckonings; a travel itinerary followed by landscape description gives way to jottings on public events. Like many authors, Sarton regarded her notebooks as loam for sowing and harvesting inspiration.

She quoted Davis, then seventy-nine: "It seems to me that persons below 70 do not fully appreciate what courage growing old requires. This is especially true of those beyond 75. That is the age, I think, when one sees the stars go out one by one. Humorously, I think of 60 to 70 as the Sunset Club, 70 to 75 the twilight and starlight club, 75 on as the Midnight Club in old age bringing a dim perception of the morning star."

a word about Yeats: The Green Helmet (1910) begins on p. 253 of *The Variorum Edition of the*

Poems of W. B. Yeats, ed. Peter Allt and Russell K. Alspach (1957, 884 pp.), which charts the alterations Yeats made to his work over the years.

later Wordsworth: Many believe that the freshest, most innovative work of the great British Romantic poet William Wordsworth peaked around 1810, though he continued to write all his life (1770–1850); only *The Excursion* (1814) to his vast "philosophical epic" was completed.

Maud Gonne . . . the Abbey Theatre: Yeats loved Gonne (1866–1953), a major source of inspiration, almost unrequitedly most of his life. A fierce Irish patriot, a founding member of Sinn Fein, and a heroically beautiful actress, she titled her memoirs *A Servant of the Queen* (1938). But in 1917 Yeats married Georgie Hyde-Lees (1893–1968). She was a "medium" only in that, to amuse her husband on their honeymoon, she attempted automatic writing—and found that, given their shared occult interests, she generated ideas and imagery on which Yeats based much of his mature output. Several plays premiered at the Abbey, founded to promote Irish works; his "system" was published as *A Vision* (1926; revised 1937).

Babette Deutsch: 1895–1982; she published her *Collected Poems* in 1969, and translated Russian works with husband Avrahm Yarmolinsky. Sarton quotes her *Poetry Handbook: A Dictionary of Terms* (1957; revised three times).

taken up by . . . Eliot: The St. Louis–born British poet and critic (1888–1965) encouraged Moore to compile her *Selected Poems* (1935), reviving her career.

Unitarian (if anything!): Sarton's affinity for this denomination began in girlhood. Nineteenth-century Unitarian theology summed itself up in five principles: "The fatherhood of God; the brotherhood of man; the leadership of Jesus; salvation by character; and the progress of mankind upward and onward forever."

Radcliffe Seminars: Sarton taught "The Art of the Short Story."

TO SIR JULIAN HUXLEY   June 22d, 1958
[Wright Street]

Julian dear, it is your birthday—that is one reason for writing to you. And I have let too many such occasions, your 70th, and your knighthood pass without a word, though you were much in my thoughts, proudly and happily. The second reason is that I read right through Pelican Politics with growing delight and amusement and then saw your signature—such a pleasure. The third reason is that I am in the middle of putting together the New Yorker sketches with some amplification and additions into a book, and so have been living in the past—and so have been thinking about you and our love affair (this will, needless to say not appear in the book! Nor perhaps will there be much about England, I am not sure yet just what I shall do—perhaps a sort of omnibus chapter of all the excitement for me of meeting people at that time, an emergence from the disaster of my theatre, but I am awfully tired of Autobiogs that just list famous people—so I lean to a final section of un-famous friends like Kot, Grace Dudley, the Longs in Santa Fe—people <u>in</u> landscapes. We shall see.)

As I cast a look back at that time when I first knew you, such a bouquet of delights, pleasures and sweet love, I am terribly aware now of how crude and young I was, and really in too narcissistic and self-intoxicated a stage to be very human. That is sad. But I did want you to know that at least now I know it, and appreciate more than I could then your dearness and kindness and love. Someday before we both die we must have a long talk. And one of the delights of getting older is just that one <u>can</u> talk in a way one never could when young—I was awfully sad that that one time when you turned up in Cambridge alone, I was not there. Juliette does not want to see me, I guess.

I am emerging from two years of depression, perhaps just that transition into middle age (I am 46 now), and personal things. But I went off on a wonderful lecture trip this spring and found myself back in my real center again, which must be poetry. Anyway all sorts of lovely things happened—I gave $1000 to an old nun in a very good Catholic college, who is that rarest of things, a true (and not sentimental) religious poet—and now she can have a year off and be free—nuns never get holidays if they are teaching nuns, and she has been stifled for 25 years. I thought of Hopkins. In this case the Mother Superior was imaginative enough to double my thousand so this could be done. Whether it was that, or writing poems again myself or just emerging at the bright end of a long dark tunnel, I don't know. But now I am happy and workful and feel centered. Also, I have bought a funny old house in a tiny village in the White Mountains as a week-end place, and a place of my very own. This all happened two weeks ago, so I am still like a newly wedded wife, <u>doting</u>—it won't be habitable until autumn as I had to have a furnace, bathroom etc. put in. It stands in a great open meadow, beside a white-spired church, a very intimate and sweet New England scene and the house about 150 years old, is modest but distinguished. Has five fireplaces, can be made light, airy, and cosy I think. I want to be able to go up there and work for weeks at a time alone. Life in Cambridge has become a bit frantic—I begin to be quite well-known and the phone rings, and you know how it is.

I think my last novel was a failure and yet a step forward—and perhaps the next one will be really good. It got awful reviews in England, but somehow <u>wild</u>—and so much the effect of a state of mind there that I could not take them too seriously. But what is happening is that, slowly, here at least I am getting a reputation not based on any single great success (which I have not had) but on the whole body of work both prose and poetry, and that is what I always hoped would happen.

So, darling, all is well with me. I wish I could see you. I just need to have a long talk with you <u>sometime</u>. Judy and I are coming to England next late June or early July and I do hope it can be managed then—but no doubt you will be in Timbucktoo!

Love and blessings from your old
May

Sir Julian Huxley: 1887–1975. Leading biologist, zoologist, educator, and philosopher, former secretary general of UNESCO; knighted 1958. Sarton first met him in Cornwall, 1 April 1936. He wrote numerous books on diverse topics.

Grace [Eliot] *Dudley:* Sarton met Dudley (d. 1950), granddaughter of Harvard president Charles William Eliot, crossing on the *Normandie* 3 April 1938, and went on to stay six weeks at her Vouvray home, broken by one week in London. "Architectural Image" (*Inner Landscape,* 1939), written at sea 5 April 1938, is for her. Intended for *I Knew a Phoenix,* Dudley's portrait and those of other "un-famous friends" were held back.

Juliette does not want to see me: In 1921 Julian Huxley had married Swiss-born sculptor and soi-disant governess to Lady Ottoline Morrell's daughter, Marie Juliette Baillot (1896–1994). Once she and Sarton met, 8 April 1936, she became and remained a central personage in Sarton's world, despite a long impasse between 1948 and 1975. See *Dear Juliette: Letters of May Sarton to Juliette Huxley,* ed. Susan Sherman (W.W. Norton, 1999). Sarton had dedicated the American edition of *Inner Landscape* to the Huxleys.

a true . . . religious poet: For Sister Maris Stella, see 29 June and 9 November 1958.

Hopkins: Religious duties and scruples inhibited the poetic vocation of British Jesuit poet and professor Gerard Manley Hopkins (1844–89); his innovative work was only published posthumously.

awful reviews in England: British novelist Angus Wilson (1913–91) said of *Birth of a Grandfather* that while "everybody is highly sensitive to the moods of everyone else, none of them know for a moment how smug and insulated they are in their gracious living," as (he claimed) in Woolf's *To the Lighthouse* (*Observer,* 23 March 1958).

TO KATHARINE DAVIS   June 29th, 1958
[Wright Street]
Dear Katharine, it is always a joy to hear from you, and as you see, I hasten to reply—though I am at the moment up to the ears in work as they want the autobiographical book ("I Knew A Phoenix") by early fall and so I am on a stiff schedule for the present, not going to Europe but staying right here to work through the summer. The book won't be out till next spring, even if I get it in by Oct. 1st as contracted for.

Before I forget, do send the snaps of Mittens—I would love to see them.

I think your idea of the old woman musing in the sun is a wonderful one. The final chapter of my new book is called "Jean Dominique: A Way of Dying"—the final section is five chapters each celebrating a friend, now dead. Jean-Do was a woman poet and teacher in Belgium whom I adored and learned much from. Something of what you suggest I may be able to get into that chapter, which is why I mention it.

The lecture trip was a wonderful experience. The two high points were Agnes Scott College in Decatur, Ga. (sometimes called the Vassar of the South)—here I found that rare combination, real fervor and a high standard of scholarship, a wonderful atmosphere of true learning and excitement about learning. I made a new friend there, Ellen Douglass Leyburn, an 18th century scholar and a great teacher. I opened their arts festival (which included a production of The Tempest and an opera by Vivaldi) with my lecture "The Holy Game"—to quite a large audience. The second great experience was a Catholic college in St. Paul, Minn., the College of St. Catherine. Here I was deeply moved by the perfect marriage of devotion and scholarship. The professors are nuns, most of whom had degrees from Oxford! Among them is Sister Maris Stella, a really good religious poet, the rarest of beings. She is 58, and I observed at once how tired she looked—they never get a sabbatical year off or even proper holidays—and she has not been able to write poems for years. So I took my courage in both hands and wrote a letter after I left enclosing a check for $1000 (all I made on those six weeks of lectures) and said that I wanted to give it to provide a year off for Sister Maris Stella, if they would double it. Of course I was afraid the hierarchy would object, but I had a charming letter back from the President, Sister William Mary, and she is to have her year. Now I hear from all sides that she looks ten years younger. I have much more feeling about helping an older person get some time, than a young one—there are so many fellowships for the young—and she has given a lifetime to her students. So this made me very happy. It is to be called the George Sarton Fellowship.

I felt more like myself on that trip than I have for two years—somehow it was like coming out of a long dark tunnel. I felt how deeply my true center is and must be poetry and when I am in that world I am myself.

Then when I got back I finally discovered the little old house in the country I have looked for since my father's death and the sad closing of his house. It is in Nelson N.H. a few miles from Dublin and all this is very new, so I still catch my breath about it. I bought it (18th century, five fireplaces) for $3900 including 38 acres of meadow, woodland and brook! But everything has to be done and it won't be habitable till September when bathroom, furnace will have been put in and a lot of inside work, painting floors, ceilings, etc. as well. However, even if all this comes to around $12,000 (including the original price) it will still be a bargain and a good investment, I hear from all sides. It has a lovely front door fan light by the way—and I can't resist enclosing snaps, but please return as these are my last copies. It stands on the tiny village green so I have lights in sight when I am there alone—but there is no shop in sight—and I feel as if buying a house were rather like getting married! I shall use it for weekends and later on to live in for months at a time, I hope, and get away from the incessant interruptions here.

I have an awful pile of stuff on my desk so must stop. But thank you for all your wise words about the novel—

and write soon again—

love to you and Helen—and I trust you are almost through the "plains of Abraham" and can rest and read poems again—

Your

May

———

Jean Dominique: Pen name of Belgian poet Marie Closset (1874–1952), founder of the Institut Belge de Culture Française in Brussels, which May, aged twelve, attended one winter; see "A Belgian School," *I Knew a Phoenix*. This new profile of "Jean-Do" became the twelfth and final memoir in *A World of Light*.

Ellen Douglass Leyburn: 1908–66. Chairman of the Agnes Scott College English department; author of *Strange Alloy: The Relation of Comedy to Tragedy in the Works of Henry James* (1968). Soon after they first met, Sarton wrote Evelyn Ames (8 June 1958) how Leyburn "in about half an hour's talk opened for me the whole mystical world . . . she had been deeply moved by my lectures—and I think we really opened some door in each other, which might be called the door into religion." Later that year Sarton included Leyburn in a notebook list of eleven "Great teachers I have known."

Leyburn did retain three poems that Sarton had written to her. "Epiphany" (written 23 May 1958) appeared in *Massachusetts Review,* Summer 1960; for "Inscription" (April 1958) and "In a High Room of Leaves" (16 July 1958), see appendix. But she destroyed Sarton's letters.

The Tempest: Shakespeare's late "romance."

Baroque Italian composer Antonio Vivaldi (1678–1741), known for concertos, wrote many operas popular in his day but rarely revived until the 1990s.

"The Holy Game": This lecture on the writing of poetry took varying forms, depending on the venue and Sarton's current concerns. A 1962 script opens with Dylan Thomas's "In my Craft or Sullen Art"; another, with her own "Prayer before Work"; a third, for the Concord and the Milton Academies rather than her usual college audiences, with Frost and D. H. Lawrence before taking off in new directions. See 27 February 1963.

Essentially Sarton identifies the holiness of this game with "selflessness . . . self discipline . . . a long silence from which a few words will spring like a jet" and likens it to "the mystic's life," with its rules, "its long arid days and nights, its long contemplations, its moments of vision. But the game is played for God and is thus without question a holy game."

"plains of Abraham": On this site southwest of Quebec City, a decisive 1759 battle won Canada for England, though both leaders—the British Wolfe and the French Montcalm—perished. Here it signifies emerging from a costly struggle.

TO CORA DUBOIS   Wed. Sept. 10 [1958] Cambridge
[Wright Street]

Darling, I have much to thank you for—the munificent boxes of kitchen herbs and things (which will not be really appreciated until I move in October 1st—and lucky if then, considering how slowly things are going), the cards and letter that tell me that you are really in the West and how consoling to be among bears and badgers, not to mention moose, and lastly and most important the beautiful gay chrysanthemum (a wonderful yellow) that was sitting in the living room surrounded by your cards and others for Judy and Judy herself visibly touched and delighted by this dear thought of yours and very cheerful—when I got back from New York last night. Now I am about to go and do various things about the party tonight, but I thought I would mention a few of the many notes I have had in my heart to tell you all these long incommunicado days.

It is good to think that when you get this you will be "home" again, settling in, making lists, and perhaps eventually to have a drink in one of your patios (!) on the rising wave of a new world and a new life.

New York was, as I knew it would be, a very exhausting business, and very little is left of me now except the need to be alone, and that fortunately will be possible soon, as Judy goes back to Simmons. Ellen Douglass and I had written enough before I went down so that, as I wrote you, it was clear that we would move into a new relationship, without love making, or decide to part. All this is so inextricably woven into my relation with you, and that seems so precarious and such a quicksand too, that I find it extremely difficult to write to you. Let me say simply that E.D. wanted to come to Nelson in the Christmas holiday and that I said no. I felt that it would take some months for her and for me to feel our way into whatever is to be, and that I at least could not afford another meeting just now. I feel as if every vein in my body had been emptied of vital essence in the effort to give enough love to make up for so much withdrawal. But that concerns me and not you. So, basta.

As for the rest, New York seemed to me tawdry and suffocating. I saw one play out of three that seemed worth the effort, the Lunts in The Visit and one that made me quite ill viz. Joyce's Ulysses, a nauseating excursion into sterile obscenity. I saw a good movie called Me and the Colonel in which Danny Kaye has at last a chance to show what he can do as a subtle and serious artist.

I had a three hour talk with Ted Amussen about the book. The conclusion we came to is that I shall hold the portraits, all of Part III of the book [*I Knew a Phoenix*] except the Two English Springs for another book and end this one with the E. Springs. I am much too disturbed about other things to care very much one way or another. The jacket on the book is handsome. It is now out of my hands, except for perhaps a week's work on the final theatre piece which may mean cutting and may mean some amplifying. I shall have to see how I feel when I get into it.

I had a lovely lunch with champagne cocktails with Louise on Tuesday who seems in fine form. She said "pain is growth" and she also said that it would be dangerous to try to embark on radical change (this is a ref. to a long letter I shall enclose) without asking the help of a psychiatrist. She said "Maybe God meant you to be a boy and it would be fatal to try to change." It was good to see her. Detached and wise and believing. Perhaps she will be able to write some poems now. She spoke of them for the first time in ages. That made me happy.

Perhaps you could find it in your heart to acknowledge receipt of a poem called The Waves which I sent you from Ellsworth on August 22nd. You did kindly acknowledge some roses, but apparently a poem is not worth a thank you. These are hard things to accept, Cora.

But I have spent the last three weeks not breaking into pieces. Your image about the jug that goes to the well until it breaks referred of course to yourself. That it might also be applicable to me cannot have occurred to you since for you (as you have so often made clear) "projecting" is a sign of weakness or folly. I think that for some time I was really intimately aware only of what you were suffering and not what I was suffering. Now as time goes on it has become clear that I too suffer and that dragonflies can be very easily smashed. Perhaps I am not after all a dragonfly but something more durable in your life since we are still in communication.

Having beaten me to my knees you now return with love, say that perhaps after all we can resume our intimacy and ask me to speak about Nelson. The last I cannot do. Not yet, anyway.

There is the word "responsibility" like a sword between us still. I did bludgeon you about Nelson and about Stanford. But why? That is the question that bothers me. Isn't it a fairly natural thing between lovers for one to wish to be where they can go together? This is the same war we had last summer. It has never been solved. Possibly when we meet in New York we can try to talk about it lovingly and come to the truth. Meanwhile I find it difficult to write to you freely about Nelson. Let me say only that it is still a chaos and I shall not move in until Oct. 1st (with Céline arriving the 3rd or 4th)—the bills mount up, and I cannot deny that since your absolute withdrawal "These were your choices, not mine, and I can take no responsibility," there has been a certain irony about Nelson for me. It is just a chore that has to be got through before I can get to work. The mystique—the invisible house, so much more important than the real one is no longer standing.

I have never asked you to get me a job, find a house, take any material responsibility either for Stanford or for Nelson. It would seem to me quite outside our relationship to do so. So what is involved is emotional responsibility. What is emotional responsibility? On my side it has been to arrange things so that you were covered, so that my coming to places where you are can be explained on the grounds of lectures, jobs etc. On your side it is less tangible. On my side it has also been to try to include Jeanne always. I feel bitterly sad about the last week-end for that reason. But there I think my resilience has really died. It was in a way I cannot quite [come] to terms with yet, traumatic. I have had several nightmares since in which Jeanne plays a part. I do not minimize what she went through either. That is why I believe that episode has closed something irrevocably. I simply haven't the courage to face anything like it ever again. "La cruche va a l'eau jusqu'a ce qu'elle se brise" does not only apply to you.

On your side emotional responsibility has involved being available to a quite extraordinary extent and at great cost to yourself. My angel, I have lately thought of this very often. What is it then about Nelson and Stanford that you feel you can't do or be? I only really ask you to be glad in each instance that we can be together. This would be an intolerable burden to place on anyone if love were not the premise. But I have always believed that it was "through the destruction of Carthage and Troy." I have believed that it was.

[closing not extant]

---

cards . . . for Judy: On 9 September, Matlack turned 60; when Sarton came home the next day, they celebrated her birthday together.

notes . . . in my heart: "You said something about my many love affairs," Sarton wrote DuBois at the start of their relationship, 1 December 1955. "They have never been light; I have always been wholly committed. They have been spiritual rather than physical adventures, in essence, and by them I have grown."

"And in case you need reassurances," DuBois wrote back, "which I hope you don't, 'anxiety that makes you hit out' does not close me from you; nor need you ever fear that I shall ever be really closed off from you, darling. There are few things in this shifting world that I can ever say with certainty. But that I could ever, in my heart, close you off, once and if only once, having known you, is inconceivable. With no possessiveness, and precisely because there is no possessiveness, you are mine forever. And for as long as you want me, I am yours."

the Lunts in The Visit: For their farewell performance, the husband-wife team of Alfred Lunt (1893–1977) and Lynn Fontanne (1887–1983) chose this translation of *The Visit of the Old Lady* (1956) by Swiss playwright Friedrich Dürrenmatt (1921–90). Lunt played Anton Schill, a man destroyed by the woman he once rejected.

Joyce's Ulysses . . . sterile obscenity: The surrealistic "Circe" chapter from the 1922 novel *Ulysses* by Irish writer James Joyce (1882–1941) had been adapted as *Ulysses in Nighttown,* with Zero Mostel as Leopold Bloom.

Comic actor Danny Kaye (1913–87) was known for his quick delivery of the trickiest wordplay.

Ted Amussen: Longtime book editor Theodore S. Amussen (1915–88) later became editor in chief for the National Gallery of Art. Sarton met him when he was 27, working for Farrar, Straus as well as Rinehart, and enthusiastic about her poetry. "He really gets the point of my kind of writing, not a one-book affair and a quick selling proposition but the slow process of a serious writer's growth." (To Bill Brown, 22 January 1945) After he moved to another firm in 1947 they remained friends.

"Two English Springs" are those of 1936, when Sarton met the Huxleys and John Summerson, among others; and of 1937, when she encountered Koteliansky, Bowen, and Leonard and Virginia Woolf. "The portraits" resurface in a 1 July 1963 letter to her Norton editor Eric P. Swenson; but eleven years passed before work resumed on what became *A World of Light*.

cocktails with Louise: When Bogan was lecturing in Austria that summer, she was delighted that Sarton wired her dark red roses for her sixty-first birthday. See *What the Woman Lived*, 12 August 1958. Bogan's poem "St. Christopher" had just seen print, and the next year she wrote "The Young Mage"; see *The Blue Estuaries*.

the last three weeks: DuBois had written her, 20 August 1958: "You are so buoyant that oscillations from hate to love, from rage to tenderness are possible. Slow tortoise that I am, I only slowly accumulate the impact of events. I live in a shell; you, in the air. I acquire through slow accretion layer after layer of conditional carapace. You, like a dragonfly, cleanse yourself from minute to minute on wings in the air. . . . Every quarrel, every scene, every rage leaves an indelible streak on my shell. . . . You can no more scoop me out of my shell than I can (or would want to) change the air in which you live. . . . As you know even better than I, love and intimacy are not equivalent. To save our love, which I cherish, it may be necessary to reduce our intimacy—"

to write . . . about Nelson: Sarton bought the house there not only as a workplace but as a haven of retreat with DuBois. A May 1959 notebook entry clarifies what Sarton wished she could tell her: "[C]ora. Here at Nelson I shall see you for the first time in a place which I cannot be 'asked to leave' or 'allowed to stay'—in which I am not helplessly in the power of an atmosphere created by others—Here I create the atmosphere—you can come or go as you choose but you cannot make me leave." DuBois had accepted a teaching position at Stanford University in Palo Alto, California; her first visit to Nelson is commemorated in the 1961 poem "Der Abschied" (The Farewell).

include Jeanne always: Jeanne Taylor, a painter, lived for many years with DuBois. *"La cruche . . . se brise"* is the French proverb about the jug translated earlier.

destruction of Carthage and Troy": Might this be from Simone Weil? or from a poem, perhaps Swinburne? It alludes to Dido Queen of Carthage, and Aeneas in exile after the sack of Troy; their legendary love was not as everlasting as Dido had hoped.

For a wry retrospective anecdote about the Sarton–DuBois relationship, see May's account of having a tonsillectomy at 50, and Cora's "stoic" response, in *Endgame*, p. 104.

[May Sarton moved to Nelson on 1 October 1958.]

TO SISTER MARIS STELLA, C. S. J.　　　9 November 1958
[Wright Street]
Dear Maris Stella,

This time I have not answered as soon as I always wish to. I spent five strange illuminated lonely days at Nelson to put in many little plants (all naked roots dangling in cellophane bags and it will seem a true miracle if any survive the winter) for a perennial border. Also I wrote the Christmas poem which is always an ordeal and it must be fairly cheerful (!) though I do not expect it to be seasonal exactly. It is more what I have been thinking about and where I am, a spiritual letter to my friends. I did, I think, an adequate poem and really got into that wonderful state of non-being where one forgets everything—a queer conversational poem which you will get at Christmas so I won't send it now. About why the form of a house can <u>inform</u> the spirit, why window mouldings create a way of life. Those five days were a test and I think I know now that I can manage there alone and do good work. Unfortunately I was getting grippe and came back to fall into bed. Now I am in fine fettle again—with a whole bevy of lectures to give in the next two weeks—and all this only to tell you why your good letter did not get answered sooner.

First things first. The poem. Beautiful. "The hollow reed unbroken" haunts me. There is everything in it, sound, meaning—such a tremendous image. My only quibble is the scansion of the next to last line. I wish a one-syllable word could be found for "stillness" and even if scanned (is my ear all off? The line seems over-long) I long for a stronger word.

Do not imagine for a moment that I think the decision to become a religious means that all problems are solved from then on in, or that it pre-supposes peace of mind, freedom from guilt, or that one is transformed into a saint by following a strict rule! Though the rule must be a support. An armature so to speak. I am plunging into the center of things—but let me first say a word about that beastly little critic on Commonweal (I do respect that journal and see it occasionally though not regularly. And I am grateful to it for a really serious review of Faithful appeared there, relating it to my other novels, a great joy.) I feel that modern criticism of poetry and poetry itself (as represented for instance by John Ciardi) is somehow all beside the point, or rather that it stops at the materialistic level. It has become an intellectual exercise and this is a contradiction in terms. I do not know Sister Maura's work but I presume that it springs from a spiritual life and is an act of the spirit. I often think that critics today have no means of coping with "pure poetry", with a James Stephens, for instance. But how hard it is! However, the question you raise is about pride. I fear that there is a pride and it often manifests itself by superiority—the superiority of the "unrecognized" who says to himself, "I am too good for this world", that sort of thing. The only perfectly humble poet I have ever seen is Marianne Moore. And, alas, I do feel that her work has been over-rated. She is a distinguished original poet, but not a great one. Only she has been puffed up, again by "clever people" who like her for the wrong reasons, as if she were a quaint antimacassar. What she really is, a <u>moralist</u>, they fail to see.

In my heart of hearts I do believe that art and sanctity can go together—because at the inmost center of art is selflessness. I often think that no unhappy poem can be a real one, but always beside the point. For at the center of poetry is always joy and praise. Do you remember Rilke's little poem that begins:

"Oh tell me, poet, what you do? I praise." ["For Leonie Zacharias"] <u>Yet</u>, without the blood in it, the conflict, the mire if you will, the art has no substance and this is the great problem. Here I am perhaps wrong for I see that I am now imagining sanctity to be pure light, a place arrived at like Heaven, and not the arduous, painful, conflicted journey that it no doubt is.

When you speak of what you went through to come to terms with teaching as "mothering" as against what seemed like a selfish pursuit of course that is what one means (even in a secular life) about the conflict between life and art and if you don't think I feel it continually, you are sorely in error! The whole trouble is that no honest artist can be <u>sure</u> that his work justifies the sacrifices made for it in just these terms of not doing the human thing—in my case, endless obligations to friends and people who depend on me in one way or another. I live each day in a state of guilt and always have to make an examination of conscience, so to speak, and somehow come to terms with this guilt every day before I can get to work. What I am bumbling to say is that just as in prayer, it would be a poor prayer which could <u>only</u> be made <u>if</u> an answer were assured. The sanctity of art seems to me just in this risk—the very humility of doing it knowing that perhaps it will all be a bungle and serve <u>no</u> purpose is where one is closest to the religious spirit in art. One side of me has the utmost sympathy and loves you for making the immense sacrifice you did when you dedicated yourself heart-wholly to teaching at the expense of poetry. But the other half of me, (I hope an angel, not a devil) <u>must point</u> out that it may sometimes be easier to do just that. <u>Because</u> in the eyes of the world "service" is always easier to understand than either art or the contemplative life. Even I in some ways find it easier to accept the religious as a nurse or a teacher than as a pure contemplative. (That is how unregenerate I am!) Art is such a lonely endeavor, between oneself and God. I do find that I constantly relate it to prayer. Oh dear, so many words to say next to nothing—and this letter has been interrupted by a visit, so I must really stop and get our lunch. But it would be good to have a real talk sometime. Dear Maris Stella, through all this rambling I hope what you can read with your wise heart is that I believe so much in you as poet that

I feel sorely tried at the thought of your being used wholly as a teacher in the service of God. And that is enough—

But I have not said how surprised I was that the house poem moved you ["Moving In"]—it was wrenched out and came out simple (which I always think means a real poem) but—well—anyway it was comfort to know it reached you. And of course those lines from Hopkins are dear to my inmost self—I do understand why you feel so close to Hopkins, and why you have a right to.

But as to my personal failure (to which you are so dear and charitable) I do know it is there. I have always <u>seen</u> so clearly what I cannot <u>be</u>. I fail all the time. But of course we all do. I do not consider myself an intolerable sinner—I always <u>hope</u>, you know, that I shall become detached. Yet when one is detached, that is also a terrible <u>loss</u>—well, I won't start on that huge theme.

It is very nourishing to be able to communicate with you on so many levels. When you make your examination of conscience do not forget what you do and have done for me, first by being a poet, then by being a true friend.

Tucson will be beautiful—and I do want to hear about the landscape. I remember sharp blue peaks on the horizon's rim and a great sense of space and lovely warm "world-mothering-air"— And I trust that the meeting in Cal will be interesting (though meetings are horrible on the whole don't you agree?) I do not like California either—I feel that what comes from there (with the exception of Morris Graves' paintings) always seems a little inflated. I have New England in the marrow of my bones, I guess. But an art without austerity does not move me. The self-indulgent in art has to be burned away just as in life and so much of the Cal art seems to me pure blowing off steam! I am probably prejudiced.

With dear love. The rain pours down. I think of you with very great tenderness, admiration, and thanksgiving always—

Your

May

Sister Maris Stella, C. S. J.: Alice Gustava Smith (1899–1987) received the habit in 1921 from the Community of Sisters of St. Joseph of Carondelet. As was the custom at this period, she assumed a new name. Maris Stella, Latin for "Star of the Sea," was an appellation of the Virgin Mary. Sister Maris Stella earned two degrees at Oxford and had already published three volumes of poetry. She and another sister inscribed *Cause of Our Joy* (North Central Publishing Company, 1956) "To MS/You have given us all great joy! Sister Maris Stella/ Sister Marie David, with the profoundest admiration for your disciplined life/ May 8, 1958."

a spiritual letter to my friends: Sarton's Christmas poem this year was "Reflections by a Fire: On moving into an old house in New Hampshire."

bevy of lectures: Over the next two weeks she appeared at Simmons College, Milton Academy, MIT, Wellesley College, and the Emma Willard and Chapin schools.

"The hollow reed unbroken": In Matthew 11:7 Jesus asks a crowd, curious about the ascetic prophet John the Baptist, "What went ye out into the wilderness to see? A reed shaken with the wind?" French religious philosopher Blaise Pascal (1623–62) developed a famous analogy from the proposition "Man is a thinking reed."

really serious review: In the Catholic periodical *Commonweal,* 8 April 1955, Frank Getlein singles out how "Sarton catches the likeness of McCarthy better than most political attempts." In the 6 December 1963 issue, Sister Maris Stella would review *Joanna and Ulysses:* "Sarton's way of seeing is poetic and uniquely her own."

For poet John Ciardi, see 8 February 1962.

The poems of Irish author James Stephens (1882–1950), often about animals, aspired to the timeless lyric; Sarton met him through Koteliansky. "James Stephens's coat was all out at the elbows and he looks like a small wizened tramp," Sarton wrote her parents, 18 April 1943; "both he and Kot are like two mad angels, delivering mad dicta about politics and the world." (See *I Knew a Phoenix,* p. 213, and *A World of Light,* pp. 179–80, 188.) "A Letter to James Stephens" concludes the American edition of *Inner Landscape.* Reviewing the British edition, 16 April 1939, Stephens wrote in the London *Times,* "The author is in love with discrepancies. . . . [She] is able to do a thing hitherto impossible—she can warm snow, and regard it and love with a passion that makes them equally lovely. . . . [S]he is passionately thoughtful. . . . [W]hatever she does is done at the stress of its own being. And she writes beautifully."

conflict between life and art: See *Among the Usual Days,* pp. 45–49, for more deliberations on this dilemma.

Tucson will be beautiful: "Amazed" at this stroke of good fortune, the sabbatical made possible by Sarton's gift of one thousand dollars (see letter to Katharine Davis, 29 June 1958), Sister Maris Stella left in August for Santa Fe where she spent three months visiting Pueblo Indian reservations, went to California in November, then on to Tucson for more Indian observation.

"world-mothering-air": Sarton plainly expected this phrase—which otherwise looks like a Native American term, or a German compound noun—would be readily recognized: perhaps it is from Sister Maris Stella's own poetry?

Morris Graves': The Oregon native (1910–2001) moved to Ireland in the late 1950s. His introspective, calligraphic work was influenced by Zen and Asian art; Sarton might have seen it at New York's Museum of Modern Art.

thanksgiving always: At Sister Maris Stella's prompting, Sarton later spoke at Rosary College near Chicago, where she met Sister Jeremy. "Apparently she regards you as a fountain of good works and simple holiness which I felt to be grotesquely to under-estimate you, if you will forgive me saying so!" Sarton wrote Sister Maris Stella, 12 April 1965. "How could you be so great if there were not some acidity and some conflict I felt like saying? Later I asked her [Sister Jeremy] why more of her poems did not deal with inner life (as I had asked you) and she made the same answer: 'We live in a community, many of whom would be alarmed or not understand'—and I thought to myself, yes, but so do we all in one way or another." For the rest of Sister Maris Stella's story, see 9 July [1978].

This "Sarton Fellowship" was a one-time stipend. Making her will in 1961, Sarton resolved to endow "two fellowships in poetry and history of science, the income to accumulate for three years so that $10,000 can be given in one lump, every three years to a poet, and every alternate 3 to a historian of science." (To Katharine Davis, 29 March 1961)

Proceeds from her 1995 estate auction were added to her savings for this purpose, and the grant was established as first envisioned under the auspices of the American Academy of Arts and Sciences. The first George and May Sarton Fellowship was awarded on 12 May 1999 at the Academy in Cambridge, Massachusetts. President Dr. Daniel C. Tosteson made the presentation to historian of science Dr. Cristina Chimisso, for her work on the French historian of science Helen Metzger. This inaugural ceremony included dinner, music, and readings by poets Galway Kinnell and Rosanna Warren, introduced by poet Frank Bidart.

TO PEGGY POND CHURCH   May 10th, Sunday [1959]
[Nelson]

<u>Dear</u> Peggy,

What a wonderful letter! I must tell you that when I read the paragraph about my poems I burst into tears—it was like a voice from far in the past and I remember that once long ago I <u>felt</u> like that, and now I seem to be very far from my real self. But I have taken the bull by the horns (if that is the word for it!) and am going to an analyst to try to find out what has happened through four years of a disastrous yet un-break-offable personal relationship which is, I truly believe, murdering me, and yet which seems in some queer way so deep and important that to break off would be to have suffered in vain. For I must believe still that there is a way <u>through</u> to the heart of the matter and that if I can find it, it will be like Beauty and the Beast.

I was so upset by what you said about your parents. I do not see how you emerged the good and true person you are. And how do people ever dare to be parents, yet you did? I mean either there is bad love or too good a love—and in either case the child is crippled in one way or another. I do not honestly think that I made gods of my parents, though I loved them dearly, but it was a long time after both their deaths when I could begin to see them clearly. Of course I loved my mother too much and was her lover against my father (with my father as rival)—one says these things so glibly but the truth is harsher and more difficult to extricate. In the end my parents became my best friends (I left home at 17, you know and hardly saw them for years, all through the theatre years)—and it is as friends that I miss them now terribly. One of the horrible truths I have recently discovered (and how illuminating that para. about Colette you sent me was in this context) is that no really intimate person in one's life can ever <u>see</u> one's work. There seems always to be jealousy or fear or the inability to communicate, so one runs with one's treasures, like children to be loved, and gets no response. But parents (at least mine did) <u>can</u> respond because, I suppose, one is an extension of them and so, at least, they are not jealous. K is not, but she is one of my few intimate friends who ever responds to anything I write. And for many years I said and felt that I wrote for my friends and if anyone else happened to overhear that was all right too. So it is now a complete reversal and I am finding it hard to accept that, amongst many other things.

But about the most important thing, the constant struggle between art and life. I do not believe any woman whether married or not, can go through life without suffering from this conflict excruciatingly. There are always the human claims which one either takes on (even writing a letter) and then feels guilt because the work is undone, or the work, and then one feels ruthless in regard to people. "Why not just live?" says my analyst, whatever that means!

Yes, I do understand I think that it was time that you left New Mexico—Oh Peggy, I am so glad that E.W. book is off your neck and so well off it, so to speak! I still feel that it was an almost impossible task which you did wonderfully well—yet somehow the silence of that woman is untranslatable, and how immensely difficult to communicate a life whose whole point was its inwardness, its communications not through words. You have made a work of art. But in some ways I hate all the time and worry it was, for I keep knowing that you are a poet. Now is there some clear time ahead?

I want to say a word, too, about K. You have been such a wonderful friend to her and always her letters after she has been with you, have the tone of someone temporarily released from jail.

Oh Peggy, to go back to my parents and yours—I used to feel that love flowed through me like an inexhaustible river because I had been so well loved. In a curious way too because my father was rather indifferent as a <u>father</u>, and I only really came to love him after mother died, but his values went deep into me. When my mother died I felt a huge relief, as if I were suddenly free and really I believe this is true whatever the relationship with parents may be. Cruel truth. But what I did, it seems, was to fall in love with someone who seems to be my father and mother all in one (poor person! What a burden!) So it was not all solved after all, but all to be begun again.

Two men are diligently washing the windows (I am having a sort of housewarming here on Saturday, 6 friends of Judy's for martinis and lunch, so all these preparations are quite festive)—I do wish you could see this house, for whatever else is wrong this is an angel, this house, and the village, and all the dear people. Today my nearest neighbors came back like swallows, an elderly lawyer and his wife [Gerald and Bertha Cobleigh] from Nashua (very local, thank Heavens!) and I invited them over to see the house which they had watched being rebuilt all last summer, but had not seen, furnished. We drank sherry and talked for an hour, and then later that dear old man trotted over with an old pair of binoculars and a bird book for me. And also told me that he keeps vast amounts of penicillin in a kitchen cupboard, in case of need, and I am to help myself! I feel greatly blessed and also very happy that K. will be here this summer. I feel it may be for her what it is to me—a fairyland of solitude.

It was Yeats who said the quarrel with ourselves makes poetry—but not, I have found out, if the quarrel is <u>too</u> terrible. I feel stripped down now to a very small core. But novels are such hard labor, and I am in the middle of one I care about deeply, but feel entirely unable to do justice to— [*The Small Room*]

Well, enough. I must go and cook something to eat. This is a bad letter but it is hard for me to write just now.

Yours with a great blessing.

Love

May

Peggy Pond Church: Born in the New Mexico Territory, in youth Church lived on the Pajarito Plateau; in 1942 her family had to leave when the federal government appropriated her father's Los Alamos Ranch School, and the area around it, for the Manhattan Project. She spent most of her life (1903–86) in the mountain country west of Santa Fe, which furnished matter for her poetry (*New and Selected Poems,* 1976). For an earlier letter, see *Letters 1916–54.*

K: Kathryn ("Kay") Martin, at that time a schoolteacher in San Francisco, had been a student of Sarton's at Boulder. For a while she lived in nearby Henniker, New Hampshire, staying at Nelson when Sarton traveled. She was a poet; her first novel, *The Departure,* appeared in 1962, when she was in her fifties. For her 1981 memoir *A Question of Age: The Dorm and I,* Sarton provided a blurb.

that E. W. book: Church's *The House at Otowi Bridge: The Story of Edith Warner and Los Alamos* (Univ. of New Mexico Press, 1960) was a brief biography of the woman who was friends with both nuclear research scientists and the indigenous San Idlefonso Indians. Sarton's acquaintance with Warner is referred to in *Letters 1916–54,* pp. 318–20.

TO KATHARINE DAVIS   July 20th [1959]
[Cornwall]
Dearest Katharine,

It was such a joy to find your good long letter when we arrived here, the bay the most wonderful indigo blue with purple streaks and across it green fields dipping down to cliffs ... after reading your suggestion of places I was inspired to set down just what we have done. If you have a map of England you will see that we covered a lot of trerritory but most of it on the west coast (Oxford Judy studied at for a year and I know [it] pretty well so we shan't go there this time). I have made very few comments on the enclosed sheets, but I think the single most moving experience was Fountains Abbey [West Riding, Yorkshire]—we were there after dinner, driving about 3 miles to the gates of a large estate, then through the park to another gate where one leaves the car. No one told us we had a 3-mile walk ahead (fortunately as we might not have had the courage and it was worth it)—one walks first along a most ravishing 18th century water garden, with a lovely Greek temple reflected in half moon shaped pools with long emerald strips of grass between, statuary etc. No flowers, just marvelous great trees. A poem. Finally after this finest walk for about a mile one sees the ruins of the abbey, immense and still. It is the most beautiful ruin I have ever seen and there is something very poignant about the complete great empty windows, sky instead of stained glass and the swifts flying in and out among the broken arches. Of all landscapes we have seen I liked North Wales best— wonderful unspoiled and without tourists. Down here in the South the roads are hair-raising.

You asked about means of conveyance. An Austin car exactly like mine was hired to meet us at the boat and that is why we drove down from Greenock and got off there instead of at Liverpool. I grazed a truck slightly the first day (because unused to left drive) but otherwise get on well. Once we got stuck on a perpendicular hill and had some anxious moments but I backed down finally, tried again, and we made it.

Before I go further, I must correct a misapprehension, namely that Kathryn Martin, the dear friend now at Nelson, is the person who did not like the novels. She loves Nelson and Union Suit whom she calls the late George Apley. She is the public school teacher. The friend who attacked the novels is another kettle of fish: she is Cora DuBois, the Zemurray professor of anthropology at Harvard (one of only two women profs and a very distinguished person indeed, was high up in the State Dept. doing policy-making work during the war and in OSS with Mountbatten). Cora is not an artist but a scientist and this perhaps explains why she doesn't like the novels—but what disturbed me is that she does like the sort of novel I like—V. Woolf, E. Bowen etc. Never mind, I am getting over that, and your letter was such a fillip.

You are an angel to have read all those sonnets and to make such heartening comparisons—The Land of Silence was barely reviewed (never in the Saturday Review, I think, or very briefly and John Ciardi wrote a really mean review in the Nation, the sort that killed John Keats). That book was really buried alive and I think my present depression is really a cumulative one—I have buried disappointment and gone ahead so many times and suddenly because I was tired, the whole thing exploded. I sometimes feel a sort of rage because I do believe in my work really—and I wonder if it will ever "get through." It is a lucky accident when someone like you who does see what I am doing <u>happens</u> to discover it.

I was very tantalized because the paragraph about Philip ends "so the boy will go to rh" and I do not know what rhn [sic] means! I do think he should be punished as things have gone too far and he has shown that he was not worthy of your interest and compassion.

I am so relieved that on re-reading Faithful seems to you not a failure, bless you.

I must stop as we are off to Mevagissey [Cornwall]—love to Helen and Mittens and with dearest love to you from

M

---

the late George Apley: Title and central character of a 1937 novel by John Marquand (1893–1960), whose mild satire often dealt with rich New Englanders; Union Suit was a cat.

OSS with Mountbatten: Office of Strategic Services. Louis, first Earl Mountbatten of Burma (1900–79), British admiral and statesman, directed World War II commando raids in Europe and became supreme allied commander of the Southeast Asia Theatre (1943–46).

all those sonnets: Probably the eleven originally comprising "These Images Remain"; Davis chose five for inclusion in *Cloud, Stone, Sun, Vine: Poems Selected and New* (1961) and read in manuscript that book's twenty-sonnet sequence "A Divorce of Lovers." Davis's side of the correspondence consisted largely of critiques on Sarton's work.

The Land of Silence: Gerard Meyer (*Saturday Review,* 16 January 1954) both praised and questioned her "neatly turned concluding line," her "quick, colloquial thrust, and the telling, sudden word that defines the moment and the scene." Poet Howard Nemerov was disappointed (*Atlantic,* September 1954); translator Wallace Fowlie singled out "The ease with which images in her poetry transpose notions" (*New Republic,* 14 December 1953). John Ciardi (*Nation,* 27 February 1954) faulted overreliance "on 'high-pitched' adjectives which have no specific sensory content. . . . Her poetry asserts pregenerated emotion—it is distinct from and inferior to the type of poetry that generates its emotion in its own movement."

Another great Romantic poet, John Keats (1795–1821), died not from harsh criticism but from his family's disease, tuberculosis.

TO POLLY THAYER STARR   Oct. 24th, 1959
[Wright Street]
Dearest one,

I am so very grateful that you called. And after writing that sentence I just sat here with the rain and wind outside, thinking and unable to say a word. Desolation. For so long your little mother has been as light as a feather, on her way, and you have been holding that feather up in your heart, keeping it from blowing away, sustaining it, and now it has gone. Now you are an orphan too, as Henry C. Greene wrote me when he was 80 and I lost my father. The really awful thing is that no one ever again is that person for whom one was the world, the <u>absolute</u> love. I suppose that love is as near to God's as we can come in human life, and so to lose it is the most poignant loss there is. I want to hold you very close and say nothing.

I feel such a failure as a friend and a person altogether, that it was very wonderful to have you say that the Phoenix meant something to you and Donald. I have been really in the darkness, darling, since last April. And I did get some help from Izette de Forest, a psychiatrist who fortunately has a place in Marlboro near Nelson. I know what I have to do and more about true love than I did, but it is very very hard to do what one sees, to become what one knows. I began to write poems in France and felt alive again, but here in Cambridge the furies are at the window—and I am way back again in the abyss. So the lectures will be a help as it is good to feel useful, and in touch with that deep spring of poetry.

I think now that after a long life it is wonderful to be allowed to go, to be allowed to die. I think your mother was ready, so for her it is good to be released. The hard thing is that we all have to go on to the very end somehow. I think of you very dearly always and wanted very much to see you last week, but the line was busy—perhaps at that very moment you were facing death.

Ever your devoted
May

Polly Thayer Starr: Boston painter and graphic artist (b. 1904), married to Donald C. Starr (1901–92); Dinah and Vicky were their daughters. Starr met Sarton through Molly Manning Howe around 1935, when Sarton was involved with the Apprentice Theatre. Fascinated by Sarton's unabashed energy and poetic sensitivity, Starr painted her in 1936 and drew her on several other occasions; a pencil sketch of her served as frontispiece for *Encounter in April* (1937). Their lifelong friendship was fueled by a deep love of literature, delight in the endless specifics of nature, and the search for spiritual integrity in their respective disciplines.

as Henry C. Greene wrote me: This story, which Sarton often told (*Solitude,* p. 178, *At Eighty-Two: A Journal* [1996], p. 205, and elsewhere), presents a conundrum. Greene died on 29 December 1951: he might have condoled about her mother's death, 18 November 1950—but not her father's, 22 March 1956. Whatever the explanation, it was plainly the kind of remark, and Harry Greene the kind of man, that Sarton's memory thought belonged together.

to hold you very close: "I feel at the moment a great invisible bond with you," Sarton wrote Starr on 6 December 1959. "I think I have never fully realized before just what 'family' means and what it is when family goes. For there is no other absolutely-to-be-trusted love on earth, and how we rebel at not being children and having to take on the whole human responsibility!"

Izette de Forest: They had only a few sessions, beginning 5 May 1959. Two years later, de Forest would write Sarton that she "found I could not put it down [*The Small Room*]. It's enthralling . . . you have seized on something emotionally real & given it a true picture."

TO ERNEST HOCKING   Dec. 24th, 1959
[Wright Street]
Dear Ernest Hocking,

Frances Pray copied for me a wonderful passage from a letter of yours to her about Shady Hill, about feeling and its importance and about "lifting all life to the level of poetry—which is a sort of imaginative religion." These words lifted me right up on their wings and healed. I saw that this was the meaning of my life and I had nearly forgotten it in a really terrible year of near despair and the end of a crucial relationship. Now on this eve of the rebirth of love and of our yearly rebirth to greater understanding of what it means, I must tell you, dear one, that words can save and can heal and that yours did.

The mystery of life is just overwhelming.

Ever your loving
May

––––––––

Ernest Hocking: In 1915, Hocking and his wife Agnes founded Shady Hill, the experimental school in Cambridge, Massachusetts, where young May received her formative education. Frances Pray, now deceased, graduated there in 1921; nothing more is known of her.

The "end of a crucial relationship" refers to Sarton's intense involvement with Cora DuBois.

TO EVELYN AMES   Aug. 2d, 1960
[Nelson]
Evie darling,

Home again with huge sighs of relief! Tomorrow is my mother's birthday and I have been thinking about her and how extraordinary she was like a small flame that veered and trembled but could never be put out. I'm now on the final stint of the novel [*The Small Room*], another two or three weeks more and then it will be done. The garden is monstrously active too—and I rush out madly to pick peas between bouts. Zucchinis reached giant proportions while I was away and now there is a positive deluge of Chinese peas (the kind you eat, pod and all)— The woodchucks have eaten the poor phlox again after it put forth hopeful new leaves...but I am resigned.

As for Rio—God, what an opéra-bouffe the Congress was. Only one speech even mentioned the theme we had come to discuss i.e. mutual appreciation between East and West. It was mostly impassioned chauvinistic speeches by small countries to prove how great their literature and how <u>un</u>-influenced by anyone else! Fortunately the Robie Macaulays turned out to be dear people. He edits Kenyon and wants to get away from so much criticism and print more poems and stories, and we could giggle together. My first fit of giggles was just after the serious opening session when they played what I thought was a Gilbert and Sullivan air I did not quite recognize and it turned out to be the National Anthem! I tried in vain to get a record of it and I know it would never fail to cheer in the darkest hour—really terribly funny and very long with choruses of young girls etc. Moravia (who presided) never appeared again after the first day, in a huff it seems. Our official elder statesman, Elmer Rice, seemed like a patient old bear who had long ago given up trying. No American spoke which was a pity, I thought—a man from Uruguay scolded me about this and he was quite right. But I turned out to be not even an official delegate and could not go over the heads of the others even if I had been prepared, and I was not. The French sent a preposterous set of second-raters whose only concern was the next free drink or meal and who screamed and had tantrums if some of us wanted to linger in a museum for fear they would miss a drink! As Robie said, "I love the French passionately until I meet one Frenchman!" The only moving moment to me was the welcoming of a coal-black new member of PEN, I mean the introduction of a new section: Côte d'Ivoire.

Rio itself is, as everyone says, in the most divine setting one could dream—really like a city in a dream with its peaked volcanic mountains, the great [statue of] Christ with arms outstretched on one of them (a truly moving sight), its endless variety of little bays and beaches and its "alabaster" look of giant white skyscrapers, all clean and bright from a distance. Actually on further thought, I came to the conclusion that it is a rather vulgar city—the 19th century architecture is just the same sort as the new only of that period, showy, without real distinction. The one good thing is the atmosphere of complete racial equality—and the way all these colors mix, play together, accept each other. But the gap between rich and poor is quite appalling—just back of the skyscrapers the "poor" live in the merest shacks with no running water at all on the steep hillsides. The transition was brought home to us when we were entertained at a country club on a "created" island near the city. A stone's throw away across about 20 feet of water was a colony of these utterly miserable peasant shacks. One felt very uncomfortable indeed.

I did have one marvelous afternoon when the Am. delegation took a bus high up into the perpendicular mountains to the fabulous eyrie where Elizabeth Bishop lives with her friend, a Brazilian whose pleasures seem to be building and then tearing down when she sees what she has designed wrongly! The house is in a tremendous site (halfway up a mountain) but did not to my mind seem to be a work of art—too pretentious—this is what I felt about Brazil in general. I liked Bishop better than I had expected to—she has a real <u>savor</u> as a personality, cool, humorous, shy, <u>real.</u> But I also felt a kind of stagnation in this life she leads, too rich somehow, too protected, like being a perpetual guest in someone <u>else's</u> life.

Well, I must stop, darling. How are you? I love to think of you on the island [Martha's Vineyard] these blessed days. Hasn't it been a wonderful July?

Love and love
M

The woodchucks: "[W]hoever said life in the country was quiet?" Sarton demanded, 2 July [1961], of friend Dorothy Wallace. "I feel in the midst of nature's <u>ferocity</u> and have just fired my first shot (<u>not</u> heard round the world, I hope!). The woodchucks have <u>returned</u> and eaten all the phlox for the X-th time. I tried a new device i.e. dried blood (literally) which you spread around your garden in a cordon sanitaire—they are supposed not to cross it but I saw a fat one not even stop to <u>sniff</u>, so that was no good. Yesterday I bought a 22 rifle—and feel like a pioneer woman as I stalk around looking for Indians and woodchucks and making loud bangs. The chances are so slight that I shall ever hit one that I have no guilt—I am convinced, since it terrifies <u>me</u> so, that the woodchucks <u>must</u> realize they are in dire trouble and so may leave. We shall see."

the Congress: The international group PEN (Publishers Essayists Novelists) held its Writers Congress in Rio de Janeiro, Brazil, 22 to 30 July 1960.

only one speech: Salvador de Madariaga y Rojo (1886–1978), Spanish writer and diplomat, "made the only good speech," Sarton wrote Rosalind Greene, 29 August 1960, "though I did not agree with his thesis (keep out the communist countries) as in an ass[ociation]. like this I felt it can do no harm to have them there—they were consistently voted down and might take reps back. In one case at least pressure from PEN helped get some Hungarian writers out of jail."

Macaulays: Anne and Robie Macauley. An author and teacher, he edited *The Kenyon Review.*

National Anthem!: In 1922 the Brazilian anthem's old music was given new words, *"Ouviram do Ipiranga as margens placidas"* ("A cry rang out from peaceful Ipiranga's banks").

Moravia: Italian novelist Alberto Moravia (1907–90).

Playwright Rice (1892–1967) was known for *The Adding Machine* (1923) and *Street Scene* (Pulitzer, 1929), basis for Kurt Weill's 1947 musical.

Côte d'Ivoire: Ivory Coast, Africa, declared independence from France in 1960.

Elizabeth Bishop: The American poet (1911–79) lived with architect and landscape designer Lota Costellat de Macedo Soares (1910–67) in a house Soares had designed at Samambaia, Petrópolis; she was involved in civil projects hampered by bureaucratic inconsistency. For Bishop's view of this visit ("I think everyone had rather a good time"), see her report to Robert Lowell, 27 July 1960, in *One Art: Letters,* ed. Robert Giroux (1994), pp. 387–88.

a perpetual guest: Bishop in turn had one reservation about Sarton. While admitting (to Lowell, as above) it might be nice to live out life in a lighthouse reading, "let us not say, to quote Miss S., 'I've fallen in love with solitude' "—one of the signature concepts for which Sarton is now renowned.

TO DOROTHY WALLACE   July 24th [1961]
at Nelson

Dorothy dear, I was amused that the Park Lane was not your dish (I wanted to ask you "Why not Brown's?" when you gave me the address)—I myself was there under most unhappy personal circumstances and thought they had perhaps colored my view, but I really thought it an awful place. I didn't want to prejudice you and the view was fine. (It was about 30 years ago, and then seemed to be full of rich travelling salesmen types et al). And I was delighted to hear what a good traveller Dan is— changing a tire, no less! Do give him my admiring congrats.

Ravens, of course! Thank you for reminding me. I am in deep mourning myself (speaking of birds) as I heard through my dreams a frantic yet feeble screaming of birds the other night and when I went down in the morning found that the phoebe nest had been robbed—no more sweet cheeping, no more dear tail-wagging parents on the phone wires and coming so close to me while I gardened that I could almost touch them. Silence. I must confess that I cried with the blow of it and the awful cruelty of nature. Now I wonder what could have done it—a snake? A rat? If Dan were here he could rig up some contraption to keep them out another time (the nest is under the eaves on the back porch).

It seems unbelievable that you are now a Greek! I shall be so eager to hear of the islands—of the weather. Is it very hot? Is the color as white and blue and brown as one imagines? I am furious that I do not have my modern translations from the Greek anthology here as there is one I wanted to send. Here, instead is an old favorite which you probably already know by heart:

> They told me, Heraclitus, they told me you were dead,
> They brought me bitter news to hear and bitter tears to shed.
> I wept as I remembered how often you and I
> Had tired the sun with talking and sent him down the sky.
>
> And now that thou art lying, my dear old Carian guest,
> A handful of gray ashes, long, long ago at rest,
> Still are thy pleasant voices, thy nightingales, awake;
> For Death, he taketh all away, but them he cannot take.
>   (Callimachus. Tr. by William Cory)

The awful typing is due to the fact that we are having the hottest and dampest day of the year so far—about 95 is my guess. I hope I am melting down like butter and will wake up tomorrow lean! I am certainly melting…

Well, to the news. The great event of these last days has been the Memorial show of Quig's paintings—how I wish you could have been there! In the first place Alex James's immense barn studio (the weathered boards turned <u>inside</u> like Hiawatha's mittens, skin side inside and fur side outside) is one of the most beautiful rooms I have ever seen—and Quig's paintings look splendid there—not a great painter perhaps, but one who could catch subtleties and nuances in a landscape (the inner face) as well as the landscape of a face— It was a long exciting day as Mildred, Barney, Helen Corsa, and I and Freddy James (Alex's widow) were all there from noon til after four—standing and propelling the hundred or more guests around. A friend of mine, Ellen Faulkner, bought one in the first half hour and a second sold that day with two or three more "considering"—so it has been a real success. It was an echt-Boston and New England affair, including a marvelous Irish biddy who has worked for the Jameses always and who told me "I love silver, copper, brass, and linen" (epitaph of an old-fashioned cleaning woman, if one put it in the past). Mildred looked lovely, so distinguished and <u>fine</u> and so perfectly herself in that rather "society" setting—ancient crones kept coming up and kissing me and making speeches "wonderful daughter of a wonderful father" said Mrs. Linden Smith (the dowager empress of Dublin)—I am always amused by the mixture of reserve and exaggeration in New Englanders—I must say that it was a huge relief to take off my dress and shoes when I got home and water the garden in bare feet. Social occasions have to be washed off me—I really loathe them. The show closes Wed—

This coming week-end is the dreaded one when ancient (83) Katharine Davis and friend come from Friday to Monday—I clutch lists of what they can and cannot eat (NO RHUBARB, NO mixture of tomato and cucumber etc) But anyway it will soon be over. Meanwhile the play creeps to its anti-climactic close. I think I have written myself out for a while so it is just as well that I am too tired to do very much these days—there will come a spurt I trust, before too long.

But it has been quite a six weeks—what with the Hopkins lecture (all done now, 24 typed pages) and also many letters to answer about the novel. It will be good to get up to Maine with Judy at the end of August—I intend to sleep almost all day as well as all night in that <u>cool</u> pine-y world.

Dearest one, a poor letter, but mine own, and bless you for your letters, so much harder to accomplish there than here—

Ever your May

Dorothy Wallace: Ardent philanthropist and patron of the arts Dorothy Colman Wallace (1913–2000), Vassar '33, was a lifelong student proud of having taken more Radcliffe Seminars than any other attendee. It was at one such 1956 course, conducted by Sarton, that the two women met when Wallace was 43 and mother of five. Here she is vacationing in Turkey and Greece with her thirteen-year-old son Dan; her husband had recently died. The Park Lane and Brown's were London hotels.

Greek anthology: Some four thousand poems of every genre, from the seventh century B.C. through the sixth A.D. This is a Victorian translation of the poet (c. 305–c. 240 B.C.) who cataloged the fabled library of Alexandria, Egypt.

the Memorial show of Quig's paintings: Sarton's Nelson neighbor and friend, Albert "Quig" Quigley, painter, stonecutter, photographer, fiddler, had died 23 January 1961; see "Death and the Maple," *Plant Dreaming Deep* (1968). For more about his artwork and his character, see "Quig, the Painter" in *A World of Light.* The show was held in Dublin, New Hampshire, at the home of the late Alexander James, son of Alice and William James, Jr. Those present included Quig's widow, Mildred, and the second of their three children, Barnabas (see 2 March 1968), and Wellesley English professor Helen Storm Corsa (see 6 August 1965).

the dreaded [weekend]: Davis came with her companion, Helen Chitty, and demands for food and drink at precise intervals precipitated a blowup. Sarton resolved, "I shall be all right when the psychic wounds heal." By 9 July 1962 Chitty had died, and Sarton wrote Davis: "It is absolutely horrendous about the will, after all you have done. . . . [P]eople are so damned rapacious when it comes to death. I saw it even when my father died and people (no relations) cheated me about his books—people who pretend to be 'old friends come to help.' I have never forgotten the bitter taste this greed left."

the play: On 14 June Sarton had begun *The Music Box Bird,* intended as a vehicle for Eva Le Gallienne, dealing with the complex emotions of four siblings coming home after their mother dies to divide up her property—in other words, with "money and its effects on people" (to Katharine Davis, 29 March 1961). Poet and playwright Archibald MacLeish (see 8 February 1962) read it and advised cutting the second act and completely reworking the third. On 27 July 1963, after the well at Nelson had "died a natural death," Sarton wrote him "[W]hat a peculiar joy it was to get right away from salmon cooking [for guests] and dragging pails of water around, and sit down and read your wonderful and exhilarating letter, . . . You are dead right, of course, . . . Since we met I have heard from the Ford people that I didn't get one of those (idiotic really) fellowships for novelists and poets who wish to write plays. My first feeling was relief." For the world premiere, see 26 October 1993.

the Hopkins lecture: Given at Johns Hopkins in Baltimore on 24 October, "The School of Babylon" discussed the "tension and equilibrium within the writing of poetry and within the poet's life." The university needed the manuscript early to have printed copies available. See *Writings on Writing* (Orono, Maine: Puckerbrush Press, 1980).

letters . . . about the novel: The cover of the 1995 Norton paperback describes *The Small Room* thus: "Anxiously embarking on her first teaching job, Lucy Winter arrives at a New England women's college and shortly finds herself in the thick of a crisis: she has discovered a dishonest act committed by a brilliant student who is the protégée of a powerful faculty member."

Anthropologist and author Ashley Montagu (see 2 October 1977) designated it "that rare thing, a perfect work of art. The human condition, here unfolded in the microcosm of a college campus, has never been more sensitively or more faithfully revealed." To Wallace, Sarton rejoiced, "Ashley is deluded but in the best possible way!" (2 July [1961])

TO KATHARINE WHITE   Sept. 7th, 1961

[Nelson]

Dear Katharine,

I'm sorry that I did not manage to answer your kind word sooner, as I wanted to tell you how sorry I am that you are not well (I gathered this from what you said about having time to read!) and how dearly I hope you will revive from whatever it is, and be your own glorious self (canning beans, being Mother Superior to a bevy of writers etc!) Meanwhile perhaps you have read my novel....

I am sorry I did not write sooner, because now this has to be a letter of farewell, a final letter, "finalizing," if that is the word, my relationship with the New Yorker, and hence, I must suppose, with you.

Dear Katharine, I am a realist. I am very well aware that snide, slick reviews such as the New Yorker gave my novel, pay off: most people enjoy a bad review much more than they enjoy a good one. Many of my so-called "friends" will be very happy because out of a hundred or so reviews from all over the country, <u>at last</u> this book is flayed. Failure is so much more gemütlich than success as I well know—I shall be well supported by my true friends. But I am a realist and I do know that review copies of books are passed out with some idea of what person and what book are in sympathy—a person who uses the word "female" in a pejorative sense (whether that person is male or female) will never give a book of mine a good review. So, someone <u>wanted</u> me to be kicked in the stomach and kicked in the stomach I was. I cannot but think that it is a pity to relegate such business to a monkey brain, for only a monkey brain would call a book "chilling" and "sentimental" in the same breath. But there it is. That review (I do not understimate the power your magazine exercises) will cost me a great deal: I have been publicly humiliated and I suppose cut down in sales by about 5000 copies.

I can make no defence. I am not even successful. I have just worked hard for 25 years at a craft. Outside provincial New York I seem, however, to have achieved something like a reputation. It is not large, but it is real. And it is dignified and self-respectful. More I have never asked.

Out of dignity and self-respect, and from the <u>small</u>, totally unimportant and quasi-unrecognized room in which I live and do my work, I must however take a stance. I am through with the New Yorker. You will not again need to notice me in any way. If there was some pretence that I was (for a brief time) "one of yours", the truth has now been made crystal clear. I never was. I am <u>not.</u> Passion and commitment "earnestness," uncamouflaged in my case by any wit or slickness, are not your dish. So be it. I have had over 100 letters from college professors (both male and female!) thanking God that someone at last is not snide about their profession— What are the values of the New Yorker anyway? This is a sorry business—

I am counting on the very long run. Although I am tired and middle-aged, I still count on it. I have never doubted for a moment that time is on my side, not on the monkey brains you hire to make your readers (who can afford to buy Rolls Royces) happy.

Goodbye and good luck, as they say.

May Sarton

Next day—I have re-read the review— Snide may be too strong a word—but at least the writer of it clearly cares not at all about the teaching profession—too bad. Forgive this outburst. I'll recover my equanimity in time, but I am angry—and I think with some reason—

---

a hundred or so reviews: The *Christian Science Monitor* called it "a mature novel that deals with questions of honesty and integrity" (24 August 1961), "graced with Sarton's fine-drawn insights" (*Kirkus Reviews,* 15 June 1961). Edward Weeks advised that "the concise economy of Miss Sarton's style is a delight to read" (*Atlantic,* January 1962), the *Saturday Review* concurring (26 August 1961): "for those who listen this novel speaks with an uncommon purity of pitch." In *The New York Times Book Review* (20 August 1961), Elizabeth Janeway found "the theme of the responsibility of the teacher to respond to her student's emotional needs as well as academic ones is superbly dealt with."

Gemütlich: German, "enjoyable, pleasant."

Only Sarton could say who "Many of my so-called 'friends' " were.

"one of yours": Despite the seven memoirs (see 30 March 1956) and one poem ("In Time Like Air") which *The New Yorker* had published, it does not seem that Sarton had any "first reading rights" agreement, such as the magazine offered authors appearing more frequently.

I have re-read the review: The brief unsigned notice, 2 September 1961, calls *The Small Room* an "absorbing but somewhat chilly novel" about "Lucy's initiation into the art and mystery of teaching." The main drawback lies in believing she "is predestined to be a great teacher, and that she has no honest choice but must exist in solitude and burn herself out in fires reserved for those who are martyred by their own genius or by their special facsimile of genius," because her only previous love affair resulted in the "abrupt and painful termination of her engagement to a young doctor." Her school, Appleton, would seem a fitting retreat for her, "peopled with clever older women," sensible and self-justified in their "monastic life," dedicated like Lucy "to a lifetime of teaching female college students." "As a commentary on the position of the intelligent university-educated woman in the modern world," the review concludes, the "book is sad, but the sadness is kept in check by the sentimental air that hangs, faintly yet uneasily, over the encounter."

White was *The New Yorker's* editor of fiction and poetry; it is not clear whether she had any foreknowledge of or control over reviews. Later this same year, after several decades' service, she retired. *The New Yorker* next published Sarton ("The House in Winter," a poem) on 4 January 1964.

TO ADA COMSTOCK NOTESTEIN   Oct. 29th, 1961
[Nelson]
Dear Ada Comstock Notestein,

I brought your dear letter up here (I try to get away every other week-end to catch my breath and bask a little in the village). I was so very happy and relieved to have it. It [*The Small Room*] was a kind of love letter to the profession of teaching, as you saw, but I was anxious both not to be snide (as so many novelists have been when dealing with college life) nor sentimental. I also was determined to stay within the college, and so made little of Lucy's love affair, though in a first version she was still very much involved with her young man. Some critics pounced on this lack of "love" but I think they were wrong; it seemed to me to split the focus. It has been very heartening to feel the response from friends of mine scattered all over the country in colleges where I have lectured; it was their opinion in this instance, and not so much that of critics in the usual sense of the word, that mattered most to me. But I had wondered whether, perhaps, you had just not liked the book, so I was simply delighted to hear. You are very good to have written Norton, as well, and even at this late date, when you might so easily have evaded that burden. I appreciate it mightily.

I am happy, too, that you singled out the first poem in Cloud, Stone, Sun, Vine. The novel has had a fine response and even a fine sale (much more astonishing), but I always feel that the poems are orphan children and I am rather nervous about their official appearance before the world on Nov. 13th. Yours was almost the first word I have had about them.

How lovely to have had five weeks in Italy! Oh, I forgot to say earlier on, that I guess the reason you became such a great administrator was just because you felt torn about leaving teaching. As I grow older and also see more and more of colleges in one way and another, I come more and more to appreciate you. In fact, I'm afraid you have become a touchstone, and that is hard on almost all other presidents! In some extraordinary way you never ceased to be yourself, as open as sunlight— one never felt the self-consciousness or the guardedness that power of this kind so often induces in those who wield it, and perhaps especially in women in administrative positions, alas. I feel privileged to have witnessed greatness in a college President (it must be even more rare than greatness in the arts!). But, lest you think, I am in any way referring to Radcliffe now, let me quickly add that I rejoice in Mrs. Bunting and all she is setting in motion. She seems a very fine choice indeed.

This letter is much too long, partly because I am rather exhausted. I love my teaching at Wellesley (two exciting seminars in creative writing with a dandy bunch of girls this year), and it is a perfect set-up for me also because I have only one semester a year there. That means that I can come up here and work or take off as I shall do in March—to celebrate my 50th birthday by a five-months trip around the world—Japan, India, Greece and home by Europe!

Blessings on you, dear Ada Comstock, and please forgive this inadequate answer to a letter which was a real event in my life.

Ever your
May

Ada [Louise] *Comstock Notestein:* 1876–1973; see note to 22 May 1955. At this time Comstock was 85.

dealing with college life: Cora DuBois likened it to *The Masters* (1951) by realist British novelist C. P. Snow (1905–80): "[T]hey both certainly make one feel the horror of the academic life and its futility." Sarton protested to Dorothy Wallace, 2 July [1961], "[N]othing could be farther from what I intended!"

By 6 May 1976, Sarton asked her bibliographer, Lenora P. Blouin, "Did I tell you that Norton is re-issuing The Small Room in paperback this autumn..at the request of several colleges who will assign it to classes," and of her many reissues it "seems to be doing the best" (11 September 1986, *After the Stroke: A Journal* [1988], p. 141). The book can be read, Nancy Porter wrote in 1994 (*Women's Studies Quartlerly* 22, No. 1–2), "as a stimulating presentation of some of the issues and realities female faculty [still] face now." Given concern about student plagiarism, the novel has become a standard text nationwide to prompt debate over academic integrity.

Cloud, Stone, Sun, Vine: This "Selected," as Sarton often dubbed it, opens with "Prayer before Work," followed by extracts from all six previous volumes grouped under eight themes, concluding with "A Divorce of Lovers" and seven poems about Nelson. Katharine Davis read that sequence in manuscript; Sarton replied (29 March 1961), "[T]he originality of these sonnets is their honesty and their 'modern' approach to age-old human problems" and "What you don't like is what I consider its strength."

Louise Bogan found the sequence too "discursive" rather than "dramatic," and thought "it should be clear[er] that your sonnets are written to a woman." "Otherwise, I think that the book *marches;* proceeds; opens out," and specifically praised "Humpty Dumpty," "Somersault," "The Phoenix," "The Furies," "What the Old Man Said," and "These Pure Arches" (*What the Woman Lived,* 31 October 1961). "On the whole, you have a *metaphysical* bent; you desire the universal behind the apparent; you have a passion for the *transcendent,*" she concluded, feeling "that your *big, unrelenting, drastic* poems (*life or death*) are to come."

teaching at Wellesley: Sarton taught poetry writing one term a year—the springs of 1960 and 1961, and the autumns of 1961–63.

real event in my life: In October 1965 Notestein, writer Kay Boyle, and Archibald MacLeish sponsored Sarton for a Radcliffe Institute fellowship, but "I did not seem to be in dire enough need." When the refusal was "explained," "I found the fog so dense that I could not even see my own shadow," she wrote Notestein (8 March 1966), thanking her for her efforts.

TO ERIC P. SWENSON   Dec. 25th, 1961
[Wright Street]
Dear Eric,

I warned you (and myself) but I must confess that Mr. Shapiro has done a little worse than even I expected—I feel as if I had had a bad <u>physical</u> blow. I feel just plain sick to my stomach. But I suppose one recovers. I am only sorry for you and for all the trouble taken—and for me, too, and 20 years work, so hardly treated. However, I have an idea that the very harshness may make some people feel prejudice of some sort at work—a lukewarm accolade might have been even worse.

This is also to say that from Dec. 27th to Jan 4th I shall be at R.F.D. Munsonville in case any good news should come up!

Love
May

Eric P. Swenson: Rinehart had published Sarton since 1948. When they did nothing to promote *The Birth of a Grandfather* (1957), her agent Diarmuid Russell (son of Irish poet AE) urged her to seek another firm. "I am very reluctant to write the break-off letter," she told Evelyn Ames in early 1958. "I know now, as I didn't immediately after my father's death, that that event has made some immense split in my inner life." While Rinehart did issue *I Knew a Phoenix* in spring 1959, *The Small Room* (dedicated to Russell) and *Cloud, Stone, Sun, Vine* were her first titles with W. W. Norton, who remain her major publishers to this day. For most of the rest of her career, her editor was Eric P. Swenson (b. 1919), whom she had met while on the faculty at Bread Loaf and who remained a staunch friend.

Mr. Shapiro: Poet Karl Shapiro (1913–2000) received the 1944 Pulitzer for *V-Letter,* having won *Poetry*'s Levinson Prize in 1942 (as Sarton did in 1994), before editing *Poetry* 1950–56. He served as Consultant in Poetry at the Library of Congress, 1947–48 (forerunner of today's Poet Laureate); in 1956, having moved to the University of Nebraska, he began editing *Prairie Schooner.*

After writing an *Essay on Rime* (1945), coauthoring *A Prosody Handbook* (with Robert Beum, 1965), and being esteemed for his command of poetic forms, Shapiro turned savagely against such formal constraints in the preface and bitter prose poems of *The Bourgeois Poet* (1964), as Louise Bogan noted (see *A Poet's Alphabet,* 1970, pp. 368–71). At the time of this letter his most recent book was the essay collection *In Defense of Ignorance* (1960). His 24 December 1961 *New York Times Book Review* piece included these remarks on *Cloud, Stone, Sun, Vine:*

> "It is pointless to be cruel about bad poetry, but sometimes there is no escape. Whatever May Sarton's other accomplishments as a writer, she is a bad poet.... Her poetry is lady-poetry at its worst—this at a time when poetry is very much the art of women.... Her poems are personal in the sense that the reader is invited to participate in the higher life, as tourists visit the house of the Duke of Bedford. But ... her high literary attitudes (Rilke and Yeats) are only hastily mastered techniques duly applied for the occasion—I am sorry to say this. I apologize."

By 27 January 1962 Sarton had "almost recovered," she informed Jean Burden. The 21 January *New York Times Book Review* had carried excerpts of five letters on her behalf, from Helen Storm Corsa, Doyle Hennessy (Brooklyn), Judith Matlack, Nyleen Morrison

(Concord, New Hampshire), and Basil de Sélincourt (see 17 October 1964). "Anyway, let us rejoice that we <u>are</u> poets—I am so dying to get back to poems I can hardly wait!"

R.F.D. Munsonville: In pre–zip code days, the Nelson mailing address. At this period, before *Journal of a Solitude* or even *Plant Dreaming Deep,* she could report (to Burden, as above) having written, "as I have done for the last [few] weeks, roughly ten letters a day."

TO JOHN HOLMES   Feb. 8th, 1962
[St. Charles, Mo.]
Dear John,

I am having a wonderful time here, in a college [Lindenwood] with a very <u>warm</u> and self-questioning Eng. Dept. (at Wellesley it may be self-questioning but it is not warm—at least to an outsider like me) and I feel useful, despite great fatigue, and happy and alive. So it is a good time to sit down in this big white room in a little old brick house (St. Charles has the Mississippi at its feet and is a charming old town of small houses)—to sit down and try to answer your letter.

Before I begin let me say that Judy looked up some old calendars and found that we did meet at least once in our place at 139 Oxford St. on Feb. 18th, 1949, to be exact. At Wright St. I have some folders with specific poems we read (at least those we handed around—Eberhart if I remember never did give us copies!) which may be of factual help. I'll take a look at them before March 4th and send you what I have.

I must first say that I was hugely relieved to have you say that you also felt woe, and condescension about your poems—all my defences got pierced, and that I had each time to remake my faith in myself—<u>but</u> that I also learned a Hell of a lot and would not have missed the fruitful pain for the world. On looking back, I seem to feel that very few of us (you and I perhaps alone) were looking for or could use criticism. And I believe it is tragic that Eberhart could not, but that Wilbur <u>was</u> "untouchable" as you say. His [Eberhart's?] poems had been refined and often would have been greatly improved (a silly word) if he had been willing occasionally to listen. I see him, smiling and beneficent, arriving with his gigantic briefcase packed with poems, all of which he would have liked to read, none of which he wanted to be criticized! I remember especially his reading the poem about all the women he had loved and how stunning I thought it was, and a poem of Wilbur's about autumn, and "Listen-citizen sparrow," and your Montaigne.

I must now confess that my first feeling about those gatherings is guilt—guilt about a specific occasion and poem. The occasion was at your house, Ciardi, Wilbur and Eberhart (I think) all there. It was when Ciardi read his poem about Dante, to Dante, which has a long epigraph quote from the <u>Inferno,</u> about the man who was pushed into the mud.

And is a plea, written in a rather sassy tone, for compassion. I think it is a stunning poem and I have since often read it to audiences—at the time it hit me hard but I reacted with anger. And I remember saying to John, "You can't do that!" and getting really into a rage about it. I was so ashamed afterwards, and think perhaps that is the root of Ciardi's unwillingness to accept me or my work as a poet. If so, it was my fault. Strangely enough, it has happened to me more than once to react with anger to both works of art and to people whom I later came to love. My tone was arrogant on that occasion. Perhaps we each have our arrogance and have to have it: mine, perhaps, has been that I have values, a skill of feeling that John in his violent power and crudeness often lacks. Eberhart's was, of course, that poetry is divine inspiration and that he is inhabited by a gust of genius which does not require him to fashion what comes to him. (I remember on one occasion that he had written five poems the night before!) Wilbur's was, perhaps, that he was the complete artificer who has achieved perfection—he may be right in this, but I have (a perhaps arrogant) feeling now that it also may be his Achilles' heel—i.e. he got there at the very beginning, but may in the years to come grow less than you and I have done and will do, so that his genius, wholly arrived, has in a queer way completely jelled too soon. I felt that his last book showed this—nothing more has happened to him as a craftsman because essentially he reached maturity at about 25 (it is the worst fate for an artist that I can imagine.) This may seem irrelevant—I write what comes to mind as I sit here.

What were our true feelings about each other? I imagine that the reason the pain was bearable was that whatever we suffered, we gathered in mutual respect, that we considered each other equals, or at least that we all thought all of us were true poets. That is why it came as such a bitter blow when John did not include me in the mid-century poets. I could not, after that, have met him in the same way or been willing to take his criticism. I realized that he did not respect me and never had, and that was to make all those evenings much worse in retrospect, even than they had been at the time. I had exposed myself to contempt without knowing it.

I do believe that Dick Eberhart, you and I, felt real respect for each other. I am not at all sure about Dick Wilbur, younger and already more "arrived" than any of us at that time, even possibly Eberhart. I am sure that John had great respect (as well as love) for you, and for the two Dicks (I wrote ducks!)—was it so painful partly because we were acting out in that small room each time, the desperate attempt to "get through" that all poets feel most of the time, here in the intense small group which was really an image of the world. Only here we met it face to face, the bafflement, the ache, the self-doubt, the self-discipline it required to sit still and sometimes be told the hard truth, sometimes not kindly uttered. The amazing thing to me is that we kept on meeting for so long at least three years I think? At one point Gray Burr sometimes attended, and once a man whose name I have forgotten who was rather chi-chi (quite well known)—I have it, Byron Vazakas. I remember veto-ing the idea that MacLeish might join us (I think I was wrong—he might have gentled the atmosphere) my fear then was that the balance would be wrong, and that he was too famous and too much our elder to appear as other than a teacher, and that we probably did not respect his poetry enough to respect this, yet would have hesitated to hurt him by criticizing him. (Am I right in that?)

[unsigned]

John Holmes: 1904–62. Poet and critic, he taught at Tufts and directed the Chautauqua Writers' Workshop. He reviewed three of Sarton's early books of poems, calling *Inner Landscape* "a passionately real record of life, of inner life and a woman who has found her-self, and is recommended as being among the really few excellent books of the season." (*Boston Evening Transcript,* 1 March 1939) His most recent collection was *The Fortune Teller* (1961). For previous correspondence, see *Letters 1916–54.* The "poetry group" Sarton ana-lyzes met for three winters during the late 1940s.

Eberhart: Poet Richard Eberhart (b. 1904) took degrees at Cambridge and Harvard; served in the Navy during World War II; worked in business; taught widely; published a long series of poetry collections, starting in 1930. Consultant in Poetry at the Library of Congress, 1959–61.

Wilbur: Poet and professor Richard Wilbur (b. 1921) is known for his mastery of complex verse forms and his actable idiomatic rhyming translations of Racine and Molière. He con-tributed witty lyrics to Leonard Bernstein's *Candide* (1956). Sarton "played fairer than the rest of us," Wilbur recalled, 20 August 1991; "she took criticism seriously, and often appeared at our meetings with poems which had been rewritten and bettered." (Quoted in the introduction to *A House of Gathering: Poets on May Sarton's Poetry,* ed. Marilyn Kallet [Univ. of Tennessee Press, 1993], p. 17.) Sarton refers to his poems "In the Elegy Season" and "Still Citizen Sparrow," from *Ceremony* (1950); his most recent collection was *Advice to a Prophet* (1961).

Ciardi: Poet John Ciardi (1916–86) served sixteen years as *Saturday Review* poetry editor and directed Bread Loaf for seventeen years. He taught at Harvard and Rutgers; *How Does a Poem Mean?* (1959) became a standard classroom text. Ciardi is most widely known for his annotated translation of Dante's *Divine Comedy,* published as a work in progress, 1954–71; complete version, W. W. Norton, 1977.

the mid-century poets: Ciardi's anthology *Mid-Century American Poets* appeared in 1950 (Twayne). It included Wilbur, Peter Viereck, Muriel Rukeyser, Theodore Roethke, Shapiro, Winfield Townley Scott, John Frederick Nims, E. L. Mayo, Robert Lowell, Randall Jarrell, Holmes, Eberhart, Elizabeth Bishop, and Ciardi himself.

Commissioned for the Henry Regnery series "Twentieth Century Literature in America," Louise Bogan's *Achievement in American Poetry 1900–1950* (Chicago, 1951)—a 111-page historical survey, with 32 pages of poetry—does not mention Sarton. Eberhart and MacLeish appear in passing; Wilbur, Moore, and Shapiro (among many others) have poems.

Invited to guest-edit the first issue of the *Beloit Poetry Journal,* Fall 1950, Sarton's "Foreword" warns that "Absolute statements about poetry make me angry. . . . A literate person who cares for poetry should recognize . . . many kinds of poetry have value." But the poets and poems she chose all had "the power to seize my imagination and take me into themselves," including, among others, Holmes, Eberhart, and Ciardi.

Byron Vazakas: 1905–87. He lectured at Harvard; was a friend of MacLeish and William Carlos Williams, who wrote the preface to his first collection, *Transfigured Night* (1947); and spent most of his later life in Reading, Pennsylvania.

MacLeish: Archibald MacLeish (1892–1982) served in World War I, started publishing poetry in 1917, gave up his legal practice to write in 1923, served as Librarian of the Congress (1939–44) and in various government posts (including Assistant Secretary of State, 1944–45), was a Harvard professor (1949–62), and wrote in many genres, including verse drama (*J.B.,* 1958, his third Pulitzer). Sarton first met him at a 1934 party (including Gershwin and Dalí) for the opening of the ballet in Hartford, Connecticut, where her theatre company, then called Associated Actors, was playing. See *Letters 1916–54*, p. 99.

Am I right in that?: Holmes died only a few months later, 22 June 1962.

TO ERIC P. SWENSON   May 7th, 1962
[On board the *SS Delos* to the Greek Islands]
Dear Eric,

Muriel [Rukeyser] sent me a cable for my birthday (50th, May 3rd) and I find I don't have her address. Could you very kindly stamp this card and send it along to Macmillan, adding their address? I hope it will not be the last straw on a busy day.

I am now rather like a boa constrictor who has swallowed one continent too many! Or like a woman who has plunged recklessly into three love affairs at once...Japan, India, now Greece. I took to my bed in sheer emotion at the <u>light</u> when I got here from the fetid heat of Bombay, but am now resuscitated. The trouble is that I am jammed full of impressions and have no time yet to get them down. I look forward mightily to the second half of this journey which begins on the 20th at I Tatti in Florence. There I shall sit in my room and think for hours and hours, I hope.

Do tell me any news. Is the second printing on the poems out? Will there be some more money coming in eventually on The Small Room? I gather that except for TLS the reviews in England took the opportunity to attack Am. education rather than reading the book, but I have not seen them and couldn't care less. I am much too busy at the moment with NOW.

Love from
May

I miss my typewriter—this is a communal one.

———

I Tatti in Florence: After the death of American art connoisseur Bernard Berenson (1865–1959), his villa became an outpost of Harvard; Sarton was the guest of the directors, Eleanor and Kenneth Murdock, professor of American literature at Harvard. He and F. O.

Matthiessen had edited Henry James's working notebooks, 1947; Sarton dedicated *Faithful Are the Wounds* to the Murdocks.

"Life here is very formal," Sarton wrote Katharine Davis, 30 May 1962. "Lady Berkeley (a former Lowell from Boston, married to Lord B. of B. square in London) to lunch, an illiterate old woman, with houses all over Italy; tonight a dinner party. I have no proper clothes, especially as it has been v. cold and find the very rich on the whole very dull. . . . Up here at the top of the house with a superb view over olive groves, cypresses and red roofs and the distant blue hills around Florence, I have a bedroom and study and vast bathroom across the hall. And I have tried valiantly to work"—perhaps on the travel poems in the first section of *A Private Mythology* (1966).

the reviews in England: The Times Literary Supplement (30 March 1962) said, "This novel is as just and scrupulous as a sonnet," while *Punch* (11 April 1962), echoing Cora DuBois, likened it to C. P. Snow.

TO CAMILLE MAYRAN   le 25 juin, au soir [1962]
[Le Pignon Rouge]   [Passages in French]
Dearest Marianne,

I wish I could recapture <u>now</u> the intense emotion and joy of all the hours after I left you, as I drove through the <u>Var</u>, and felt poems welling up—and tasted all the wonderful treasures of those days at the Mas, remembering each hour and turning it over in my heart and mind. The angels were with me as I turned off the road and climbed up a hill to a tiny village (Fox-Amphoux) where I happened on a perfect auberge— small, beautiful, with a little terrace looking down over fields, wild flowers on the table—and where I began to make notes furiously, as I ate my lunch. I drove on to Vence and there also found a quiet place—an immense terrace looking down over hills and the Mediterranean—and there I stayed the night and worked all the next morning at a poem. Somehow it has not quite come out as I hoped—but perhaps tomorrow morning I can work at it again. At any rate, I'll put this word in the mail so you will know that I am safely here.

At last we had time to truly know each other—time to talk of the past, to bring back to life the <u>spirit</u> of Pierre Hepp. I came away from those few days dazzled by the tiny flame inside you, so real and so very pure, which always flashes out again after so much anguish, so many losses—how wonderful you are, my friend! And I can see you alone, at night, on the broad terrace with all the countryside at your feet, considering the stars (I was haunted all that last night, until the moon went down, by this line from [Charles] Baudelaire—"Listen, my beloved, hear the tender night advance," since I was so fully conscious of your <u>presence</u> below, and the perfect communion of our hearts across that total silence)—and I can see you that morning, reading Pascal at dawn, and perhaps writing something deeply <u>thought</u>, after your morning tea. It's impossible to <u>explain</u> how all that makes me seem to live beside you—to feel the wellsprings of my life slowly being reborn—poetry itself—thanks to how permeated I feel by the ambience of you and your precious Mas.

Everything about those days was rich—I recall the benevolent impressions of the variety of human lives you showed me—the two sisters in their ancient house, Maurie Mauron, the bourgeois vine-planter who has found his true calling far from the factories, the Bellinos, and that outsized woman with the rough voice but <u>kind</u> face, who came to help out in the garden. But most of all I recall our two walks out on the heights, making for the towers—the first night and the last, thyme beneath our feet, with the rice fields reflecting the heavens here below—the skies patterned like silk, the rock slabs where we lay down. All of that stirs within me—and <u>reverberates</u> like music. And I recall as well our simple, perfect meals.

Here I'm in the room I always have—and I look out on the orchard below where two white pigeons stroll on velvet grass. Never have I seen this garden (always a poem) so beautiful. We had tea yesterday under the apple trees—accompanied by Franz the goose and his wife, two brown ducks, a little rooster, a grey guinea hen, two dogs, and the Persian cat—my mother's best friend, now seventy-nine although she looks sixty, oversees this little world like an abbess (I'm in the middle of reading <u>Les Deux Mondiales</u>—very striking)—I feel at the deepest level the hold Europe has on my being.

And so—how can I return thanks for your being <u>yourself</u>? For that has been the great revelation of these past few days for me. Thank you, dear dazzling heart, for the <u>light</u> you shed.

That's really all that I can say. Unfortunately I arrive here with a hideous migraine (the result, I think, of the change in pressure in the plane, a terrific heat-wave then a chill wind, plus the time-change) and got a phone call <u>at one in the morning</u> from New York (!), a friend who had just broken up with his partner and wept—from Oxford, another friend also in distress, and a Swiss woman (I don't know who, since she never called back after having tried to reach me just before my arrival)—then a pile of letters which I must answer—I've spent the whole day trying to dispatch all these human responsibilities before getting back to the poem, tomorrow.

June 26
And here is the first version of the poem I worked so hard on, but which is not yet altogether <u>there</u>. Alas! ["Joy in Provence"]
With great tenderness

from your
May

Camille Mayran: Mme. Pierre Hepp ("Marianne"), 1889–1989. French writer; winner of the Prix Femina-Vie Heureuse for her novel *Dame en Noir* and the Prix du Roman de L'Académie Française for *Histoire de Gotton Connixloo, Suivie de L'Oubliée* (see *At Seventy: A Journal,* p. 86, on the latter). Sarton first met her at the Huxleys', in 1938 or 1939; though they saw each other rarely, they became intimate through letters about their respective work.

Mas: Although Mayran lived in Strasbourg, she had a *mas* (French, "farmstead"), Mas du Planète, Bouches du Rhône, St. Gabriel-par-Tarasçon in France.

Pierre Hepp: Camille Mayran's husband, whose death resulted in part from "the too hard labor expended in trying to rescue part of his library from the rubble" of the Mayran family home in Tarasçon, destroyed by American bombers. See *At Seventy,* pp. 282–84.

my mother's best friend: Sarton was visiting Céline Limbosch at the family home near Brussels, where she had stayed as a girl. See the poem "Franz, a Goose" (1959) and, for a photo of Le Pignon Rouge, *Endgame,* p. 31.

Les Deux Mondiales: French, this (partial?) title might refer to "The Two World Wars."

TO LOUISE BOGAN   Sept. 4th, 1962
[Nelson]

> "Noli me tangere; for Caesar's I am,
> And wild for to hold, though I seem tame."

Dear Louise,

It is good to think that you too are seeing the autumn light on the fields, the long shadows—I am tired from writing you so many letters in my head. This time perhaps I shall mail what has troubled me for long.

We have known each other now for quite some time. It began when I wrote you in <u>1944</u> (I think) and asked you to read poems at the Public Library in N.Y. and you said you could not appear in public—that is how long ago it was! Then I was angered when Radcliffe did not get you the audience you should have had some ten years later. I did what I could about that. It is the poet whom I love, as you know. So we entered upon a friendship, begun as more than that on my side, but fruitful and dear at any rate for many a year since then.

But I am now clearing the decks for some years of true inward work and I sense the stresses of it more than ever before. In this state I find that I have to be careful. I shall not bore you with a long lament about my position in the <u>world</u> of poetry: it is certainly a peculiar one. But I have no doubts about my position in relation to <u>myself</u> as an instrument for poetry (for better or worse, and whether I ever 'succeed' or not). I find, for instance, that the Shapiro review coming as it did after such a long sustained struggle (20 years of it) did break some spirit in me. No doubt in the long run I shall see that this was right—that I had to withdraw whatever little antennae had been out towards the world of poetry, that I had to "give up" once and for all the hope that I might be <u>heard.</u> The hardest thing I have ever had to do was to read poems shortly afterward at Rutgers. But I did it, and I shall be able always to do it now. In this way my poems do not altogether go unheard. They are read, as the three editions of the selected [*Cloud, Stone, Sun, Vine*] show. They are read and they are heard, though not by the critics; they are even celebrated here and there, though not by the anthologists. Many people never have even that consolation. I do not really complain, but I have come to see that I cannot afford to expose myself at all in places and among people where the <u>world</u> of poetry operates. This is a neurosis, if you will. Neuroses are always defences, I suspect. I have to defend myself somehow against rage and despair (those two sides of the same coin).

Now the troubling thing is that you are my dear poet, but you are also—alas—a critic. I find that this makes for ambivalence in my feelings toward you, and even hostility. When the Shapiro thing came out, I wrote you, "The hardest thing to bear is that I shall not be defended." I meant defended by my peers. And I was right. Save for Basil de Sélincourt, voice practically from the tomb.

You told me once that Babette Deutsch (whose work you do not really respect, or so you have said) badgered you into getting her into the Academy. I have never in my life approached anyone of influence to work on my behalf, and I never will. This is pride, false pride perhaps. But if this pride implies choices, as I suppose it does, then I have to choose not to see people of influence because it is just too upsetting. That whole miasma rises up and blurs the relationship.

What to do? I felt that the only thing was to be honest with you and tell you that I have to suspect you as a critic, or cease to believe in my own work.

I am a wounded bear, my dear, and I just must go on somehow and not be prevented from what I can do. When I see you, the wounds begin to bleed and I want to roar with misery. I can't help it.

> "I leave off therefore,
> Since in a net I seek to hold the wind."

But to the poet, most loving greetings,

Your
May

I've begun a poem on the great <u>Indian</u> plain ["The Great Plain of India Seen from the Air"]—

"Noli me tangere: This letter opens and closes with lines from "Whoso List to Hunt," by Sir Thomas Wyatt (English, 1503–42). The sonnet delineates the speaker's frustration at striving but failing to capture a hind; about its neck, "graven with diamonds in letters plain," are these two lines which cite, out of context, the words Christ speaks to ward off Mary Magdalene after His resurrection: "Touch me not" (John 20:17).

it began ... in 1944: Sarton and Bogan's first brief exchange was in April 1940 (*Letters 1916–54,* pp. 164–65; *What the Woman Lived,* p. 207). On 15 February 1953, Sarton gave Bill Brown a lively exasperated account of the Radcliffe reading (*Letters 1916–54,* p. 332), lamenting that only "about 30 people showed up—most of them my students at that." Sarton never wavered in her belief that, as Elizabeth Bowen phrased it, "One must regard oneself impersonally as an instrument." (20 November 1974, *The House by the Sea: A Journal* [1977], p. 28)

Babette Deutsch: See note to 29 September [1957]. A decade earlier, Bogan's estimation was not so harsh: she wrote a promotional "remark" for Deutsch's critical survey *Poetry in Our Time,* a very rare favor (*What the Woman Lived,* 23 March 1952).

In the Winter 1954 *Yale Review* (43), Deutsch said of *The Land of Silence:* "The lack in these poems seems to be due to Sarton's inability to be severe with herself." That same volume found Bogan, in *The New Yorker,* highlighting Sarton's "mature power of recognizing the heart of the matter and expressing it in memorable terms" (27 February 1954).

When *In Time Like Air* appeared, Bogan—in her sole other published review of Sarton's work—contended that she "does not subject her material to the crucial tensions usual in modern poetry, but it would be a mistake to place her at a remove from the moderns, since her wit and insight are sharply complementary, while her subject matter is . . . timeless. . . . She is contemplative and exploratory." (*The New Yorker,* 22 March 1958)

Just as the notice for *The Land of Silence* was not retained for *Selected Criticism* (1955), so this one was not added to *A Poet's Alphabet: Reflections on the Literary Art and Vocation,* ed. Robert Phelps and Ruth Limmer (published posthumously, 1970), which included the previous volume and significant writings since; Bogan had approved the choice of contents.

the Academy: As a distinguished elite of fifty or fewer members selected from the National Institute of Arts and Letters, the American Academy of Arts and Letters at this time had few women members. In 1969 only two of nine were poets, Bogan and Marianne Moore. See *What the Woman Lived,* 10 May 1969.

most loving greetings: Bogan's 6 September 1962 response did not explain why she had not protested the Shapiro review or grapple other issues raised here. She regretted that her professional side dominated Sarton's view of her and predicted that "we shall be poet-friends (or just human friends) once again. Get all the bear into your work! Get all the bitterness too. That's the place for it"—yet another conviction about which the two poets differed.

Why Bogan would not state more often in print what she told Sarton about her poetry in private is difficult to determine. Perhaps her reluctance stemmed from a concern that, should she give praise once to someone so attached to her emotionally, she would be expected to do so henceforth.

TO ROBERT FROST   Jan. 16th, 1963
[Wright Street]
Dear Robert,

I had the pleasure of meeting a man who sees you every day (your anesthetist) the other night, so I got it from the horse's mouth that they are having a hard time keeping you down—no surprise to me, I may say. Anyway it occurred to me that I would do my bit in preventing you from rushing around by sending you this little sketch of my father. It might absorb your interest for a few minutes...I remember that you read the Greek science book. In it he is rather hard on Plato and you will see a certain mellowing in this respect, in some quotes from the journals.

I was happy about the Bollingen. Some honors are nicer than others. Ever so much love, dear Robert,

from
May

Robert Frost: Shortly before 15 July 1928, budding poet May told her mother that Agnes Hocking of Shady Hill School had promised "Next time Robert Frost comes to Cambridge she is going to have me meet him. Isn't that exciting?"

For a later encounter, see *Letters 1916–54,* 19 March 1954, written to Frost on the eve of his eightieth birthday banquet at Amherst. "I enjoyed myself in a feminine guise," she wrote Bogan (27 March [1954]); "it was enjoyable to look pretty and to be almost the only woman among 100 men." But "There was a good deal of 'standing in awe' all through the proceedings," which made the occasion memorable but "sad": "I felt terribly sorry for Frost, his lonely eminence."

"Tomorrow night," she wrote Katharine Davis on 22 March 1958, "I have the nerve-wracking chore of introducing Robert Frost in Sanders Theatre to the Harvard students—it is rather like introducing God and I have been lying awake at night worrying about how to do it gracefully."

this little sketch of my father: "An Informal Portrait of George Sarton," *Texas Quarterly,* V. No. 3 (Autumn 1962); reprinted in *A World of Light.* Frost had recently read *Hellenistic Science and Culture in the Last Three Centuries B.C.,* which George Sarton had completed just before his death in 1956.

the Bollingen: Frost, the most acclaimed poet of his time, learned on 3 January 1963 that he had won the Bollingen Prize for poetry; Bogan and Richard Eberhart were on the five-member committee. On 7 January he had suffered a pulmonary embolism, not his first.

Ever so much love: Born 26 March 1874, Frost died 29 January 1963.

On 3 February Sarton wrote a note of condolence to writer and Bread Loaf director Theodore Morrison and his wife, Kathleen, Frost's lifelong friends. His passing was "as if some cliff had fallen into the sea. I found myself more moved than I had expected, and in tears when I read somewhere that R.F. 'had a long poem running through his head'——now out somewhere in space where we shall never read it."

TO CAMILLE MAYRAN   10 February [1963]
[Nelson]   [Portions in French]
Dearest Marianne,

I do believe that's the name which fundamentally suits you best...by the way, that "R.F.D." in my address means "Rural Free Delivery" and the farmer who's also the "mailman" here brings me, along with letters, cigarettes or milk if I need them. This place is so humane! I've been here alone for a week—a very cold week (several nights it's been twenty below), and the house makes extraordinary thunder-like noises due to the cold. Would you believe, the nails pop out of the walls (the whole place is wood) with bursts like gunshots. Was I ever startled! I feed hundreds of birds and a very wild cat who looks me straight in the eyes from just the other side of the window-pane, then runs if I open the door— but he comes back later to eat what I put outside for him. Everything that dares to stir, in this world of ice and snow, becomes very dear; you watch everything warm-blooded with bewildered tenderness—how can they survive, the birds, the squirrels, the cats?

But always the transition from my out-going world to this inner one is difficult—and this time I have had a stupid week because of a sort of grippy cold, and also endless ennuis with my car—which has become a sort of cranky beast in my mind—but I have spent hours and hours waiting in dank garages while one thing after another was replaced—now, at last, I think the beast must feel better—anyway it did start today. On other days I have had to be towed several miles—all the men carry chains in their cars to help each other out in this village, so one is always helped.

Anyway I have worked hard and well at the little childish donkey book, and I have begun to feel the detachment, the timelessness of this place for me...as if slowly the immediate tensions relaxed.

How grateful I was to have your letter—to be reminded of Joubert (to have this link between you and me, for Joubert is one of the two or three people I really want to <u>know</u>, to have as a friend, if there were a Heaven where this might be possible—Joubert and Tchekov).

But I have not begun to write this evening, in the silence, really to speak of me or of you, but of Noémie and this really intolerable burden that she carries ... May I speak quite honestly? I know I may, but I hesitate. I have been on both sides of this sort of relationship myself. I was always "in love" with my teachers and I am sure that I asked an awful lot of them—not to the point of this poor girl, who is in a sort of madness, but still, I know the <u>flame</u>, how it burns and how it aspires and how it really destroys. I do not believe that it is really <u>kind</u> to allow a flame like this to go on devouring the air which it needs to live. It was Volta Hall who said to me once in a situation not wholly unlike Noémie's "It is a bottomless pit. The more love you pour in, the deeper the pit becomes." And the more demands there are! There is no "love" of the kind that poor child wants except between equals. So I feel that what Noémie has to do, however cruel it may <u>seem</u> is to be frank, to say, "You are devouring me and I cannot give you what you need." Begin at least to see her <u>less</u> rather than more often, not answer letters. Be brutally honest. "The only way I can help you in your life is to detach you from me"—any bread that she's able to offer will never satisfy this starveling. Such is the truth as I see it. On the contrary: crumbs only leave this half-crazed girl even hungrier. It is just here that I feel religion and the <u>willed</u> religious attitude can become a romantic delusion...one does not really give anything worth having if one gives only out of pity. I really can't bear to think of Noémie being literally exhausted by this girl. It is wrong from every angle. It is wrong for the girl, because it simply excites her more and more after a false god—false because nothing can be built on a purely one-sided relationship. The only answer that can be made to such passions is, "some people never feel so deeply. For you who do, there is a great responsibility not to make your feeling a burden. Life itself will one day give you the chance to give to someone else what you wish to give to me."

I know that this sounds cruel, but in the long run, it is kind. Someone has to <u>break</u> the tension and only Noémie can do this by being apparently cruel. Curiously enough, my experience has been that the facing of reality, the shock of it, sometimes at least becomes a sort of relief. Noémie has gone as far as anyone could and that has not worked. Now I feel that she has to confront reality with this girl. The worst thing the girl has done is to use her conversion as a "force majeure," unconsciously of course, but it is none the less (to my way of thinking) a sin. The true way of sublimation must be outside the relationship itself. Religion, yes, but not to go to Mass together! You will think I am very cruel, but I know what I am talking about, believe me. Quite unconsciously the girl tries to induce <u>guilt</u> in Noémie. "I ask nothing, only to be with you" etc. But all the time she <u>is</u> asking a great deal and taking a great deal, with no right to do so. If she loves someone so passionately who cannot love her in the same exclusive way, that is tragic. But to be tragic it requires a facing of reality. Tragedy can be noble. It is something one "faire face à"; but at present the girl's "passion" is a self-indulgence for which Noémie pays.

Next day

A soft snow falling, so it is like being in a cocoon. Throughout the night I thought over what I wrote earlier, and asked myself whether I had the right (moreover, whether I had the wisdom) to speak with such assurance. Still, isn't it true that one of life's miracles (borne out over and over by psychoanalysis) is that every relationship between two beings is bound by an emotion of <u>communion</u> different from any other—no doubt some basic patterns are well-known to the analyst, but there are always myriad variations in the pattern, and it is exactly those variants which make life mysterious.

I know this girl has mentioned suicide—and there lies the risk Noémie dare not ignore in resolving this matter. To me it seems that she must speak out with a tough directness—show that she understands very well the <u>temptation</u> of suicide, that everyone goes through it, <u>but</u> that under circumstances such as these it would equal an assault against the loved one, a punishment. "Every suicide is a repressed murder."

If only she could tell this poor girl, "Look, wait six months. After six months both of us will see things more clearly. Then I can become the true friend that I cannot be right now."

Basically what I'm thinking—and this is hard to say—is that Noémie, through pity and in total good will, has let herself be led too far into an instance of folie à deux. The power of such a passion leads us to feel false guilt—we haven't given enough, we haven't loved well enough or purely enough, (without self-centeredness), etc.—but our actual guilt lies in not having the courage to cut to the quick <u>in order to cure</u>.

Dearest, forgive this outburst which (as I'm sure you know) arises from much painful and slowly-won understanding of my own suffering. Tell Noémie anything you wish that might help—and only what seems best to you. I have merely answered your question as best I can.

I very much hope that now, through contemplating the sea and the sky and the weather, you can rediscover that inner thread which has been severed by your anguish for your sister—that the dawning of spring in the days ahead will bring you joy in your work. I read with the greatest emotion what you said about me—and about yourself—in this last letter. I too believe that's the truth—that what will save me from becoming a truly <u>impossible</u> person (immoderate emotion, anger, passion etc) will be my intellect and the exertion of <u>thinking clearly</u>.

Dearest, I will write better next time.

Soon, I trust. Your letters flood me with light and I am much in need of that just now.

Most tenderly,
May

P.S. I'm sending a profile I've written of my father.

———

thunder-like noises: See "The House in Winter" (1964). The "donkey book" was *Joanna and Ulysses* (1963).

Joubert: French moralist and aphorist Joseph Joubert (1754–1824). Sarton asked Bill Brown (8 August 1945) to try to get hold of Joubert's *Pensées* while in Dijon, where Brown was stationed in the Army: "He is practically my favorite philosopher and says wonderful things about poetry and writing especially."

Volta Hall: Sarton's psychotherapist, Dr. Volta Hall, died suddenly in October 1962 at age 52; she had been consulting with him since 1959. See "Death of a Psychiatrist" (1964).

Noémie Hepp was Mayran's daughter, who, having attended a convent school, became a schoolteacher.

not to make your feeling a burden: "Perhaps the greatest gift we can give to another human being is detachment. Attachment, even that which imagines it is selfless, *always* lays some burden on the other person. How to learn to love in such a light, airy way that there is no burden?" (*Solitude,* p. 210, 15 September 1971)

force majeure: an occurrence that could not be reasonably foreseen or controlled once it occurs.

faire face à: faces up to.

repressed murder": Sarton's version of a key concept from French writer and thinker Albert Camus (1913–60) and his meditations on suicide in *The Myth of Sisyphus* (1942).

folie à deux: A technical term in psychology; literally "double madness," defined by Merriam-Webster as "the presence of the same or similar delusional ideas in two persons closely associated with one another." It also carries the sense that one person's weaknesses or obsessions or even virtues interlock with the other person's opposite qualities. Here, Noémie's well-meaning pity connects with the girl's wish to retain an emotional hold on her chosen beloved (Noémie) through religious ties and threats of suicide.

anguish for your sister: The situation referred to is not clear.

profile . . . of my father: Later that year, in responding to "An Informal Portrait of George Sarton," author Helen Howe (see 4 December 1963) said: "I feel like Edward Everett Hale writing to Abraham Lincoln after his Gettysburg Address! WHY am I floundering among pages and pages and pages of writing—when you in those few pages, written by an <u>artist</u>, have created—no less than a work of art—and one worthy of your father!" Four years later (27 December 1967) Howe would reaffirm "How proud, how proud both your parents would be of you!"

TO SIGNI FALK   Feb. 27th, 1963

[Nelson]

Dear Miss Falk,

Your letter of Feb. 23rd reached me today, having crossed one I sent off a few days ago. I am amenable, up to a point. Let me say first that I usually do address the whole student body at some point in these visits and that I have done so at large, not very highbrow places like Southern Illinois U. (where my predecessor the week before had talked about baseball!). The risk one takes in being absolutely oneself and in not compromising is a definite risk. On the other hand, I object violently to the state of affairs where poetry is something for "specialists, people interested in poetry"—and one reason I put myself through these yearly lecture trips is because I am trying to <u>break out</u> of the groove and pigeon hole. Since 1940, when I began to read poems at colleges as a regular thing, I have become more and more convinced that the <u>fear</u> that something will not get over is destroying our culture. I believe myself that the general public is consistently under-rated. The proof is Robert Frost.

On the other hand, where R.F. did have a magical way of communicating even with a very large audience, on a very personal level, many poets and scholars (as you say) don't even try. I am no Frost, needless to say. But I speak to people, not to specialists. I was, as you know, in the theatre for six years instead of going to college, and this has helped me learn to "project". I would rather give your football player the best I have to give, and believe he can rise to the occasion than to feed him exhilarating pap. What I would like to do is give at the Wed. convocation a lecture called The Holy Game—it runs about 40 minutes. I do not use many of my own poems—and it is an impassioned explication and defence of poetry. Why write it? Why read it? What values does it represent? <u>What goes into it</u> if you are a poet. It ends with Wordsworth's "Toussaint." Would you be willing to let me try? Of course it will not perhaps reach every single person in the audience. But I would consider it worth doing if it reached four or five of those who came under duress and might perhaps leave with their eyes opened.

Before your letter came, I had packed up two printed lectures of mine, given in the last few years. The Writing of a Poem (which Scripps printed in a booklet) is more technical than The Holy Game, but it did not fail, even before student convocations (at DePauw for instance). The H. Game is simpler, and more dramatic perhaps.

However having made my plea, I would be willing to try to write something—on the theme "Books that change lives"—It will mean a week's work and I must say I would rather not have to do it. The kind of book I have in mind is V. Woolf's To The Lighthouse, Isak Dinesen's Out of Africa, Simone Weil, [J. D.] Salinger [*The Catcher in the Rye*], Cry, The Beloved Country [Alan Paton]—books which enrich and extend experience itself, so that one is a different <u>person</u> for having read them.

I hope to get all the work done on the lectures by Feb. 15th so may I hope for a speedy answer? Also to my letter which crossed yours about the Tuesday schedule?

I'm sure you are doing the right thing in meeting the students halfway! I'm against pompous scholarly lectures which are better read than spoken. Lecturing is a kind of dramatic performance and if it is not that, does not exist as an art (apart from the written lecture meant to be read not heard.)

Most cordially yours

Signi Falk: Signi Lenea Falk, professor of English at Coe College, Cedar Rapids, Iowa, 1947 to 1971; for Twayne's United States Authors series, she wrote on MacLeish and Tennessee

Williams. She had doubts about Sarton's plan to read her poetry to an assembly "of students from English classes, but also football players, physical education majors, or boys in business administration" because "I do not want to risk a good thing, take any chance that those who are really interested in poetry will be disturbed by those who are not" and so proposed a smaller meeting.

The Holy Game: See note to 29 June 1958. In this version Sarton emphasizes that the "holiness" lies not in "amazement at one's own cleverness, but absolute concentration on the subject; that implies selflessness." She stresses that "the joy of creation" has to be earned through discipline. "But when it has been earned, then sometimes a work of art is sent down through time to restore, console, and help man to free himself. Let us end with Wordsworth's great poem," the 1802 political sonnet "To Toussaint l'Ouverture." Born in 1743 to African slave parents, as Haiti's governor Toussaint resisted Napoleon's attempts to reinstate slavery; sent to France, he died in prison in 1803.

The Writing of a Poem: See *Writings on Writing.* After prescribing the poet's mental preparation, Sarton talks the audience through her work sheets—from the first line "given" by the Muse to the finished product—for "Truth" (*The Land of Silence,* not reprinted) and "On Being Given Time" (a longer version, later cut down on MacLeish's advice for *In Time Like Air*).

"Books that change lives": Probably descended from her 1962 essay "Books with a Lasting Effect"; see note to 27 November 1955.

Simone Weil: French thinker and religious writer (1909–43); see note to 4 March 1970. It is her essay "The Iliad, or the Poem of Force" that prize student Jane Seaman plagiarizes in *The Small Room.* Sarton frequently used Weil's statement "Absolute attention is prayer" to illustrate the degree of attentiveness with which the poet must see and hear.

Lecturing is . . . performance: For almost five decades Sarton derived much satisfaction (and an important part of her income) from crisscrossing the country, reading and commenting upon others' work as well as her own, to convey the importance of poetry in a civilized existence. Only age and illness made her give up these enriching, exhausting journeys, and even then she did not surrender: in spring 1995 she read her latest poems for the New Hampshire Public Television video *May Sarton: Woman of Letters.*

TO ERIC P. SWENSON   May 10th, 1963
[Nelson]
Dear Eric,

I am in such a state of exhaustion (just back from a gruelling lecture trip) that you must regard this as just a quick response to your good letter—I shall be thinking about it seriously in the days and weeks ahead. And I think it would help if you could (as I suggested to your secretary) telephone me sometime next week at your convenience.

Please send back the ms. as I have sent my only other complete copy to England.

My first feeling is that you are asking me to do more with a simple "tale" than I really conceive of its holding. However, I do agree that there is something unfinished or too abrupt about it as it now stands. I feel myself that the "human relationship" which might serve to prove

Joanna's rehabilitation must be that with her father. You say that she must come back from the island with more than a mere healthy donkey—but nowhere in your letter do you mention that she is a painter and that what really happens on the island (with the help perhaps of the donkey and the freedom to paint) is that she becomes a real painter—by that I mean, that she opens up a new dimension for what was merely pretty in her work before. It is this the father senses—so he is able to treat her as an adult with respect and this changes his whole relation to her and hers to him. The richness of life possible to a solitary person was one of the things that interested me in this tale.

You say "somehow she has to come off the island and go back to Athens with something more directly meaningful than a well donkey and the pleasure that has given her"—but you fail ever to take into account that she comes back a painter and that is the whole point!

The donkey is not, as I see it, a catalyst between her and humanity but rather between her and some inner starved person who is the artist.

Anyway I am grateful for this very thoughtful letter—grateful to have you for an editor. I must however add that I have been warned by both [Victor] Gollancz and Basil de Sélincourt that American editors are prone to manipulate their author's work too much—to read into a ms. another and perhaps better book, rather than to take what is before them. Keep in mind that this is a tale, not a novel. That it is not pretentious nor has it a moral. That said, I agree that as it now stands something doesn't quite happen perhaps that would make the whole thing jell. The question of J's age may have some significance—what if she were 40 instead of 32? Possible?

Let's talk on the phone—by the way, I can't get at this till after June 6th probably—as I have a commencement address to write and the usual intolerable mass of correspondence which accumulates like the plague when I am away for a month.

I'm awfully happy anyway that you think to publish. It would break my heart to be severed from Norton just when I seem to have found the perfect publisher!

Love and many many thanks for your thoughtful helpful letter—

Love from
May

---

a simple "tale": Joanna and Ulysses: A Tale of 127 pages was published later that year.

The question of J's age: Joanna turned out to be 30.

a commencement address: For Beaver Country Day School, Cambridge, Massachusetts.

TO EDMUND WILSON   July 7th, [1963]
[Nelson]
Dear E.W.

Just a brief <u>Huzzah</u> that your contributions to the U.S. are regarded as equal to a 5-Star general! Good news—bless you.

May Sarton

What fun it will be in Sept. to see that collection of diverse people of distinction in the White House—

———

Edmund Wilson: The polymath man of letters (1895–1972) had been awarded the Presidential Medal of Freedom, the country's grandest civilian honor, for converting "criticism itself into a creative act, while setting for the nation a stern and uncompromising standard of independent judgement." Wilson attended a White House dinner in May 1962, but his published journals do not mention his presence there in September 1963.

"Daddy was rather amusing about Wilson and Genesis—'elementary, my dear Watson' was what it amounted to." So George Sarton's daughter wrote Louise Bogan, 17 May 1954, concerning one of Wilson's many forays into fields new to him, chronicled in *The New Yorker*; Bogan had known Wilson well for years. "He feels that Wilson is a bit over-impressed with his own very slight knowledge of Hebrew and draws some rather far-fetched conclusions. I suppose I shall have to read it after all." The article in question is included in a reissue of Wilson's writings on such matters, *Israel and the Dead Sea Scrolls* (Moyer Bell Ltd., 2001).

TO WILLIAM JAY SMITH   Sept. 17, 1963
[Nelson]
Dear Bill,

Now I know what we were celebrating! So happy to see you have one of those rich Ford grants—I had hoped for one myself, but I guess a Sarton added to a Swenson and a Sexton would have been a bit much—anyway I shall be excited to see a play by <u>you</u>! Many thanks for letting me join in the fun the other night—It was heartening—

Yours ever
May Sarton

———

William Jay Smith: b. 1918; writer, translator, teacher, Democratic member of the Vermont House of Representatives, Consultant in Poetry to the Library of Congress (1968–70), and poet; he wrote many successful volumes of poetry for children. As an old friend, Smith would preside at the Academy of Arts and Letters memorial for Louise Bogan.

a Swenson and a Sexton: Poet May Swenson (1919–89), after a fellowship-sponsored European trip, had just published *To Mix With Time: New and Selected Poems*. Poet Anne Sexton (1928–74) had most recently published *All My Pretty Ones* (1962), sequel to her first collection, *To Bedlam and Part Way Back* (1960). Bogan's *New Yorker* review of the two new books (*A Poet's Alphabet*, pp. 431–33) was titled "No Poetesses Maudites."

[Wright Street]
Helen darling,

In the midst of the gloom it was so wonderful to hear from you, and so dear of you to take time off both to read and send a word about my book to Norton—as well as writing me such a heart-warming appreciation. More about that in a minute—when I came to the part about Johnnie Ames, I burst into tears: somehow I missed the papers (perhaps I was in Nelson) and had not known of it, and now I have just called Moll [Howe] so at least I can share in the grief at the memorial service (perhaps you will be there?) on Saturday.

"The beginning of age," you say and I feel this too so much. I am surrounded this fall by very old querulous friends, so I feel quite senile myself a good part of the time! Oh dear...I hear Johnnie's wonderful ripple of laughter, a sort of <u>chuckle</u>, as the happiest of sounds—it was always there like a saving grace in the background of life, for he was not a foreground figure for me (we did not know each other well as you and he knew each other), such a <u>dear</u> man. I hate to think of what these last two weeks must have been for you, just one long <u>knell</u>. I had not expected to be so utterly dismayed by the Kennedy tragedy, but like everyone else it has been a time of real grief that does not go away. I wake in the middle of the night and wonder what it is that is so awful—and then remember.

So I feel very deeply your loving kindness in responding to my little book at such a time. I loved your saying "fable" for that was what I felt when I heard the story from my Greek guide—that it was like a myth, a form into which I could pour many things I had long wanted to say, about the woman alone, about the artist and about what animals do for people.

All the <u>facts</u> about the donkey (his shaking his head on the pier, eating hats et al.) were told me; also the <u>facts</u> about the mother's death—all the inwardness I suppose was what I brought to it. You know, it sold first to Ladies H[ome]. Journal for $10,000 so I was able to send my guide a large sum and I spent the summer giving money away (a wonderful feeling but I am relieved to be poor again)—rebuilt a neighbor's house in Nelson and all sorts of things like giving <u>all</u> of Beatrix Potter to the Nelson library—One little boy had been taking Peter Rabbit out <u>every</u> week (it was the only one they had)—

I want to hear about <u>you</u> and please please let me know ahead and let's make a date in January (I am up at Nelson for part of the month—when do you come?) I long for a real heart to heart talk about everything. Old friends become increasingly <u>dear</u>—bless you.

                                        Ever your
                                        May

Helen Howe: Helen Huntington Howe (Mrs. Reginald Allen, 1905–75), writer and mono-loguist who performed throughout the U.S., as well as in New York and London supper clubs and theatres. Her father, Mark A. de Wolfe Howe, author or editor of more than forty books—"the tireless biographer"—is the central figure of *The Gentle Americans, 1864–1960: Biography of a Breed* (1965), his daughter's literary and social chronicle of Boston, in which Sarton is mentioned. Mr. Howe considered any stretch of time during which one of his three offspring did not appear in print as a sign of the decline of American letters. What Sarton called "that brilliant trio of Howes" also included Helen's writer brothers Quincy, a radio commentator, and Mark, a professor at Harvard Law School. Through Polly Thayer Starr, Mark met and married Molly Manning; see 5 June 1967. All were friends of Sarton's.

Johnnie Ames: John Worthington Ames, Jr. (1897–1963), architect, studied at the École des Beaux-Arts; was wounded in the French Army; and was an intimate friend of the Howe family. He was Polly Thayer Starr's first cousin. When Ames died, Helen Howe wrote: "Father's death was the end of my youth—this, the beginning of age."

the Kennedy tragedy: On 22 November 1963 President John F. Kennedy was assassinated in Dallas, followed by four days of nationally televised coverage—Lyndon Johnson's taking the oath of the presidency, the capture of Lee Harvey Oswald, his murder in the Dallas jail, the President's lying in state at the White House and the Capitol Rotunda, the funeral Mass, the procession to Arlington, and the graveside service with the final playing of "Taps."

all of Beatrix Potter: This would have meant all twenty-three diminutive volumes written and illustrated by the British storyteller and Lake District sheep farmer (1866–1943), published by F. Warne & Co., 1902–30, including the first, *The Tale of Peter Rabbit.*

old friends: Howe had once written Sarton to express "how deeply I value all you are and have been not only to me personally but to our little frost-bitten corner of the world [Boston]. . . . I still treasure the lovely picture of [actress Eleonora] Duse [1858–1924] as a young girl you gave me when I gave my first London recital [as a monologuist], writ-ten in your hand in a corner 'force et confiance' ['strength and confidence']. That I should give a good performance, with the highest possible goal in mind, you seemed to count as important in the scheme of things, and not just the gratifying of some personal whim of my own."

TO DIANE DIVELBESS   Jan. 1st 1964
[Nelson]
Dear Diane, I only came up here on the 30th to discover the wonderful package, full of fun and glory...and it was a blessing. We had a queer Christmas overshadowed not only by Kennedy's death but also by the death of a young girl who was buried on the 23rd, the day her engage-ment was to have been announced—it all happened in 10 awful days while we stayed suspended on her every breath (she was the daughter of a dear friend of mine and the granddaughter of another dear friend and she herself had had a hard life as her mother died of cancer, was divorced when Eve was a small child—we all felt she had at last come into her own and was to marry just the right man, a young Doctor)—I am try-

ing this week to write an elegy for her—what else can one do? But it is hard going. I play Gluck's Orpheus and cry but so far, no poem. The muse turns her back.

Besides that tragic event, it seemed to me I trundled about from one hospital and nursing home to another, as so many people were ill.

Nevertheless, the tree in our house in Cambridge was exquisite and we had a series of small parties and saw old friends peacefully. Anyway it was wonderful to have a second dear Xmas up here. The carousel is my joy—it sits on top of an old fashioned revolving bookcase beside my desk, and when I swirl it round to find a book, the horses and tigers fly out—lovely! Also it stands just below a terribly funny Indian painting of the God Ganesh (the elephant god) [of wisdom and good luck] with his attendant mouse—and together they are charming.

I sat right down and read Leonard Woolf's piece—and was grateful to him and to you for sending it. There has been so much <u>clouded</u> about Virginia's madness that this perfectly realistic, tender and honest coming out with the truth about it, is a relief. I did know the photograph, and it is one of the "mad ones" but this is such a wonderful reproduction of it that I began to like it. I feel it was a tremendous gift for you to give it up, dear, and I am grateful. But maybe you would like it back—maybe it might induce a painting? If so, let me know and I'll send it.

By the way, if you happen on the December Harper's Bazaar do look at the baby owl, a full page in color to advertize a jewelled frog it holds in its claw—I love it passionately. (Owl not frog!)

The book I laid away in mothballs was some portraits, including one of my mother, portraits in prose and I am sure my agent was right about it. Anyway I am now pondering a new novel, very different from anything I have done, a sort of picaresque novel about what the woman poet does for a Muse—it may die before it is born, but I plan to begin when I come up here for good in Feb, and we shall see.

Despite the really horrendously full life you lead this year you sound in wonderful form. I loved the description of your father's trek to the dances, and of your own watching the church being re-plastered (if that is the word) and all those people who got made presents are lucky—I forgot to mention the beauty of the wrapping of my present, those blues and greens, lovely.

I must now return to the struggle with the recalcitrant Muse—after Feb. I'll be more human and can write letters, so do write again in the spring. I hope you like J. and U.—it is really a sort of fable and I rather like it myself. It has had good reviews and seems to be selling, despite <u>no</u> ads—or only one too late to do any good. I do not like the illustrations

at all. The donkey should have been much smaller and with more delicate feet and Joanna herself more boyish and the little boy much
younger. Also those <u>awful</u> hands with the flowers!

Happy New Year! I feel that it will be somehow …work well flourish
and be happy…

Yours with grateful love
May

––––––––

Diane Divelbess: b. 1935; painter, Professor Emerita, California State Polytechnic University;
presently a full-time artist. When Sarton delivered "The Writing of a Poem" at Scripps
College, Claremont, California, Divelbess was an undergraduate there and wrote an account
for the college paper, *The Associate* (22 March 1957), "May Sarton, Master of Poetic
Frankness."

The lecture demonstrated the ruthlessness necessary to make sure that a poem's original
intention triumphs, no matter how many revisions it must undergo. Just as striking to
Divelbess was the mien of this "strongly framed and strongly featured woman, with a shock
of steel gray hair and the two most piercing-penetrating eyes God could grant … a pacing
dynamo," who did not scruple to voice dismay "concerning Scripps' method of caring for
guests on campus."

Sarton stayed with her when she returned in 1963 to give "The Design of a Novel,"
drawing on her experience writing *A Shower of Summer Days* (1952), *Faithful Are the Wounds,*
and *The Small Room* (see *Writings on Writing*); in 1966 Divelbess visited Nelson. To this editor, she writes: "I knew her to be very kind, wise, generous to a fault, intense and absolutely
hilarious"—the latter trait hard to document, but attested to by many friends and passing
acquaintances alike.

death of a young girl: Eve Morgan, daughter of Francesca Greene Morgan and granddaughter
of Henry Copley and Rosalind Greene, had died after eight days in a coma following a suicide attempt. See *Among the Usual Days,* p. 262.

to write an elegy: This same day, after ten drafts, Sarton did complete "Elegy for Eve," unpublished; see appendix. The final stanza likens the poet, addressing the deceased, to Orpheus,
singing to his dead Eurydice. Sarton was listening to the opera *Orpheus and Eurydice* (1762)
by Christoph Willibald Gluck (1714–87) as she worked.

Leonard Woolf's piece: Since Woolf was in the midst of writing his five-volume autobiography
(1960–69), this article was probably incorporated in *Beginning Again: An Autobiography of the
Years 1911–1918,* pp. 75–82. There he charts his dawning awareness of Virginia's equivocal
mental health and describes in detail the causes and symptoms of her breakdowns and the
contradictory medical counsel received over the next thirty years.

It is not known which photographs of Virginia Sarton regarded as "mad." (For the
story of some forty shots taken 24 June 1939 when Woolf was definitely *angry* at the photographer, Gisèle Freund, see Hermione Lee, *Virginia Woolf* [1997], p. 650, and related
photo-insert.)

the illustrations: The *Ladies' Home Journal* used Sarton's own snapshots; for the book, she
sent Eric Swenson postcards bought in Greece to help the artist, thinking them preferable
for that purpose. James J. Spanfeller illustrated the Norton version, with the "awful hands"
holding flowers as the frontispiece; for the British edition, John Murray employed David
Knight.

[Nelson]
Dearest Le Gallienne,

That was such a fine time with you last Sunday—I'm only sorry to have missed Evensen, but I was in a delirium of fatigue because of all the people seen during the holidays...I get stretched out into too many directions. But now I have been here safe and warm for five days, I begin to feel like myself.

I have been thinking much about the problem of getting a really good history of the Civic into the works before it is too late, and it occurred to me that one avenue of approach might be first of all to gather together short chapters of reminiscence from a whole group of people who were involved, who would each tell what seemed significant to him. This should be done fairly soon as people are dying all the time—couldn't you hand over the job to someone like Ruth Norman? Possibly a letter from you yourself should be sent out, giving some idea what you have in mind. The people who come to mind are not only members of the company, such as Jo (who should certainly be asked) Beatrice de Neeregaard, but also technicians like Thelma, apprentices like Buzz Meredith, Howard da Silva, Helen Walpole (now a successful TV writer!) Arnold (I forget his last name) [Moss]. If these personal essays could then be added to a perfectly cold chapter of facts—numbers of plays, titles, finances etc. you would have in your hands the raw material for a future historian. You must try to get down at least a chapter yourself, of course. My feeling is that this must be done fairly soon—in fact that it should be done this year. I wish that someone from the audience, from among the "regulars" could also be found who would be able to say what the theatre meant to that particular faithful and fervent group. It may be that you know such a person?

By the way, I sent off the play [*The Music Box Bird*] to your friend in N.Y. Many thanks for the suggestions.

I do plan to come to "Sea Gull" Friday night and will come backstage about 8:15—it is rather scary because of that Cerberus but I'll try to screw up my courage.

Dearest one, all love and blessing in the New Year, from your old

May

Eva Le Gallienne: See note to 3 July 1955. As Le Gallienne did not save Sarton's letters, this is one of the few extant. *At Fifteen: A Journal* includes two transcripts, one from shortly before 17 February 1928 (also in *Letters 1916–54*), and one "purely business letter," 1 April 1928. For poems young May wrote for and about Le Gallienne, see *Catching Beauty: The Earliest Poems, 1924–1929,* ed. Susan Sherman (Puckerbrush Press, 2002)—henceforth *Catching Beauty.*

Ruth Norman: Business manager of the Civic and assistant to Mary Benson, general manager; together they looked after the company's finances. Among the company members who made a lasting impression on Sarton were Howard da Silva, now a veteran stage actor, and Burgess "Buzz" Meredith (1908–97), actor and director on stage and radio, in television and films. Josephine "Jo" Hutchinson (1904–98) and her mother, Leona Roberts, acted in the Civic's permanent company. Hutchinson had been an intimate of Le Gallienne's; she remained devoted for the rest of her life, even after Le Gallienne left her for Marian Gunnar Evensen (1892–1971), with whom she shared a home for 37 years.

"Sea Gull": Le Gallienne, touring with the National Repertory Theatre, was directing her translation of the 1898 comedy-drama by Anton Chekhov (1860–1904). In Greek mythology, Cerberus was the savage three-headed dog which prevented the living from crossing the threshold to the underworld; here, a theatre security guard.

TO JEAN BURDEN   Feb. 15th, [1964]
[Nelson]
Dear Jean,

A beautiful blizzard is in progress—sheer Heaven as the house becomes a cocoon and I feel absolutely protected from interruption! Am in a wild state of work—both the novel and poems plunge in at me and I am almost afraid of the double burden, but the flood is fine while it lasts—and no doubt it won't be sustainable forever!

Your poem about the window is a beauty—it hit me where I live in a lovely way. Thank you. Last night I went over to see Louise Bogan at MacDowell colony and took your book to her—I thought she might <u>there</u> give it a second look. I admire her greatly but I do think that as a critic she rarely goes out toward the young unless they seem to be about to be in fashion. That is an awful thing to say, but I became disillusioned some years ago—she is a true and wonderful <u>poet,</u> of course. An incorruptible and wise <u>person</u>—yet power does corrupt something and she has had that job for 25 years, too long for any one critic to hold the fort in any such important place in my opinion. Bury this of course. But just as an example she has not reviewed Muriel Rukeyser for years and years and this is just plain unfair. The really Hellish truth for women poets is neither men <u>nor</u> women poets really like them. It is just about 50 times as hard for a woman as for a man, I am convinced of that.

You kindly ask about J. and U. Yes, it is out and called Joanna and Ulysses (has sold close to 9000 copies so far.) Norton put a huge half-page ad in the Sunday Times a couple of weeks ago so I think they may believe it still has a short run ahead. John Murray will do it in London this fall; German rights have gone through. That little donkey is getting around! The reviews were wonderful, even the New Yorker did not say "sentimental" but praised the style. So I feel vast relief as I expected to be torn limb from limb.

I enclose Perley Cole—on re-reading I did not feel it perhaps quite right for Yankee so shall not be surprised if you decide against it. But do keep it if you do want to publish (my last copy so please return if not) also enclosed another little lyric.

Love and blessings
May

Jean Burden: b. 1915; poet and poetry editor at *Yankee* magazine. Her 1974 anthology *A Celebration of Cats* contains four of Sarton's feline poems not included in *Poems 1930–93*; her critical work, *Journey Toward Poetry* (1966), mentions the Sarton-Shapiro ordeal. From Burden's most recent book, *Taking Light From Each Other* (1992), *At Eighty-Two* reprints "Lost Word," pp. 128–29.

MacDowell Colony: The writers' retreat in nearby Peterborough, New Hampshire. Bogan was probably reading proof for *The Journal of Jules Renard* (1964), which she had translated with "Elizabeth Roget" (Sylvie Pasche—see 10 February 1970), and preparing for her year as visiting professor at Brandeis University. Bogan does not seem to have reviewed Burden's 1963 collection *Naked As the Glass*.

not reviewed . . . Rukeyser for years: 1939 was the last time Bogan gave Rukeyser's work substantial consideration (see *A Poet's Alphabet,* pp. 229–30); disliking her brand of socialist poetics, the critic refrained from further comment. Sarton's loyalty to Rukeyser, and her conviction that politics could indeed have a place in poetry, reinforced her disappointment for years. See also 15 February 1976.

To judge whether Bogan rarely went "out toward the young unless they seem to be about to be in fashion" would require surveying all her published criticism, collected and uncollected. Having been *The New Yorker's* poetry critic since 1931, she was admired or disliked but not feared, and never trimmed her views to be "fashionable." What matters here is Sarton's enduring certainty of one hurtful but unshirkable truth: that Bogan did not like her poetry as much as Sarton dearly would have wished.

praised the style: The *New Yorker* (21 December 1963) liked the "gentle, unsentimental prose that is beautiful to read," leaving *The New York Times Book Review* (24 November) to say "It may be slight and occasionally sentimental but . . . Sarton knows how to be tender, romantic, melancholic, and amusing all at once."

Perley Cole: "A Recognition, for Perley Cole." For the sequel to this submission, see 22 January 1965.

love and blessings: Of a visit to Pasadena by Sarton in the 1980s, Burden recalled to this editor a book signing that "attracted a crowd that stretched from the store halfway around the block. She wanted to see the gardens at the Huntington so we drove over—and all the top echelon was waiting for us, lined up to shake hands with her as though she were visiting royalty—which of course she was!"

TO LOTTE JACOBI   Feb. 24th, 1964
[Nelson]
Lotte dear,

I have been thinking of you so much—and hoping that the New York trip was successful and happy in every way. Since I got here on Feb. 5th I have been lifted up on a stream of fire—and have been working 10 or 12 hours a day at my desk—the new novel in the morning and poems in the evening. I have not even seen my neighbors! Of course this always means for me a wild seizure of the imagination by a <u>person,</u> in this case (as always perhaps) an impossible one who has not sent one word of response to 20 poems! Always a woman, of course .... So I am in a queer naked inspired state. Now I am off to Cambridge (tomorrow unless we have a storm) until Sat. but I want very much to see you—what about Sunday March 8th early in the afternoon? I would leave here about 2:30 to get back before dark?

A drunken message at the end of the morning!

Love always from
May

Lotte Jacobi: German-American Lotte (Johanna) Jacobi (1896–1990) was known worldwide for unpretentious portraits of the famous—Einstein, Frost, Moore, J. D. Salinger, Paul Robeson, Eleanor Roosevelt, and many others, now in permanent museum collections here and abroad. She moved her studio from New York City to Deering, New Hampshire, in 1955; Sarton started commissioning publicity shots from her soon after. Her work adorns many Sarton books and dust jackets—*Joanna and Ulysses, Plant Dreaming Deep, Journal of a Solitude, Recovering,* and the study of Bogan in *A World of Light.*

To Eleanor Blair, Sarton exclaimed how remarkable it was to have had "a whole career in Germany before 1933 [actually 1935] and then to remake it here as a refugee . . . [including] one-man shows at the Museum of Modern Art. . . . She is very good at getting money for other people, far better than getting it for herself! She asks $125 for a portrait sitting at which she takes anywhere from 30 to 50 shots—this is about one fifth what [touted celebrity photographers Bradford and Fabian] Bachrach would ask and she is about 100 times better (and more famous)." Blair was another photographer who served Sarton well; see 5 August 1967.

lifted up on a stream of fire: "If only my talent were at all commensurate with what I <u>feel</u>!" Sarton lamented to Rosalind Greene (23 February 1964); "ah, there's the rub!"

TO CAMILLE MAYRAN   10 March [1964]
[Nelson]   [portions in French]
Ma grande douceur,

I am writing, like a figure in "Winter," by the light of an oil lamp—in the middle of a blizzard (the power went out, which means the central heating too, but I have a wood fire and for some reason I'm in the process of cooking pears in their skins—living like Crusoe suits me fine!) Since last night it has snowed and blown without stopping, some twenty-four hours already—and today is the "yearly Village Meeting" which I will go to on foot—everyone in a good mood because of the storm, the superhuman effort made to get there from far off, in cars, etc.—a very human atmosphere...

This big chunk of your life, with the close-ups it provides, has moved me so much—I was quivering by the time I let fall the last of these precious pages, these drops of blood..you have done a great thing, the only thing which could possibly put me back in the center of life; you have stripped away the sense of isolation, of madness, of strangeness and mystery which had become, I must confess, somewhat frightening.

And what is more, you have given me other manna—very much needed—since one of my torments is that I dare not show these poems, except a few—since the subject is only too obvious, or the object I should say—and I feel trapped two ways, by the affection which cannot be delivered to the person who has stirred me so, and by the fact that what attracts me as a poet must remain hidden.

The true story (which is not the one I'd imagined) continues to be extremely perplexing. Two weeks ago I came down from my ivory tower to the city—in part to attend a lecture at the college given by one of our most illustrious female authors, Eudora Welty. I did not go in order to see the person who had struck me with lightning, but there she was—and for one instant I was beside her while leaving the hall—without looking at me she said, very quickly, in a tone of simple politeness, "Nice to see you here, May" and then she disappeared into the darkness. I spent the night at the home of two quite charming elderly women, one of whom will soon retire as Dean of Faculty—they having asked me in an endearing fashion which quite surprised and touched me, I must say, and they treated me like the child of the house. The next morning I went to chapel—each Wednesday the President speaks to the students—I had never gone before since I'm not usually on campus that day. Chapel is not compulsory and I was very much surprised and grieved because the place was nearly empty, perhaps 15 students and as many faculty in a hall that seats hundreds! The President spoke very movingly about the strikes of Negro students to get fairer treatment in Boston—it was to take place that day—and she spoke to her own college as to whether they should take part or not—and I thought it was a noble 5 minutes, leaving it all to the individual conscience, at the deepest level and ending with a short, but moving prayer! I had parked my car just behind hers outside the chapel. When she came out, she came to me and said, "May, I have not had time to open personal mail. I have not read anything you have sent." Then she said, "you mustn't send me any more flowers"—I protested that the order for flowers for her desk once a week had been given and it would be hard to now cancel it. And she said, "Well, then I'll enjoy them," smiled, and got into her car.

I must say that I had imagined every possible rebuff, but I had not imagined that she would not read these poems and it was a very hard blow. I was crying so much I had to stop the car when I had got off the campus and could draw to the side of the road. So, there it is. My first feeling when I had calmed down was that this was a lie—that she must have read them, but I now believe it to be true. And it shows also what a driven life she does lead, unhuman. I have written <u>no</u> letters, only sent the poems as I wrote them—and each might take 30 seconds to read!

I had really felt a kind of participation mystique between us—something I know you understand (and you say as much at the end of your letter)—I do not believe that such a thing happens only from one side, except in the case of a teacher, for the student does <u>see</u> the mystical person in the teacher in a way the teacher rarely can in the student. What I am now trying to understand is what to believe has happened, will happen and what I am to do with it all! At any rate, a certain suspense, a certain tension which was becoming dangerous for me I think, has been broken. I know that time is involved and patience—perhaps one day months from now I shall hear something. Perhaps I never will. Is it conceivable that she would <u>never</u> read the poems?

Meanwhile I wrote an open letter to the students for the student paper asking them seriously to re-consider whether the fashion for not going to chapel might not be cutting themselves off from the spiritual source which they complain is lacking. They do complain and I believe the reason they do is that this great woman does lock herself away in some way that is finally sterile. I realize as I think all this over that in the nearly four years I have taught in the college I have consistently tried to understand a lack, a lack of <u>joy</u> and then to do what I could about it—one of the first "contacts" I had with the Pres. was about a battle between the editors of the student paper and herself and she was coldly angry with me for trying to make a bridge. Of course I am now terrified that my letter may do no good, but I had to write it. There was something heartbreaking to me to see what she <u>did</u> give that day to the empty benches ....(the college is over 800 girls so 15 is really rather few to reach).

Now I am writing poems called "Letters to Myself"—as soon as I have some copies I'll send them. They are less good than the others—it is as if that high-tension wire which was set up so mysteriously had gone slack. I have lost the sense of myself in some queer way...Oh how mysterious it all seems to me!

I am glad you are going to Paris—to steep yourself in your true life (one of your true lives, since there is also the Mas)—As for that great poem about the sea, you may need to hunt far and wide—I have to believe that there must be some editor who can appreciate it at the <u>Mercure de France</u> (which comes out abroad as a weekly—["hebdomadaire"]—is that a word in French? It always makes me envision some prehistoric <u>animal</u>)—

Do keep the poems—later tell me which ones seem to you to speak as poems—I am so in the dark!

Love and blessings, magnificent you—
May

Ma grand douceur: "My great 'sweetener' " (sweetheart).

like a figure in "Winter": Many artists have done series on "The Seasons," and Sarton may be thinking of a calendar illustration for December; the scene also recalls an intimate interior by French Post-Impressionist Édouard Vuillard (1868–1940), whom Sarton had admired since at least 1943 (see *Letters 1916–54*, p. 216): *Two Women Under a Lamp* (1892).

Crusoe: Hero of *The Life and Strange Surprising Adventures of Robinson Crusoe, a Mariner* (1719–20), the novel by British writer Daniel Defoe (1660–1731) about a shipwrecked man who survives on an island twenty-four years by using his wits.

Eudora Welty: 1909–2001; renowned for her intense stories and novels of her native Mississippi and her 1984 memoir, *One Writer's Beginnings*. Welty is the only author to be granted, while still living, her own volumes in The Library of America (1998). Elizabeth Bowen formed a close friendship with her.

the person who had struck me with lightning: Margaret Clapp (1910–74), scholar, history instructor at the Dalton School, Columbia University, and Brooklyn College; wrote the Pulitzer-winning biography *Forgotten First Citizen: John Bigelow* (1947). As eighth President of Wellesley College, 1949–66, she edited three essays on *The Modern University* (Cornell Univ. Press, 1950).

two . . . elderly women: Keats Whiting, dean of faculty and professor of English, and her companion, Marguerite Hearsey. "Like the child of the house" translates *comme enfant de la maison*—that is, they took her in as one of their own, and made her feel young again.

participation mystique: Perhaps best rendered as "psychic rapport."

never read the poems?: Speaking of *Cloud, Stone, Sun, Vine* in 1961, Clapp wrote Sarton, "I am delighted to have your poems, some of them old friends, some new to me . . . and to have them from you. But 'not to rebel against what pulls us down' ['Somersault,' 1958]—this is not in this world. Maybe in another era we can argue it out, for now, I have time, alas, not even to rebel. I am convinced that discipline helps, but grace is what matters. And contrary to the fathers, I suspect grace, though it cannot be earned, must be earned to be conferred." (*Recovering: A Journal* [1980], 28 September 1979, pp. 210–11)

TO ERIC P. SWENSON   April 10th, 1964
[Wright Street]
Dear Eric,

I am well aware that what I sent you needs some thinking about.. and I thought that might implement our discussion on the 24th if I sent you and Diarmuid [Russell] some of my present thoughts about it and thought aloud a little about what this book [*Mrs. Stevens Hears the Mermaids Singing*] really is.

What really interests me here, I suppose, is to explore some of the rare kinds of love which are written and talked about very little, or only as symptoms of neurosis, which provide the creative intersection.

I have just come back from lectures at the U. of Pa. and I was appalled at the state of alienation of the students I saw—their short stories could be epitomized by one about a 50 year old "failure" who goes off to Mexico to build a pyramid in the desert all by himself. When I asked "why did this guy never marry?" the boy answered, "I never asked myself that question." Relationship terrifies unless it is a simple sexual exploit (usually read about rather than experienced) etc. Feeling terrifies. Our society is impoverished I am more and more convinced by a <u>fear of feeling</u>. I myself am very tired of relationships reduced to sex.

This is to put the book in a social setting—I would like to suggest that "peak experience" is of great variety and what is always involved first is the imagination.

I have also long wanted to write something about the woman as creator: a lot of nonsense is talked about this and it is constantly talked about in texts of all sorts, books like Friedan (so superficial) etc. Why is a woman writer different from a man writer (and vive la differ-ence!)...this may seem rather "special" but it is my experience that the subject fascinates the general public, at least would fascinate my public, which seems to be roughly 10,000 people out of 200 million. If you think in terms of Mary McCarthy's audience, all my books have been total failures but you and I know that this is not true. So let us forget for a moment about reaching the <u>mass</u> audience. At some point the established writer can afford to give himself his own book, the one he always wanted to write, but didn't quite dare to—this is it for me. (Woolf's [1931 novel] <u>The Waves</u> is a comparable example from the history of lit.)

This said....I think I have a clue as to the trouble with what I have got down. The "peak experience" (there are 6 in a hundred pages) is taken at the peak each time, the cream skimmed off and the reader not enough involved because it is so compressed. What if each of these episodes were extended to say 20 or 30 pages each? This would greatly reduce the pro-portion of talk between Hilary and the interviewers in relation to the body of the book. By the way, Judy has read the ms. and did <u>not</u> feel that the interviewing part was boring (much to my surprise); she is a rather severe critic and not apt to be enthusiastic.

When I first started thinking about this book, I thought of it in terms of a picaresque novel with a woman as hero—that picaresque in terms of <u>inward life</u>—I also foresaw a good deal of change of scene. As I have designed it there is an episode in Japan, not yet written.

I very much want to keep the hero an <u>old</u> woman. I know this presents problems. I have even thought of having the whole book one day in her life as she <u>expects</u> the interviewers and to have the book end where it now begins (no interview takes place but she has prepared herself by re-living her life so to speak)— But this would <u>lose</u> the chance for the reader to see her as she now appears to strangers. It was the contrast between what was uttered and what was felt which seemed to me to be a fruitful juxtaposition.

The final epiphany, by the way, is a young Finnish boy who wants to write poems (the coming full circle from her own wish to be a boy in episode <u>one</u>) and with whom she now, at 75, identifies. When she and the interviewers go up on the moors in Part III, the boy appears like a wild animal and runs away...

I now think there must be one "lived-out" love affair with a man, possibly older than Hilary in which the reasons why she does not write poetry are experienced by the reader. (This might be her marriage about which there should be more. I realize too that there must be a good deal more about the parents.)

To sum up, what has got down on the page looks now like a kind of schematization of what now must be written, but I do not despair yet. And I hope we come to some fruitful meeting of minds of what <u>is</u> possible, without your believing the whole thing beyond the pale.

See you both on the 24th at that elegant place at 12:30.

Love from
May

---

books like Friedan: Writer and feminist Betty Friedan (b. 1921) reawoke the American women's rights movement with *The Feminine Mystique* (1963), attacking the status quo notion that women can achieve fulfillment only as homemakers or child-bearers. When published by Norton, Swenson sent Sarton a copy; she thanked him for a "rewarding, illuminating book—my mind has been running along the same track for some time, and I feel in my students (girls [at Wellesley]) the fear of commitment. . . . How fine if she could, single-handed, make the revolution!" (30 January 1963)

Despite Sarton's later reaction against it, the book did "<u>begin</u> a change of outlook for us all": in 1966 Friedan founded NOW, the National Organization for Women. See *At Eighty-Two,* pp. 72–73 and 83, for renewed enthusiasm about *The Fountain of Age* (1993).

Mary McCarthy's: 1912-89; woman of letters, polemicist, sharp-tongued wit. She achieved a best-selling succès de scandale with a roman à clef detailing the fates of eight Vassar girls of the class of '33, *The Group* (Harcourt, Brace & World, 1963); it became a notorious film. For a time McCarthy was the wife of Edmund Wilson.

TO LENORE STRAUS   Oct. 17th [1964]
[Nelson]
Dear Lenore,

I finished the book last night...it is a moving record, and curiously enough, most moving in regard to your marriage. But it is somewhat marred by the romantic aura (which may be merely verbal) with which you surround Norway, sculpture, and Zen. I think these are not convincing as written partly because they are too generalized. When you talk about sculpture you talk in vague mystical terms..and alas I have heard a lot of this about poetry and states of mind from bad poets. The parts about Norway (except in the one instance of the hard, pained face of one man you met there) seem to me a dream rather than an actual event. The truth in literature is conveyed by minute particulars, not by generalities. The truth about any art lies in great part in its craft aspects..that is why we have so little of value on the arts themselves. An exception is Matisse and another, Auden, who says (I think I remember correctly) "Poems are made with <u>words</u>." (not with fine feelings etc.)

You talk rather a lot about choosing deliberately the hard materials to work with, marble, granite or whatever. But the talk about it is strangely fluffy and blurred. You have asked me to be honest. What troubles me about what I have seen of your work is that the face is always (apparently) the same face (your own?) and the hands always the same hands. There is no visible growth or change to accompany your own changes. The effect of the "noble figure" is, for me, blurred in a strange way. The effect is of narcissism.

Now this is strange because you yourself do not communicate this at all, as <u>yourself</u>. Why does it come into the art?

The best book I ever read about Zen was Herrigel's on the Art of Archery ..I believe we spoke of it the first time we met. It was totally convincing to me and taught me a great deal. It sounds as though you had come to a crucial place.. a wonderful place..where you will no longer have to please anyone, even your Zen master (as you tried too hard to "please" your husband and thus achieve your will to make the marriage work) but will find yourself alone with the reck [sic]. I feel you have been too content with the struggle, though this sounds odd, and have not demanded enough of yourself as a sculptor in terms not of mysticism but of the actual problems themselves, problems of design, tension, balance, all the rest of it. I am going to get to work now, but will re-read this tomorrow and add. It is so good that I feel free with you to say what I really feel and think, and know that you will take it as meant.

                                    [Closing not extant]

Lenore Straus: Born 1910, sculptor Lenore Thomas Straus was also the author of *Stone Dust* (1969) and the artist's memoir Sarton comments on here, *The Tender Stone* (1964). Her marriage, during which two children were born, lasted two years.

Matisse and . . . Auden: French painter and sculptor Henri Matisse (1869–1954) began as a Fauvist, with "savage" colors and rough brushwork, before developing his bold, joy-centered style of painting and decorative work. His writings and remarks on art have been issued in various editions.

Writing Bill Brown on 27 January 1947, Sarton remarked how "Matisse begins with a literal rendering of an object or a person and then gradually reduces it to its essence, drawing by drawing. That is the way I write poems, but many people carry the changes in their heads and many painters, I'm sure, make the abstraction in their heads, too. It's all fascinating." After visiting his Chapelle du Rosaire at Vence (1948–51), she wrote Katharine Davis that it provided "pure radiance and joy, a truly religious place and so exciting that a contemporary achieved this." (5 December 1954)

British-born poet W. H. Auden (1907–73) devoted several essays in *The Dyer's Hand* (1952) to the intricacies of craftsmanship.

For the Herrigel, see note to 27 November 1955.

TO BASIL DE SÉLINCOURT   Oct. 17th, 1964
[Nelson]
Dearest Basil,

It seems ages since I have heard from thee and I hope it doesn't mean that you or Jay is ill. Letters are a huge effort I know! Anyway I wanted to commune with you briefly about The Little French Girl which I have just read with much delight (and often moved as well) for the first time. When oh when will literature come back into these gentle human pastures again, or has that style, that vision of life gone forever? Just before I read it, I had struggled halfway through Saul Bellow's new novel Herzog. I do respect him as a true artist but the content of this book, a long ramble inside the usual non-hero's mind, could fill about 100 pages and it is 500! The critics have been <u>rapturous</u>. I simply cannot understand it. By the way, a little thing I loved in the Fr. Girl was a description of cat's paws as feeling like rasberries in your hand (so true!).

I am feeling cheerful again because the big bulk of the novel [*Mrs. Stevens*] has gone to the typist—I am keeping the short final section about 50 pages at most and probably less, to revise at Yaddo where I go Nov. 10th for a month of concentrated work with no responsibilities. The poor pussies will languish in a kennel, but I think it may be good to take a month's break about now....I may get back to poems, and shall take books on Japan and India with me. Now those images should be distilled and I think I tremble on the brink of utterance—however the Muse cannot be commanded and may refuse to appear! We shall see. Anyway I shall be getting a book of poems ready—an odd book, no very personal poems for a change, a section of animal and people poems, a Nelson section, a section of travel poems so to speak. I am thinking of calling it Voyages, Discoveries (subtitle, New Poems by M.S.) What do you think? The problem is that the book has no central idea really. But to call it just New Poems seems a little arrogant as if everyone were waiting as they might be were I W. H. Auden or Robert Lowell.

The chief news here is the continued drought. I have just heard that two more neighbors' wells have gone dry in the last few days. Mine had about 6 feet (it is normally 21) a week ago—we have had no real rain, by that I mean more than a night of rain, for 6 months, since mid-April. The waiting begins to be quite nerve-wracking and now the trees are beginning to shrivel and I fear for my little fruit trees—especially the plums which bore magnificently for the first time this year. It is awful to see the leaves shrivel instead of turning and falling. I take no pleasure in going out as I alway [sic] have to witness some dying plant in the garden. However, I did put in 500 bulbs, including 100 bluebells in the little wood below the garden, hoping they will spread and make a real english bluebell wood down there eventually. It was strange to plant the bulbs in <u>dust</u>, for that is what the earth is like. I think I shall have to contemplate an artesian well next spring, but it is a very risky affair as you know and one must be prepared to shell out up to three or four thousand bucks, which I simply do not have this year. I did finish Mildred's house outside—one wall was still to do and this is a great satisfaction, almost as good as water. But the waiting for rain has I'm sure added to all the usual tensions and we are all at nerve's end around here now. Perley is digging a well but could not get the people to come until Nov. 15th—that is how busy they are. I am grateful to him for doing it this fall as he would be glad to sell me water and bring it if I really get desperate (and that would help him pay for the well so we would all benefit).

The English elections have been almost obliterated here by the two dramas of the Chinese bomb and Kruschev's being out in Russia—I expect you are sad to see Douglas-Home go (a very gentle and dear man I feel) but I believe maybe Labor may do a better job in some ways. Here of course we tremble before the dreadful possibility that Goldwater <u>might</u> win—the recent scandal around one of Johnson's aides has not helped and could turn into a kind of Profumo thing I fear. Also Goldwater is trigger-happy about Russia and if the Russians and Chinese now get together, some people might foolishly want him rather than Johnson, the "appeaser."

What a world!

Anyway despite the drought the autumn has been radiant—superb color—now the leaves have almost gone, but that means that the hills are revealed again, so another beauty takes their place. I was much encouraged when a dear friend, Ellen Douglass Leyburn, from Atlanta, came for a few days (she is doing a book on Henry James' tragic sense of life) and read the ms. of the novel—she was really tremendously impressed. I can't tell at all yet of course, too close to it, but I think it may be my best novel .... though it will I fear shock some people. You will perhaps hate it but I hope not, dear Basil.

J. and U. comes out in England in Nov. Murray believes it will sell. Let us hope so! It might bring us <u>water!</u>

Love and love

M

Basil de Sélincourt: 1873–1966; literary critic for the London *Observer*. Wrote books such as *Giotto* (1905), *William Blake* (1909), *The Enjoyment of Music* (a Hogarth Essay, 1928), *The Religion of the Spirit* (1929), and *Towards Peace and Other Essays Critical or Constructive* (1932). Through her friend Richard Cabot, Sarton first met de Sélincourt in May 1936 at his home in Kingham, Oxfordshire; she visited him often in the years following. A great supporter of her early work, he found her poetry "a tool . . . searching to the point of ruthlessness, and very delicate"; the poems of *Inner Landscape* tell the story of "human passion, unique, holy and unforgettable" (2 April 1939). *Cloud, Stone, Sun, Vine* was dedicated to him; he appears among the "Ghosts and Guests" of *Plant Dreaming Deep*, pp. 158–60, photo on p. 152.

Jay, his second wife, had been a dear friend of novelist Anne Douglas Sedgwick (1873–1935), his first wife. Sedgwick had been taken at age nine to England, where she lived the rest of her life; her 1924 novel, *The Little French Girl*, presents a Jamesian contrast between French and English standards of life.

Bellow's . . . Herzog: In the 1964 best-seller by Saul Bellow (b. 1915), the hero deals with the dissolution of his career and marriage by writing letters to all the dramatis personae of his life, letters he does not send.

Yaddo: The estate endowed by Katrina and Spencer Trask as a working community for painters, sculptors, composers, and writers in Saratoga Springs, New York. To writer Mary Elsie Robertson (8 February 1987), Sarton made light of this, her one visit to Yaddo, in the last six weeks of 1964. Rosalind Wilson (b. 1923), daughter of Edmund Wilson and actress Mary Blair, "for some reason disliked me and attacked me unmercifully at every meal. Why did no one pull her down? It was extremely painful. But the nice thing about winter is that the group is small and if congenial that is homey. I had Mrs. Trask's room in the winter house with a life size statue of Pallas Athene in it," no less, while Wilson "had the dressing room and we shared a bathroom. Maybe she resented my having the big room though hers was far cosier...anyway she used to lock me out of the bathroom!"

New Poems: Neither brilliant erratic Robert Lowell (1917–77) nor Auden ever issued a volume entitled only *New Poems*. Sarton chose, with a nod to Yeats, *A Private Mythology*.

Mildred . . . Perley: Sarton had paid for repairs to the Quigleys' house. The life of legendary scyther and jack-of-all-trades Perley Cole (1887–1970) is chronicled in *Plant Dreaming Deep*, pp. 106–17; his death, in *Solitude*, pp. 20–24.

two dramas: After being charged by his opponents with hasty decisions, phrase-mongering, etc., over 14 and 15 October, Soviet Union Premier Nikita Khrushchev (1874–1971) was deposed. The day before this letter, 16 October, China had exploded its first atomic bomb.

Douglas-Home: After Conservative Prime Minister Harold Macmillan resigned on 19 October 1963, Sir Alec Douglas-Home was named to succeed him. The Labor party won a majority in the House on 15 October 1964, and its leader, Harold Wilson, became prime minister.

[Barry] *Goldwater might win:* The conservative senator from Arizona (1909–98) was the 1964 Republican presidential candidate; "the Profumo thing" was a recent British politician-prostitute scandal.

The Great Society program of Lyndon Baines Johnson (1908–73) realized many of the Kennedy administration's proposals for social, educational, and civil rights legislation.

you will perhaps hate it: Trying to disarm de Sélincourt's probable rejection of the book's themes and implications, Sarton wrote Jay de Sélincourt, 6 May 1975, "[A]s I wrote I went through it pretending to be Basil! One thing I did was to eliminate the . . . [ellipses] wherever possible you may be glad to hear! I also took out 'passion' and 'passionate' wherever possible as it seemed rather too much 'passion'!"

TO MURIEL RUKEYSER   Oct. 27th, 1964
[Nelson]

Darling, I am such an oaf! And it was so <u>good</u> to hear your voice—and to know that slowly all goes well and your courage and patience are being rewarded.

It is very delicate & pale here now, Novemberish, now the leaves have fallen and the sky seems very open—and I can see the hills all around, also a rather rotten looking red moon these nights rises up late. I seem to be in a weakened and idiotic state of being sleepy all the time, sort of sickish after really a very long bout with my usual nose & throat trouble (since July). I was so ashamed of my behavior on the phone that I have made all sorts of resolutions, including not smoking to see if that will help—It is now 9:30 and I have not had one yet, but no doubt this state of grace will not last!

I am also, I suppose, like a drug addict being given the cold turkey treatment—it was so wonderful, miraculous to be carried off on a great tide of poetry in February & March—and a very little, just a lunch every six months, or a phone call [from Margaret Clapp], would have kept me going indefinitely. I feel <u>deprived</u> and the only way to handle things has been to close off poetry—or it closed itself off, I guess. I cannot believe that I was in that glorious state with poems just pouring out such a short time ago—but anyway the novel is nearly finished and will be when I leave Yaddo. That, too, is a cause for anxiety as I am dealing with an old woman poet and trying to talk sensibly about what it is like to be one—the hazards, above all the fact that the Muse is feminine—once more, I suppose, really about the <u>price</u> of any truly creative life. The old girl is triumphant of course and no self-pity—a character, as they say! I feel fairly sure it is the best novel I have done—but it will expose me to a lot of stupidity and perhaps even cruelty and I must confess I dread it all rather. Only I had to write it and to stand where I stand. And if I who have no family cannot say these things, who can? The novel is called The Interview—the core of it is a sort of Paris Review interview—with digressions by the old woman into her dreams & memories, which are not spoken aloud.

I think the real reason I cried when I heard your voice darling, was that I had just read a terribly needling letter by a friend who was disturbed, I guess, by my own anxiety about this book and so needled me. "Is it a confessional? What is your motive in writing it? Did Judy retire a year early because of it?" (Preposterous) But it was rather like asking some guy on the last lap of climbing Everest, wrapped in his sleeping bag at 50 below zero, whether he had really thought out why he was climbing it; and had perhaps better give up! The person who wrote the letter also suggested that I might lose friends by publishing it. Well, I realized then that Nelson does give me a kind of strength I never had before. My life is really posited here on solitude—the village itself will not read what I write, and takes me as I am—from here I should be able to afford to be absolutely honest.

But one does worry and I often feel like a deer, wild-eyed in the wood, waiting to be hunted down.

Today Perley Cole is here putting wood ash on the rocks, and fertilizing everywhere—I am always happy when he is on the place, working so deftly and slowly and well though he is 77 now. He says wonderful things such as "two heads are better than one, especially when one is a sheep's head."—or "so and so knows as much about farming as a goose knows about Jesus." He makes me keep quiet when he has things on his mind by shouting "Court's in session. Now you listen to me!" And soon he will be in a for a glass of sherry.

Thank you, angel, for calling—I'll do so from Yaddo or before—let us keep in touch on the perilous marshes of middle age.

I feel I have not been the support I meant to be in your ordeal, but I have been sort of knocked about, rather like an animal disappearing into its hole to get itself well—I know you understand.

Many, many hugs.

M

Muriel Rukeyser: Poet, 1913-80. Wrote critical study The Life of Poetry (1949); worked in photography and film; engaged in political protest all her life, from the Scottsboro Boys to the

Vietnam War. An intimate friend, she encouraged Sarton's writing while they worked in New York at the Office of War Information, where Sarton wrote documentary scripts and Rukeyser headed the poster department, after completing her biography of mathematician and physicist Willard Gibbs, *Willard Gibbs: American Genius* (1941). "Among other things," Sarton remembered (*Recovering,* pp. 220–21), "I learned from her that loafing is not a crime, . . . Work, I discovered early on, excuses one from some sins."

For Rukeyser, Sarton wrote "Letter from the Country" (1942, unpublished; see appendix), "Song" ("No I will never forget you"; see *Selected Poems,* 1978), "O Who Can Tell" (1948), and "Poets and the Rain" (1950). See *Letters 1916–54* for a previous letter and for Sarton's comments on Rukeyser's wide-ranging, ardent, rough-hewn, often topical poetry. At this time her most recent publications were translations of Spanish poets and her own collection *Waterlily Fire* (1962).

did Judy retire . . . early: Matlack seems to have retired from Simmons College in 1964, aged 66; the New Criticism was strongly in vogue, and she was considered somewhat old-fashioned. She promptly took up a one-year stint at Douglass College. Within another two years she would become increasingly forgetful, and depression would begin to set in.

the perilous marshes: Despite having suffered two strokes by the late 1970s, Rukeyser remained active. Her *Collected Poems* appeared in late 1978; see *Recovering,* pp. 225–27, for an October 1979 dinner honoring her—with "that wonderful Buddha smile"—at which Sarton and other poets spoke in tribute.

TO LOTTE JACOBI   Nov. 17th, 1964
[Yaddo]

Dearest Lotte, a yellow piece of paper for a somber November day! How sweet it was to catch that glimpse of you on Sunday, the last good thing that has happened to me for ages it seems—

First that night my English agent called and was very un-pleased with the novel, did not, in fact say one positive word, so I arrived here rather knocked down, and began to remake my own thoughts about it and to get into it again. I have to <u>create</u> it now and not worry too much—

Then on Saturday when I had just begun to settle in to this vast room (as big as my whole house and very gloomy though it is painted white, very dark pine trees all around, as silent as a tomb), I had a formal letter from Margaret Clapp to say that I shall not be re-appointed to my job. It was a nice letter (cold as always) no mention of the poems of course but she did take pains to let me know that the decision was by a committee and had to do with the new curriculum—I suppose courses such as mine are "out". I gather some people tried to get me back for just next year and she was on their side, but they were voted down. It is, of course, a serious blow.

1) Personally excruciating. I shall never see her again

2) the money—$4000 for four months, not easily found

3) I loved the work and I think last year I had become a rather exceptional teacher—certainly the letters from my students about the course

tell me so. They are still deeply moved by what we accomplished together.

I cannot remember as bad a blow since my theatre failed 25 years ago—though this is a less <u>public</u> humiliation. I have been quite sick over it, not able to eat etc. but today I have "gone through" the grief and feel a new strength.

In the long run, in the light of eternity, it may be that it was too rich a job and too much security for a poet to have. I shall be poorer and freer now. I have got back some human dignity for I realize how humiliating it was to be always sitting in an ante-room waiting for someone else to tell me whether I had a job or not each year. Now I command my own life and to Hell with <u>them</u>!

Did I tell you that I decided to dig a well just before I left? I got a man who was supposed to do it this week and paid him a little in advance to seal the deal. And we planned where it would be. I would not have dared do it now with no job ahead, but I am glad I did.

So that is all my news. Has it rained there?

Love from
May

---

my English agent: Patience Ross, of A. M. Heath & Company, had been Sarton's British agent since the mid-1930s. On 24 April 1947 Sarton wrote Judith Matlack, "Afterwards I went to see my agents who live in a sort of cubby hole, I mean their office is there—Patience Ross talks very fast and never stops and never stays on one subject more than a second." For a 1986 Christmas message from Ross to Sarton, see *After the Stroke,* p. 210.

Diarmuid Russell had also decided *Mrs. Stevens* did not "work"—" 'a disquisition on love and on the sources of poetry done with great understanding and delicacy, but not a novel,' " Sarton told Diane Divelbess 28 December 1964. (See *Encore,* pp. 91–92, for Sarton's further recollections on this point, and of Russell himself [d. 1973] : "His introduction [to publishers] carried weight.") "I have a wild hope [Norton] might publish it, as I suggested, as a <u>non</u>-novel, as some other animal. But I expect the worst."

what we accomplished together: "Each person must handle failure in his own way," Sarton would write to Margaret Clapp on 11 December 1964. "Mine is to imagine at least that my life is predicated (as yours is, I know) on being a giver not a getter." *A Private Mythology* was dedicated "To my students at Wellesley College, 1960–1964." Poems inspired by Clapp ("Jonah," "Easter Morning," "The Muse as Medusa") were held until *A Grain of Mustard Seed* (1971), with seven others among the "Earlier Poems" of *The Silence Now: New and Uncollected Earlier Poems* (1988); see also note to 31 January 1966.

my theatre failed: After struggling with poor attendance and financial difficulties in the wake of the Great Depression, her Associated Actors Theatre folded in 1935.

"gone through" the grief: By 2 June 1965, Sarton was able to write Ada Comstock Notestein: "[D]o not imagine that the chip on my shoulder is heavier than a butterfly! Even though the butterfly does seem to rest there, willy nilly."

Love from May: Many of Sarton's recipents in this two-volume selection receive only token representation of correspondences sustained sometimes over decades. So with the letters to Jacobi (see also 24 February 1964); these two women never fell out of touch. *At Seventy,* pp. 69–73, provides a photo of them together and a lively narrative about a 1982 visit to Star Island, New Hampshire; *Endgame,* pp. 24–25, provides a final testimonial after Jacobi's death. A 23 December 1970 Christmas note from Sarton expresses something essential about both the season and her friend and can stand proxy for all the letters left out:

"I have the vision this Xmas that we all make our way toward that manger through pain and loss and old age and in some curious way we go to worship love reborn, not in the Babe, but in the Old, who just like the holy family are those in this civilization least recognized, and that from them comes the holy light. Among all my friends, dear shining heart, I feel it is you who most exemplify the life-giving, life-enhancing <u>riches</u> that the old have to give…and it is partly because (of course) you are not and will <u>never</u> be old." (23 December 1970)

TO ROBB SAGENDORPH   Jan 22d, 1965
[Nelson]
Dear Robb Sagendorph,

Of course no poet expects to live on poetry (except perhaps as a lecturer rather than a writer) but considering your present circulation and the amount of advertising you carry, I must say I think a check for $5 for a poem of 55 lines (mine in your January issue) is just a little worse than nothing. You deprive me of the pleasure of giving you a week's work for free, and you pay me at the rate of about one penny an hour. At the time the New Yorker had about your circulation it was paying $4 or $5 <u>a line</u>. Poetry Chicago which hardly makes ends meet does a good deal better than you do.

Is it not really time, as we enter the Great Society, that poets in the U.S. were treated as members of the human race?

Yours sincerely,
May Sarton

Robb Sagendorph: 1900–70; founder of *Yankee* magazine. The poem was "A Recognition, for Perley Cole."

Yours sincerely: Eight days later, Sarton recalled how transgressors once were punished by heaping atop the head "Coals of fire! Thanks for the generous check. Of course The New Yorker is in a class apart (no other magazine I know of distributes the profits among its writers), and poets never complain because they have such a hard time that they would be grateful (and are) to be published for no pay at all. My battle is not for me, but for poetry itself, the orphan child of nearly all journals . . . Yours cordially."

Sagendorph and poetry editor Jean Burden visited Nelson on 1 October 1967. "There is no one to take her place," Burden wrote in the December 1995 *Yankee* eulogy of Sarton, claiming that "May didn't need the Pulitzer Prize nor the National Book Award. She had her rewards, not always easy to define, but in the long run infinitely more important."

Feb. 7th, 1965
[Nelson]
Dear Eric,

The telephone is a bad thing because one is taken by surprise—I felt the pressure on you and I was not prepared quite for the new title. I have been thinking it over and I would like to make one last plea for

Mrs. Stevens Hears The Mermaids Singing

I have tried out this title on quite a few people and all were enthusiastic. Yesterday Emery Neff (former Prof. of comparative lit. at Columbia) was here for lunch and I tried both on him (your version and mine)—he was absolutely violent against The Mermaids Singing—it sounds like any other semi-poetic novel, sensitive, delicate, fem. writing etc. Mine, he felt, had more reverberation. I myself see now that what it has is irony. One does not expect any "Mrs. Stevens" to hear any mermaids, so there is that slight double-take which makes a title stick in the mind. (Emery said, but this is perhaps too special a reaction:"You see what you are doing is putting together Virginia Woolf and T.S. Eliot, and it is very intriguing") We have to work on the premise that this is not everybody's book. Therefore why not go all out for the kind of reader who will appreciate it and that reader would not go for The Mermaids Singing. I feel it is ambiguous, raises expectations which will not be satisfied, is a lure without being a precise enough one.

I know what a bore it is to have authors yapping at your heels and what all those discussions take out of you when there are a million other things on your mind. BUT a title is awfully important. I know you will agree on that.

If, after this, Sarton's last stand, you still want your title, I'll hold my peace and not sue you for defamation of character!

The point is not that mermaids sing—the point is that some people hear them, and some do not.

Love from
May

Woolf and . . . Eliot: Emery Neff and his wife, Frances, were long-standing treasured friends who lived fifteen miles from Nelson in Westmoreland, New Hampshire; the three visited about twice a year. Neff's point: Sarton's preferred title links one woman's experience of one ordinary day, subtly and sentiently presented in Woolf's 1925 novel *Mrs. Dalloway,* with the yearning for out-of-the-ordinary experience represented by the metamorphosed muses of Eliot's 1917 "The Love Song of J. Alfred Prufrock." Near that poem's conclusion, the speaker wonders whether he can violate social conventions, now that he has heard the siren song of a life beyond convention—in Sarton's story, the artist's life:

> Shall I part my hair behind? Do I dare to eat a peach?
> I shall wear white flannel trousers, and walk upon the beach.

I have heard the mermaids singing, each to each.
I do not think that they will sing to me.
But they sing to Mrs. Stevens, and she writes down her re-creation of their songs.

TO ROSALIND GREENE   Feb. 10th, 1965
at Nelson (and winter again!)
Dearest Rosalind,

The only trouble is that there is <u>too much</u> we have to say to each other! But how great it was to see you, as the outdoor light ebbed and the firelight took over the wonderful room ... next morning I stopped briefly at Anne Thorp's and heard all about The People's Theatre and the performance (inter-racial) of Obey's Noah, which I had dreamed of doing 25 years ago with my little group .... it is very moving to watch from the sidelines you and Anne, each consumed by this "new world" we are making in the U.S. at last. I wish I had heard more about your Roxbury venture, which means that I missed hearing really about what most concerns you. But here anyway is a small check, a token rather than anything it should be. That will save your addressing one envelope anyway!

I felt when I left that I had been clumsy (as usual) in a great many ways and I lay awake pondering on why I am such an oaf. I know I should not have ostentatiously tried to help lift things for you, but darling, your spirit has wings and I just <u>hate</u> you to be troubled with pain—and I know it is there, so I just instinctively move—and then I didn't do the one thing I could have, to carry out the heavy tray! Then, much worse, I spoke about my solitude and how I had learned that no one could help—when <u>you</u> had been perhaps the one person who kept on making supportive gestures during that dark time, and when you yourself were a thousand miles away with a thousand other concerns. How stupid can one be? I suppose what I was trying to say was just that I have (I think) settled for a curiously solitary life where far from meaning little, friends are <u>everything</u>, for what I meant was that in the old days I always imagined <u>one</u> magic person would be the solution to anguish and loneliness. I was thinking of lovers, not friends! But I did not make it clear.

I suppose the strangest thing about my life is that it has to be such a mad risk—I <u>don't</u> help people as you do nor give time to what is so important just now. I have to try to believe that somehow my work will help people understand each other better—the responsibility is awful, the self-doubt excruciating. If I fail, then I shall have failed <u>entièrement</u>—that is all I meant really when I said, "I faced that this was my agony and I alone could handle it"—the <u>handling</u> being the ability to continue to create somehow and to keep the demons of doubt at bay.

When the novel looked like a failure I was very frightened because I thought I had perhaps reached the end of what I could do as a writer—at the same time as a teacher. But they were both things that I had somehow to make peace with <u>alone</u>. I feel it more just now, because I realize that the truth can hurt, is dangerous and it is better that no one come anywhere near me. Being a poet and the kind of person I am makes me far <u>more</u> of a leper than any Negro ever was.

But what I have to do, I think, is to withdraw more and more, in order more and more to be able to give. If there is arrogance here, believe me, Rosalind, it has been paid for and will be, in much anguish of spirit. But at least here in Nelson I am accepted as an eccentric—there are many of different kinds around—I am not sneered at as I may well be "outside in the world" when this novel comes out. It is a great protection for my soul.

But oh at the same time (and I never forget it) how lucky I am, to have freedom, to have time, to have friends—and to have Nelson! Here in the end I shall do my best work and I believe it is still to come. Perhaps the novel was only a block in the way and when it is out, I can begin at last to write about this village, as I mean to do.

I want to copy out for you a poem I may already have sent you—it was written long ago to Saunders Redding, a Negro writer at (I can't remember the name of the college at the moment)—it is in Va. a Negro college. I think I shall put it in the new book, one of the few "personal" poems this time.

That is all.

Dear love from

Your ancient battered friend
M

---

*Rosalind Greene:*1885–1975. From her earliest years Sarton shared Greene family outings and grew up with the four girls, being especially close to Katrine. Having nursed acting ambitions herself, Rosalind greatly supported Sarton's early theatre efforts: 6 November 1933 finds Mabel Sarton writing, 'Mrs. Greene is a host in herself. She frightens me with her efficiency. She is in Boston locating halls for your second performance."

"I am going this afternoon to a gathering of a clan, under a cherry tree, all the Greenes (COPLEY-Greenes as they like to be called)," Sarton wrote Bogan in 1954. (This is the same Copley as in Copley Square, Boston.) They were "a rather formidable family of high-powered women who have a rather peculiar neighing laugh so I hope it will be outside where this is more bearable. I shouldn't say mean things about her," but that same year a journal entry (6 January) recounted a conversation with Anne Thorp about Greene, "the way in which her praise is always somehow a denigration." Greene's daughters, of whom she demanded much, felt this keenly. "She spoke of mother [Mabel Sarton] always as CHIEFLY a gardener. Of Anne (who resents this) as 'good to her friends' and the way she fixed one with her glaring eye and said 'Take care of yourself.' "

"She lived consciously by the device of noblesse oblige, by the aristocratic ethos," Sarton wrote later—the conviction that "Noble birth imposes the obligation of high-minded principles and noble actions." But "noblesse" could take less benign forms, as in the 1935 débâcle that finally killed Sarton's Associated Actors Theatre, which Radcliffe had agreed to sponsor. Having recruited former Shady Hill director Katharine Taylor to support her, Greene visited president Ada Comstock Notestein and threatened to tell the trustees about lesbians in the company, somehow not implicating Sarton herself; Notestein was unwillingly forced to revoke the underwriting. (See *Encore,* pp. 81–82, for this episode.)

Nonetheless, "Song for Rosalind" (1942) was written for her (see the appendix to *Letters 1916–54* and a 1951 letter), as was "For Rosalind on Her Seventy-fifth Birthday" (first published 1971). Greene wrote evocatively of Sarton's poetry. After Christmas 1961, to counteract the Shapiro review of *Cloud, Stone, Sun, Vine,* Greene echoed the words of "Beloved May": " 'Time slides away, and how are we to taste it?' And surely we can taste it only, because as a queer grace in the confusion of the slow evolution of man, Poets are born and show us how to find 'Beautiful Pauses!' "

Earlier, 6 November 1953, Greene singled out from *The Land of Silence* such poems as "The Swans," "Villanelle for Fireworks," "The Sacred Wood," and "Provence": "As you see, the poems of visual image captivate me. Your gift, in this realm, is rare—extraordinary. I have always cherished the belief that you and your father are Arabs—the black Belgians (I knew a handsome hawk-profiled Belgian poet when I was young) are, I think, part of the Spanish-Moorish inheritance. And that brilliance of the visual image, as in Persian miniatures, is quite unique."

For Greene's own attempts at poetry, see *House by the Sea,* pp. 93–95; for her character, pp. 81–83. Greene is a difficult person to sum up; it was while trying to write her portrait for *A World of Light* that Sarton came to realize "The past is a minefield."

Anne Thorp: Friend of the Sarton family, Anne Longfellow Thorp (1894–1977)—granddaughter of the poet—was young May's inspiring teacher at Shady Hill, as testified to in *At Fifteen* and the poems written to her in *Catching Beauty.* A 1929 letter to her appears in *Letters 1916–54; Solitude,* pp. 172–73, sketches her personality. In 1965, as she did each summer, Sarton spent a few weeks with Judith Matlack on Greenings Island, the home of "the most beneficent person I have ever known" (to Kay Martin, 5 August 1965).

Obey's Noah: Noé (1931), a wittily poetic treatment of the Noah story by French playwright and actor-manager André Obey (1892–1975). The People's Theatre seems to have been a community drama group.

Roxbury venture: Greene was deeply involved in some youth sponsorship program the exact nature of which is unclear—except that Sarton wrote concerning it: "I was thrilled that the Stokely Carmichael day in Roxbury turned out to be a kind of intimate rejoicing rather than an angry mob."

copy out . . . a poem: "Conversation in Black and White, for Saunders Redding," first published in *The Nation,* 1 November 1958. Sarton met Redding at the Hampton Institute in Hampton, Virginia, when she spoke there on 21 November 1957. "We had a long talk," she wrote Evie Ames, 12 December 1957, "and I felt so the pain always under the surface and how it <u>must</u> be talked about."

TO DOROTHY WALLACE   [12 April 1965]
[Beloit, Wisconsin]
Dorothy darling, how splendid to find your letter here (brought over from Rockford) when I flew in through El Greco skies just before a tornado hit near Monroe and knocked down 50 houses! The wind was ter-

rific but, unaware of danger, I was simply in delight at the great moving skies…no damage here. I have felt terribly cut off from you lately and it was like an act of God that I could not seem to reach you by telephone, or a Kafka story—so great joy at your word. This is before I have been to Rockford but I am writing now as there won't be a free hour probably after today until I am back at Nelson on Easter day—but I'll write as soon as I can a play by play description and I shall be very discreet about The Goldwater caper.

It seems unbelievable that when you open this you will be in Jerusalem! "If I forget thee O Jerusalem!" And I think perhaps you are having a great time, for once with no family on your mind, a free agent, the great Lion roving alone..I trust by now several distinguished men have told you you are beautiful and adorable and that you have dismissed them all with a royal look?

As for me, this is the longest (not in time but in effort somehow) lecture trip I can remember and I long never to go out again, but I think perhaps I was too tired when I started out after this gruelling year..and also had flu the week before which didn't help. Shades of it pursue me (I had 101 fever in Chicago day before yesterday but am revived now at the dear Chad Walshes here)—There have been some golden hours, nevertheless—one at the Philadelphia zoo where I watched entranced a young lion playing exactly like a pussy cat with his tail and leaping about in what appeared to be pure self-delight. And the aviaries there are just like the garden of Eden, with waterfalls and little pools and groves of bamboo and camellia trees and many brilliant birds all together—I wanted so much to be a bird for a while and there sitting and singing safe and calm. Instead I spent a day in bed weeping from sheer exhaustion and even thought of taking a plane home and going to a hospital but I got over that panic and since then things have gone better. I was really overworked at the U. of Pa. and also irritated by the indifference and lack of talent of the students. No medical student could get away with such laziness, and surely young writers should be equally on the qui vive, if not more so. But there were a couple of dear boys, one really talented one. They all responded wonderfully to watching an ancient woman pour out her blood before them in daily ovations, without the slightest idea what this sort of performance costs, nor that it should be deserved.

Well, anyway it was finally over and I fell into a wonderful Catholic college at last as usual revived by the innocence and the discipline, was allowed to attend compline (these were Dominican nuns) which is like a slow pavane—they walk around with candles, bowing and kneeling in a lovely slow rhythm. Soul could be visible and I felt at home. Everywhere (at Rosary, too) it is most moving to see how students are moving quietly in to the great work before us: in every college students are tutoring Negros in the city slums, for instance, and all speak of what a nourishing exchange it is—and what an eye-opener for them. No one expects quick results. Here at Beloit one of the girl students worked in Harlem last summer and discovered a Porto Rican boy and persuaded the college to take him on a scholarship though he was utterly not able to pass the exams—he did very badly at first but in this last term got straight A's—so it just <u>shows</u> what can be done when caring and faith can rouse latent intelligence and overcome the despairing protective apathy so many have fallen into.

I can hardly wait for this week to be over and to be home again—and by then you will be <u>almost home</u>—I have an idea that I missed your birthday this year somewhere along the way. But one day perhaps we can celebrate a joint one—and meanwhile, darling, many loving thanks—for your letter and for you and for opening the door at Rockford.

Ever your
May

[*Beloit, Wisconsin*]: En route to Rockford, Illinois, where Wallace had encouraged her to speak, Sarton visited Beloit College, just north of the border into Wisconsin, to see her friends the Reverend Chad Walsh and his wife, Eva; a known poet and author (1915–91), he was professor of English there thirty-two years. In 1965 he edited *Garlands for Christmas: A Selection of Poetry,* including Sarton's "Nativity: Piero della Francesca." Monroe is to the west.

El Greco . . . Kafka: Turbulent grey and sulphur cloudscapes are prominent in paintings by Spanish artist El Greco ("The Greek"), 1541–1614.

The tales of Austrian author Franz Kafka (1883–1924) feature characters trapped in waking matter-of-fact nightmares.

O Jerusalem!": Wallace, widowed for six years, had joined an archaeological study tour led by renowned biblical and Ugaritic scholar Cyrus Gordon (1909–2001). Sarton was reminded of Psalm 137:5: "If I forget thee, O Jerusalem, let my right hand forget her cunning."

overworked: For two weeks Sarton prepared and taught four weekly meetings of two hours each at the University as well as speaking at the nearby Baldwin School.

Catholic college: Rosary College, in Forest River, Illinois; see note to 9 November 1958 for her encounter there with Sister Jeremy. Dominicans are a mendicant order dedicated to teaching.

Compline, 8 or 9 P.M., is the seventh and last of the Church's canonical "hours," each hour having its own particular prayers.

The pavane (from "Padua," Italy) is a stately sixteenth-century court dance or the slow duple time music for it.

I missed your birthday this year: An anomaly, as Sarton kept careful notations of friends' birthdays and was committed to remembering them. Twenty-eight years later, as her contribution to the birthday albums daughter Connie Wallace Gordon was preparing for a gala 1 March 1993 celebration, Sarton wrote "An Eightieth Birthday, for Dorothy Wallace," dated November 1992; see appendix. *At Eighty-two,* pp. 113–17, recounts a reunion of the old friends that October.

[Nelson]

Dear Richard,

The book is a treasure! I have lost myself in good dreams of next spring—and it came at a good time, as I have had rather a hard and exhausting spring so far ... first there was a gruelling lecture trip in late March and April (I got home for Easter) which took me to Chicago and Wisconsin and Philadelphia. For the first time—I have been doing this for 25 years—I felt simply too old and tired and it was all a huge sterile effort, not helped by a bad attack of grippe so that some of the time I was speaking with a temp. of 100. You ask whether I know the MidWest—indeed I do. You see, there are literally hundreds of colleges and state Universities there and for years I have been somewhere there in the spring—in Southern Indiana and in Iowa the spring is heavenly—there are wonderful woods <u>full</u> of every kind of wildflower including my favorite hepaticas—but also anemones, Dutchman's-breeches, every sort of violet, trillium—

The one good thing about my trip this time was to learn how many many students from all the colleges (including Catholic ones) are volunteer tutors now for Negro children in the big cities. The "movement" is far more serious and sustained than just the dramatic "marches" show. I feel myself that this country is getting back its soul—and thanks to the Negro. For the first time since the Spanish Civil War the students are really involved.

But I longed to be home again, and arrived the Sat. before Easter, more dead than alive, only to find that one of my cats (they were both in a kennel for a month but there was nothing else to do) was very ill indeed—so instead of sleeping for days and gardening and in general restoring my depleted forces, I have been a night and day nurse to the poor little creature. It has meant getting up at six to get household chores done in time to drive her 5 miles down to the Vet's for daily injections—feeding her every hour with a medicine dropper, forcing pills down her throat, wiping her face (the disease is numinitis—and it is a disgusting one as the cat's mouth, eyes and nose are all full of mucous). It is now the 16th day of this ordeal and last night she got up suddenly (she sleeps beside me) at three A.M. and staggered to the kitchen and began to <u>eat</u>—I nearly cried with relief. So I think the worst may be over at last.

The spring is very late here—at least two weeks late—not a leaf out yet, although the lilacs are showing little leaf-buds at last—a few daffodils and crocus in front of the house are out. But the grass is still gray. However I have begun to sow the vegetable and annual garden—

Thanks again for the grand book, just what I yearned for. Give May my love and tell her I am delighted the check came in handy.

Best wishes to you all—
Cousin May

———

Richard Pipe: A cousin by marriage, over ninety at the present time. His wife, May "April" Dorling, daughter of Alice "Gram" Dorling (Eleanor Mabel Sarton's first cousin) and sister of Ruby, Evelyn [Mann], Arthur [Rose], and Ivy [Eastaugh], was one of the cousins in England who took the infant May in as a refugee in 1914. Isobel [Strickland] is one of the Pipes' three children. Richard Pipe and Sarton held similar political views. He had been the left-wing leader of the Ipswich dockworkers before he retired with his wife to Dakons, a large country house outside Ipswich; he wrote extensive pieces of local interest for the paper there. Sarton always sent her cousins generous checks at Christmas; the book was probably a pictorial volume on Britain, a present for her fifty-third birthday.

the Spanish Civil War: In the 1936–39 conflict, conservatives overthrew the Second Spanish Republic, with devastation and death tolls hitherto unknown in the country's history; it initiated a right-wing dictatorship that did not end until Franco died in 1975. From all over the world volunteers went and fought, and intellectuals took sides, including Ernest Hemingway, George Orwell, Auden, and Rukeyser, among many others.

numinitis: Pneumonitis, a feline disease now preventable by vaccine. A week later, after being fed dextrose in a medicine dropper, Fuzz-Buzz finally responded to cortisone.

Cousin May: Sarton never fell out of touch with the Pipes; see *Endgame,* pp. 197–98, and *Encore,* pp. 229–30, for visits in spring 1989 and March 1992 respectively.

TO BASIL DE SÉLINCOURT   June 24th, 1965
[Nelson]
Dearest ones,

Not only have we had a great storm of rain, white foaming waves of it so one felt one was under the sea for hours, but your long-awaited word about the novel came this morning. First let me say how very grateful I am for Jay's word about it. You can understand now, no doubt, why I was reluctant to send the proofs long before I knew Basil (the darling) would be in no state to read them....I sensed that this book would be a shock to him. But I was a little dismayed to have Sodom and Gomorrah thrown at me! (I am smiling as I write this).

Dearest Basil, please look into your heart and discover whether you really believe the Almighty would have consigned Socrates and Shakespeare to the flames? Both, if you remember, wrote eloquently of the love of boys....and in fact long ago Julian Huxley told me when we talked about this, that all through nature there is a definite regular percent of "deviants" from very low-grade creatures like slugs up to the higher mammals. So it looks as if it really were a part of this mysterious creation from the start. In human terms my guess is that the creative nature is itself and in itself a marriage between masculine and feminine (as everyone must be to some extent) so we find a great many artists, poets, painters, composers who lead lives out of the ordinary. The sadness is that these people have been so cruelly persecuted....just as cats were burned as witches in the 17th century. What has to be fought (although my novel is too special to do so in any universal way) is the tendency to lump all these people as criminals. Some are criminals, no doubt of it. But then there are many heterosexual criminals too—pimps, prostitutes, thieves etc. The necessity for concealment, hence for dishonesty, leads to criminal lives often. I simply do not believe that there is danger to "society" or that there would ever be enough such people to tip the balance away from normality for the vast majority (It is not a contagious disease).

I am sure you have never considered how many people you admire are this way—[composer] Benjamin Britten comes at once to mind, for one. The writers (women) Sybille Bedford, H.D., Bryher; the composer Dame Ethel Smyth. I could make a long list but it seems pointless to do so. Not only [André] Gide, but Julien Green in France. Proust.

Until now the literature has emphasized the criminal types—and recently there have been some horrible examples. My own feeling is that where sex is exploited (by any sex) without love, it is always criminal and disgusting. And in some ways my book is a reaction: what interests me is the imagination. And I have waited until I had a firm reputation and had written enough books which show that I understand and am for the normal human situation, so that this should take its place in the series of novels as one out of nine or ten. I felt it would be dishonest not to come out into the open—that this was mandatory for my own true relation with myself. And now it is done, I doubt if the subject will come up again in any future work. The new book of poems, by the way, has no love poems in it, and this also is deliberate.

I got it off yesterday and enclose a sample.

Please forgive this long screed—I do so wish we could talk. It was most moving to have a page in Basil's own hand and I know what an effort it must have been—

How lovely the garden sounds! Thank you, dear Jay, for telling me just how it looks—and for being able to visualize Basil's days, savoring the leaves, the light and shadow, petals, birds .... my garden, too, is just glorious—a paean of peonies, roses, iris and now the Oriental poppies—pale pink with shaggy black hearts—

And now the book is off, I can catch up at last with all I laid aside, and make some order out of the chaos on my desk. Judy has just been here for a week, and is settling back into Wright St. after her year away—and we go off to Anne Thorp's island on Aug. 1st for two weeks of real holiday.

All blessings and love

Your old battered

M

P.S. I have tried to decipher Basil's last word but am stuck—"much love to you and your remaining wings"? It looks like. But can it be?

Sodom and Gomorrah: In Genesis 19, these two Cities of the Plain were destroyed by heavenly brimstone for persisting in their sexual proclivities. They also supply the title for the fourth volume (1921–22) of *À la Recherche du Temps Perdu* (*Remembrance of Things Past*, or *In Search of Lost Time*) by Marcel Proust (1871–1922), which spotlights modern-day French descendants of those cities.

This letter is Sarton's urbane, coaxing response to de Sélincourt's prejudiced denunciation of the homosexual themes quite openly addressed—for mainstream fiction, 1965—in *Mrs. Stevens.* (Homosexuality was not legally decriminalized in Britain until 1967.) Rather than dictate his censure, de Sélincourt was sufficiently stirred to write a page by hand, despite his physical debilitations. *Mrs. Stevens Hears the Mermaids Singing* is dedicated "To The Muse."

TO HELEN STORM CORSA   Aug. 6th, 1965 c/o Thorp
[Greenings Island]
Darling,

It was an act of love to write that difficult letter and believe me I know it. Many thanks. It made me wish we could talk and yet I think maybe we are each too prickly still (for various reasons) to do so in the clear peace which one hopes may some day come to us. . . and after all, life with no controversy or reason for disagreement would also perhaps atrophy in the end. I learn a great deal, though painfully, this way.

Naturally I am sad that you did not like the novel—but not too surprised. I care what you think. It may be that in ten years I shall see it as you do, and you must forgive me if I cannot do so now. If I did, I would not have allowed it to go out to the public. I expect I may get some bad blows from the reviewers and I cannot deny that I am very anxious, as I know you are. But in the deeps of my being, I am at peace—and every day more aware of what a load off my mind there is. For I have been preparing for this book for nearly 30 years, although I could not write it until after the episode of Margaret Clapp—for it is that episode which forced me to come to terms with the Muse once and for all, and to recognize what she is—never to be "known", never really to be loved as one loves someone with whom one lives through a great deal—but the catalyser. So, although it may seem immature to you, for me both the episode and the book have been a major turning point in my life and in my work.

It is this about which I really wish to speak with you now. It is significant that <u>after</u> finishing the novel I was able to come to a real break through on new poems—poems also held back for three years—in a new <u>style</u> and that this book of poems contains no love poems. It is also significant, I believe, that only after the novel was finished did I begin to see ahead into the next fifteen years of my work in terms of a series of novels which will be in no way autobiographical—and to which I look forward because in them I can I believe make a rather valuable statement about life in the United States—and never before had I a social milieu complex enough, ranging about enough kinds of people and lives, to make this possible. Also I wasn't ready as a person or as a writer.

I feel very solid about my life these days. I do not foresee any other intimacy—as you know, solitude has become precious to me, and I am now able to have it at Nelson and <u>also</u> to share it, as I have done this summer with at least three separate people whom I watched revive and able to do good work of their own there. I am beginning at last to be the giver and not the taker .. and if this is late in life, still it is not too late.

Judy and I seem to come to a deeper and deeper understanding and to enjoy each other more every time we are together—as here [Greenings Island] now. As at Nelson this summer.

The break with Wellesley, so painful at the time for several reasons, seems to me now a natural and good part of the big life line—I shall not perhaps be teaching as much after this fall. As far as Margaret goes, I have the warmest feeling—I know she is there, I am sure she is fond of me (it was kind of her for instance to acknowledge the book and say she will read it, and I know she will not mention it again, but I understand—all that is accepted and understood and under my belt. And in ten years or so, I know too that I shall see her and that we will be able to talk.)

There are many big efforts ahead to be made, but I feel capable of handling them. And even if reviews on this book are bad it will be over in about two months and behind me. I shall not be publishing anything of the new novels for three years and by then whatever bad press there was will be forgotten. There is a mountain of other work on which I stand.

I'm sorry I used the word "had" about Cath. It was indeed clumsy but I am glad I did it as it brought forth a fine and moving statement from you. I do have an inkling of what you have fought through to <u>be</u> and I am staggered and overwhelmed to think what it has cost—but all worth it, because you come clear into your real self and that is so visible and audible in this letter.

I wish I had Henry James by me to dig out the quote about "We do what we can—we give what we are—and the rest is the madness of art" or something like that. In any total opus the failures have their importance and if this book is one, it was, I think necessary for me at this stage. The risk is and was immense. "But there's more enterprise in going naked"—and, as you know, <u>disguise</u> is not in my ethos, never has been, never will be. So help me God. (here I think perhaps there is a real difference between the artist and the critic: the critic does not have to give himself away. The artist (especially the woman artist) does have to.

I know that you are truly concerned about the effect the novel may have on my life and on my professional future, so let me comfort you with a couple of statements from recent letters about it. This from Gunther Neufeld (art critic and German Jewish friend from way back:)

"I've just finished Mrs. Stevens (couldn't stop till I'd reached the final word)—it is a <u>beautiful</u> book, and I love it. . . How warm it is, and deeply moving. The central problem, if such it can be called—woman's creativity—emerges in a transparent light, not from cerebral abstraction but from life passionately lived."

And from Agnes Sibley (who teaches at and got me the job at Lindenwood): "it is so completely different from any of your others and yet it has even more power. It seems to me that it involves the reader in life in quite a new way—not so much story, not so much identification of the reader with the characters, but yet he (the reader) is forced to ask himself questions, such as the ones Hilary so relentlessly asks herself—what are the sources of <u>my</u> conflicts, how can I resolve them etc. As to the homosexual aspects, which so worry you, they seem to me much less important than the fundamental questions you raise, about how one can become whole, how to live as a woman in the modern world, how unify life and art."

And this from my religious friend—mother of six—the painter [Mary Campbell], "I feel it is not given to any artist, or any person, to really know how wide or how prolonged or in what way the works of his life will affect other people—how many or where or whom— It is no longer your province, I think, to estimate and expect any sort of reliable or even sensible answer once the work is done and out. Isn't this so? It is my own opinion that your work (and this novel is like the foundation of all the past—it <u>glitters</u> in its truth!) will have long and deep strength and its reverberations will go right on moving and lifting and saving people. It is a <u>saving</u> book, May."

Ruth Harnden, on the other hand, agrees (more or less) with you— It's time for a drink and I'll spare you more. I'll be thinking of you on Aug. 21st and meanwhile, most gratefully

and with much love

Helen Storm Corsa: The sole member of the Wellesley faculty who Sarton felt truly welcomed her, she was one of the five whose letters the *New York Times Review* excerpted to protest the Shapiro review. Having met Sarton in spring 1960, Corsa brought her cello to Nelson that summer and spent many weeks helping in the garden. She inscribed her 1964 study *Chaucer: Poet of Mirth and Morality* (Univ. of Notre Dame Press) "To May, with many thanks for sunlit hours in Nelson and its 'garden of such prys/ But it wer the verray paradys'/ Love Helen/ March 1964." Though she was not a muse, Sarton would later write Evelyn Ames (29 October 1966) that "Helen has been here for ten days, a most re-assuring time—I have begun to think for a while I simply could not believe that a happy love could be <u>real</u>. But now I do!"

sorry . . . about Cath: Apparently Corsa's psychiatrist. "You say I 'have Dr. Cath.'. . . If you mean that I have a loving, supportive, all gentle father you are <u>quite</u> mistaken," Corsa had written. "He is an austere, strict disciplinarian . . by hard, anxiety-ridden work I have learned . . mature values. I do not 'have' him in any sense."

Henry James: In the 1893 tale "The Middle Years," the novelist Dencombe says, on his deathbed, "A second chance—*that's* the delusion. There never was to be but one. We work in the dark—we do what we can—we give what we have. Our doubt is our passion and our passion is our task. The rest is the madness of art."

The "enterprise" quotation is from Yeats's 1914 poem "A Coat," *Responsibilities.*

Gunther Neufeld: An old writer friend, fellow refugee with Belgian roots who lived with his wife, Rose, in Concord, Massachusetts; they often house-sat in Nelson.

Agnes Sibley . . . Lindenwood: She was "the dear person who leapt into the breach when I lost the Wellesley job," Sarton wrote Basil de Sélincourt, 23 July 1965, "and persuaded the President [of Lindenwood]. . . to make me that grand offer for the autumn." By October she was writing Judith Matlack: "the albatross continues to be Agnes, who is a dear, but terribly dependent."

Ruth Harnden: See note for 6 June [1957].

TO ELIZABETH BOWEN   Aug. 25 [1965]
[Nelson]
Dear Elisabeth,

It is autumn here suddenly. John Meixner harried and harrowed me for half a day yesterday about you and your work. He is, as critics go, intelligent and able, but I had terrible nostalgia for you when I went to bed, finally in a state of exhaustion and illumination (self-illumination!). He told me that Bowen's Court has been torn down: he described it. Howard Moss had told me, but somehow I could not register or believe it. Now I have to. He [Meixner] told me that you think I am "cheeky" to have written about the house in that long ago novel. I suddenly realized that that was a true comment, but it had never occurred to me. I am sorry. I would however, probably do the same thing again.

But what I cannot believe is that you and I have ceased to be friends. Elizabeth, all around me, friends are dying now (I am 53). I have just come back from a day in N.Y. to see one, just my age, whom I do not expect to see alive again. I see nothing that passed between you and me, or between me and the world about you which justifies this cancelling out. And in my heart of hearts I simply <u>do not believe</u> in it.

So—I am moved tonight to speak to you once more about this house. About this village. This house is for solitude and work and I have done good work here; also I have lent it to people when I am away who have always <u>felt</u> the atmosphere very strongly. The village (I am right on the Green) is so silent, so remote, so peaceful. The house is so comfortable, light—5 fireplaces—snug, warm in winter, full of light, books, big tables, to work at. Bathrooms. Furnace. Easy big room where I cook and live. It is beautiful. Also there are planes twice a day to and from N.Y. No one around here would have the remotest idea who you are, as Mrs. Cameron. My local friends would welcome and cherish you as they do all my friends, and leave you alone to work, as they do me. I wish very much that you could come here when Judy and I go to Europe next spring (to celebrate her retirement) mid-March until mid-June. I would leave you my car (without one one cannot live here as there is no store except a small one two miles away—I do a big shopping and errands and have lunch once a week in "the town," Keene, N.H.) The pussy cats (2) would welcome you in lieu of me, and a neighbor would look after them when you wanted to go to N.Y. I would so hope that anyone you wanted to see could fly up—it might be a good place for you. But I know so little of your life now, I hardly know to whom this is addressed—a swanlike person with whom I fell in love thirty years ago, an old <u>friend</u>, a writer whom I have long admired, the wife of Alan whom I loved dearly. Elizabeth.

I suppose I was cheeky when young. Now I am rather old and battered, un-successful, full of works and patience. You would hardly know me now. Yet I have come into some sort of plane on which all goes well. I am happy and at peace. Just now an apple fell down with a huge, terrifying thud (I always forget how loud it will be when the first one falls). I am off in two weeks to a three month job as poet in res. at a small midwestern college. A new novel comes out soon—then new poems. I do not expect an answer of course. But please think about next spring.

Elizabeth Bowen: For previous correspondence with her, see *Letters 1916–54*. John Meixner was the "young scholar" who suggested she resented Sarton's recasting Bowen's Court as "Dene's Court" in *A Shower of Summer Days*; but her own letter of praise for the novel disproves that theory. See "Elizabeth Bowen," *A World of Light*, pp. 209–10. Poet and critic Howard Moss, *The New Yorker*'s poetry editor from 1950 until his death in 1987, wrote about Bowen for the magazine. Sarton wrote "Because What I Want Most Is Permanence" (1953) for her.

Bowen's Court, near Kildorrery, County Cork, had been finished in 1775 and kept in the family since; but after the death of husband Alan Cameron (see 24 February 1973), Bowen could not maintain the large house and demesne with what she earned by writing and teaching. Sold, it was torn down in 1960. See her family history *Bowen's Court* (1942; rev. ed., 1964). Like other celebrated women of that period, "Mrs. Alan Cameron" sometimes found her married name a useful camouflage.

nothing . . . justifies this cancelling out: "For the last twenty years of her life I did not see Elizabeth," Sarton says in *A World of Light* (p. 210). Bowen died in 1973; there was the 1955 stay at Corkagh House (*World*, pp. 206–08), then Sarton's last visit to Bowen's Court in 1957, when she lost ground to the "charming and beautiful young Californian," Miss Lovelace (*World* pp. 208–09), akin to her own younger self.

"It is one of the unfair facts of life," observes Victoria Glendinning, "that people who are greatly loved and valued can afford to behave much more unpredictably than other people without in any way jeopardising their position: indeed it can even enhance their value." (*Elizabeth Bowen: A Biography,* 1977, p. 241) Possibly; but Bowen staunchly believed in loyalty (see her 1950 essay on "Disloyalties" in *Seven Winters and Afterthoughts,* 1962) and would not have severed a longtime friendship over this seriocomic interlude. True, for some reason Sarton "had become a second-class citizen in Elizabeth's province"; perhaps a future biography will clarify the older woman's motives. But as for thinking about "next spring," Bowen did not visit Sarton again.

During World War II Bowen served as an air-raid warden in Regent's Park, her neighborhood in London, ensuring that the blackout was observed and pedestrians went to shelters when sirens sounded. Her short stories of the Blitz, *The Demon Lover* (1946), and her novel *The Heat of the Day* (1949) attest to her undaunted courage and capacity for observation. In recognition of their earlier rapport, see the appendix for a poem Sarton wrote for her in 1947, "After the War, for Elisabeth."

TO LOUISE BOGAN   Oct. 25th, 1965
[St. Charles, Mo.]
Dear Louise,

I was awfully glad to hear, but am a little surprised that you apparently never received a letter I wrote a few days ago, immediately on reception of yours, where you thought you might move. It was addressed to Louise **Bogan** (not Holden and that may be the trouble) I'm sorry for I wanted you to know how very much I think of you every day sending little butterfly messages—and when I wrote then I was not quite such a heap of exhaustion as I am today.

I also sent ages ago also to L.B. a little funny stained glass pendant thing to hang in your window, so I begin to feel rather Kafka-ish and baffled....

It's good to know that you like the Doctor, as you told me in your first letter and that in this one you seem less felled by your fellow inmates! Also that you are off tranquilizers—I am <u>on</u> them as I try to survive the sneers which pile up on Mrs. S. (The N.Y. Times was not bad but the heading was "Down Memory Lane with Hilary"—how cheap can you get as you would say?) Someone called Rennert gave it a great sneer in the Herald-Trib and accused me of being in The Establishment. This is rather like telling Christ in the wilderness that he is a notorious

winebibber in the dens of Athens—(I do not mean to sound blasphemous but can hardly think of a strong enough metaphor for my isolation has been complete for <u>years</u> and I have suffered so much from it)
The Sat. Review was even worse—there have been some very good
ones, but not <u>one</u> intelligent one. I keep thinking of Robert [Frost]'s
> "No one can know how glad I am to find
> On any page the least display of mind."

Of course I have laid myself open—I hope never to live through
another three months of torment such as these. I begin to feel quite paranoid. And it is like swallowing glass after glass of poison—just absorbing
it makes my whole physical being ill for days and is so exhausting and
wasteful of energies I need here for work. I wish I could go to Nelson
and bury myself for months and even years in <u>silence</u>. I am just deathly
tired of the struggle—it is now the 17th time I have come up to that fir-
ing line with the best I have to give and I have never got through.

What makes for further depression is that Ellen Douglass Leyburn,
my dear friend from Atlanta, is now in the death throes of cancer—I
heard her voice for the last time on Sunday when she said she had no
longer the strength to answer (as I can well understand, but it was my
only way of keeping in touch as she can't write). I have cried so much in
the last 48 hours that I can barely see. So you see, dear heart, I fear I am
not much <u>help</u>—except I <u>am</u> here, and fond, and dismayed that you
have not got my messages along the way.

The classes go well enough and are a distraction, I suppose. I pine for
solitude which is really my element these years— The autumn is very
lovely here—gentle like England. But hardly any birds sing—I miss the
birds. And go to the Zoo to cheer me up. Here is a poem about bears
["Bears and Waterfalls"] which I trust will seem a bit more like a letter
than this poor wail—

We'll <u>survive</u>, darling!

> Ever your
> May

Holden: "Louise Bogan stood for public reticence," Ruth Limmer reminds us in her introduction to *What the Woman Lived*; from July 1937 onward she lived on Manhattan's 169th Street
where, despite her divorce, "the slit beside the bell in her apartment house read 'Holden.'"

fellow inmates!: Suffering from clinical depression, in June 1965 Bogan checked into the New
York Neurological Institute, where she had sought help during her first breakdown. ("I
refused to fall apart," she wrote 11 April 1931, *What the Woman Lived,* "so I have been taken
apart, like a watch.") In September 1965 she returned to Bloomingdale Hospital, White
Plains, where she had gone after her second (and last previous) breakdown in 1933; she
remained there until December.

For despite a summer respite, by 28 August she had to remind herself of her "consistently *optimistic*" outlook over the past three decades: "I have surmounted one difficulty after another; I have *worked* for life and 'creativity'; I have cast off all the anxieties and fears I could; I have helped others to work and hold on. Why this collapse of psychic energy?" (*Journey around My Room: The Autobiography of Louise Bogan: A Mosaic* by Ruth Limmer, 1980, p. 174, a passage that should be read in full to understand the woman Sarton was striving to exhort.)

sneers . . . pile up: In "Down Memory Lane with Mrs. Stevens," *The New York Times Book Review* said, 24 October 1965, "The plot is deceptively simple, the mood subtle, the feeling intense." But in *Book Week* (24 October), a supplement distributed by the *The New York Herald Tribune* to various big-city newspapers, Maggie Rennert scolded Sarton for "bruising English grammar and felicity as grievously as any beatnik without offering either freshness or meaning or the thrill of rebellion." Ruth Brown, in the *Saturday Review* (23 October), found the style "sensitive to the point of fussiness, and totally without humor."

One of the most positive appraisals came from Sarton champion Eugenia Thornton (*Cleveland Plain Dealer,* 10 October): *Mrs. Stevens* is "a small classic; perfect in form; high in feeling, truth, and reverence for the best to be found in all things and all relationships." Reviews in Britain the next year were much more appreciative.

Christ in the wilderness: In the Gospels, Matthew 4:1–11, Mark 1:12–13, and Luke 4:1–13 tell how Jesus went into the wilderness and fasted forty days and was tempted by the devil, who offered among other enticements worldly authority in addition to worldly acclaim.

We'll survive, *darling!:* On 3 November 1965 (*What the Woman Lived*), Bogan wrote from White Plains: "Dear May, how wonderful it is to be unburdened by depression once more! To be at the mercy of that *oppression* is one of the most frightful experiences possible. . . . Write again!"

TO MADELEINE L'ENGLE   Jan. 13th, 1966
[Nelson]
Dearest Madeleine,

I knew Jan. 13th would bring some good news—and it was wonderful prayer answered to have your letter. Last year on Jan. 12th I thought 1) that I would have no job for the year ahead as Wellesley College had dropped me, 2) that Mrs. S. would not be published as both Diarmuid and my English agent, a woman, did not like it at all 3) well-drillers had been here for weeks drilling for artesian water because of the drought— and used dynamite, roughly, far too strong a dose and had just covered the snow white newly painted house with thick black goo. But on Jan. 13th I heard that Norton loved Mrs. S. and would pay $3000 advance; the well drillers struck water at 80 feet—unheard of luck, and I had a nibble of a job which turned into a splendid poet in res. job for $5000 for ten weeks this fall! I shall never forget that day—I nearly had a heart attack from sheer relief.

But Jan. is apt to be a hard month—do you agree?

It is so grand about the new adult book—I shall be waiting so eagerly to read it! Then I was very happy to hear you had that good time with Jo and Le G. I saw her in St. Louis for a wonderful evening (though she had an abscess under one eye and was in great pain, poor dear) and thought she was miraculously right as The Madwoman. Unfortunately I then saw her as Hecuba in The Women of Troy and simply loathed the whole production. It confirmed my belief that the Greek plays must be stylized, the actors wearing masks if possible—the alternative, which Peggy Webster (who directed it) chose, is to create gigantic <u>human</u> figures who then almost inevitably overplay. Le G. played Hecuba as a wild old woman not as a Queen, grieved so loudly for one hour and three quarters that the audience was left stone cold. I had said I would go back[stage] and she was actually dismayed that I was not in tears, and I just couldn't conceal my lack of feeling. Lay awake all night and wrote her a long letter about it—probably a mistake, for she never answered. She is, I think at her best, by far the greatest actress I have ever seen (and I have often said so) but also she can be one of the worst. I wish I knew what you thought of that production, but don't suppose you will see it. The chorus was very good and very well directed, but I thought everyone else just awful.

It is very grim about the strike. I feel for all the theatre people and especially for Hugh—what wretched bad luck! I had some of the same as Mrs. S. came out during the paper strike—and was never reviewed at all in the daily N.Y. papers which have usually done well by me. So there was nothing to counteract really devastating <u>sneers</u> in Time, Sat. Review and the Trib Books which goes to Washington, Chicago and San Francisco as well, as you know. I did persuade Norton to run a full page Ad before Xmas as a sort of consolation prize but sales are low, 6700 up to now. I am sure you know that it was a terrible anguish to write that book and I suffered the pains of Hell over the reviews all fall—but I do understand why it did not please. It really is a very uncomfortable and uncomforting book—naught for your comfort. And that is why it was so hard for an optimist like me to come to terms with. Someday we must talk. I know there are grave flaws—but I do want so much to know all your feelings about it.

And there is just a chance that we might, for today also Norton called to say that PEN is giving a party for the book of poems, A Private Mythology (poems about the trip around the world I took to celebrate my 50th birthday—and rather deliberately <u>no</u> personal poems this time) and this is to be—the party, I mean, either March 21st or March 28th— I presume I can invite friends and maybe you and Hugh and I could have dinner afterwards? Of course, these are never very human occasions—I already dread it in advance, but it would be human and lovely to see you.

Before I forget, The Music Box Bird got into the final 5 in a contest for some organization in Evansville, Ind. but did not win. But the sweet man who runs it liked the play so much (and wanted it to win) that he is trying still to get a production for me somewhere...A movie co. keeps taking up the option on Joanna and Ulysses (the people who made David and Lisa so I do hope they can raise the money eventually to do it)....

But I feel emptied out at the moment and what I most want is a year off, as I now plan a whole series of novels, not at all like Mrs. Stevens, about a village like this one—a cross-section of matriarchal families, from every "walk of life." The great thing about Nelson is that at last I have American roots in a place where I know all kinds of people. I think I had, once and for all, to say what I said in Mrs. S. to be free to do this other, much more universal job. But I need a year or two now just to think and read and cogitate and make notes ... and even a life as comparatively simple as mine gets pretty complicated as one reaches the middle years and so many people depend on one in one way or another. I am appalled to see how much it costs me to live, and it is scary as it all depends (as for you and Hugh) on pretty constant creation.

How lovely your writing place sounds—lovely and useful too. I mean to other people as well as to you. I am sure you cast a rather special light on the books in that library and have more "influence" than you can know!

Of course the best would be if you and Hugh and Jo and anyone else around could come up here sometimes—then we could really talk, come and go, feel free as birds. It is a most beautiful "lost" village, with hardly anyone in it except me and a few dear neighbors, in winter. In summer it becomes quite social, but I have firmly kept out and never accept invitations. It would cease to be what it is for me, haven and escape, if I once began the cocktail round.

In my deep inner self, I feel very lonely, and have dark rages about not having had any recognition, despite the 17 books...I feel just like the animals in Alice shouting "prizes, prizes!" I want the long struggle to come out somewhere. I rage because I know by the fact that my books have constantly to be re-bound, that I am <u>read</u> in the public libraries all over the country. But I have never really got through—how does one cope with this? By just silently going on, of course. And as for private life, solitude has become my "grande amie"—but there is dear Judy in Cambridge who understands all this, but is there, and has been for the 20 odd years of our life together. We are going to Europe in April to celebrate her retirement from teaching—she is 13 years older than I.

Well, this was meant to be a real letter, but I am all at sixes and sevens and it is not. The teaching job paid well but was totally exhausting and I feel like the ancient mariner—although I really only want peace and quiet, and would not stay the parting guest! But how good to be in touch with you again—permanent friends grow more precious every year. Don't they? Dear love and blessings.

Your

May

Madeleine L'Engle: b. 1918. Author of novels, poetry, memoirs, books for children; particularly known for her 1963 Newbery Award–winning fantasy *A Wrinkle in Time,* which had three successors; spiritual counselor, theologian, writer of religious works. *The Arm of the Starfish,* her "new adult book," had just come out.

water at 80 feet: or 90 feet (to Rosalind Greene, 14 January 1965), or 86 feet (*Plant Dreaming Deep,* p. 241).

The Madwoman: Eva Le Gallienne had been playing the antiwar eccentric, *The Madwoman of Chaillot* (posthumously produced, 1946), by French dramatist Jean Giraudoux (1882–1944).

In the Trojan War tragedy by Greek playwright Euripides (c. 484–06 BC), Queen Hecuba goes mad when Achilles slays her son Hector and drags the corpse by chariot around Troy's walls three times.

Margaret "Peggy" Webster (1905–72) staged and acted in New York productions (including Paul Robeson's 1943 *Othello*) and became the first woman to direct (briefly) at the Metropolitan Opera.

Hugh['s] . . . *bad luck!:* Hugh Franklin had been appearing as D'Artagnan in John Whiting's play *The Devils;* though the play had been expected to run through the summer, the recent New York City blackout and transit strike had forced it to close.

counteract . . . <u>*sneers*</u>*:* On 1 October 1965, *Time* summarized *Mrs. Stevens* thus: "Hilary gushes about lyrical art and Mar moons about his poetry and love for a sailor. Nothing else happens," though the critic suspected Sarton used the book to justify her own life through her heroine's. It is salutary to remember that Mrs. Stevens's fortunes soon would change, when Sarton's novels and poetry were taken up by the critics in the academy only a few years later.

movie . . . *option:* No movie has yet been made of *Joanna and Ulysees; David and Lisa* was an acclaimed 1963 film by Frank Perry.

a whole series of novels: Here begins the evolution of the project that resulted in *Kinds of Love* (1970).

your writing place: One of L'Engle's most recent books is *My Own Small Place: Developing the Writing Life* (1999), about her refuge, Crosswicks Cottage.

"prizes, prizes!": After running an inconclusive caucus race, Wonderland's talking creatures want to declare a winner. The Dodo pronounces, "*Everybody* has won, and *all* must have prizes," and they surround Alice, the sole human, demanding them. (See Chapter 3 of *Alice in Wonderland* [1865] by "Lewis Carroll," Charles Lutwidge Dodgson (1832–98), British author, mathematician, and Oxford don.)

For a partial list of Sarton's honors to date, see 12 March 1968; the latest would soon arrive from *Virginia Quarterly,* which awarded her the $250 Emily Clark Balch prize for nine poems, written for Margaret Clapp. As she wrote Rosalind Greene, 27 June [1966], "[S]ome of what seemed like waste has been salvaged."

Nowadays the New England Poetry Society, which honored her with its Golden Rose in 1945, offers "The May Sarton Award ($250): Given intermittently to a poet whose work is an inspiration to other poets. Nominations accepted."

the ancient mariner: Central sufferer in the 1798–1817 narrative poem by another great
Romantic poet, Samuel Taylor Coleridge (1772–1834). He can ease his pain only by telling
his story over and over to any passing listener, such as "the parting guest," who at the end
turns away from the wedding feast.

TO LOUISE BOGAN   Friday Feb. 11th, 1966
[Nelson]
Dear Louise,

Oh, how glad I was to have your word—I took no joy in the book [*A
Private Mythology*] (although Norton has done such a lovely job) and
decided that until a reader or two has breathed life into a book it is a
blue baby... so bless you for writing at once. That was a true act of
friendship when I can sense that you yourself hover still on the border
of depression (though manfully staying on the positive side). I am sure it
is true that what you miss is poetry—and that is a dark absence which
no one who is the poet you are, could bear without real suffering. My
darling one, you must believe that poetry is hiding just behind the
kitchen door and waits only for you to lift your little finger to steal in
and stand, like a small shy child who hopes for attention, at your side.

It seems to me that what God asks you to do, by constantly raining
down depression, is to settle in and write some imitation poems as bait
for the big fish in the subterranean depths. What it is like in your cocoon
of the morning depression—or just a simple free verse poem about
cooking an egg! would be quite wonderful under your ministrations. A
bitter ironic poem about the people who (God save their souls) are not
depressed these days ....memories of that chipmunk at Pete; look on it as
a game of solitaire, just because once in to a simple exercise you will find
that you forget everything else for an hour or two... I now hear a deep
sigh breathing out from you...then sigh it out in a poem.

It is very sad about Dr. Wall—perhaps he is just old and tired like you
and me and cannot be quite so there as he once was, at your side. But
Poundstone (can that be a real name?) Stones by the pound seem hardly
right for a man whose business is to provide bread for a stone, and not
the reverse, but I gather his name does not describe him, Thank God. It
is so awful that I cannot send you a huge bunch of spring flowers as a
valentine—but I am (with infinite pain) trying to turn my grasshopper
self into an ant self, to pay my huge incursions into capital ($5000) to
pay the damned income tax, plus what they say I owe on 1963...I am
just not allowing myself any extravagance until that money is paid back
into the fund. I get scared to death when I think how I have depended
on an infinite capacity for sustained creation. And it is pushing my luck
now when I thought I was too tired to do anything for a year to be

writing furiously for money...I have sold one piece on "The Pleasures of Non-Affluence" to Woman's Day (!) for $750 and just sent off another about buying this house which they asked for, so I have hopes. On Monday I shall plunge like a salmon going upstream to lay an egg and <u>die</u>, into a children's book which I hope to finish before we go to Europe April 1st. In a way the old gambler in me rejoices in the chancy business it all is...but I have to laugh when I think that I had imagined this time as two months of rest and meditation!

It is thawing here now—so queer to see patches of earth—I had forgotten what it looks like. And I am off now to take Mildred into Keene to do her weekly food-shopping, and when I come home I intend to make a beef stew for Perley, whose wife [Angie Cole] is dying...and who may sell out. He has grippe as well, so the poor old man is very depressed. He broke down and cried bitterly in my kitchen the other day. When a man cries, it sort of breaks one's heart.

By the way PEN is giving one of their so common parties (I mean they give them often, not that they are vulgar!) for me on March 28th—Norton has set up some interviews and stuff as well so it is going to be rather tense and rushed. Do you go to those parties? Would you come and then to dinner with Madeleine and Hugh Franklin and me?

She writes childrens' books—won the Newbury Award—and is an old Civic Rep. friend, and he is a very good actor who was knocked out of a job by the paper strike. They are very civilized and dear people, both—do say you will!

I am very cross because Mrs. Stevens is not even in the final lot for Nat[ional]. Book Award—I knew I couldn't get it, but I have nearly always been in the final 6 or so. I feel very bitter inside. The day the poems came I had an infuriating letter from an unknown asking me why my books always disappointed her—why I could not repeat that "perfect" book,—of all things—The Fur Person! If only people had any idea what a letter out of the blue can do of devastation and joy-killing! I remember V. Woolf on this when we talked—the terrible power of the anonymous reader who so often only writes to tear one down. When you are just managing to survive by the skin of your teeth anyway, that unknown who tries to make you lose your grip, finger by finger. Such people are murderers, and they do not even know it in their smugness.

I say <u>don't</u> give up your apartment this year—wait it out—see, feel your way. Live for that core in yourself now that is poetry—and to Hell with things! All will seem easy once you are back in the true groove where you belong. Any chance of your coming to the [MacDowell] Colony this summer?

Oh dear, I have to go now. Somehow we must manage a meeting

when I am down—for instance, the party is at six—come and have tea in my room at the Roosevelt before it? And then come <u>with me</u> to the party? (I would be covered with glory!) I'll phone you later on when I know about plans more definitely—

Off to the wars now!

Ever your devoted

M

---

poems as bait: Since it was Bogan who once encouraged Sarton, when blocked, to write "imitation poems," which might by surprise turn into real ones, it is "ironic" that the younger woman now urged her to write "about cooking an egg"; on 9 April 1955, *Saturday Review* published a poem (uncollected) she had written for Bogan, "Easter Egg."

Pete: Peterborough, New Hampshire, site of the MacDowell Colony.

Dr. Wall . . . Poundstone: Dr. James Wall, who treated Bogan during her 1933 breakdown and advised her since, was five years her junior; see Frank's *Louise Bogan,* pp. 193–96, for his valuable counsel. She found her new physician, Dr. Bruce Poundstone, "really intuitive, sharp & with it" (p. 397), though to ease her symptoms this time required not psychotherapy but shock treatment.

an infinite capacity for sustained creation: Sarton would tease Ashley Montagu, 2 October 1977, about possibly tiring of "book-a-year Sarton," but from 1955 onward, any year without one major publication was often followed by a year with two, not taking into account her growing professional correspondence.

"The Pleasures of Non-Affluence": Woman's Day, June 1966. It opens with Sarton shoveling snow, pondering the purchase of a snowblower, but "Women make good gardeners because they like to cherish and watch things grow. They make poor mechanics because machines never grow; they only deteriorate and exasperate their owners." The first of Sarton's two books for children was not published until 1974.

Live for . . . poetry: As Sarton had urged, Bogan did make an effort to write more poetry. On 6 February 1966, she translated a rondel from the fifteenth-century French, "Cleanse and refresh the castle of my heart / Where I have lived for long with little joy"; see *Journey Around My Room,* p. 182. She once observed that Sarton kept the Hell out of her poetry—whereas to produce her best work Bogan often had to lift the lid off hers. She had used her earlier psychiatric ward visits in one of "Five Parodies" (December 1938): see *The Blue Estuaries* for "Evening in the Sanitarium: Imitated from Auden." Now, for the only two new poems she seems to have ever completed, she drew upon her most recent harrowing experiences, though the "Psychiatrist's Song" is strikingly empathetic and tender. As for the "small shy child" who waits "to steal in and stand . . . at your side," that is exactly what befalls the haunted person who hears "Little Lobelia's Song."

TO POLLY THAYER STARR   Feb. 17th [1966] Thurs. Eve
[Nelson]
Dearest Poll,

If I go on much further, you will wish you had never invited me to lunch! But oh dear me, it is a <u>great</u> comfort that you liked the poems.

"The Turtle", by the way, is in the new book and "Baroque Image", neither of which could be related to a specific person. I suppose I have waited partly because it has all been such a mystery and I seem to hear an inner voice saying "wait"—The hardest thing to bear was really that I had accepted that the whole thing was some sort of madness on my side ... that my strong sense that the silence <u>was</u> a speaking silence was illusion for the final angry poem was two years ago, as you noted. Then the absolutely astounding announcement of the early retirement last August set up a whole new suspense. I really cursed that day. At the moment I feel completely blocked, stifled might be a better word. It is infuriating because I believe I could have lived on very very little, perhaps two lunches <u>a year</u>. The only word I have had was a single line acknowledging receipt of Mrs. Stevens (which was dedicated to her as you no doubt observed). But even that sent my spirits soaring for a while.

I sent the poems the other day, which are dedicated to my Wellesley students, but there has been no acknowledgement. Darling, I have 50 here, but when I made the lists of old ladies and people in Europe they all went—I just hate always having to give my books to people whom I don't really want to give them to! But I am so broke that I made a firm rule this time that except for the first three or four, I must resist sending it to friends who can afford to buy it. Will you understand?

What troubles me now is simply that until July when I shall make one last effort to see her, I just have to wait—and that waiting is just a limbo. After three years of it, I feel like a desert at the moment... when <u>one</u> drop of rain would make the whole garden burst into bloom! But I have figured out that M. will only write me if the matter concerns the college. In the one letter she wrote when she said "Someday I will retire and then I shall look forward to seeing you in Florence, Hong Kong, or Tyringham or Nelson"—<u>that</u> letter—the only communication I have had except two telephone calls I made (she then stopped answering) since Feb. of 1963—was to acknowledge the final settlement between the college and my lawyer about a $20,000 bequest to Wellesley in my will. I suppose all I have to do is bequeath another 20,000 and I might extract <u>several</u> syllables—it is to laugh! Well, I am a fool. But the flood of poetry was wonderful while it lasted...and I regret nothing.

But now I feel very old and battered, I must confess. Mrs. Stevens is, I believe, rather a cold book. It was an agonizing re-appraisal, in which I cut out the whole <u>romantic</u> for what seemed then the truth of things. It was my way, I suppose, of trying to understand and to forgive M.— "The Muse does not respond—she goes her way—"

Here I am working furiously hard,—when I am through I play music and weep gallons of tears, but not for any Muse, just because I long for

God and cannot utter that name without beginning to cry so much that it is better not to.

I am terribly curious about "What other way is there than love?" Don't recognize it—is it my line? When? I forget everything—but I do not forget you—

You ask about plans. I'm up here trying to pay off the income tax until late March—then there is a party for the poems at the PEN in N.Y. on March 28th. Judy and I fly to France (I'll come home and leave with her from Boston on the 1st) for ten weeks—I'll be back here at Nelson June 15th. For the whole summer except two weeks in Maine (Aug. 1st to 15th). Surely somewhere along the line I can get you up here over a night? I long for you to see the place...and to have time to talk. It's high time!

Well, I have sold (I think) two short pieces to Woman's Day for $1350 and now am embarked on a fantasy, a fable, some sort of short eccentric book called Mr. Thimble Hare and the Maiden Porcupine (I am the maiden Porcupine but I trust no one will recognize me!) which might bring in some money. The supreme irony of all this is that I had counted now on two months of no effort, just to sit and weep about God, and write poems.

Do read, by the way, the Fitzgibbon biog. of Dylan Thomas. What a tragic book! What a tragic sad man! So self-indulgent and so endearing, and such a genius—but if he had had just a grain of New England in him, he might have survived. One feels so for his wife, too. Like living with a crazed animal.

It seems to me that the one important fact of our era is the loss of an intimate sense of God. That is what has undermined us. The loneliness. Of course, I know I am talking to a believer and I envy you. I believe in some supreme Mystery, but that is [as] far as my crippled legs seem to carry me. I am helped by some friends—notably Camille Mayran, a great French woman who has never laid a hand on me—I mean because she is a Catholic—has not tried to convert me—of the gentlest sort (there is a poem to her in the book too ["Joy in Provence"]) but who does live in the place I long for—here is a paragraph from a beautiful essay she sent me recently about the miracle that reflection (a tree in water, for instance is): "Ce petit appât d'un reflet d'étoiles m'a tirée hors de ma vie dans ce suspens de l'étonnement où m'apparaissent à la fois les infinies distancers et les infinies liaisons. Tout ce qui existe ensemble est pensé ensemble; le miroir qui nous impose cet espèce d'arrêt— comme d'un animal en présence d'une odeur, d'une couleur qui fait appel à ses secrètes sensibil-ités—le miroir creuse en nous ce blanc, ce vide sacré, cette attente qui est notre seule manière de penser la Pensée qui contient tout."

It sometimes occurs to me that I am a terribly serious bloke!

And by now you are tired of this letter and so am I.

But the great thing, dearest Poll, is to be friends again, which means sharing the really important things. I brood a great deal about your feeling that you have to be cook on that d—— boat! An unhappy cook is not a good cook. Period. Why force yourself to what is not necessary? God designed you to <u>paint</u>!

> Ever your devoted ancient friend
> May

---

the poems: "Turtle," unlike "Baroque Image," was not retained for *Poems 1930–93*.

early retirement: It had been reported that Margaret Clapp had resigned from Wellesley to direct a college for young women in South India. Sarton had still not received acknowledgment of a gift sent for Christmas 1965—a large star crystal, accompanied by this note:

"A star crystal seems to me to be like love—many-faceted—and why they occur, in nature, in their odd forms, no one knows. A perfect star crystal is almost unknown. And depending on where the crystal is, it will emit different colours of the spectrum. It is hard to place it so that a pure white light is obtained. When the sun is not shining, the crystal emits no light—but one knows that, nevertheless, it is all there, in the crystal, only waiting for another day. None of it is ever lost; only waiting to shine out under propitious skies.

"Finally, crystal is pure and hard. But little scratches mar it very easily.

"There is very little personal in this. This is a simile that has occurred to me, and that I wish I were brave enough and pure enough to live by. I think that perhaps you are. In any event, please keep this and, if you are ever sad or feel forsaken or lose faith, perhaps you can look at it and think of these feelings."

The crystal was engraved with these words—a one-line poem, as it were, perhaps by Sarton herself: "An inward music is just within reach."

I sent the poems: Referring to the hardbound copies of *A Private Mythology*.

Tyringham: Clapp had a house in Tyringham, Massachusetts.

"What other way is there than love?": The first line of Sarton's unpublished "The Diviner" (1934?); see the appendix of *Dear Juliette*.

Mr. Thimble Hare: After "Thimble" had turned into "Trumbull," *Miss Pickthorn and Mr. Hare: A Fable* came out in 1966, with illustrations by James Spanfeller again.

the Fitzgibbon biog.: The authorized biography of the Welsh poet (1914–53), *The Life of Dylan Thomas* (1966), was by novelist Constantine Fitzgibbon. Caitlin Thomas (1913–94) had written *Leftover Life to Kill* in 1957; *Solitude*, pp. 30–31, quotes Bogan's review (see also *A Poet's Alphabet*). Caitlin likened life with Dylan to "raw, red bleeding meat." As he lay dying, comatose, she burst into his hospital room and, finding another woman there, fought with bystanders and bit an attendant.

"Ce petit appât . . . contient tout": "This tiny lure—a reflection of the stars—is what has drawn me outside my life, suspended aloft in astonishment, where I can perceive, simultaneously, infinite distances and infinite connections. All that exists as one is one in thought; the mirror which brings us to this sudden halt—like an animal put on the alert by a scent or a color which calls into play its secret senses—that mirror cracks open inside us this wide white sacred emptiness, this expectation which is our only means of thinking the Thought that contains everything."

cook on that d—— boat: Donald C. Starr (1901–92) was an avid sailor and owned many boats throughout his life. *The Schooner "Pilgrim's Progress"* (The Peabody Essex Museum, 1996) is his account of sailing around the world on an eighty-five-foot schooner in the summer of 1932. Polly Thayer Starr did continue to paint until poor vision made work impossible; her paintings are in galleries and museums across the country. In the 2001 Boston Museum of Fine Arts exhibition *A Studio of Her Own: Women Artists in Boston 1870–1940,* Starr was the only living artist represented. Her 1936 painting of Sarton (see letter of 3 July [1994] and note) was widely used to promote the show, and was reproduced on a vertical banner hung between the columns of the Museum's front entrance.

TO KATHARINE TAYLOR   May 5th, 1966 R[h]odes
[Le Pignon Rouge]

Dearest Katharine, it was so heartening and dear to have your word for the birthday of this ancient girl! Yes, it has been a great journey of wonders—the Gorges du Tarn like Chinese landscapes in the pouring rain, the Dordogne almost impossibly green, sweet and peaceful with the birds singing their airy songs all day and all night, the wonderful rich rivers flowing fast (there's been a lot of rain here) and there we had two days of warm sun and could wander in the meadows finding wild orchids and all sorts of exquisite small spring flowers. But for me it has been curiously shadowed...we both had the flu in St. Paul (where we did have three weeks and cooked for ourselves and were near dear friends) and it has hung on in colds and general wan-ness...the trying to absorb so many deaths close to me this year...and now finding Céline suddenly a very old lady and this house and garden which I realize now has been the one stable thing in my life since I was seven, about to be sold and broken up because it is just too much for her. However, it is at its most radiant now—and I take comfort in Franz, the goose, now 22(!), still followed everywhere and talking raptly all day long to his faithful brown spouse. The lilies of the valley brought here from Wondelgem are in flower—the garden a sort of poetic ruin, but still very lovely—so, one more farewell. Also, on another level, I found here rather a shock as the real Joanna of my story has been got hold of by a shyster Greek lawyer and they are trying to get money out of the movie people and threaten a suit, which will be passed on by the movie people to me: it could be a dirty and expensive business, but I try to forget it as I can do nothing until I get home. And meanwhile it may be possible to buy them off (the movie firm is at it now). But it is very dis-illusioning and bitter as a taste in my mouth. I wish you could get right away to some place without a phone for a week or so—What a year it has been for all of us! How precious [under?] its griefs and disasters the sure touch of old friends, bless you—Take care of yourself.

Your devoted
May

Katharine Taylor: 1888–1979. Successor to founders Agnes and Ernest Hocking as head of the Shady Hill School (1921–49), where young May received most of her formative education. Taylor encouraged Sarton's earliest poetry, for which she served as the first major muse. See *Catching Beauty* as well as *At Fifteen,* and the title essay of *I Knew a Phoenix.* A 1928 letter to her appears in *Letters 1916–54; Recovering,* pp. 243–44, offers an extract from a 1947 speech Taylor gave to parents about intellectual discipline. After retirement she devoted her time to children's causes at home and overseas.

Sarton and Judith Matlack were touring the Côte d'Azur in the south of France, before ending up at the Limbosches' in Brussels.

dear friends: Sarton saw Sybille Bedford and Eda Lord, among others, in St. Paul-de-Vence; the picturesque twelfth-century fortified village with ramparts, terraced on a ridge above the Riviera, was home for Annie Duveen Caldwell.

so many deaths: Ellen Douglass Leyburn, Basil de Sélincourt, Katharine Davis, "Aunt" Mary Bouton (Cambridge family friend), and Katrine Greene. On 11 March 1966, the day Katrine died of cancer, Sarton wrote her mother, Rosalind, "I read over the so vivid description—the brilliant eyes, the thin person they look out of, the hair like a halo, and electric. . . . [W]hen I asked about plans at New Year's she said, 'Oh, I shall be back at work in March.'. . . I have no sisters or family. K. has been that. You are all my family and have been for many many years. . . . Not enough has been said about death—or about life for that matter. We live in this great mystery."

Commiserating with Polly Starr after the suicide of a friend's husband, Sarton wrote (27 September 1966), "I suppose death is the great drama, yet I feel more that life is...we have to try to 'make happen' the image of the self we have projected on the screen of eternity. There must be an image of grandeur, even though we fail every time to meet its reflection. We have to live in the light of eternity—where every act is symbolic as well as actual. This seems to me 'the great drama' which is always tragic because no one of us can meet the image he has created for himself in that light."

Wondelgem: Sarton's Belgian birthplace and home for her first two years. See *Endgame,* p. 87, for a photograph of "Franz, a Goose" (1959) with Céline.

TO RACHEL MACKENZIE   July 27th, 1966
[Nelson]
Rachel dear,

I hate to do this to you—but Winifred Wilkinson is a most remarkable woman whose first novel (written when she was over 70) made a huge success in London, published by Gollancz—God in Hell. She sent me the enclosed odd piece and asked me to send it to the New Yorker, just on the chance. I shall make no comment, save to say that she is a good writer at her best.

She has also published a volume of short stories, by the way.

Any word you might have the generosity to write her which might be helpful would be an angelic deed. She and Walter live on a pittance with great style and courage.

How are you? It seems years since I have heard. I am in a dell, depressed because overtired. But I have made a firm decision to take this year off and stay put. Judy and I came back from ten weeks in Europe in mid-June and I faced then that the depletion in me was real and has been going on for a long time. Luckily a funny little fable I wrote last spring will come out before Christmas and may bring in some money, and as soon as I am better I want to write a book about this house. Norton is putting the new poems into paperback in the winter. Twayne is doing a book on me for their series of American authors—I was surprised and delighted! So things mull along ...

Animal life surrounds me here—a raccoon comes about midnight to pick up a snack of four chocolate biscuits I put out to keep her from attacking the garbage cans; a deer and doe live in the woods below the house; the phoebe who nests under the porch eave has just safely flown her three babies ... and of course my own wild animals, the pussies, are in and out of the house all day and all night. At three A.M. Scrabble leaps onto the screen at my window (I sleep downstairs) and crucifies herself there until I rescue her!

Ever so much love, darling..I'll tell Winifred not to expect a quick answer. They go to Paris Aug. 30th but I'm sure mail will be forwarded from the address on the piece.

Your
M

––––––––

Rachel MacKenzie: Novelist (1909–80). Though plagued by ill health for much of her life, she was a well-loved fiction editor at *The New Yorker*, working with such authors as Isaac Bashevis Singer, Bernard Malamud, Saul Bellow, and Philip Roth.

Winifred Wilkinson: A Quaker friend of Judith Matlack's and an underrecognized writer, whose work Sarton thought brilliant. Gollancz brought out both *The Doc and Other Stories* and *God in Hell* in 1964. The novel, issued in the U.S. as *Even in the Depths,* tells "of a Polish boy saved by an old woman from death during the destruction of Warsaw during World War II."

depletion was real: Returning to the demands of the mail and the garden at Nelson, Sarton felt "for a brief week that I could not cope with such a place alone any longer... dreaming of a bare cell with not a flower in it!" she wrote Rosalind Greene, 27 June [1966]. "Such are the delusions of fatigue...for of course the place is what keeps me going."

Twayne['s] book on me: May Sarton (1972). "[T]he person chosen will be ideal," she assured Greene (as above), referring to Agnes Sibley, her friend at Lindenwood College. "I have seen the general plan and glow with delight that someone sees that the whole work (poems and novels together) adds up to a vision of life."

TO ANNE SEXTON [Sept. 13th, 1966]
[Nelson]
Dear Anne Sexton—

Quite a thrill for this old raccoon to find your new book "Live or Die" in the mailbox! I appreciate very much such a gesture. Your talent has always filled me with questions, alarms, self-doubt, makes me re-think where I stand about poetry (thank God I'm not a critic!) and it is certainly a live one, bless you! Now we have had the Inferno and the Purgatorio may we expect the Paradiso one day?

> Grateful thanks
> May Sarton

Anne Sexton: Poet (1928–74). A student of Robert Lowell's, she taught at Boston and Colgate Universities; *Live or Die* won the 1967 Pulitzer. One poem reproaches poet Sylvia Plath (1932–63) for having gone ahead alone "into the death I wanted so badly and so long," though the circumstances and motivation for Sexton's eventual suicide were quite different from Plath's. For Sarton's estimate of their work, see 24 December 1970. Here she hopes that like *The Divine Comedy* (c. 1308–21) of Dante (Italian poet, 1265–1321), Sexton's Hell and Purgatory will eventually yield to a vision of some sort of Heaven.

Bogan also received a signed copy of *Live and Die.* "O why can't I write psychotic verse!" she asked Ruth Limmer, 19 September 1966, *What the Woman Lived.* "Neurotic verse pales into insignificance beside what those girls—Sexton and Plath—can (could) turn out."

TO BEVERLY HALLAM   Oct. 28th, 1966
[Nelson]
Dear Bev,

Such a good letter, I am off to Cambridge for a little break and when I go even for two days it seems to be a major operation! But I did want to send a word in answer to your good letters... and I do intend to drive over maybe some Sunday after Xmas (I go down to Cambridge from Thanksgiving through Xmas, but then settle in here for three months peace and quiet) and meet your friend and have more chance to talk about the real things.

The news from Eugénie is better—her husband will recover and is home now. But the poor maid is dying so Eugénie comes home from a day at the hospital to cope with that tragedy. I don't know how to "explain" her exactly—she is just a very old friend of mine who has always been there, so to speak. Her daughter is a good artist, does big panels (abstract) in enamel, is married but without children. E's son [Eric] has four children, though, so there is plenty to keep her busy as a grandmother. She has a great feeling about art, absorbs it like a sea anemone, listens so acutely one finds oneself saying unexpected things. She was thrilled by our day with you!

Oh, I know about cooking (such a splendid lunch you gave us) and in fact this is the big problem for me of living alone—if I invite people they want to see me, but they also expect to be fed and between cooking endless meals and talking I am a dead duck after 24 hours. A new meal looms up just after one has cleared away the one before! But you must come over and see this place before too long...yes, it is insulated—I have sheet rock (painted white) everywhere and it does a fine job. I have an oil furnace and am warm as toast and very inexpensively so—also 5 open fireplaces, a great joy.

You are sweet to remember about the dying friend—there were two and both died just before we went to Europe. I think the shock and grief—and long waiting, for it was in each case a slow business—was why I was so depleted during that whole trip. I have lost so many key people in my life since I moved in here 8 years ago that I sometimes feel like a <u>survivor</u>.

What I am working on, now, by the way is a book about this house [*Plant Dreaming Deep*], non-fiction, but eventually I may pluck up enough courage to enter in that wilderness, untamed as yet, of some novels about N.H.

Now I have to make a confession—I have violent feelings against playing around with flowers to make them into faces etc. (will you ever forgive me?) The reason, as far as I can make out, for this reaction is exactly the same as when a young poet compares a birch tree to a slender young woman (that happens all the time!) because things are <u>themselves</u>; nature in all its aspects is so complex and so beautiful that humanizing it, diminishes the glory, brings it down to human size—is (for me) a bad joke, not a good joke, I had to say this because I can't keep anything back from your honest eyes.

Which leads me into what humour is anyway—but no time—however, there is <u>black</u> humour (Daumier, the war cartoons of Goya, for instance) and there is tender humor like Sholem Alacheim which makes us love human beings more for laughing with them; there is grotesque humour (Breughel), but all these have to do with <u>people</u>. Let me make a wild generality and say that we are allowed to laugh at ourselves but not at God.

Hope you'll want to fight back! I need to learn—

Off to the city now—

So much love, Bev, it's good to know you are there—

Your
M

P.S. Of course you're a genius whatever you do!

————

Beverly Hallam: Painter, lecturer, and professor at the Massachusetts College of Art, Beverly Linney Hallam (b. 1923) first encountered Sarton's work when Inez M. Atwater, Hallam's colleague at LaSalle Junior College, took her to hear the 1953 lecture "Journey toward Poetry." Later Elda Robb (one of Judith Matlack's circle of friends, "The Fish") introduced her to Sarton.

news from Eugénie: For Eugénie Dubois, see note to 18 June 1957. In September she visited Sarton at Nelson, and they called on Hallam in Ogunquit, Maine; but soon afterward her husband Jean suffered a stroke, forcing Dubois to return to France.

humour: French artist Honoré Daumier (1808–79) was renowned for satiric illustrations scourging the judicial system and social injustice.

The Disasters of War (1810–14), by Spanish artist Francisco José de Goya y Lucientes (1746–1828), has rarely been equaled for indicting state-organized butchery.

Russian-born Yiddish humorist Sholem Aleichem (Sholem Yakov Rabinowitz, 1859–1916) wrote the Tevye stories, which formed the basis for the 1964 Harnick-Bock musical *Fiddler on the Roof.*

Flemish artist Pieter Brueghel (the Elder, c. 1525–69) was known for peasant scenes, hallucinatory fantasies, and allegories of human self-deception, such as his 1568 painting *The Blind Leading the Blind* into a ditch.

TO CAMILLE MAYRAN   13 May [1967]
[Nelson]   [Portions in French]
My great friend,

As you no doubt know, I wrote Noémie right away and told her how happy I was that this good news had come <u>at last</u>—and I am delighted to read, in her reply, that she hopes to come to the U.S.— For myself, I am so discouraged at the state of my country that it did me good to learn that she would love to come here! (I'll answer her letter soon—how wonderful if she could stay a weekend at Nelson along the way!)

For me this is a difficult time. I read with distress what you told me about your own aging—I write that word but cannot connect it with you at all—except that I <u>understand</u>, since I see with astonishment how much heavier I am becoming, and me only 55! Perhaps something of the sort is only natural at an age which everything in our civilization tries to postpone—an age with hours for musing, taking life perhaps a bit more spontaneously, where one can work or let a book fall aside, whenever the spirit wills it—[where friends akin to] Marie Closset can drop in for brief visits—it's that, more than anything, which you lack, my dear soul, it's this solitude not nourished by friendships deeply rooted in the past...at bottom you are <u>in exile</u> and it seems to me a great pity.

I had to smile at your evocation of my return—for I came back to three inches of <u>snow</u> (we have never had such a horrible spring), then hail, rain, finally hard frosts which killed half the garden, rain again—today at last the sun has come back, but with a high wind—and it is still very cold, freezing at night! Somehow the hosts of daffodils have survived and are beautiful just the same, but moles have eaten 200 tulips I planted, and altogether, the garden is not going to be much this year, I am afraid.

I still have the big reading in Washington next week—and then at last I can rest. It is high time, as I feel rather ill and queer, I am so tired. Also discouraged—I was really shocked and made ill by the atmosphere in which I found myself both in Kentucky and in Baltimore—in Kentucky I was with very rich people who condescend to Negros—I woke in the night murmuring to myself "love them to death"—and that is just it. They love the dear old Negro as long as he is willing to remain a dependent child; as soon as he wishes to grow up, they fear and hate him. And blame all the "trouble" on agitators from the North. In Baltimore I was driven to the Negro college by a woman I had never met before (but has written me for years, very irritating letters, I must say) and she simply came out with it and said "I hate the Negros—I despise them" etc. When I came back I felt as if I were full of <u>mud</u>, of hatred, of horror...I had to face how far we have to go and also that the South is a wholly different <u>ethos</u>—I felt more homesick there than I could ever be in India or Japan, I am sure. Yet the speech in Baltimore went awfully well—to a mixed audience. At the end the Negro head of the English dept. (the meeting of College English profs from all over the region took place in a Negro college) got up and said "I love you, Miss Sarton!" The spontaneity of this was really so <u>dear</u>, it did me good. My speech, on revision as creation, followed on a terribly dull one by a famous critic, Cleanth Brooks. It was rather fun for me to see the audience wake up when I began!

Then I was again comforted by the Negro chauffeur who drove me to the airport—I told him how nervous I got before a lecture, and he said "When you are scared, just take a deep breath—it helps" ..it was said in such a fatherly way (and so true too) that I was very touched.

The Negro has, I believe, so much to teach us—of warmth, of how to cherish, and how also to <u>laugh</u>—if only the hatred does not become so bitter that we can no longer teach each other anything. It was the fear of that that chilled me to the bone. I wanted to write a poem, but was at once faced with the hideous appalling avalanche of mail, requests to read. God knows what! I feel sometimes that I shall never write a poem again, since I never foresee getting through what is on my desk.

I did finish reading the translation and have sent Marie a warm letter and about ten pages of suggested changes (no about 6, I guess) all of which concerned the <u>meaning</u>, not the style in French. For that, I am not competent, but it is really not very good. Never mind—from what you say the chances of publication are slight indeed (as I always thought). I did not mention what you told me, about its having been sent back from Plon—what about Feux-Croisés? I thought that might be a possibility, if I remember something you said earlier.

The other thing that makes me feel ill and have bad dreams is the horrible Vietnam war—if I could write some poems I would feel better.

And perhaps I can. Anyway I am going to rest for a week after Wash.—I bring Judy and the cats up on the 20th for a week or ten days—then she leaves the cats in their summer palace and goes home—but I hope we can have some peaceful days together...

I must now dash off to town, taking an old neighbor [Bessie Lyman] to the Doctor (she who had an eye operation) and get some food in as an old friend [Polly Thayer Starr] is coming for 24 hours tomorrow—a great joy as she has never been here, yet I am so tired that I dread it a little—never mind all will be well.

Forgive this desperate badly written thing, but at least it is a way of keeping in touch—dear heart—

Ever your
May

Next morning—more cheerful because three good things happened yesterday afternoon! I decided to give myself an hour off from the desk and went to the woods to look for arbutus—an exquisite sweet-smelling tiny flower which grows <u>under</u> dead leaves and always seems like the resurrection—I found a lovely bunch. When I came home Perley Cole's son (a shattered man of 50 [Parker Cole] who came back from World War II mentally ill, poor fellow—he is very <u>gentle</u> and totally silent) gave me a bluebird-house he has made and would not let me pay for it (it will be put up in an old apple tree near the barn) and finally in the evening Trumbull Hare banged on the door, smiling with triumph, to bring me the first trout he had caught! The country does always comfort in a wonderful way.

---

how much heavier I am: "I am ten pounds too heavy too!" Sarton commiserated with Beverly Hallam, 10 March 1966. "Never mind—who wants to be a stick?"

Marie Closset: The real name of poet "Jean Dominique"; see note to 29 June 1958.

Washington . . . Kentucky . . . Baltimore: Two Kentucky engagements in late April were followed, 6 May, by the College English Association conference at Morgan State College, Baltimore. Sarton spoke on "Revision as Creation: The Growth of a Poem"; see *Writings on Writing*, pp. 59–66.

Critic Cleanth Brooks (1904–94) taught at Yale and collaborated on the classic texts *Understanding Poetry* and *Understanding Fiction*. Sarton's experiences on these two visits crystallized into "Night Watch" (1969).

On 18 May she read for the National Foundation of the Arts and the Humanities in Washington, D.C., at a presentation ceremony where she (along with poet Robert Duncan, among others) received a grant—in her case, funding time for the project that became *Kinds of Love*.

reading the translation: It would seem that Marianne "Marie" Dubois was attempting, with Mayran's assistance, to translate Sarton's 1946 novel *The Bridge of Years*; the main characters are based on Céline and Raymond Limbosch. After that version was rejected by one French firm Sarton suggested another; but it would be twenty-six years before her first book publication in France—see 13 July [1992].

Trumbull Hare: The fictional name Sarton assigned to the Nelson neighbor portrayed in *Miss Pickthorn and Mr. Hare* as the shy man with a child's awareness of the world's unexpected beauties.

TO SUSAN HOWE VAN SCHLEGALL   June 5th, 1967
[Nelson]
Sukey dear,

Thanks for your wonderful letter. It moved me to tears for I met in it so many of my own feelings. I guess children always feel as you do—if I had only had <u>time</u> to show him or her what I really felt! We all suffer remorse and perhaps it haunts us forever, but I suppose what happens is that one tries to give to others what could not be given in time to the beloved person. The relation between parents and children is really so horrendously delicate and difficult—for every child in a way has to murder its parents to <u>exist</u>, fight for its own life. This is cruel, but is a fact, I guess. (murder is a rather strong word, but I hope you know what I mean by it).

But what made me weep bitterly was your sentence about "the world just doesn't contain those totally honest people any more. Things have gone so wrong." Yes, but I don't believe there ever were a great many people or even more than a few like Mark, your father. In every age, there have been a few saving graces. He was one, in this dirty time. There will be others, others perhaps influenced by him, students of his, and perhaps you can give little new Mark some of that courage and honesty. I have just written a word to that brave Captain Levy who has got three years at hard labor for refusing to teach Green Berets—he is very young, but there is he, with the shining courage to stand up and say <u>no</u>.

> Defenceless under the night
> Our world in stupor lies;
> Yet, dotted everywhere,
> Ironic points of light
> Flash out wherever the Just
> Exchange their messages:
> May I, composed like them
> Of Eros and of dust,
> Beleaguered by the same
> Negation and despair,
> Show an affirming flame.

Perhaps our greatest responsibility toward parents is after their death in what we make of ourselves and our children. I have no children, but how often have I remembered my father (a pure man like yours in a world of operators) and chosen the unpopular road, supported as if he were there to beam his great smile at me.

Now I have just re-read that vignette of Mark cooking meals on the boat and standing looking out in his battered white hat—thank you, darling Sukey, for giving it to me.

Someday I hope you can come here with your husband and little Mark—is your daughter [Becky] with you? I know so little really, but I feel we are in touch on a deep level now and that will <u>keep</u>. No need to answer this, but it comes with a vast hug from this old raccoon in New Hampshire—you are a grand person, Sukey.

Love from

May

Your mother and Helen [Howe] came to lunch on Friday and we had a good long talk—I was glad to get to know Helen a little—

Susan Howe van Schlegall: "Sukey" (b. 1937), sister of Fanny, niece of Helen Howe, daughter of Mary "Moll" (Manning) and Mark de Wolfe Howe (1906–67), the Harvard law professor and civil rights activist for whom Sarton wrote "The Rock in the Snowball," first published in 1971.

On 5 March 1967, she wrote Mary-Leigh Smart (see [2 October 1972]) about attending "the funeral of one of my dearest friends, that great man, Mark Howe. He was the essence of New England at its best, and I shall be haunted by his deep set blue eyes and that straightest of looks as long as I live. He was only 60 and died in a few minutes of a heart attack. It has made me feel clouded by gloom...hard to blow away."

Captain Levy: Dr. Howard Levy was drafted into the Army as a captain, at Fort Jackson, Texas, without receiving customary military instruction; his refusal to compromise his conscience caused Col. Henry Fancy to escalate charges against him to court-martial level. For Sarton's crackling satire on "The Ruminations of Colonel Fancy," extant only as a heavily corrected and uncompleted draft, see appendix.

Defenceless under the night . . . show an affirming flame: The final stanza of "September 1, 1939" (first published in 1940) as it appears in *Collected Poetry of W. H. Auden* (1945).

as if he were there: To see George Sarton "beam his great smile," turn to E. Mabel Sarton's photograph on p. 140 of *At Seventy.*

TO CAMILLE MAYRAN   29 July [1967]
[Nelson]   [Portions in French]
My dearest Marianne,

What a joy, this letter fragrant with the atmosphere of Florence! I clasped it to my heart with such contentment, also happy to know that this ambience lightened for a little while Noémie's concerns about the huge task of preparing for the new term. I wish I could send you the huge lily, green at the back of the trumpets (there are 6) snow-white inside with vermilion stamens and pistil, which stands on the mantel

here in my study, in a Chinese jar with pale blue and deep blue del-
phinium. What a glory!

I shall go on in English for it is the end of a long day and my tongue
stumbles searching for words in French. Of course I was immensely
touched and pleased to hear that you and Marie had gone over my suggestions together; I had so hoped that you would help. I shall not say a
word about the new hope, and I myself have given up any idea that
there is a possibility long ago. Nothing that I write seems to have any
relation to the world as it is … I feel so old-fashioned, darling! I am sure
you are right about the word "murderer" as too strong. I'm sorry that
you do not feel with me about the real point of the book [*The Bridge of
Years*]—although it is surely about marriage as well! But I am not alone
in feeling what I feel about the moment when the child suddenly real-
izes that he cannot attack his father or mother, as he used to do, because
he must support them because he sees that he can hurt them too much
i.e. the roles are reversed—(I have witnessed this at the Limbosches in
Belgium, for instance, and also at the Huxleys, and I felt it very much in
relation to my own father). But I may have expressed it badly in the
book—I must think about it.

I have been in a long doldrum, hardly functioning as more than a
gardener lately—the weather is very damp and hot, the worst summer
we have ever had here, after the bad spring too. The only saving grace
is that there is plenty of water! But slugs eat everything—and today,
final horror—a woodchuck came back and ate half the annuals, especially my beloved shirley poppies, so airy and fragile, which were just
about to flower. I had planted the seeds, doggedly, in a cloud of black
flies, on my knees…and was so proud to have done it against all the
odds. Now, all gone! I am stupid to care so much. What does it matter
compared to the agony of the cities? The Vietnam war? Or even De
Gaulle's really intolerable arrogance in Canada? Of course that comes
out of 1940—but does he not remember that in France's darkest hour
it was England who offered France a complete partnership? Now he
wants to keep England out of the Common Market—in her darkest
hour. Everywhere there seems such lack of generosity…in our own
Congress, despite all the horrors, they have just voted down a bill to
exterminate the rats in the slums! The Senators made jokes about it!
So funny it seems to them that Negro babies cannot be left alone or
they may be bitten by rats! As you see, I am in a state of black rage
about nearly everything.

But I escape into reading the history of the villages around here and
make notes and dream of those novels … one of which I shall begin in
late October…it is fascinating stuff, primary, in the sense of primitive, in

many ways, but what courage those people had! And what a sense of their destiny and of its responsibilities! "What do you raise on your cold rocky pastures?" a Southerner asked Daniel Webster and the answer was, "We raise men."

Meanwhile, just to blow off steam I am writing a series of non-poems based on items of news in the papers...ironic ballads. I enclose one, of which the last line does not quite work yet.

Since I wrote the verse, I have read the book of which the review had moved me so much—a remarkable and compassionate work, compassionate also toward the die-hard Southerners whose whole ethos is being rocked, who are afraid too. The psychiatrist who wrote the book has followed these children for five or six years, as they grow up. Everyone thought Ruby, for instance, would be marred by the terrible war she fought alone, going to school each day with armed guards, and meeting a crowd of screaming women, but the <u>fact</u> is that perhaps the fact that she could act, that she could play such an important role has not made her bitter at all. However, I wrote the poem before the riots— and I think, in essence, it is true. The hatred is now coming out and must come out perhaps before the first step toward a constructive meeting of the races can take place. The Negro is becoming an adult at last. He no longer lives a secret life under a facade of "Yes, Suh!" I have been thinking so much about violence...wanting to write a more serious poem on the subject. Violence is <u>final</u>, that is what is so terrible about it. Violence is <u>forever.</u>

But life interrupts these days. Perley Cole, the old man who has helped me make this place what it is, and who is now 77, is ill. We had a talk and agreed that whatever happens, he must give up hard work. This turns my world here upside down and I am exhausted by the sheer physical work I now have to do alone. This dear, but <u>very</u> tempestuous old man, ran away from the hospital last week—so I persuaded him to go a long way to a Doctor he had faith in in a different city—drove him there, and next week will take him to another hospital. Perhaps there they will discover what is wrong. He is hemorraging and has lost a lot of blood. But I have now lost two days at my desk and have had to add a lot of outdoor work to the usual stint, so I feel rather exhausted again.

Even before Perley became ill I had decided to leave here in 10 years, sell the house, and move to a smaller one nearer Judy. I shall then be 65— and want only to write poems (the novels, d.v. will be written by then) and live a peaceful life without too many demands of garden and estate. I felt like a prisoner who is given a reprieve when I realized that I do not <u>have</u> to go on being worn down by my idiotic passion for the garden.

The effect of exhaustion is to make one egocentric—I long to talk about Florence with you. I devoured every word! But I find it hard to express my feelings tonight.

Let it rest on the joy your letter brought me, dear friend....

Ever your devoted
May

P.S. I heard indirectly that Margaret Clapp returns from India next month and had there "an exasperating and frustrating year"—I must confess that I was rather glad! I think she was not <u>at all</u> prepared for the experience, inwardly or in any way.

———

Daniel Webster: New Hampshire-born lawyer and statesman (1782–1852) who served as congressman from Massachusetts and in other government posts; noted for his oratory.

non-poems: Among other topical pieces, the first section of *A Grain of Mustard Seed* includes "The Ballad of Ruby," "The Ballad of Johnny (A News Item)," and "Easter, 1968"; these were not retained in *Poems 1930–93.*

Amidst a 1960 New Orleans desegregation struggle, six-year-old Ruby Bridges became the first black child to attend all-white William Frantz public school; despite harassment and death threats, Ruby still walked to school, her unintimidated courage depicted in one of Norman Rockwell's most memorable images.

before the riots: Forty people died as a result of race riots in Detroit, July 1967.

tempestuous old man: Writing to Eleanor Blair, 8 November 1966, Sarton narrated how she had "stopped in at Perley's to tell him I had borrowed a heavy stapler (for the waterproofing paper that winterizes all the edges of the house) and hoped he could do that job when he came also for the rubbish. I found him in the back room, sitting back to me, and realized soon that he was in one of his black rages. . . . [He] said 'May Satrun'—that is the way he pronounces my name—'I'm through. You can get somebody else. This time I mean it' etc. Well I begged him to tell me what I had said or done to upset him, but it was no use and finally he became insulting about me as a woman and that I could not take. . . . I realize that Perley has been under a lot of strain but this is the second time in a month. . . . It's just not a good state of affairs." Despite trusting and treating each other as friends, they had a good deal to bear in one another.

d.v.: Latin, *Deo volente,* "God willing."

the joy your letter brought me: See *Solitude,* pp. 193–95, for a 27 August 1971 letter from Mayran, with Sarton's translation and reaction.

Clapp returns from India: She had completed her term in India with the United States Information Agency as a cultural attaché.

TO ELEANOR BLAIR   Aug. 5th, 1967
[Nelson]
Darling,

First of all, happy Aug. 8th and happy year, in which you will (I trust) see yourself in print as a professional photographer in two books by

M.S.—and perhaps as an author too if the history piece on Wellesley gets published, as it should! I am simply astounded when I realize all that you accomplish, as these days flow through my fingers like water with so little to show. It was simply an inspiration to make the big effort of hauling the lawn-mower up here that weekend—I am very happy with mine and feel confident because of what you showed me. But that is the least of your imaginings and the wonders you perform on my behalf, darling!

Now about Saturday—we'll look for you anytime you arrive from 11:00 on and have a picnic lunch (very simple) ready. Don't bring too much food—there will be cold roast beef, zucchinis of course from the garden; coffee, tea, milk, cat food, other supplies like a small steak or chops in the freezer, bread, butter—all staples, in fact. And, as you know there are cans of corned beef hash, baked beans, cold ham on the shelves if you get stuck.

I have had a dithering week because of all day spent with Perley on Tuesday and all day Thursday spent writing a 12-page critique of that thesis on the Civic which I have been laboring through—it depressed me as the tone is patronizing and the fellow never captures what the Civic was to New York, because he had to rely entirely on the critics—I wish he had talked with some of the people who came regularly and made the audience a distinguished and endearing group. The most irritating thing was the pseudo-sophistication, and inaccuracy of his language i.e. he called the Civic "déclassé" twice! An absurdity. I talked to Le G[allienne]. on the phone and she also had been very disappointed and distressed, but she does take all these defeats with superior balance and courage. I felt woe because all that greatness finally gets pinned down in a stupid man's tome—which may become the source for other books.

Perley has an ulcer and will go to a specialist in Hanover (after I leave probably) and his daughter [Mary] will see that he gets there. They may have to operate but I think diet may do the trick. I myself feel relieved that it is nothing worse, but I may be over-optimistic. In some ways it is a relief not to have him around and I am certainly saving a lot of money—Trumbull Hare cut all except the back which I had done, very well, for $2.65. I paid Perley for at least two half days work which is $12 every week! Perley's spirits are good—I think he is relieved to have laid down the burden of hard work at last. He does a little mowing on his own place.

The garden book you gave me is wonderful! I have kept forgetting to thank you—and for so much else! Let's hope Saturday will be a good day and not too hot. Dearest love until then—

Here is your birthday present! With a huge hug of love—

M

Eleanor Blair: 1894-1992; 8 August was her birthday. A former copy-editor for Ginn, Blair became "more than anyone the 'friend of the work,'" offering a "sensitive editing eye" to *Plant Dreaming Deep* (*Solitude*, p. 140), "typing, editing, and believing in *Kinds of Love* during the long struggle to get it done" (p. 105), since as Sarton admitted to her (20 February 1967), "I have a sort of inbred violence against detail (so unlike my father in this)—it creates awful frustration." *The Poet and the Donkey* (1969) was dedicated to her.

Blair's photographs enhanced not only *Plant Dreaming Deep* but the celebratory selection of poems *As Does New Hampshire* (William L. Bauham, Publisher, 1967; paperback, 1987). Lotte Jacobi thought her photo of Perley Cole with his scythe "was great!" (reproduced in *Solitude*, p. 20). Sarton agreed, writing Blair on 8 November 1966 that it "brought tears to my eyes—it is just perfect, the sensitive hands, the intent tilt to his head and the tension in the shoulders—and the whole composition against trees and flowers is just perfect!" Blair was to house-sit at Nelson while Sarton and Judith Matlack made their summer visit to Anne Thorp on Greenings Island.

thesis on the Civic: Paul Cooper had sent Sarton his 1967 dissertation "Eva LeGallienne's Civic Repertory Theatre," Graduate College of the University of Illinois. He may have meant that the Civic appealed across class lines, but rather than "classless," "déclassé" signifies having lost worldly status or intrinsic quality.

$12 every week: Cole's two half-days of four hours each would equal $1.50 an hour; the 1967 federal minimum wage was $1.40 ($6.83 in 1998 dollars). Though keeping tabs, Sarton was not stingy when hiring local workers. However, by 13 May 1968 she was informing Beverly Hallam, "Had to fire Trumbull Hare, who never did any work except when dead drunk and last time appeared with an even more drunken friend who leaned and tottered on the shovel like a Shakespearian clown and I had to pay him as well! Perley has come back. . .and already the place looks as if someone cared."

TO KATHARINE WHITE   Nov. 6th, [1967]
[Nelson]
Dear Katharine,

Rarely, rarely comest thou spirit of delight! But I spent an hour of pure bliss in bed last night like a bear with a pot of honey reading your piece on arranging flowers—the bliss came from many things, unexpected such as dear Kilvert making his unexpected appearance, or Herrigel (her husband's book on Zen in the Art of Archery [Eugen Herrigel, 1953] is practically my Bible about almost any human effort from writing poetry to teaching, but I had not read hers and now shall)—but chiefly from the immense relief it is to find someone talking <u>sense</u> on this prickly question. I feel quite sick if even anyone uses this word "arranging" flowers now because of the truly appalling things done in its name by people who apparently love neither flowers nor any human habitation where such things might be placed...you hit the nail on the head so <u>nicely</u>! (I did laugh about Zen and zat too and in several other places) But best of all I loved all the evocations of childhood rooms and flowers...

It made me long to see you and just <u>talk</u> about flowers—I think I really have my peculiar garden only to keep four or five bunches of flowers going indoors from May till the frost here—and I've just come back from Amsterdam where I saw some sort of autumn show of "arrangements" mostly awful, but there was <u>one</u> low bowl stuffed full of purple, lavender and white autumn crocus that I shall never forget—in fact I have since on a modest scale had the same on my desk these last days, for the autumn crocus get broken off by raking at this season, and now I know just what to do with them. Well, I won't launch into the tome which floods my mind as a result of reading you—just many, many thanks and how I look forward to Part II, dear Katharine.

How are you and ineffable E.B. White? (do not dare call him "Andy" of course as I never had the luck to lay eyes upon him)—

I am in a laocoön struggle to write a series of novels about N.H.—I got a big grant (National Fdn.) to do it and have been reading local histories all summer and filling out cards full of sense and nonsense, but I now face the dire business of conjuring up this world—it begins in 1842 and at this rate will go on forever, though my intent is a series of quite short rather lyrical books on the subject of how people deal with failure, for this is failed country....well, enough, think of me groaning at the desk every morning for four hours and you will understand why extreme pleasure is rare these days—

Thank you for giving me that pot of honey

> Your ancient bear
> May

---

spirit of delight: This "Song," c. 1820–21—by a fourth great Romantic poet, Percy Bysshe Shelley (1792–1822)—is known by these, its first two lines, often quoted at this period by Sarton.

White's "Flower Arrangers" was one of a series of horticultural essays in *The New Yorker* that after her death E. B. White gathered into *Onward and Upward in the Garden* (1979).

Kilvert: Robert Francis Kilvert (1840–79), a Welsh clergyman whose shrewd humorous *Kilvert's Diary: 1870–1879* (1944 ed.) Sarton read with delectation in 1952.

Sarton's affinities with Gustie L. Herrigel are evident in this extract from her *Zen in the Art of Flower Arrangement* (1958): "[B]ehind everything that can be visibly represented [in flower arranging] there stands, waiting to be experienced by everyone, the mystery and deep ground of existence. . . . Not the slightest intention of arranging [flowers] 'beautifully' must disturb this self immersion."

Amsterdam: Sarton had seen the Netherlands that fall while visiting Baroness P. J. (Hannie) Van Till; see note to 2 September 1968.

a laocoön struggle: Named after the mythical priest of Apollo, squeezed to death with his sons by sea-serpents while sacrificing to Poseidon, god of the ocean. Here it signifies being trapped in the toils of an overwhelming situation. Sarton wrote Bill Brown, 8 November 1967, that her working title for this saga about "how people deal with failure" was *The Cold Winter.*

March 2d, 1968
[Nelson]

I was awfully glad to have your letter—(so heartening!). I realize that anyone who comes in from outside to a town like Nelson and then writes about it (though I did wait nearly ten years!) will be suspect to most inhabitants! I hope you liked what I said about Quig and your mother. (The only thing Mildred has said is that she was humiliated by one sentence at the beginning when I describe water coming through the roof and dirty dishes, but I think this is unfair since there is such very high praise of her and of Quig all through the book except for that one sentence. I had not sent you the book because I was so deeply hurt by this and other things which perhaps one day we can talk about.)

I wish we could sit around and talk—the trouble is that Mildred wants, of course, to see you when you come up and I do not want to take you away, but maybe one day you and [wife] Nancy could come over for a drink by the fire, as Quig used to do.

I can well understand that you left here in bitterness. I have felt that bitterness, too. But I came here as a free person to make the life I could myself choose, and when I was (so to speak) a person in my own right. Everyone has to break away from family at some point, I'm sure. It is wonderful that you have done it, you alone in the family, and with Nancy's help have made a viable, rich, fruitful life of your own. I feel so proud of you, Barney—and I think I have some idea of the <u>cost</u>. But that is the past. It is behind you, and now perhaps Nelson can be something else—less bitter. I do hope so.

It may interest you, however, that the theme of the historical novels I am trying (desperately) to get started on is how people deal with <u>failure</u> and that the deeper I go into the past the more I am aware of how <u>thin</u> (in some ways) the life has been here.

Oh well, bless you for writing—please do not mention anything in this to your mother.

Love to all three

Your old battered
May

———

Barnabas Quigley: b. 1936; one of the three Quigley children, along with Terence G. and Thomasa, "Tami."

humiliated by one sentence: Page 74 of "Neighbors Happen," *Plant Dreaming Deep*, describes the Quigleys' house one rainy autumn day before Sarton moved into her Nelson house: "The roof leaked; a pail stood on the long trestle table covered with unwashed dishes; there was a pile of lumber in one corner, and one wall was unfinished. A violin lay on one chair and a pile of laundry on another."

Writing Polly Starr the summer before, 25 June 1967, Sarton recalled Mildred's saying "'the only thing I can do for people is to clean their houses' and the way she cleans is like an artist, and with so much love. I begin to cry as I write this because I feel so discouraged about myself and the little I manage to do…don't laugh—but I have so much 'going for me' as they say, and she has so little. As I told you, I'm sure, the greatest value of this place for me is the sense of proportion it has given me because I am surrounded by such hard-working and poor people. It is a constant lesson."

Perhaps that explains why Mildred shunned cleaning her own house; perhaps such words could hurt her chances for employment which a widow might need, for people in Nelson plainly did read what their "local bard" wrote about them. Everywhere else Sarton writes tenderly and lovingly of the whole family; but human nature being what it is, these lines were what stayed with Mildred. Sarton is buried beside Quig in the Nelson cemetery.

TO GRANVILLE HICKS   March 3rd, 1968
[Nelson]
Dear Granville Hicks,

It was splendid to learn that we have shared many of the same experiences just 100 miles or so apart—you and your wife must come and see me if anything brings you into New Hampshire in the summer.

Your review meant a great deal to this old porcupine, and also brought back an earlier debt I owe you for the wonderful push you gave to Faithful Are The Wounds some years ago.

Let me slip into the envelope with this the little book I brought out last year to help celebrate our bi-centennial—I have become a local bard and enjoy it very much.

Sincerely yours,
May Sarton

Granville Hicks: Author and Marxist literary critic (1901–82) who resigned from the Communist party after the USSR-Nazi Germany nonaggression pact. He wrote novels and an autobiography; as a contributing editor to *Saturday Review* (1958–69), he praised *Plant Dreaming Deep* (17 February 1968) as "tenderly poetic though not sentimental," "a well-wrought book about a woman living alone."

an earlier debt: Reviewing current political novels for *The New Leader* (28 March 1955), Hicks pointed up how Sarton surrounded "Edward Cavan with a group of intensely and admirably realized characters" in order to explore "the deepest problems of identity, friendship and love. . . . To the sensibilities of a poet, she adds sharp powers of observation and a fine sense of structure. Thus her book belongs to the small group of novels that transcend the public events with which they deal." His 7 October 1957 *New Leader* review of *Birth of a Grandfather* was headlined "Some Good Fiction Which Won't Get the Popular Attention It Deserves."

a local bard: The subtitle of the original edition of *As Does New Hampshire* reads "For My Neighbors at Nelson on the Occasion of the Bi-Centennial, 1767–1967."

[Nelson]
Officers of the Poetry Society of America:

I felt real dismay when I read Louis Ginsberg's sneer at two books of mine in the yearly review in the Bulletin. Just what have I done? Am I anti-semitic? Hardly—one of my cousins was tortured to death in the Belgian resistance and that resistance was chiefly in defence of the Jews. Why do I need to be crucified? I alone treated with contempt, patronized? Why does the Society choose as its official critic a man who appears to be illiterate? I presume that he did not mean to say what he did, that Louise Townsend Nicholl has an "envious" reputation?

Mr. Ginsberg introduced every poet except me with some mention of his or her achievement. In my case alone, the membership is merely informed that "May Sarton, we are told, was born in Belgium." Is it implied that I have lied about my birth, as well as being a bad poet?

I have refused from the start to be a critic or reviewer. I hold that no poet should take a position of such power, because power does corrupt. I have paid heavily for this stand, no doubt; I have no regrets. But I am deeply wounded that in the Poetry Society of America (where presumably my work is known) I should have to bear this sort of attack.

I have had no "influence" ever on my side. On the work alone I have been given a Guggenheim fellowship in poetry, a Lucy Martin Donnelly Fellowship (Bryn Mawr) in the novel, an Hon. Litt.D. from Russell Sage, an Hon. Phi Beta Kappa from Radcliffe College. I am a fellow of the American Academy of Arts and Sciences. I was one of the first twenty American writers to be given a $10,000 grant from the National Foundation of Arts and Humanities. And I believe I am the only writer ever to have been nominated as a candidate for the National Book Award in two categories (novel and poetry) in the same year, 1957. But the only thing Mr. Ginsberg felt he could say about my work or me was that I was reported to have been born in Belgium. (If this really were the whole story, then might he not have given me credit for writing in English, rather than in French?)

One cannot answer a critic. But may one not beg a reputable Society to choose its yearly critic with more discrimination? I do, at any rate, have the right, I am sure, to ask to be quoted accurately. Mr. Ginsberg found one line in two books of mine that he could praise. In his version the line does not even scan. His line reads "With our neighbors we come now to exchange our solitude." The line reads "We come now to exchange our solitude." (I might add that out of context it communicates nothing whatever).

I have had many blows, too many. I have been nervously ill for months. I have kept alive hour by hour and day by day against terrible depression. When a knife in the back is as unjustified and random as this, when it costs what it does, what is the justification? I am not young. No man is my enemy. I have 20 books on my record. I am told that the record is distinguished as well!

Yours in <u>anguish</u> of mind.
<u>May Sarton</u>

The Poetry Society of America: Founded in 1910. Members have included Frost, Moore, Langston Hughes, Edna St. Vincent Millay; members today include Adrienne Rich, Robert Haas, Sharon Olds, and recent Poet Laureate Stanley Kunitz. Besides issuing publications, the Society holds readings at their Gramercy Park quarters in New York City and grants awards to new and established poets, such as Elizabeth Bishop, E. E. Cummings, Robert Creeley, and Robert Pinsky.

Louis Ginsberg: 1896–1976. A traditional poet, high school teacher, and socialist, he reviewed for *The Times Literary Supplement* in the late 1950s and early 1960s. His radical Communist wife, Naomi, went tragically insane in early adulthood and was memorialized by their son, visionary poet Allen Ginsberg (1926–97), in "Kaddish." For a time, starting in 1966, father and son gave joint poetry readings.

tortured to death: Jean Sarton, George Sarton's first cousin, died in November 1948 as a consequence of his treatment during World War II. On 18 January 1946 May Sarton wrote S. S. Koteliansky that he had "proved himself a hero and was terribly tortured but did not tell anything. He will never be well again, poor man. . . . It is so moving to think of these poor human beings who seemed to be so little and then found in themselves the heroic qualities they did not imagine they possessed. Jean Sarton was one of those."

"The Tortured" was written for him in 1946; he also inspired her play *The Underground River* (New York: Play Club Inc., 1947). Set in German-occupied Paris, it examines the moral responsibility of the oppressed to resist and of the artist to take action against oppression.

Louise Townsend Nicholl: A New York City poet who, in the 1920s, worked for a time in the same office as Margaret Mead, Léonie Adams, and Bogan; she also served on the nine-member editorial board of the little magazine *The Measure*. Nicholl's *Collected Poems* were published in 1953; her most recent book was *Blood That Is Language* (1967).

on the work <u>alone</u>: Sarton refers to these awards: The Guggenheim Fellowship, 1954. Bryn Mawr Fellowship, 1953. Russell Sage degree, 1959. Phi Beta Kappa, 1955. American Academy of Arts and Sciences, 1958. National Foundation of the Arts and Humanities, 1967.

National Book Award: In 1958, *The Birth of a Grandfather* (1957) was nominated for the novel, and *In Time Like Air* (1958) for poetry.

"to exchange our solitude": From "The Annealing" (1967), *As Does New Hampshire*; not reprinted.

in <u>anguish</u> of mind: This letter, from the archives of Boston University, was sent.

TO LOUISE BOGAN   Sunday March 31, 1968
[Nelson]
Dear Louise,

So good to see a bit of literary criticism in the New Yorker again, and especially from you. I was very pleased. Have been meaning to write, but life is absurdly full considering that I am doing nothing serious, just puttering about like a character in The Wind and the Willows.

You started a long train of thought about Virginia Woolf when you called. I do understand the reaction now to an over-estimate in some ways. But can you name a novelist today for whose next book one waits with such excitement because you will have no idea what it will be like? The daring of her experiments, Orlando, The Waves, To The Lighthouse, the fact that she never let the mold stay to be used again..this is already a sign of genius. Some of these experiments were failures, but all were extremely interesting. People blame her for not being [James] Joyce— why should she be? She was not experimenting with language so much as form and there is a real distinction here. That is all what critics look for. But what about the common reader? I have yet to find a woman writer who can illuminate in just this way "ordinary life" or any one who has stated what women's lives are, the complexity they have to weave together, the harmony they have to make out of the emotional chaos and physical disorder of "family life," the art this takes. She has done far more in a real, unblinking coming to terms with the woman than all the Betty somethingorothers [Friedan] and their "feminine mystique." It is not a sentimental view! Or a "feminist" view—the novels. But for the common reader, perhaps her greatest gift (comparable to Emily Dickinson) was to make the ordinary things of life, a woman knitting a sock, a certain light on the grass, marvelously new and touching. In one of the fan letters I have had recently, a woman writes "I've found through the years as my family responsibilities have increased that I must put a ban on my reading or I become too restless to stick to duties. But two people I can always read..Virginia Woolf, because of all her awareness of small things, which is contagious and I then notice all the small glories of my daily life. And you" etc. (underlining mine) It is easy to be patronizing to this gift as it is easy to sneer at the saints, but I do not believe it is nothing to give back courage and to illuminate daily life for those (most of us) close to despair all the time. The word is "life-enhancing." I shall have more to say when I am dead (that is meant as a joke). Helen Howe is here for the week-end and I must take her to see some new lambs) ...I do hope we can talk one of these days. You were so dear to call!

Did I tell you the marvel that has taken place in my doldrum? I am now rescued forever, it would seem, from teaching or lecturing and can become a <u>rich</u> recluse in Nelson, because Family Circle was so delighted by the new book [*Plant Dreaming Deep*] that they are contracting for a monthly column about country things, anything I choose. The pieces are just three double-spaced typed pages each and I love the form, rather like a sonnet in prose, and find that I have immense stores of things to say which do not fit into novels and cannot be made into poems when the fires burn so low...I have written 6 in a month, with great joy. They pay $1000 apiece. So I am sending Mildred to Florida on a holiday with her grandchild [Miranda, "Randi"] and all sorts of plans buzz in my head...the contract is for 6 months and then we see. They want it to be permanent...I now remember that I mentioned this because you said Maidie knew the magazine. Please forgive this burble. Oh Louise, the pressure is off at last, the terrible pressure to create and earn...and already I begin to feel dim stirrings of the novel, of poems, when I am deeply and altogether rested. It will still take some time.

Mud season now, one snow drop by the granite step, one blue primrose under some hemlock boughs ...

Dearest love and bless you for being there, <u>my</u> poet.

Your
May

E. Bowen will have a big new novel called Ida Trout—(This is not right but Trout is) I'm so excited! Heard it indirectly—She has been so <u>silent</u> I was anxious.

---

criticism in the New Yorker: The 30 March 1968 omnibus review "Verse" covered eighteen titles–translations (Homer through Nelly Sachs and Christian Morgenstern); three books on Ezra Pound; collected poems by Moore and Auden; new voices such as John Berryman and Anthony Hecht; and Elizabeth Salter's *The Last Years of a Rebel,* a sad and frightening chronicle of Dame Edith Sitwell's "obsessive preococupations."

Bogan's final *New Yorker* piece (28 December 1968) was devoted to a study of Keats and books by six young poets.

This note, in keeping with several others, is indebted to Claire E. Knox's bibliography *Louise Bogan: A Reference Source,* Scarecrow Author Bibliographies No. 86 (Lanham, Maryland, and London: The Scarecrow Press, 1990), a valuable resource for detailed documentation on Bogan's publications and thus her career.

The Wind [in] *the Willows:* The 1908 fantasy by Scottish writer Kenneth Grahame (1859–1932) features well-to-do Rat and Mole and Toad (of Toad Hall)—human in all but bodily form—pursuing droll, inconsequential adventures.

Virginia Woolf: Bogan was collaborating with professor and Woolf scholar Josephine O'Brien Schaefer on an afterword to the 1968 Signet paperback of Leonard Woolf's 1953 selection *A Writer's Diary.* Bogan once complained to Sarton about "people *mooning* over" Woolf (*What the Woman Lived,* 21 September 1955). But this essay, one harbinger of resurgent interest in

Woolf's life and works, concludes: "*A Writer's Diary* explains so much of the unforgivable—the lady's prejudices and ignorances, the ambitious woman's jealousy, the neurotic tricks of the rejected child—that at the end there is nothing to forgive; and, for any writer, worlds to learn."

Woolf wrote two volumes of essays addressed to *The Common Reader* (1925, 1932), a phrase taken from British man of letters Samuel Johnson (1709–84). Bogan had also written about Emily Dickinson (1830–86), poet extraordinaire.

Family Circle: Sarton would write a dozen monthly articles (June 1968–May 1969) for this popular magazine, which millions purchased from checkout-counter magazine racks. Topics (often assigned) ranged from "Riches Beyond Measure" through "The Mowing, Before and After" to the last, "Living with a Mountain" (Mount Monadnock, New Hampshire). After two six-month contracts, the column was not renewed.

Maidie: Maidie Alexander Scannell (b. 1917) was Bogan's daughter by her first husband, a professional Army man, the German-born Curt Alexander (1888–1920); she was Bogan's only child.

Mud season now: A particularly depressing time in New England; see "Mud Season" (1961).

my poet: By this time Bogan had drafted and revised but not finished her final poem. See *Journey Around My Room,* pp. 183 and 185, for the transcription and holograph of "December Daybreak."

Bowen . . . Trout: Eva Trout or Changing Scenes (1968) was the biggest and most ambitious of her ten completed novels, featuring a larger-than-life heroine and Bowen's only use in fiction of America.

TO CONSTANCE URDANG   May 14th, 1968
[Nelson]
Dear Miss Urdang,

Unfortunately the April issue of Poetry reached me with pages 44 and 45 blank, a nice gift from the furies. Long ago when I was young and tried to forge out a stance for myself which would reduce anxiety as much as possible and above all keep me from ever occupying a position of power such as you assume as a critic I made a vow that I would <u>never</u> review, and I have held to it. It is interesting to note how Olympian a tone you assume when you have never published a single book, and thus never met a single critic. So you will of course laugh when I tell you that this review coming upon others, Karl Shapiro (of the Selected Poems), the ubiquitous [John] Ciardi long ago..and the feeling I had had for years that I was trying to be heard by pushing up the gravestone laid on my mouth by the facile, the irresponsible, and the truly careless critics such as you..has brought me once more close to suicide.

I ask you just one thing. If the "educated middle class" at which you sneer, values my work, but if, as you suggest <u>what</u> it values has "no value for literature," how can you defend your own reviewing for Poetry? Who reads Poetry except the "educated middle class" for God's sake? And isn't it amazingly snobbish for a <u>poet</u> or a would-be poet to divide people into <u>classes</u>? Is literature today which has "value" being written only for the "uneducated lower classes," if I may use your terminology? And just who falls into this category as writer? I suppose that man whose name I have forgotten whose poems sell by the millions and who strums a guitar...and who has not, as far as I know, been reviewed in that upper-middle-class-literate-however valueless magazine Poetry.

If you will re-read "A Village Tale" and "The Death of the Turtle" in the animal poems, or any other, I think you will have to admit that they are not for children. I wish they were. Children are good readers of poetry because they come to it fresh, generous, and without the need to sneer.

Thank you for pointing out some pretty odd rhymes. That was helpful.

Otherwise, I must say damn you to Hell for a snob first, for a cruel sneerer second, for wishing apparently to drive a perfectly innocent hard working, unknown, unrecognized, desperate person to suicide, a person 56 years old, who has never had a break, never. I hope with all my heart that you learn to endure all this yourself, that you are given a stone for bread, that you nearly starve in order to go on writing, that finally you are given the sour accolade you have given me by some young woman who is on the point of publishing her first book...

I am <u>read</u>, Miss Urdang—that I know (By C. O.'s and G. I.'s too, and by college students, and by what <u>you</u> would call the "illiterate masses"— but not by the critics—)—and I am published by a discriminating publisher—but <u>across</u> the barrage, believe me—

Your

<u>May Sarton</u>

Constance Urdang: b. 1922. Poet, novelist, editor, and critic, after several years in U. S. military intelligence during World War II she worked in publishing and at universities. In 1976 the Natinal Endowment for the Arts would award her a grant; she had published verse in *Poetry* at least a decade before reviewing *A Private Mythology* ("Gregor, Sarton, Vazakas").

Urdang notes that certain of the animal poems ("Franz, a Goose," "The Horse-Pulling") ought to attract children; but questions if serious poetry can accommodate such rhymes as "hurtle"-"turtle" or "Te Deum"-"museum", saying that although Sarton elsewhere breaks out of strict form, she has not made full use of the possibilities of free verse.

The rest of the review makes curious reading. Urdang calls the book "fluent, fluid, humble with a humility not entirely false, cultivated rather than worldly, civilized, and accomplished." But since "the most distinctive quality of our time" is a "rejection of the traditional virtues," no (true?) poet wants to be saddled with such attributes now. Though the qualities these poems embody "are still valued in real life by the educated middle class, they no longer have value in literature."

One cannot tell whether she is endorsing, deploring, or merely recording this cultural change, which sounds rather dated another generation later. The tone almost suggests veiled criticism of "poets" who reject such traits and those who claim "literature" no longer values them; but it is hard to tell. Urdang does not use the phrases "uneducated lower classes" or "illiterate masses"; Sarton is suggesting she well might.

that man: In the late 1960s, books of poetry by Rod McKuen (b. 1933)—*Lonesome Cities, Listen to the Warm*—were released in tandem with LPs featuring his haggard singing and recitations of crushingly sincere verse against orchestral backdrops and nature's sound effects. Despite substantial if fleeting commercial success (Frank Sinatra devoted an album to his work), he was almost uniformly derided by reviewers.

<u>May Sarton</u>: "C.O.'s": conscientious objectors; in this case, to the Vietnam War. This letter was sent.

TO POLLY THAYER STARR   Sept. 2d, 1968
[Nelson]
Dearest Poll,

Just sent a p.c. to Hingham where I imagined you might be to say to watch TV (if possible) Thurs. Sept. 12th at 7 P.M. for that half hour Profile of me...channel 5, Boston, right after Cronkite. Did you see the one of Sam Morison? I thought he was wonderful..this one may be awful (I haven't the foggiest idea what they will do with the 9 hours of shooting and recording and have only a dim memory of anguish about the whole thing. It was the day the donkey came, and poured rain and I was so worried about her that I finally wept bitter tears and the director relented and helped me get her into the barn. The adorable creature leaves to go back to her tiny stall at the Warner's tonight or tomorrow..she has saved this summer for me. In fact I am writing a little book [*The Poet and the Donkey*] of which she (called Whiffenpoof in the book) is the heroine. She makes Whiffenpoof-ish noises, strangled screams which I suppose are brays, whenever she sees me. And she was so lame she could hardly walk but now runs and leaps like a dog. Snap enclosed.

Oh, I do hope you can come to Mt. Desert..it sounds such a lark, and I do want you to meet Hannie..she really is an angel, and will by then have deserved a break as she is marrying off her younger boy Sept. 9th, had a big show of paintings at Veere, is painting the portrait of an Admiral, has ten people to dinner on no money about every day as far as I can see, and <u>never</u> gets tired (I must say I am sometimes full of dread, but it is only three weeks)..how she manages I do not know. Then the Queen is always calling up and she has to go to tea when she least wants to etc.

Well, it has been one Hell of a summer here..I guess I have had about 100 guests, all told, some for the night, others not. Besides those invited, I was in a state of siege in July and until we went to Maine because so many people came to see Nelson and the house because of the book and I began to feel like an animal in a zoo (but <u>what</u> animal?). Esmeralda, the donkey, was the only real help, as stubborn, cross, and difficult as I, and often as hysterical (the sounds she makes!) She was a soul sister all right. Now an English friend [Jane Stockwood] arrives Sept. 18th for three weeks and Hannie on Oct. 3rd for three weeks...but after that I am going into a profound hibernation of sleep and work, I hope.

Have you seen the Family Circle pieces? They seem to be making their way and I get sweet letters from v. simple people..also about three a day still about Plant Dr. Deep. I have begun to feel like Grand Central Station..too dispersed and always responding like a machine. Let us hope it will end soon.

Well, I found the dem. convention a real trauma, except for the Kennedy film which certainly lifted the atmosphere for a while. The scenes of police beating up peace marchers made me sick. And when Humphrey quoted St. Francis, I turned the thing off and went to bed. Judy was here those days to hold my hand..it would have been awful alone. However, I agree that McCarthy really won in some ways, won on the unit-vote ("we freed Texas", as he said), and forced Johnson not to run..the sad thing was that the peace plank got voted down.

I thought there were a lot of fine faces on the floor and awful as it was, it was alive compared to the Rep. convention. Real issues were faced and openly discussed. Where we go from here I cannot imagine..

I'm off to see Le Gallienne early tomorrow..she had a bad heart attack months ago, and this has been long planned. Just over night. I would not do it for anyone else, as I am really dead tired and this letter reeled off the top of my poor old bean. Maine [Greenings Island] was the one break...I was so relieved to be there and not here that I wrote 50 pages of the little book, wonderful relief to be working again. "Happiness is not a warm puppy. It's work" as Will Hawthorne said the other night on the phone. (He has just been made Master of Churchill College in Cambridge..the husband of my darling old friend, Barbara, from Shady Hill)

You just must come to Maine.

Sorry this is such a burble.

It brings much love. Have you been painting? It is so grand about raising all that money. We did not do very well, but apparently the ads (with names of distinguished women from many towns and cities in N.H.) were effective, I am told.

A hug darling,

Love
M

P.S. Had a lovely day with Helen [Howe] on the island—

Hingham: Starr inherited her childhood home, Weir River Farm, in Hingham, Massachusetts, from her mother.

half hour Profile: WHDH–Boston had taped the interview on 23 May; Sarton watched it at the nearby home of Helen and Robbins Milbank, who had a color television.

Harvard professor and historian Samuel Eliot Morison (1887–1976) won Pulitzers for *Admiral of the Ocean Sea* (1942) and *John Paul Jones* (1959). "May Sarton's prose is equal to her poetry. Need I say more?" he asked on the dust jacket for *Plant Dreaming Deep.* "In both she has described the wintry scene in Northern New Hampshire better than anybody except Robert Frost."

Hannie: Among other achievements, the baroness P. J. "Hannie" Van Till (d. December 1986) survived four years in a Japanese prison camp on Java during World War II. Her hostess at tea was Queen Juliana of the Netherlands, who ruled 1948–80. Sarton wrote "Dutch Interior: Pieter de Hooch (1629–1682)" (1970) for Van Till; see *After the Stroke,* pp. 214–18, for reminiscences and a photo of her working at her press.

Veere is a very old town on the Veersche Meer, in Zeeland Province. Mount Desert Island, like Greenings, is off the coast of Maine.

seen the Family Circle pieces?: Elizabeth Bishop had seen them: "I was in the Supermarket (I love to go there to read the packages, it is just like a library, really) and I saw a number of *Family Circle* with 'Marianne Moore on Baseball' on the cover & of course I bought it. May Sarton, Truman Capote are also in this number. I think it must be getting to be the fashionable publication." (to Marianne Moore, 10 October 1968; *One Art,* p. 499)

Bishop would have read "Memorable Gifts": the best "are works of imagination. They come with the giver's signature on them, wrapped in a personal magic. . . . We can bring back the fresh glory of the Christmas Star . . . by loving not only the people to whom we give but the gift itself." Moore was a noted baseball fan; Capote may have written about Christmas too, a favorite subject of his.

the dem. convention: Having won five early primaries, Eugene McCarthy lost four to Robert F. Kennedy; after Kennedy's assassination 5 June, Hubert H. Humphrey—who had not run in the primaries—became Democratic presidential nominee. During the convention, brutal clashes between demonstrators and the Chicago police were telecast worldwide. Humphrey narrowly lost the election to Nixon.

For St. Francis, see note to 11 February 1970; he is popularly known for having preached to the birds.

"not a warm puppy": Adapted from the 25 April 1960 *Peanuts* strip by cartoonist Charles Schulz (1923–2000); his 1962 book was titled *Happiness Is a Warm Puppy.* For the Hawthornes' role in Sarton's life and work, see 14 July [1975] and 12 March 1979.

raising all that money: In her sole foray into fundraising, Starr let Eugene McCarthy give a speech in her studio.

TO BEVERLY HALLAM   Feb. 8th, 1969
[Nelson]
Dear Bev,

ARE YOU BETTER? I am worried....but I think much is exhaustion, i.e. the old carcass demands rest and makes up a symptom so you can get it. How I admire your orderly mind that gets the files straightened out...and makes that wonderful Mexican journey on tape with pictures. I must see it (Incidentally you should sell the idea of a mixed-up mad travelogue to the Smothers Brothers...grat.)

I have dear friends, new, at Orono Maine. Ash and Mary Campbell. She is a humble painter (I mean she has not shown) and he is a prof, in the engineering school [University of Maine]..they have six remarkable children, all doing Peace Corps or things like that. Send me an advance notice of the show, so I can remember to tell Mary to get in touch. She is very tense, but really a great woman. One of the greatest I have ever known, and that is saying a lot. Ash is wonderful, too.

About Phoenix, too bad you bought two. The new edition is unchanged, except for pictures, that was the point, Norton's idea, and they have done a dandy job, I think. The response is good so far, thanks to my friends like you (who buy two copies!)

I did laugh about Dudley [a dog] and his educational toy..I have about decided that my only friends shall be animals, not people. Animals are better. They do not give advice, for one thing. I blew up and cried awfully when I went to see some old friends yesterday (what a mistake) and broke down trying to explain how awful it is for me that Judy can give me no support at all (after all we have lived together for 22 years and she is the only family I have)...before I had even told some of the things that are hard to bear, the wife was telling me "you must be serene" and I hit the ceiling. Cried hysterically half the night. I am so damned lonely Bev, but there is no solution..I can't work with anyone around and it is clear that it was a fatal mistake to go out for lunch twice last week. I see no one for weeks on end, but that is better than these débâcles which only cause guilt and despair. I am such a mess. Anyway the parrot [Punch] is a comfort..any living thing that does not explain what I ought to do or be, is a help. Good Christ, let them be inside my skin and bear the tensions (and not be an alcoholic) for even an hour and they would not lightly tell me "you must be serene." I'll be serene when I am dead and not before.

I agree with you about handwriting...mine, for instance, shows incredible anguish, so I show it to people as little as possible. I am sure this anguish goes back to infancy..being driven out of "home" when I was two, shunted around for two years in England...all that. It makes the poet, but it's Hell to pay just the same. That is what people do not realize...the immense losses,..by the time I was 40 I had lost every one I ever loved except Judy. Sure, I go it alone...better for the work, but Hell on the person. Sometimes I think all God asks of us is to listen...not give advice..just listen to the rage, despair, the sheer human woe all around. I do it a lot through letters. I know what other people's Hell is. I listen and I answer.

About T[rumbull]. Hare...I imagine he is taken care of by Welfare...someone is doing it, not me.

Thank you for listening, dear Bev,...I guess that is what I need too. It has not helped to have that murder in Cambridge just a block away from Judy (who is apt to leave her key in the lock).

Anyway, thanks to Norton's taking the donkey book, and what F. Circle owed me, I am solvent for about 6 months. It is expensive living here in winter..$75 for heat last month, 60 for birdseed(!) but what would I do without birds? and 80 for telephone (But what would I do without friends?)

Oh dear...forgive this typing...I'm a wreck. Tell me how you are...but no compulsion, for God's sake! Take it easy if you can (how can one?)

Love anyway
M

P.S. Thanks for <u>photos</u>—all those smiles cheered me up!
P.P.S. Thank Mary-Leigh for her sweet word—I love you both—even all <u>four</u>—how are the dogs?

---

the Smothers Brothers: Tom and Dick, a comedy musical duo; their variety show exasperated television censors with its controversial satire about politics, the Vietnam War, the sexual revolution, and other late-1960s topics.

Ash and Mary Campbell: Ashley Campbell formerly taught at Tufts University.

Phoenix . . . new edition: After the success of *Plant Dreaming Deep,* a Book-of-the-Month Club selection, Norton added archival photographs to these autobiographical essays—pictures of small Mabel Elwes, young Eva Le Gallienne, Lugné-Poë, Wondelgem, etc. Though the text was reset from the Rinehart edition, only a few small changes were made.

Judy can give me no support: Plant Dreaming Deep, published in early 1968, was "For JUDY, *who believed in the adventure from the start."* On 29 January 1969, very shortly before this letter to Hallam, Sarton wrote Matlack using the Quakers' second-person familiar: "As for why I love you, it is because you understand everything, my darling, as no one else does, and I am always happy and at ease with you as with <u>no one else</u>. . . . When I explode it is because I can't believe that you can be as passive (otiose?) as you are, and also I suppose, feel that you could make more effort, for <u>your own sake</u> rather than mine. And I feel you are doing just this. . . . Do not be anxious about thee. Thee is a treasure!"

Nonetheless, memory loss depressed Matlack further; having to find a nursing home for her seemed inevitable, eventually. "But at present Judy wants to stay where she is and I feel human dignity is involved," Sarton wrote author Ilse Vogel (see 17 October 1969) on 21 June 1969. "She is now seeing a doctor and they are trying massive vitamins and tranquilizers also. Let us hope she can have a few more years as an independent person."

there is no solution: On 29 May 1967, Sarton had written Hallam: "I am wearing permanent sackcloth and ashes because of the awful things I say and do, my tears, rages and general behavior lately of a child just teething, but maybe it is the process of growing a huge wisdom tooth which will make me gentle, wise, loving, patient, etc. till I die. Let us pray."

TO THE REVEREND MARY UPTON   April 1st, 1969
[Nelson]
Dear Mary Upton,

I live with your Nelson church, as an inspiring ark..I must look at it a hundred times a day and always with worship in my heart. It is a sturdy and splendid support. Yet I am not a member of the church. And I feel, after more than ten years here, that I have to tell you why. All churches are in peril. Your congregation does not include many people around here who might be drawn in, who like me yearn to worship God with their fellows as they now must alone.

What is wrong? I felt it first at Ma Tolman's funeral and again yesterday at Fran Tolman's funeral. I felt it with even greater impact on the day of your sermon that opened our bicentennial celebrations. On that day you chose to attack conscientious objectors, surely a day when reconciliation was mandatory. A minister of the church <u>today</u>, so narrow and self-righteous that he or she cannot imagine that Christ himself might well be a conscientious objector simply drives people away to commune with Him alone. Compassion and love, without these, no church can long survive. But you even read the Gospel in a tone of voice that seems to fling it at us...you <u>sock</u> it to us and so we go back to read the Bible alone. I have known too many instances here in the village where it would have seemed the minister's job to console. Instead you <u>judge</u> and choose to show your judgement by your absence. This is a serious charge. I have waited many years to make it. But I have been deeply hurt in my spirit by what appears to come from your pulpit..self-righteousness, narrowness of spirit and a visible <u>hatred</u> of the congregation when it contains many people who are not members (as at funerals that bring the whole village together.)

There are few women ministers. Women in the ministry have a peculiar responsibility..In Maine I know one who fills seven churches. Why should we here in this beloved village have to suffer the indignity of a pulpit from which love does <u>not</u> flow towards every living creature? I do not speak for myself alone. You must know that your lack of compassion is notorious.

I do not say things behind people's backs, without <u>also</u> speaking out to the person involved—things of this gravity. But I am deeply troubled.

Yours very sincerely,
May Sarton

Upton: The Reverend Mary Upton was born Mary Brakeiron (c. 1912) in the Pennsylvania mining country. In Nelson she met Richard Upton; once married, they lived in nearby Harrisville. For thirty years she was minister of Harrisville, Nelson, and Chesham. In the winter there was one service for all three villages, on a rotating basis; in the summer, there were services in two of the churches each Sunday, in rotation.

Yours very sincerely: This letter was sent.

TO PEGGY POND CHURCH   May 10th, 1969
[Nelson]
Peggy dear,

What a wonderful letter! It came at a perfect time as I have been rather ill and took the day off, just dozing, so I could absorb it and savor it slowly and think about it happily for most of the day. It brought back Santa Fe so vividly and Haniel [Long] ...I felt terribly homesick! I was so touched by your telling me the dream and then picking up Plant again and finding that bit about solitude which I had forgotten. If I ever get through the monstrous novel I am wresting out of my exhausted psyche now, I want very much to do another and much more personal book about Solitude, a sort of notebook. This novel has nearly killed me..I got a huge grant to do it on, so I feel obligated but I feel that the material is not really mine so the struggle is fierce..and it has about 40 characters..about a village like this. It was to have been historical but after reading for a year and making a start, I <u>knew</u> I could never do it, so it is now a novel about the interchange between summer people and the natives (I hate the word, but you know what I mean) and how they have enriched each other. This subject has been dealt with humourously before, sneering etc. on both sides, but I feel myself that it has been a great cross-fertilization and that is what interests me. The central figures are two women, one a rich Bostonian who comes for summers (and spends a first winter in the village at 75 when the book begins) and a farm woman.. and their friendship is what links it all together. Enough of this borning subject. (I meant <u>boring</u> but the typewriter wrote <u>born-ing</u>! So I'll leave it like that—) I expect it will be a year before I am out from under. I have written Part I in rough and there are three more to come. (About 600 pages in all, I fear, so it looms before me like a huge mountain still to climb..those promises to keep before I sleep).

What a strange feeling to be the subject of a biography...I do hope the person who wishes to do it is worthy and I suppose by that I mean percipient enough to both read and write between the lines..But you are ready to "give your life" now to someone only I wish you would write it yourself! Have you ever thought of that? It could be a great book, as you have contained and used so many lives, wife and mother, all the part before your marriage on Los Alamos, but also you have been a poet and prose writer, and a lover, so it is a more whole life to tell than might be true of me, for instance. And would have great value to so

Granny Elwes with May at 4 months.

"It made me homesick for England . . . you know my mother was English, an Elwes from Suffolk."

Eleanor Mabel Sarton.

" . . she was like a small flame that veered and trembled but could never be put out."

Sarton with Irene Sharaff, Florence, 1932.

"those wonderful discovery days in Paris—Belguim and Italy"

Credit: Paul Child

Edith Forbes Kennedy.

"... *of blessed remembrance.*"

Credit: Harriet Burkhart

Alice and Haniel Long, 1953.

Credit: May Sarton

Elizabeth Bowen, Bowen's Court, 1952.

Courtesy: Estate of May Sarton

Pencil sketch of Elizabeth Bowen
by May Sarton.

" *. . a swanlike person with whom I fell in
love thirty years ago, an old <u>friend</u>, a writer
whom I have long admired . .*"

Charcoal drawing by
Polly Thayer Starr, 1966.

*"One ancient nun took one look at my
hair and said with a gleam in her eye, 'Ah,
that's what I can do.'"*

Courtesy: Polly Thayer Starr

Credit: May Sarton

Judith Matlack and Céline
Limbosch, Belguim, 1966.

Credit: Lotte Jacobi

Sarton, 1965, photographed by Lotte Jacobi.

Bill Brown, Santa Monica, 1967.

"our friendship . . . will be known surely after we both are dead"

Sarton with Perley Cole, March 1968.

Judith Matlack and Anne Thorp, Greenings Island, 1976.

May Sarton, Wild Knoll, 1974.

Credit: Lotte Jacobi

Huldah Sharpe, c. 1978.

Credit: Alan L. Katowitz

Sarton at Bookshop on the Square,
Cleveland, December 1978.

Courtesy: Estate of May Sarton

Charles Barber at Wild Knoll, July 1982.

"You will always be here with me
As long as I live,
A towering figure of love."
        —"Elegy: Charles Barber, 1956–1992"

May Sarton, Monhegan Island, Maine, September 1982.

Eva Le Gallienne, c. 1980s.

*an "astonishing genius for
all aspects of theatre"*

Sarton with Sylvie Pasche
("Elizabeth Roget"), April 1984.

Courtesy: Christopher de Vinck

Christopher de Vinck, Sarton, Fred Rogers,
at the 1985 filming of *Mister Rogers' Neighborhood*
episode, "Making and Creating."

Courtesy: Estate of May Sarton

With Doris Grumbach, 28 September 1985.

Credit: Stephen Trefonides

Polly Thayer Starr, c. 1975.

*"the most unaffectedly humble
person about your work that we
know"*

Honorary Doctor of Humanities, Bucknell College, 26 May 1985.
Sarton, 3rd from left. Carolyn Heilbrun, 5th from left. Vartan Gregorian,
6th from left.

Sarton with Lotte Jacobi, 7 December 1986.

*" . . you who most exemplify the life-giving, life-enhancing
riches that the old have to give . . "*

Sarton at York, 1988.

*"I still see the gentle smile on her
radiant face."* —Dan Wallace

With Nancy Hartley, March 1990, Multnomah
Falls on the Columbia River, Oregon.

Credit: Paul Dahlquist

Sarton, 31 March 1990.

Credit: Kennebeck Journal

Sarton, 1992.

"I hope you like this strange ecstatic photo of me."

Credit: Edith Royce Schade

With Carolyn G. Heilbrun at Westbrook
Conference, 14 June 1992.

"my literary guru"

Credit: Waltraut Schenke

Beverly Hallam and
Mary-Leigh Smart.

Credit: Jack Barnes

With director Erika Pfander, at the world premiere of *The Music Box Bird,* 8 October 1993.

Courtesy: Estate of May Sarton

Solange Sarton, 1995.

"My dear twin . . . very glad to have this photo in the big handsome coat!!"

Credit: Nancy Hartley

70th birthday, 3 May 1982.

Credit: Susan Sherman

83rd birthday, 3 May 1995, with Edythe Haddaway.

"83 is too old, but it turned out a brilliant, heart-warming day."

oct. 1, 1924

Dear Barbara, how are you? I am very
well. We are in Ipswich with Grannie.
    This is what I am writing for, that mother
told me just the other day that Joan Hocking
was often rather left out of things at school.
Mother said that aunt agnes told her once
that Jeannie said that when she walked
home from school she was safe with Joan
and May! She said that with others she
was not sure that she wasn't going to be
left out. Won't you please try and bring
her into things? She is always giving
things to other people so I have sent her
a little doll I dressed too.
    How are you getting on at school? I
will start in Belgium as soon as we
get there. We went to Wembley and
Westminster abbey and the Parliament
Houses it was a strange mixture
wasn't it? Please show this letter
to albie ~~boy~~ but not to anyone else
    with much love from your best friend
                    May

1924 holograph; see note to 12 March 1979.

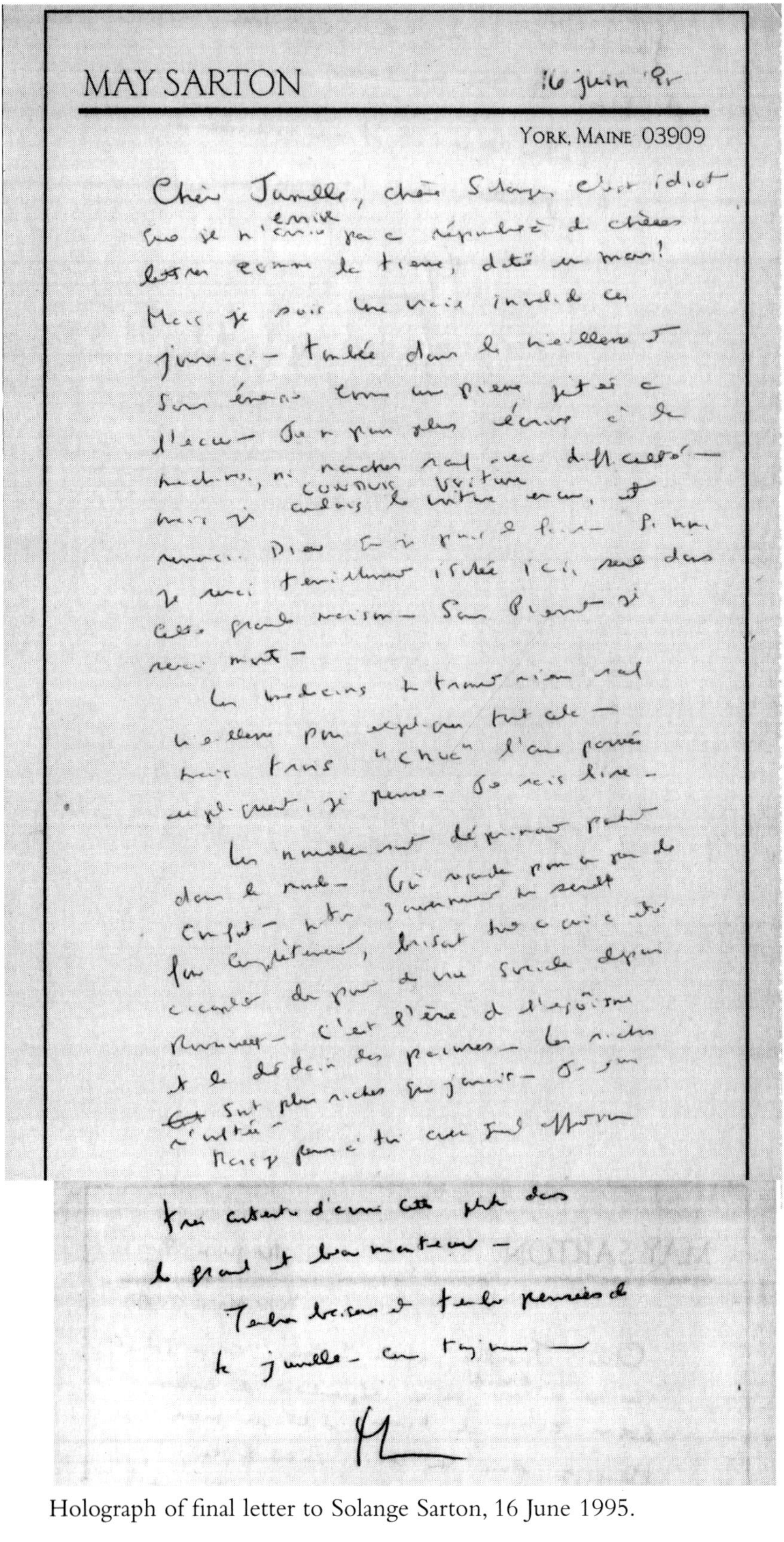

MAY SARTON

16 juin '95

YORK, MAINE 03909

Chère Jumelle, chère Solange, c'est idiot

Holograph of final letter to Solange Sarton, 16 June 1995.

many women who struggle on...Plant has brought me too many, far too many lives pouring themselves out and I am more aware than ever before of the dreadful loneliness <u>within</u> many marriages. Lately two women began to write me a letter a day (imagine inflicting that on a stranger!)..each is a fine person, but it is too much for me. I think I got sick (fearful nervous indigestion for three weeks so I am done in now) just from the pressure of trying to be so much to so many people and at the same time lift a whole world (the novel) out of me.

I got into a kind of panic because I felt the well so low and could hardly draw up a cup of water for a friend out of it. But then a sort of miracle happened. After twelve years of anguish and loneliness..two devastating affairs of the heart...the true person suddenly swam into my ken. It has all happened in the last weeks..and very ironically I had filled my calendar with guests as the garden is so lovely now, masses of daffodils under the frail transparent new green of the trees..no leaves yet, just flowers. I am now being reborn through love.

Meanwhile my life companion, dear Judy, has just been here for a week. I have anxiety about her as she is losing her memory. Her mind is clear about everything except the simplest practical matter, so being with her is a little like being with a dear beloved child.

I so agree about being "wrong" rather than touched by most of what goes on in the world. Lately I read poems to raise money for that wonderful Dr. Gatch in South Ca. He lifted me up because he has shown that <u>one person</u> can still move mountains despite all the bureaucracy..he fought it out alone, for the sake of starving Blacks in his county, lost his white practice and finally has become seriously ill himself. But he has made the plight <u>known</u>..we raised $500, so it was worth doing though I could hardly stand I was so ill that night.

Your letter made me feel sure that you are in a state of special grace, dear friend, and that means the difficult book on Mary Austin will be wonderful.

This is all I have strength to write.

Much love
May

Plant: It might be noted that *Plant Dreaming Deep* does not signify "A plant [noun] dreaming deeply" in winter, or whatever. This injunction to plant [verb] oneself in a specific physical place, take root in a native soil, is drawn from Sarton's translation of the sonnet "Heureux Qui, Comme Ulysse . . ." by French poet Joachim du Bellay (c. 1522–60), beginning "Happy the man who can long roaming reap" (1966). The passage concerning solitude begins on p. 92.

the monstrous novel: On 28 March 1968 Sarton had confessed to Church that her "series of historical novels" had reached "an impasse. After trying and trying and sweating out 130 pages, I began to weep and howl whenever I sat at the typewriter and just had to stop. It is very scary as I have never before had a block like this. My agent laughed and said all writers do, so I wait…and hope." At 464 pages, *Kinds of Love* is Sarton's largest single imaginative effort.

promises to keep: Sarton's condensed remembrance of lines from Robert Frost's "Stopping by Woods on a Snowy Evening," *New Hampshire* (1923): "The woods are lovely, dark and deep, / But I have promises to keep, / And miles to go before I sleep, / And miles to go before I sleep."

Dr. Gatch: A general practitioner who attempted to remedy the dire problems of malnutrition and its consequent diseases on both sides of the racial divide in Beaufort County, South Carolina. Sarton not only gave a reading on 27 April at the college in Keene but rallied her friends to his cause. On 9 April 1969 she wrote Ilse Vogel, "Bless you and thank you for responding so sweetly to the appeal for Gatch. Did I tell you he is now himself in hospital with under-nourishment and worms and exhaustion." "[I]n spite of promises of free food from the Senate Committee on Health and Welfare it is all held up again," she wrote Beverly Hallam, "and it is a moral issue with me to show fast that someone cares." See *Solitude,* pp. 18–19, for Sarton's comments upon his fate; see the appendix in this volume for her tribute "The Precious Seed, for Donald Gatch, Beaufort County, South Carolina."

Mary Austin: "I never met Mary Austin," Sarton wrote Church, 28 March 1965, "but of course her legend was everywhere when I first came out [to Santa Fe]." A novelist, dramatist, and memoirist, Austin (1868–1934) married a teacher who hid his hereditary illness; their only child was an imbecile. An unconventional feminist and mystic, in 1896 Austin left her marriage for an artists' community, working for women's social reforms. After a 1923 breakdown she settled in Santa Fe, where the Indians became her special care.

Church's book, *Winds' Trail: The Early Life of Mary Austin,* ed. Shelley Armitage (1990), appeared posthumously.

TO NANCY HALE   August 10th, 1969
[Nelson]
Dearest Nancy,

In a week I'm off to Maine for a much needed rest, so I am answering your letter pronto. It seems wonderful that we are in real touch again after all these years . . and I feel that we are, through these two books of ours. Where to begin? Your letter made me happy and made me long to talk. . .this A.M. I have written twelve letters ranging from one to a Black young man in trouble (but he reads poems and asks me "are all poets honest and loving?") to a friend in Cal, who has just lost her mother, to friends in Europe (one 86 [Camille Mayran] and still so young in spirit). . but none was one I wanted to write as I want to write to you. Only I am tired now.

First about your mother. I did not really know her as you think I did, Edith Kennedy of blessed remembrance, asked me to lunch with her and did it in such a way that I knew she was bringing me a rare treasure (you know her genius for just such encounters. . and by the way, I wish you would write something about her some day) When I said "elusive" in that review, it was what I felt. The exterior was formidable . . not cold, but somehow one felt daunted. Maybe you hit it when you talk about the <u>immense</u> secret person, the ego at the bottom, the artist. That person did not reveal itself in a social situation. One saw the beauty, the <u>style</u>, the touching modesty, shyness too. . one wanted to know <u>more</u>. I have thought a lot about my mother recently and certain things have revealed themselves only lately. . I adored her. I suppose she is what drove me to love women rather than men (also because I suffered so much from my father's ego and his ignoring of <u>her</u> needs, unlike your dear father). . but what I have come to see was that there was very little <u>physical</u> warmth. I needed to be <u>hugged</u> and never was by either parent. My mother and I became intimate friends, but it was never physical. I say this because in your mother I felt an almost invincible shyness about giving herself away. .hard on a child, I should imagine. Certainly you and I were both tremendously <u>loved</u> only children. . but something was lacking. Any physical thing, even going to the toilet, was somehow difficult, embarassing. .no? The mysteries of one's parents sex life! I mean, this does haunt and trouble. Your mother seemed to me inviolate and no doubt my mother did also to outsiders. (She loved my father passionately as your mother did your father. .yet. .what? I feel shy of the question.)

Digression. .I had to smile at your query "how often do you read a review that sounds as if it were about the book you wrote?" <u>Never</u>, is my answer. For instance, Plant was reviewed chiefly as a book about a <u>house</u>! Luckily the reviews were favorable. .and now people are discovering it for themselves because it was named one of the 40 best books of 1968 by the ALA [American Library Association] so all the libraries have it. No, it did not sell well. .about 13,000. What is <u>that</u>? Nothing. But you and I have the same problem (except for your [1942 novel] <u>Prodigal Women</u>). .books don't sell of a lit. sort <u>unless</u> they are taken by a book club, and publishers don't advertise unless a book has been picked. There are millions of people who would wish to read Life in the Studio <u>if</u> they knew it existed. .I mean people outside the Eastern coast who do not read the Times. About photographs. .it is <u>too bad</u> there were none. Norton told me that photographs by the new method (not inserted on glossy paper but printed on the same paper as the text) are not that expensive. They have just re-issued I Knew a Phoenix with photographs and it's a lovely book in this new edition. .maybe I must send you one. I will!

And now to the Real Thing. .about solitude. About this I hope we may write each other more letters. .if I ever finish the albatross of a novel that is round my neck now, I want to do a much more <u>naked</u> book than <u>Plant</u> about it, to be called <u>Inner Space</u> (maybe I already spoke of this?) I learned about solitude the hard way in quiet desperation. .I came here to this house to have a place for my love to come to, and then she never came. She sneered at my work always and it was a deadly and nearly killing ten years..but what it brought me as an un-imagined by-product was the courage to live alone and the immense inner excitement and reward of solitude. (Just now in the last four months the Right True Person—a student of Fredson's—Marion Hamilton—Do not tell him this—has come into my life..almost a miracle as I am 57! And at last this is a happy house..but I shall always live _alone_..my friend is head of a school and we shall meet when we can, but not live together.)

You speak of solitude, yet you are married. I think I do understand this. It is what comes to me in innumerable letters from married women in their fifties and sixties..one of the things I hold _against_ the U.S. sense of values or whatever, is the vacuum of those years for many women..imagine if you were _not_ a writer! Somehow this civilization is not one because maturity is to be discarded and every attempt is made to "stay young". Who wants to? Only the sad immature who must have their hair dyed and their faces lifted. In Europe the mature woman, mature in every sense, is a _treasure_, not something to be discarded because she does not look like Twiggy!

Oh dear...I have had three drinks to write this letter at all, and it is time I ate something and had a nap in the rain.

One more thing about your mother. In the last years in Charlottesville she answered my Xmas poems with always _dear_ messages. I felt more close to her than ever before.

Isn't it great that Bill is married, happy, and has found his _voice_ not only as a writer..but simply to be _heard_ in ordinary human conversation?

Dear Nancy, write again when you feel like it. Let us take this communion at its flood, not hold back, exchange, be ourselves. Yes, it is true that "to go in is to come out" or vice versa. I take people in..but that means that, in a way, every meeting is a kind of collision. My only law now is "never see anyone except in depth." Social engagements bore and exhaust. Only the real meetings count, but they are costly.

So much more to say, but I am dead. If you feel like it, write to c/o Anne Thorp, Greenings Island, Southwest Harbor, Maine 04679. What are you working at now? Please think about Edith K[ennedy]. as a subject! I'll be on the island from Aug. 21 to Sept. 5th.

Oh, I wish we could meet.

love and blessings,
May

P.S. Must get the Bhagavad Gita—do _not_ have it—

Nancy Hale: This Boston-born fiction writer (1908–89), whom Sarton met through Edith Forbes Kennedy, was Edward Everett Hale's granddaughter. Her just-published memoir, *The*

Life in the Studio, described growing up as the daughter of Philip Hale (1865–1931, student of Monet, distinguished teacher of drawing and painting) and Lilian Westcott Hale (1880–1963, celebrated portraitist). Sarton reviewed the book in *The New York Times Book Review,* 27 July 1969.

Edith Kennedy: Edith and sons Fitzroy, Edmund, and Robert, were also Cambridge friends. Sarton wrote "Evening Music" (1950; last reprinted in *Selected Poems,* 1978) for Edith, who remained a great friend and influence; see the profile of her in *A World of Light.*

your mother . . . my mother: During summer 1953, Lilian Westcott Hale moved from her long-time Boston home to Charlottesville, Virginia. On 2 August Sarton wrote her, recalling how "last year I cleaned out the attic in my mother's house—going through piles of letters and photographs and above all, the piles and piles of her beautiful designs [for clothing and furniture], trunkfulls of them, each with a card for the colors. I feel that it was like what you are doing...[in] your house and all it had held of Mr. Hale and of you and of your life together and his work...You are wise I am sure not to hurry things—though I think that means self-discipline, for part of one wants to just throw everything away and turn one's back on it forever, in one violent gesture."

a review . . . about the book you wrote?": Even sympathetic friends could approach Sarton's books from the wrong angle. As Sarton defended to Helen Storm Corsa (27 February 1966), "A work of art must be criticized within its own premise. Poet and Donkey is a small light book . . . [that] matured, so to speak, through years of agony. . . . I solved the agony by borrowing a donkey and concentrating on something (someone) outside myself. . . . I learned to smile at my own neurosis and foolishness, and in so doing was able to be reborn. . . . The book has to be seen as a small graceful thing, that was able to be written only after much work on the self. Hence its intimate triumph (triumph for me as a poet and human being). There are people who can take these oblique lessons or fables better than a more serious and anguished presentation. . . . You have judged it as if it were Job. Now Job in me has spoken but for me the work of art is a way of solving. . . . [T]he writer I had in mind as an exemplar for this book was E. B. White. Charlotte's Web is a light book that smiles, but it contains wisdom. One does not ask such fables to be St. Augustine's confessions."

a place for my love: Referring to Cora DuBois. Hale's husband, Fredson Bowers, chairman of the English department at the University of Virginia, was renowned for his work in textual editing.

Twiggy: Professional name of the big-eyed blonde waif of a model (Lesley Hornby, b. 1949) who personified London pop fashion in the 1960s.

Bill is married: William Wertenbaker, Hale's son by a previous marriage.

Bhagavad Gita: This ancient "Song of the Lord" is a Sanskrit poetic dialogue between Lord Krishna and Prince Arjuna on the eve of battle, stressing devotion to selfless action. Hale had noted how this "New Testament of Hinduism" supported Sarton's theory that, since failures can potentially nourish the soul, "success" or "failure" are mere by-products of what truly counts, the goal one is trying to achieve.

TO BEVERLY HALLAM   Aug. 15th, 1969
[Nelson?]
Dear Bev,

Your self portrait is neither that nor <u>Sea</u>, nor <u>Seal</u>, but (how could they get it so wrong?) a portrait of May Sarton, about to be carried to an insane asylum on a stretcher! It's a masterpiece and will come in handy for publicity purposes as I am signed up with Colston Leigh (the N.Y. agent) for lectures in 1970–71..this will surely drive away any bidders and be just right, as I don't want to do it anyway, but signed up for purely money reasons—will need some.

It always gives me a lift to hear from you on your tide that rises and rises and apparently never <u>ebbs</u>...though I guess it does now and then, when you get overtired as you must.

I am now a total wreck since I have not had a break except for week-ends for exactly a year and have sat on my tail here (or entertained visiting firemen as I did all last fall, no rest) for a full year. IT IS HIGH TIME for a break. Meanwhile the gremlins are crawling around making everything as hard as they can for me to get off..for instance I bought a Westinghouse four-hole toaster for my tenants (a woman with two children) who come on Sunday to take over. It refuses to work on the 2d day (You <u>can't</u> be sure if it's Westinghouse apparently). So back to Keene with it in the boiling heat. The septic tank has rebelled, this time against the water-soaked earth (the rainiest July here in memory) and is now being dug out and vast trenches all across the back lawn..the devastation comes now, and the BILL later. Also I have the worst go of nervous indigestion I ever had, and thought it was a coronary last week when it began..then I had such violent headache I thought my head would explode and imagined a brain tumor was growing. Take another look at that seal and you will see that it is an exact portrait of me.

ANYWAY, all is well because of Marion whose plane back from Europe I meet on Monday if I can stand up..then on Wed. take Judy to the island.

I have written a lot of poems..also got on with the novel, now into Part III and it should be finished in rough by Xmas, a very long haul, I must say..like running a race every day for a year..I guess I am best at <u>shorter</u> spurts! The donkey book will be out in October..from what I saw of the illustrations they are <u>awful</u> (and I sent them your lovely photos, hoping the artist [Stefan Martin] would see them)..in Maine I intend to get a new book of poems together, Bears and Waterfalls (no new ones, they're for later). I mean no poems written these last months..but none has been published in a book before.

Title for novel? I am stuck..I wanted Old Devotions but everyone says (and they are right) that it sounds like a 17th century book of sermons, so no go. The idea is really the inward journey to a village and the thing that comes closest to describing it I found in Robert Graves, to wit

> The untameable, the live, the gentle.
> Have you not known them? Whom? They carry

Time looped so river-wise about their houses
There's no way in by history's road
To name or number them.

I wish I could get a title out of that, but I can't seem to. What amuses me is that it is a sort of apologia for this <u>not</u> being a historical novel and I might use it as an epigraph anyway.

Wish I could think of a title for you....wish you could just use that whole list you sent me..why not?

Don't worry about not painting, for God's sake..you are on a great creative tide..there will be time later on for painting. As for an island in the South Seas (did you mean that or West Indies?) it seems rather far away to commute from but sounds dandy.

I can't make it this fall, by the way..awful..but I have lectures at the end of Sept. (Chicago and Milwaukee, to help open the art center there. Fortnightly in Chicago..then I must settle into a long work at the novel without interruption except to see Marion. Love is glorious but it sure is hard to fit in..but when this book is done I shall have time again at last. Want to do a book called Inner Space about solitude and this place..more naked and deeper than Plant, on a different level, more about <u>inside</u> me.

That is all. I talk about myself, but I <u>read</u> you, dear Bev, with the liveliest interest and please forgive the silence..it was not my fault.

It was so splendid about the show at the Point..never did anyone deserve success more and my old heart beats a little faster for the joy of it..

A hug and love to you both..keep in touch..

Your

May

Address till Sept. 5th c/o Anne Thorp, Greenings Island, Southwest Harbor, Maine

---

your self-portrait: An elaborate joke based on the title and subject of a work by Hallam.

Colston Leigh: Sarton stayed only briefly with this well-known lecture agent, finding she preferred to manage her own bookings, as she did the rest of her life.

visiting firemen: Sarton used this term when describing the staccato explosion of summer visitors upon her—often well-known writers—and the ensuing meals in which she would wind up embroiled.

Her tenant with offspring was painter Anne Woodson, who became a dear friend; Woodson's partner, Barbara Barton, was commissioned by Sarton to sculpt the phoenix that marks her grave.

Sarton makes play with the appliance maker's slogan "You can be sure . . . if it's Westinghouse."

Bears and Waterfalls: This became *A Grain of Mustard Seed* (1971), dedicated "To M.H.H."

an epigraph: Sarton did introduce *Kinds of Love* with this extract from "Through Nightmare" by British man of letters Robert Graves (1895–1985), author of the autobiography *Goodbye to All That* (1929); the historical novel *I, Claudius* (1934); an inquiry into the nature of the Muse, *The White Goddess* (1948); etc.

open the [Milwaukee] *art center:* Another expansion of the Milwaukee Art Museum on the Lake Michigan waterfront, originally designed by Eero Saarinen (1957).

TO ILSE VOGEL   Oct. 17th, 1969
[Nelson]
Ilse dear,

For some reason it is a grieving autumn...for you, the loss of your mother, but also the [Vietnam] war, I think really eats into the heart, and at our age losses are constant. Poor Perley Cole is dying in the hospital, such a tiny frail bird all at once..Lotte Jacobi has been very ill. Yet the leaves have never been more glorious..such transparent marvelous light everywhere. I had forgotten how at this season, the house feels dark, <u>because</u> the color is all outside and every window frames this glory.

By a strange coincidence a very old lady sent me yesterday a letter my mother had written her friend (who died 6 months ago) about the death of an aunt. I read this letter with tears streaming down my cheeks, thinking of my mother..and it seems the one thing I can send you, thinking of <u>your</u> mother.

May 4, 1930
"Dear Miss Holman,

I sit down to write to you almost instinctively because my thoughts have over and over been reaching out to you these last three days, since I knew that your aunt was at death's door. We can none of us regret that she has passed beyond it..and yet that passing brings always something so tremendous, so <u>pregnantly silent</u> that it is as if our very selves strained our spiritual ears for some message, strained them with painful intensity. It is difficult then to turn back to all the fuss and striving of every day's life filled with clamorous voices and demands, none of which seem important compared to that still, quiet message.

These are not just "words" I am sending you. You do know me well enough to believe that the only worthy thing I can find to offer you, is some sharing of a similar experience? I have only had this strange feeling that if only I could be given time and peace and aloofness in which to listen that some tremendously important thought—the very meaning and essence of life—is there near me, hovering in the silence. So I am hoping that you will have had a few quiet hours before Monday comes with all its everyday burdens. You have had many trials to meet and have plenty of courage and poise to meet them with and I admire you for it.

Affectionately yours,
Mabel Sarton

I had thought that surely this autumn you and Howard would come to see me here..but as I told you, I have been quite ill, in hospital..and very driven by the novel. This Hell will be over by December I think...what fun if you could come at Xmastime, yourselves..instead of only a magic package under the tree! Judy will be here then. And the pussies for a week.

I am off for the week-end now but did not want to go before sending a word. You have been so much in my thoughts.

Ever your poet
May

Ilse Vogel: Ilse-Margret Vogel (1914–2001), born and raised in Germany, helped establish the Rosen Gallery, the first contemporary gallery in postwar Berlin. She came to the United States in 1950 as director of New York's New Art Circle gallery and worked as a toy designer and illustrator. In the early 1960s she started writing books for young readers based on her life under the Nazis.

"I have always felt that these autobiog. books of yours were very much like poetry, a distillation of memory," Sarton would write her on 15 November 1987. "[W]hat looks like ordinary material for children actually is very daring and unconventional extending the boundaries all the time, and extending the deep awareness also. (My work, too, looks conventional but is not!) So it is not surprising that you have had a special kind of response from children themselves."

Vogel's recent titles at this time were *The Don't Be Scared Book* (1964), *1 Is No Fun But Twenty Is Plenty* (1965), and the Little Golden Book *When I Grow Up* (1968). Her husband, noted artist Howard Knotts, would provide the illustrations for Sarton's *Punch's Secret* (Harper & Row, 1974).

Miss Holman: Not yet traced; probably a colleague of Eleanor Mabel Sarton's at the Winsor School. For four other letters by Mabel Sarton, see *Recovering*, pp. 70, 146–49; see also note to 8 June 1985, to Peggy Pond Church.

TO SYLVIE PASCHE ("ELIZABETH ROGET")   Feb. 10th, 1970
[Nelson]
Sylvie dear,

I cringe at the thought that you had to be the one who found Louise, dead, and alone in her apartment. I tried to get you on the phone but learned it is unlisted and then finally, after 24 hours, talked with Maidie

[Scannell]....after calling God knows how many people in vain..the obit. I saw (in New London, Conn) was so vague, it was very disturbing.

Now I am home again...I feel more than ever how precious your steadfast, unsentimental, loving friendship meant in these last years of growing depression...it is so very good that <u>you</u> were there.

It is not a moment for a long letter. I am sure you are very busy helping Maidie with all that clearing out the dear apartment means. Do not answer this. It is only to thank you and send love and blessings and this unworthy poem.

I look forward to your book!

Let us keep in touch.

Love from May

Sylvie Pasche: Louise Bogan met the novelist known as "Elizabeth Roget" (1900–90) at the MacDowell Colony in 1958. Pasche's first language being French, she and Bogan translated extracts from *The Journal of Jules Renard,* the incisive and witty French man of letters (1864–1910). Her forthcoming novel was *Shagbark Hill* (1970), set in Pennsylvania.

the one who found Louise: On the afternoon of 4 February 1970, receiving no answer after ringing the bell to Bogan's apartment, Pasche used the key given her and found her friend in the bedroom, dead some hours from "a coronary occlusion." A funeral in Manhattan two days later was followed by cremation.

unsentimental, loving friendship: During the late 1960s, Bogan increasingly found her *New Yorker* reviewing a torment. On her own initiative Pasche alerted Bogan's old friend, writer William Maxwell, an editor at the magazine; supported by her psychotherapist, Bogan decided to leave her post. See Frank, *Bogan,* pp. 411–13.

this unworthy poem: Written that same day, "Elegy (for Louise Bogan)" first appeared in *A Durable Fire* (1972).

TO MARIANNE MOORE   Feb. 11, 1970

[Nelson]

Dear Marianne,

One becomes a survivor. Louise's death...it must have hit you hard as it did me. If the hippies wish to reject our world (and why wouldn't they?) surely they must see that order and clarity of a superior kind are involved in making a new one...heroism such as St. Francis showed when <u>he</u> rejected a society.

I feel lonely and rejected in spirit. I think of you. I have not communicated because I know you are snowed under (even <u>I</u> am).

But thank God you are there.. your presence in a recent New Yorker made this old raccoon happy.

Love from
May

St. Francis: Here the saint appears as a young businessman, sobered by experiences as a prisoner of war, renouncing his inheritance to espouse poverty, tend the sick, and propagate orthodox Catholic teachings, founding the Poor Clares and the Franciscan orders.

Why "the hippies," just past their prime, should be linked with Bogan's death is unclear. Moore died 5 February 1972.

TO MARION HAMILTON   March 4th, 1970
[Nelson]

Dear heart, I have been trying to find something to send you, a poem in answer to your splendid letter that has made me think a lot..I knew, of course, that you would find it hard to accept the image of the little book..the poet replacing his impossible muse by a very real ass! and I was very touched that you had copied for Emmanuel a page about the poppy…the point is, I think that there is a real difference in our natures that makes certain intuitions invalid on either side. You do not, I believe, have a physical sense of "the creature" or only as dross, never the pure gold…you live on a plane where creature things, animals, even plants if it comes to digging about among roots with bare hands, the physical food that nourishes people (and which is always mystical for me i.e. when I feed a friend, I give him as if an intimate part of myself "This is my body. Take and eat" are the words, I believe, of the communion in church???)..you are always somewhat dismayed by the <u>physical</u>. Simone Weil was of your kind..but I have a hunch that she would have been in far deeper <u>communion</u> with the workers in the fields whose life she shared at one time if she had literally "broken bread" with them.

The thing that moved me so deeply about the sheep mother, was her physical tenderness (so unexpected in a sheep) and that <u>physical</u> sound she made. When I went back to Italy after World War II I was really overwhelmed by the way fathers hold their children, the warmth of physical communion in Italian families..I felt that by comparison, Americans were in some way <u>arid</u>, afraid, of being whole men. Afraid of <u>hugging</u> a child. All of this, I fear, seems to you in some way not "evolved", animal in fact.

You do not identify with animals..thus you never understood I think what I suffered for that poor dog your father had, the misery of that animal. But even in the Catholic church (which denies a soul to animals) there are saints who exemplify a tenderness towards the whole creation…St. Francis, of course, St. Anthony who took a thorn from a lion's paw.

Your nature is contemplative, I feel..and one contemplates a flower, meditates upon it in a way that one cannot an animal, at least one for whom one is <u>responsible</u>. I think I see love as action, rather than as contemplation…"what ye have done unto the least of these ye have done unto me" is the only thing I truly can say I <u>believe</u> of Christ. I mean, this is the one <u>command</u> I truly understand.

I feel that you lump animals (the care of them) with <u>material</u> things i.e. less than spiritual. But I feel that everything is or can be illuminated by the same Creative Presence if one sees it there..even a stone. In some profound way perhaps I feel that animals are one of our ways back to the primitive in the sense of <u>close to God</u>. Also in the sense of being "natural" as we, with our complexities are no longer. So, I believe they can help us to be more fully human. We are not, I think, meant to be gods..that idea seems blasphemous to me…but we are meant to become as fully human as possible, as "creaturely" as possible. The poem, even, depends on concrete physical images to convey soul.

You would say that instinct is animal. I would say that it is sometimes divine and that by covering over natural instinct we sometimes protect ourselves from real experience and take refuge in metaphysics. You will not have forgotten St. Teresa's remarks that she needed good strong girls in the convent who could scrub floors and as for the mystic, that would come naturally.

The celebration of a "natural" world is what makes Hopkins the supreme poet he is. By some misery of chance I have lost my Hopkins Collected poems..reread the one about Elwy, thanking his hosts.

So…to get back to the book…Andy has been deprived of his power to <u>act</u> as a human being by the impossible muse and must find some means of renewal..he rejects the contemplative if you remember (learning Russian or about mushrooms) and, instead, borrows a sick donkey and learns "donkey". There is a passage where he does not prod the beast but stands beside her and waits that is crucial (for the author) i.e. one who has <u>willed</u> learns not to will, but wait and to feel with a fellow creature. A donkey is the most cursed and beaten animal in the whole world..but it was on a donkey's back that Christ entered Jerusalem.

> "Fools, for I also had my hour,
> One far fierce hour and sweet..
> There was a shout about my ears
> And palms before my feet."
> (G.K. Chesterton, a Catholic)

Since then, legend tells us, every donkey wears a cross on his back. And it is a fact that every donkey does. The animal world teaches us among many other things, fidelity and patience and loving kindness.

What would you say, for instance about the sheep dog in Scotland who stayed with the body of his master for a whole winter (what did he eat? How did he survive? Who knows? but it is a true story) and was found in spring still there…nearly a skeleton? when the master died in the mountains alone. Animals, are often far better (gooder) than men. We can, I am sure, learn much from them.

That we also exploit them is another matter.

Well, this is no argument. I wish you to understand that we are different natures…each has its supreme value and reality. You are a mystic and a philosopher…I am a poet and a realist (believe me, they go together). The French are not, I believe, by nature, poets..the English are. The English are not by nature metaphysical..nor philosophical..the French are.

So at the moment, the French (Pompidou) are outraged by the American reaction to the selling of planes to Libya (when everyone knows they will be used against Izrael) meanwhile refusing to deliver planes paid for by Izrael to that beleaguered country. I wonder what France would have said of Germany if the Germans after World War II had refused to come to the peace table? The Arabs who did not deny that their aim was to exterminate Izrael and then were beaten, will not come to the peace table. Pompidou is an intelligent man. The fact that he refused to condone outrage in these circumstances seems to me quite mad. It is a physical matter of survival..and (for that matter) surely the French oil interests in Libya can hardly be called metaphysical. Sorry to bring this up but I am sick at heart, sick to the marrow of my bones at the horror of national power in relation to human situations in our time. The U.S. in Vietnam.

[remainder missing]

Marion Hamilton: At the time this letter was written, Hamilton was a school administrator.

Emmanuel is unidentified; see *The Poet and the Donkey,* pp. 119–20, for the "page about the poppy."

communion in church: Christian liturgies of communion descend from the four Gospels' variant tellings of the Last Supper. Sarton comes closest to Matthew 26:26: "Jesus took bread, and blessed it, and break it, and gave it to the disciples, and said, Take, eat; this is my body."

Simone Weil: See note to 27 February 1963. A brilliant and precocious student, the Jewish Weil was strongly drawn to Hellenic spiritual traditions as well as to Catholicism. While teaching philosophy in a girls' school (1931–38), she sought to validate her social activism by undertaking factory work (1934–35) and studying its psychological impact; after the Germans occupied Paris in World War II, she worked in southern France as a farm servant. She went to the front in the Spanish Civil War, and then dedicated herself to the Free French effort. Sustenance and the lack of it, spiritual and physical, were a lifelong preoccupation. Painfully aware of the suffering around her, she grew to regard it as a means of uniting spiritually with God.

"Her life is almost a perfect blending of the Comic and the Terrible, which two things may be opposite sides of the same coin," wrote Flannery O'Connor, whose fiction about belief and unbelief affected Sarton strongly. The complexity of Weil's thought cannot be condensed into a footnote; see *Simone Weil: A Modern Pilgrimage* (1987), by Robert Coles, and *Simone Weil* (2001), by Francine du Plessix Gray. Sarton would cite Weil the rest of her life.

the sheep mother: At a lambing on 8 February 1971, Sarton hoped "to hear again the extraordinary throaty, hungry sound the mother makes when she licks her lamb for the first time" (*Solitude,* p. 106); but that ewe was silent. The image persisted: see "The Cossett Lamb" (1985).

St. Francis . . . St. Anthony: To honor his empathy with the natural world, in 1980 St. Francis was named the patron saint of ecology. The Franciscan "hammer of heretics," St. Anthony of Padua (1195–1231), is patron saint of "the lower animals" and often shown in art with a donkey. It was St. Jerome (c.341–420), translator of the Bible into Latin (the Vulgate), who "took a thorn from a lion's paw," taming the animal into a faithful companion. The name of Sister Jeremy at Rosary College (see note to 9 November 1958) derives from his.

"what ye have done": Shortly before the Last Supper, Jesus discourses on the Last Judgment and the separation of the sheep from the goats. Unto those who gave food, drink, shelter, clothing, moral solace, and comfort to the needy, the King shall say, "Inasmuch as ye have done it unto one of the least of these brethren, ye have done it unto me" (found only in Matthew 25:40).

St. Teresa's: Teresa of Ávila (1515–1582), seeking to hew closer to the order's original intent, founded the Discalced (barefoot) Carmelite order, both female and male. She became the first woman Doctor of the Church and combined intense mysticism with earthy teachings.

Hopkins: See note to 22 June 1958. His poem, "In the Valley of the Elwy," Wales, dates from 1877.

To Basil de Sélincourt, 5 December 1965, Sarton wrote she would soon make her last "speech in Chapel [at Lindenwood College] and am taking as theme Hopkins' poem 'The world is charged with the grandeur of God' ['God's Grandeur,' 1877] and talking about how the only way we can praise Him, know Him is to <u>look</u> at his creation, which is not necessarily visible in churches, alas. A simple flower growing out of an infinitesimal seed being so much more miraculous as poetry, chemistry, mathematics, physics than any flight of two astronauts into space can possibly be."

on a donkey's back . . . Christ entered Jerusalem: That He should do so fulfilled the words of the prophet Zechariah. This marked the start of His final ministry in that city, in the days leading up to the Crucifixion. The ass is mentioned only in Matthew 21:2–5.

G. K. Chesterton: In *Endgame,* pp. 94–95, Sarton prints all of "The Donkey" by this prolific British man of letters and Catholic polemicist (1874–1936)—along with a photo of her and Esmeralda, a.k.a. Whiffenpoof.

(Pompidou): At this time, Georges Pompidou was president of France (1969-74), carrying on De Gaulle's policies. The snarled international debate Sarton alludes to, wherein "developed nations" justify selling war-waging materiel to "rogue states" or unstable regimes, continues to this day.

Her odd spelling of "Izrael" here is baffling as it has no special significance save that "s" versus "z" sometimes gave her pause, and she almost invariably spelled Elizabeth Bowen's name with an "s."

TO BILL BROWN   June 24th, 1970
[Nelson]
Dearest Bill,

Wonderful to hear..your letter came on a good loose-end day so I am answering at once. E. Blair has been here for two nights helping me punctuate my new book of poems, which is now almost ready to be typed. It is rather somber, no love poems this time, but I intend to bring out a book of all love poems (shades of Robert Graves!) to celebrate my 60th birthday in a couple of years, so am holding them back now. The book will be called (this one I mean), A Grain of Mustard Seed.

Oh dear, my heart sank when I read that Paul is signed up for life and you cannot move East after all. But one must go with Fate and not against it..and now you know the future you can surely find a wild place to live in somewhere in the hills, and looking for it should be fun. I loved those cats, especially the tail seen emerging below a hat behind a cat..and the kitten bringing violets! All I really want to do is write children's books..did you see that E.B. White has a new one out about a trumpeter swan?

I heard from Janet..have not seen her new book..will avidly read if you will send. But I feel she may be producing too much..how far away New Zealand seems..winter there now, and I guess the transition must be hard for her. She is certainly an authentic genius ...but I do understand that it's not easy for you that you have become a kind of personal focus for her. What a responsibility!

Hope you decide not to go to Princeton...I agree with Aunt Amy, but it is hard to think of your father facing that aggravating gradual weakness of Parkinson's. Is there not a magic drug now that has worked wonders? His doctor must know about it. Imagine being 91!

I have been reading Aldous Huxley's letters..really rather boring, I think. (So far anyway, about a third read). One gets glutted with the famous people..they were all snobs of course. I really do not believe that I am..I mean after I wrote that phrase I wondered. Maybe I am not because I fear and hate the world and suffer too much from competition, so the reason is not a noble one. But I cannot manage the worldly things..Lael Wertenbaker is a neighbor here and had sent to me her new novel in proof for a blurb. It is so embarrassing I could not do it, lay awake for two nights..as it seemed so pretentious not to. What does my opinion matter? Then someone told me a school bought any book I recommend.. so I felt I had a responsibility to literature as well as to a friend. Wrote Lael an agonized letter which she has not answered..and I feel like a fool.

Norton thinks my novel is superb...but they have named it Kinds of

Love .. a title that describes it well, but not as the common reader might be led to think i.e. it is not lurid and the kinds of love that of a married couple 75 for each other, that of a crazy man who is in love with woods and animals etc. The trouble is that even after the huge advance I know they will not push it unless a book club takes it and the chances are so slim. In April and May I went into a real tailspin when I realized I would have to produce something else _fast_ or be dead broke in January. I am not a factory. But I was in a state of extreme psychic exhaustion..had been taking Ritalin, an amphetamine, I now read, under a Dr.'s prescription but I think I really forced the psyche at the end. I begin to feel better and more able to cope at last.

Joan Baez...I too saw a resemblance...I think she is a fine person. I saw her the other day on the David Frost show. Some of what she said seemed to me not realistic, a kind of revolutionary _patter_, a little too easy, somehow. This came through about Hitler, say...but I am in no state to argue this. I feel she does a lot of _good_, and what more can be asked?

The interesting thing is what will happen when (if it ever does) the [Vietnam] war _ends_? So much motivation is there because of the hideous war. Will it, can it be carried over later into the very hard patient work required to solve the problems inside the country? The thing that disturbed me on the Frost show was Baez' lukewarm appreciation of Gandhi _because_ he was a leader. My hero is Martin Luther King...no amount of soft idealism will make a whole city of Blacks walk to work for a _year_ to desegregate busses, for instance, as he did in Montgomery, without leadership.

On a deeper level than anything so far in this rambling letter...I have been depressed also (apart from the state of the world, depressing enough) because after a lyrical year of passionate love, I begin to see the problem and to suffer from my life of scattered weekends with Marion. The shock came when I realized that an old friend of hers (much like Judy in my life) was coming from Scotland for the summer...i.e. she gives five weeks to this, and _we_ have two. I went through the depression alone as May is in any school a time when the head is consumed by present obligations...to the point that M. did not _write_ to me for five weeks, though we talked often on the phone. If I go there I am living her life not mine...finally, I came to see that my loneliness (acute and awful) was really a loneliness for _myself_ and what I had to do was get back to my blessed solitude. My motto, the opposite of dear Forster's, has become "only _disconnect_". It has to be done, at least for the present, or I shall not survive. M. comes here July 24th for two weeks...perhaps then we can find a more viable mode of being together. She talks a lot about feeling "married" to me but when the chips are down, this proves not to be true. It is certainly one of the hazards of homosexual unions that one cannot be before the world. So, if I go <u>there</u>, say for a month at a time, there would be gossip—and she can't come here.

Judy is losing her memory...has just been here. I feel oppressed by the horrors of old age. The one great visible joy has been the garden..full of god-like presences of white peonies and iris (one <u>black</u> one was really tremendous)....

That is all, dear Bill..it does me good to commune with you. But feel no pressure about answering. Only when the spirit moves...

Always your old
M

Bill Brown: Artist and amateur musician William Theophilus Brown (b. 1919) was Sarton's lifelong friend. She first met him by chance in 1939 at the home of Harrison Smith, noted editor of *Saturday Review*, on the eve of their both sailing on the *Normandie*; they met again on that ship's last voyage back to America. "Unlucky Soldier" was written for him (1944, *The Lion and the Rose*, not reprinted). His work is now nationally known and shares artistic affinities with Richard Diebenkorn, David Park, Elmer Bischoff, and Paul Wonner.

Brown and Wonner (b. 1920), who is considered one of the most important representational painters working today, met during art school in 1952. At this time they were searching for a place to settle far from a city.

Robert Graves: See note to 15 August 1969; his *Love Poems* had appreared in 1969.

E. B. White: His third and last book for young readers was *The Trumpet of the Swan*.

Janet: Sarton agreed with Brown (13 February [1970]) that New Zealand writer Janet Frame (b. 1924) "is the absolute pure authentic thing and [I] shall <u>devour</u> the novels," which at that time included *The Rainbows* (1968; U.S. *Yellow Flowers in the Antipodean Room*). Her troubling family and mental history is related in her autobiography, *Angel at My Table* (also a film by Jane Campion); see also Michael King, *Wrestling with the Angel: A Life of Janet Frame* (2001), dedicated to Brown.

Writing Sarton about first encountering Brown at the MacDowell Colony in 1969, Frame said, "Knowing Bill has been the chief experience of my life: I feel this must be true of everyone who meets him." She found *Plant Dreaming Deep* "like a poem in that it names and makes alive every stick, stone, creature, season, silence, sound, feeling that belongs, invited or uninvited, to the story of the house, or perhaps it is these that are the host, with the house and its story as the guest."

Aunt Amy: Brown's aunt, Amy Loomis, almost ninety. Both his mother and father died early the next summer. See *Solitude*, 8 July 1971, pp. 177–78.

Huxley's letters: The Letters of Aldous Huxley, ed. Grover Smith (1969). Despite impaired vision, this Huxley (1894–1963, brother to Julian) became a prolific critic, satirist (*Brave New World*, 1932), and essayist (*The Doors of Perception*, 1954, about his experiments with mescalin).

Lael Wertenbaker: Lael Tucker Wertenbaker (1909–97) was a reporter, screenwriter, and foreign correspondent. She worked for *Time*, as did her husband, Charles; her best-known book, *Death of a Man* (1955), recounts his battle with cancer. Among her novels are *Lament for Four Virgins* (1950) and *Afternoon Women* (1966); this one is unidentified.

Ritalin: Before its current use for treating attention deficit disorder in children, the brand-name drug Ritalin was prescribed to combat mild depression, emotional volatility, and impaired concentration in adults. While it belongs to the same class of central nervous system stimulants, it is not identical with amphetamine. More sophisticated antidepressants have since been developed.

Joan Baez . . . David Frost: Singer-songwriter Joan Baez (b. 1941, to a Quaker background) came to prominence in the early-1960s folk boom thanks to her pure soprano and her social activism; in 1965 she founded an Institute for the Study of Non-Violence. On this National Public Television talk show, hosted by British interviewer David Frost, Baez was promoting her recent album, *One Day at a Time,* and discussing the incarceration of her husband at the time, draft resister David Harris.

Gandhi . . . King: Inspired by Thoreau's civil disobedience, Indian spiritual figure and nationalist Mahatma Gandhi (1869–1948) in turn inspired African-American civil rights leader Martin Luther King, Jr. (1929–68) with his policy of nonviolent agitation to bring about social change.

the opposite of dear Forster's: The passage, from Chapter 22 of *Howards End* (1910) by British novelist E. M. Forster (1879–1970), reads in full: "Only connect! That was the whole of her sermon. Only connect the prose and the passion, and both will be exalted, and human love will be seen at its height. Live in fragments no longer. Only connect, and the beast and the monk, robbed of the isolation that is life to either, will die."

Back on 13 February [1970], Sarton observed to Brown that her "blessed solitude" was in fact "really an immense crowd and just that is, perhaps, the point."

only when the spirit moves: The Sarton-Brown correspondence, rich with resonances of five decades, will eventually merit a volume of its own; this letter is but a signal instance of their exchanges during this period, of which Sarton said, "Every letter he writes is a literary masterpiece." After an eight-year lacuna beginning in 1984, the letters resumed; see May 1992.

[*Journal of a Solitude* begins 15 September 1970.]

TO KYOKO NISHIMURA   Oct. 11th 1970
[Nelson]
Dear Kyoko,

The autumn has come suddenly and now all at once after three days of golden splendor all the leaves are falling and I feel I shall be buried...a thick gold carpet surrounds the house. It is raining. In the Japanese jar on my mantel here in the study (the Tokinoma of the house) I have branches of barberry and two marvelous starlike deep red chrysanthemums (like daisies) with greengold centers, and a single spray of peony life, a wonderful strange pink...I wish you could see it! I hope you have autumn flowers now in the blue jar we found together in Kyoto....

I am sure you miss your garden but perhaps the apartment is comfortable..is there a park nearby where you can take the children? Now I see that you do have a place there where you can plant flowers..wonderful that the soil recovered and now the plants are happy again.

I am sorry I did not manage to write when you were alone but by now the family is reunited and you must have been happy to see Mitsuo [her husband] safely home again!

Splendid that Sugio can swim..bravo! How I wish I could see him and Makiko who can speak whole sentences (that is brilliant for a 2-year old I think).

Yes, I have a big novel coming out this autumn. Kinds of Love. It deals with a village like this one and is really about old age. I think..you will enjoy it, I hope. Will try to get it to you for Christmas. New poems come out in the spring, so my work goes well...especially as it looks as if this novel might be a best seller (let us hope)..Reader's Digest has taken it for their book club so I shall make some money in any case [$15,000]. I hope to have a whole year of peace as I am writing now a journal of solitude..Inner Space and need long times of meditating as well as writing.

But I have been very depressed and lonely..it is not easy living alone here at best. It is v. hard to get any help in the garden and sometimes I feel it is too much. Now I have been greatly helped by a psychiatrist..also I have a good new friend whom I see for weekends now and then, but strangely enough it is her presence, far away yet near, that has made me feel so lonely. I am sure you understand this, dear Kyoko..how often I think of our wonderful time together!

With much love as always and do write soon again.

With a kiss from your
May

Kyoko Nishimura: Sarton's guide in Japan, 1962. See "Kyoko," "Inn at Kyoto," "An Exchange of Gifts," and the other Japanese poems which lead off *A Private Mythology.* In 1963, during three months in the United States, Nishimura (b. 1938) visited Nelson, and spent two nights at Wild Knoll in 1984. "Both times I visited her alone," she recalled, 10 December 2000, and they "talked about many things, visited neighbors, ate lobsters, walked around her place and had a very good time, as if we were mother and daughter." For recollections from 1991 of "Kyoko," that time in Japan, and a 1962 photo of May in Kyoto, see *Endgame,* pp. 237–39 and 243.

the Tokinoma: Traditionally the Tokonoma is a small, slightly elevated, sacred corner or alcove in a guest or master bedroom, reserved for a work of art, a scroll suited to the season, or arranged flowers.

do write soon: At a time when Sarton was nearly unknown in Japan, Nishimura taught *House by the Sea* in English at a junior college. Years later, *Solitude* became a best-seller in Japan, a fact Sarton lived to enjoy; see note to 13 July [1992] for other translations. In "May Sarton's World" (*Kyrsha American Literature,* 1979), Nishimura links those two journals with *As We Are Now,* which she calls the culmination of forty years' writing, "full of indignation at the debasement of human dignity and compassion toward the oppressed."

[Nelson]

Dear Dan,

In the first place for God's sake...you must get used to the way I fade out after a few hours of intense communion such as we shared...I am just quite suddenly "gone" like the Cheshire cat, a wan smile remaining suspended in the air. I keep our day with me like a talisman of the fact that whatever our failings as human beings...and I feel mine very much these days...such communion is occasionally possible and when it is, it is a sort of miracle of light and love. It was not so much anything we said as the sense I had that we recognized each other that first time..as fellow sufferers, I suppose..but also as two people with something like human genius at our best..and that when we are together it doesn't matter a hoot in Hell what we say, something like communion is going on all the time. Still, we said a lot.

Well, here is your letter. I feel great pity for Jean because she has made herself a painful bed in which she must lie. But I am relieved, Dan, that you have made that hard but necessary break. It does not, necessarily, mean forever. But I rather hope it will be. You have too much to give to be battered and crippled by a person who does not know how to give and who is..at present..out for herself alone. (Forgive this sententious remark!)

But I never saw a more radiant and less crippled person than you are now..and I keep a very vivid image of your head against the soft gold outside, a Renaissance portrait of someone better than a prince, a totally sensitive human being with immense gifts in his hands. Wish I were a painter and could paint you like that...maybe someday it will be a poem.

I am sure these days ahead will not be easy. Please phone if the spirit moves, or just drive up on a Sunday..(but phone first..I may be away over the 24th and leave for lectures on Nov. 2..Dallas and Shreveport). As for me, dear heart, I am sort of on the rack too...but an easier one than yours I guess, because Marion is a truly loving person. Only she has no time to "take in" what is happening to me or to herself..this causes a great deal of pain. For example I sent her some poems that came out of a true act of the spirit, to "let go" my infant dependence...they had been wrung out of a lot of feeling and thinking...I called at 7:30 one night to ask whether they had reached her and she was furious and said, "I just got in" defensive but it is tough. However, I should know by now that my poems reach strangers almost never the person I am hoping to reach.

> "Those who suffer see the truth; it has
> Murderous edges. They never avert

The gaze of calculation one degree,
But they are hurt, they are hurt, they are hurt."
(last stanza of a poem by Dick Eberhart)

[letter incomplete]

———

Dan Wallace: Son of Dorothy Wallace (see 24 July [1961] and 12 April 1965). His sister, Connie Wallace Gordon (1944–2001), was the "Girl with 'Cello" (1971); see *Plant Dreaming Deep,* p. 157. For Sarton's account of his 13 October 1970 visit and their discussion of "loyalty," see *Solitude,* pp. 43–46; for a consideration of his involvement with "Jean," see pp. 74–76, 5 January 1971.

"May was always intensely curious about my experience of life," Wallace recalled in December 2000, particularly about "the development of my relationship with and attitude toward women. I remember one visit in New Hampshire [perhaps the one in *Solitude*] when she was particularly supportive of my emerging consciousness. She played me George Harrison's 'Something in the Way She Moves' as an example of how men might relate to women. I still see the gentle smile on her radiant face as she listened to it."

Sarton alludes to another song by Harrison (1943–2001), "My Sweet Lord," in *Solitude,* p. 99. "Something" appears on the 1969 Beatles album *Abbey Road.* In the 1993 poem "An Eightieth Birthday: For Dorothy Wallace" (see appendix), Sarton greets Dan's mother with the title of another song from that album, also by Harrison: "Here Comes the Sun."

the Cheshire cat: In Chapter 6 of *Alice in Wonderland* (see note to 13 January 1966), the "Cheshire puss" is a tree-perching grinning feline that can vanish and reappear with startling suddenness; but at Alice's request it fades away gradually, leaving "a grin without a cat!" Sarton's penchant for the Alice books goes back to girlhood; see 14 February 1928 in *At Fifteen.*

these days ahead: Wallace took an M.A. in education; spent a year studying theology at Oxford; married, had children, and taught public school in Maine before moving to Salt Lake City. ("He's going to become a great teacher," Sarton predicted, *Solitude,* p. 43.) For his last visit to Sarton in May 1991, see *Encore,* pp. 33–34.

a poem by Dick Eberhart: " 'The Full of Joy Do Not Know; They Need Not,' " *Collected Poems 1930–1986* (1987).

TO KAREN O. HODGES   Nelson Christmas Eve 1970
[Nelson]
Dear Karen, what an event your grand letter was, and is, as I reread it this morning while we sit inside a huge cocoon of white thick furry snow falling, as it has been since early last evening..it is truly a white Christmas here! About 12 inches so far is my guess and it's still coming down...luckily I got in food for a week yesterday. We have plenty of wood..and the faithful gas tank men have just trundled a huge cylinder through snow way above their knees. Judy and the pussies are here for this week and my parrot, Punch, is talking away..the snow must look rather improbable to his bright round eye!

Of course I long for a snap of you, all three. Emily must be talking by now..and I want to see what she looks like!

I am now going to run through your letter and answer it as each rich paragraph is read, so if there are non sequiturs you'll understand <u>why</u>. I haven't read the Scott Nearing book but mean to. I have an idea that they lead a far more rugged and outdoorsy life than I do! I sit at my desk many days and only go out to get the mail in. .and that looks like a lazy life but you know that it is very intense inside here. A lot of hippies have illusions that they can live off the land with no idea of the <u>hard labor</u> that costs. Still, it is worth a try..and some may find that physical work is what they want. I wish them well. I wonder whether your little sister (is she Dennis's sister?) will make it…is she married?

Your house sounds great..and what fun to be a householder, put down roots, grow things..do you have a garden? After all the apartment years it must be a good feeling to own a little "forest". Yes, having money is good, but as you say, has its dangers..money is such <u>power.</u> One gets spoiled very fast..I know that I am when I think back to the days [in Cambridge, Massachusetts] when Judy and I had one drink a week on Saturday night and lived on baked beans..a roast was a rare occasion! Glad you feel young and adventurous rather than suburban and settled as a result of a little ease..you and Dennis will always know how to use money, I feel. Travel seems one of the great ways of spending..I remember a Boston banker telling me after my father died and I had a little money, "Don't buy a house. Travel!" Actually I did both, as you know. But he said "travel will give you memories you can feed on forever after"..it was rather surprising coming from this rather square character. It is startling to hear that your friends feel old or fear the best years are over..I have quite the opposite view. And incidentally the big novel <u>celebrates</u> old age..more vivid yet balanced than any other time of life, I believe. I am 58 now, believe it or not (I don't) and feel younger and somehow more fertile than ever before..and I am in love and very happily with a wonderful woman, head of a school. It has made a big difference to my state of mind. Well, it is high time that we tried to change the American ethos in respect to maturity.

Have you read The Greening of America by the way? I do not feel out of tune with a basic revolt against purely material values and a longing for life with some meaning other than asking what one's pension will be when one gets a <u>first</u> job after college! The thing I cannot go along with is such permissiveness toward joys that have to be earned..poetry being an example. I mean a great gush of emotion, like an orang outang beating its breast and screaming does not appear to be satisfactory to me, either as reader or as creator.

Well that brings me to the crucial and best part of your letter..about what stopped you as a poet just at that moment of flowering..I agree that it is terribly hard to be a woman and a poet, a mother-and-wife and a creator at the same time, in the same complex of life. But it looks as if you were about to get it all into harmony and when you do I know the poems will flow in..it sounds as if already that was beginning. I suppose one purely mundane problem is how to get enough consecutive hours to concentrate..when Emily goes to school, that should make a real difference and give you mornings for yourself.

I agree about Women's Lib but the trouble is the awful <u>hostility</u>. Men and women must be able to live together in amity without murdering each other and it seems almost as bad for the women to murder (or wish to murder) the men as the other way around. There is no doubt that men in general (bless Dennis for being different) are terrified of women as creators and really don't want them to be artists. I am back in psychiatry (I did get terribly suicidal last fall) and have found a miraculous old woman, Marynia Farnham, who retired to Brattleboro, an hour's drive from here. I found her in the yellow pages if you can imagine such a folly! In two months she has helped me to conquer rage (which risked destroying my new great love) which has been with me since infancy..We talk about a lot of things..amongst others, women of course. She thinks that men are jealous of woman's primary creative power..feel left out of "creation" since women bear children and are at the center of it..and hence are outraged when women <u>also</u> enter their fields as artists or whatever. This makes sense to me. She also has said many times that women are stronger than men.

It <u>is</u> a damned shame that your psychiatrist was a male Freudian..I can imagine the harm he did. But now you can see it all more clearly, you can banish him from your ethos.

I cannot read Sylvia Plath as I also cannot read Anne Sexton. I feel these poets are self-exploitive and never go deep enough into their metaphors to learn anything from the unconscious. There is, for me, a radical difference between nakedness and transparency. Nakedness embarrasses the reader or (sometimes) may make him feel superior, "She sure is a talented <u>crazy</u>"..but a good poem must be true for all sexes, it seems to me. Love has no sex. and maybe sexuality per se does not belong in poetry which is a matter of essences. (I am just thinking aloud so if this sounds arbitrary, it is not meant to be). I do agree about love..and also I feel that only when in love do we really <u>pay attention</u> in the deepest sense to another human being..and that is why it is so enlarging an experience.

For Heaven's sake never think I am not passionately interested in all you have to say! No apologies..the fact is that I am only interested in just such letters, rare as they are, and I demand relationships in depth. I see no one really with whom I do not have a relationship in depth. I have no social life at all. I resent all superficial talk except maybe with workmen, the road agent who drops in for a drink during a snowstorm and beams at me and tells me the village gossip. But that is elemental and real.

I think you were right to go to graduate school..and I have no memory of my angry letter. I guess I was angry to see so much potential going to waste.. but a time of indecision, an identity crisis as Erikson would call it is the very stuff of maturity. Everyone has at last one..and I am inclined to believe they come at about ten year intervals. I was in the midst of a big one when I decided to come up and live here alone, of course. It has worked out well..although I begin to think it is an un-naturally lonely life.

On the other hand, I can only do what I do with solitude by paying for it with times of extreme and suicidal loneliness I guess. My next project is a journal of solitude..I am in it already but the fall has been very frustrating for various reasons and I've been away too much..lectured in Dallas in October etc. (I found Dallas horrendous..all those immaculate lawns with not a single leaf allowed to rest on the grass!)

And you are dead right, dear person, that I shall never be frightened away from you. You are very dear to me..as I write I see your face so clearly!—and very proud of you. I guess you have no idea what a remarkable critter you are and maybe that is just as well.

Do read Kinds of Love..I want you to and to know how it strikes you, honestly. It got a murderous review in the N.Y. Times.. just said I was a bad writer and the book no good. But it is selling very well..I think people are relieved to find real people they can like in an unsentimental novel. And also a celebration of old age as an adventure and challenge. It is surely for the over-30's..but I think you may like it as you are an ageless person, as I have always been myself. I mean you were old, when young, and now perhaps begin to be young as you grow older.

Well, I had better make Judy a cup of coffee. One of the reasons for my depression is that she is losing her memory, really a premature senility..and it is rather like living on a quicksand. She always was my rock and now there is none. The entire absence of family in my life is queer..but Judy is dear although forgetful..I cannot trust her to do anything as she forgets in the middle, leaves the gas on etc.

Have a happy new year..and may the poems well up now..

A hug from your old racoon
May

Love to Dennis—and Emily!

Karen O. Hodges: Poet (b. 1943) and Jungian analyst now in private practice in Charlotte, North Carolina. She was Sarton's student in creative writing at Wellesley College in the early 1960s, where a friendship began. Dennis Buss was her husband from 1964 to 1983, and Emily their oldest child; they lived in Dallas, Texas.

the Scott Nearing book: Leader of the "back to land" environmental movement, Nearing (1883–1983) lived in a stone house he and his wife Helen built on a 140-acre Maine farm. *Living the Good Life* (1954) chronicles his attempt to farm outside the New England cash-crop economy. One of Hodges's sisters-in-law was involved in a similar experiment at this time.

Sarton comments on Helen Nearing's 1991 memoir of the couple's life together, *Loving and Leaving the Good Life,* in *Encore,* pp. 166–67. For Sarton's 80th birthday, Nearing wrote from the Netherlands to salute "A great lady and human being."

The Greening of America: A hotly-debated best-seller by Charles A. Reich (1970), the paper-back's blurb read: "There Is a Revolution Coming. It Will Not Be Like Revolutions Of The Past. It Will Originate With The Individual And With Culture, And It Will Change The Political Structure Only As Its Final Act. It Will Not Require Violence To Succeed, And It Cannot Be Successfully Resisted By Violence. This Is The Revolution Of The New Generation." A twenty-fifth anniversary edition appeared in 1995.

Marynia Farnham: Psychiatrist (1899–1978). After training here and abroad, Farnham worked in New York City as a pediatrician until turning to psychiatry in 1935. Though in general practice, she specialized, as professor and attending physician, in treating children and ado-lescents. She and Ferdinand Lundberg wrote the controversial *Modern Woman: The Lost Sex* (1947), which asserts that limiting women to the roles of nurturer and homemaker has only made them, and society at large, miserable. In *Solitude,* pp. 112–13, Sarton quotes and dis-cusses the book.

"Of course the therapy is about done," Sarton admitted to Beverly Hallam (2 March 1971), but "I keep on because I need to talk with someone in my own language and there is no one here…but I knew we would be friends, that ideal friend I have missed since Jean Dominique died, the older woman sophisticated, understanding, full of life…and Marynia has been such a delight."

Sylvia Plath . . . Anne Sexton: See [13 September 1966]. Sexton had published her own *Love Poems* in 1969, followed in 1971 by the influential *Transformations,* her radical reworking of fairy-tale motifs. Plath was then known only by her accomplished collection *The Colossus* (1960) and the posthumous *Ariel* (1965), in which her verbal and rhythmical virtuosity gal-vanized classical themes into lacerating modern utterances.

Some rough distinctions: For Sexton, the poem was a means for expressing and explor-ing pain. For Plath, the poem was a triumph over pain through language. For Sarton, the poem was a record of the triumph over pain and the triumph itself.

never go deep enough: In *Solitude* (p. 31) Sarton wrote about poetry as "a kind of dialogue between me and God," which "must present resolution rather than conflict. The conflict is there, all right, but it is worked through by means of writing the poem. Angry prayers and screaming prayers are unfit for God's ears."

Erikson: Danish-American psychoanalyst Erik Erikson (1902–94) endeavored to make psy-chiatry take more account of social and cultural pressures; his division of life into eight stages (*Childhood and Society,* 1950) was applied to psychobiographies of Luther and Gandhi. Sarton had recently read Robert Coles's *New Yorker* profile of him; see *Solitude,* pp. 59–60 (17 November 1970) and, for further reactions to Dallas, pp. 49–52.

a murderous review: Richard Rhodes's *New York Times Book Review* appraisal (29 November 1970) is summed up by its title (no doubt given by an editor), "How the Summer People Learned to Pass the Winter." He faulted the style, found the content "flabby," thought the characters lifeless: "Perhaps the flaw is that she tells us of feelings rather than showing us." Again Eugenia Thornton was laudatory in the *Cleveland Plain Dealer,* Nancy Hale praised the book's "depth and breadth of feeling," and *The New Yorker* (December 1970) approved: "We watch with fascination as Miss Sarton builds her huge portrait of a joyous and generous spirit who is doomed, even in old age, to suffer the pain of bewildered love." But it was the *Times* review Sarton remembered.

may the poems well up: Hodges's response is excerpted in *Solitude,* pp. 70–73, with Sarton's additional remarks.

TO KAREN O. HODGES   Feb. 14th, 1971
[Nelson]

Dear Karen, this is not an answer to your rich, thought-making wonderful strange letter about K[inds]. of L[ove]…but only to send quickly some spring flowers in the only form I can..a check. It is too beastly that you have had these bugs out there in what I should have thought such a healthy clime! Please get a large bunch (if such a sum is enough..alas it probably is not!) of freesias and daffodils and tulips and iris and things..and revive..

I am off on a lecture trip next week for a week, hence no time for a proper answer. Also I have had a body blow so awful that I felt at first like a torpedoed ship..my wonderful Dr. Farnham is going to live in Mexico for good..she doesn't leave for 6 months..but as my main reason for going to her was my neurotic anxiety that everyone is going to die or go away, that nothing lasts, and considering that Dr. [Volta] Hall (my former Psyc) <u>died</u> suddenly of a heart attack..you can see that it is traumatic. Perhaps the very violence of my reaction will help us get at the roots of the old enemy <u>angst</u> once and for all.

Just a couple of rebuttals..who do I write for? Certainly <u>not</u> only for women..I guess I write for sensitive human beings wherever they are, however young or old, and of whatever sex. But I do <u>not</u> write for academic critics, that's sure. Nor do they like what I write. It is a mutual lack of interest. The day your letter came or in the same week, I had three from men, all very different sorts of men..one was a soldier whose profession is high school teaching (math) in a little town in Maine. He said in part "I felt so much a part of the lives of these people that when I finally closed the book—sadly—a part of me seemed to end." The second from a strange young man in Wichita connected with the Arts Ass[ociation]. there, who had just lost his job "Yesterday, I closed K. of L. my heart filled with love for you. It has proven to be a solid friend, close to my side these past dark days. I really do not believe I would have made it without complete despair if I hadn't had the companionship of your book. You just can't imagine how much I learned from those pages and how keenly it helped me to understand something of my own situation and my relationship with others." The third a long hand-written one from Samuel Eliot Morison, the historian, which ends "All yankees should be grateful to you for this deep and perceptive book."

It is very childish of me to tell you this..only I can't get stuck with a "for women only" label. I think one has to write from wherever one is without thinking too much about what sex one is..we're all <u>human</u>, after all.

I think what has been wrong with my work before is expressed by Jung when he says, "One does not become enlightened by imagining figures of light, but by making the darkness conscious." I have "sublimated" a lot, including family life..as you point out. But at least in this book there is darkness and I do not believe it is sentimental.

I don't think you should be upset about the poems..you are conflicted in a <u>stopping</u>..way, but you are on the point of breaking out of it I feel..and this was clear in some of the poems. V. interesting about Dickinson.

Well, more when I can..please forgive this and bury your nose in a daffodil..I was immensely pleased, honored, delighted and altogether "sent" to have such a long letter about K. of L.. For God's sake stop under-rating yourself and recognize that <u>anyone</u> would be flattered by so much attention. I can read your handwriting perfectly.

Best love, dear heart..

May

---

send . . . flowers in the only way I can: This spontaneous Valentine Day's gift cannot but call to mind Sarton's lifelong habit of generosity. After a stroke of good fortune on 15 February 1928, teenage May rated her happiness "perfect": "I wish I could give out some of it or all of it to a thirsty heart" (see *At Fifteen*). Forty-two years later she would liken herself to "a child who runs about saying, 'Look at this treasure I found! I am going to give it to Peter, who is sad, or Betty, who is sick'" (*Solitude*, p. 45, 17 October 1970). "Being very rich so far as I am concerned is having a margin. The margin is being able to give."

Even when the margin nearly vanished, Sarton was forthrightly openhanded all her life, sending packages to friends overseas during World War II and the austere period afterward; bringing those Europeans to the United States for visits; recommending refugees for teaching positions at colleges where she had spoken; supporting organizations whose aims matched hers, such as the ACLU; assisting, among others, the Quigleys, Dr. Gatch, the Sisters of Mercy, Sister Maris Stella—the list of those she helped goes on.

Samuel Eliot Morison: See note to 2 September 1968. As early as 1938, when Sarton was 26 and immersed in reading the American women poets just preceding her, he claimed she had "already beat Elinor Wylie by a mile."

Jung: This quotation, with other extracts from Jung and reflections upon them, can be found in *Solitude*, pp. 110, 147–48.

TO MARYNIA FARNHAM   March 25th [1971] after my call
[Nelson]

Dear Marynia, I have so much to say and it is none of it easy. But it was, as I hope I conveyed to you just now, of course a consummation devoutly to be wished for that you come into my house and feel it, as I believe you did. I was very frightened when Mildred Quigley long ago said to me "It has not been a happy house." That seemed at the time like a curse, but I have come to understand that it was the truth. A place of great psychic tension and near despair where I have battled most things out alone and have created a great deal that gives comfort to others... a letter today from a woman whose husband had a stroke, about Kinds of Love says

"Of course we shall never be the same people again, but our acceptance is tinged with more gaiety and optimism, and we are more firm in our nervous systems than we could be without you and the Chapmans."

It is not fashionable these days for art to give comfort, yet I believe that is greatest [sic] it must always <u>transcend </u>and thus do so.

I have wanted to write a poem yesterday and today that had to get pushed aside so that I could answer most of what has accumulated lately on my desk..the poem will be some day about your combination of fervor and detachment, for I <u>saw</u> suddenly that it is just that that has, of course, spoken with such unmistakable authority to me. <u>Detachment</u> is what I still have to learn, so that I am less torn apart by the <u>slightest</u> human contact. Who can add to Eliot's "teach us to care and not to care"? ["Ash Wednesday"] But I would wish to do so not in a <u>religious</u> context.

I wonder whether you see the N.Y. Review of Books? There have been a series of three dialogues between Robert Coles and Dan Berrigan (I have felt that Berrigan was arrogant but this forces me to recognize something else) of which I have only seen the second.. somehow I must have thrown away the issue that had the first one in it. It raises very serious questions about the psycho-therapist...who on the whole helps patients to bear the status quo. (I do not argue this..only it feeds in to a lot about the times and how any human being tries to handle so much reason for despair with some reason for hope) and this second part ends with Berrigan saying that he would mistrust vast approval when he did various things that were utterly against what most Americans believe and he ends "My friends are often struggling against considerable odds; <u>what</u> <u>they</u> <u>offered</u> <u>me</u> <u>was</u> <u>a</u> <u>certain</u> <u>light</u> <u>that</u> <u>emanated</u> <u>from</u> <u>their</u> <u>lives.</u> In one way or another they said to me: you are somewhere and we are somewhere and you come and tell us what you have finally decided, and we will stand with you as best we can." (underlining mine)

I believe that you understand that, exactly as I do. And perhaps the most precious thing that we share is some given sense of each of our lives as primarily concerned with giving. . . so your coming here had many elements in it, as I need not tell you. I do not know how long I can stay here even though I am aware that it means something to a lot of people I do not even hear from, and so many from whom I do, that someone does stay on the edge of nowhere, someone who maintains what is essentially the life of the spirit, outside all the cadres, and who listens and answers. But in some very deep, secret part of myself I feel spent. That, I suppose is what frightens me when a great deal of feeling flows in. . .you said "I will talk to you." Please remember that.

Sometimes I am overwhelmed by the feeling that all I have created here has been a substitute, an ersatz thing, but who knows? Anyway I spent a very extraordinary hour and a half while the light slowly blazed up and went, yesterday afternoon, waiting for you to come. I really saw the physical world in all its mystery and beauty because I did not do anything but wait for you and experience it in long series of notes on light and shadow. . . so, you see your gifts are many, even in raising expectations that are not realized at the moment.

But how splendid of you to arrive this morning! You are such an odd and endearing person . .all that talk about dogs masturbating reduced me to tears of laughter as I drove to Keene. And the BOOK was a great joy to read on my return. . a little marvel.

I am glad you told me about your having to clean the parrot's cage at 8 [years old] as it explains your dim view of parrots. Also I am glad you told me about your daughter . . . I hope so much that she will come to wish to adopt a child//some parents are doing this deliberately because of the population explosion . . . well, I have much more to hear and to learn about you.

Poor Mrs. Tedford, whatever will she do when you go and she can no longer say "WE—have the New Yorker?" I suddenly see that it is a real liberation that nobody can say that "we" about me in Nelson. And in Guadalojara it will be a different kind of "we" from the people around you. . . I will come and see you there if all goes well, and we will have long talks.

Why is this such a long letter I wonder? Only to make some transition from you to Marion [Hamilton] . . . another very deep and fulfilling world to which I now go with a full heart and much thanksgiving to be alive.

I hope the sun was brilliant on your journey and on your homecoming and that the gardenia will flower for your return. I'll be thinking of you very happily and very tenderly.

[no closing or signature]

a consummation . . . wished for: Hamlet III.i.62–63, quoted out of context. The visit inspired "The Consummation," first published in 1977.

Robert Coles and Dan Berrigan: Now professor of social ethics at Harvard, Coles is known for many books linking literature with psychology, as well as landmark studies about children, such as *The Moral Intelligence of Children: How to Raise a Moral Child* (1999). Sarton read and referred to his work frequently.

Like his brother Philip (b. 1923), Daniel Berrigan (b. 1921) is a Roman Catholic priest; both were imprisoned for destroying Maryland draft registration files, resulting in Daniel's one-act play *The Trial of the Catonsville 9* (1970). A teacher, poet, and author of over fifty books, Berrigan views his social activism as a function of his Christian responsibilities: see his 1987 autobiography *To Dwell in Peace.*

edge of nowhere: In the chapter thus titled of *Plant Dreaming Deep,* Sarton gives an estimate of her work and her career, as it stood in the late 1960s—after *Mrs. Stevens* but before *Solitude.*

your daughter: Farnham and her husband Charles Nisom had a daughter and a son.

TO ROBERT FRANCIS   June 12th, 1971

[Nelson]

Dear Robert Francis,

It has been an event for me to read The Trouble With Francis (wonderful title). I keep The Orb Weaver [1960] with a very few other books of poems that I turn to often..Frost, Wallace Stevens, Yeats, and a small volume by Frances Cornford. The test is whether one <u>goes back</u> to poems, don't you agree? I go back to yours.

I guess what moves me so much about your life as man and as a poet is that it has close parallels to my own. I too have worked as poet anyway with a great silence around me as far as serious critical appraisal goes. I have had to reach my readers like a secret agent, over or under all the usual channels. I have had to battle the anger this causes, and my coming to Nelson, a small village near Dublin, and in so doing really and deliberately "leaving the world" has been of enormous help. I now believe it may be a kind of freedom to go about one's business in peace, unrecognized, as it were. In the very long run any success devours...and perhaps also corrupts. I do have a problem that perhaps you do not. The novels and autobiographies elicit huge amounts of mail and these past few years I live a sort of agony of "responding." I feel that if one has written a thing that deeply moves someone, one has no right not to answer..but then how to keep so many "friends" at bay? They know me but I do not know them. That is the real trouble. The other problem is psychological..the work of answering is the work of Sisyphus, for even when I take a whole week off to answer, by the time I have done so, a new pile is there, waiting. When I get seriously overtired this leads to real depression and a wish to die.

I found the chapter, Eros, a masterly piece of honesty and clarity. I have lived with the same problem, and like you, did not (for many reasons) "come out" into the open until my parents were dead and until I had made a reputation as a serious writer and published fifteen or more books of poems and novels. Then I did with a novel called Mrs. Stevens Hears the Mermaids Singing. It got a jeering press, but has slowly made its way, and seems to have been of some help. I have never regretted publishing it, in fact it cleared the air for me.

We are different in that I have never led as rigorous a physical life as you do. I am ashamed of earning more...but I do garden and divide the days between indoors and out. Perhaps one day I could drive over and see you or vice versa. But that is not important. I only wanted to send you a firm handclasp, to say thank you for being there, and for writing the poems, and now this splendid, acute, reverberating autobiography. I shall have it in my mind for many years to come, and shall "spread the word" about it all I can.

Sincerely yours,

Robert Francis: Massachusetts poet and essayist (1901–87); Sarton is commenting on his autobiography. They may have first met at Robert Frost's eightieth birthday banquet (see note to January 1963); a "Seating Arrangement" shows them sitting at the same table. *After the Stroke,* pp. 263–64, cites passages from Francis's poetry and entries from *Travelling in Amherst: A Poet's Journal* (Rowan Tree Press, 1986); he spent most of his life there. "Francis was a solitary, lived on next to no money, grew his own food (he was a vegetarian) and had very little success. 'What is more ludicrous than a successful poet,' Louise Bogan used to say."

Wallace Stevens . . . Cornford: Stevens (1879–1955) wrote poetry of great rhetorical and musical fluency ("Sunday Morning," "The Idea of Order at Key West") that charted the interplay between the world of the senses and the world of imagination.

The epigrammatical poems of Frances Cornford (British, 1886–1960), collected in 1954, were a lifelong delight to Sarton; *Recovering,* p. 139, reprints "Epitaph for Everyman."

the work of Sisyphus: In Greek mythology, as punishment for offending the gods, Sisyphus in the underworld was condemned to roll a huge stone up a hill only to have it roll back down again, forcing him to start over and repeat the sequence for all eternity.

TO BEVERLY HALLAM   Aug. 6th [1971]
[Nelson]
Dear Bev,

The only grief of the perfectly Grand WOW of a day, was that we had to give you up to the Art Ass. for part of the time! Marion was in a great state of exhilaration at meeting you and Mary-Leigh ..equal with the joy and excitement at seeing the place and now she has just been studying a map and says that Wild Knoll is only 5 miles farther from New

London than Nelson is..and of course it is much <u>nearer</u> Cambridge than Nelson is..

I felt badly at not looking more attentively at your world in the studio, but we were all too keyed up, I think, to be able to <u>contemplate</u> anything by the time we got there.

I don't know how to say what I feel without treading in dangerous places where the subconscious has its lair..but I can say that for both you and me I know there is a frightful tearing up of roots to be done <u>before</u> the fruitful time of beginning to use a new environment for work can begin. So we will be in a limbo for a while..and you far more so. What I dread for you is the consuming work on detail of building and planning, for it is bound to go on for a year or more. But you must hack out firm days where you simply do not <u>think</u> about the house (easier said than done) I think I know you as I do myself, in the sense that my rest is my <u>work</u>. The exhausting days are when I can't get at it. But in the silence when I am writing, I get centered and all the dispersals of life center around that inner place. And can be better dealt with afterward.

The lunch was superb!

Mary-Leigh is an angel.

I am blest indeed in you both and in this immense radiant meadow and ocean which I go to sleep visualizing..I begin to love the house too.

Written in a wild rush just to say THANK YOU (and let nothing you dismay.)

M

V. happy to have <u>The Way</u> back again!

———

Wild Knoll: Sarton had committed herself to moving from Nelson to this gracious house in York, Maine, on the 40-acre property recently purchased by Mary-Leigh Smart; Smart and Hallam had commissioned an architect to design their adjoining houses to be built on the waterfront.

Wild Knoll, which sits back from the ocean, was built by the Reverend Julian K. Smyth and completed in 1916. After Smyth's death his daughter, Miriam, a decorator, inherited the house, filled it with antiques, and later sold it to Urbain Robert of Boston, the last owner prior to Smart. It was doubtless the Reverend Smyth who named it Wild Knoll.

<u>*The Way:*</u> Hallam had offered this Oriental-style monotype to Sarton in gratitude for *Mrs. Stevens Hears the Mermaids Singing*; it had been borrowed for a major retrospective of her work at the Addison Gallery of American Art in Andover, Massachusetts. On 4 May 1971, leading up to the opening, Sarton had written her: "I am thinking of <u>The Hallam</u> who is about to look back on all her incarnations…Maybe you will be so overwhelmed by your own genius that you will have to rush away…and begin painting in an entirely new style! Maybe you will just feel very quiet at the center…waiting for the angel to seize you by the hair. Maybe…you will be just plain astonished at what you have accomplished and full of joy that so much is already there <u>forever</u>." In the years since, Hallam has exhibited and conducted demonstrations

throughout the United States, concentrating on vast dramatic floral paintings executed with an airbrush. These and her earlier works are showcased in *Beverly Hallam: An Odyssey in Art* by Carl Little (Washington, D.C.: Whalesback Books, 1998). *The House by the Sea,* for which Hallam provided the photographs, is dedicated to her and Mary-Leigh Smart.

TO THOMAS C. BARNES   Sept. 26th, 1971
[Nelson]
Dearest Tom,

There seems to be a darkness everywhere...Attica hangs over us all for one thing. Maybe it is a time when everyone has to wait and be terribly patient while some new hope is able to grow inside us, strong enough to change this arid world. I am really glad to hear that Jamie is taking his time to make this life decision...the hardest thing is to hold a decision in suspense, I know well, but he is wise.

As for you, you have waited long and I dearly hope and trust that you will have good news soon and be able to begin to live your real life. Meanwhile say to yourself that healing yourself and growing strong again is the first thing asked. I am glad you have flowers to look at. On my desk I have a whole bunch of late roses with lovely names, especially Souvenir de la Malmaison, also White Wings (a single rose with very dark red stamens, lovely), and dear old Queen Elizabeth, very fat and pink.

I am going through a very hard passage in my personal life. It is the end of a relationship in which I have invested a very great deal, and even into psychiatry to change myself into a more worthy person. I did change. But I have come to see that we are too destructive and have hurt and been hurt beyond what can be mended. It is a little like dying and it is all I can do to pick flowers, wash dishes, maintain life here...yesterday I couldn't eat at all and wept floods of tears. Today I begin to find my self again, and to believe that God has always meant me to be alone. His will be done.

Dear boy, it is very precious to me to know that I am in your prayers, as you in mine (though mine are awfully unorthodox).

Tell Jamie, Mauriac is one of my dearest authors..I am glad to have this one in English. And the book you sent which I have not yet really got into...and all your loving thoughts, bless you, go into my heart.

Your
M

Thomas C. Barnes: Barnes first wrote on 20 May 1970, after reading *Plant Dreaming Deep;* on 21 July 1970 Sarton replied, "It is dear of you to offer and wish friendship. I don't have a lot of men friends and it sounds good. But...500 or more people feel that I am an intimate because they know my work...I write about 100 personal letters a week...out of a sense of responsibility and in God's name, so to speak…So, let us be friends with a full understanding that communication may not be frequent…" But they did write consistently from then on. "T and J" had visited Nelson on 29 August 1971; see *Solitude*, pp. 197–99.

Attica hangs over us: On 9 September 1971 inmates at the Attica (New York) Correctional Facility, revolting against long-standing mistreatment and overcrowding, took forty-two officers and employees hostage, threatening murder if attacked. The standoff lasted five days; lawsuits continue to the present.

His will be done: Barnes's response moved Sarton, on 17 October 1971, to "wish I could feel the presence of Christ as you do. I must confess that I have a far greater sense of God than of Christ. Perhaps I am not really a Christian but a Buddhist! But I am truly with you in understanding that we cannot rest in or on human love."

Mauriac: Devout Catholic writer François Mauriac (1885–1970) worked with the Resistance during World War II and won the 1952 Nobel Prize in literature; his stark novels deal with the psychology of sinners struggling with faith. Sarton was greatly influenced by his style of *clarté,* emphasizing directness and transparency.

[*Journal of a Solitude* ends 30 September 1971.]

TO ROBERT O'LEARY   Sept. 7th, 1972
[Nelson]
Dearest Bob,

How hard it is to be our age, when one by one, friends disappear as if great cliffs were eroding and falling into the sea—leaving less and less terra firma! This is sad news about Leonard..you do not say whether he had had a long illness or whether it was sudden. I am touched that he spoke feelingly of Kinds of Love … and especially glad that you saw him as recently as a month ago. But oh, it is hard, dear friend.. I feel with you, deeply. And with Roberta to whom I shall write today also.

It is far too long since we have met…I did not even know about Eleanor's second operation. Is all well now? Will she be able to see all right in time? It seems absurd that you have been through this long ordeal together without a word from me.

I too have been going through an ordeal, torture one might say. I shall put this letter in with the new book of poems. There is a section at the end about my former psychiatrist Marynia Farnham: She became my only real friend around here..but when I got back in June from teaching two months at Agnes Scott in Decatur Ga. she had become senile and paranoid, turned against me, is under the influence of a truly wicked woman (whom I sent to her as a patient, ironically enough). It has been a very bad and frightening business..I was threatened with commitment! Had to get a lawyer..my intimate letters were taken to lawyers and their loving content subjected to sneers and threats. I feel this house is like a house where the Gestapo has operated…the walls are covered with blood, metaphorically speaking. I have never before met <u>evil</u> in my life and I know that it cannot be fought and that it wins...though not in the very long run, one must hope. I have been close to madness and/or suicide... but I have <u>worked</u> to save myself and now I am through the worst.

Norton will publish a journal I kept here for a year, next spring. (They are enthusiastic about it, a relief). Now I am writing at full speed a novel about the awful nursing home where Perley Cole died..a short <u>blow</u> of a book about how the old are treated in the U.S. [*As We Are Now*] In it I have been able to transpose much of my agony. I know a lot about mental torture and those who suffer <u>helplessly.</u>

In May I leave Nelson forever. I am selling the house and going to York, to live the end of my years by the sea. Renting a wonderful house there from dear friends who will be nearby. Nelson has been a rich experience but frightfully lonely..so I look forward to the move.

I hope to move Judy to an apt. near me at the same time. Her memory fails fast and she, too, has been too lonely.

Bless you..a hug from your old raccoon

M

Robert O'Leary: The O'Learys, Robert and Eleanor, both writers, were Cambridge neighbors; Robert met Sarton in spring 1933 when his brother and Leonard Mikules were members of her Appentice Theatre. (Roberta was Mikules's wife.) O'Leary shared all his work with her, and wrote a one-act play (unproduced) dramatizing an episode in her life in Paris on the eve of World War II. His 1987 story collection, *Heaven Has No Yesterdays,* was dedicated "To Eleanor Ruggles, Friend of Poets, and May Sarton, Poet and Friend."

the new book of poems: Published in June, 1972, *A Durable Fire* was dedicated to Farnham. It concludes with six poems for and about her, grouped as "Letters to a Psychiatrist."

Another book of poems was also written for her: *Bridge Over Troubled Water* (September 1971–March 1972) includes eleven poems, the thirty-five sonnets of the title sequence, and a two-poem epilogue. Sarton typed it herself "in an edition of two copies," numbered and signed. Selected sonnets had periodical publication in 1973 and 1975; in *The Silence Now,* eleven were published as "Over Troubled Water."

TO MARY-LEIGH SMART   Sunday Eve [Oct. 2, 1972]
[Nelson]
Dear Mary-Leigh,

At last here I am! And it is a perfect radiant autumn evening. Guests have come and gone. Tamas [the Sheltie] is quietly chewing a rubber bone...

It made me very happy to hear you say that you still feel I am the person you want at Wild Knoll..and partly because I am a gardener. How heartening a word! I have written White Flower Farm to order a few pink, white and deep purplish blue phlox to replace those that have reverted to that bad magenta. (Raymond had already weeded those front beds when I went back next day and we had a good talk about what can be done now.) He will till the picking garden this fall, and again in the spring and he will put in the bulbs if I can't get over when they come. We made an agreement that I pay him $3 an hour for things that he would not do for you. This is for now. What should go into the contract eventually is that I pay half his usual salary for pruning etc. and then anything over that that I want done. I gave him a check for $30 to go along with.

I called the Mr. Fogg at Sanford Mills and ordered the carpet, wheat color (really a soft melonish yellow) $500, but it will make a big difference to that room. The thing is that Mr. Fogg would like to come and measure in more detail. I gave him a rough estimate of 28 feet by 15 (as the room is nowhere wider than 15 because of the indentation of fireplace etc.) Would it be possible for you to phone him or your cousin's wife do so when it would be convenient for them that he come? The number is [ ]. There is no great hurry but I may have overestimated and it could bring the price down some. I don't suppose it would take more than a half hour. It would then be saved and they would install sometime in April if that is O.K. (I get very excited when I think of it!)

At Margeson's I ordered a small Chippendale sofa for the cosy room (a thin rather elegant stripe of white, soft green and soft orange) and a larger sofa for the big room with a lovely bright blue tweed in rough stripes...rather daring but it should look handsome. I hope. Also a really good desk, my first in my whole life. I think I deserve that for 26 books written at inadequate tables. It will be quite wonderful to have my work place upstairs and out of sight!

Malcolm is putting record shelves into the cupboard on the ocean side up there, and a louvered cabinet against the chimney wall for storage for papers etc. He is building bookcases for the small room between the bedrooms on the second floor, and covering the two French doors in the big room downstairs with a material (to be painted to match walls) that will hold a painting on each space in winter. (These covers will be removable for summer). And he is making a plant place for the window in the cosy room. (I trust none of this will radically disturb your cousin?)

And all this just to let you know what the plans are. Of course you must say nay to anything that might trouble you for any reason.

As I told you on the phone, I am relieved not to buy. There was an element of pride, ownership in the possibility, but I think it's really far wiser and simpler to make it a rental affair and it's a big hunk of capital to lay out for me at this time in my life. As for the rent $225 is generous. But as we said, you do have a good reliable tenant and a gardener, and it is a year-round proposition. I must try to believe that I am paying my way, or almost!

As for your adventure…so much more risky and costly…I hold my breath and say little prayers that all will be well after all you have been through, with costs rising astronomically as new plans are made. "Les aventures sont aux aventureux" and I feel the big risk <u>will</u> pay off in years of happiness and joy right on the rocks… "et la mer, la mer toujours recommencée" right at your feet. At least it must be a mighty relief to get the "go" sign. I do <u>hope</u> the final estimate from the electrical engineer comes through…and so let me know how things stand. By the time you get this, the bulldozers may be there and the foundation being dug…hurrah, if so!

I always love being in your house, so full of many kinds of life..as for my bad behavior. There is no excuse. I will make none. I have these fits. Thank you for still wanting me to come after witnessing Vesuvius in action! And I have the secret will and hope that when I am out of this nightmare here and settled by the calming ocean, with you, my good friends, nearby, I shall overcome at last what has plagued me and those who love me all my life.

Meanwhile all blessings and love to you both—

––––––

Mary-Leigh Smart: Mary-Leigh Call Smart (b. 1917), widow of actor, painter, sculptor J. Scott "Jack" Smart (a.k.a. "The Fat Man"), collector and patron of the arts, founder with her husband and later president of the Barn Gallery, Ogunquit; serves on boards of museums and other nonprofit organizations; member of the Maine Arts Commission Museum Panel, the National Committee of Wellesley College Friends of Art, and the Skowhegan School Maine scholarship jury.

Raymond: Raymond Philbrook (1913–2001) worked as a gardener and handyman for many in the area, including Smart and Sarton. The minimum wage had risen only from $1.40 in 1967 to $1.60 in 1972 ($6.24 in 1998 dollars); Sarton's $3 an hour more than kept pace with the rate of inflation. Sometimes he wrote the poet a poem as well; see *House by the Sea,* p. 43.

A native of Kittery Point, Maine, Philbrook lived all his life in the hundred-year-old house in which he was born. On a final poignant visit to Wildknoll in the fall of 1994, Philbrook was accompanied by his companion and caregiver, Madeline Gavin. His guardian angel during his last years, she organized an unforgettable memorial service in the barn at his birthplace.

your cousin's wife: David and Rebecca Linney were then living at Wild Knoll; local craftsmen were employed to make the alterations. Sarton was always to be grateful for the modest rent.

"Les aventures . . . la mer: "Adventures are meant for the adventurous." "The sea, the sea, forever rebeginning."

Vesuvius in action!: Smart made a comment over dinner at her house that Sarton interpreted as disparaging the English, her mother's people, triggering an outburst.

love to you both: The House by the Sea is dedicated to Mary-Leigh Smart and Beverly Hallam. See *Encore,* p. 243, for an April 1992 photo of Sarton and Smart together.

TO MARYNIA F. FARNHAM   [5 October 1972]
[Nelson]
Darling,

What joy to be able to write to you! It would be fine if we could just let these last 7 months (yes, that is how long it has been since I left you at the Cosmopolitan Club) drop away gently, as the leaves go, without grief, to make loam for another spring. But seven months in any life represents a lot of growth and change. ..I feel quite light and airy with all that I have let go, all that has slipped away, to leave me feeling rather naked as far as human relations go, but clear in myself, ready to go on alone as I must do.

Bill and his friend, Paul Wonner, moved in yesterday to a house between Dublin and Pete, so for the first time in my 15 years here, I have very old good friends near by. I have known Bill for 30 years, and as artists (he is a painter) we have grown along side by side, meeting rarely, but always with joy. I can hardly believe that he will be here at my side this winter, and I wish you could meet him. Perhaps, in time, that will be possible. He is a musician as well as a painter and was an intimate friend of the Stravinskys'. Studied with Hindemith at Yale. Like me he is unfashionable (has reacted against the abstractionists) and has had a struggle.

These days I split between getting to the end of the short novel laid in a nursing home..the end is very hard to get at, as Caro, the leading character burns the place down. To find the exact psychological balance between despair and such violent action is the problem and I have not yet solved it. The other half of the day I spend upstairs sorting and arranging hundreds of letters, journals, draughts of poems etc. which a man is coming to assess Oct. 24th and which I hope to get out of here (sealed till 2000) before I go to York May 1st. It will be a relief! But what I dreaded so much, that long look back into my life, that enormous freight of people loved and loving, has proved to be clarifying and helpful. I have felt like a leper since you cast me out. But I see now that I have been greatly loved, and by great people...and somehow it has helped me to get a balance again. On one of the very worst days I was reading through a folder of Marianne Moore's letters and came upon this. "You make beauty from ashes. You affirm and transcend." That helped.

This last month I have been able to read seriously again. The most important thing has been Freud—<u>Living and Dying</u> by Scurr. I found it deeply moving and also illuminating. I suppose I have been what my father called "a bushman" about Freud, ignorant and prejudiced. But the unremitting honesty of his self-analysis hit me with great force and opened the way for much fruitful thinking and slow self-understanding and self-pardon. This has really been the chief event of the last month and it is why I called you to say that I am crystal clear, as far as getting rid of poison goes. I tend to believe the worst about myself and have gone through a lot of guilt, some of it un-necessary, I have come to see. I have come to understand, with the help of Freud, that my long sweat of panic, the fear of being committed was of course my own fear of madness. And the fear of madness is knotted into the old problem of anger. This has still to be solved, but I do not despair.

In somewhat the same way from a different angle I have been absorbed and taught a lot by the two volumes of Lash on Eleanor Roosevelt. In her of course the ability to handle pain and always make it into a key toward further giving fills me with excitement—the adventure of life itself.

The Virginia Woolf biography I <u>devoured</u>—have ordered three copies, one for you, from England. I'm dying to talk with you about it. And now I am reading Rozhak Where the Wasteland Ends..this, I fear, will affront you. But, despite the journalistic style, I am glad someone besides me believes in the mystical approach, even to political reality—and its plea for a return to the Romantic point of view. This pleases both the natural raccoon in Sarton and the mystic in Sarton and seems rather heartening.

Norton will publish the journal in April. They are pleased. I really have no idea what it is like as I had to cut all passages about you as psychiatrist (There had to be either more or nothing, I felt) and Marion appears as X, faceless, sexless, place-less, occupation-less, rather too abstract a figure! What is left at least Norton thinks is great..and we shall see...

Tamas is asleep in his pen. It is far too late in the morning for me to get to work.. but I had to celebrate your assent [to receiving] a letter. And now I can start the day in a state of unusual happiness.

With love as always

[no closing or signature]

Marynia F. Farnham: See note to 24 December 1970. Sarton had not been fully aware to what extent her psychiatrist was then slipping into senile dementia. It took much time, anguish, and money for Sarton to unsnarl herself from the resultant personal, literary, and legal entanglements. See *House by the Sea,* p. 239, for the Cosmopolitan Club incident.

Bill and . . . Paul. . . moved in: Although just granted tenure at Santa Barbara, Wonner quit the job, and he and Brown moved back East to Peterborough.

Stravinskys' . . . Hindemith: Russian-born composer Igor Stravinsky (1882–1971) deeply affected the entire development of modern music; he was married to Vera, whom Brown continued seeing long after her husband's death. And he remained close friends with the prolific and versatile German-born composer Paul Hindemith (1895–1963) even after the Hindemiths left New Haven and returned to Europe.

man is coming to assess: Carolyn G. Heilbrun (see 24 February 1973) initiated the purchase of Sarton's papers, assessed by Herbert Metzendorf, for the Berg Collection of the New York Public Library, where they now reside, available to scholars.

before I go to York: "I sold the house last week!" Sarton exulted to the Reverend Thomas Barnes, 27 October 1972. "I sold it for $40,000 instead of $45 because I loved the young couple so much and they <u>felt</u> the house as no one has—babes in the wood, they are, married only since June. He is an apprentice cabinet maker, such a right profession for the owner of this house to be. They were modest and open-eyed, noticed every detail. And for me of course what a relief not to have to show it any more!"

After moving in, Mark and Nancy Stretch discovered, etched onto a windowpane near the front door, Sarton's translation of Du Bellay's sonnet "Heureux Qui, Comme Ulysse," done soon after she had moved in. To protect it and ensure it stayed with the house, the Stretches had the pane removed and framed. Once they "took possession" they phoned York. Sarton told them, "Leaving Nelson was one of the saddest days of my life," since "No other house will ever appeal to me as much as that one did." See "House for Sale: Poem on a Pane of Glass," *Yankee* (March 1995).

Scurr: Max Schur, M.D., *Freud: Living and Dying* (1972), is a recounting of his later years by Freud's personal physician.

I do not despair: See the refrain to "What the Old Man Said: For Lugné-Poë, founder of the Oeuvre Theatre in Paris" (1940): "but he did not despair."

two volumes: Probably *Eleanor and Franklin* and *Eleanor: The Years Alone* (W. W. Norton, 1971 and 1972), by Joseph P. Lash.

Quentin Bell, *Virginia Woolf: A Biography* (1972); Sarton was reading the two-volume Hogarth Press edition.

Theodore Roszak, *Where the Wasteland Ends: Politics and Transcendence in Postindustrial Society* (1972).

TO HELEN HOWE   December 27, 1972
[Nelson]
Dearest Helen,

Your letter was my best Christmas present..and came on the dreariest of days, the day <u>after</u> Xmas when exhaustion and quiet desperation set in! I am so very happy and proud that you liked Kinds of Love..in fact I have been waiting hopefully for ages for a word (though I quite understood why you put off reading it). No one but you is interested in what went into writing it, so I shall indulge myself by answering your questions..in the first place I wanted too a historical novel and spent a year reading town histories and gleaning facts. I wrote 200 pages laid in the early 19th century and then realized that it is quite beyond my powers to deal with history. I mean I was constantly bogged down in material detail..what people ate, wore etc. and felt like a person feeling his way through <u>fog</u>. But at least the final book maybe had a kind of richness under it. Only you know how awfully hard it was and in fact, now two years later I still feel exhausted in my head.. I was enormously helped by Eleanor Blair (a former copy editor) who made a card index of characters and noted pages where they were mentioned and went over the ms. with a fine toothed comb for any mistakes in <u>time</u>, age of characters etc. (I am very bad at all this because it bores me).

The town is really a mixture of Nelson and Dublin. Christina is more a Dublin person and was somewhat based on Rosalind Greene (I used to stay with them in Dublin as a child.) Because of the journal people think she is I, but that is not true at all. Sev. people have expressed dislike of Ch. by the way. The only characters direct from life are Ellen (my Quigley neighbor), Old Pete (who appeared earlier in Miss Pickthorn and Mr. Hare) and Nick..though his violence was not in the prototype <u>at all</u>. I'm glad you felt the young lovers were real.. I found that rather hard to do. The boy was somewhat inspired by a hippie who stayed here a couple of days..

All this really to say don't give up on your novel. I'm sure that a "time off" often pays..it all comes into focus suddenly. I shall be waiting to read—with the keenest anticipation.

You know from Polly [Thayer Starr], I expect, that my private life has been nothing but anguish for a year due to the senility of the two people closest to me.. Judy and Marynia Farnham, my former psychiatrist who has become paranoid and threatening..it is hard to describe what a quicksand one feels under one's feet when one's psychiatrist, the one person you trusted, tells you and others that you are a filthy, dirty and dangerous person. I finally had to get a lawyer. (At one point she threatened to commit me and at times I believed I would go mad, and twice nearly committed suicide.) My sanity has been saved by a darling little dog, my first, a Sheltie called Tamas. He and my cat, Bramble, sleep on my bed..for months I couldn't sleep so it has been a huge comfort to have animal tender warmth close to me. Judy is always loving, thank God, but terribly exasperating..so I live in a constant state of guilt. She cannot do the simplest thing..for instance, I asked her to get some nuts out of a cellophane bag and put them in a bowl...only to come back and find her busily <u>shelling</u> them! I got her all dressed to go out to Xmas dinner in a new suit and blouse I gave her—she looked so sweet.—and she came down <u>as we were to leave</u>, having changed into a dirty blouse and shabby old suit. I lose my temper of course and that makes me feel even worse.. well, we managed to have a fairly good Xmas, tree and all. I take her home tomorrow.

I feel terribly desolate and orphaned these days and get frightened because I have to produce so much to live. Two books will be out this next year, A Journal of Solitude in April and later on a short bitter novel about how the old are treated in nursing homes. I wrote it fast and with passion as I was able to transform some of the mental torture I have suffered in it..it is written in the first person by an old woman who is "put away" and abandoned. (By the way, I found first person fascinating and much easier than I had imagined it would be from the technical point of view).

I am so frightened of premature senility..and the worst thing is that I can never again get psychiatric help. I have been too battered and frightened by Marynia.

Anyway the move to York is sure to help. My address after May 1st will be Wild Knoll, Godfrey Cove Road, York, Maine.

I may be in N.Y. at the end of January..maybe we could have an hour's talk. It would be an oasis to this ancient starved camel.

Meanwhile thank you and bless you for writing as you did and when you did..

And all wishes for a big last heave on your novel and my having a chance to read it...

Much love, dear Helen—

Your old raccoon

M

P.S. Kinds of Love was shattered (as far as ads or selling) by a very stupid and cruel review in the Sunday Times. I expect you saw it? I did make money because Reader's Digest took it for the condensed books..but Norton would have pushed it, I believe, if the Times had come through... oh well, it's all a roulette game. The Berg collection has bought my "archive" for $19,500. I am very happy about it and it gave a boost to the ego..the papers were assessed at that price but I never thought they would pay it. So I creep on inch by inch..and have much to be grateful for.

Blair . . . made a card index: Like a vast nineteenth-century novel, *Kinds of Love* offers, in the front, a list of "Chief Characters"—"The Living" and "The Dead."

battered and frightened: Reviewing 1972, "the year of the descent into Hell," in a notebook entry on 2 January 1973, Sarton concluded: "A year of extreme pain, but also a year of growth. By no means a lost year."

last heave on your novel: Whatever Howe was working on seems never to have been finished since from this time onward her health worsened.

TO CAROLYN G. HEILBRUN   Feb. 24th, 1973
[Nelson]
Dear Carol,

What a comfort to set down here as though flowers strewn on a grave, something about Elizabeth Bowen for you. As I play the Fauré Requiem..and the light so brilliant outside. Tamas has stopped barking, thank goodness. So many images rush about in my mind...

When I first knew E. she was on the brink of great fame and lived in that wonderful Regent's Park Terrace (a little way down from H.G. Wells on a corner, 5 Clarence Terrace) [London]. John Summerson took me there first... I see white peonies on the mantel and a very large very stiff Regency sofa where E. liked to lie stretched out, and looked small because the sofa was so large. (On purpose?) Sometimes late at night she went and got a bed pillow and lay with her head against that..the image is exact for part of her genius lay in this mixture of formality and formal occasions and complete <u>un</u>selfconsciousness—she had very large hands and wore heavy bracelets. But these large hands were used in strangely incomplete tentative gestures in the air as she talked..and of course half the charm of her talk was the slight stammer (which bothered audiences but in private was extremely charming, at least to me). Also that rippling laugh that accompanied the wit of David Cecil or Isaiah Berlin. Androgynous she certainly was...she carried as a millstone round her neck a woman called Bea whom she had had a love affair with and who always seemed to be <u>looming</u> as a threat, a drain..someone who goes on making demands long after the affair is over. My guess is that Bowen had affairs with women before she had affairs with men, within her marriage. Certainly she was enormously sensitive (as I am) to emotional <u>atmosphere</u>—our brief love—well, later about that.

Like Bloomsbury (of which she was never a part) she was extremely frank about her own love affairs, at least with me. and about other people's. And her genius was to make a complete nobody like me (I was 25 or 26 and had published only one slight book of poems [*Encounter in April,* 1937] when I first knew her) feel understood and cherished. I have sometimes wondered what my value to her could have been, unlicked cur that I was, and I guess it was primarily <u>social</u> at first i.e. I was an "attractive" young female to strew in among the stars at dinner parties, very much like the flowers on the mantel, for purely decorative purposes. But we did, very soon, become friends. She was glad that John S. was falling in love with me...because she didn't like someone else he had been attracted to (not the woman he later married)..

I simply quiver with remorse when I think of all that I accepted then without realizing what managing a life like hers <u>cost</u>. Alan seemed to be at first a figure of fun..but later when I sometimes went off with them on a Saturday for a picnic in the country, and we all lay on the grass and snoozed after lunch, I sensed that his value was a <u>cosy</u>, natural relief from all the glitter and brilliance around her. He and I sometimes went to the zoo alone to look at the great cats..all of which reminded Alan of Elisabeth—panthers, lions, tigers...and it was true that she resembled a large beautiful CAT. His affection for me took the form of making me into a small cat whose ears he liked to caress. Perhaps also he enjoyed talking about Eliz to someone who clearly loved her as he did..and yet was not quite IT for her in some ways. One did not get the sense that he was unhappy (and I doubt if he knew about the love affairs, strangely enough) but rather that he was deeply enamoured and slightly in awe of her talent, at the same time teasing her about practical matter—they carried on a lively flirtation all the time in which his attacks, always about nothing really, were met with rueful admitting that she was at fault..She played the role of the wife to perfection. (But a scene I relate in The Single Hound [1938] came from something she told me..when she was so in love with Sean O'Faolain (sp?) and his cruel letters came, and she and Alan were having breakfast in bed, when she read them, and had to pretend nothing was wrong.

She talked about T.S. Eliot and the frightful strain of his visits at a time when he was clearly attracted to her but <u>never</u> could come to the point...long tense hours...you can imagine! (I am sure he appears in Death of the Heart as the lover of Anna).

I have a sudden insight that in some ways we were at the same place in our lives as women when I first knew her i.e. she was suddenly famous, adored, in full flower as a writer of genius..and this was not at all the case when she and Alan lived in Oxford (he was a civil servant in the dept. of education) and I, who had been immersed very young in enormous responsibility in running my theatre company, was suddenly and for the first time at 25, simply an attractive young woman in love with <u>life</u>. It was a flowering time for each of us, though in different ways.

I really got to know E. the next year (after those first dinner parties) when I rented Conrad Aiken's house in Rye and lived there for some months with an odd crew of women who shared the expenses..some from my theatre and from the Civic, one an intolerable young woman [Elizabeth Johnson] who had just graduated in the first class from Bennington. Elisabeth came down more than once for week-ends with us...I still wonder why she wanted to! Once there was a full moon and we slept together. The next day she went to France...to meet Sean..and that was the end of that. (The letter about this is at the Berg). It was a great shock to me of course. (See Single Hound). But what really bound us together in friendship finally was this: it is a scene related in Mrs. Stevens. I came home severely wounded. I told the story to Edith Kennedy.

[incomplete]

Carolyn G. Heilbrun: Scholar and author (b. 1926), known for biographical studies (*The Garnett Family,* 1961; *Christopher Isherwood,* 1970); best-selling critical works (*Toward a Recogniton of Androgyny,* 1973, and many others to be cited in succeeding notes); and, as Amanda Cross, eleven campus mystery novels (1981 Nero Wolfe Award). Her latest book is *When Men Were the Only Models We Had: My Teachers Barzun, Fadiman, Trilling* (2002). The first academic to take pronounced interest in the work, in November 1970 she sent Sarton an essay on Bloomsbury; see *Solitude,* pp. 63–65. An April 1971 visit (pp. 134–43) solidified a friendship that resulted in Sarton's naming Heilbrun her literary executor.

the Fauré Requiem: The 1887 setting of the mass for the dead by French composer Gabriel Fauré (1845–1924). In a 1988 interview: "[I]t's such tender requiem and it's such a consoling requiem that I've found it very valuable as the losses pile up. And I think I first began to play it when my mother died, which was a long time ago, thirty-five years. It reminds me of her."
Bowen, born 7 June 1899, died 22 February 1973.

Wells . . . Summerson: British man of letters H. G. Wells (1866–1946), famous among much else for his "scientific romances" (*The War of the Worlds,* 1898), collaborated with son George Philip Wells and Julian Huxley on *The Science of Life* (1929) and *The Work, Wealth, and Happiness of Mankind* (1932).
In 1936 John Summerson, already an architectural historian and critic (see 17 June 1992), had the apartment next door to Sarton's in a Taviton Street rooming house. He played his harpsichord while she wrote; they became lovers; he introduced her to Bowen. See *I Knew a Phoenix,* pp. 200–02, 215–17.

Cecil or . . . Berlin: Two Oxford dons: David Cecil (1902–86) wrote elegantly about British literary figures; Isaiah Berlin (1909–97) wrote profoundly about political philosophy, especially liberty versus free will in unfree societies. See *Endgame,* pp. 264–66, and *Encore,* pp. 72–73, for Sarton's observations on Cecil's life and personality.

"Bea" was Beatrice Curtis Brown, sister of literary agent Spencer Curtis Brown, whom Bowen asked in the mid-1950s to serve as her literary executor. In 1975 he edited the miscellany *Pictures and Conversations,* titled after her unfinished autobiography, and including the first chapter of what would have been her eleventh novel, *The Move-In.*

Bloomsbury: No one paragraph can encompass this group of like-minded friends, circa 1910–40, many of whom (such as Virginia Woolf) at one period happened to live in London's shabby-genteel Bloomsbury district. The common reader's best guide is *Bloomsbury* (1968), by Woolf's nephew and biographer, artist and author Quentin Bell. Woolf did visit Bowen's Court once, and Bowen stayed with the Woolfs at Rodmell in 1940 and 1941; see Victoria Glendinning, *Elizabeth Bowen,* pp. 122–26, for more about their friendship.

Alan: The straightforward and convivial Alan Cameron (1894–1952), whom Bowen married in August 1923 and regarded as her bedrock all his life, served with distinction in World War I, then rose in administration at the BBC. His 1935 appointment to the School Broadcasting division took them from Oxford to London. For his teasing of his wife, see Glendinning, *Bowen,* p. 132.

Sean O'Faolain: Irish fiction writer (*Midsummer Night Madness,* 1932, etc.) and political biographer (1900–91). His take on Bowen's work can be examined in *The Vanishing Hero* (1956), "Elizabeth Bowen: Romance Does Not Pay." See pp. 168–72 of *The Single Hound* (1938) for the novel's transposition of the scene Sarton relates.

the lover of Anna: Curious readers may be able to descry Anglo-Catholic poet and critic T. S. Eliot in novelist St. Quentin Miller, Anna Quayne's co-conspirator. It is he who announces—in this classic 1938 novel of innocence betrayed, set largely in Regent's Park— "This evening the pure in heart have simply got us on toast."

Conrad Aiken: Prolific poet, novelist, and critic (1889–1973), who owned Jeakes House in Rye, the Sussex seacoast town where Henry James died. For the "odd crew of women" (which included Margaret English and Kappo Phelan) and Sarton's measured estimate of Bowen, see the *World of Light* profile. *Letters 1916–54* has a contemporary letter, 25 September 1937, about the interconnections between Bowen, Kennedy, O'Faolain, and Sarton.

The scene fictionalized in *Mrs. Stevens* seems to be Hillary's remembrance of Willa MacPherson, pp. 134–46.

[incomplete]: In her 1990 essay collection *Hamlet's Mother and Other Women,* Carolyn Heilbrun devotes a chapter to "May Sarton's Memoirs." Considering the *World of Light* portraits of Koteliansky, Bogan, and Bowen, she finds their most impressive feature "the energy with which these individuals are imbued by Sarton's love for them, and our sense of how she vibrated to the personalities of these three figures, and was made to suffer with and by them as only those who dare love and friendship can suffer. One truth among the many Sarton teaches us is that, lightly as the words love and friendship are tossed about in connection with the merest lusts and acquaintances, love and friendship are rare experiences whose cost is great."

TO THOMAS C. BARNES   Sunday March 11th [1973]
[Nelson]
Dearest Tom,

Last Sunday…how far away and yet how close it seems…we were at Gethsemani among the beautiful round "knob" hills, in your heart's place, and I was so happy and at peace to be with you there. This is the first day since I got back when I could recapture a little of that..so here I am to send love and blessings.

It was wonderful to have an hour alone in your and Jamie's nest..to look at the books, the works of art, to really appreciate the lovely, cool ordered atmosphere you have created..the sumptuous flowers. As I write I have a vivid image of those red tulips in my mind! What a triumph is the compact kitchen! Thank you for inviting me to stay with you, dear heart. It was a wonderful and life giving time for me.

Then I was so happy to be with those adorable Niles'—the whole atmosphere there so alive and real. I really felt at home with them..a very interesting and thought-provoking contrast for me with Carolyn Hammer's which had (for me) a curious deadness, a death-in-life quality. But it takes time to know people and I make no judgement, of course. [Victor] Hammer's drawings are exquisite, the paintings with their high gloss do not appeal to me in the same way, nor the "imitation" icons..every artist takes with him into his own work influences from the past, his "chosen" artists or period, but when the modern work becomes a true work of art it is a synthesis and not an imitation. For me, Hammer fails when he <u>imitates</u> Renaissance painters or earlier painters of icons. Eric Gill (about whom the same might be said) at his best achieves a synthesis. Pure imitation is always vulgar in some strange way..for example <u>imitation</u> Victorian lamps. Well, you can say I have very definite ideas..but they have come from an enormous amount of seeing of paintings in Europe and all over..I do so wish you and Jamie could go to Florence, and to Chartres..and to London..you seemed to brush Europe aside as though you <u>knew</u> a great deal that no one can know who has seen only reproductions or photographs. The very stones of the little streets in small Italian hill towns have been walked on for 1000 years..the sustained human work and breath breathes through it all. Well, you can see that it was all a rich experience for me..I sent Carolyn a copy of A Durable Fire, by the way, and also to the Niles.

Thank you also, dear Tom, for taking me to the Greeks..I loved it there and being with you in one of your haunts. I can see how you have in such a short time already "lived your way" into people's hearts. Really it is awful that I never saw the bank except in its glittering outside. But I simply feel that it will not be an abiding place for you..but only a way of waiting out time and earning a living until the right work comes to you and an angel leads you there, as if by accident. For surely that is how it will happen..not by your will. You will be <u>chosen</u>—

Meanwhile how great that you have helped Jamie find his own course. It was just a joy to see that radiant face. The man exudes happiness..he is so huggable because of it! And I know how much you have done to make this happen for him.

I seem to be in a state of exhaustion again, so this is not a good letter, after all. But at least there is better news of Judy. She has seen her doctor and the family have come to a decision to have the coloured woman who cleans for her (an old family retainer) come three times a week now, wash out her underwear, cook a hot meal etc. This is a huge relief to my mind..I always leave Judy with a dreadful woe inside me. It is witnessing the slow, inexorable disintegration (not her fault) that is so hard.

In case I did not give it to you, my phone number in York will be [ ]. The dear card! I was so glad to see your hand in the mail yesterday.. Dearest love to you both.

Ever your old raccoon,
M

Gethsemani: Thomas Merton's Trappist order, Our Lady of Gethsemani, Kentucky. This American religious and writer (1915–68) garnered much acclaim and criticism during his life, and even more posthumously, for poems, essays, and journals on the monastic calling, especially his autobiography, *The Seven Storey Mountain* (1948). See *After the Stroke,* pp. 207–08, for extracts from his *Thoughts in Solitude* (1968).

Niles' . . . Gill: John Jacob Niles (1892–1980), renowned as a field collector of traditional folksong. Eric Gill (1882–1940) was an English sculptor, engraver, designer of fonts, and writer who led a life of some emotional and erotic complexity, his religious works notwithstanding.

you will be chosen: On 11 May 1973, Sarton again recalled "what [Thomas] Merton told you, that your mission was to work in the world..wherever you are." By 10 June [1979] she could say "you are leading a very creative life, creative in a life giving sense. And it is [a] selfless kind of giving, too, which carries out your Christly vocation in the secular world," even though "Some part of you lies unused."

Some years later Barnes sent her his photograph: "I have had it up on the mantel here since it came," she wrote from York. "There is so much humor and wisdom in this face, and it is so penetrating a look that I feel myself being discovered." In 1987 Barnes was ordained into the priesthood.

glad to see your hand[writing]: Until the end of her life she kept a card Barnes sent her, 7 March 1989, on the bureau in her bedroom, like a memorial card. It said, in part, "You know, May, your poetry, novels and your journals—your endless correspondence, your entire response to the authenticity of your life, your presence to the endless letters that pour into your life are parts of a 'ministry' that is in some ways as authentic a mission as any ordained minister. In fact, there is no question in my own mind that you are as much a priest as I am, and that so often I have been nurtured at the altar of your writing as any communicant kneeling at the communion rail in their place of worship. So much of what I give to others either in the pulpit or in the counseling room has germinated out of something you have said or written about over the past several years, taking root in me."

[May Sarton moved to Wild Knoll on 27 April 1973.]

TO NANCY HALE   June 23, 1973
[York]
Nancy darling,

You can hardly imagine what a lift your letter gave me..the first word I have had on that book from "outside", and I am so grateful that you read it so fast and managed to send Norton a word in the midst of settling in at Howlets. Before I forget, I had the same problem here of a cleaning woman (this is a huge house) and finally found the perfect solution i.e. one of those firms that open cottages and do odd jobs. They bring all equipment, wash floors, vacuum, do a very thorough job (much more so than any cleaning woman I have ever had) and you do not have to have a "social" relationship. I have them every two weeks and it is $25 each time, but that is nearly what I paid Mildred Quigley and she <u>never</u> washed a floor and spent about one hour out of three in conversation over coffee! (I am very fond of her, of course, but this is so much more efficient). This might work well for you.

As usual when I hear from you, how I wish we could talk! I moved five weeks ago and am in Heaven..a gloriously ample lovely house on the most miraculous site, combining as it does all the charm of wild woods and woodsy paths at the back and a great open view to the sea at the front..a very gentle view because I look down a long green field, then ocean..no rocks in sight, though they are there below out of sight. When there is a storm the surf showers up over the green. Tamas can go free all day and he and the cat and I have two walks a day, one to the ocean and one to the woods. I have not yet started any real work (thank God with two books out this year I can wait a while) and that sometimes worries me, but it has been a big transition..so..let us hope I'll have an idea eventually.

Distance from Marynia Farnham and that long ordeal has lifted some of the blackness—I have not had one single moment of nostalgia for Nelson or regret, just relief to be <u>away</u> at last. I feel the tranquilizing effect of the sea already.

And this brings me to your glorious word about the novel. Of course Caro is I and it was written out of all that agony..transposed. But I was made to feel a pariah..I was made to feel "dirty"..I was cast out, as it were, and isolated. I feared madness etc. So it was all given me, I suppose. (I mean in the good sense of a gift of understanding through pain. Is there no other way?) I loved using the first person for the first time in a novel.

I can't resist sending you Journal of a Solitude..it has come out to a dull press and good letters, as usual. This is <u>not</u> for a professional word, dear person and good friend, but to read for pleasure at leisure—and feel no need to write about it at <u>all</u> while you immersed yourself in the final push on Cassatt. That is a book I look forward to with keen anticipation..and it should have a special <u>value</u> now, at this time when women are thinking so much about the artist in themselves and how to find fulfillment in a new way. (Curiously enough I am getting many letters from young women about the Journal and all say the same thing, "I met there an old friend who turned out to be myself.")

It is foggy and very humid here today. I am sitting in my study on the third floor and look out into ghostly trees, the ocean is there only as a <u>sound</u>.

Judy is now permanently in a nursing home. You can imagine my woe about it after reading the novel! But after 6 weeks there (and two here with me) she begins to feel at home and said to me this week when I ran down to see her..it's in Concord, Mass.. "I could not be in a better place." She has a room of her own and bath of her own, that is the great thing. I have her very old pussy here..she lives upstairs in my study and also has a private bathroom!

So that's the news..you simply must come here..for sheer beauty of place it would be hard to match (except for Folly Cove and some parts of Cornwall)..it is two hours from Peterborough in case you are going to MacDowell and could stop off...

Much love, dear heart..what a blessing you have given me!!

Your old May

Nancy Hale: See 10 August 1969. Howlets was the Hales' home in Folly Cove, Rockport, Massachusetts.

I'll have an idea eventually: In time, these strolls would spark the idea of Sarton's second book for children, *A Walk Through the Woods* (Harper & Row, 1976) with Tamas and Bramble, illustrated by Kazue Mizumura.

your glorious word: Hale had written about *As We Are Now:* "There is so much of insight, intuition, understanding, suffering, and wisdom in it . . . your best novel, if only because of the eerie, paradoxical objectivity it has."

Unlike *Kinds of Love, Reader's Digest* did not take it for their condensed books, writing to Eric Swenson, "It is one of the most wonderful novels we have ever read…but too grim," Sarton had reported to Thomas Barnes, 11 May 1973. " '[T]oo close to the bone' said one of the magazines..so I fear it will not sell. I mind because I have a message in this book…"

"This novel is my J'Accuse," Sarton stated in press releases for the book, against maltreatment of the elderly in substandard unmonitored "homes." She was referring to the 1898 denunciation by French novelist Émile Zola (1840–1902) in defense of army officer Alfred Dreyfus (1859–1935), imprisoned for treason on false charges motivated by anti-Semitism, later pardoned, then cleared. For readers not yet familiar with *As We Are Now,* the opening paragraph characterizes this "short blow of a book" like a slap:

"I am not mad, only old. I make this statement to give me courage. To give you an idea what I mean by courage, suffice it to say that it has taken two weeks for me to obtain this notebook and a pen. I am in a concentration camp for the old, a place where people dump their parents and relatives exactly as though it were an ash can."

a dull press: The trade publication *Publishers Weekly* (19 February 1973) had called *Solitude* "honest to the point of bluntness," likening Sarton to a New England Colette. Heartier reviews came somewhat later. *Choice* (10 September) said "the person revealed is closer to Hilary Stevens" and would "come as a surprise to those readers who romanticized her and failed to note the signs of fire." In *America* (1 September 1973), Margaret Ferrari promised that "It offers convincing and intimate contact with a middle-aged woman's 'dark night of the soul.'"

Sarton dedicated the book to Eric Swenson.

Cassatt: Hale's *Mary Cassatt: A Biography of the Great American Painter* (1844–1925) would appear in 1975.

TO NANCY HALE   July 4th [1973]
[York]

Dearest Nancy, I was about to answer your first note about the Journal when the second came! The two have given me to think..one thing, are you aware that the Journal though only just <u>out</u> was written in 1970–71? I revised it of course..a journal written for publication is a work of art of a rather special kind, (the novel was ever so much easier to write by the way), and in this instance I was deliberately trying to scotch a false image of me which comes to me through letters. I wanted to make clear that, whatever the calm of art, the person struggling to create it is very imperfect and vulnerable and has not "arrived" in an inward sense. The risk was that a book designed to give aid and comfort to my friends might easily give aid and comfort to my enemies.

The journal would have been better had I been able (as I did in the original version) to keep in the fact that I entered therapy with Farnham the day after I began it, or two days later, after the reading at the Unitarian Church. (All the part about "letting go" happened through therapy.) I had to cut all that because at the time of publication she was threatening me and had become senile. X also demanded cuts. The miracle is that any-thing survived at all! Perhaps one can only tell the truth in fiction and that is what you really are saying. .but I now get a lot of letters from people who say it is as though they were talking to themselves. The fact is that very few people ever can be honest <u>at all</u> with themselves..this is what is so awful now with Watergate as a public example.

I am always glad to hear what <u>you</u> really think by the way..bad or good, praise or "criticism"..it is always valuable because I know you are <u>inside</u> the work. The "criticism" that causes my rage and despair is stupid public criticism in newspapers..there is nothing whatever to be learnt, for instance, from Karl Shapiro reviewing my selected poems with the words "May Sarton is a bad poet". It was in the Sunday Times and it simply was an awful blow that had to be recovered from as a blow. A piece of very bad luck. The same with the Sun Times review of <u>Kinds of Love</u>. Carol Heilbrun who is my literary guru (and will do a critical biography eventually) teases me and points out that you get good reviews if you butter up the right people and that I have never done that and am "loveable" in consequence but must accept that if you don't play the rotten game, you can't win. I did not believe this at first but it is at least partly true. And not for wholly wicked reasons i.e. if you give me a rave review of a book I am just naturally and humanly going to read your next work with a sympathetic eye! (I have always refused to review in my own fields.)

What you said about anger interested me enormously. After all the

Farnham horror I tried to analyse myself in some imaginary interviews with an imaginary psychiatrist..this is not for publication, but for my own understanding. I think I came to the right conclusion that it is the infantile response that makes the anger, "I want whatever it is <u>now</u> and if you don't give it to me I'm going to fling myself in a mud puddle in my white fur coat" as I did when I was two because I wanted goldfish I saw in a window and were refused them. The intensity of the wish for love (which is there later as you surmised) and the fury when it seems to be denied, etc.

I have read Francis Wickes, but I did not like the book which was written in her old age and much revised by Muriel Rukeyser..<u>she</u> was a great person and a great therapist, though, and if you knew her as such you probably could read the book in a rather special way. But I do believe that one changes one's life through writing..the writing, the work of art is always a little <u>ahead</u> of where one is or can be as a person, it seems to me. It is a vision of the possible.

Anyway, darling, I glow with your praise (very nice that about Conrad) of the novel..it was wrenched out of so much pain. I am proud of myself in a good way..and perhaps all the Hell produced some very real <u>growth</u>, so it is partly better than the journal because two years of great stress and growth intervened.

Forgive this long letter..but it's really just to say thank you and for making me think over all this. Damn it, I wish we could talk.

I am now in an orgy of ordering plants for this garden, tree peonies among others. The best thing is that I have a real gardener here, a perfect angel, a whimsical, knowledgeable troll of a man [Raymond Philbrook] who loves chocolate cake (so I am learning to bake cakes for the first time in my life).

Much much love..and so many wishes for the happy and exhilarating end of the Cassatt book.

Your old
May

Watergate: During the 1972 presidential campaign, five burglars were arrested in the Democratic party headquarters at the Watergate Hotel in Washington, D.C. By early 1973 they had been linked to the Nixon White House; the ensuing scandal exposed the Republican administration's illegal attempts to undermine its opponents, amid general deception and corruption.

my literary guru: It was in the introduction to *Writing a Woman's Life* (W. W. Norton, 1988) that Heilbrun was able to look back and claim that "the publication of *Journal of a Solitude* in 1973 may be acknowledged as the watershed in women's autobiography."

the Farnham horror: Sarton later overcame it sufficiently to visit Marynia Farnham at her

Brattleboro, Vermont, nursing home twice a year, though her former analyst did not always recognize her or respond. See *House by the Sea,* pp. 121–22 and 171, for their 1975 encounters.

imaginary interviews: "The Imaginary Psychiatrist: A Journal" is a twenty-page typed manuscript Sarton later dated "Sometime in 1972—in Nelson." She means to speak as if in a series of hour sessions with a psychiatrist "neither man nor woman, a disembodied soul." Her overriding concern is anger, "a problem I have struggled with since I was born," "the wicked and destructive side of the animus that is also (in its positive side) the creator."

She narrates "three recent examples" of explosive fury—against a loved one; against a good if not a dearest friend; and against one of her closest intimates. The links among anger, grief, guilt, and immaturity are explored with scathing self-honesty; the perils of self-right-eousness are exposed as perhaps the most dangerous failing of all. She finds that, in her case, all these shortcomings can only be "transcended through poetry." Yet even there lurks a risk, the work's being exploited as an excuse for inexcusable behavior, which "A healthy ego would not need to justify itself." Her anguish erupts from the clash between perceiving what she should do and finding herself unable to do it.

Sarton had intended this self-interrogation to consider the whole "Farnham horror," but she never went on.

white fur coat" . . . goldfish: For the childhood tantrum about the coat and the puddle, and more on anger in general, see *Solitude,* pp. 27–29. Later young May did have a goldfish, kept in the living room where George Sarton worked at his desk, but his concentration was so disturbed by the fish's almost inaudible noises that she had to move it elsewhere.

Francis Wickes: 1875-1967, analyst and disciple of Jung; her works include *The Inner World of Man* and *The Inner World of Children.* For her, Rukeyser wrote "Voices of Waking for the Eightieth Birthday of Frances G. Wickes," in *Body of Waking* (1958). Sarton asked Wickes, 13 December 1963, for a referral to a therapist suitable for her old friend Barbara Runkle Hawthorne; see 12 March 1979.

that about Conrad: Hale told the anecdote where writer Joseph Conrad (British, b. Poland, 1857–1924), reading the paper at breakfast, fulminated against a review of his new book. When his wife asked, "Darling, couldn't you just perhaps <u>learn</u> something from the criticism?" Conrad shot back, "I don't want criticism, I want praise."

TO ILSE VOGEL   [October 12, 1973]
[York]
Dear Ilse,

I know you want the best for me..and so you try to <u>pretend</u> that "the Times "loves you". At one time I did some reviewing for them, but <u>only</u> of books not in my field. I have always refused to review poetry or novels. It is a matter of principle with me because I know what a racket it is, and how dangerous that kind of power is if one wants to keep oneself pure. George Woods is a sweet creature and I loved reviewing children's books as I did for a short time for him. After the review of Kinds of Love I with-drew. This was a major work and they (not he but the editor of adult book reviews) treated it badly. I felt the only thing I could do was <u>vanish.</u> The Times loves me? Since Faithful Are the Wounds they have consistently kicked down my work, sometimes brutally as the Selected Poems ("May Sarton is a bad poet") sometimes with contempt (As We Are Now). They never reviewed the Journal. They have not reviewed any book of poems since the Selected. They never reviewed "Mrs. Stevens" etc. To say that the Times "loves me" is therefore not a kindness. It simply rubs salt into the wounds. I am a realist and I know exactly where I stand. They reviewed Plant Dreaming Deep kindly and that, for nineteen years is the only kindness I have had from them. It is ages since the daily Times has reviewed me, by the way. The last was Shower of Summer Days.

If someone beat one physically over a period of 20 years and a friend insisted "but they really love you," one would react either with anger or with deep depression. I am sorry but telling nice lies to be helpful is not helpful. It is to break down the small wall of personal dignity one has managed to build against despair. "The dark is light enough" and better than artificial light. I have lived with it and done my work. The whole thing has been a long bitter struggle.

Now what is happening is on an entirely different level. i.e. I am being "publicized" on TV as a personality. I am finding a way, I suppose, to get through directly to people without the reviewers and/or the critics. It is fine and I am pleased about it. Ten minutes on the [NBC] Today show may seem short to you, but it has taken me forty years to make it and to me it seems quite grand. They rarely give a poet a chance.

What means a great deal to me is your faith in me and your support and I'll never forget that dear package of books you sent to put under the tree…and then we met..and all the wonderful words of support. That is what means something, more than I can say. But do not, please, tell me to make me "happy," that the Times loves me. It is not meant as a cruelty, but it is cruel, and that is that.

I have been away so much I have not yet packed the Collected Poems [1930–1973] for you, but they are here and I hope to do it tomorrow so this can go with it.

I think I'll be off the roller coaster at the end of May..Judy comes for a week the 14th—before that, a time at Lawrence Academy in Groton [Massachusetts], a book-signing etc.

Love from May the dangerous raccoon—
P.S. What news of Ilse's book? Eric Swenson's daughter read Punch [*Punch's Secret,* 1974] to him and she loved it—

Ilse Vogel: On 11 October 1973, Vogel attended a party at Harper & Row's new quarters, where George Woods, a *New York Times Book Review* editor, mentioned that "I" or "we love May Sarton." Vogel phoned Sarton the next morning and repeated what she had been told.

reviewing children's books: Sarton occasionally wrote for the *Times* over the years; here she refers to omnibus surveys of ten children's classics (5 May 1968) and of "Poetry for Children" (29 September 1968).

Kinds of Love: See note to 24 December 1970.

Faithful Are the Wounds: See note to 10 March 1955, to Evelyn Pember.

Selected Poems: (Cloud, Stone, Sun, Vine); see note to 25 December 1961. Sarton's last published reference, in the journals, to Karl Shapiro's review appears in *At Eighty-two,* p. 84, 15 October 1993.

The following *New York Times Book Review* assessments are identified by date and author.

As We Are Now: 4 November 1973, Ellen Douglas. Sarton "is an honest writer. She has created a convincing record of evil done and good intentions gone astray." Douglas faults the overuse of "intensive adverbs like 'rather,' 'certainly,' 'very,' and 'awful,' " which weaken the effect, but finds nonetheless that "the novel is a powerful indictment."

Journal [of a Solitude]: 13 May 1973, Phyllis Meras. "Sarton is more a poet-philosopher than a naturalist, and her references to flowers and seasons are backdrops and atmosphere for the agony of fading love" and other strong feelings. "Sometimes her attempt to exorcise troubled emotions seems mannered and excessive."

[no] *poems since the Selected: A Private Mythology.* 13 November 1966, Joseph Bennett. "Sarton's poems about India are remarkable for their savage brilliance. She was offended by India, and unprepared; her response has the power of resentment and struggle. The poems about Japan and Greece are . . . [like] notes thought out in advance."

"Mrs. Stevens": 24 October 1965, Ray Corsini. "Sarton has handled the theme, the mystery of the creative impulse, well. . . . The music of Miss Sarton's prose leaves compelling echoes in one's mind." See also 25 October 1965 and note.

Plant Dreaming Deep: 4 February 1968, Brooks Atkinson. "In this sensitive, luminous book Sarton writes of her house that reflects her tastes and style—immaculate and orderly, traditional, basically austere with overtones of grace and charm. There is pain in her book . . . that as a writer she is not recognized and that literary critics stand between her and her public. But there are also joys. . . . Love is the genius of this small but tender and often poignant book by a woman of many insights."

the daily Times: Sarton draws a distinction between notices in the daily edition and those featured in the weekly *Book Review.* At that time the *Review* was but another Sunday supplement; only several years later was it made available by separate subscription. The Sunday *New York Times* was air-freighted to major cities across the country for weekend sales and thus seen by a great many more readers than the weekday reviews; but Sarton's tone suggests they held more cachet for her, signifying that a new book was a "newsworthy" event.

On 23 August 1970 another supplement, *The New York Times Magazine,* featured a photographic essay by Lisa Hammel, "There . . . Stood the House," about the place in Nelson, captioned with extracts from *Plant Dreaming Deep.*

[A] *Shower of Summer Days:* 26 October 1952, John Nerber. The reviewer ranked the book among the best of her notable novels, convinced it solidified "Sarton's unmistakable authority. Violet is never reduced to the novelist's mercy—she is so complete. It is a first-rate literary creation."

But despite the positive reactions of many *Book Review* notices, Sarton's memory was colored by those less sympathetic.

Ilse's book: In 1974 Golden Press published Vogel's *Daisy Dog's Wake-Up Book.* In *Endgame,* p. 184, Sarton underscores that her old friend "Ilse is a person with a genius for friendship." Vogel's 1992 memoir *Bad Times, Good Friends* recounts how, in Berlin 1943–45, she and a network of friends hid fugitives from Hitler before she herself escaped.

TO ANGÈLE OOSTERLINCK-BAELE   24 October [1973]
[York]   [In French]

Dear Angèle,

Yesterday your letter of the 14th arrived with its sad news..sad in one way, but perhaps not altogether <u>too</u> sad..that poor Cécile is finally at peace. I was touched to hear that she was wearing the nightgown I had given her on her final voyage. Most of all I am consoled by the thought that your long and costly self-sacrifice has ended at last. How good and compassionate you have been..undertaking the difficult daily task of caring for this poor invalid! God bless you.

The photo touched me deeply..Cécile's expression, hinting at a smile, brings her vividly back to me the way she looked when I was a child. Many thanks.

My handwriting's bad today, because three days ago I fell and bruised three ribs..it has made me ache day and night, and stooping to put the cat's and dog's dishes on the ground is torture. It's nothing serious, but I was already quite exhausted, and now I feel broken in pieces..just imagine, since moving in I have had a guest every three days, more or less, for five months! All my friends have come to see the new house, which is big and handsome with a large terrace in front..then a long lawn..then the sea. After a very hot and humid summer, the fall has been marvellous..the blue sea crashes before me.

My latest book is doing well..it deals with a poor old woman in a nursing home.

A big hug for you, dear Angèle. Please convey my sympathy about this passing to all the family, and accept my deeply-moved gratitude for all that you have done for our Cécile..

Always your

May

———

Angèle Oosterlinck-Baele: Daughter-in-law of Cécile Oosterlinck, little May's nanny in Wondelgem, before World War I.

final voyage: "Soon we must set sail / On the last mysterious voyage / Everybody takes / Toward death. / Without my ship there, / Wish me well." From the title poem of *Coming into Eighty* (1994).

the photo touched me: See *Among the Usual Days,* p. 33, for this cheerful 1967 snapshot, and a winter 1912 picture of "the way she looked when I was a child," with infant May on her knee.

All my friends: Early visitors to Wild Knoll included Judith Matlack, Ilse and Howard Vogel-Knotts, Eric P. Swenson, Carolyn G. Heilbrun, Mildred and Tami Quigley, Eleanor Blair, Camille Mayran, Vincent Hepp, Mary Tozer, Lee Blair, and Elizabeth Voelker.

my latest book: As We Are Now had been published on 23 September 1973.

TO ISOBEL STRICKLAND   Jan. 13th, 1974
[York]
Dear Isobel,

It's four below zero here to day, after three snow storms in a row and I look out across an ermine field to a shining dark blue sea..glorious! The house is fairly warm, especially up here in my study on the third floor, but it costs a fortune to heat! So far we have been lucky as December was unusually warm, but I expect we are in for real winter now. I am told the sea tempers the cold so I imagine it will not get much colder than this ever. (In Nelson it went to 20 below more than once.)

The calendar is simply beautiful..I have never seen one with more charming photos and it's such a treat to have 24 instead of 12! And I plunged into the magazine with joy and am taking it down to Judy tomorrow when I hope I can get to see her..the weather made it impossible last week. We had a lovely Xmas week together here..a huge tree in the big library, and even stockings to hang on the mantel that some kind friend sent, all filled. Judy seemed better rather than worse..perhaps because I had bad flu while she was here, so she made an extra effort to help me, and even made my bed (her own idea) every morning. I had flu for six weeks. .an awfully long pull..but am now at last really well and back at work. That is the good news and a good way to start the year.

I worry an awful lot about all of you..England is going through a terrible time. I have no confidence in Heath (maybe you disagree?) who seems rigid and punitive, when the reverse is surely needed. But at least I suppose he is honest which cannot be said for our dreary and dangerous Nixon. He has created a climate where no one believes anything he says and many people (I am not one of them) think the oil crisis was simply made up by Big Oil to cash in huge profits. They are certainly profiteers and should be curbed, but there is no doubt that we have all squandered power (and the U.S. more than anyone) and must pay for extravagance now. It is very good for Americans to learn to be less wasteful..and already the low speed limit of 50 even on thruways, has brought the accident rate down!

I feel very happy and settled here now..and relieved that I have begun to work seriously since the New Year.

                                        With love and thanks from
                                        May

Isobel Strickland: English cousin, and daughter of Richard and May "April" Dorling Pipe; see 2 May 1965.

Heath: Named prime minister in 1970, Edward Heath (b. 1916) tried to tame high inflation by wage limits, which turned unions against him; a fiasco with the miners' union

(November 1973–February 1974) forced the country into a three-day workweek. Britons did not have to endure his tenure much longer: the next year he ceded Conservative party control to Margaret Thatcher. Still politically active, in fall 2000 he oversaw the election of the new speaker of the House of Commons.

the oil crisis: Tightening of production by OPEC led to stringent curtailment of America's petroleum usage; conservation measures included reduced public lighting and turning down thermostats in government buildings. For the first time in U.S. history, gasoline passed $1 a gallon, about $3.65 in 1998 dollars.

TO DOROTHY HEALY   May 5th, 1974
[York]
Dear Dorothy Healy,

(Or is it Healey? I wasn't quite sure of the signature) How dear of you to write me such a marvelous letter about the brief TODAY show thing, and to do so under the shadow of such terrible pain and loss. Tom's suicide came to me with the still poignant memory of Ernesta Greene, who at exactly Tom's age did the same thing and also destroyed all her letters and papers. This was thirty or more years ago and was my first intimate knowledge of a suicide. The waste seems unbearable and all is mystery. You are rare and marvelous to be able to respond so warmly to my poems under these circumstances…but of course the only possible thing to do is what your are doing, making a learning <u>haven</u> for others like Tom, bless you.

You must forgive a brief word. I am snowed under and on a roller coaster of public appearances till the end of the month. I'll be on Book Beat May 12th by the way, a full half-hour interview for which I went to Chicago weeks ago.

With every warmest wish and more than I can possibly put into words of sympathy.

Yours
<u>May Sarton</u>

––––––––––

Dorothy Healy: 1914-90. Curator of the Maine Women Writers Collection at what was then called Westbrook College, Portland, Maine (now University of New England, Westbrook Campus). On 13 March 1974 Sarton reminded her that Louise "Bogan was born in Maine—and surely should be on your list," since "she was such a wonderful lyric poet." Sarton gave a benefit reading for the Collection in May 1982.

Ernesta Greene: One of the four Greene daughters; see note to 10 March 1955, to Evelyn Pember.

The Healy's youngest child, Tom, had been working on his painting and writing in San Francisco. He "was an extremely sensitive, creative young man, the intellectual among our children. He loved books, being a profound and discriminating reader, music, art, philosophy, history," Healy wrote Sarton, 2 May 1974. But having destroyed "every personal thing in his possession," at twenty-six Tom committed suicide on 19 March 1974, after "trying to find his way in this world which was so alien to him."

"My heart aches and I know now that the grief will always be there," but "I am writing you all this because you are a poet." Healy wanted Sarton to know how much "What the Old Man Said" had touched her, wishing "too that Tom 'did not despair' but the young are so vulnerable."

Book Beat: To promote *Collected Poems 1930–1973* (1973), Sarton was interviewed by author and journalist Robert Allen Cromie, host of NET's *Bookbeat* since 1964.

TO ELIZABETH GRAY VINING   July 21, [1974]
[York]

Dear Elizabeth,

I loved the Whittier! I hate to have it read as it gave me many happy thoughtful hours in the companionship of that dearest of men. You have brought him so vividly to life, have made one see how much he has to tell us <u>now.</u> Here is a hero for the times. The gentle passionate believer. I wrote your publicity person at once..and no doubt you will see what I said. Hope it helps.

It is moving to consider how much sisters meant both to Wordsworth and Whittier, isn't it?

My only criticism would be that here and there brief descriptions of women overused the words "gay" and "sweet" ..I feel your copy editor should have caught that ahead of time.

I grapple every day (between very hard work now to finish the novel [*Crucial Conversations*] by next week when J. and I go to the island) [Greenings] with the philosophical question as to <u>why</u> the American people are not more outraged by Nixon's devious and dishonest ways. No one seems to care very much about the Constitution and the dirty strategy of accusing everyone else of being partisan is having its effect. A strange very troubling time in our history surely.

Well, thanks for saving me for hours from these black thoughts!

Love and blessings
M

―――――――――

Elizabeth Gray Vining: Writer and Quaker (1902–99). In 1952 she published *Windows for the Crown Prince,* of Japan, whom she served as tutor, 1946–50; also well-known for children's books written as Elizabeth Janet Gray. Sarton had reviewed her autobiography, *Quiet Pilgrimage,* in the 22 November 1970 *New York Times Book Review;* here she thanks her for the juvenile biography *Mr. Whittier.*

American poet and abolitionist John Greenleaf Whittier (1807–92), born of Quaker stock, was as popular as Longfellow; he is now remembered for his country idyll *Snow-Bound* (1866) and ballads: "Of all sad words of tongue or pen / The saddest are, 'It might have been.'" Vining also wrote *The Taken Girl* (1972), about a boardinghouse servant who falls in love with the poet.

how much sisters meant: Dorothy Wordsworth (1771–1855) had an intensely vivid eye for nature and the poor; her journals often inspired her brother and spiritual soul mate William. For a period Whittier lived with his mother (d. 1857) and beloved younger sister (d. 1864).

Nixon's . . . dishonest ways: "It is very sinister to see all these nice-looking 'clean-cut' men in their thirties admitting to the vilest misuse of public power without apparently much guilt. They confess now to save their skins," Sarton wrote Archibald MacLeish, 30 June [1974]. "As for Nixon. . . what frightens me is that I do not believe for a moment that he feels <u>any</u> guilt at all. He is a true 'manipulator' who is able to be dishonest with his <u>own</u> soul as with anyone else's. That <u>scares</u>, doesn't it?"

Between 27 and 30 July 1974 the House of Representative passed three bills of impeachment against Nixon; on 9 August he became the first president to resign the office.

TO ANN MCLAUGHLIN   July 30th [1974]
[Greenings Island]
Dear Ann,

I am grateful that you let me see Carol Houck's letter..I thought it very sensitive and helpful, about the best such letter I have ever read in fact; it's too bad that Norton came that close to a contract, but maybe HM will see the light. Meanwhile how brave of you to go in for a doctorate at American …it sounds like a good not too rigid program, and based on the splendid "Lear" essay you wrote, I feel sure you will do distinguished work.

Kot did talk a lot about KM..and I have always felt that her letters to him showed what a good influence on her he was..alas, horrible J.M. Murry to whom Kot lent her letters after her death for the Selected Letters Murry published, <u>destroyed</u> quite a few, presumably those adverse to him. Kot always hated him and this was he felt quite in character. Have you read LM's book? This is the most illuminating one written on Mansfield, the most understanding perhaps. Kot always said LM was a great selfless person..who never defended herself against Murry's meanness of spirit, and only wrote this book when she was very old. Do get hold of it..published in London a year or more ago. If you can't I'll lend it to you.

I'm a total wreck at the moment, having arrived here with awful poison ivy on arms <u>and</u> with my back "fallen out" or whatever that pain at the small of the back means. Can't stoop or turn over..I'm with dear Judy here, who is losing her mind and the scene last night with me on my bed unable to move and she unable to find her nightgown or toothbrush..all this by candlelight..was quite funny had it not been so sad.

I guess I am exhausted after finishing a new novel last week..I get into awful panics because I cannot be ill as there is no one to take care of me. It's a strange feeling. But luckily I am a monster of good health on the whole.

Forgive this small word..you are such a great person, dear Ann..I treasure your friendship and Charlie's.

Dear love to you both.

M

Yes. I'm <u>very</u> happy by the sea—a dream really—
P.S. I was on the Today Show May 2 for the Collected Poems. Great fun!

———

Ann McLaughlin: Born 1928, McLaughlin did earn her Ph.D. from American University in Washington, D.C. At this time her husband Charlie was editor-in-chief of the Frederick Law Olmsted Papers at the Library of Congress. Sarton wrote "Epithalamium" for their wedding, 14 July 1952 (see *At Eighty-Two,* pp. 40–41); when both spouses contracted polio in 1955, Sarton read poetry in the hospital's respirator ward. Charlie's mother Eleanor married Kenneth Murdock; see note to 7 May 1962.

Carol Houck (later Carol Houck Smith) was an editor at Norton who returned the manuscript of one of McLaughlin's books; it was not Houghton Mifflin ("HM") but John Daniel and Company, Santa Barbara, California, who published *Lightning in July* (1989) and several novels since.

KM: New Zealand-born author Katherine Mansfield (1888–1923) wrote intensely perceived, keenly worded short stories of striking modernity. After she died young of tuberculosis, her husband, British critic John Middleton Murry (1889–1956), fostered a doctored version of her achievement and character through his editions of her literary remains, now being re-edited. S. S. Koteliansky was an intimate friend of the couple.

LM was "Lesley Moore," real name Ida Baker; the sometimes stormy relationship between her and Mansfield began in childhood. *Katherine Mansfield: The Memories of LM* appeared in 1971, when Moore was 83 (Sarton says, *Solitude,* pp. 178–80). The standard biography portraying all these figures in depth is *The Life of Katherine Mansfield* by Anthony Alpers (1980).

[*The House by the Sea* begins 13 November 1974.]

TO EVELYN AMES   Feb. 24th, 1975
[York]
Evie darling,

What an event your marvelous letter of the 16th was, written that day of Julian [Huxley]'s obit in the Times. I had seen his face on the screen the night before and knew of course why, at once. Such things are a shock even when one has hoped and prayed for the person's release from physical and mental disintegration…it's much harder to imagine anything after death in such cases, and I have been thinking a lot about <u>that</u>, of course. But it could be, couldn't it? that the soul, freed of that decaying animal, soars away..that it has been stifled and swaddled in the last years. One thing the biography of Aldous did for me (Sybille Bedford) was to move me extremely at the way in which Aldous helped Maria to die, during the last hours (of course he had refused to admit she was ill for a year before and dragged her about Europe), and in which then A's second wife did the same thing for him. "Let go..let go.." he said to Maria as he sat beside her...and one senses that he, the supreme rationalist, really did think that death was a hard passage through into something not just dust and ashes.

I had an amazing letter from Francis Huxley to whom I wrote my dismay about the atmosphere at tea in October..he really said it was "war to the death" between them, a frightful situation. I suppose extreme dependence does cause hostility on both sides. Thank God, it is over. But I'm afraid it's too late in Juliette's life for her to remake it. She does not communicate with me so I expect no answers to my cable and letter, but if you do hear anything, please let me know..in some ways I hope she will leave that house, shadowed by the hospital now, and a lot to carry without help. The garden will be the hard thing to leave.

Oh darling, so many deaths! Céline...my mother's oldest friend and the only person who remembers my English grandfather [Gervase Elwes] (he died when mother was 19), also died..she was 93..time to go, but I felt my childhood had just fallen into the sea forever.

Then dear Helen! Again the shock of reading that in the paper..we had a lovely time together last summer when she took me over to Eleanor Belmont's to read poems..Helen was having an awful time try-ing to write about Mark, whether to make it autobiog, how to use the letters and so on. I think she made herself ill over it..she had a break-down during writing her best book, The Gentle Americans, as you remember no doubt. In a way, you know, I understand wanting that for-mal funeral..I felt bitterly that the day of my father's funeral at Appleton Chapel, there was a really immobilizing blizzard and many people on their way from New Haven and even Chicago and N.Y. never arrived..and I felt so sad. I wanted it to be a real festival in his name..a gathering to honor the triumph of the life, not so much the death. Perhaps Helen felt that. It is good that you were able to be there. (I mean, for her sake) But one does want to weep—and the atmosphere must have been very cold indeed not to.

I too think about death a lot, of course. I get a little frightened of falling and not being found..I mean, for days. Poor Tamas and the cat! There has been a rather awful change in one's view of life..I mean, even that the work might go on and still be useful. Now there is the very real possibility that man himself may be on the way out. So we live among dying illusions.

Then why so happy, one might ask? I am so glad, Evie, we feel the same way, released, fulfilled, not deprived by coming old age. That is how it should be..and of course we have been lucky to stay well enough. With me it is that I am letting go gently of compulsiveness and I quite often now just don't <u>push</u> when I begin to feel tired. I used nearly always to go a little beyond that point...

Nature is more and more beautiful and comforting. I just do not know what I would do without Tamas, and Bramble, and the constant stir of wings at the bird feeder, and the daily excitement of watching the sea in all its moods...I really feel I am in Heaven.

Lindisfarne? I want to know more, never heard of it but how does one?

I'm glad you are writing poems..one must at every stage..I am not at the moment, but I think after this book of portraits I may take 6 months off and just meander about and write poems, if they will show themselves...I did make a start at one about "The Gentle Revolution" which must be on the way if we are to survive.

I'm really dazzled at how much is happening through womens' lib, not so much all the blare (Ms. I don't like really) but the deep digging into what woman really is..and here we begin to realize that even Jung spoke from a masculine prejudice. There is a book called Women and Psycho-Analysis which contains a rather interesting chapter analyzing Jung from a feminist point of view. What I see all around me is how marriage is changing for the better. .how much young men enjoy what used to be called women's work and is now seen as <u>human</u> work (such as changing a baby's diapers).

Well, it's time I stopped and went for the mail through a driving rain..I rather like it, and Tamas loves it.

I wish I were coming to New York! Long to see your beautiful face and talk at last..but we will, somehow..

Meanwhile all blessings and love
M

Julian [Huxley]*'s obit:* For more about his life, see the letter of 22 June 1958 and its notes.

the biography of Aldous: Sarton had been reading the two-volume 1974 British edition of *Aldous Huxley: A Biography,* by Sybille Bedford. Huxley's wife, Maria Nys, died in 1955; he married psychotherapist and author Laura Archera the next year; he died in 1963. See *House by the Sea,* pp. 46–48 and 55–57, for Sarton's commentary.

the atmosphere at tea: Francis and Anthony were the two sons of Aldous's brother Julian and his wife, Juliette. In *House,* p. 48, Sarton described this October 1974 visit as marred by a "sad and confined, ungenerous and bitter" air.

Céline: Some profiles of longtime associates were held back from *I Knew a Phoenix* (see note to 10 September [1958]) for a later volume, proposed in July 1963. Only now did Sarton revive what became *A World of Light: Portraits and Celebrations* (1976), one of which memorializes "Céline Dangotte Limbosch." For more about her, see note to 18 June 1957, and *House by the Sea,* pp. 70–72, 95.

Helen: Helen Howe's testament to her father Mark A. de Wolfe Howe was never completed. "I have never known a more conflicted writer," Sarton regretted, in *House by the Sea,* pp. 62–63. There she describes the 1974 reading she gave at the home of Eleanor Belmont; for her, see 15 December 1975.

Lindisfarne or "Holy Land" is off the coast of northeast England. In 635 a monastery and church marked the arrival of Celtic Christianity in Britain; religious retreats are still held there. The Lindisfarne Gospels, dating before 700, is an illuminated Latin manuscript now in the British Museum, a masterpiece of Celtic art.

"The Gentle Revolution": Intriguingly, what began as a poem metamorphosed into a commencement address delivered at Clark University, Worcester, Massachusetts, 11 May 1975. (See *Encore,* pp. 315–16, for the sudden bout of laryngitis that heightened the reception of Sarton's speech.) "New Year Poem," first published in *The Silence Now* (1988), turns the concept back into poetry.

Ms. [Magazine]: The periodical, and Sarton's opinion of it, changed with the years; for its 1982 interview with her, see note to 13 July 1984. In the 1990s *Ms.* took note of the three last journals as they appeared.

analyzing Jung: Women and Analysis: Dialogues on Psychoanalytic Views of Femininity, ed. Jean Strouse (1974, reissued 1985), presented "ten key essays about women by major figures in psychoanalysis, with specially commissioned responses" as counterpoint.

TO ASTRID LILJEBLAD   Feb. 26th, 1975
[York]
Dear Astrid,

You can hardly imagine what a blessing your letter was! Very few people know that Julian's death was a grief for me, in the first place... and then I saw him last October in London, a crotchety, senile old man of 87, and it was a terrible shock. So your vision of that Grundlsee summer brought back something precious.

Unlike you I felt especially the second volume of the Autobiog, was boring, partly because it read like an "official" biography..so little of the reality of breakdown (he had several and many shock treatments) or what was going on inside him is mentioned. The fact that none of the women he loved is ever mentioned seemed to me not to do what he no doubt intended make his marriage seems very fine (as it truly was) but to diminish it.

Now you have helped me to remember his generosity, his marvelous vivid enjoyment of life, something boyish and exuberant that was very touching. His fascination with birds was so delightful..I am glad you saw him in that aspect. Another moving thing is to see how his two sons have each grasped a part of what he had to pass on..Antony is a great expert on plants and flowers. I am just reading his last book (fascinating) called Plant and Planet. Francis, the younger, is a distinguished anthropologist and has just published a book on The Sacred. (This I have ordered but it hasn't yet come).

His wife, Juliette (very much as was Aldous Huxley's wife, Maria— ~~was~~ is (she is still alive) an extraordinarily marvelous person, very subtle and imaginative, a slave to his difficult temperament. Without her he could not possibly have survived, let alone accomplish what he did.

It is good to think of you and Sven. I wish you had told me more about how you both are. I think with distress at how ill I was with flu in Pocatello so missed some of what I would have enjoyed there. But it was great to see you both again.

I am happier than I have ever been because this is such a beautiful place..a big house with a marvelous view over a long field to open Atlantic ocean..I watch the sun rise every day over it, tremendous and tranquillizing. Also at long last it seems my work is getting through. I have a new novel coming out in May (not my favorite..it's about a divorce) and am now working very happily on a group of portraits of people who influneced me, A World of Light. I have my first dog, a Sheltie, Tamas, and a cat Bramble who is his great friend. We take a long walk together, all three, every day..

With loving thoughts and thanks,
Your old May

---

*A*strid *Liljeblad:* The Liljeblads, Astrid (b. 1909) and Sven (1899–2000), first saw Sarton in summer 1937 at Sommerheim, Seeblick am Grundlsee, Austria. Sven had a carrel in Harvard's Widener Library beside George Sarton's long before they truly became acquainted with May in Cambridge, 1947. For some years the Liljeblads taught at Idaho State University in Pocatello before returning to their native Sweden. For an extract from Astrid's letter, see *House by the Sea*, p. 80.

the Autobiog: Julian Huxley, *Memories:* volume 1, 1970; volume 2, 1973.

Plant and Planet: By Anthony Huxley (1920–92), a 1974 general-interest treatment of the plant world's "evolution and relationship with mankind, and the importance of its existence for our survival." (Tuesdays, which brought the "Science Times" section of *The New York Times,* were always an event for Sarton.)

The Way of the Sacred (1974) by Francis Huxley (b. 1923) considered "[t]he rites and symbols, beliefs and taboos, that men have held in awe and wonder through the ages," amply illustrated. Francis Huxley contributed the foreword to *Dear Juliette,* which illuminates Sarton's relations with the entire family.

accomplish what he did: By 23 May 1975, Sarton had written "a short tribute" to Julian Huxley. In summing up "such a complex genius," "The first word that springs to mind is 'generosity.' When we met, I was twenty-five and Julian was fifty, but he treated me as an equal—what could be more generous than that?" She closed by quoting from his poem "The Old Home"; see *House by the Sea*, pp. 88–91.

TO KAREN O. HODGES   March 8th [1975]
[York]

Dear Karen it's one of those times when I'm overcharged by events and experiences I have had no time to digest..<u>four</u> of my dearest friends (all in their eighties except one) have died in this past month..a huge part of my own past just fallen away. A lot of human responsibilities have descended also plus the work which is pushing <u>me</u> and I do need to get it down in this state..so you must forgive the pause before answering your letter of Feb. 23rd which has been much in my mind under all the rest.

I think about your problem re plots or "event" in the novel. It has been my experience that if the situation is dramatic enough plot will sort of come naturally..an illness, a death, a move to another city, a marital collision..any of these can set off the concentric circles which become "action" if you will. For instance, in your own life (not that you are using that, but as an example) your arrival into Denny's family and the first stay with them in Vermont would precipitate a huge amount were the central character a young woman like you. I do believe that if the first page is right, the whole novel flows from that.

To give you an idea let me take my own novels because I know them best. In Shower of Summer Days the "situation" is the <u>return</u> (from Burma) of an Anglo-Irish couple to the ancestral home in Ireland of the wife, with all the reverberations of the past for her, the strength of the house and its traditions against the ebb and flow of human affairs, notably the arrival out of the blue of an intransigent American niece who hates everything at first.

In Faithful, the novel opens with the suicide of its protagonist.

In As We Are Now, with the arrival in a nursing home of its protagonist.

In all these <u>shock</u> of one kind or another precipitates action.

(By the way I was fascinated by your analysis of your mother's changeable temperament and all you have learned to deal with as you have grown up.)

I am cross with Dennis because he did not want to see what Belgium had to give..such as paintings by the Flemish painters. That seems to me as narrow as a person who refused to go to a bird sanctuary because he or she demanded "art". But your analysis of Denny in relation to clients and co-workers (in Belgium too) was fascinating. The novelist in you is a very cogent observer!

To go back to the novel, it is possible to write a whole novel as a monologue of course (Camus, The Fall) but frightfully hard I would think. No, the thing is to invent an incident which will precipitate strong feelings and/or action in your characters. An example from a recent letter of yours Denny's bringing home guests at an inopportune time..That kind of thing (in a novel) could become the last straw and precipitate divorce. I think perhaps events you consider "trivial" are really the stuff of human comedy or tragedy and therefore not trivial.

Since I know so little of what you are trying to do, what the theme of your novel is, I don't know really what more to say. But even if you are often interrupted, even for several days, writing a little <u>whenever you can</u>, and trying to do it quite spontaneously i.e. do not analyse <u>before</u> you have something on the page. The point of writing often is that little by little the subconscious will open its treasure and you will write something that surprises you by its truth and/or reality. Don't censor <u>too soon</u> is what I am trying to say. It is here that the transition from the analytic work on the doctorate back to pure creation is, of course, a hazard. You have to quell the critic while you create. The critic comes back later on, in revising of course.

Dear Karen, I am too tired to write properly today...I hope the spring is bringing you a charge of energy..(but it may well have the opposite effect). As I ponder all you say I keep feeling that you and Denny <u>are</u> a most remarkable pair and even the battling keeps you alive and constantly adding to your store of "experience", the mine from which the novelist draws up coal or gold.

It's a gray day here...a gentle day—soft gray sea over the sad brown field, all the snow has melted. I dread the lectures ahead and uprooting myself from what has been a very good thrust of work for two months or more. But possibly living wholly in the past as I have been doing for the portraits in the new book, might become obsessive. I'll be torn back into the still alterable <u>present</u> soon enough.

Much love, dear person.

Your May

Do you have a library near by? Elizabeth Bowen's last book, Pictures and Conversations (just out) reprints her truly marvelous "Notes on the Novel." These are the most helpful remarks I have ever come upon when writing a novel. I strongly advise getting hold of it.

---

dearest friends . . . died: Helen Howe Allen, Céline Limbosch, and Julian Huxley had been followed by Rosalind Greene, whose funeral was 6 March 1975. For Sarton's immediate reaction to her death and an account of the funeral services, see *House by the Sea,* pp. 81–84. That journal also chronicles her struggle to write a *World of Light* profile of Greene: "what a heroine she would have been for Henry James."

Denny's: Dennis Buss, Hodges's husband at this time.

The Fall: English title of *La Chute* (1956), the last novel that Albert Camus lived to publish.

the lectures ahead: After speaking in North Carolina and Washington, D.C., in March, Sarton visited the University of New Hampshire, Bates, and Ohio Wesleyan in April, then New England College and Clark University in May.

Pictures and Conversations: The 1975 collection reprints Bowen's 1945 "Notes on Writing a Novel." Filled with stimulating and useful observations, it reappeared most recently in *The Mulberry Tree: Writings of Elizabeth Bowen* (1986), ed. Hermione Lee.

TO LENORA P. BLOUIN   Sept. 15th, 1975
[York]

Dear Lenora,

Sorry to be so late in answering yours of Aug. 23rd..I have not had a day to myself for weeks. Now at last this week opens up as a work week, and it is glorious weather too..the best of New England is autumn. The sea becomes dark blue, sometimes almost purple, "the wine dark sea" and the air is crystal clear. The only trouble is that any day now frost will take the garden. I can still pick wonderful bunches.

Now to answer your queries: Yes, I well remember the Library of Congress record. It was made when Dick Eberhart was there. Harvard University also has a very good record which friends have occasionally got reproduced by Fassett in Boston for $12.00. (wish Caedmon would do one commercially).

I tried to find my OWI material..it's somewhere in the files or I might have sent it to the Berg Collection, but I don't remember doing so. I wanted to see exactly which films I had written the continuity for..TVA you have seen. We did one on the N.Y. schools called "All the Children". Is that the other you sent for? I think there is a third about a small town (the director was Steinberg? Was that his name, the man who brought Marlene Dietrich over) Extraordinary about Hymn of the Nations..I remember absolutely <u>nothing</u> about it!

I'll be returning Lesbian Images with this letter. I had ordered it at once when it was announced in the Times but my copy only came the other day, so I was very grateful for the loan of yours. I agree that it is serious and interesting. My quarrel is simply that Rule seems only inter-ested in that subject. Her own novels apparently deal with Lesbians. Only about 10% of my work does and this has been quite deliberate. I want to appear as fully human and to respresent all people, young, old, lesbians, homos, married, solitary, etc. I have never been a proselytizer (sp?) or on the defensive. I do not believe that being in love with the same sex stretches the person as being in love with the other sex does. The danger is narcissism. So I had mixed feelings about what Rule said about "Mrs. Stevens." My original title for Mrs. S. was "Naught for Your Comfort" by the way. Then I found it had been used in a fine book by an Episcopal minister on South African prejudice.

I <u>was</u> upset by the Times ad on the Rule book. In the first place I am the only living writer she chooses to talk about, and it is a little hard on me. Why didn't she do Djuna Barnes, I wonder?

Thanks for the tip on Godwin's The Odd Woman. I'm snowed under at the moment but will keep it in mind. I'm about to begin the Edith Wharton biog that sounds so good. I have the Auden..I order these books at once from Hatchard's in London. I thought it was fascinating, the Auden. As you say, it nearly does the job of a biog. and does it very well.

I am feeling better but awfully driven..the summer is always hard because the garden is nearly a fulltime job, plus innumerable guests..no solitude or nearly none is possible..now I hope to get at the new book seriously and finish it by Christmas..then a long open 6 months for poetry, I hope.

I was very pleased by Anne Lindbergh's praise of me in her intro. to Gift from the Sea, reprinted by McCall's in the Aug. issue..not for the bibliography. I am simply mentioned among "brilliant" women of the day with Elizabeth Janeway and Florida Scott-Maxwell.

Don't worry when you have to give full time to the job..the bibliography gets richer all the time and there <u>is</u> time.

Warmest good wishes
May

Lenora P. Blouin: Blouin (b. 1941), who took two master's degrees at San Jose State University, was in the midst of twenty years' service as librarian with the San Jose public library system (1976–96), the last ten as head of reference. She first read Sarton in 1968, and started research for a bibliography in 1972. The two women did not meet until June 1978 when, after speaking in Berkeley, California (see 9 July 1978), Sarton invited Blouin to dinner. Now a member of the National Coalition of Independent Scholars, Blouin has begun a bibliography of works by and about Adrienne Rich, among other projects.

Library of Congress: Sarton recorded 16 poems there on 20 January 1960 during Richard Eberhart's tenure as Consultant in Poetry (1959–61). The Harvard LP of seventeen poems was made 10 October 1962. In 1987, Caedmon did issue a recording of Sarton "Reading Thirty Poems." Others have been produced by the Academy of American Poets (1984), Watershed Tapes, Washington, D.C. ("My Sisters, O My Sister," 1984), and Columbia's American Audio Prose Library (1987, excerpts from *Solitude* and *As We Are Now*), to name a few.

OWI material: Sarton's 1943–44 scriptwork for the Office of War Information included *The Valley of the Tennessee: The Story of the TVA* and *A Better Tomorrow: Progressive Education in New York City*, both with Irving Jacoby, released 1945.

Vienna-born director Josef von Sternberg (1894–1969), who came to the States as a boy, brought actress and singer Marlene Dietrich (1901?-92) here in 1930.

Tenor Jan Peerce, the Westminster Choir, and the NBC Symphony Orchestra, all conducted by Arturo Toscanini, performed the 1862 *Hymn to the Nations* by Italian opera composer Giuseppe Verdi (1813–1901), with narration written by Sarton, released 1946.

Lesbian Images: Jane Rule's 1975 book (reissued 1982) measures her own responses to lesbian experience against those of Colette, Vita Sackville-West, Willa Cather, Bowen, and others.

Rule regards Sarton as caught in a double bind: longing to be alone in order to write, she also wants "to cast another in the role of listener," a role she is weary of playing (pp. 164–74). Rule regrets that Sarton's Freudian views make her tag traits masculine or feminine rather than human, but the way she presents sex in her work proves Sarton's respect for women.

being in love: "Being in love," Sarton had written Karen O. Hodges on 20 March 1974, "is how one <u>learns</u> about other people, the huge imaginative leap into another's way of being, and also how one learns about oneself. . . . I would condone any relationship if real love is involved (even incest), condone any sexual aberration I mean, if there is <u>love</u>. For it is love, and hence the imagination, that separates man from rutting animals."

about "Mrs. Stevens": In mid-1974, Norton had reissued *Mrs. Stevens* in hardback, with an introduction by Carolyn G. Heilbrun (reprinted in *Hamlet's Mother and Other Women,* 1990), and a paperback edition the next year. Heilbrun contended that "The quality of the relationships, homosexual or not, like the active role Hilary played in them, are more important than the sex of her particular muse."

"Naught for Your Comfort": 1956, by Trevor Huddleston, who was persecuted by the apartheid government for crusading on behalf of South Africans in shantytown Johannesburg. In 2000, Nelson Mandela unveiled a monument to him in Huddleston's home city of Bedford, England.

Djuna Barnes: 1892-1982; author of the enigmatic psychological novel *Nightwood* (1936). Writing Blouin on 6 May 1976, Sarton added, "I'm afraid I am rather wary of overt 'lesbian novels'..so few have the slightest literary value, *Nightwood* and the novels of Mary Renault being exceptions"—pen-name of Mary Challans (1905–83), British-born writer known for vivid reconstructions of the ancient Greek world and the classic gay novel *The Charioteer* (1953). As for the once-notorious 1928 book by Radclyffe Hall (1886–1943), "*The Well of Loneliness* is a turgid self-pitying novel. The whole aspect of woman trying to be men is now quite old-fashioned it seems to me. That is pathetic and suggests immaturity and a kind of narcissism I find boring. 'John' [Hall's male guise] in her tuxedoes etc."

The Odd Woman: Gail Godwin's 1974 novel.
   R. W. B. Lewis, *Edith Wharton: A Biography,* 1975.
   Stephen Spender, ed., *W. H. Auden: A Tribute* (1975), includes contributions by Hannah Arendt, John Betjeman, Joseph Brodsky, Cyril Connolly, Christopher Isherwood and others, with many photos.

"brilliant" women: In a 1989 *New York Times Book Review* piece, Janeway (author, b. 1913) judged *The Fur Person* (1957) one of the two best cat books ever written. Reviewing *Birth of a Grandfather* (*New York Times Book Review,* 8 September 1957), she found it less successful than *A Shower of Summer Days:* "Sarton needs to see her male characters in male terms, a task not impossible for a creative writer." For her review of *The Small Room,* see note to 24 July [1961].

Florida Scott-Maxwell: Florida-born author and Jungian analyst (1883–1979). Her 1968 meditation on aging, *The Measure of My Days,* has remained in print since publication. Sarton cites it in *House by the Sea* (pp. 104–05), *Recovering* (pp. 123–24, 134), and elsewhere. In a 13 November 1983 letter to Peggy Pond Church, Sarton laughed that "in my innocence five years ago I wrote a piece for the [*New York*] *Times* in which I speak of old age as 'ascension.'" ("More Light," 30 January 1978: "As power diminishes, we grow toward more light.") "Now I am more realistic" and, opening Scott-Maxwell, Sarton found:

   "'Think of others' we were once taught. 'Adapt, adapt' we are told. But it is a coward cry, for he who after cruel buffeting wins to aloneness learns that life is a tragic mystery. We are pierced and driven by laws we only half understand, we find that the lesson we learn again and again is that of accepting heroic helplessness."

An undated reply from Scott-Maxwell to Sarton catches the older woman's tone and slant: "Your letter was delightful to receive, wise, or agreeing with my own thoughts, which makes us both seem wise, and your arrow of insight not a thread off center when you say we are monsters, as well as gods of course, at seconds"—that moment by moment the behavior of human beings can switch from the monstrous to the divine.

the bibliography: Blouin's first edition appeared in 1978; she then updated it for Constance Hunting's *May Sarton, Woman and Poet,* 1982. The second edition, surveying all Sarton's life-work, was published in 2000 as Scarecrow Author Bibliography Series No. 104 (Lanham, Maryland, and London: The Scarecrow Press). Scores of footnotes throughout this volume are indebted to this indispensable guidebook for Sarton scholars: details of hard-to-find interviews, précis of reviews and critical analyses, complex publication histories of individual poems, and much more.

Blouin has since contributed the cover article to the December 2000 *Bulletin of Bibliography* (Vol. 57, No. 4), "'The Stern Growth of a Lyric': May Sarton, Writing Poetry/Writing About Poetry, and Major Critical Responses to Sarton's Poetry—A Bibliographic Survey."

Blouin has also posted on the Internet, as part of the University of Pennsylvania's Celebration of Women Writers (ed. Mary Mark Ockerbloom), the succinct biographical essay "May Sarton: A Poet's Life," which can be accessed at http://digital.library.upenn.edu/women/sarton/blouin-biography.html.

Blouin has plans under way for a Website devoted to Sarton and Sarton studies.

Meanwhile, Sarton is making inroads elsewhere on the information highway. The on-line December 2000 issue of *O: The Magazine* (www.oprah.com) offered this "O to Go e-card":

"There is only one real deprivation, I decided this morning, and that is not to be able to give one's gifts to those one loves most."

—May Sarton, *Journal of a Solitude* (p. 191, 16 August 1971)

Users could send either the print version or an audio clip with the extract introduced and read by Oprah Winfrey. If known to hundreds of thousands of readers before, Sarton can soon be accessed by millions.

TO ELEANOR BELMONT   Dec. 15th, 1975
[York]

Dear Eleanor Belmont,

I read Amy on the plane to and from St. Paul, Minn. the other day, and how much I enjoyed it! One of the joys was to find you flitting in and out of its pages—I had not realized that you and Ada Russell had been such dear friends and colleagues on the stage.

I think Jean Gould has done a splendid job, open and truthful, and that the book will send readers back to the poems which should now be rediscovered. In a way Amy Lowell's masterful personality and plugging of her own work (as well as that of the Imagists in general) got in the way of a just appreciation. She was "oversold"..do you agree?..and then the reaction set in. It is really time now that her publishers brought out a Selected Poems and all those to Ada will be accepted now in a new way. Ms. Gould has also made one feel what immense courage A.L. had..altogether a splendid biography.

I'm awash in Christmas but wanted to send a word of thanks now that I have read the book.

It is hard to soar above the really horrendous state of the world, but for a little while we shall soar on the wings of that ever-renewed hope that Christ brought with him..yet, it is terribly painful that <u>religious</u> wars are again tearing the world apart.

Well, dear person, thanks for your light—

and love from
May

Eleanor Belmont: Philanthropist Eleanor Robson Belmont (1878–1979), wife of financier August Belmont, named a Triple Crown Winner, founded the Metropolitan Opera Guild, and left her estate to the Belmont Fund, in the New York Community Trust, to aid young musicians and house the homeless. As an actress she inspired Shaw's *Major Barbara,* and had known Ada Dwyer Russell, Amy Lowell's companion from 1914 until Lowell's death in 1925. After Sarton read at her home, Belmont sent her *Amy: The World of Amy Lowell and the Imagist Movement* by Jean Gould (1975). At present no separate volume of Lowell's poems seems readily available. Belmont's own memoir, *The Fabric of Memory,* appeared in 1957.

Sarton had written Katharine Taylor, 23 October 1975, about going "to St. Paul to receive the Alexandrine Medal (given to distinguished women) by the College of St. Catherine," Sister Maris Stella's school. "It pleases me that this is a Catholic College. Rather surprising."

A few years earlier, after the innovations of Vatican II—and after Sarton had started cropping her hair—she was able to report to Beverly Hallam (13 May 1968) "a great success" after another reading at a Catholic institution. "[A]lways go over big with the nuns and it was fascinating to see them experimenting with dress, some wear just ordinary tailored suits and no coif at all..one ancient nun took one look at my hair and said with a gleam in her eye, 'Ah, that's what I can do!' "

hope that Christ brought: The contradiction between the promise of Christmas and the state of the world at Christmastime never ceased to trouble Sarton. *At Eighty-Two,* pp. 146–47, reprints the poem she sent out for "Christmas, 1993": "Bullets rain all day / On Sarajevo now."

TO CHARLES BARBER   Feb. 7th, 1976
[York]
Dear Charles,

I was so happy to hear at last! And so much sooner but just as your letters came, came also the ms. of my book with a lot of queries to pon-der..my editor comes next week to talk it over. (It will be out in September after you get home, since you ask so kindly). The changes are really not much but they involve "telling more". and that I am reluctant to do, so I have to find ways around obscure passages. This book was my invention as a way of avoiding talking about love affairs, to bridge the gap between I Knew a Phoenix and Plant Dreaming Deep. And I do think it works. So I am not going to be pushed. Anyway my editor is a dear and and will always let me do what I want after he has said his say.

I'm thrilled to hear that The Bald Soprano, after all your hard work, was a rousing success. Bravo! Then I was galvanized about the week in Cyprus. for a painter friend of mine from Michigan, Catherine Becker (married with small children) was there staying with an American diplomat—she was appalled by the embassy life..did you meet her? Your description of you and the gilded youth and your high-jinks make me laugh terrifically and remember exactly how I did such things years and years and years ago. The group is a very dangerous thing, isn't it? I mean people egg each other on and one feels so "in". But it is a dismally depressing scene when set against the true suffering and nightmare beyond the embassy gates. I was <u>shocked</u>. No wonder Americans are hated everywhere. (I mean the Embassy, not <u>you</u>.)

The thing that delighted me in your letter was your wish to come to grips with studying..and Brown sounds dandy. (Of course I'm pleased because it's so near here, not more than two hours so I'll see you occasionally, I hope). This is such a dull letter that I'm going out in the ten above zero sunlight and walk Tamas and will go on after lunch..yes, we have had a very grim winter so far, deadly cold, gale winds (the wind chill has been fifty below zero often) and very little snow, though what there is is still piled around in frozen dirty piles because it has never melted since Xmas. Whereas you will be seeing daffodils by the time this arrives, or nearly..primroses...Oh dear me! Bluebells in the beech woods.

Later
Evelyn Pember hated Crucial Conversations .. she wrote me one of her violent letters. But I don't like the novel much myself and I am always amused by her because her opinions are authentic, however crazy at times (such as her conviction that the whole of Bloomsbury was "second-rate"). She has never liked any of my novels anyway and has not seen the autobiog. books I think. I guess she has never forgiven me for writing her a long (meaning to be helpful) criticism of an unpublished novel of hers..she did publish one or two and they were not very good. But this is an elemental person and one has to love her, quand même. I'm glad the Sayces are proving such good directors or whatever they are called..I liked them a lot the one time I met them after a poetry reading at N.E. College.

Well I have been slowly, like an ant, writing poems since January first, notations rather than poems..but I shall keep at it for 6 months and hope in that time for a breakthrough. At any rate I enjoy even these uninspired struggles <u>tremendously.</u>

New lectures begin..I go to Notre Dame the 18th for five days..a good group will be there for their literary festival (I'm the only woman)..I probably wrote you about that? In March I go to Manhattanville College and in April to the University of Oklahoma for three days and later on to Vassar and then to Clark U (where they are studying "Mrs. Stevens" in an English class). At Vassar it will be the psychology dept. with the English dept. I always dread these excursions into public life but I guess I would become too neurotic and self-enclosed if I never got out of here. It is lonely and at times I get dull from lack of outside stimulation. My life at the moment could not be more different than yours.

So I feed on letters and books..am now reading Golda Meir's Autobiography. What a great woman! But all it does is to create frightful woe and anxiety about what next..how is Izrael to survive? Although I see no one for days at a time, and sometimes believe I am turning into a dog or a cat, I am stretched out into the world all the time..and I cannot say that my meditations are cheerful.

Are you writing poems? Have you found a friend? Duncan? The move out from campus sounds good..but why are you a vegetarian? Admirable, no doubt, but can you live on vegetable marrow? Blake and Auden sound a fascinating mixture. You may explode!

Do write soon again. You really have an obligation to keep this old raccoon amused in the long dreary winter cold. While I have been writing this, the lights went out for a half hour. Now it is snowing.

With much love from
M

I'm glad Miss Pickthorn pleased you!

Charles Barber: Charles Andrew Barber (b. 1956) first met Sarton on 17 April 1975 when he was a student at Ohio Wesleyan University, where she delivered the Carpenter Lecture. After a summer's work as a lifeguard to earn passage to England and attend New England College Sussex there, he visited Sarton on 12 September 1975 en route (*House by the Sea*, pp. 144–46). Here she replies to his letters from Europe.

The Bald Soprano: Absurdist 1949 farce (*La Cantatrice Chauve*) by Romanian-born French playwright Eugène Ionesco, filled with tourist-phrasebook non sequiturs and pseudologic to demonstrate life's irrationality.

See *Recovering*, pp. 162–63 and 174–75, for artists David and Catherine Becker (later Catherine Claytor) and their two daughters.

Evelyn Pember: See 10 March 1955. "I've not met with the Rodmell folks for months," Barber had written, 25 January 1976, but "I am going to definitely pin them down, for they keep offering to introduce me to Duncan Grant, Barbara Bagenal, Peggy Ashcroft on and on—but then never follow through. So I suppose I should initiate some initiative, no? (When are you coming over for a visit?) I'm fascinated by your suggestion that Trekkie Parsons and Leonard [Woolf] were lovers. Did you really get that impression?" (See *Love Letters: Leonard Woolf and Trekkie Ritchie Parsons, 1941–1968,* ed. Judith Adamson, Chatto and Windus, 2001.)

quand même: even so, in spite of everything.

The Sayces, from New England College, Henniker, New Hampshire, were running the British program: "They are like second parents to all 150 of us here," Barber reported. "Everyone loves them, and vice versa." He signed off: "Have you seen Rollo May's new book, *The Courage to Create?* How is it? Give your house and grounds and ocean a big hug because I love them. And what of you? Write and tell all.

"With much love from Charlie"

notations rather than poems: This would seem the first stirrings of *Halfway to Silence* (1980).

Meir's Autobiography: Russian-born Golda Meir (1898–1978) emigrated at three with her family to Milwaukee; strong-willed and drawn to Zionism, she left home at 15, and ended up Prime Minister of Israel, 1969–74. See *House by the Sea,* pp. 200–01, for Sarton's consideration of her memoir, *My Life* (1975).

Blake: Another great Romantic poet (1757–1827), William Blake published his lyrics (*Songs of Innocence and Experience*) and Prophetic Books (*The Marriage of Heaven and Hell, Jerusalem*) in his own vividly hand-colored "illuminated" editions.

Do write soon: Soon Barber found himself anxious to return to the States, wearied by "being stared at constantly, the butt of unfunny cross-culture jokes" (*House,* p. 220). "I used to get into awful rages," Sarton replied, 16 March 1976, "when people said (as a compliment after running down Americans) 'Of course you are not an American, are you?' And I would shout that I am and proud to be."

TO HUGH MCKINLEY   Feb. 15th, 1976
[York]
Dear Hugh,

If I may call you so? You can hardly imagine how welcome was your understanding word about Crucial Conversations, as I am recovering from rather a battering in the English press plus angry letters from friends who <u>hate</u> Poppy etc. (Auberon Waugh did quite a lethal job in the Evening Standard but it was so long and hateful that I truly believe it will make some readers go out and buy the book). Thank God you understood the point about Poppy ..she is never going to be a great sculptor but she feels <u>herself</u> when she is working at it. And what point would the book have had she been made to be a genius? In that case she would never have married Reed in the first place and certainly left him early on had she done so. I am really surprised to see how ingrained is the idea <u>still</u> that to feel a responsibility towards one <u>self</u> is somehow immoral. If Poppy had left Reed for a man everyone would have accepted <u>that</u>. I believe we are on earth to make our souls and it is not immoral to feel one can do that best alone. Of course I look forward to your review. And am very grateful that you took the time and energy to write one. Where does it come out?

Wonderful that you got to Vienna. I wonder whether Muriel Rukeyser, the poet, and an old friend of mine, was there? She is Pres. of American P.E.N. I believe..haven't seen her for years. I used to feel her poetry was too fulsome, but compared to the hogwash now being called poetry over here, it has begun to shine in my mind.

No great poems being writ..but I am slowly making what I call "notations," very plain and exact. I rather like them..it's a new kind of poem for me..when I get a few typed up I'll send.

Of those you sent "Who's I" struck me of course..and "Victim's Day!" Bravo!

We have had a truly fierce winter, way below zero most of the time with high wind bringing the wind chill to fifty below zero! So life has been mostly a struggle to survive. Walking my dog at times was an ordeal on glare ice roads..but spring is coming—already the skies are a tender blue, though the earth is iron hard. I am off next week to a poetry thing at Notre Dame University .. Galway Kinnell, Louis Simpson, Robert Penn Warren and Borges will be there, too. I think it will be fun. But I am scared as usual.

Warmly yours,

M

Hugh McKinley: Anglo-Irish poet, lyric tenor, Baha'i teacher, literary editor, and reviewer for the Athens *Daily Post* (d. 1999). His collection *The Transformation of Faust, and Other Poems* (Ipswich, England: Golgonooza Press) appeared in 1977.

Auberon Waugh: 1939–2001; acerbic novelist, reviewer, and columnist on politics, society, and wine. *House by the Sea,* pp. 198–200, includes a lengthy quotation from the serious Christian-era novel *Helena* (1950) by his father, satirist Evelyn Waugh (1903–66).

Notre Dame: Sarton's visit is recounted in detail in *The House by the Sea,* pp. 205–08, 224. Aside from Argentinian man of letters Jorge Luis Borges (1899–1986), the other speakers— Robert Penn Warren (1905–89), Stanley Kunitz (b. 1905), Louis Simpson (b. 1923), and Galway Kinnell (b. 1927)—were all Pulitzer-prizewinning poets, Warren and Kunitz Poets Laureate, with Sarton the sole distinguished "outsider."

Writing on 23 February 1976 (probably to Camille Mayran), Sarton says she felt nervous at being asked to read, for the first time, from *As We Are Now.* She was buoyed by the standing-room-only crowd, "by the unexpected laughter at certain passages (one when Standish shouts 'shit' (merde) when the minister first comes to see him), another when Caro says 'old age is not interesting until one comes to it'..I ended with Standish's death.... [T]he whole audience <u>stood</u>, still applauding.... It was a real <u>festival</u> of the spirit."

[*The House by the Sea* ends 17 August 1976.]

TO RUTH LIMMER   Sept. 19th, 1976
[York]
Dear Ruth Limmer,

I was so relieved and happy to have your good letter about the Bogan portrait—I was afraid you might not think it authentic. I'm pleased that you singled out that "snow fence" image, as I believe it is accurate.

Of course I'm abashed at the stupid mistake about Institute and Academy. (Institute sounds small and academy, large, to me as a member, among <u>hundreds</u>, of the Academy of Arts and Sciences..maybe that is how I made the mistake). That will be corrected in the second edition as the advance sale, before any reviews, is already 8000. Thanks for the offer to help <u>assassinate</u>!

I ponder on hermetic and hermitic..maybe neither is quite right. For Louise was not really a <u>hermit</u>, was she? Perhaps in the back of my mind was also the secondary meaning of hermetic .. magical. i.e. reclusive and magical. I love to think about words. Thank you for suggesting that I do in this case.

I never knew it was Livermore Falls, such a strange town, a manufacturing town full of Canadian French. Did Louise note any memories of it in "the long prose thing"..and is there enough of that to be published?

This is a dull letter because I am somewhat confused and muddled between letters about World of Light and my own difficult final revising of my next book [*The House by the Sea*]. It is just a little too much all at once. Plus lectures looming...

But thanks immensely for the good word. I had been quite anxious about your response.

Kind regards,
May Sarton

P.S. The Berg Collection is having a show from Sept. 28 to Feb. of new acquisitions—called "Arrivals"—There will be <u>6 cases</u> from my archive—I have no idea what, or whether letters from Louise are among what they have chosen—

———

Ruth Limmer: Former professor of English and program planner for the National Endowment for the Arts. She met Bogan in June 1956, when the poet received an honorary degree at Western College for Women in Oxford, Ohio. She is Louise Bogan's literary executor.

Bogan's "life-enhancing qualities were often defenses, carefully placed and designed 'snow fences,' such as those New Englanders dispose to keep the snow from drifting dangerously and cutting off roads." "Louise Bogan," *A World of Light,* p. 227.

Institute and Academy: From the larger National Institute of Arts and Letters, not more than fifty members are selected for the American Academy of Arts and Letters; Sarton had confused the two (p. 229), belonging herself to the American Academy of Arts and Sciences. (It was in 1976 that the first two organizations were amalgamated into the 250-member American Academy and Institute of Arts and Letters, from which the fifty-member American Academy of Arts and Letters is drawn.)

hermetic and hermitic: Bogan, the "charming companion," seemed at ease in the world, "but under that acquired layer of 'wise living' she was hermetic." The paragraph on p. 230 exploring this trait also alludes to her "pathological faithfulness" to her husband, Raymond Holden, and breaking a writer's block with "imitation poems"—signaling that Sarton's rich essay should be read complete, to begin understanding the complicated relationship between these two poets.

Sarton dedicated *A World of Light* to Carolyn G. Heilbrun. The title is from Henry Vaughan's 1655 poem that begins "They are all gone into the world of light / And I alone sit lingering here."

Livermore Falls: The small Maine mill town where Bogan was born on 11 August 1897. Her fragmentary memoirs were incorporated in Limmer's "mosaic" of her unpublished work, *Journey Around My Room.*

kind regards: A scene in the *World of Light* profile (p. 221) describes the two poets, with Sarton driving in New York City, trying to recall an A. E. Housman poem; Sarton misses the exit again and again and, laughing, they cross and re-cross the George Washington Bridge three times. Sarton's last published reference to Louise Bogan, in the journals, reviews their relationship from the perspective of 2 June 1992 (*Encore*, pp. 308–12), and prints the poem they were trying to reconstruct, "I to my perils / Of cheat and charmer."

Sarton many times expressed the hope that someday her correspondence with Bogan would be published in full; and, as with the Bill Brown correspondence, it merits a volume of its own as an unprecedented exchange of views between poets of strong views and character.

TO KEITH FAULKNER WARREN   Dec. 15th, 1976
[York]
Dear Keith,

We shall soon be in daily communion as you struggle with your memoirs (I am so happy you are doing that!) and I plunge into a new novel in a state of fear and trembling..but I look forward to it after a much-travelled autumn. However, we both know that writing is extremely hard work. Take it a page at a time is my advice.

I was very touched by Barbara's 1937 remarks..I too love maidenhair ferns, and, I think the kind of beauty she exemplified in her own distinguished way. In fact I read it with tears brimming my eyes. You and I also share something only you and I can know the depth of..watching a loved one fade away yet still live. Of course Judy is still aware and I do enjoy having her with me for the holidays..they would be excruciatingly lonely without her. I seem to live among ghosts these days. A sentiment which became vivid in New York the other day when I went to see an exhibit at the Berg Collection where there were 6 cases of stuff I had sold them..letters to my parents, a journal I kept when I was in high school [*At Fifteen*]: letters from great friends like Bowen—I felt I was already dead and looked at those cases from an infinite distance. It didn't help that several friends from the past turned up for the party, looking a million years old!

The check! It is a real boon and I thank you most heartfully for it. I have been nearly done in because a lecture I gave in Minn. supposed to be paid for with $750 turned into $500 after the tax was taken out. And the new Maine income tax is retroactive so I had to pay $900 more this year than I thought, a deadly blow. You will be glad to hear that I am now being sensible (rather late) and am saving $3000 a year in a retirement fund—that is non-taxable when put in. You pay the tax if and when you take it out. That should reduce my huge fed. income tax some.

On this mundane note, cheers and hugs,

and so much love, dear man,

Your devoted
May

P.S. We'll read the New Yorker renewal in bed with our stockings on Xmas morning—

––––––––

Keith Faulkner Warren: 1892–1987; Judith Matlack's brother-in-law, married to her older sister Barbara; father of Timothy Matlack Warren, Sarton's executor.

so much love, dear man: The first of "Two Birthdays," written "for Keith Warren at eighty," was published in *The Silence Now.*

TO SYBILLE BEDFORD   Jan. 10th, 1977
[York]
Dear Sybille,

I am so grateful that you wrote me the whole story. I didn't answer at once because Christmas intervened with people pouring in and out every day, and also a wish not to plague you with letters. It touched me what you said of dear Jane [Stockwood]..I felt just what you describe last time I was in London. She is a secret person but as you say full of treasures of understanding and kindness, percipient kindness.

It is just a month since you wrote, and today we are having a wild blizzard, tons of snow falling through a whirlwind, then a few hours ago it changed to rain, and now I hear it will soon freeze meanwhile immense waves pile up at the end of the field and break into fountains, white fountains over an ermine field. I love it best here in winter when there are no guests and for the first time in 8 months, I have an empty calendar before me until March 30th..bliss.

Your telling brought back very vivid memories of my mother dying (it was cancer of the lung) and that she, too, never talked about death. It is wonderful that you were able to stay with Eda at night at the hospital, and thank you for telling me all that you did, the room with a view of the river, flowers and friends, and Eda never losing her beauty to the end. Only one thing troubled me..I'm not sure it is true that it is harder for those who have gone. "Missing the light," you said.

Jan. 11th

I stopped there, unable to find the words. It is dusk now—we have had a huge snow storm that ended in violent rain and then glare ice as the temp dropped to below zero. At least no one can get in and I am (oh dear I see now I said all this yesterday! Please forgive.)

Once in a while something really happens on TV and sometime last autumn I heard a Dutch woman speak, a doctor or nurse (?) who has had much experience of death and the dying—she said that people who come back from death, as sometimes happens, have had what seems extraordinary experience of <u>light</u>, and do not wish to come back. She said she was afraid of saying too much about it for fear it would cause multiple suicides..and really she was so convincing that I felt it lift a great weight off my chest. For the first time since I was a small child I <u>believed.</u> The woman is middle-aged, not at all cosily religious, quite matter of fact. It was impressive. That is why, I suppose, I questioned your saying what you did.

I am glad to know that you love the house you are in and that it has a garden. I hope you can work at something soon, but I know too well how the absence is always there when you lift your head.

Dear Sybille, bless you for your letter. It was awfully good of you.

Much love always
May

I keep a good memory of our last meeting..Eda so tired and so kind to come to supper with you at Jane's. I'm so glad I did have that last glimpse of you together.

Sybille Bedford: Anglo-German woman of letters (b. 1911), known for her travel writing, her biography of Aldous Huxley (whom she knew intimately), the 1956 novel *A Legacy* ("of the rich and titled in pre–World War I Germany"), and *Jigsaw: An Unsentimental Education: A biographical novel* (1989).

For Jane Stockwood, see note to 6 June [1957]. Eda Lord was Bedford's longtime companion who had recently died.

a Dutch woman: Probably Swiss-born Dr. Elisabeth Kübler-Ross (b. 1926), famous for working with the terminally ill. Her first book, *Death and Dying* (1969), proposes a multistage grieving process and provoked worldwide debate. For a backlash against this attitude, see 12 March 1979.

TO MORGAN MEAD   March 27th, '77
[York]
Dear Morgan,

Spring in the air at last! We had the worst storm of the year just as the crocuses were opening, a very few early ones, and I was without power for 24 hours, a rather interesting experience as it made me aware of how dependent we are on furnaces, dishwashers, water etc.! Luckily I had a sterno and could heat a cupful of water for coffee or soup. There was about that in the taps. The animals kept me warm and cheerful..it would have been very disconsolate and frustrating without them.

I'm glad someone heard the [Studs] Terkel interview [December 1976]. He is such a wonderful man and we had great fun. Actually a friend heard it in California too.

I think you are quite wonderful to have told your mother, but how difficult! If it would help you may tell her about me (or give her "Mrs. Stevens"). I have an idea that I can be useful because I am not what ordinary people think of as a "deviant," and am respected etc. Little by little she will come to see that such a life may have real quality and be productive (even if not producing children) But give her time..one always has to remember that people who have not had this experience of love are terribly frightened of it (because partly they appear to have wild sexual images and do not think of love so much as that in the context). I am very angry with Erica Jong because in her new awful novel she has a horrible sexual scene, cold sex between two women..this is really to betray lesbians. My guess is she made it all up to be in fashion and it will delight men and also women who fear the lesbian and want to be told it is disgusting. The book deserves the bad reviews..but of course she'll make a million!

How marvelous that you have saved $5000! I am sure your decision to take a year off without any job is right. You must do it now while you are still free..and the plan to be in N.H. part of the time delights me of course for I can hope to see you! Then London where I think you can find a dreary furnished room for not very much money. Any room with a table and a bunch of flowers is enough! The only trouble with the winter is that you can't sit in the parks..that is what I loved best about London, to sit in a park for hours, watching the people, reading, and making notes for poems or stories...It's very good indeed to have those encouraging notes from the New Yorker!

The House By The Sea, that journal, is coming out late this autumn..you asked about it.

As for my novel [*A Reckoning*], now 200 pages long, it is still a kind of nightmare, an obsession, but not a good one. I have real fears that it is a total dud. But somehow I have to keep plodding on, page by page..the chief character is dying, as I guess I told you. Luckily if this fails I have a really good idea for another one, to write as a novel the life of my amazing friend, Anne Thorp (she of the island), who has just died. It would be called The Magnificent Sinster (Spinster! Sinster would be quite off the mark in this case).

It's been a long siege alone here this time..and I'm glad to be off to Nashville now for five days to catch a glimpse of spring, and give a lecture or rather read poems about gardens at a women's club. But I am going really because it's a chance to stay with a good friend.

So that's all for the moment..I'm afraid I feel more like a crumbling stone wall than a rampart!

A hug from
May

Morgan Mead: After he wrote her about *Kinds of Love* in 1974, Sarton invited Mead (b. 1950) to York and immediately recognized he was "one of my people," as she expressed it in 1979 (*Recovering,* pp. 57–59, 130–31). "Yet there must be nearly forty years between us, nothing at all, when it comes to essences." Eldest of six, and in her opinion a fine writer, Mead was most of all "a born friend."

Erica Jong: Woman of letters (b. 1942); she wrote, of *A World of Light,* "May Sarton is a national treasure." *How to Save Your Own Life* came out in 1977. Pages 68–69 of *Recovering* offer a much more nuanced view of this incident, while pages 225–26 provide a warm note about Jong herself, when she and Sarton met by chance at the Pierre in New York before a dinner honoring Muriel Rukeyser in 1979.

take a year off: Later this year, when Mead was studying in England, Sarton arranged for him to call on Juliette Huxley; she gave him bed without board so he could have a place to write.

a good friend: "I feel born again," Sarton wrote Catharine Claytor, 24 April 1977, "but just as vulnerable as a small baby." "A miracle has happened and I am writing poems again—that means (for me) a person on the horizon, a muse again at last," Sarton wrote Karen O. Hodges, 1 May 1977. "[S]he is coming here for the first time on May 5th for four days. You can imagine how agitated and in suspense I feel in a quite absurd and juvenile way." This was heiress Huldah Sharpe, "The Queen of Tennessee," her home state, whose "perfect example of androgyny" Sarton found endearing (she wrote Charles Barber). "[S]he designed her own wedding dress and told me 'I want to look like a boy cardinal.' " Sharpe served as the muse for *Halfway to Silence* and as the basis for Ned in *Anger* (1982).

a hug from May: For several years Mead alternated between real estate and teaching English in the upper grades (see *At Seventy,* p. 307); at present he is dean of students at the Buckingham Browne & Nichols School in Cambridge, Massachusetts. *Encore* (pp. 189–90) recounts a January 1992 meeting: "His eyes light up when he talks about [teaching] and how interesting and exciting his students are to him. . . . This man is a born teacher and loves it."

TO THE REVEREND RICHARD HENRY   May 2d, 1977
[York]
Dear Dick,

What a rich compendium of things you sent! First, I am happy about the vita nuova.. I had sensed in some subterranean way that you had about sucked that orange dry in Denver and perhaps also vice versa. I just wish Salt Lake City were not quite so far away! But I hope the holiday just before the move may bring you here..I'll be back from Europe Aug. 26 I think. Did I tell you I am going over for a month, partly to get away from visiting firemen here and to take a real break from the novel too. The best thing will be one week <u>alone</u> on Sark [in the Channel Islands], with an expedition from there to the Durrell Zoo I trust.

Naturally I was extremely grateful to have your sister-in-law's thoughts about terminal illness and how it can best be handled..what a superb person! but what spoke to me even more because I have so many problems of the same kind was the love letter from your parishioner, if that is the word. How can we understand the dreadful mystery which comes out of a passion for someone who does not share it? And why does such a person (I have been one myself!) always have to believe that if he or she feels so much the object of this passion must return it and just be refusing to admit it? The burden these things lay on one is truly HUGE isn't it? One is always in the wrong. They are the true believers, the radiant beings who are in love..I have to laugh because a woman about my age, married and with children grown up has been writing a letter a day for about a month. I tried a brief answer to say "Don't project your needs on me" but nothing appears to work. She has lost forty pounds, she says, and blames me for "rejecting" her while I on my side grow fatter and more morose under these attacks. It happens about once a year. Eventually she will stop. And she is at least not to be seen..I can imagine how very hard such things are to handle when your adorers are sitting just under the pulpit every Sunday! The immense illusions at work..

Is that why you sent the letter? To let me know that you know..

May 3rd

A perfect day here with garlands of daffodils all over the field and a gentle blue sea...such joys!

For a moment let me go back to the above. All these people really are emotional blackmailers. One is always being made to feel guilty. The tender heart forces one to give what one can and that is nearly always fatal! And I am especially susceptible because I have suffered in their way, as an unrequited lover. Well, it's wonderful to be a requited lover for a change..at last the whole trauma of Marynia Farnham falls away, and poetry, at long last, is with me.

Dear Dick, the phone keeps ringing and I had better get this off..

Next time you are near, please come here.—maybe soon?—in the fall

Love M

---

the Reverend Richard Henry: b. 1921. Ordained in 1946, he became an honorary Doctor of Divinity, Meadville Theological School, University of Chicago, in 1970. He was minister of the First Unitarian Churches of Denver (1957–77) and Salt Lake City (1977–86).

vita nuova: Italian, for "new life," familiar as the title of Dante's sequence of poems and prose meditations on love, c. 1293.

back from Europe: "Belgium was hard because so many friends are dead," Sarton wrote Eleanor Blair on 5 August 1977 about this trip. "But I did have one wonderful walk with Eugénie [Dubois] across lovely fields of standing grain, barley and wheat with lines of poplars in the distance and tasted my earth again. Then J[acqueline]. Limbosch (Céline's youngest) took me on the last day for a long walk in the great beech wood and that was simply glorious despite the cold gray weather. . . I had three long visits with Pauline Prince in her nursing home. . the last of those intimately connected with Jean Dominique to remain alive."

A brilliant teacher of literature at the École Normale and one of "Les Fidèles," Marie Closset's intimate circle of friends, Pauline Prince wrote Sarton interesting, philosophic let-ters about her work; see *At Seventy,* pp. 65–66. She regarded Prince as "such a remarkable person and so cruelly treated by life, I cannot understand it."

the whole trauma: Farnham died, age 79, on 29 May 1978. See *Recovering,* pp. 105–09, where Sarton reconsiders their relationship and prints two unpublished poems, "A Birthday" and "The Place Beyond Action"—presumably succeeding "The Action of Therapy," one of the "Letters to a Psychiatrist" in *A Durable Fire.*

next time you are near: House by the Sea, p. 20, records a 16 November 1974 visit to York by Henry; Sarton "was troubled by something frail about him." On 7 October 1995, at the Nelson Congregational Church, he conducted Sarton's memorial service.

TO ASHLEY MONTAGU   Oct. 2, Sunday 1977
[York]
Dear Ashley,

I'm dismayed that you never got a copy of A World of Light. If you haven't yet ordered drop me a p.c. and I'll send you a copy. Maybe I thought you might be getting tired of book-a-year Sarton! Actually I am determined now to take a year off after a novel about dying is revised..it will be published late next year, and for 1978 I am going to keep quiet except for poems, friends, gardening, love.

Yes, no doubt G.S. feared Mabel's death but he let her cook dinner every night (not even a single day off!) without ever taking her out. If his fear had turned into some kind of practical love that might have helped her...oh well, he was a dear man as I say in A World of Light. Peace to the dead. Yes, I have read you On Being Human.. and now have just been galvanized by your answer to those who wish to make man naturally aggressive and wicked. Bravo! To be good we have to believe we are good..and that the wicked sides are aberrations. I have always believed this and been accused of being a sentimental idealist, as G.S. also was I must remember.

Now you can laugh at me because after all those wise, whistling-in-the-dark words in the journal, I am in love (a miracle) and so am able to write poems again. It is really like being reborn.

Yes, I well remember those "merry" occasions after a disaster but you have to remember that the relation with the children was complex..Katrine really hated Rosalind [Greene] and kept her at bay when she (K) was dying, as she refused to have her mother "run her death" as she had Francesca's. Someday we must talk about this. I withdrew the portrait of Rosalind from A World of Light because I felt I had not sorted it all out..and perhaps that could only be done in a novel.

To answer your question about the woman's movement. In the first place when I was young it was hard to be a woman poet because women poets were jealous (Louise Bogan did not notice me in the New Yorker except with a short squib and we were good friends) and male poets hate women poets. ..at least they dislike women poets who talk about feelings. Elizabeth Bishop and Marianne Moore are exceptions and both good poets but each rather impersonal and witty. Since woman's lib there is a real sense of a sisterhood, of women helping each other. Secondly and more importantly, I came out as a Sapphist (V. Woolf's word and the only elegant one, I think, for the lesbian) long before it was fashionable and when it cost me several jobs, so I am a kind of hero now. I suppose I represent a "role model" in that I am not an alcoholic and lead a respectable life in the country and produce a lot of books. So I'm a dear old grandma who can be safely loved and admired. It's really very moving..when I read poems in N.Y. last spring for the first time in 20 years, the audience was so excited and loving that I was in tears at the end..a standing ovation, but all the way through laughter, applause, and the most intent listening I have ever experienced. They knew the poems by heart. This is quite new for me and awfully touching. I have been in the wilderness so long and still am as far as "the establishment" goes. But I am happy and free of all that now..it's better to be loved than famous.

Poor Marjorie [Montagu's wife]! What a horrible fall...yes, I try not to run to the phone! Please give her my love..

And a hug to you.. you are dear to have written that good long letter.

Ever your old

M

Ashley Montagu: British-born American anthropologist and educator (1905–99), noted for his popular writings in his field and on other scientific matters, such as *The Natural Superiority of Women* (1953) and *Science and Creationism* (edited, 1984). In 1950, the year *On Being Human* was published, he also crafted UNESCO's "Statement on Race," promoting ethnic equality. He was an old family friend of the Sartons'.

TO SISTER ALICE GUSTAVA SMITH, C.S.J.

[York]   Sunday July 9th [1978]

Darling one,

At last here I am to commune with you a little . . I wonder what "the shakes" are, but whatever they may be in some ways I am relieved that you are in a place where help is at your side. On the other hand I can imagine the wrench it was to leave the community where your heart has been rooted for so many years. The address suggests that you are quite near by, so I trust your friends can easily drop in to see how things are with you. It was an awful pang to read that my books (yours) have gone to the library.. but I am happy that Sister Mary William [convent president] is pleased. She wrote me a sweet letter. At any rate you will soon have a new one which comes out in the autumn, a novel about a woman dying of cancer, called *A Reckoning*. It is not a depressing work, I believe. It is about dying as the last great adventure.

Everything is very lush and green here now. . roses in profusion, peonies just over. I spend a lot of time watering and I love doing that. It helps me to re-center myself after a very dispersed and dispersing spring. But all things are good just now.. it is marvelous to see the work getting through at long last. When I spoke at Radcliffe two months ago, they expected at most 50. . but messengers were sent to the President's house where I was dining to warn us that we couldn't possibly get in by the front door, there was such a mob! In fact 500 people squeezed, even standing in the windows outside to try to hear, standing in the hall at the back, sitting on the floor around my feet. . and 200 had to be turned away! I have not seen this kind of audience, loving and expectant, since Robert Frost, so it was quite a thrill. What delights me is that the establishment is unaware I exist . . it is the students who know and who read me and that is very satisfactory.

Now I am just back, as I wrote you, from a gruelling week at Thomas

Starr King school of religious leadership in Berkeley (they are Unitarians). They had asked 8 people over 60 from different fields to each hold a seminar on their own lives, work, and beliefs. Most of my group which met in the morning, also attended Howard Thurman's seminar in the afternoon .. that marvelous 78-year old black mystic and I seem to have said many of the same things, so it worked well for the 17 in our group. I'll never do it again but it was worth doing once. And it was moving to see how my open self and open work broke open things in the group and in the end we did, as I had hoped, create a real spiritual communion out of shared experience. It was two hours each day for five days, so you can see it was quite exhausting. The people were two male and two female ministers, two religious educators, a psycho-therapist, and the rest laymen, young and middle-aged of both sexes. There was among them a remarkable blind woman around 50.

Now at last I shall be here in peace for a while, except for the visiting firemen who pounce at this season.

One point about the Unitarians. I find them a little sentimental, perhaps because the emphasis is almost entirely on human relations. God appears to be absent, or they are afraid both of His absence and His presence. We had a 15 minute chapel every morning, but not one word of the Bible was ever read—the music was mostly "popular" such as Day by Day [from the 1971 musical *Godspell*], that sort of thing, all very well, BUT . . . I got quite cross when one day one of the T.S.K. staff chose part of a sentimental child's book as the text. The idea, I suppose, is to make us feel like children again, wide-eyed before the wonders of nature. But I found the means trivial and I resented it. I said so afterward to this woman minister and she was very angry and said, "You deal in words. I deal in people", so that was that. I had begged her to use a psalm in the next chapel!

I hope that in time someone will come to whom you can dictate a word or two. . . Are you still able to read, for instance?

Dear heart, I feel cut off, and need to know a little more when you can. Meanwhile my love and thoughts run to you, as always

Your

May

And I look forward to seeing you in the fall when I come to St. Paul (Nov. 13th and 14th) to speak at Macalaster and also at Unity Church.

Sister Alice Gustava Smith: Formerly Sister Maris Stella; see 9 November 1958 for the first part of her tale. After the Vatican II reforms she resumed her baptismal name and retired from teaching, with honors, in 1971. At this time she was living at "Bethany," the retirement home for nuns of the College of St. Catherine, on Randolph Avenue in St. Paul.

Howard Thurman: Theologian, poet, and civil rights advocate (1899–1981), Thurman taught at Howard University (1932–44), was dean of Marsh Chapel at Boston University (1953–65), and helped found San Francisco's Church of the Fellowship of All People. His many books include *Jesus and the Disinherited* (1949), inspired by Gandhi and an inspiration to Martin Luther King, Jr., Maya Angelou, Vernon Jordan, and Jesse Jackson. In 1953 *Life* magazine named Thurman one of the twelve greatest preachers of the twentieth century.

my . . . open work: During this week Sarton spoke about her poem "The Absence of God."

seeing you: It is not known whether Sarton was able to see Sister Alice on this trip; word from her came at Christmas 1980:

> "Dearest May, I read & reread (with my uncooperative eyes) Recovering—to me a comforting book & very revealing of a great soul. I trust you are not struggling with Judy this year—but how great of you to try! I live in a house with many Judys—Poor darlings & I wonder how long I shall know the score—Winter came gradually but it is here to stay. I hope this makes sense—it comes from a shaky old girl. Love & blessings, S. Alice S M S that was."

But Sarton did see her at Bethany in April 1983, when visiting St. Paul to speak at Unity Church: "She is having a hard time, but it was clear to me that she will die as she has lived—with a core of radiant light at the center" (*At Seventy,* p. 328).

Sister Alice Smith lived until 1987.

TO CONSTANCE REVERE MATLACK LLOYD

[York]   Sept. 11th, 1978

Connie dear,

What a sweet surprise to find a note on Judy's door for me and the marvelous macarroons, spelled wrong I see. It is so like you to do this for me.. you are just about the most thoughtful person I have ever known, and you do everything with such grace. I had meant anyway to write you this afternoon to thank you for the elegant lunch..it was a delightful sendoff to our journey, and I had to hide the chocolates after we arrived as Judy was about to devour the whole box. She came back again and again to your card which I had set up against the lamp on the table. She really did seem a little more alive to what was going on this time, in spite of several disasters and the bed soaked each night, but it was well worth all the trouble..and she did run away with Tamas next morning and was brought back by a kind neighbor [Sylvia Frieze]. Everyone watches out for her around here now, so I'm less anxious. It's so good for her to "escape", you know, that I am rather glad when I can't find her.

We had a little snooze together, Tamas, she and I, on my big bed, and that felt good and homey.

Forgive the bad typing..I'm rather pooped and depressed, I must confess.

A big hug from your old

M

P.S. I have frozen the macaroons for Huldah who comes Sept. 29 for a few days—

Constance Revere Matlack Lloyd: Mrs. Edward Lloyd (1902–99), Judith Matlack's younger sister.

[*Recovering* begins 28 December 1978.]

TO NANCY HALE   March 1st [1979]
[York]

Dearest Nancy, I have just unearthed your letter of (ai mi'.) January 14th, but I know you understand. I have been working furiously hard at a novella to keep the wolf from the door and letters have piled up. The great good news in your letter is that you are halfway through a big novel! I thought at once of The [Prodigal] Women, how good that was, and how much more you have to say now because you know so much more. I shall be very eager to read it eventually…

Thank you for all you said about A Reckoning. After four months since the mean review in the Sunday Times they finally printed a long letter in my defense by the LeShans. He is a psychiatrist who works with the dying and is convinced that the search for identity goes on to the end—anyway he compares me to Tolstoy (The Death of Ivan Illitsch) [1886] and it was a little balm. Better be over-praised than under-praised! The reviewer's answer to his letter was quite idiotic and will do her no good, I'm glad to say.

You asked about the genesis of A.R. and whether it had depressed me the writing of it..the truth is, Nancy, that I <u>was</u> dying, but not physically. I felt I was coming to the end of everything and it was a kind of preparation for me for the final letting go. Then halfway through I fell in love and began writing poems again and felt reborn. A strange sequence. All the characters in it are invented except Sybille (Rosalind Greene) who is perhaps the least realized in the novel. There seems always to be a censor at work when one bases a character too closely on a real person.

Nice things have been happening..two different outfits are to make a documentary film (one is a videotape, the other a movie) on me wandering through my life here, reading poems and so on. Did you see that marvelous documentary on Georgia O'Keefe? I saw it twice and each time felt renewed and more alive. I hope mine may be almost as good..almost because she is, at 90, still a great beauty! Also Paris Review is coming to do an interview next week. It is a joke because I have already done that interview in Mrs. Stevens. The girl who wrote me and will be the interviewer has such erratic handwriting that I wonder whether she is able..but we shall see.

Yes, I think you are right when you suggest that I am too "readable" to please the critics. There is method in my madness as I have tried to eliminate all cleverness (as to style) and to achieve something completely transparent and <u>plain</u>. The daylight. This is not fashionable. I felt that at the end in her last books Bowen had become extremely mannered to the point where she was constantly stopped by her stylistic idiosyncrasies. But at her best, how wonderful. Did you read the biography? I felt that it was accurate but somehow did not make one go back to the <u>work</u>, as a good biog of a writer should.

Well, I must go down and walk Tamas, my dog, and Bramble, my cat who always comes along, keeping her distance and racing up trees while Tamas trundles off into the woods after imaginary birds and beasts.

It is good to be in touch again, dear Nancy. Who is there but you who remembers Edith Kennedy and so much else—and who but me remembers your mother as vividly as I do?

Much love—
May

I love it that your typing is just as erratic as mine!

A Reckoning: In the 12 November 1978 *New York Times Book Review,* Lore Dickstein thought the novel's treatment of both cancer and homosexuality ineffective, "marred by Miss Sarton's style, which tends toward the ready cliché" and "the edge of sentimentality." Sarton's ability to credibly invoke one person's sensibility does not suffice in a story where "separate voices and the fabric of their lives are necessary to create a world outside the main character."

Writing in the 25 February 1979 issue, Eda and Lawrence LeShan state, "It is our feeling that Miss Sarton has written a truly magnificent book ... that ought to be read by anyone who works with the dying. ... Miss Sarton's character was finally able to discover and face who she was—the most real person in the very center of self." (For the LeShans, see [2 July 1992].)

Reviewing the contretemps from the perspective of 12 September 1991, Charles Barber took the long view: "I don't think people need to wrestle anymore with 'the critics'—this has been done already. Plus, it gives (lends) them a power they don't have in the long run. Not the power you have."

videotape ...movie: She Knew A Phoenix (1980), produced by Karen Saum, directed by Elaine Goldberg; *World of Light: A Portrait of May Sarton* (1979), produced and directed by Martha Wheelock and Marita Simpson.

The 1977 documentary on painter Georgia O'Keeffe (1887–1986) was by Perry Miller Adato.

This *Paris Review* interview never saw print.

in her last books: Sarton probably had in mind Bowen's *Eva Trout* (1968), in which subject and treatment are equally audacious.

Victoria Glendinning's *Elizabeth Bowen: A Biography* (1977) prompted the paperback reissue of all ten novels, with Knopf bringing out the *Collected Stories* in 1980. It remains the standard biography and a model of the brief modern literary life.

TO KAREN O. HODGES   March 12th, 1979
[York]

Dear Karen, what an angel you are to have taken the time to write that long and terribly good letter about the LeShans view of A. Reck[oning]. (he is a psychiatrist who works with the dying, mostly dying of cancer and has written a lot about the search for identity up to the end.) I suppose the danger if one has come out as a lesbian is that this is going to be read into everything. .I do not agree with LeShan on the point that "Laura took a wrong turning and chose safety etc." when she married. There was never any idea on either Ella's or her side that they would ever live together or be lovers. I said this in so many words. Ella, too, married. What they did wonder at the very end is whether it would have been better if they had been lovers, and Laura, I think, says "we had the best of it."

This is not a matter of sexual passion but of a strong identification with each other. The reason Laura is kind to Harriet Moors is because of what happened to Laura's older sister and that long ago aborted love affair—but I can see that someone wanting to believe that Laura should have been a lesbian because I am, might use this as evidence.

It happens that there is an Ella in my own life. We were "best friends" in grade school..she married an englishman and is now Lady Hawthorne, perpetually in hospital with asthma, a kind of psychological mess I'm afraid..three grown-up children..but the most original person I've ever known. We meet rarely but when we do we speak our childhood language, a highly inflected invented language of our own, and <u>always</u> feel as though we had come home. I can imagine very well longing to see Tioga (that is her name in our language and is also my name in our language) if I were dying. I have always felt we were twins and she might have been an artist..she seems to be a genius <u>without</u> a talent, a disaster. She is terribly funny even when in despair and we laugh till tears roll down our cheeks. (I should have used that laughter in my book, but I forgot it). The point is that I never felt the slightest sexual pull toward her nor she to me. We each lived a life the other one might have lived, she a wife and mother, I, a writer. (This is not true of Ella and Laura.)

The reason I didn't want them to be lovers is that what I had to say is on page 243… "what women can be for each other" and haven't been partly out of fear. The last thing I want to suggest is that "lesbian" is better or even a good idea unless it is absolutely what the woman <u>is.</u> A lot of letters suggest that most women get all this and are not disturbed. Many heteros have written me about the book.

The most exciting thing that is happening from the woman's movement is "bonding". Men have always had it...Denny has it with the people he takes out to dinners etc. but women have had no way to do it, women in general, after college and after marriage.

In Worcester where I read poems the other day, I took an extra day to sign books to help a Women's Bookstore that is having a hard time. I thought I might pull some people in who didn't know it existed. It was a lovely place and so many women came to thank me..women, holding the hand of a small child, nuns..young women, and all spoke of what a wonderful "center" the bookstore is. The nuns love it (I guess they know plenty about male chauvinism!) The atmosphere was full of love and light and humor.and I really wish it were nearer here and I could drop in.

Laura I think comes to see as she dies that women..her mother, her younger sister Daphne, her daughter, have been the unsolved relationships, that it is they she has to reckon with now. Rather little seems to have been written about all this, strangely enough..I mean in fiction.

Today I had a letter from a head nurse in Vancouver so succinct I'll copy it: "The human and artistic integrity of A.R. is a reprieve. I am afraid we were almost Kubler-Ross'ed to death. Thank you."

Well, we are both about to disappear as you face all these guests..how awful to have a family of four for a week-end and then Denny's sick mother for two weeks! Oh, to be nearer by and take her off your hands for a day now and then..grand that Emily likes the therapist and that Denny is coming round.

Interesting that his mother is so interested in theatre..she and Emily may have a bond there??

I'm reading Flannery O'Connor's letters, absolutely wonderful.

Spring will blow your mind any day now, I think..here it is bitter cold again but I picked some pussy willows and there are snowdrops out— we had rain for seven days, now high wind and 20 again.

I feel sure you're right about Dickstein and lesbians as she had a very gentle praising review of Pearl Buck of all people in last week's Times book review, nary a mean word.

I'm in a dither myself about leaving..and trying to write a final scene in rough of the novella so it will have some wholeness when I go back to revise. It is quite bad, I fear, but must try at least to make to better.

Much love, dear Karen..you are a trump to write me at such length and so wisely.

Your
May

Lady Hawthorne: Barbara "Tig" Runkle Hawthorne (1912-92) had been Sarton's best friend at Shady Hill School; their secret tongue was called Oyghee. On 14 July [1975] Sarton had written Hodges, concerning *Crucial Conversations:* "I based Poppy somewhat on one of my dearest friends, a brilliant woman (who wanted to be a singer) who has never said an unoriginal thing yet has been a total failure as a wife . . . Her husband who is a brilliant engineer (they wanted him to be Provost of MIT) and now Master of Churchill College in Cambridge, was recently knighted. Barbara has humanized Will and he loves her, but how he <u>can</u> when she is anything but a helpmeet I do not know. She could not even manage to have water boiling for his tea when he came home. I think she was afraid to leave him (when it was still possible. She is my age and it's too late now), but their marriage has been a war. The three children seem to have survived even though B. is always 'away' in sanitariums or under treatment of one kind or another."

we were twins: When they were ten or eleven, young Barbara took May to her family's Unitarian church; for Sarton's recollection of this formative experience, see *After the Stroke,* pp. 151–52, and *At Eighty-Two,* pp. 94–95. Hearing of Hawthorne's death in June 1992 prompted Sarton to add, concerning the flap about *A Reckoning* (*Encore,* p. 330), "I think I might say categorically that one does not usually fall in love with the 'best friend' who goes back to the fourth or fifth grade in school."

Seven years after Hawthorne died, Shady Hill classmate Mary Dewing Morain (sister of Abbie Dewing) sent this editor a letter found among her own papers from Sarton, age 12, to their childhood friend Barbara Runkle, dated 1 October 1924, Ipswich, England. (One thinks of a line from *The Magnificent Spinster,* p. 192: "What is not destroyed is perhaps deliberately left to be discovered in time.") It is reproduced here as characteristic of Sarton as both girl and woman, a testament to a truly lifelong friendship.

> Dear Barbara, Oct. 1, 1924
>
> how are you? I am very well. We are in Ipswich with Grannie.
>
> This is what I am writing for, that mother told me just the other day that Joan Hocking was often rather left out of things at school. Mother said that Aunt Agnes told her once that Joanie said that when she walked home from school she was safe with Jean C and May! She said that with others she was not sure that she wasn't going to be left out. Won't you please try and bring her into things? She is always giving things to other people so I have sent her a little doll I dressed too.
>
> How are you getting on at school? I will start in Belgium as soon as we get there. We went to Wembley and Westminister Abbey and the Parliament Houses it was a strange mixture wasn't it? Please show this letter to Abbie but not to anyone else
>
> with much love from your best friend
> May

O'Connor's letters: The Habit of Being: Letters of Flannery O'Connor, ed. Sally Fitzgerald (1979).

TO PEG UMBERGER July 16th, [1979]
[York]
Dear Peg,

I loved your letter written during the garage sale! Wanted to answer right away but I am pulling myself up from a mastectomy three weeks ago and writing is still quite an effort, so my desk is a mountain at the moment. I'm so pleased that you discovered Shower and liked it so well..it almost made Book of the Month club (was shoved aside at the last minute by a political book) and I have often wondered how that might have changed my life had it happened. Of course the house is Bowen's Court and the husband bears some resemblance to Elizabeth's, but Violet is not E. at all (except for the moths!) but was based on the mother of an english friend of mine, who was what the English call "a lovely." Bowen's Court has been torn down, so I am happy that I wrote the book to celebrate it, so long ago.

I suspected that something was wrong before I left for England in May, but I was determined to have that trip, and also to let the people making a documentary film interview with me have the week they needed, and I'm awfully glad I did wait. The trip was just perfect, a very peaceful and dear time, partly because I was determined to tame this tiger in me and accept things as they are. A barge on the Thames is the most restful form of travel imaginable..we generally docked in open country and could take a long walk in the gloaming. In the mornings they took us on delightful short trips in a minibus, ending up at some delightful old pub for a drink before lunch on the barge. Then around two we went sailing slowly down the river, sitting in the prow in deck chairs..perfect peace. Sark was perfect, too, with picnics high up on the cliffs, in fields of bluebells looking down on the gulls sailing the wind currents far below..it is a magic island and reminds me of The Tempest. We ended with a one-day visit to Gerald Durrell's zoo on Jersey..such a moving place where every glorious bird and animal one sees is an endangered species so it is very poignant.

The film is going to be beautiful, a poem. And the crew of six were so sensitive I felt myself able to be myself to the fullest extent, as, alas, I can never be with Huldah so it was with a sense of fulfillment that I went into the hospital the day after reading poems in Camden to raise money for a Shakespeare theatre there. I had a modified radical mastectomy of the left breast..luckily the left, as I could drive when I got home after only 8 days in hospital. I have been alone here for the past two weeks or more and can do everything except pull weeds. The body is a miracle in the way it goes about healing itself—and of course one gets enormous support from friends after major surgery. Mental anguish such as I suffered last year is incomparably harder to handle in every way..and then it is so lonely.

Yes, the reading at the Library of Congress went well but nothing like the huge audiences I had in Berkeley and San Francisco the month before. Also there are always two readers..they put me first and I was so afraid of running over my time (though the audience was clearly there for me, not for the playwright who followed) that I felt cramped and did not do as well as I can do under different circumstances.

I had decided before the op. that I would take a year off from public appearances..and in many ways this is a year of transition. The only work in hand is a Journal which I had called Recovering before the operation, and now I am recovering from that, too, so it works.

I'm convinced that the mastectomy was psychosomatic and came from too much pain and buried anger last year. Perhaps it can be a kind of exorcism.

Oh, the poems! There is a whole book of which the one you liked is one and I hope to get it to Norton by fall. But the whole struggle with H[uldah]. has stopped the flow now and God knows when I'll write another poem. I tore up the novella I wrote in Jan. and Feb.

Don't give up on that piece that came back from Yankee. There are several journals who might snap it up..one is called Country Living, I think. Yankee is inundated with material these days..it does not mean that the piece is not good!

I've run out of energy..

Much love

M

Peg Umberger: Friend of the work and, at that time, director of the Iroquois Indian Museum of New York State. See *At Seventy,* pp. 106–07, where Sarton calls her "one of the few of my friends who can laugh at me (gently)." She had written Sarton about *A Shower of Summer Days.*

a mastectomy: Writing critic Henry Taylor (see note below), 2 August 1979, she assured him that "The operation went off well. . a modified radical mastectomy of the left breast. As one in eighteen women go through this brutal assault I can't feel too sorry for myself. . and everyone rallied around to help me. The little hospital here [in York] is friendly and efficient. . my room was a bower of flowers."

except for the moths!: Of which Bowen was, surprisingly, quite afraid. Near the end of the *World of Light* profile, Sarton remembers her in a variety of settings, concluding with her "standing in the long windows of her bedroom at Bowen's Court in an ecstasy of terror about the moths."

can never be with Huldah: "Maybe it is that, old baby that I am, I had somehow hoped that Huldah would be a kind of wall against woe or a large mother-bear," Sarton wrote Charles Barber. "I suppose I had hoped that someday we could live together, but I could never fit into that social scene."

On 28 April 1979, Sarton had recalled (to novelist and publisher Dorothy Bryant) how "just at the time A Reckoning was clobbered last October [1978] my lover told me 'we are too old for love-making' and withdrew. . . . She cannot ever say a tender word, never looks at me with love..I am not such a sexual person that <u>that</u> matters, but the reason given for withdrawal (not the true one but a defence because she is frightened of her own sexuality, afraid of letting go, of letting life flow, must <u>control</u> everything) has had a <u>withering</u> effect. We are about to go to England for 2 weeks..and what I have to be is loving and charming and ask for nothing."

Sarton returned from this trip with "a sense of coming home to <u>me</u>" so strong that she wrote Sharpe a breaking-off letter; but by 8 October 1979 she was explaining to Catharine Claytor that "I feel she can be the central person"—"how I need that, and how loathe I was to think of someone new, for I must love someone, you know."

the playwright: Romulus Linney, author of *The Sorrows of Frederick* (1966), *Jesus Tales* (1980), and various plays.

Sarton was escorted to the Library of Congress by critic Henry Taylor (b. 1942); in 1986 he won the Pulitzer for *The Flying Change*. Taylor also introduced her reading, at the request of poet William Meredith, then Consultant in Poetry. Sarton thanked Taylor by letter: "What a golden evening it was at the [Cosmos] Club! I felt so Washingtonian and privileged and sort of in the ambience of my father who often was invited there when he was in Washington so it had a special aura for me." Though the Club had extended its reach over the past sixty years, it was founded by a group of scientists (Taylor wrote this editor), and George Sarton would have been welcomed there.

Taylor had supported her work since at least 1971: in the *Collected Poems 1930–1973* he found "Overall, there is a didactic tone that makes her unique; didacticism with a positive quality and within the historical bounds of poetry." By 29 May 1976 Sarton could write him about the astonishing attention she was now receiving at colleges: "[Q]uite a new experience for me to have students quote the poems by heart and ask about some statement on page so and so of the Journal. . . . I seem to have become a kind of exemplar and it is really terribly moving. . . . I tell you all this, dear Henry," because he had been such a friend of the work: "In fact you stuck your neck out, bless you!"

Oh, the poems!: Serena Sue Hilsinger and Lois Brynes's *Selected Poems of May Sarton* had been published in late 1978, offering a 206-page sampler grouped around various themes—"The Composed Imagination," "In a Dirty Time," "Invocations and Mythologies"—including several poems Sarton did not retain in *Collected Poems 1930–1973* or had not reprinted since publication.

In this letter Sarton is looking forward to what would become *Halfway to Silence* (1980).

I tore up the novella: That is to say, she set it aside. The 115-page manuscript of *We Aren't Getting Anywhere* opens with the lament "It's awful to be only eighteen," and chronicles Susie's miserable visit on a Maine island with rich relatives who make her feel always in the wrong. (See note on p. 308, *Dear Juliette*.) It had been years since Sarton discarded a sizable piece of work into which she had put much effort.

[*Recovering* ends 30 November 1979.]

TO KAREN O. HODGES   Sunday Jan. 27th 80
[York]

Dear Karen, I am in a hopeless state of confusion and disorder trying to get squared away so I can, at long last on February 1st, enter the uncluttered timeless land of creation again and start a new novel. Meanwhile I scrabble desperately about trying to get the photos for the new Journal [*Recovering*] decided on and placed, and the permissions (endless boring details) at least organized so someone at Norton can write the necessary letters to publishers. I have read four novels in proof since I got back and written blurbs..the last one is very dull and long, but I know the author, a man, has had a discouraging time..and I wanted at least to read it to the end, always hoping it might jell. Letters pile up..but that is my recurring problem. The point of all this complaining is to explain that your last letter deserves a long answer. I found it extremely fascinating and, as always, made me think hard and feel, too. In case you have forgotten it was about sexuality.

I agree with you absolutely that sex must have sheer fun and laughter in it (your image of two puppies tugging at a stick made me laugh) as well as that other dimension of communion on a rather deep level. I always felt with Julian that the actual consummation became great, <u>impersonal,</u> something that took us both into the heart of the universe. Making love with a woman is never that great for me. It is always personal..one does not forget the person in some great transcending wave. Its quality is in its tender exploration of the other, and the giving of one's <u>self</u>. I am saying this very badly but wanted you to know. What remains a mystery to me is why sexuality seems necessary for me if I am to write poems. It is a terrible deprivation. On the other hand I found the sexual times with Huldah very exhausting..we both looked exhausted the next day! Maybe that is where age does play a part. But we made love every night when we were together..I wish we could get back to it, <u>now and then</u>, but I fear she is armed against it now. .and could wither me with a word. There is for me no other activity in which I both lose <u>and</u> find myself so completely..except in the creation of a poem and maybe that is why they are closely allied.

I have been sick, I think with pain and anger..an attack of diverticulitis. It is because Cora, my former lover (Divorce of Lovers was about her) who years ago said to me "As far as I can see nothing you have ever written has any value"—and ever since has received each book with some kind of put-down. When I had her invited to see a showing of the film about me in Cambridge, I warned myself that she was bound to be mean spirited in response..but what she said was worse than I could imagine, to wit "there is too much of you in the film." Since it is a portrait of me…and in a way a <u>testament,</u> this is tantamount to saying it would be better if I did not exist. I heard her say this before I went to Switzerland but after I came back it was a slow burn and finally I had a bad attack of diverticulitis which I lay to it and my despair of her ever <u>seeing</u> me as in any way beautiful or valuable. Her friend agrees with her and wrote me "I am a visual person so I enjoyed the flowers and sea.." as if a human face were not also worth <u>seeing</u>. It is quite absurd to have gone into such a tailspin but I finally wrote them a breaking off letter. I feel "wasted" by the whole stupid business. And it is time I stopped hoping for what will never happen. I mention this because it sounds a little like what your mother does to you..some infernal kind of put down that kills joy. Does she know she is doing it?

This is a stupid letter and I am in a stupid state. So I had better send it off, chiefly to send you the enclosed contest slip..they ask me to spread some around and you are the best poet I know.

I liked both poems you sent but they did not get me on the pulse as some of yours do..Maybe partly they have a slightly "literary" flavor which seems less immediate than others of yours..a slightly Shakespearean air..I wish Wedding Gift were in form..it almost asks for it, to my ear.

Well, forgive this horrible mishmash. It brings much love anyway— and how I enjoy your ruminations. They bring me to complete attention at once.

love
May

Divorce of Lovers: The twenty-sonnet sequence in *Cloud, Stone, Sun, Vine*. On 28 January [1983], Sarton explained to friend of the work Doris Beatty that these poems were not about Judith Matlack. Rather, they conerned "a five year love affair which happened while I was living with Judy (I must hastily say that we had not been lovers for years as that end of things was not really right for her, so though we lived together in real <u>love</u>, I went my way and had love affairs, mostly in Europe)..I went to Nelson while that love affair was ending to have a place for my love to come..she almost never came there. A strange story. I mean in the end the solitude was what I needed. . .There was no such tension between us [Matlack and Sarton], ever, Judy was not primarily an intellectual and never tried to beat me down. (It just shows what I have to fear from biographers!)"

despair of her ever <u>seeing</u> me: Easier relations were in evidence on 8 September 1982 (*At Seventy*, p. 147), when Sarton lunched with DuBois and Jeanne Taylor: "I do not see many old friends these days and treasure the tranquil conversation, the autumn sunlight, and the not unhappy knowledge that we are all three in the autumn of our lives. So much does not need to be said, so much can be taken for granted." See also *After the Stroke,* pp. 22–23.

But "I believe the writer, especially the poet, has one supreme responsibility," Sarton had written Peg Umberger (25 July 1973), "to be absolutely honest." She told this editor, 22 April 1989, that "Cora knew she didn't have a great imaginative grasp—she called herself 'Herr Professor.'" Sarton felt their communion had finally lapsed when DuBois declared she did not care for "enthusiastic people."

I enjoy your ruminations: Hodges continues to write about her field, Jungian psychology; her latest publication is "Women, Depression, and the Soul-Image," *Spring: A Journal of Archetype and Culture* (Woodstock, Connecticut), Vol. 65, Spring and Summer 1999 (issue on "Lost Souls").

TO HULDAH SHARPE   Feb. 13th, 1980
[York]
Darling one,

I must write just a word before I get to work. Poor Amber and poor you! But it is comforting to think that mistreated dog had a year of love and a taste of what life can be for a good dog. I do feel a little relieved that you are not in for another long nursing job—and excited to think that a relative of Scottie's may be there when I come. The Clarksville kennel, if I remember, was where Scottie came from? I know you thought there was some connection.

It appears to have been a winter of struggle for you so far and I just hope there may be an early spring to make up for all the shovelling and wear and tear on slippery roads. I know you rather enjoy ordeals but I do <u>not</u> enjoy being anxious about you while they are going on!

I feel rather tired this morning, though again it was a most beautiful sunrise, with the new moon very bright against a lavender sky when I got up at 6:15, then a rosy dawn, "the rosy fingered dawn" gilding the edges of the small window panes, and catching the prism so it flashes (that ugly pink thing does not seem to work very well).

Lee seems now on top of things, happily working at tiny animals in clay, one of which she sent off to you yesterday (open it very carefully or it might break) and determined to get up here at long last to inhabit her own house by March 1st or so. Meanwhile she makes vegetarian casseroles for those two old ladies, one of whom has been in hospital for a cataract op., and cuts wood for them and brings it in as the other one is very arthritic. No doubt having someone to think about and help is the best medicine. If only the furies who seem always to be at her window, keep away for a while!

Poems are coming in for that issue of Beloit I am editing..I am very tired of simple declarative sentences and pure description in free verse. And I hate rejecting but little by little I hope to have a good issue in hand. One day I'll go through all your poems again and choose one, if I may? I have till July so there's time.

Poor Martha [Wheelock]! In L.A. her briefcase was stolen out of the car, the only thing that was stolen..and it had the first chapter of her thesis in it and all her notes for other chapters..it seems too strange for a thief to take it and nothing else. But they are having a triumphant time with the film..I've had quite a lot of mail about various showings in Cal. and now on their way home they show it in Santa Fe. There is a chance it may get onto Hugh Downs show, Over Easy (national TV about old people, not exactly what I might have chosen.)

It is now nine and I must stop this babbling on.

Your flowers did my heart good, made it beat a little faster, and now rejoice my eyes—the combination of yellow tulips and lavender freesia is perfect in mother's wide-mouthed Venetian glass which works well when the tulips begin to bend so gracefully as they fade...

I'll print a few more hearts on my lion when I see her again..it feels a long way off, but we are getting there!

> All love from your
> [a heart]

Maybe your letter will come today—

Lee: Artist and friend Lee Blair (d. 1998).

that issue of Beloit: Sarton guest-edited the first issue of *The Beloit Poetry Journal* (Fall 1950); see notes to the 8 February 1962 letter to John Holmes. Her fall 1980 preface mentions her hope of presenting "an entire issue of poems using meter and rhyme." Instead, she "had to settle for substance and grace without supreme tension of release." For this thirtieth anniversary number, Sarton included work by (among others) Evelyn Ames, Jean Burden, M. F. Hershman, Karen Hodges, Jean Clark Lieberman (a Shady Hill classmate), and Henry Taylor, but none by Sharpe.

TO PAUL REED   March 6th, 1980
[York]
Dear Paul Reed,

I have been in a quandary about answering your last letter because, frankly, I know so little about you! Can I be honest? Do you really have any idea what goes into a good poem or story? So many people have illusions about a possible talent and so little awareness of what the competition is. Being a published writer is a little like being an Olympic gold medal winner..that is the competition, only one has to do it over and over again.

It may be that the novel, which sounds autobiographical from the title, may be "your thing." But I was dismayed at how (honestly) bad the poem you sent is. The first stanza, broken down, is grotesque. No good poem, a highly structured thing, can be compared to <u>cream from a bottle</u>. What in hell does "thick" writing mean? My poems are neither "diffuse" nor "sweet." A good metaphor has to be able to stand intellectual analysis on both sides, the metaphor itself <u>and</u> what it stands <u>for</u>. The cream suddenly turns into a translation of earth-dreams!

It looks to me as though you were trying to get published before you were ready. Do you get any criticism from a critic-friend you can trust? Have you ever joined a writing group?

I think of those lovely flowers and all your kindness and am grieved to write such a letter to you. But I want to help. You are in for a lot of rejection (and that is good for no one) if you don't learn to be more self critical.

I'm off for two weeks to Fla. and Tenn. after getting 100 pages down of the new novel [*Anger*], so am a little frantic..

All warm wishes from your friend
<u>May Sarton</u>

Paul Reed: Author (b. 1956) who initially wrote Sarton in 1978 about *House by the Sea*, the first of her books he had read. He took his M.A. in social anthropology from the University of California at Davis.

Olympic gold: Sarton increasingly found younger artists, such as Reed, appealing to her for encouragement or advice; she never underplayed the difficulties. To Catherine Claytor (then Becker) she wrote, 28 September 1978, "[Y]ou are right to refuse to be mediocre, to wish to make a total commitment, to insist that the artist in you must be recognized and accepted (first by yourself). But don't panic because you are not 'great' right away…more and more I feel great art is made small step by small step. What you ask will be given if you are patient with yourself. . . . you are an artist and it will all happen, if you get at it slowly, lovingly, inwardly."

all warm wishes: By 1984, Reed had written *Facing It: A Novel of AIDS,* and was well launched on a productive and noteworthy career. (See 24 June 1989.) Receiving her copy, Sarton was "touched by your mention of me in the front. It is a splendid job, bless you, and will help a lot of people in the hetero world who have never imagined what AIDS has been for the homo world . . . help because you have brought it all down to the human plane." It is widely acclaimed as the first published novel about the epidemic.

TO WILLIAM HEYEN   Sunday, June 1st, 1980
[York]
Dear Bill Heyen,

Last night I read the Swastika Poems through and lay awake a long time thinking about them and you and the immensely difficult spiritual journey they represent. You know I expect that I was born in Belgium, and that we were driven out by the Germans in World War I, so in a way my journey parallels yours but from the opposite direction. I have had to journey deeper than an ingrained hatred of the Prussian to where when it came to the holocaust I could go deep enough to accept that we are all responsible, and every one of us might have been caught up in the machine. You will find two poems in the Selected [*Poems,* 1978] I sent you, "The Invocation to Kali" [1971] and "The Tortured." The latter stemmed from the torture (and later death) of one of my Belgian cousins, the failure of the family whom everyone looked down on. Then he stood up under torture and did not tell. It took me three months to find a way to talk about this. I believe that poetry is the healer..in one sense because it makes it possible (through music and form) to look at the un-endurable.

You do this in these marvelous poems. So many people still will not "take in" the holocaust. I bless you for them, and for sending me this present when I needed it badly. I get hundreds of poems in the mail, nearly all bad free verse and self-indulgent. Very few true poets care enough to send me their work. I am a sort of Dodo, I think, buried centuries ago by the literary establishment. My poems are not even reviewed these days. But that doesn't matter now..I am getting through just the same and have standing room only audiences when I read! I am not complaining, but wanted you to know that your gift was precious.

It's a hard time here for several reasons.

I am glad you are there.

Gratefully yours,
<u>May Sarton</u>

William Heyen: b.1940; poet, editor, instructor of English at SUNY, Brockport. Sarton quoted his poem "The Field" in *Recovering*, p. 12; "Harpoon" would appear in *Encore*, p. 225, and page 129 of *At Eighty-Two* attests to her admiration of Heyen as a poet.

he stood up: For Jean Sarton's story, see note to 12 March 1968 and *After the Stroke*, pp. 211–12. (Heyen's poem "Lord" appears on p. 220.) Sarton contributed a blurb to *Falling from Heaven: Holocaust Poems of a Jew and a Gentile*, by Heyen and Louis Daniel Brodsky (1991), which included *The Swastika Poems* (Vanguard Press, 1971), as "Part One: The Village."

glad you are there: Sarton and Heyen did not meet until 5 May 1982, when he came with publisher William Ewert and a friend to Wild Knoll; see *At Seventy*, pp. 18–19. That visit inspired Heyen's poem "May Sarton (1912–1995)" (published by Ewert, 1999) from *The Angel Voices, A Poem*.

Heyen and Mary Elsie Robertson interviewed Sarton on 3 November 1983; see Earl G. Ingersoll, ed., *Conversations with May Sarton* (Univ. of Mississippi, 1991), henceforth "Ingersoll's *Conversations*." Recalling Bogan's remark about keeping the Hell out of her work, Sarton admitted it "haunted her," until "At some point the iron went into me, and it was first shown in *As We Are Now* and *Crucial Conversations*. I began to look at the dark side in those two books, and in the poem 'The Invocation to Kali.' "

TO PAMELA ASKEW   July 6th, Sunday [1980]
[York]
Dear Pamela,

Unbelievable that your letter that made me so happy, happy because you liked the Poussin poem, is dated May 14th nearly two months ago. That is simply an example of why my life at present fills me with despair, and all I can think of is Empson's "the waste remains, the waste remains and kills."

You can hardly imagine what a lift that letter of yours gave me—I meant when I spoke of the poem as a start, not that it was not finished, but rather that I hoped to go on and deeper in to the painter and away from myself in other poems. But I am caught in a very pressured summer here and creation is rather far away these days, in another country. I have been working hard to finish five big lectures I have to give at the U. of Maine at the end of the month on the writing of poetry. Yesterday with the help of ritalin (which I use in emergencies but not as a general rule) I finished the third, "Form as Freedom." But I am flogging a dead horse these days.

Anyway the garden is glorious and in better order after a great battle to weed and mulch the annual beds. The Japanese iris elsewhere is about to come into flower, such beauty and the field in front of the house is now rippled by wind, sumptuous green waves of long grass..it makes me laugh that people think of me as sitting quietly observing and enjoying all this while as a matter of fact I am running all the time <u>against</u> time.

I read "The Angelic Consolation of St. Francis" with great interest, but because those painters do not touch me as Poussin does, it was less of an event than your notes on Poussin—or I was not quite in the mood, perhaps. By the way, I have often been inspired by painters especially by Piero della Francesca..the frescos at Arezzo made me rethink everything about art when I saw them. There is a poem about that called "Nativity" [1957] (though there I used the nativity in the National Gallery in London). Someday we must talk about painters, or rather <u>go on</u> talking—what fun!

But surely we shall meet again and I'll be a better correspondent after this horrendously busy and depressed summer...

Yours
May

Pamela Askew: Professor emerita of art history, Vassar College. Among other works, she has edited for the National Gallery of Art, Washington, D.C., *Claude Lorrain, 1600–1682: A Symposium* (1984) and has written a detailed study on *Caravaggio's Death of the Virgin* (1990). "The Contemplation of Poussin" leads off *Letters from Maine* (1984). Sarton's mood made her think of a villanelle by British critic and poet William Empson (1906–84).

five big lectures: These dealt with "the Ars Poetica, one a day, with an hour and a half seminar for writing poets every afternoon," Sarton wrote Sylvie Pasche, 24 July 1980. "It seems quite impossible to me at the moment, but I expect to revive like an old fire horse who hears the bell when I get there." From 25 to 28 August she was "due to exude wisdom for the Methodist ministers at their yearly retreat (!)."

"[I]t turned out to be an epiphany," she reported back to Pasche, 7 September 1980. "[T]he ministers, many of them quite young in outlook were deeply moved and said I had given them back the gospel (!) although I did not mention God or the Bible" but simply suggested "that poetry heals because it makes it possible to look at the unbearable."

Poussin . . . Piero: French painter Nicolas Poussin (1594–1665) was renowned for scenes drawn from biblical and classical themes; Sarton's poem dwells on one of his bacchanals.

Piero della Francesca (c. 1420–92), Italian painter known for religious works and aristocratic portraits. Seeing the Arezzo frescoes the first time "was a glorious surprise," Sarton wrote to her father (12 September 1954), "really the most grave and perfect <u>splendor</u> in their cool spaciousness and strange characteristic cold blue, greens and a queer dark Siena red." "It was like a religious experience," she later recalled to Ilse Vogel, 15 January 1969. "The necessity for space, for silence, (within the poem or the painting), the strange coldness which is also so <u>moving</u>."

TO FRED ROGERS   Aug. 14th, 1980
[York]
Dear Fred Rogers,

A little miracle took place yesterday as I was sitting, a little lonely and scared, in the hospital waiting to be called for the first of a series of radiation treatments I am in for. (Sorry about all the "littles"! I guess I feel a little diminished!) I had the mail with me and opened your letter..it just seemed too good to be true that I had a letter from Mr. Rogers and that Mr. Rogers has read Sarton and liked her. It was such a blessing!

When I came home I turned on the TV at five to renew our acquaintance. I need not tell you that it is not only little children who find a pool of peace and understanding in that half hour. I used to watch often in Nelson on winter evenings (at this season I am apt to be out in the garden at that time). Anne Thorp (who appears in Journal of a Solitude) when she was in her late eighties and a child again watched you every day, took off her sneakers when you did, and looked at you and all you did or said with eager love. It is very good news that you are or will be doing a show with old friends in it.

So, all things considered, I am sending a donkey to Nantucket. I hope you haven't read this one [The Poet and the Donkey]. You will recognize me in the guise of Andy..may it give you some moments of pleasure.

And do not feel the burden of an answer on your holiday, for Heaven's sake!

Love and thanks
May Sarton

Bless Eda and Larry [LeShan] for making the connection!

――――――

Fred Rogers: b.1929; creator of Mister Rogers' Neighborhood, which ran for thirty-three years before its final episode was taped in November 2000. The series lives on in rebroadcasts.

making the connection: Five years later, when she visited Pittsburgh during a book tour, Rogers "put me into a segment," Sarton wrote Char Radintz, 4 October 1985. "[T]he whole atmosphere in the studio was so gentle and loving it was quite amazing. We had to go over it three times, nothing written, so it was different each time…and 'we' were Fred and me and a dear young man poet who comes in at the end and joins us on the porch. It took 5 hours in all!"

The episode, "Making and Creating," was first shown 6 February 1986. The young poet was Christopher de Vinck; see 20 March 1988. For Radintz, see 12 June 1988. Sarton felt that Rogers, despite the demands upon him, "manages the human and the intimate with such grace" (Endgame, p. 53). When he phoned New Year's Day 1994, she admitted being depressed (At Eighty-Two, p. 187), saying, " 'I am eighty-one, you know,' and he laughed and said, 'Everyone all over the world knows you're eighty-one.' "

TO ANNE ALVORD AND EDITH ROYCE SCHADE

[York]   Jan. 29th, 1981

Dear Anne and Duffy,

I am delighted to hear that you will use My Sisters, O My Sisters as a jumping-off point for discussion..and by all means make copies, for those present. Before I forget on page 75 of Collected Poems [*1930–1973*] there is a bad misprint. Line 7 should read "In the warm light" not "in the pure light" (the underlining is not meant to be in the text, only to draw your attention to that). The historical context of the poem has some interest, though I trust it transcends a point in history. At that point (long before militant feminism) [1946] I felt that American women too often dominated and even looked down on their husbands as not really "with it"..and by so doing had given up asking "greatness" of men, and by doing that had limited their own growth. This is an unfashionable view but I think it remains true though the feminists in your audience will rise up! (the other side of this not dealt with in the poem is American men's fear of the strong woman, especially the intellectual woman. Moving as I did at that time between Europe and the U.S. I had felt that in Europe I did not have to pull any punches, that European men enjoyed my powers but American men were afraid..I could be "a whole woman" in Europe and not over here.)

The first part deals exclusively with the woman as writer, poet. The woman artist has always had problems, God knows. What I was getting at was that now the woman poet could hope to be less of a "monstre sacré" and become a good poet and a fully developed human being, not asserting herself as somehow apart from every other woman, but be a fulfilled woman and a fulfilled artist. This is very optimistic and I might be less optimistic now. (See "Mrs. Stevens" written much later which deals expressly with the woman as artist, I think passages from this novel would come in handy in your discussion.) Of the eminent women novelists today, for instance, Eudora Welty never married, has no children; V. Woolf and E. Bowen, married, no children: ditto Edith Wharton. Willa Cather never married. Of the painters you would know as well as I or better, Cassatt never married, Georgia O'Keeffe has no children and so on. The point here is not that they are unfulfilled human beings but that dedication to an art and bringing up a family are hard to manage.

Part II really goes on to talk about the woman in every woman, artist or not, the sense of what a woman as nurturer can be, the actual physical happy being a woman, and what it means to the woman, and what it can give to a lover or a child.

"Wise as the serpent and gentle as the dove" comes from the Bible but I don't know where [Matthew 10:16]. My father used to say it to me with a twinkle in his eye when I set out on my adventures when I was young. The serpent is not evil—

"The deathly bone" ..I hate to analyze but I think the deathly bone represented the intellectual side of man which a woman's touch can help him integrate with his physical being. "Deathly" as the skeleton without flesh, without feeling.

Part III suggests the dangers of being a woman, of going too far onto the nurturing-mothering side where it stifles the life of children and husband. I was partly reacting (in the whole poem) against easy sex, sex as simply pleasure, instead of only when the God is present, when its sacred side (which is love) is present. This was a period of growing sexual permissiveness, at the expense of spirit, I felt. Sex as a gift to the "poor small god of pleasure" I saw as a danger because it reduces a tremendous experience to something petty.

Part IV is fairly clear..the last part does perhaps come back to the woman artist, who will be fulfilled and find her greatness, not by denigrating that of men, but by balancing it with her own. We grow together, not at the expense of one sex, (I agree about Yang, Yin..but this is where an interpreter—you—can help elucidate by bringing in your wisdom and expertise.)

My morning is almost gone..and I'm working hard again after almost a year of illness.. So I must send this off now.

Let me know how it all goes. All warm wishes

May Sarton

Anne Alvord and Edith Royce Schade: Alvord and Schade gave numerous presentations of Sarton's work at libraries throughout Connecticut and elsewhere.

Alvord was a schoolteacher, a member of the Glastonbury Board of Education. As a graduate of Yale Divinity School, she is now ordained in the United Church of Christ Congregational, and is pastor of a Housatonic, Massachusetts, parish.

Schade is a professional portrait and illustrative photographer, with many publishing and exhibition credits. She also uses her work for such civic causes as environmental protection, as first-prize awards from the Connecticut Audubon Society attest.

"monstre sacré": In a documentary about French singer Edith Piaf, an associate described her by using the word *monstre,* but Sarton thought the proper term *monstre sacré.* "There is no English equivalent," she writes (*House by the Sea,* 11 March 1976, p. 214), "but I think it means someone larger than life, set apart by genius, whom genius has made impossibly difficult, as well as impossibly marvelous." Here, Sarton implies that women poets can now begin to be accepted as whole human beings and as women, not as extraordinary grotesques, set apart from humankind.

TO JACQUELINE LIMBOSCH 16 August [1981]
[York] [In French]

Dearest Minx,

I don't know why tears come to my eyes after calling you by our childhood nickname (which you used to sign your sweet letter of July 31st) but no doubt it's because it made me think of our long life side by side..and now I believe we have become real friends who share memories going far back—what riches there are in the past!

On the whole your air-tour must have been enriching, but I understand quite well the exhaustion you felt setting out, the poignance of being away from your native place! Like you, I am always overwhelmed in Europe, by the memory of my travels there with Judy, the irreplaceable friend.

I hope you found Eugénie [Dubois] in good shape? certainly happy to be leaving for Marianne's [Camille Mayran]. I'm sad that the rain prevented my making the acquaintance of those three hens, but it was good to see <u>her</u> anyway, glowing and wise as always.

It hasn't been a nice summer here..humid, cloudy, grey weather, so that I almost never wake to see that blue ocean which I love. The arbutus in the garden is mildewed, and I feel a little mildewed too, alas. I've had too many people here as guests passing through..and I have to fight for time to work, though I hope that after September 1st I'll recapture my solitude and some peace. Happily I won't be giving any more poetry readings till April.

But there are good moments all the same, especially when I can write <u>one</u> page which seems to me satisfactory..the book is starting to take on a life of its own..it's a good sign when I write things without being aware of it—that is to say, which come straight from the subconscious to astonish me! As with all my books this novel is a big risk, and as always I suffer from anxiety and panic..at least I'm not like the ram of Marthe and Madeleine (do you remember) "miserable with well-being."

How I reveled in picking flowers at Nicole's—and I have many other fine and tender recollections of my visit, which I think of in bed after a long day—

Let me give you a big hug my dear—drop me a line when you feel like it—

Your
May

Jacqueline Limbosch: Died November 2001. Claire, Nicole, Jacqueline, and Jacques Limbosch were the children of Céline and Raymond Limbosch; Jacques died in a 1935 skiing accident. The Limbosches were Sarton's second family, with whom she spent much of her child-hood in Europe. At this time, Sarton had just returned from three weeks abroad.

"miserable with well-being": Possibly a reference to the old fable about a donkey that, torn between a pile of succulent hay and a bucket of delicious oats, starves from indecision.

TO CONSTANCE HUNTING   Jan. 21, 1982
[York]
Dearest Constance,

What a day was yesterday when the two pieces came and were devoured like manna from Heaven! I was delighted by the originality, the unexpectedness of The Eccentric Biography..very wise of you to omit private life altogether! I love the quotes from George Sarton and how beautifully they are used. My only query would be a perhaps too great emphasis on joy—the opening sketch has the unadulterated joy of the <u>memory</u> as told by her mother,..Wondelgem in retrospect became a lost Eden, but it was <u>lost</u>. Most of my work has been charged by the necessity to deal with pain, to come to understand, and then to make something flower from it that was <u>not</u> negative. The much-uprooted child longs for roots (in the first years of my life we were uprooted from Belgium, then from England, then from Washington D.C. to Cambridge.) My mother was ill (after the death of a little boy) and I was taken from her twice during my first two years. I learned very early how to make very quick roots and attach myself like a limpet to people simply in order to survive. All this does not have to be said in so many words, but somehow suggested nonetheless. I think the weak place is the last few lines of page 8. They are elegant stylistically but perhaps a shade too light? I hate to have the last page altered, yet again here I feel perhaps the emphasis is too great on my father's joy in my birth, and I winced at the last line, since it is clear my father and I had a hard time as father and daughter, and he did not understand me at all! If the wonder endures it is partly because it was tested again and again by failure, lack of recognition disastrous love affairs, uprootings etc. For years the split between Europe and America was so intense that I did not know where I belonged..I really only became American when I got the Nelson house and had, for the first time, a home of my own. I was then 45.

But think this over and if it doesn't work for you to change it..I shall still be happy and fulfilled and infinitely grateful for what is on these pages. I am sure you were right to go for <u>essences</u> rather than biographical particulars.

I was dazzled by the prescient precise analysis of the poems—no one has seen the value of certain irregularities as you do here. I was especially pleased by the remarks about "Now I Become Myself." [1948] I love how you use my mother's embroideries, but here again I wonder whether that paragraph would fit better within the analysis of form and whether at the end some space might be given to <u>content</u>. The discipline has been not only that of saying or how to say, but of how to deal with feeling itself, the discipline of learning more and more how to be honest. "What had to grow has been allowed to grow" ["In Suffolk," 1978]. I wish the section on the poems could end with a poem of <u>substance</u>. "Death and the Lovers" [1958] might do it. Control as far as form goes has deeper meaning when what is being controlled, and come to terms with by means of creating the poem, has in itself a certain harshness or depth. Form consoles while it clarifies: "The Sacred Wood" [1953]. Coming where it does I don't think "the risk is very great" at the very end is quite right: the embroideries do not take the deep risks that some at least of the poems do. (The first stanza of "The Invocation to Kali" for example.)

Do you ever answer your question on page 2 "Is May Sarton not only too sober but too serious?" (There are humourous poems after all)

Well, dear heart, cast all this aside if it does not make sense to <u>you</u>, the admirably sensitive critic.

I am happy as a lark with both pieces as a matter of fact, and I understand exactly what you mean when you talked about "enjoying watching my mind at work." I and a great many other people are going to enjoy that!

With grateful love

M

Am sending these both as you may need them—

———

Constance Hunting: b. 1925; poet, professor of English at the University of Maine, publisher and editor of the Puckerbrush Press and *The Puckerbrush Review. At Seventy,* pp. 185–86, reprints a poem from her 1982 collection *Dream Cities.*

To honor Sarton's seventieth birthday, Hunting was editing the collection of essays *May Sarton: Woman and Poet* (Orono, Maine: National Poetry Foundation, 1982). It includes three of her own: "May Sarton: Reaching the Lighthouse" (in which she quotes Sarton: "Those things that alone can give value to our life must be won, and won again and again") and the two discussed in this letter. "An Eccentric Biography" takes its departure from Sarton's "Autobiography of Moods," an essay written at sixteen. In " 'The Risk Is Very Great': The Poetry of May Sarton," Hunting identifies its three main attributes: form, precision, and ease.

the death of a little boy: Young May was sent to stay with friends in Yonkers, the Baekelands, at the end of Mabel Sarton's difficult pregnancy in 1917; Alfred, born in Cambridge, Massachusetts, near the end of August, lived only five days. Two letters from this time open the 1986 selection of her mother's *Letters to May*; see note to 8 June 1985 for details about that book.

TO CHARLES BARBER   Feb. 4th, [1982]
[York]

Dear Charles,

We are having a one day respite from the worst winter I have had
here in 10 years..I even have my window open and the sun is out after
48 hours of heavy rain on top of glare ice and two feet of old snow. It
will be a joy to walk Tamas for a change in the reviving gentle air.

What a stoic you are to have managed that awfully hard work at the
Strand! Of course I shall be anxious now to hear what Phelps has to say
about the Cocteau, but whatever he says, splendid to hear it is completed..and even more important I want to hear Mabou Mines' reaction,
I wish I had seen the Colette.

I saw Barbette once..absolutely amazing! So slender, beautiful and
feminine that when he took off his wig at the curtain call it was a terrible shock. Your idea about Colette's presence somewhere in a corner
sounds delightful, by the way. How inventive you are!

Are you having fun acting? Send me a program sometime so I can get
it all straight, who you play, what the company is called etc. As for
Repertory the problem seems to be that you need a permanent company of distinction who can each play varying parts and who will stick
together. Because the theatre is now or never it is very hard to keep
actors who have a big success and then are bought by Broadway or the
movies. And you can't even blame them! Their time is as short as art
goes as the life of a mayfly in the natural world.

It's too bad about Bill Alfred's play..I gather Dunaway was wonderful,
but the play didn't really function. He is such a darling man I hoped it
would be a big success. (I think of him always feeding caviar to his big
black dog at tea and having the courage to bring his very non-U parents
to Cambridge to be near him and never apologizing for them..saintly in
the snobbish Harvard environment).

The Dinesen letters were my book of the year..how it shows what a
work of art is and how distilled out of misery and snobbism and everything else Out of Africa was. Her delight in killing animals and her
snobbism (imagine saying, it was worth getting syphilis to be a
Baronesse!) are her only flaws. What courage and wisdom otherwise!
She has always been a hero for me—

Brideshead is my one great pleasure these days when I am on a diet
to lose 20 pounds and depressed because the novel is finished and I feel
empty. But I agree that Sebastian is wrongly cast..the wrong features. He
might be a grocer's son!

Anger won't come out till early '83, a long wait. But now I hope to
write a few poems..March 6th I go to Captiva for ten days rest from

Maine winter and struggle..and on April 1st go on the road most of the month starting in St. Louis but mostly in N.E. ($8000 for a month is not bad for an aged bird!)

Well off I go into the air..this is an awful letter because I spent half the morning doing figures to find out why my bank balance was way off. It now seems that they were changing computers the day I deposited $3500 and it never got registered! Christ, what are computers for? (if you remember your Amy Lowell)

Love and hugs
M

---

hard work at the Strand: Barber worked at the famous and famously huge Strand Book Store in New York, while pursuing the theatre. "The [Jean] Cocteau" and "the Colette" seem to refer to dramatic presentations about these French writers, whom (among others) the late Robert Phelps edited and translated. Mabou Mines is an ongoing experimental company based in New York which specializes in Beckett and exploratory productions of the classics.

Barbette: A legendary trapeze artist of the '20s and '30s, Barbette performed in dresses and wigs until, as a grand finale, the circus's patrons would be astonished when it was revealed that she was really a he. (Note adapted from Jeremy Iggers's descriptions in the 22 February and 17 May 2001 issues of the Minneapolis–St. Paul *Star Tribune*.)

having fun acting?: At one point Barber directed an all-male cast in *As You Like It,* in keeping with the custom of Shakespeare's time.

Bill Alfred: Playwright and Harvard professor of English, William Alfred (b. 1922). In 1965, at the American Place Theatre, Faye Dunaway starred in his production of *Hogan's Goat.*

the Dinesen letters: Letters from Africa, 1914–31, ed. Frans Lassons, trans. Anne Born, 1981. *At Seventy,* pp. 266–69, provides a longer consideration of Dinesen, her work, and Judith Thurman's classic *Isak Dinesen: The Life of a Storyteller* (St. Martin's Press, 1982).

Bill Brown gave Sarton a Cecil Beaton photograph of Dinesen taken three days before her death, her face "suffused in an ineffable smile, the smile of one who has suffered everything and accepted everything" (p. 269). For one version of the poem Sarton tried, for years, to write about this image, see appendix: "The Blessing."

Brideshead: The new Granada Television production of Evelyn Waugh's *Brideshead Revisited* (1945) aired over many weeks, with Anthony Andrews playing Sebastian Flyte.

Anger won't come out: In fact it was published fall 1982. In *The New York Times Book Review* (17 October 1982) Sheila Ballintyne intriguingly viewed the novel from the perspective of *Recovering,* the journal just preceding it, concluding: "Considering the enormous scope of her work and the number of people it has reached, it is clear that May Sarton's best work . . . will endure beyond the influence of particular reviews. . . . She is a seeker after truth with a kind of awesome energy for renewal, an ardent explorer of life's important questions."

Captiva: A barrier island and bird sanctuary, just next to Sanibel, off the west coast of Florida; the nearest big city is Fort Myers. In earlier years Sarton had visited poet and civil rights activist Marion Cannon there; now it was the winter home of Adelaide Cherbonnier.

your Amy Lowell: Lowell's 1916 poem "Patterns" ends with the speaker saying her lover has died "In a pattern called a war. / Christ! What are patterns for?"

Love and hugs: See *At Seventy,* pp. 85–87, for Barber's July 1982 visit to York. Nineteen when they met, he was then twenty-nine, and "Life has not been easy on that innocent face." Having confronted the hard facts of theatre life, he was returning to his writing.

[*At Seventy* begins 3 May 1982.]

TO ADELAIDE CHERBONNIER   June 8th, 1982
[York]
Dear Jabber,

We were cut off but I didn't want to call back since family were there and you had just finished dinner...or not quite. On and off all night I was thinking of you, "now you are an orphan too" as an eighty year old man wrote me when my father died.

You must feel deep down happy because you accomplished what you meant to do so well..take care of your father in the most sensitive and practical way, with so much imagination, to the gentle end you had hoped for. That was a long sustained journey you made with him. That it has now ended and what you most feared, yet hoped for, as his strength waned, has happened, you must feel a lot of things all mixed up together. But how rare a daughter you are to have accomplished what you did! I have said it before but will risk repeating it that I had a great lesson in love when I was with you and I'll never forget it.

I'm so happy I met your father, experienced his courtesy and sweetness, saw the twinkle in his eye! And I like to think of you going out to the farm tomorrow.

I hope you can sleep a lot now and let future plans come naturally in time. Not forced to do anything fast. But do think of coming here for a few days in August, will you? Almost any time would be all right here, except the 3rd, my mother's birthday when I'm going down to see LeGallienne. You know the wonderful Civic production of Alice in Wonderland with Richard Addinsell's music is to be revived and open in N.Y. October 26th? (I'll be in Vancouver, alas). Someone has come forward with a million and a half to do it..that is what it will cost! Someone who saw the original production and loved it. I am so happy for LeG.

I have been panting through May and until now because things piled up so.. but after July there will be a break. And after the big speech at the Unitarian Assembly June 25th I can breathe better .. I am scared to death about that. I more or less planned it yesterday, though, and feel a bit less panicky as a result.

Oh those bears! What a <u>marvelous</u> present! Bears sleeping, bears lumbering around, bears in pools, bears together and that wonderful sleeping scene at the end. I shall never have enough of those BEARS!

A quick letter because I'm driven as usual .. people come to record a poetry reading and for an interview later this morning. Thursday for four days a young woman who is doing her PHD thesis on my novels. The worst has been being unable to garden because of the incessant rain..but this afternoon I hope to get the tuberous begonias I have been growing under lights in the cellar <u>in</u> and just being outdoors and getting my hands in some earth will be reviving.

Your garden must be beautiful now?

Do write when you feel like it and think about August!

A big hug
M

Adelaide Cherbonnier. b. 1926; patron of the arts and faithful friend, Cherbonnier had served on the American Repertory Theatre board and knew Le Gallienne. Her father had been suffering from Parkinson's. "Jabber" was her lifelong nickname.

going down to see Le Gallienne: Sarton writes about their visit in *At Seventy,* pp. 110–12: "We have been friends for fifty-three years."

Alice in Wonderland: In 1930, Le Gallienne and Florida Friebus adapted the two Alice books for the stage. Classically trained composer for films Richard Addinsell (1904–77) is best known for his *Warsaw Concerto,* centerpiece for *Dangerous Moonlight* (1941). *At Seventy,* pp. 227–28, gives details of this production, done when Le Gallienne was eighty-four: "[T]he ring in her voice makes it very clear that she will not be downed."

PHD thesis: This was Betsy Swart; see *At Seventy,* pp. 65–68.

TO DORIS GRUMBACH   July 22, 1982
[York]
Dear Doris,

And now for you and me, and my unjustified and harsh attack on you a year ago. Since I wrote which seems ages ago though I expect it was not more than 24 hours I have been wrestling with forgiveness and atonement between you and me and also as philosophical concepts. I do not believe one can atone for such an outbreak, or that one can forgive it. It is like a schism in the human compact. But atonement, or atone, goes back to "at-one" (middle English) according to my dictionary..and perhaps that is the clue for me in my present condition which resembles that of Mr. Head in "The Artificial Nigger" [Flannery O'Connor]..please read p. 88 of Journal of a Solitude where I quoted the passage that haunts me.

I cannot atone for what I did that night, but I can perhaps in time be "at one" with you, and that is a matter of abnegation first and of understanding you as well as myself. It is very hard for me to confess what I am about to confess but I think I have to do it if clarity between us is to be reached. I have envied you and envy is the worst of all emotions except jealousy.. they are closely connected of course.. because it cannot be sublimated. Most pain can be sublimated and most of my work has been an attempt to do so. When Chamber Music came out it received everything I have wanted and have never had..universally admiring reviews, translations into many languages including French, and lots of money. Your publishers gave you a party (no publisher has ever done that for me). But you also have six daughters and a grandson. Moreover you are a power in the literary establishment. (If I envy that because it makes some things easier for you in getting your work through to the public, I also know that when I went to Nelson I deliberately chose to close myself off from other situations, stopped reviewing for the Times etc.). I am ashamed of that envy and actually no longer feel it. But I did feel it.

Do I come through to you as suffering from "pride"? In your letter you suggest that I do. That I justify bad human actions by my work, or a talent. But the curious thing is..and I have never entirely understood it..is that I have always felt I had to <u>atone</u> for whatever talent I have by doing a great deal for other people—far from using a talent to justify I have felt that I had to "make up" for the luck of having it, by extreme acts of generosity, by giving about two thirds of my life to helping people, often people I do not know personally and then who get adopted into my extended family, and by depriving myself both of time and money. Why does having a talent create guilt rather than pride? I do not know. But you have sometimes said you feel it too when we have talked.

Dear Doris, I have the most fresh and revitalizing memories when I think of that Easter week we shared and you gave me..and I know (I think) a little of what such generosity cost you. It was a beautiful week..unforgettable going to Mass with you (for once I did not leave a church in tears, a Godless orphan) the exquisite drive through the arboretum..oh those brilliant azaleas among the flights of white dogwood) the remarkable play about the deaf (almost never do I go to the theatre and to be there with you was a blessing) and most of all, the days when I read Cather and you were working next door..such a sense of peace in its most active mode. What was painful and did take something out of me was that irresponsible and truly wicked story about torture which affected me like a rape of my psyche and I am not sorry that I made the effort to speak out. Was I wrong to do that? I do not believe so.

You have over the years done everything you could to help my work..from that first wonderful P. [paragraph?] in the New Republic about <u>As We Are Now,</u> on.

It is good that you have found a true communion religiously speaking..you have been on a journey inward this year, and if part of that journey has resulted in your writing me such a gift of a letter, I am deeply touched. Earlier in this summer I spent 4 hours with Lotte Jacobi (now nearly 86) on Star Island [Isles of Shoals, New Hampshire] where the Unitarians have conferences. I went because she said it was Paradise..and there I too felt I had found a community and shall go back for a week next June. A seal was set on this later when I gave the Ware lecture at the Unitarian National Assembly and was introduced (to an audience of 2000) as "our poet." Also the Women's Fed. of the U.U. gave me that day their Ministry to Women award. "For your courage, honesty, and the healing power of your work." Some day tell me why the religious organizations (from Catholic to Unitarian all down the spectrum) recognize my work as valuable, but the lit. establishment does not. But at 70 it all does seem to matter less…

Well, dear Doris, I shall write again soon..you have broken a dam and I hope you will not feel drowned by the result.

I love you and honor you today more than ever

Your old contrite

M

Doris Grumbach: Woman of letters and former National Public Radio book reviewer (b. 1918) whose works include novels (*The Magician's Girl,* W. W. Norton, 1986; see *After the Stroke,* pp. 250, 252–53); memoirs (*The Pleasure of Their Company,* 2000); introductions to novels by Willa Cather and Edith Wharton; and *The Presence of Absence: On Prayers and an Epiphany* (1998).

Chamber Music: Grumbach's 1979 novel; for Sarton's reaction at the time, see *Recovering,* pp. 95–96, 178.

done everything you could: For a time Grumbach was a *New Republic* editor; her 13 October 1973 review of *As We Are Now* claimed: "Everyone ought to read and live in this book for a while, especially the young." A general appreciation (8 June 1974) admired Sarton's career and character, "serene-seeming despite her declared traumas." In *The New York Times Book Review,* 27 April 1975, Grumbach found *Crucial Conversations* "not prime Sarton, but then we are still waiting for what we have always expected she would do some day and has not yet quite done." Considering *The House by the Sea* (*Los Angeles Times,* 27 November 1977), Grumbach remarked that "Sarton is a curious literary phenomenon," whose stature is best measured by the staunchness of her loyal readers. Pointing out Sarton's lapses into sentimentality and "effusive prose" (the overuse of "lovely," for instance), Grumbach nonetheless rated her writing convincingly evocative.

the Ware lecture: Earlier speakers included Rollo May and Martin Luther King Jr.; Sarton may have been the first woman to deliver it, reading poems around the theme "The Values We Have to Keep" at Bowdoin College, 25 June 1982. (The Cambridge [Massachusetts] Forum has issued a recording of this speech; Sarton includes poems that illustrate her title.) *Ms.* magazine and Maggie Kuhn, founder of the Grey Panthers, had been previous recipients of the Ministry award.

religious organizations … the lit. establishment: "When two Methodist pastors called … I asked, 'Why me? and what do you want me to do?' 'Talk about vulnerability and self-healing,' and

I knew I could," she wrote Evelyn Ames (17 June 1982). "But I felt I must be sure they knew so I said, 'You know I am a lesbian.' 'No problem,' they said. Boy we have come a long way since I published 'Mrs. Stevens' to nothing but sneers!"

When the University of Maine—"the establishment" in another form—gave a launch to Constance Huntings' *May Sarton: Woman and Poet,* "it was like a travesty of Academia at its worst," Sarton wrote Sylvie Pasche (31 August 1982). "Hugh Kenner, that grand panjandrum of Joyce critics was there by accident and sat opposite me at the luncheon. He and a scholar from U. of Wisconsin, dragged in too, spent the whole lunch talking about what house Bloom lived in in Dublin!"

Her first visit to H.O.M.E. (Homeworkers Organized for More Employment) in Orland the next day revived her. "[D]id I tell you of what Sister Lucy is doing in that very depressed area of Maine? Building houses for the poor, educating, lifting the whole region. . . And I shared Mass that evening before supper with six of the community. . . I have never taken communion before. They asked me to read a poem during the Mass. That was the 'real thing' and not the champagne luncheon the day before." See *At Seventy,* pp. 124–33, for the full account.

Your old contrite: For Grumbach's August 1982 visit to Wild Knoll, see *At Seventy,* pp. 113–14.

TO DORIS GRUMBACH   January 3rd, 1983
[York]
Dearest Doris,

How fine it was to have an elegant present from you to lay under the tree..I love those Caswell Massey creations (and their catalogues) but have not tried <u>almond</u> before..then there was your charming card as well. Many thanks.

It was a good Christmas here with my friend Lee Blair who had made me a beautiful crèche, a copy of one at the Met, and who was a relaxed and happy guest. And people came in in small groups for champagne in the afternoons. But I had heard on December 22 that Judy died that night in her sleep, and although we have all prayed that she might go in peace at last, the actual finality of her death threw me. I guess I had to mourn because while she was still alive even grief was in limbo. She is the only one of my loves with whom I had a home for many years..and perhaps the only one who really understood me. We lived in amity, how rare that seems. Pat Carroll who called me from L.A. ended her call with "Happy grieving," a rather characteristic remark..I begin to experience the truth of it, now the good memories flow back. But something precious has gone <u>forever</u> and that is still hard to know.

I am now intoxicated by three months of solitude ahead..after 8 months when I have hardly called my soul my own, it is hard to adjust to such bounty of time..will I ever not feel pressured? But now the pressure is fruitful at least as I shall get back to the novel, and deepen the journal (altogether too busy and staccato until now)..and the poems still come although I think my muse is withdrawing. That is understandable.

She has a very full life and a nine to five job..but at least she opened the spring for me after the sterile and exhausting summer and I am grateful for that, whatever happens now.

When do you go to Iowa or did I dream that you are going there again? I think of you like a runner in [the 1981 film] Chariots of Fire, working too hard—but surely this year will see Willa [Cather] off your back (and it will be marvelous) and then your imagination will be free to fly to LLangollen. I hope it will be a very oog and (I wrote <u>oog</u> for <u>good</u>, oh dear—but maybe oog is O.K.) fruitful year, dear Doris. I send very loving thoughts as always,

your old
May

P.S. The one bad effect of a new muse was to make me feel aware of imminent death (in a few years, I think)..I mean there is not longer much <u>time</u>. I had somehow not faced that fact till now.

I hope the tiny beautifully presented book of poems reached you safely? They gave me <u>no</u> low numbers which was rather mean. But I loved having any to give away..such a small edition.

Caswell Massey: America's oldest chemists and perfumers, founded 1752. The reference here is doubtless to one of their soaps.

Judy died: "But the tree, quite magical this year, became a kind of memorial tree, all lit up for Judy," Sarton wrote Ilse Vogel, 8 January 1983; and on 15 January, to Sylvie Pasche, "[N]ow I begin to remember the good times, the wonderful Christmases, our trips to Europe (twice to the Dordogne) and the remarkable woman she was, a great teacher (the English novel) as I hear now from many people and knew anyway."

For how Sarton learned of Judith Matlack's death, and the subsequent trip to Nelson to visit friends who remembered her, see *At Seventy*, pp. 211–16. *Endgame* contains further reminiscences (pp. 68–70, 98–99), with a photo of their home at 14 Wright Street on p. 69. Soon after this Sarton wrote the poem "Mourning to Do," and the unpublished "Requiem for Judy"; see appendix.

Pat Carroll: The actress; see *At Seventy*, p. 219, and 18 March 1994.

my muse is withdrawing: Elizabeth Bristowe, clinical psychologist and consultant in gerontology, inspiration for "Letters from Maine," appears in passing throughout *At Seventy*. "The guardian angel has seen to it that my muse is 2000 miles away (in Victoria [British Columbia]) and in love with someone else," Sarton wrote Sylvie Pasche, 21 November 1982. "She is 57, a grandmother and a gerontologist by profession (I have to laugh at that it is so appropriate considering my age). I feel sure that a real love affair is beyond my strength now . . but to be writing poems is <u>bliss</u>." A "central person, however impossible . . . makes all the difference."

But by 16 June 1983 she told Pasche, "The blight is clear. My muse from Victoria descended for 48 hours . . . an extremely odd visit as she seemed so full of hostility that I dared hardly utter a word. . . . I haven't a clue as to why she came . . . . Luckily the weather was perfect and she spent most of the one day we had lying out on the terrace. . . . It is all very well to say 'good riddance' but it is hard that the poems are cut off." Bristowe reappears briefly in *Endgame*, pp. 134–35.

Llangollen: Town in Wales, an allusion to Grumbach's next novel, *The Ladies* (W. W. Norton); see 15 September 1984. For Grumbach's journal entries concerning an abandoned book about Willa Cather, see "An Aborted Project," *The American Scholar* (70:1), Winter 2001, pp. 133–34.

book of poems: William B. Ewert had issued fifteen new poems as *A Winter Garland*, designed by Michael McCurdy, in an edition of 186, initiating Sarton's series of special publications and broadsides with Ewert.

TO SUSAN KERESTES   Sunday Jan 30th [1983]
[York]

Dear Susan,

I woke up this morning before sunrise thinking about you and our good talk. I am so glad you wanted to tell me about your traumatic experience at fifteen..as I thought it over it seemed a right intervention of fate that brought your parents into touch with the murdered girl's parents, so that you were forced to take some action to heal them of the not-knowing…and also because you are now ready perhaps to come to terms with what you had to block out then. Please don't imagine for a moment that I am necessarily right in what I thought when I woke up..but I'll tell you for what it is worth.

It seemed to me that you now have first of all to forgive yourself for running away, that some of the unresolved anger is really directed against yourself. I think your creativity is closely allied with this awful experience, that somewhere deep down you are trying to be reborn by means of it, and finally by transcending it. A whole difficult but necessary and inspiring spiritual journey has to be involved—and at twenty six you are ready for it. (Some of this in my mind today has come from reading Matthew Fox in a book called A Spirituality Named Compassion (which he allies closely with creativity)..he says "creativity is about overcoming fears by entering into them and spiraling out of them."

What I would like to see melt in you is some defensive hardness which at present makes a wall between you and poetry, between you and your deepest most authentic self.You are such a dear person..I am so glad you came and we talked.

Dear Susan, I love you and I want to see you writing the real poems..set free.

Well, on into the jungle of correspondence..I don't write the novel on the week end so try to answer a lot of letters and clear the decks. Thank goodness three grueling hours with IRS found me white as snow and owing nothing. But I resent the hours I spent sorting out the papers! However the young woman who officiated was sensitive..warm and efficient. I kept contrasting her attitude with that of the kind of bureaucrat, brow-beating and <u>in</u>human, I would have met in Russia or any fascist country and was very glad to be an American of the USA!

With my love,

> your old
> May

———

Susan Kerestes: Kerestes, a poet, then twenty-six, was working on a nearby sheep farm; she had visited Sarton a week earlier. See *At Seventy,* pp. 248–49. This letter typifies Sarton's level of concern for people she was fond of, even when they were not closest friends.

Matthew Fox: Sarton responds to Fox's 1979 book in *At Seventy,* pp. 256–57. In accord with her own adherence to the principle of rebirth, she found "most important his plea that less emphasis be laid on the Cross and more on the Empty Tomb"—" 'Behold, I make all things new.' " (Revelation 21:5)

[*At Seventy* ends 2 May 1983.]

TO POLLY THAYER STARR   July 26th, 1983
[York]
Dearest Polly,

How fine the Hermitage Diary sounds..I've seen reviews of the other book about anger which, I take it, takes the view that anger is bad physically and mentally for the angry one. But does she also suggest that controlled anger can also wreak havoc..I feel sure my mother died of repressed anger against my father (to protect him she more or less killed herself). But I do know that expressed anger is very harmful to other people..on the other hand, repressed anger is also harmful to other people as I learned with Huldah who was <u>punishing</u> without ever losing her temper. You can't win!

As for sales I think your friend exaggerates. My novels sell only around 20,000. And it is a great mystery to me how many people seem to read them..but I guess it is through the libraries, bless 'em.

What a pang I felt about your eyes! But if laser does the trick and it sounds as though it has, then God be praised. What an ordeal it must have been, though, and so scary. It made me laugh and cry when I read your phrase "It is an amazing thought to me that <u>everyone</u> now living has got to find their way out." You are right that Judy did not suffer in the last years..I think she did when she knew she was forgetting things and felt bewildered and was so brave about not complaining, and there is a very sad poem about the loneliness of this in a handwritten book of poems she left me in her will.

I am encouraged about my own death by the presence of hospices..there is one in York. People are really helped in very dear and sustaining ways these days..I wish Helen [Howe] had had that sort of help, as Molly told me she was terrified of dying. The comfort is, of course, that so many people have gone before..and one must look at it as a natural thing, the most natural thing in the world and go with it, as I suggested Laura did in my novel [A Reckoning]. How many letters I get telling me how it is helping people..that is a good feeling.

But I am rather cross and overwhelmed these days, too many people. Yesterday Sally Fitzgerald [called] to bring a Japanese woman who teaches American writers in Japan. Do you know Sally? Her husband has just divorced her for a 20 year old woman—he is 70! It seems so cruel I can hardly bear it. I had not met her before. She said she knew Moll and had met you.

The new journal and soon a new book of poems go off to Norton..the journal has gone and they like it, thank goodness. It is not at all the journal I intended..and I have grave doubts as to its worth. Now I am getting back to the novel about Anne Thorp—but oh how I long for some uninterrupted time!

Much love

M

The Hermitage Diary: The Hermitage Journals: A Diary Kept While Working on a Biography of Thomas Merton, by John Howard Griffin (author of *Black Like Me,* 1960), written at Gethsemani Abbey, Kentucky. The biography was left incomplete; this book was published posthumously in 1981 in its stead.

the other book about anger: Carol Tavris's *The Misunderstood Emotion: Anger* (1982) remains in print today.

the most natural thing: "[S]o many people look serene and joyful in death that it makes one wonder," Sarton had written Starr on 23 March 1983. "My own feeling has always been that the last great mystery must not be probed in advance. When we get there we'll know, and we can't know before. Does one really want to go into another life? Will the struggle and anguish all begin again? without darkness? I felt very strongly when my mother died and I saw her that she simply was not there, and so it seemed she must be somewhere else. But who knows?"

Sally Fitzgerald: 1917–2000. Friend of Flannery O'Connor (and like her a devout Catholic), Fitzgerald edited her essays, letters, and The Library of America volume of her writings (1988), and was completing O'Connor's authorized biography when she died. In later years a research scholar at Emory University, she had been married to professor and classical translator Robert Fitzgerald (1910–85).

Dear Connie,

I have now spent a half hour trying to find your letter in the melee without success! So I shall just write and at least catch you up a little with things in this mad house. Yesterday the Times sent a photographer and interviewer and they stayed over two hours..both were very intelligent and nice, but I was hysterically tired at the end. Last Saturday as you know I was in ~~Atlanta~~ Augusta (!) [Maine]..some of it great fun, staying at the Vaughans in Hallowell was pure pleasure, so rare to be in a house lived in since the 18th century by the same family, beautiful, lived-in, no "interior decorating"..lovely people. But the audience that night appeared to be chiefly congenital coughers. I did not get through a single poem without horrific interruptions by coughs. I literally <u>prayed</u> inwardly "let me have just one poem without a cough"..Not a large audience and I am spoiled for I was cross. However, I behaved, I am glad to report, like a perfect lady—at least till after it was over when I complained loudly about the coughing. Why didn't those people leave? From there I came home over night and then went to N.Y. City to receive an award from some organization to protect the old..If you live long enough you get a Tiffany clock, so stick around. There are 9 women ranging from 68 to 94 and all achievers. It was rather fun. I was badly introduced by [feminist author] Kate Millett who had only read Journal of a Solitude and said I was "urbane, civilized and witty"(!); for that audience some word about As We Are Now was mandatory. There were so many speeches I just read one poem, the unicorn one from Paris Review (which is out, by the way now.) and people were really moved. Alice Neel, the painter, who had been quite huffy till then said it was worth the whole thing to hear that poem.

The light here is so beautiful I just ache not to be here much of the time..upstate N.Y. next week. Then at last a break till Thanksgiving.

Anyway I have been immersed every night in Vanessa Bell and am dying to talk about it with you. I expected to find her loveable but somehow Virginia seems far more so..it was strange, too, to read that she seemed not at all grief stricken at V's suicide. It was Julian of course, his death, that broke her heart. What is moving is the absolute dedication to her painting..and also that she managed to be such a good homemaker if that is the word, as well. BUT she had servants!

This afternoon come hell or high water I must get the tuberous begonias out of the ground and in their winter bed of peat moss..all I dream about is next year when I shall be here and not on the road. I have not had a cigarette for 6 weeks at least..it is a triumph, but I just feel listless and exhausted and may decide it's not worth the cost..we shall see. I do not crave a cigarette. I just crave to feel more alive and competent.

Love

M

---

the Vaughans: This visit marked the beginning of her friendship with Maggie Vaughan; for her photo, see *Endgame,* p. 275. Sarton wrote "The Skilled Man" (1985; *The Silence Now*) for her husband, William Loring Vaughan (1917–88).

organization to protect the old: The Avon/COCOA Award—an award from the New York State Coalition of the Council for Older Americans, underwritten by Avon, the cosmetics company. At the Lincoln Center Library and Museum of the Performing Arts, 24 October 1983, nine "pioneer women" were honored, including Alice Neel, Betty Friedan, and Sarton. Friedan (see note to 10 May 1963) predicted "a new movement in human maturity." As part of Sarton's biographical sketch, the printed program quoted the opening paragraph of *As We Are Now;* see note to 23 June 1973.

the unicorn [poem]: "Who has spoken of the unicorn in old age," #7 of "Letters from Maine," *The Paris Review,* Vol. 89 (1983).

Unconventional portrait painter Alice Neel (1900–84) often depicted her subjects, famous and not famous, in the nude (including herself, age 81); her work is at the Metropolitan and the Whitney in New York, and many other museums worldwide.

Vanessa Bell: Frances Spalding's 1983 biography of Virginia Woolf's sister (1879–1961), the painter who was married to Clive Bell. One of their two sons, Julian (b. 1908), was killed on duty as a volunteer ambulance driver in the Spanish Civil War, 18 July 1937. "I shall be cheerful," Vanessa said, "but I shall never be happy again." Virginia died in 1941. Before World War II, and the advent of many modern appliances, even the most modest families in Britain could afford household help.

love M: As publisher and critic, Hunting continued to add to Sarton studies—considering her poetic output to date for the *Dictionary of Literary Biography* (1986) and identifying it as "a poetry of praise" (" 'Years of Praise': The Poetry of May Sarton," 1992). As one editor to another, Hunting celebrated "May Sarton, Editor of Vision" (1994) for her edition of her mother's letters, and her analyses of her own poetic worksheets. The last two articles can be found in Hunting's *The Experience of Art: Selected Essays and Interviews* (Orono, Maine: Puckerbrush Press, 1997). See *Endgame,* pp. 271–72, for Sarton's pleasure in a March 1991 visit from Hunting.

TO TIMOTHY WARREN   December 29th, 1983
[York]
Dear Tim,

Because this is chiefly to tell you how moved I was by the huge check from Judy's estate, this is addressed to her executor..but of course it must be shared with Phyllis. I think you know..I hope you do..that one of the precious things Judy left me besides that rich treasure in dollars was her family. I just can't tell you what it means to me to be included and our luncheon was one of the dearest events this Christmas, as it has been over the years. Keith is such an angel..but it is partly because you have been able to give him such a cherished old age and done it with such tact and imagination.

In a world where families break apart like Venetian glass and no one picks up the pieces, you and Phyllis have created such a life-giving and life enhancing one that it seems a miracle.

Well, I dashed off to the bank like a millionaire and put the check into my money market savings account which gets a little over 9% and I can draw on at any time. What a great feeling! Judy was a very careful person about money and I honor that..she would have been proud and pleased to know she could give such a gift to me and members of her family. But I am glad, too, that we had some extravagances—especially our trips to Europe!

Feldene is helping my arthritis and my awful cold is better so I am starting back into my own work..the Thorp novel—in better fettle than when I saw you.

The darling cat-box is still on the mantel in the library but will eventually make its way, purring no doubt, to the table by my bed and contain the precious feldene.

I forgot to ask Annella [Brown] about Dover and you..but shall when I see her next .. she told me on the phone she had just spent $100,000 on Art Deco jewelry! (But she will resell and make money on it, no doubt.) I was appalled and said so through my laughter which peals out whenever she boasts as she does often, about money. But she is a truly kind woman nonetheless.

Dears, may it be a very happy New Year! Let me know where you have decided to go for a holiday..

Ever your old
May

The photo shows my quiet desperation!

Timothy Warren: Timothy Matlack Warren is the nephew of Judith Matlack and Constance Revere Matlack Lloyd, son of Keith Faulkner Warren, and president emeritus of Warren Publishing Company, publisher of *Honey in the Hive* (see 1 September 1987). He served as the executor of Sarton's estate, as well as Judith Matlack's.

TO MARCIE HERSHMAN   July 13th 84
[York]

Dear Marcie, splendid to get a letter full of good news yesterday! Page 375! I have stumbled into about Page 250 but I fear it is the dullest book I ever wrote, and just horribly difficult. The problem now is that the narrator must <u>not</u> grab the reader's attention at the expense of the central character, yet to some extent her knowledge of Jane Reid (ALT's name in the novel) [*The Magnificent Spinster*] has to come from problems of her own...even saying this much at 7 A.M. helps me to focus, so <u>thanks.</u>

Great about your holiday on the Cape with the right person this time. I hope the weather which has been pretty damp and dismal here until yesterday, holds and you have wonderful picnic and beach days. But just being "away" together will make it memorable. I hope you are happy about Ferraro? It does seem to bring a little sparkle to the deadening Mondale campaign. <u>I</u> like M but no one else seems to and he has a singular capacity for <u>not</u> exciting the viewer. What did Gore Vidal say? something like, "A magnum of chloroform". Ferraro is a pro and seems to be on the right side as far as South America goes which is a relief.

As for France it was so beautiful, Marcie..the European roots in me were nourished by those fields cherished and tended for hundreds of years, the old farms (limestone with red tiled roofs) and on every hilltop a chateau or castle, as in a fairy tale. When I got back I realized the rest it was to be in a place where the eye rests on beauty everywhere...no motels, road signs, shacks, land gone to ruin, second growth etc.

BUT Dr. Brown was rather a fiasco. I knew we were not soul mates but I did not expect her to be so bored that she hardly listened to a word I said, talked incessantly herself about "Allie" (Alice Lowell with whom she lived and with whom she had a Louis XIII house there). .she is such a materialist. I just felt like a fish out of water as far as our relationship was concerned. My guess is that her macho personality only gets involved if she is chasing a woman. When I asked her one day why she never listened to me, she said, "because I have read everything you have written so I know it all" which is quite ridiculous of course. But it did make me feel rather <u>diminished</u> and perhaps even <u>finished</u>. She made me feel very old and unattractive in fact and that was hard because I know it is not really true.

Anyway it was wonderful to come home and settle in and know I shan't have to move for a while, and even then not to give a reading. . I did give a last one for a year after I got back from the State Poetry Societies' nat. convention in Ohio. That was even more depressing than Annella. Mostly women who write poetry instead of playing bridge or quilting, have no interest in an established poet, I felt (and I am not even that, really)—I had to listen to two hours of second-rate poetry, poems that had won prizes and which were with <u>one</u> exception either prose or awful poetry. The second rate <u>kills</u> any impulse to write.

But even with my doubts about this book I am happy to be working again and must, this minute, get right down to it.

Much love and all wishes for a very happy time on the Cape.. and all luck with the last third of the novel!

Your old
May

P.S. Did you see the full-page ad for <u>At 70</u> in the Sunday Times June 17th? I was <u>pleased</u>—

———

Marcie Hershman: Novelist and poet. Her profile, "May Sarton at Seventy: A Viable Life Against the Odds," appeared in *Ms.* (October 1982); see *At Seventy,* pp. 104–05. "I'm not a genius," Sarton said, echoing Hilary Stevens. "I have a talent, several talents, that I have fought for, and discipline myself to, and tried to fructify—if that's the word—and the results are good." The "second wave" of her career was brought about by *Mrs. Stevens* in tandem with *Journal of a Solitude.*

Ferraro. . . Mondale . . . Vidal: Democratic presidential nominee Walter Mondale (b. 1928, senator from Minnesota) had chosen Geraldine Ferraro (b. 1935, congresswoman from New York) as his running mate, the first woman to be picked for that position. American gadfly of letters Gore Vidal was born in 1925.

Dr. Brown: Dr. Annella Brown, president of the medical staff at Milton Medical Center outside Boston. She had initiated a friendship with Sarton based on the work, as well as a shared affection for the Dordogne region of France, which Sarton and Judith Matlack had enjoyed visiting. For their initial lunch on New Year's Eve before 1983, see *At Seventy,* pp. 220–21.

the last third of the novel: Thinking it "a work of genius," Sarton wrote a blurb for the jacket of Hershman's first published novel, *Tales of the Master Race* (1991), which deals with the horrors of life in German cities during Hitler's reign; see *Encore,* pp. 72–74. Hershman's other books include *Safe in America* (novel, 1995) and *Speak to Me: Grief, Love, and What Endures* (2001).

TO DORIS GRUMBACH   September 15th, 1984
[York]
Dearest Doris,

What an event when, at last, The Ladies came to the door and with what eagerness I have spent the last two nights reading it before I went to sleep..I am touched to be mentioned in the dedicace, touched and astonished. And before I go into the content let me say what a beautiful piece of bookmaking it is—the jacket just right, with the best portrait of you I have seen, and the book itself beautiful. That engraving on the title page, jacket, and presenting each chapter quite perfect. You must be pleased! It will surely persuade the right readers to buy when they see the landscape and those two haunting figures...

You have made <u>your</u> Ladies immensely interesting and vivid, but I must confess that they are not <u>my</u> ladies. Was Eleanor really such a choleric macho person? Was there never gaiety or laughter between them?

Marriage has its prickly moments and often more "crises" than theirs appeared to have had, but aren't there often private jokes, too? Neither of them as we see them here _ever_ laughs. And was it only their "strange union" that brought so many statesmen, intellectuals, poets to their door? I was fascinated to learn that Sarah was the garden planner, the outdoor master of the place, and that suggests qualities of imagination as well as mastery of a skill rather rare in a woman (it comes again at Sissinghurst). Well, you have given me a rich feast to meditate upon and I am grateful. I now opened to Page 37 and see there _is_ a little joke about donkeys there.

The episodes with Margaret are charming..but I missed the cat sitting at table to lap a saucer of cream with them at tea time!

I love the description of them as seen by the villagers on page 101. and Eleanor's reflections about herself on page 82—wonderful.

I am happy when I think how many people who have never heard of them will now meet The Ladies.. and, as I have felt from the beginning when you first told me you had embarked on it, I feel sure it will be a best seller—and it should be.

It's raining—we need it badly, but it is rather dismal, just the same. I am in the final throes of the Spinster and in a state near exhaustion these days. Maybe it is a good thing that Alan [Eastaugh], my English cousin, comes here Sept. 24th for three weeks as I shall not be able to work then quite as hard. But I still hope to have it roughed out by the time I leave for Belgium Nov. 12th.

At 70 has been taken by Quality Paperbacks [Bookclub] which is good news, I think..and is now off the best seller list after six weeks on and off it. It is number 8 in Washington D.C., I just heard, and as it stayed below 13 in the Times, that is good news also. But you know that book is far away and long ago for me now...

Has the semester started well? Are you working away at the new novel? Good to be away for a while from carpenters and painters. I keep in my heart the hope I may see you really settled in and come down in the spring for a brief visit. Ah!

> Much love from your old
> May

---

the dedicace: Grumbach's novel bears the dedication "For My Friends," including "May Sarton, who talked to me about the Ladies."

your Ladies . . . my Ladies: Eleanor Butler and Sarah Ponsonby, mid-eighteenth-century Irishwomen who declared their love for one another. Their home, Plas Newydd, in

Llangollen, Wales, became a gathering place for intellectuals; Sarton and Judith Matlack visited there in July 1959. Grumbach calls her book a "fiction about the Ladies of Llangollen, not in any way a history." The standard biography is Elizabeth Mavor's *The Ladies of Llangollen: A Study in Romantic Friendship* (1971, reissued 1999).

Sissinghurst: The elaborate formal gardens created at Sissinghurst Castle, Kent, by British poet and novelist Vita Sackville-West (1892–1962), intimate friend of Virginia Woolf.

TO LOLA L. SZLADITS
[York]
Dear Lola,

January 3rd, 1985

What a lovely way to start the New Year to read the New Yorker profile of you—and to know a lot more about your life and dear husband than I ever hoped I might! You have managed to hide behind the WORK (and what a great work it is!) but I among many, no doubt, am delighted to see what made you what you are. Dear Lola, long may you reign!

I have been meaning to write for another reason. In November I flew to Belgium for the celebration of my father's centenary at the University of Ghent, to read a couple of poems for him, and to listen to some very moving speeches, especially a wholly charming one by that angel, Robert Merton. The logistics were rather mismanaged but they did put on a tremendously interesting exhibition called George Sarton's European Roots. I am hoping to extract some copies of the printed text. It ran the length of a very long hall, on both sides, ten foot screens covered with excerpts of letters, photographs, portraits of intimate friends etc. and was really a novel in itself. You know G.S. wrote a short (very romantic) imaginary autobiog. when he was twenty or so, called Vie d'Un Poète, and had it privately printed. I have always liked the idea that I was living one of his imaginary lives! Now it is even stranger to realize that I am a few months older than he was when he died. I tell you all this because I know you admired George Sarton. No one in the field has matched his learning <u>plus</u> his humanistic vision since.

Things go well here except for the incredible clutter that pours in here and has to be answered. But at least The Magnificent Spinster, a long novel about an old friend which nearly finished me before I finished it, is in the works and will come out in September. Norton is enthusiastic and gave me a big advance. And I go into this year not under pressure for the first time in ten years as I am refusing public appearances until September...ah, time to think for a change! Meanwhile nice things happen...a whole seminar on May Sarton at the University of Maine, ditto at Trinity College (there by a man who is a psychologist and the theme was "identity"), a PhD thesis in the works at Harvard. It is all coming out in my old age, as fifty years ago, an Italian painter who read my fortune in the Tarot cards, told me it would. It has been a long haul.

Dear Lola, may it be a great year for you personally and for the Berg! Things have certainly changed for the better at the Library haven't they?

Love from your old

May

––––––––

Lola L. Szladits: 1923–90. Curator for twenty years of the New York Public Library's Berg Collection of English and American Literature, where Sarton's archive is housed along with those of Herman Melville, Walt Whitman, T. S. Eliot, James Boswell, Elizabeth Barrett Browning, W. H. Auden, and many others. Szladits wrote on Virginia Woolf and initiated the Berg's purchase of Woolf's diaries and other papers from Leonard Woolf. She was married to Columbia University law professor Charles Szladits (d. 1986). Whitney Balliett's "City Voices: Lola Szladits" appeared in the 31 December 1984 *New Yorker.*

Robert Merton: Historian of science, recipient of a MacArthur Foundation award; in 1997 his son Robert C. Merton shared the Nobel Prize for Economics. Merton himself was a colleague of George Sarton's, a lifelong friend to him and May. "He was not a very good father you know," she admitted to Merton, 29 June 1984, "but in the end he was proud of me as I certainly was of him and after my mother's death we became good friends. The great bond we shared all three was certain <u>values</u> ... I am lonely for their values."

On 19 February 1988, while dealing with unpleasant medications, Sarton wrote Char Radintz that she would "just have to 'bear and grin it' as my father said when he had frightful pain one night and I was called at 2 A.M. It was gallbladder. It was very dear that he could joke while in such pain. I often hated my father because of my mother, but he was a mensch."

no one ... has matched [him]: In Ghent, Sarton also met Eugene Garfield, president of the Institute for Scientific Information (Philadelphia). On 11 August 1985 she wrote him that his article "The Life and Career of George Sarton: The Father of the History of Science" (*Journal of the History of the Behavioral Sciences,* April 1985) was "the best, most cogent, and generous estimate of Sarton that has come to my attention.... [S]hortly after his death there was a tendency among historians of science to denigrate and make little of the achievement. My father was an innocent and more sophisticated people found it easy to belittle. You have set all this to rights."

fortune in the Tarot: See *Encore,* pp. 189–90, for the tale of how Sarton as a young woman had her future foretold by the Italian painter Cagli: "You will have hard times but everything will come out at the end—money, fame, love." The image of working out a game at solitaire found final expression in "A Fortune," *Coming into Eighty.*

changed for the better at the library: This refers to Vartan Gregorian's presidency at the New York Public Library, and his support of Szladits and the Berg, both morally and financially.

TO MICHEL THIERY   March 10th, 1985
[York]
Dear Michel,

I was delighted to hear that you had been enjoying the books I sent! Of course I looked at page 215 and was amused to find that bit about envy and gratitude..amused because I so often do give large sums away and then become panicky..I have just done so, so it rang a bell.

I do dream of coming back, for perhaps a week to be in Ghent in peace with you—go for little walks and drives, find my own roots. And, as I think I said when I was there in November, I plan to do this when I am 75, perhaps in late May of '87..it is coming very fast! The years simply rush away when you are my age.

I have not thought about a portrait of Raymond [Limbosch] partly because I wrote so fully about him and Céline in my novel The Bridge of Years [1946]. I have no copy to send you but I think it will be out in paperback in June and I'll send it then. In the novel I made him a philosopher—who perhaps should have been a poet whereas I think he was a poet who should have been a philosopher! I'll put in the envelope with this a tiny essay Céline asked me to write and then had printed after his death. You may not have seen it? The tragedy of Raymond was that Céline, to help him of course, <u>paid</u> to have his books published— this is fatal if one is to be taken seriously by the critics. Well, we'll talk about all this when I come.

I can't tell you how I look forward to it and how happy I am that we are friends..a wonderful piece of luck that we found each other at last.

As for me now, I am having a hard time because I had to have all my teeth extracted two weeks ago and then got flu. The new method is to put the new ones in at once, and everyone says I look exactly the same. But inside I feel 100 years old and it has been traumatic. Perhaps the flu accounts for the low state of mind.

I expect spring is there..and today it feels like it here, though there is snow on the ground.

Love to you both from
May

Michel Thiery: b. 1924; his family had been friends of the Sarton's during their pre–World War I days in Belgium. Gynecologist and longtime department head of obstetrics at Ghent State University, he is now professor emeritus, with many professional publications. Much interested in the history of medicine, he serves on the board of the annual journal devoted to George Sarton's work, life, and legacy, *Sartoniana*, which began publication in 1988.

Thiery had referred to a passage in *The House by the Sea*, pp. 215–16, where psychologist Melanie Klein's book *Envy and Gratitude* prompted Sarton's complex reflections on giving and its discontents.

a tiny essay: The ten-page "In Memoriam," dated 30 July 1957 and written in French, issued by Willy Godenne, Brussels, in an edition of two hundred.

we are friends: The reader will have noticed that, however much Sarton mourned losing old intimates, and maintained many connections over decades, she never stopped reaching out to make new friends; and drawn by someone so "direct, eloquent, courageous, and honest" (in the words of Thiery's 1996 *Sartoniana* tribute to her), new friends came.

Wondelgem, Belgium, where Sarton was born on the Botestraat ("Boat Street"), is now part of Ghent. Thiery informed this editor that, as of 19 May 1999, the town council had renamed a nearby street in Sarton's honor. A City of Ghent sign-plaque proclaims in Flemish: "May Sarton Street / American author / Wondelgem 1912–York (US) 1995."

TO PEGGY POND CHURCH   June 8th, 1985
[York]
Dearest Peggy,

I was immensely heartened by your litany of the daily interruptions that keep you..as they do me..from all you really mean about your life. And I was deeply touched by what you said, too, to me "and you, even at such a distance have always been a part of me." I feel safe with you which may sound odd, but rather few people understand as you do what I am all about and it is a <u>comfort.</u>

The sonnets are moving..nowhere except in Meredith has a poet celebrated the struggle in a marriage? The long term making concessions and even compromises to maintain the deep core. You have done it. My favorite at present is number 8, also 12..and I had tears in my eyes at the final one. It is remarkable that your marriage <u>held</u>..I felt you were in some ways deprived. I have felt that about my mother also but now reading her letters I have at last come to understand that theirs was a "marriage of true minds"..they shared so much. And it has been a healing for me to realize this because perhaps I knew too much about what she suffered from his inability to talk about money or ever give her enough to run the household. Money was the dragon in their marriage..it just hurts to think I could now give her ten thousand and not miss it! But that, I suppose, is why I give so much away and do it really in her name. For she was a fountain of giving...

I have been awfully depressed which is why I have been slow to answer..it is all because of those devourers of time and energy. However I am over the worst and becoming rather ruthless about not answering. The annuals are in at last..that became acute frustration because every time there was a perfect day someone was here for tea or supper, and when I had a free afternoon it always rained! Now what I have decided is to give myself two mornings a week for <u>me</u>—and I have written a poem and am at work on another as a result. So this is the way to handle the interupters. Could you do that yourself? Take two days a week and simply refuse to see anyone those days? It is amazing how much more cheerful and less badgered I feel as a result.

The tree peonies are about to flower in fact one white one is out..a godlike flower, really to be worshipped. But the iris has done badly. What a philosopher one has to be to be a gardener at all!

It makes me so happy to have five copies of your book to give..I hoard them waiting for the right person. But I did give one to a professor (woman) at Bucknell University..where I got my 12th doctorate the other day) who had had to have her old dog put to sleep. She was very moved by that poem.

It is now time for me to take Tamas for our daily walk. It is a very slow walk as he has to stop to smell all sorts of things and also to eat grass. The cat comes along and races up trees, and I enjoy walking so slowly and "taking things in." The lady slippers are out now in the woods, such magic. And the beech leaves are that brilliant green. Of course I may decide to take the other walk, down the grassy path to the ocean where we are bombarded by swallows who nest in the banks above the rocks. The cat miaows with rage when they do that!

Do write when you feel like it, precious friend, precious poet.

Ever your old devoted
May

––––––––––

The sonnets: The Ripened Fields: Fifteen Sonnets of a Marriage. Sarton is likening them to the sequence of fifty quasi-sonnets by Victorian poet and novelist George Meredith (1828–1909), "Modern Love" (1862), an unidealized depiction of a marriage disintegrating.

reading her letters: Sarton was in the process of selecting fifty letters out of hundreds, covering thirty years, which the Puckerbrush Press brought out in 1986 as *Letters to May* by Eleanor Mabel Sarton (1878–1950). In thanking Constance Hunting on 3 June 1986, Sarton quoted Polly Thayer Starr: "If ever there was a labor of love this is it!—the beautiful format—it gives it a kind of fragrance as if it were a flower, a white lilac, or lily of the valley." For the cover, at May's suggestion, Nancy MacKnight adapted a design by Mabel Sarton.

ruthless about not answering: Sarton agreed with friend of the work, massage therapist Phyllis Price (27 April 1985), that letter writing "is a lost art and I do love writing to friends. That I am rarely able to do these days . . . . [Instead] I am asked to connect in depth with someone who knows me well through my books but whom I do not know. . . . [Y]ou cannot give to thousands of strangers and have any creative self left. Isak Dinesen at one time had as her motto, 'Je réponderai,' 'I will answer' and I took it for mine. I have not failed many but I sometimes think that I have failed myself."

Yet she concluded by rejoicing that Price had sold her first poem: "Bravo! I sold five sonnets to Poetry when I was 17 and I remember the thrill of that small check and that I bought Katherine Mansfield's letters with it and a book of drawings of Isadora Duncan. What will you do with yours?"

precious poet: November 1986 found Sarton returning to the Santa Fe area after forty years to give readings (*After the Stroke*, pp. 187–95); there she heard that Church, who had been going blind, had recently died. A "last poignant poem" of hers is printed on p. 190; in 1993, Red Crane Books in Santa Fe brought out *This Dancing Ground of Sky: The Selected Poetry of Peggy Pond Church.*

TO J. PARKER HUBER   Thanksgiving Day
[York]   [28 November 1985]
Dear Parker,

Your dear letter—and it is dear—has been on my desk for a long time because I was out in Cal. when it came and I have only just unearthed it from the vast pile on my desk. It is snowing and I wonder if you are risking the climb of Monadnock today—and rather hope not! I have given up driving to Lewiston and shall simply give thanks for a very welcome day of solitude and communing with friends by letter.

It makes me happy that you saw what I was trying to do in the novel [*The Magnificent Spinster*], that it really spoke to you—what a blessing, dear Parker! It was so hard to do I gave up twice and still cannot really believe it is any good. But I have had some fine letters and one or two perceptive reviews.

I too have had a wild autumn but it is beautiful to have such huge audiences and such loving ones..the Smithsonian sold out weeks before I read there and the same thing happened in San Francisco (Arts and Lectures) in November. It is fun, as well as the hordes of people at book signings, but it does somehow leave me in pieces. Oh, I am glad for this quiet day alone with snow falling...a way too to mourn Bramble. I had to have her put to sleep ten days ago. The house feels so empty. Only Tamas and I are left now and who will go next? He is well, thank goodness, and so am I. But Bramble .. she and I had a deep bond. Tamas loves everyone, but she only loved me, the wildest cat I ever had. Never again will she leap in my bedroom window and purr and purr at my side all night. It has been a hard loss and I have cried a lot. But life goes on.

Your teaching schedule sounds horrific, the sheer energy involved..but it sounds as though you had found the clue for your own future in psycho-synthesis. All that you tell me about it sounds good. And you have so much to give. It is grand to know that you and Foster will follow Muir in the high Sierras in July. Oh boy!

Yes, let us try for a time together in late December..no, that won't work. But in January after the 14th maybe. Give me a ring..when Christmas is over.

Meanwhile love and thanks

                                                        Your old
                                                        May

J. Parker Huber: Huber edited a special issue of *Thoreau's Journal* (2, No. 4, March 1982) to mark Sarton's receiving, from Eastern Connecticut State College, the 1981 Richard D. Perkins Memorial Award, honoring "people whose work and creativity arouses in us a deep respect for human greatness." (See *Encore,* pp. 154–55.) In "A Magic Encounter with May Sarton" at Wild Knoll, he writes that "Her literature nurtures a nation." "I have great admiration for this man," Sarton wrote; see *At Eighty-Two,* pp. 145–46, for his intense response to *Among the Usual Days.*

perceptive reviews: The best came later. Leona Fisher, in *Belles Lettres* (January–February 1986), declared that "Befitting her unique subject, Sarton has created a fresh form . . . a narrator who writes a novel, celebrating her teacher/friend without violating her privacy"; Sarton added a separate section to this review in which she discussed the challenges involved. Valerie Miner, in *Women's Review of Books* (December 1985), noted how this innovation provided "a testimony to independence; an enlightening portrayal of old age; a celebration of friendship and an engrossing story." In *The New York Times Book Review* (11 May 1986), novelist Margaret Atwood cited it to show that women's friendships are "now firmly on the literary map as valid and multidimensional novelistic material."

It is pleasant to note that Sarton appeared and read in company with Atwood, Robertson Davies, Michael Holroyd, and Julian Barnes at the Wang International Author's Festival, 17 October 1989, in Toronto.

[John] *Muir:* Scottish-born American naturalist and writer (1838–1914), who devoted his living to saving the natural beauties of the West from despoilation; campaigned for the establishment of Yosemite National Park; and was instrumental in founding the Sierra Club.

TO SUSAN SHERMAN   [8 December 1985]
[York]
Dear Susan,

I wish I were keeping a journal and could put into it the MENU..what a scene in the wonderful Volvo you and I eating caviar and goat cheese and cherries and smoked salmon and French bread and superior wine and coffee and crème brûlée (the best I ever tasted).. I got on the plane just in time almost the last person on, so all went well. I just hope the women at the Club were chastened by my tears and treated you better than they did me as I left!

I am sending you 1) in a roll, a beautiful large rendering of Shell.. 2) one of a very few bound copies of the original Winter Garland in a very special edition that came out before Letters from Maine 3) the special edition of Absence, not made out to you so you can sell it! All of this will keep you from ruin, I hope, when that bookseller lets you know they exist.

What I loved best was seeing your class room, a kind of refuge and bower, so expressive of you, no wonder the students flock in. It reminded me of Jean Dominique's atmosphere in her class room.

I came home to five disasters among friends of mine which meant immediate response and I simply cried with exhaustion all day yesterday—but the worst is now done and I can begin to concentrate on Xmas.

Love and blessings—
M—

Susan Sherman: Sherman had been reading Sarton's work for years before writing her in 1979; Sarton kept that letter and the two women first met in 1983 at Wild Knoll; regular visits followed. On 25 January 1987 Sarton asked if she would "look at" her papers in the Berg Collection of the New York Public Library. Sherman continued to teach while researching the archive, publishing three volumes of new material by 1997; that year she left teaching to devote full attention to editing Sarton's unpublished work.

[8 December 1985]: On 5 December, Sarton gave a reading at the Riverdale Country School, New York, where this editor taught English. The following day she read at the Poetry Society of America; after a book signing on 7 December, Sherman drove her to La Guardia Airport while they shared a picnic in the car.

rendering of Shell: "Shell," from *A Winter Garland,* was printed in 1982 as a broadside by William B. Ewert in an edition of one hundred, with typography and wood engraving by Michael McCurdy.

Absence: First published by Ewert as a 1984 broadside with a cover photo by Lotte Jacobi.

[May Sarton had her first stroke on 19 February 1986.]

[*After the Stroke* begins 9 April 1986.]

TO SISTER JEAN ALICE   October 21, 1986
[York]
Dear Jean Alice,

I feel frustrated because I have a poem brewing about you all but I came home as usual to what feels like a ton of bricks on my head, the everlasting demands in the mail, the friends with whom I must keep in touch such as Juliette Huxley, about to be 90, Pauline Prince in Belgium nearly 90. If one only had two or three lives going on at once!

The autumn is at its height here now, such glory, and today a silvery ocean with its own radiance, gray shot through with floods of sunlight here and there.

Yesterday I sent off tons of books to you—perhaps more about penguins than you wish to know—but I knew I must do it at once or never. The book of Selected Poems is for you yourself, all the others for the community and so dedicated.

How can I tell you what it meant to me to be "taken in" not as a stranger at the gate in sore need (as I was) but as an intimate and loved friend. I felt the peace in my bones and am meditating on what a life of prayer does to one who is part of it even for a few days. But I must try to write the poem and that will say what I have in my heart.

It is not a lucky thing for me that a guest arrives this afternoon for a week..one of the Nicholas Nickleby company which has just closed in N.Y.. Pat Keen is brilliant and dear, loves the animals BUT is a non-stop talker and I am exhausted just thinking of it. I shall have to make my escape because there is so much on my desk and I shall be glad to see her, I know, once she is here for tea.

I suppose if I were to count them up that this four days and nights with you are among the most precious events of my life. You may be sure, and please tell the sisters so, that they will have a lasting beneficent effect. I am so blest, dear heart—And send oceans of love.

Forgive this awful letter. More to come.

Your old
May

Sister Jean Alice: Sister Jean Alice McGoff, OCD, then Prioress of the Carmelite Monastery, Indianapolis. On 11 October Sarton had a book signing at Butler University sponsored by The Hermitage, with a reading the following day. Sister Jean Alice, who used *Journal of a Solitude* in the order's meditations, invited her to stay at the monastery. Sarton replied, "I am so happy that you will take me in, happy and honored, I must add, for I know the atmosphere of silence and meditation will be a homecoming for me, as it always is, among a religious community." For a full account of her visit, see *After the Stroke*, pp. 164–70, 259–60; and *Endgame*, pp. 105–06, for a postscript about a visit to the order by writer Alice Walker, delighted to succeed Sarton.

a ton of bricks: Sarton does not mention, in this list, news about her visit to Massachusetts General for a cardiac evaluation. "I had hoped for a pacemaker," she wrote to Edith Royce Schade the next day, 22 October 1986, "but they found the heart's atrium too weak for the preliminary operation which would have been necessary."

more about penguins: A favorite story of George Sarton's (told also by James Thurber and others) about a little schoolgirl's book report on "a book that told me more about penguins than I wanted to know."

Pat Keen: A member of the Royal Shakespeare Company, touring the States with their large-scale adaptation of the 1838–39 Dickens novel; see references throughout *After the Stroke.*

More to come: Sarton always treasured this friendship, and found it "a true blessing" when Sister Jean Alice visited York in 1987. For observations on her "spontaneous soprano"—"It's like a bird"—and her avocations after her tenure as prioress, see *Endgame*, pp. 109–11, 338–39.

"The poem . . . in my heart," "Guest of Silence," was written in December 1986; see appendix. In 2000, Sister Jean Alice sent this editor a copy of a magnificent little chapbook titled *God in Ordinary Time: Carmelite Reflections on Everyday Life*, by "The Carmelites of Indianapolis." Printed on the inside front flap is "Guest of Silence."

Another sister, writing recently, admitted that "while May was not always 'quiet,' she never was less than a joy."

TO EDITH ROYCE SCHADE   February 13th, 1987
[York]
Dear Duffy,

I meant for you to keep the photo.. but you have your own so I won't send it back. I think the series [of presentations] you are doing on myths should make for a lot of good exchanges.

I'll enclose a copy of Rolfe Humphries' wonderful poem on Proteus because it had a great influence on me..Although the poem Proteus of mine [1971] does not show it, but it might enrich discussion on that.

The Phoenix, poem [1956] is not about me, but was written after Matthiessen's suicide and someone said it is really the whole novel Faithful Are The Wounds. But it's also about my own anger as well as his..(so you are right.) I had been thinking a lot about all that, how difficult he was, making a guest in my house cry because he savagely attacked her about a political election where he was far on the Left.

If you read Birthday on the Acropolis [1966] I think you should read it all. This is a philosophical poem really..which means from or toward the balancing of the self..and what that costs in detachment only comes through in the final stanza. "I suffered from the archaic smile."

The message of At Lindos [1964] is really Gandhi's "all religions are true," we are quick to look down on people who take a less arduous path than ours, but sometimes they may get closer to a truth that way..anyway it is the unexpected validity of <u>both</u> that interested me.

The Furies [1958] is not about anger at all, but a complex in which falling in love with false gods (the wrong Muse, <u>Ambition</u>, what is glamourous but not real in fact). When I say the furies have been attentive I think I had in mind T.S. Eliot's image in one of his plays [*The Family Reunion*, 1939], of the furies at the window.

You have totally misunderstood The Country of Pain and tried to sweeten what is an extremely bitter and deliberately negative poem which has to do with sensuality rather than love, sex rather than love. There is nothing in it about "overcoming dark powers." I think it is one of my best and most truthful poems and hope you will not sentimentalize it. "Manic depressive Eros" is a good ironic description of passionate love that goes sky high but ends in depression.

I am terribly pressured these days so forgive the bluntness of this—I am really happy about what you are doing. Let me know how it goes.

Nancy is typing the new journal and I am revising as she types..it will end Feb. 21st, the anniversary of the stroke. There are three huge boxes of letters that should be answered but never will be as I write ten letters a day simply to answer the <u>day's</u> mail.

Glad you have another corgi..I may get a wire-haired miniature dachshund whom I shall see Feb. 21st at H.O.M.E. There the manager [Sister Lucy] breeds them. I will have it in May to train. I'm off to Cal. in April for a last tour. Love from

M

P.S. The poems bear a good deal more <u>analysis</u> and thinking than you have had time to do maybe? Every word counts.

Rolfe Humphries: 1894–1968; teacher, translator of several languages, longtime friend of Louise Bogan. Like Sarton and Robert Francis, he was among those attending Robert Frost's eightieth birthday banquet in 1954; see note to 16 January 1963. "Proteus, or, The Shapes of Conscience" appears in his *Collected Poems,* 1965.

Let me know how it goes: After many years' work, Schade published *From May Sarton's Well* (Goodale Hill Press) in 1994. "Schade has composed a set of her impressive photographs to communicate the light and shadow of my view of life," Sarton wrote for the jacket, 29 June 1994, "and accompanies the photographs with a text culled from my works to communicate this vision. The book is a stunning addition to the Sarton canon. I am grateful."

To structure the book, Schade devotes a section to each of Sarton's "delights of the poet": "light, solitude, the natural world, love, time, creation itself." Schade's evocative pictures enhance, counterpoint, and comment upon Sarton's words in a genuinely original combination that honors both artists. It is still in print; see www.goodalehillpress.com.

Nancy is typing: In 1979, while working as librarian at Pease Air Force Base in Portsmouth, New Hampshire, Nancy Hartley began typing Sarton's manuscripts; soon she became full-time assistant and archivist. *Endgame* is dedicated "To Nancy Hartley, who has worked for me for thirteen years as secretary, librarian, and devoted friend of the work. Hail and Farewell!" Humorous and acute, Hartley proved herself invaluable, and remains so.

[*After the Stroke* ends 21 February 1987.]

TO ROBERT O'LEARY   September 1st, 1987
[York]

Dear Bob, I have been thinking of you so much lately and will tell you why in a minute, that it was with special joy that I opened the package from Vantage [publishers] and right to the dedication to Eleanor and me! How touched and honored I feel, dear Bob, and I have been reading you each night before I go to sleep. You certainly rouse and keep intense interest with each of these stories. I think my favorites are perhaps the first one, no, <u>The Genial Current</u>, <u>Hennie on the Census</u> and <u>Rosalie</u>, <u>Come to the Fun Fair</u>. Thank God you are not a fashionable minimalist! I feel <u>you</u> in every word. .I mean your sensitivity as a person and dearness. It is a fine book.

The reason I have been thinking of you...and Eleanor of course...is that I have been working all summer on an informal portrait of Judy which her family will publish (not a commercial venture). She left me in her will a large book in which were about 100 handwritten poems by her. They are rather strange and in some ways wonderful and I decided to weave some of them into the portrait and then at the end offer a small selection of the best as poems. All are very interesting as autobiog and memory. And as I was looking into folders marked Judy for this work I found your wonderful letter written me after her death. I end the portrait by quoting a few lines from it, to wit "Judy lives forever in my heart. Her charm and intellect and humor and absolute goodness make her 'honey in the hive of memory.'" Hope I have your permission to do so? I may call the whole thing "Honey in the Hive."

It will go off to Judy's family in a few days..and we'll see what they think. They may want some changes or cuts. I found it extremely hard to do and wish it were more deserving of Judy, but I did my best.

In Feb. of '85 [1986] I had a mild stroke followed by months of fibrillating heart for which the medicine made me extremely sick so I was in and out of hospital for 9 months..but I am well now and the journal I managed to keep after April (two months after the stroke) will come out in early '88 called <u>After the Stroke</u>. I feel very well now and am dying to get to a new novel [*The Education of Harriet Hatfield*]..

Life is always a little too full here in summer when everyone comes to Maine and my big garden takes its toll of rather reduced energy—after all, I am 75 now!

Much love and warm congratulations, dear heart,

Your old
May

Robert O'Leary: See note to 7 September 1972.

100 handwritten poems: "I haven't a clue as to when she began this [collection] or when it ended," Sarton wrote, 23 January 1983, *At Seventy.* Judith Matlack "had an amazing gift for evoking sights, smells, tastes that bring back whole areas of childhood, . . . She was intensely aware of nature in all its forms . . . But there are constant references to pain, to mental anguish, to the silent acceptance of pain. All of this appears to relate to times before we met." See note to 6 June [1957] about Matlack's early life.

"Honey in the Hive": Judith Matlack 1889–1982 was published by Warren Publishing Company, 1988. The phrase from which the title is taken comes from the Massachusetts Unitarian clergyman Theodore Parker (1810–60). Prose, letters, and poetry by the two women are artfully juxtaposed to create a living memorial.

An introductory tribute by Sarton is interspersed with four of Matlack's poems and Sarton's "A Retirement for Judith Matlack," not reprinted elsewhere. Matlack's twenty-one-page portrait of her father, "Charles Matlack: An Impression," is followed by a letter from her to him and her lengthy poem about a trip to London. Sarton then adds a remembrance of her memories of Judy and their happy, nurturing times at Anne Thorp's on Greenings Island.

When she became unable to care for herself, Matlack went to live in the Walden Home at Concord, Massachusetts. A letter by her, written from there, is followed by a note found after her death, revealing that she was more conscious than anyone suspected about the gravity of her mental decline.

Sarton writes: "The deeper I went the more I became aware of the greatness and singular originality that lived in Judy, how little 'show,' how much depth and capacity to grow and to handle disaster, what courage she showed all her life and not least when she was incapacitated and not herself. Even there the dignity of her bearing and the beauty of her face in old age, even as the mind collapsed, revealed the remarkable soul within."

The book concludes with eleven of Matlack's poems including "Thunderheads," "At Dawning," and "Sorrow Will Keep."

TO CHARLES BARBER   December 8th, 1987
[York]
Dearest Charles,

I simply ache all over when I think of your life devoted to such a painful cause that keeps you in a perpetual state of rage, and sometimes I wonder whether writing it out in a book might not in the end be your best way of contributing..anyway I admire your guts and courage more than I can say. And of course it is making you a part of a community in a new way, that way of service, understanding, and hope when things are grim.

Before I forget, I have looked high and low for your shirt and cannot find it anywhere in the guestroom. Here is a check for $25 to replace it if you can.

I am into the Christmas frenzy—the only thing I enjoy is having all the dear faces come up to my mind as I write the address on cards..but it all is a bit too much. Tomorrow night I read poems to raise money for Amnesty International in Cambridge. And last Tuesday and Friday I was at Clark Univ. my only public appearances I hope for this and next year..there it was rather interesting as we were three old women being honored our works having been studied in one class of 75 for a semester..Gwendolyn Brooks, the black poet, and Tillie Olsen. I made a real new friend in Gwen, and Tillie is an old friend but an impossible woman who always talks too much in a pious inflated way that makes me crawl. I read all new poems in the last two years and it went well. And I stayed with Sue and Lois who edited the Selected Poems and treat me like a very dear mother so I feel cherished in a lovely way. They even gave me a velvet elephant because, they said, missing Grizzle [the dachshund], I would need something to hug. How rare in my life these days this atmosphere is. They have an old 1740 house almost empty of furniture and so, very peaceful. And five cats who gather at five around an enormous plate to eat a whole big can of cat food.

My novel is waiting for Xmas to be over but is now 100 pages and rather to my surprise seems to be turning into a novel about homophobia. Perhaps it is my way of marching...

Grizzle kisses you and Pierrot loves you from a distance and I send a huge hug

Your old
May

I <u>hated</u> not seeing you again in the fall—Are you really well again?

---

a painful cause: Barber had been taking part in efforts to combat human rights outrages in Argentina; now he was involved in caring for friends with AIDS. In *Encore,* p. 130, Sarton speaks of the impetus behind her 1987 poem "AIDS," which she and others read to great effect at fund-raisers to fight the disease.

Brooks . . . Olsen: Gwendolyn Brooks (1913–2000) won the Pulitzer in 1949 and was Illinois' poet laureate since 1968, amid other honors. She wrote some thirty books of poetry; her most recent at this time were *To Disembark* (1981) and *Blacks* (1987). *Selected Poems* came out in 1999.

On the dust jacket of *Poems 1930–93,* Brooks said, "May Sarton is a Survivor, spiritually as well as physically. Her poetry, too, will survive, attesting to the fact that a woman of magnificent radiance—a Truth-teller!!—was and is Here."

Feminist essayist and fiction-writer Tillie Olsen (b. 1913) is the author of *Tell Me a Riddle* (1962), *Silences* (1978), *Mother to Daughter, Daughter to Mother* (1984), and other books. She was married to activist Jack Olsen, who died in 1989.

For Serena Sue Hilsinger and Lois Brynes's *Selected Poems of May Sarton,* see note to 16 July [1979].

really well again?: Barber had been diagnosed HIV-positive. Battling her own ill health, Sarton wrote him, 28 July 1988: "[W]hat a horror you have been through and once more come out brave and alive and yourself. It is a great wonder and makes the hair on my head stand up as for a great poem.

"There are a few small rays of light in the general delay and ignoring of Aids by the gov. . . . But it has been a dirty degrading business and I understand very well your rage as one another of your friends and many other talented loveable people are swept away. The attitude of your landlords is typical, I fear. But maybe they will not put you out. They may get so fond of you that [they] do not want to let you go!"

Barber took her suggestion about "writing it out," and by 6 May 1990 she marveled: "The miracle is that you have managed to write these simply <u>excellent</u>, moving, funny, true pieces about living with Aids. Looks like a book to me?" In a happier letter from 8 July [1982], Sarton had recalled how their friendship began when "you bicycled through Ohio Wesleyan in the rain with poems about V. Woolf. Don't forget that you are in a way a messenger from the gods..what a responsibility!"

TO CHRISTOPHER DE VINCK   Sunday, March 20th, 1988
[York]

Dear Christopher,

The first day of spring and it is snowing lovely soft flakes, so I am in a kind of cocoon. Your book came yesterday..what a blessed event in this house! I sat right down and read half before lunch and then finished it in bed last night. No one will read this book without being deeply moved, and perhaps even changed. A minor wonderful moment when your son says "I liked that beetle," but all through is woven a particular relation to and encompassing of what love is all about. Oliver is the message but you are the loving, subtle messenger. No wonder you have had so many letters, enough but not too many so you could not answer them all—that is my plight, as you know, and the endless anguish and guilt that I cannot.

But the marvelous thing you did was to connect with a few parents who have had the experience of an Oliver and then to visit with them and let them also add to the gift. Peter Guilbault's letter left me in tears and then tears of joy to know by the end of the chapter that a little girl, Katie, has been born.

I have an epileptic friend, Jamie Hawkins, who worked for years with a state-run house where people like Oliver were taken care of..her patient was a man of 21 whose age would never go beyond six months. She talks about her work just as you do about Oliver. But she was fired because of the seizures though none had done any harm to anyone but herself. Now she longs to be back in the work she seems destined to do and if ever she gets the right treatment for her own disability she may be able to. Luckily she lives with a friend and their two dogs and is herself sheltered lovingly these days. We have corresponded for years and once she came here with her friend. She had a seizure and was lying on the floor partially lifted by her friend, unconscious, eyes closed. Tamas, my Sheltie, showed deep concern, and finally pushed his head through the friend's arm and licked Jamie's face..she came to and smiled. I miss Tamas terribly because he had a caring soul.

I am alone here after 8 months of very intense work on a new novel, and a new book of poems. Off on Thursday (March 24th) to N.Y. to sign books, the new journal After the Stroke at Three Lives bookstore at 7:30 P.M. March 25th. I just mention this knowing the chances you could come are slight. Far better if you can, as you suggested, come here and see me sometime, perhaps this summer.

Meanwhile I'll enclose the reprint of a little book of poems from the N. Hampshire years..I am rather fond of it and am happy that Bill Bauhan wanted to bring it back. I have run out of copies of the new journal, alas. You know all about wanting to give your book to all your friends, but that is not possible..50 have flown away of mine in these past weeks.

I am going to England for 12 days on March 31st—mostly to see one of my dearest friends, now 92, Juliette Huxley. She was wonderful when I was so ill kept me going with marvelous letters...now suddenly (and why not?) she feels old and cannot write that sort of letter, so we shall talk..in little times of an hour or so, not to tire her.

It is such a joy to think of that Kentucky magazine bringing me a bouquet of poet friends in May. Very glad you will be flowering there. Is it the poem "To May"? I liked that a lot, and the Watteau one.

We have so many bonds, and not the least is your Belgian heritage..I had forgotten that. Someday you and Roe and the children must go there and feel the wind and look at the extraordinary skies..and maybe float on a canal for a few days..

This is rushed off, so forgive its flaws..and just remember it is a warm hug of love and admiration, as the words are irrelevant mostly—

from your old
May

Fred Rogers birthday today as I feel sure you know—

Christopher de Vinck: Poet and high school English teacher, who met Sarton while taping *Mister Rogers' Neighborhood* in 1985. He had just sent his memoir about his brother Oliver, *The Power of the Powerless* (1988). See *Endgame,* pp. 42–43, 53, for his June 1990 visit to York, when de Vinck was preparing *Only the Heart Knows How to Find Them: Precious Memories for a Faithless Time* (1991).

a little book: A 1987 reprint of *As Does New Hampshire* (1967) by William L. Bauhan, Publisher, Dublin, New Hampshire.

that Kentucky magazine: The *Kentucky Poetry Review: May Sarton Issue,* vol. 24, no. 1 (Spring 1988), represented forty-one poets, including de Vinck's "Surely East to West" and poems by Jean Burden, Constance Hunting, and Marcie Hershman. Also included were a transcription of the 1983 Heyen-Robertson interview (see note to 1 June 1980) and editor Joy Bale Boone's "An Appreciation of May Sarton":"Her poetry often brims over into her prose . . . where words are splendor." Six new poems not otherwise collected were accompanied by Sarton's "A Note on Lyric Poetry":"The pure lyric is never in fashion and never out of fashion. It stands outside time, embeds itself in the memory, and has the power to haunt."

a warm hug: In 1994, Sarton likened de Vinck to Romantic essayist Charles Lamb (British, 1775–1834), "that delightful humor and gentleness" being "rare in any age"; she wrote a blurb for his new collection, *Songs of Innocence and Experience: Essays in Celebration of the Ordinary.* See *At Eighty-Two,* pp. 209, 215, and 289–90. His most recent books include *Threads of Paradise: In the Fabric of Everyday Life* (1996) and *Book of Moonlight: Why Life Is Good and God Is Generous and Kind* (1998).

TO SUSAN KENNEY   April 23, 1988

[York]

Dearest Susie,

The book is tremendous .. I have been absorbed in it for a week since I got back from 12 marvelous days in England. But I am paying for that good time with congestive heart failure again and the old rascal is fibrillating..I thought that was cured for good, so it is a shock. Never mind, I expect they'll pull me out of it and meanwhile it is Heaven to have doctors and the hospital within ten minutes drive..I am lucky.

All the above to explain why this is not going to be the letter you deserve. I shall just jot down what comes to mind..above all what grips the heart is what a true marriage is (and how rarely told these days)— the love making for instance which I often do not like in fiction I found absolutely right and satisfying as was also the parts when you are inside the husband, a tour de force at the beginning of the book and whenever

you do so. Every single word rings true. And I can see why it was necessary that you translate these seven years of hell into a work of art, that
you <u>had</u> to do it. But you not only had to do it but managed to do it
superbly. That is the triumph of course.

Another thing I found wonderful was your ability to deal with Sara and
accept that she (you) is a very remarkable woman. You never make her less
than she is. Of course the humor is wonderful..the pages about insects in
the old house, the horrendous days of clearing out things..among other
things I suddenly saw why you had had to move into town and into a
newer house. I went through much of this in Nelson.

Then the key to it all is the metaphor, perfect all the way, carried out
to the limit, of Sailing. I dislike sailing so I was gratified to find Sara did
too. But as a metaphor it does work and adds a dimension the book
would lack without it.

Well, it is a triumph and I am a lame old donkey adding my praises
to—thank God!—the splendid reviews. I used to know C. D. B. Bryan
so it was fine to find his in the Times.

Thank you, dear Susie, for writing this book, for giving it to me, and
know I think of you and Ed almost every day but do not call because I
myself have come to dread the phone..

With much love and admiration—when shall we ever meet again?

> Always your old
> May

Susan Kenney: b. 1941; novelist and creative writing instructor at Colby College. Her husband, E. J. Kenney, wrote the brief critical study *Elizabeth Bowen* (Bucknell Univ. Press,
1975). Sarton's friendship with them and their two children, James and Anne, went back
many years; see *House by the Sea,* pp. 139–40, 262-63, 283–84. Susan Kenney's earlier books
include *Garden of Malice* (1983), *In Another Country* (1984), and *Graves in Academe* (1985);
here Sarton responds to her newest novel, *Sailing.*

C. D. B. Bryan: Sarton met him in May 1971 at a Miller and Rhodes writers' conference in
Richmond, Virginia (*Solitude,* p. 152): he had "all the charm of the young Englishmen I used
to see in London, elegant and fair, open and humorous, the sharp edges refined."

ever meet again?: They did, on 28 July 1993 (*At Eighty-Two,* p. 18). By then Kenney had published *One Fell Sloop* (1990), and after a long illness her husband, Edward James Kenney, Jr.,
born 1942, died in December 1992.

In "May Sarton's Journals and *A Reckoning:* An Appreciation" (*Puckerbrush Review,* 10 no.
2, Winter 1992), Susan Kenney characterizes how Sarton uses her different journals for different purposes, and asserts that these books include some of the best descriptions written
about the daily experience of illness.

[York]

Dear Char, Your letters bring me riches and I am so glad when I see your hand in the mail..delighted about your new friends Al and Alda, almost like relatives who understand what your life is all about and can help. In this last letter you tell me a little about your parents' visit..it made me sad. Sad for them that they cannot see what good values you are sharing with the children, how hard you work and yet how aware you are of all the blessings around you—what birds! I am envious, although in May the bird feeders are glorious with two pairs of orioles who came for a half orange I hung out each day, and dozens of gold finches who will stay all summer. The orioles are now nesting I expect and have disappeared.

I've said this before but some day you are going to put Hay River Notebook together and get it published as a book. How much you manage to read! I find Brookner well written but somehow one does not care much about her people. I am in a doldrum right now, reading Archibald Macleish's letters which seem rather old fashioned. He was a most loveable person, generous, the best host I have ever seen as he made each person at the table feel important and knew how to draw them out. But somehow he never solved the conflict between being "a public man", and a very successful one, and being a poet, the latter what he wanted most. It is clear at the start that marrying put a spoke in the poet's wheel almost at once as he had to make money. It was a wonderful marriage in many ways. He was surely "taken care of" in the best most feminine ways, but he was also I think in a gilded cage and sometimes rebelled against it. Ada, his wife, really gave up her career (as a singer) for him. The letters give me something to think about.

But it is a meazley time here..I have very little energy, pay a high price even for a short visit. This is because after a week in hospital and another cardio-conversion which did not take, I am told I simply have to live with a fibrillating heart forever. It means getting used to feeling exhausted all the time and so far with very little joie de vivre left. I am back at the novel as I am determined to finish it this summer somehow. I was not able to write at all for six weeks because my heart was beating so fast. It is down to 80 now, thank Heavens.

Without Nancy and a woman who comes once a week for 6 or 8 hours in the garden [Karen Olch], I really could not manage. The only good thing, I have have [sic] stopped writing letters and have no guilt (for a change). it is a great relief.

But I begin to see that three flights of stairs which I go up and down about 40 times a day is a lot for me and the place is a lot, too. Now I have had to haul hoses around all afternoon as it is so dry..dry but beautiful and cool. This morning I got up late around seven, washed my sheets and made up the bed with fresh ones, washed two pairs of blue jeans and some shirts too and hung them up. Put out the bird feeders and filled them, and now it is after ten and I am really longing to go and lie down!

However this coming week will be interesting, for Jean Alice the former prioress of the Carmelite Monastery where I stayed arrives on Wednesday for three days. Then on Sunday I drive her, a five hour drive, to Burlington Vt. I have arranged a book signing there. It is at 7:30 that night with a dinner before but we'll make an early start so I can have a long rest before. They are very excited about my coming, it seems. Jean Alice will be an easy guest and I am starved for conversation..she will fit in, I know. Nevertheless I dread the effort, the meals etc.

I hope Jackson will be chosen as vice president. But I'm not sure Dukakis will risk what it risks. Jackson would bring in millions of votes but also lose millions of votes. Let us hope he gets it as he deserves. I do admire him.

I am very sick about this country, the more so since reading the horrendous facts about the CIA teaching the contras [in Nicaragua] and Duarte's soldiers how to torture..in Honduras. Also it is unbelievable to have to admit that we do this and always have, that the fear of communism has corrupted us to the bone. And most Americans know nothing about it and could care less. Quite reminiscent of the Germans under Hitler. And Reagan's lies about the Indians in Moscow. I am sick of politics.

Well, I must stop. There is one more letter I hope to achieve this A.M.—I used to think nothing of writing ten. Now one a day and two on Sundays is about it.

I wonder whether I shall ever feel like myself again. It may well be simply old age that is with me like a plague.

Much love and admiration always and Bravo for painting the rooms on top of everything else.

> Ever your old
> May

Char Radintz: Wisconsin diary farmer, political activist, and friend of the work, Radintz (now known as Charlene Stellamaris) regarded Sarton as not only a friend but a mentor. See *At Seventy,* p. 270, and *Encore,* pp. 61–62.

Hay River Notebook: A series of articles Radintz had written over the years, chronicling her adventures and misadventures in agriculture.

Art historian Anita Brookner (b. 1938) has published a well-honed novel each year since 1981, her best known being *Hotel du Lac,* 1984 Booker Prize winner. The distance between her and Sarton can be measured by Brookner's pessimistic observation that "what is lost, even well lost, can never be repossessed. That, after all, is the meaning of experience."

Macleish's letters: R. H. Winnick's 1983 edition, *Letters of Archibald MacLeish 1907–1982.* Sarton had written Signi Falk on 13 October 1963 about visiting MacLeish at Uphill Farm, his home in Conway, Massachusetts. Though happy, this reunion, after ten years, made her "feel freshly that too much money, too much of an 'establishment' (secretaries, a cook, a waitress, et al) is not really the right environment for a writer. It is enormously seductive, of course, and Ada [Hitchcock, m. 1916] is a master at creating this sort of life—Not that one must hug anguish and poverty to one's breast, but rather that one must in no way be 'set apart' from ordinary human life."

Thirty years later, 24 July [1992], Sarton wrote Christopher de Vinck how pleased she was that MacLeish "encouraged you when you were starting out..such an incredibly generous man. He was very kind to me when I was a lowly instructor at Harvard and he was Professor of Poetry. But do not envy him..I think he was caught between worldly ambition and poetry and never entirely fulfilled his gift. I may be wrong...But I think maybe your basement room is richer ground, austere though it is."

a fibrillating heart: Eleanor Mabel Sarton also lived with such a heart, and died of lung cancer.

no guilt (for a change): See "Guilt," *Coming into Eighty.*

Burlington . . . book signing: After the Stroke had recently been published. The signing was at Chassman & Bem Booksellers, the reception at the home of Deborah Straw and Bruce Conklin. Among much else, Straw has written about flowers and animals in Sarton's work, poems for Sarton, and the 1991 essay "Tea with Virginia: Woolf as an Early Mentor to Sarton" (*Virginia Woolf Miscellanies,* ed. Mark Hussey and Vara Neverow-Turk, Pace Univ. Press, 1992).

Conklin took many fine photos of Sarton—see especially *Encore,* p. 75, "May, Cybèle, Susan"; the front of Ingersoll's *Conversations* (see note to 1 June 1980); and the happy woman who adorns the cover of *That Great Sanity* (see note to [3] May 1992, William Drake).

Jackson . . . Dukakis: African-American leader Jesse Jackson was not chosen by Massachusetts Governor Michael Dukakis as his running mate for the Democratic presidential ticket, but Lloyd Bentsen was nominated instead; they lost to George Bush, Sr., and Dan Quayle.

admiration always: In July 1995, on the day before Sarton found herself having to make what would be her last trip to the hospital, despite being as sick as she had ever been, she summoned the resolve to write Char Radintz a note, barely legible, the last note she ever wrote. Radintz came from Wisconsin to attend Sarton's memorial service.

TO EDA LESHAN   January 16th, 1989
[York]
Dear Eda,

Such good news on every side! The wonderful advance reports on Larry's book and that you may be syndicated all over the place after the ten weeks try..how can they resist? I swallow all this good news like a magic medicine for depression. Of course January is always a low month, but I have lost my will, so at midnight I imagine some task I shall do next day and then when I get up there is no energy at all and making my bed feels like climbing Mt. Everest.

BUT last night, by the grace of God, I plunged into this masterpiece In Search of Myself and Other Children, and it was balm, and also stirred this lethargic old crocodile up so today life looks possible again, thanks to you.

It is a brave book and full of useable truth. I felt so proud that we are friends as I read often with tears in my eyes. The fear of permanent separation certainly created the trauma of my early childhood when I was torn from my mother so many times when we were refugees..when she died I was forty and felt immense relief that I would no longer ever wake in tears imagining she was dead. But all <u>she</u> went through as a child lives in me and the pain never ends. Anyway bless you for bringing me this book when it was most needed. It was sent by a fan in Michigan, so odd a coincidence!

Lovely to be in Holland in May..I would be for The Hague which is very elegant compared to Amsterdam though less romantic and of course there is the great Museum there..but in May surely gardens and tulips! And Africa in July, Oh boy!

I go to San Francisco April 2d for a last performance at the City Arts in Lectures (where they sell out for me three months ahead) and it will be easy as it is an open interview, not a performance and I'll have a chance to say goodbye to many old friends in Berkeley.

The MLA day when I was honored in New Orleans at their yearly meeting was OK and did one illuminating thing for me i.e. there were excellent essays on my work but when I got up to read from the new poems, the air was charged in a wholly different way. Art was so alive compared to criticism.

Norton sent the final 150 pages of the novel with copywright [sic] queries on Christmas Eve! But at last it's off our hands. My fantasies have been chiefly murder of the copywright editor and her literal mind. Every image was queried. If I had said, "that was another kettle of fish" she would have said "There has been no mention of your eating a kettle of fish!"

Lots of love
M

P.S. 76 is too <u>old</u>. No fun—

Eda LeShan: Psychologist, syndicated columnist, playwright (*The Lobster Reef, A Gift of Time*), and author of such books as *When Your Child Drives You Crazy* (1975), *When Grownups Drive You Crazy* (1988), and *It's Better To Be Over the Hill Than Under It: Thoughts on Life Over Sixty* (1990). Writing in her *Newsday* column, (7 May 1988), LeShan said that *After the Stroke* "makes one believe in reincarnation, but only during one['s] lifetime."

After he offered help, Sarton briefly consulted with LeShan's psychologist husband, Lawrence. He worked for many years with cancer patients and wrote *You Can Fight for Your Life: Emotional Factors in the Treatment of Cancer* (1978) and *Beyond Technique: Psychotherapy for the 21st Century* (1996). For both LeShans, see *After the Stroke,* pp. 119–20, 127–28.

mother . . . lives in me: Writing Dorothy Wallace, around 1959, Sarton said: "[H]ow closely intertwined lives that have touched closely remain ever after death. Sometimes it seems to me that my mother looks out of my eyes."

too old. No fun: Sarton's inbred optimism would not let her remain downcast long. "I have just been to Providence R.I. to be hooded with my 16th Hon. doctorate," she wrote Robbie Robertson, 25 May 1989. "Providence College is run by the Dominicans so the commencement was very colorful . . . they in their long white robes with black velvet stripes on the arms, and the two bishops present in their crimson and purple. One of the other people hooded that day was an entrancing old Buddhist who sat in his chair . . . in the lotus position . . . a beautiful presence who was addressed as 'Venerable'." Sarton felt that the Catholic orders "seem more open, relaxed, and full of joy than their Protestant equivalents. . . . I wanted to steal my lent white robe of course."

TO PAUL REED   Saturday, June 24th, 1989
[York]
Dear Paul,

What an angel you are to have taken the time and trouble to write me such a grand letter about the novel when you are battling to help Tom through this awful passage into death. I can imagine very well how heartbreakingly hard it must be, to try to stay cheerful and helpful for him while you yourself are on the edge of breakdown from the stress. I have such a vivid memory of our lunch here and the rather casual way he said he had Aids. But there is hope if he can hold out a little longer. My dear friend Charles Barber has had Aids for nearly three years (was in hospital in London for three months with that deadly pneumonia). He gets some awful infection and is in hospital and then I hear "I am well and taking ballet lessons"— Luckily he, just as you and Tom, is in a city with a great support system. I hope you do have friends to help, to relieve you. What a rotten business it is. I shall be thinking of you every day now, sending supportive messages through the air.

I am very tired of being 77 already—the trouble is my spirits are fine but the old bod is shaky and I fear falling and have awful little energy..letters don't get written, nothing gets done. It is depressing. However I tell myself that not many old women of 77 write a novel..

Now you ask about signing..I'll be glad to sign this novel if you will send it along, but 8 more I can't do! Wrapping and unwrapping, lugging to the P.O. lugging up and down three flights of stairs to my study, all that is a little beyond me now.

Much love and all the support I can give.
May
Yours is by far the most cogent I have had, bless you.

---

such a grand letter: Reed had written Sarton about *The Education of Harriet Hatfield.* In 1988 he had published his second novel, *Longing;* earlier for the (San Francisco) *Bay Area Reporter,* he had reviewed *At Seventy* and *The Magnificent Spinster.* Of that novel he noted (26 June 1986) how, "at long last," she "does not shy away from love between women," and claimed the book was "May Sarton's crowning achievement, a thick novel of hearty themes, rendered evocatively, lovingly, and with great care and craft."

In his letter of 19 June 1989, Reed told Sarton that the new novel "was wonderful! The narrator is such a warm, endearing character, and . . . your discussion of the issues came right to the point—we are talking about <u>real</u> people, with <u>real</u> lives, who ought to be able to love in any way they feel is right. . . . [It] is the love, the passion, that matters." Affixing "labels" to people is "very troubling, because it has created in the minds of so-called 'straights' the idea that same-sex passion belongs to a distinct, separate and 'different' <u>kind</u> of person. And dividing people into categories, with better and worse 'ratings,' is the foundation of bigotry."

battling . . . through this awful passage: In 1984, alongside his pioneering AIDS novel *Facing It,* Reed had published *Serenity: Support and Guidance for People with HIV, Their Families, Friends, and Caregivers* and became a well-known AIDS activist.

support I can give: Reed and his companion, Tom Gates, had a happy visit to Wild Knoll in 1988; in his letter quoted above, Reed said, "I thank you most for the frank discussions in <u>Education</u> about death and dying. This is the most difficult thing to sort out, and if I may be so self-pitying, at age 33, I don't feel well equipped to deal with this." Gates died in January 1990. "[Q]uite a <u>radiant</u> person I felt—and I'm glad he thought of me too as a friend," Sarton wrote Reed, 2 February 1990. After taking in his description of "those last peaceful hours in the afternoon sunlight" she wept, remembering how "having to be Tom's nurse was hard on you, and in this letter it is so clear that you 'measured up.' "

Reed's later struggles with pneumonia, experimental medications, and other obstacles are chronicled in *The Q Journal* (1992; see *Endgame,* p. 333), *The Savage Garden: A Journal* (1994), and *Back From the Brink* (1996): "I'm a cat with about 900 lives." Late 2000 saw publication of his third novel, *Vertical Intercourse.* He died on 28 January 2002, aged 45.

TO TED ADAMS   Sunday, Sept. 25th, 1989
[York]
Dear, dear Ted,

Your wonderful letter made <u>me</u> cry. It seemed to justify the awful effort it was to write the book [*The Education of Harriet Hatfield*] because I was sick so much that year, and now I am 77 I know I could not do it. But it is, as you guessed, a kind of testament in which I said a lot of things that have been on my mind for years. The original title was Exemplary Lives, and your perfect devotion to Johnny in the hard last years was the kind of relationship I wanted to make homophobes see. So little written today about all this is more than sex. I wanted to get away from that into the central truth of communion between human beings, gay or not. For it is rare in any case.

How beautiful those last words of Johnnie's to you are. It made me think of one of the last times Judy was here. Alzheimers causes its victims to repeat the same thing over and over. But that day I was very touched because the repeated sentence was "You'll never know what you did for me." And remembering this as I read your letter made me feel I must send you the portrait of Judy that her family wanted me to do and had beautifully printed [*Honey in the Hive*]. It was very hard to do because forcibly as a "family thing" I could not be absolutely honest about some things. Still, I think I did make her come to life and the family was very pleased.

Old age is not as one supposed is it? Of course you are younger than I am, but I resent never feeling well and having so little energy—and because so many of my friends were older than I, black holes appear every day it seems to me, where some dear beloved being has vanished. I am going to London Oct. 3rd for a brief week in order to see Juliette Huxley—she is now 92, the last of my muses to be still alive. And she is still adorable.

I can't tell you what your letter meant to me.

All blessings and love

Your old
May

Ted Adams: Business manager of Sarton's Apprentice Theatre during the early thirties, when he was just out of Yale; later a writer and director.

Exemplary Lives: Writing in *The Times Literary Supplement,* 9 March 1990, Victoria Rounding discerned that Sarton's main concern in *Harriet Hatfield* was to depict "exemplary lives. . . . Lives of people who have attained an inner wholeness, and who are able to give of themselves freely to those they come in contact with."

what your letter meant: The two friends had not seen each other for many years prior to their July 1993 luncheon; see *Endgame,* p. 57: "What is it that makes Ted so loveable and life-enhancing? I think it may be because he is filled with love and curiosity about people of all kinds and with an interest that spills over. . . . He bubbles with energy and love of life, full of laughter and amusing gossip, and his unfailing joyful appreciation of his many friends. . . . He asks for nothing except to be accepted as himself. That in itself is rare." Adams died in 1995.

TO JANINE WETTER   Nov. 24th, 1989
[York]
Dear Janine,

I am delighted to have your thesis—an excellent job. It was especially interesting to read your quotes which so often foresaw where I find myself now on this journey toward death, for at 77 I am very much aware of the diminished energy and have been both ill and depressed. But it was cheering to see that I did know what I was talking about!

One bad mistake. I was not Bowen's lover for five years! I was honest about her in the portrait of her in World of Light. We were lovers for exactly one night in 1938, but friends for ten years at least. I admired her tremendously and treasured her friendship and her kindness. She reviewed most of my books as they came out before World War II. She often stayed with Judy and me in Cambridge.

About interpretation I have a few things to suggest. The word "privileged" you use about my life. I wonder why. Whatever I have I have <u>earned</u> myself in a very hard way, by writing 45 books undeterred by bad reviews (most writers would have committed suicide. The odds against me were immense, no college education, no person of power in the literary world behind me since London in the thirties). It has been a long tough struggle and I did not make money till after I was 65 with 30 books behind me. Until then I taught, did public appearances etc. to eke out a living somehow. I was never <u>not</u> anxious about money. If I were "privileged" why then would so many women feel me as their intimate friend, women of all ages and certainly not usually "privileged" themselves—The privilege for me was having such marvelous parents.

Never do you suggest <u>why</u> my work is so loved, why the letters pour in every day. The two things women tell me is 1) "you have helped me center myself" and 2) "You have empowered me."

Never in this essay do you talk about style or art. Why do I admit to feeling rotten in the last journal? Because I have above all tried to be honest in the journals, never to build myself up (as Anaïs Nin did always) but always to communicate the human being..a person who has had a stroke would never identify with a writer who did not admit to discouragements sometimes. And they do—

You have granted me neither talent nor courage. That is too bad. So many women live alone these days and draw strength from what solitude asks and can give. They read the journals and are illuminated. Lastly, the "deer lick" which is also a poem in my last book, The Silence Now ["Salt Lick"]. I get letters every day about my work and they are not as much to praise it (those I don't answer any more precious as they are) but to ask something of me and above all to share their own lives and problems. I cannot be interested in the lives and problems of hundreds of strangers. I spend nearly all my creative time <u>responding</u>. The creator is buried now and I have often believed that I shall literally die of it.

Anyway I am delighted to have your cogent work in the files with several others...thank you for all the time and caring it took.

> Gratefully yours,
> May Sarton

Janine Wetter: Her master's thesis was entitled *May Sarton: Perspectives on Aging and Dying.* She supplied this letter for publication.

Increasingly, after the 1986 stroke, when Sarton was deeply stirred or distressed (see [24 December 1990] and 31 January 1993), she might begin a letter with one intention and then be unable to sustain it to the end. The reader is asked to recognize that the writer is speaking the truth about her mood, moment by moment, as she addresses each topic, however incongruous the result may seem.

"privileged": She was the only child of two loving if imperfect parents, one an artist, the other a Harvard professor—who gifted her with lifelong optimism and a burning sense of mission.

She was well-acquainted with money worries, but never endured severe want or mistreatment or misfortune. These advantages could be construed, by a great many of the less fortunate, as constituting an obvious case of "privilege."

I have . . . tried to be honest: In fairness to Wetter, it should be noted that her essay does not deal with "<u>why</u> my work is so loved," or "talk about style or art," because those were not her main concerns.

Anaïs Nin: Paris-born American author (1903–77) of highly wrought poetic fiction. Her legendary lifelong diary, begun in 1914, was edited by others for publication from 1966 onward, bringing her equivocal notoriety.

TO VINCENT HEPP   December 29, 1989
[York]
Dear Vincent,

You cannot, perhaps, imagine how precious our friendship is and has been for me over the years—Your Paris letter of [8] December reached me yesterday (with 28 others—the amount is what makes me ill—but yours is precious and I have read it several times, although—or perhaps <u>because</u>—I had flu over Xmas and feel shaky and depressed—

There is a wound in this precious friendship as there was finally <u>fatally</u> in relation to your mother—The trouble for me is that I am a whole person and cannot separate what I believe from what I do as a writer or live as a woman. It is interesting that in my long correspondence with your mother, its charm, its wonderfully generous appreciation of the poet in me, never did she speak to me of any suffering—children starving in Ethiopia, Blacks deprived of all dignity in South Africa—she seemed immune to any imaginative <u>sharing</u> with the poor, the outcasts—the deprived. I am a democrat, not because being so does <u>not</u> include "the notation of the heart" but because it does.

If I am a Christian it is because of a single statement made and believed by Christ: "What ye have done unto the least of these, ye have done unto me" [Matthew 25:40]—The Republicans believe and have always believed that the "least" would benefit from what the rich have as it would "trickle down." Our infant mortality rate is very high. The lack of child care centers is appalling—no Western European country treats its poor as badly as we do. None has as serious a drug problem—

But I am deeply touched that you speak of yourself and the USA as "we". You are identified. You feel <u>with</u> and I envy you that.

We must not be separated, dear Vincent. I think our last meeting was painful—I let you down.

But I hold you in my heart as very dear and nonesuch—No one is there who resembles you—

It is moving to think of Florence and Guillaume both married—

Guillaume a few days from now. I see they have married very different people—May they both be happy in the Vita Nuova—

I hope you can decipher this—Anyway it brings my love and admiration.

Ever your old crazy
May

I feel terribly old and frail, and never well—

––––––––––

Vincent Hepp: d. 1997; married to Christiane. Son of Pierre Hepp (see note to 25 June [1952]) and Camille Mayran, who had died in April 1989. Pierre was buried in Versailles, Mayran in Strasbourg amid in-laws unknown to her. Vincent's 1975 Christmas wishes appear in *House by the Sea*, p. 174; *Recovering*, pp. 211–16, recounts an October 1979 visit from him and Christiane two years after the sudden death of their son Oliver, twenty-four.

over the years: A January 1983 stroke left Hepp blind in one eye; see *At Seventy*, pp. 234–35, 241, 290–91. Writing in commiseration after Sarton's stroke, he described his own (worse) experiences (*After the Stroke*, pp. 45–46).

immune to . . . sharing: Sarton remarked upon this flaw back on 9 March 1976, in *House by the Sea*, pp. 212–13: "For almost the first time in our long correspondence I feel an abyss between us . . . there is too much on which we profoundly disagree, too much that she cannot accept about the world as it is now." Speaking of Watergate, Mayran had said " 'Of course we in France have always separated morality and politics,' " Sarton quoted to Charles Barber, 16 March 1976. "Yes, indeed!" Sarton continued. "And that is what is wrong with France." But she hardly knew how to write a truthful reply that would not injure in return, and "why offend a very dear old friend." Mayran died aged 100.

"the notation of the heart": In the letter to which Sarton is responding, Hepp wrote (in English) that he had hoped their "rare visit would take place on what we do have in common, which has to do with the heart, and 'the notation of the heart' as Thornton Wilder described literature." (American playwright [*Our Town*] and novelist, 1897–1975.) Hepp, like his mother, differed sharply from Sarton about global responsibility.

both married: His daughter, Florence, mother of twins Baptiste and Oriane, died in 1997. His son Guillaume is married to Brigitte. Hepp was "very happy with both unions. And if as Jorge Luis Borges says, Hazard and Destiny are synonyms, I like these hazards (why does the English language believe that hazard only means danger? and chance means luck?)" See *Encore*, p. 249, for Hepp's reaction to the birth in early 1991 to Brigitte and Guillaume of a daughter, Sophie Marie.

[*Endgame* begins 3 May 1990.]

TO MARTHA HALL WHEELOCK AND
MARITA SIMPSON   July 11, '90
[York]

Dear Martha, dear Marita,

I read the script yesterday afternoon and think it is good and will work. I do have a few suggestions. Over all Marita's dialogue is weak, her action excellent. Her sense of the camera etc. But for instance "You are my American mate" (Alex to Caro) is simply ludicrous.

These are my suggestions

CARO 1) It won't do to have Caro wear "sweats". The whole point of her misery is in part that she is a lady. Her speech is different from Harriet's, her whole being is of a different breed. I feel her relation to Standish is 1) friendly in a humorous way. They understand each other 2) when he is dying, primarily maternal. I do not see her getting into bed with him. But stroking his forehead and kissing him like a child, he the child. 2) curiously enough you keep Caro as I wrote her in relation to Anna. and all that part rings true as a result.

STANDISH He is reduced in this script to simply curses..why not make him a little better when he establishes a relationship with Caro, teases her maybe and she, him. His cursing is wrong because is it such trite cursing. Can't you think up some imaginative curses that would make the audience laugh or cheer?

THORNHILL Why make him into the old trite idea of a minister? I am proud of the fact that he is not. It is also that the final scene when Caro talks about forgiveness and he is so wise, be believable and touching.

ANNA Everything with her is very good and right.

Are you under the illusion that the only way to reach the general public is to write down to the level of a 10 year old? That would be a stupid mistake. What makes Hepburn so effective? That she is a lady whether in the African Queen or "Who is Coming to Dinner". So is Joanne Woodward. In the relation to Anna you do the classes thing very well indeed. and a wonderful part for someone.

It is not by being trite that you will get through. It is by being original and real. I do think it can be a fine film or TV hour and thanks for all the hard work.

                                                                M.S.

———

Martha Hall Wheelock and Marita Simpson: Coproducers of two videos about Sarton. They edited *World of Light* (Ishtar Films, 1979), published in book form as *May Sarton: A Self Portrait* (1976). Sarton wrote about making the film in *Recovering*, pp. 40–41. So did Wheelock in "May Sarton: A Metaphor for My Life, My Work, and My Art" (*Between Women*, ed. Carol Asher, Louise De Salvo, and Sara Ruddick; rev. ed., 1993, with a foreword by Carolyn G. Heilbrun); Wheelock had done her dissertation on Sarton. After the premiere their subject exclaimed, "It's amazing how much you captured of me." *World of Light* was followed by *May Sarton Live!* (Ishtar Films, 1992), a 1987 poetry reading; see *Encore,* pp. 328–29, for Sarton's first viewing of the video in July 1992.

Ingersoll's *Conversations* includes Wheelock's interview with Sarton after an awards ceremony, 10 April 1987, which Los Angeles mayor Tom Bradley proclaimed May Sarton Day.

Sarton is writing to give her reactions to a proposed screenplay for *As We Are Now;* the project remains a possibility.

Hepburn: Connecticut native Katharine Hepburn (b. 1907) starred with Humphrey Bogart in *The African Queen* (1951), and with Spencer Tracy in *Guess Who's Coming to Dinner?* (1967).

TO ANTHE ATHAS   [December 24, 1990]
[York]
Dear Anthe,

How to answer such diversity? From the incredible Glenlivet. (But Glenlivet will have to wait till I am working and <u>well</u>) I have heard of it but never had a bottle, such extravagance!. and I have at last been able to take a swallow of drink after months when it tasted awful in my mouth..the sweat shirt made me laugh and think of a summer day.

Then there is your letter and the poems and the Peanuts which I too am a fan of..and a marked passage from Kinds of Love which made me wonder. Are you suggesting that my estimate of much of the poetry that comes to my desk is evidence of a generation gap? You question the last line of a poem which to any sensitive reader came very clearly from deep and excruciating personal experience. It is not the place to ram down my throat what <u>you</u> believe, is it? Let me tell you something. Almost every week I get a letter from someone about that poem. It has helped people die; it has helped those nursing the dying. It has been read at funerals. It is built into the lives of many people who have seen death. It is treated with respect. It is not a poem to be argued with. Here is what I experienced; you have every right to your opinion but not perhaps to question my rightness in what I felt on my pulse when my mother said "Take the flowers away". The poem has, I might add, nothing whatever to do with life after death.

Now we come to Cornelius [from *Kinds of Love*]—there is, in case you don't know, no generation gap between the readers of my poetry (much of it in free verse) and their response to me. It floods in and about 30% of the letters I get are from men and women under thirty. Now I am almost 80 my poems change lives as do my novels. And they will <u>after</u> my death—

Dec. 26th

I'm again in a bad place of torment and pain so have to give up trying to write a real letter...but at least I did two paragraphs, more than for months was possible.

I do not think you read Wyeth's Christina painting and the slight breeze in a window accurately—you have to impose "a more encouraging alternative"—what arrogance! Must art be "encouraging?"

As far as the bits and pieces of writing that you enclosed I have to say that there is not <u>one</u> original phrase even..everything is half borrowed, even the concepts are. You are a fluent writer who relies a lot on those surface images that come to the surface when one is about half present. My father was a great historian so you really cannot explain triteness and dullness by a historical background. His style is so alive, never trite. All good writing has the same qualities. I have never heard a good writer boast of being one. For any serious writing there is so much anxiety and doubt that has to be overcome..As for being an essayist, take a look at Thoreau who never said a dull or trite thing in his life. These may seem harsh words Anthe but I told you I think of you as a life force but I also think you exploit "personality" at the expense of style and substance. The latter are what make for good writing whether as history, essay, poetry, or memoir. Mere ease and fluency are not really advantages. They lead you to draw false conclusions.

Oh dear, do not give me up, cross porcupine..I love the life force but I would like to see it find true channels, not surface escapes...

May it be a very good year, Anthe..the life force always wins in the long run, you know!

I'll be here watching as you find yourself and the "good writer" you will become —

> Ever your
> May

Anthe Athas: Teacher of history and philosophy, and friend of the work. She supplied this letter for use in this volume.

the incredible Glenlivet: The fabulous Scottish whisky that appears in extravagant advertisements in *The New Yorker.* Sarton was known, among her friends, for liking good scotch.

the last line of a poem: "A Hard Death" was sent as Sarton's New Year poem in 1950 but not published until *A Grain of Mustard Seed* (1971). It concludes: "Only the living can be healed by love."

Wyeth's . . . painting: Christina's World (1948), the famous image by realist painter Andrew Wyeth (b. 1917).

TO JERRI HILL   March 25, 1991
[York]
Dear Jerri—

Your letter is a severe blow, and was totally bewildering to me until Susan told me she had heard me scream (in the hall) "It's Hell! It's Hell!"

Old age plus illness can blot memory out. All <u>I remember</u> is asking you just to hang up my damp pajamas. I had been in pain since 4 A.M. and was going to put in a suppository, and waiting had been rather excruciating. But was the scream directed at you? I can't believe that. It was directed at the hellish life I have led for 6 months. I went into my room then and cried.

I have the greatest respect for you and am grateful for all you brought to this house—the plants, Pierrot and I will miss you.

But I could not beg you to come back, as it might happen again. Extreme pain does not create good behavior. Very old, sick people had better be left to die as best they can.

love,
May

Jerri Hill: Hill was a young aide Sarton hired to help her, after Susan Sherman returned to teaching in late January 1991; Hill had written to say she could not work for someone who screamed at her. Sherman had been up for the weekend when this scene occurred. For further reflections, see *Endgame*, pp. 293–96.

[*Endgame* ends 3 May 1991.]

[*Encore* begins 5 May 1991.]

TO NANCY MAIRS   Saturday, Sept. 21 [1991]
[York]

A letter from you is such an event. I hope you can imagine that..and now I can type (I couldn't when I was so sick) even though I am a bad typist, I am more legible that way than by handwriting. It is no good to say how marvelous it is the way you seize life, how incredibly alive to everything you remain, no good because the wicked truth is there that one only gets worse, I gather, so that cry of hope that you be out of it before you are totally crippled went deep into my heart. But there are no words and all I can do is rejoice that you are on earth and that I know you a little.

Of course I devoured the english journal..it made me very homesick for England..you know my mother was English, an Elwes from Suffolk, and I have distant cousins in and near Ipswich with whom I correspond. One thing about the english..my cousins were farmers, small shopkeepers etc. not upper class at all like the Elwes branch of the family..but all are so civilized compared to the American equivalent it amazes me. One cousin [Alan Eastaugh] who had a small "convenience" store, was very musical, educated himself, does jackets for books and records. He writes wonderful letters. Luckily before I became quite so ill and frail I invited three cousins over, for two weeks each on three summers..I'm so happy I did. For now I fear I'll never get over..but you never know!

I was amused at all the description of food in the journal..most people travelling never find out that a good meal is possible in England. I know the Cotswolds well though not as well as you do. I used to stay in Kingham where Basil de Sélincourt lived. He was my best critic and gave me one of the few really great reviews I ever have had on the poems..we became friends and I stayed there quite often. I became enamoured of shirley poppies because he had a whole bank sown with them, such a brilliant sight, a soft brilliance. Since then I always sowed them.

My great news is that a biographer has turned up who seems right to me and will not publish till after my death—she has about 5 years of reading to do anyway—the archive at the Berg Collection is <u>immense</u>. Margot Peters..she wrote an excellent biog of Charlotte Bronte. It is a relief to be sure now after talking with her for two hours, one hour each day for two days. One hour is all I can manage as I get dizzy and queer. I liked her, thank God!

Lately my life has seemed to be too much for me, such a clutter of people and things and the endless demands in the mail. I mind because I am so inadequate these days. I wish I could just look at the ocean, dark blue today.

It is wonderful that George is managing without chemo. And back teaching. What a brave man! Oh dear, I wish you were nearer by and I could see you both and we could talk.

Much love—and do send a poem or two when you can. I look <u>forward</u> to writing the Guggenheim—am honored to be asked—

Your old
May

Nancy Mairs: b. 1942; author of *Plaintext: Deciphering a Woman's Life* (1986), *Remembering the Bone House* (1989), and other books. For Sarton's consideration of *Carnal Acts* (1987), about how Mairs deals with multiple sclerosis, see *Endgame*, pp. 104–07. In a *New York Times Book Review* of *After the Stroke* (27 March 1988), Mairs had thanked her "for the complicated joys of your companionship."

Suffolk: The landscape and skies of this part of England, which Sarton called "Constable's country," had profoundly haunted and moved her since infancy; see "In Suffolk" and her mother's letter, dated 4 October 1934, in *Letters to May*.

an excellent biog: *Unquiet Soul: A Biography of Charlotte Brontë* (1975) had followed *Charlotte Brontë: Style in the Novel* (1973).

What a brave man!: In December 1990 Mairs's husband George had undergone surgery for stage-IV melanoma. Sarton saw them both at Wild Knoll in August 1992 and July 1993 (see *At Eighty-Two*, p. 18). Nancy has since written *Ordinary Time: Cycles in Marriage, Faith, and Renewal* (1993), *Waist-High in the World* (1996), and *A Troubled Guest: Love and Death Stories* (2001). George has now retired from teaching, and the couple continues to appear throughout the country at conferences dealing with the end of life.

TO GERTRUDE SHERMAN   December 29 '91
[York]
Dear Gertrude,

I want you to know in case you think I don't know that I do know I am the luckiest person in the world to have been sent your daughter as a guardian angel—and that she surely is! What a beautiful, peaceful Christmas we have had among astonishingly brilliant sunrises, and at evening an adorable small tree glowing.

If only you were here, as well as my mother, we would hold hands and dance our joy.

My love and gratitude flow to you with Susan—

May

———

Gertrude Sherman: 1901–97; mother of Susan Sherman, editor of this volume who, in addition to weekends and other academic breaks, had spent the two-week Christmas holiday with Sarton.

TO MARGOT PETERS   [14 March 1992]
[York]
Dear Margot,

I cannot talk with you after these two meetings until you have read the work. The reason is that once you have read it you won't have to ask most questions and you will not make superficial and troubling mistakes in the remarks you make and the questions you do ask.

I gather I am the first subject who was alive when you wrote the biography so any generalities you wish to indulge in just don't work in this case. When someone tells you they risk nervous breakdown and you say they are ornery, it is such a merciless comment that of course it makes me shut up like a clam. One more such statements [sic] and you will have lost me as a source. I am a free woman. I am not your slave/ I still have a life to live and poems to write.

My autobiog is in the books. Novels not journals.

Examples:

The Single Hound. Mark is me of course. Doro is Jean Dominique. The painter is Elizabeth Bowen.

The Bridge of Years. The whole book is the world of Limboschs, Celine and Raymond are the chief characters. I do not appear as a character. But here is the Europe [where] I was at seven for a year and at 14 for a very important year.

Shadow of a Man: Francis is I. Solange is Juliette Huxley and a description of our love affair. Fontanes is Lugne-Poe who you find also in the Paris year in I Knew a Phoenix.

A Shower of Summer Days

The house is Bowen's Court. Violet is not Elizabeth Bowen but her husband resembles E's husband, Alan Cameron.

Faithful Are The Wounds

Based on F.O. Matthiessen's suicide. I did not know him well. Everyone else is made up which no one at Harvard believed. Harry Levin who thought he was Goldberg tried to wreck me in every possible way. I can never speak at Harvard for instance.

The Birth of a Grandfather

Sprig is based on Richard Paine, an old Bostonian who supported my theatre company and was a real friend. The other characters are inventions.

The Fur Person..Judy and me and Tom Jones our cat. I am Brusque Voice.

The Small Room much of me as a young professor at Harvard is in the chief character. Otherwise all the characters are invented or composites.

Joanna and Ulysses—

A true story told me by my guide in Greece. It is dedicated to her. The trip around the world, alone, to celebrate my 50th birthday by climbing the Acropolis (see poem) cost $5000. . .Ladies Home Journal bought J and U for $10,000 so once more daring something paid off.

Mrs. Stevens

I am Mrs. S. twenty years older than when I wrote the book. I did this to make for distancing and to avoid ordinary love making which I hate and have never done. I mean I do not like sex in novels. Dorothy is Cora DuBois, the lover of A Divorce of Lovers (poems) a famous cultural anthropologist Zemurray Professor at Harvard. A 5 year love affair that ended in my leaving Judy and going to Nelson. Willa is Edith Kennedy.

Miss Pickthorn and Mr. Hare

Miss P a caricature of my lonely self. Mr. Hare a portrait of the man who lived in a shack across the street from my house but I made him a little more fey than he really was. However when the trout were sown in the brook and the season was open he always brought me four or five little trout on a fern leaf for my breakfast . . . delicious.

The Poet and the Donkey

Andrew is me of course. It is all true. When I was so hopelessly in love with Margaret Clapp, President of Wellesley, I borrowed a donkey from the Warners who was terribly lame and healed her and myself in the process. The afternoon chase all true and hilarious.

<u>Kinds of Love</u> It is really what Nelson was for me. The protagonists are invented. Ellen was based on my dear friend across the Green, Mildred Quigley.

<u>As We Are Now</u> The nursing home a real one where I went to see Perley Cole when he was dying. A woman like Caro wandered around crying and was sneered at by the horrible fat woman and her slave. It haunted me.

<u>Crucial Conversations</u> . . . all the characters are invented.

<u>A Reckoning</u>—Laura's mother is based on Rosalind Greene.

<u>Anger</u> I am the singer, Ned is a portrait of Huldah Sharpe and much of the dialogue actually took place.

<u>The Magnificent Spinster</u> really a biography of Anne Longfellow Thorp adored friend, at whose Greenings Island in Maine Judy and I spent nine summers for two weeks or so each. Anne had been my teacher at Shady Hill school and became a dear friend both of me and especially of my mother. The writer of the book is not me as is evident nor is her lover who dies, Judy.

<u>The Education of Harriet Hatfield</u>

I am not HH. She did not have my conflict between art and life. Other people in the book are invented.

All the nonfiction is autobiog. Have you read <u>Writings on Writing</u>? Any of the books of poems? <u>Plant Dreaming Deep</u>? The journals, all of them?

[not signed]

Margot Peters: Former professor of English at the University of Wisconsin-Whitewater, Peters holds a Ph.D. in Victorian literature. Her earlier books include *Bernard Shaw and the Actresses* (1980), *Mrs. Pat: The Life of Mrs. Patrick Campbell* (1984), and *The House of Barrymore* (1990). She had written Sarton that she would like to write her biography; Sarton responded, "You are not the first and won't be the last." In September 1991 Peters came to York to meet Sarton, then went to New York to be vetted by Carolyn Heilbrun. Contracts were signed late that winter, and she began the book in February 1992, making her first working visit to Wild Knoll in March. Sarton envied her research trip to Europe; see the appendix for a poem, dating from this period, wishing she were "In Belgium Now," country of her birth. (In her previous letter to Peters, postmarked 2 March 1992, Sarton had signed off as "Your Ornery May," an adjective Peters repeated but Sarton did not remember.)

never speak at Harvard: On 18 April 1993, for its Spring Benefit Reading, the New England Poetry Club would nonetheless sponsor "American Icon May Sarton" at the Harvard Science Center; Sarton was introduced by fiction writer and poet Marge Piercy.

Richard Paine: He had always been fond of Sarton and supportive of her work. His wife Ellen was Grace Dudley's sister; see "Grace Dudley Eliot: Le Petit Bois," in *A World of Light.*

climbing the Acropolis: See "Birthday on the Acropolis" (1966).

borrowed a donkey: Esmerelda; see *Among the Usual Days* p. 119, for a photo of her; *Endgame,* p. 94, for Poet and Donkey.

Have you read . . . all of them?: That Peters had not yet read all the work made Sarton skeptical; though she wanted and tried to like Peters, she remained ambivalent to the end. For Sarton's misgivings about the biographical experience, see *At Eighty Two,* passim; for Peters's views, see the 13 April 1997 interview by Lois Blinkhorn in the *Milwaukee Journal Sentinel.* ("She was so alive. She lived more in a week than I did in a year.... I was fascinated by her.") Knopf published *May Sarton: A Biography* in March 1997.

TO SUSAN SHERMAN   25 March [1992]
[Durrants Hotel, London]
Darling one, it is a strange journey out, as both Maggie and I feared lots of bad luck—Our luggage was lost in NY for 3 hours, the taxi could not find the Holiday Inn. Next morning it was snowing hard—the plane had to be de-iced twice, and was scary. But the taxi did meet us in London, there were flowers and messages for me—and we have our familiar rooms.

Monday I saw Juliette—she was very confused and said so—She finally went upstairs before lunch—I had lunch with Chris, the new housekeeper—and learned a lot—among other things that there will soon be no money and Francis may take Juliette to New Mexico and sell the house—She would die I think. But that is what she needs now—to be let go. It was a terrible shock for me to face her being not herself—

I forgot to say that on the plane I had a terrifying episode—garbled speech, felt insane—it lasted about 2 hours—I thought I would have to come home right away—it was a tiny stroke I presume—brought on by the stress of Kennedy—Poor Maggie was terribly worried but kept telling me "It won't last. You will be all right." And finally I was—and everyone so kind in England. Everyone at Kennedy had been rude and awful—they told us our luggage might have gone to South Africa!

Spring is here but it is very cold—So we have not sat in Juliette's garden for more than a few minutes—

I miss you and home and can't believe we have only been here 4 days—it seems a month—

We did go and see the ducks yesterday—and on Sunday we hear Beethoven's Emperor—with Alan.

A book signing and a play on Saturday—interviews tomorrow—it is an easy and interesting schedule and I shall enjoy it—
A heartful of love—

[a heart]

Alan . . .a play . . . A heartful of love: For Sarton's retrospective on this visit, see *Encore*, pp. 226–30, 235–36. At the theatre they saw Brian Friel's *Dancing at Lughnasa,* then Shaw's *Heartbreak House* (1913) with Paul Scofield and Vanessa Redgrave. At Festival Hall she, her cousin Alan Eastaugh, and Maggie Vaughan heard (according to the journal) the Haydn Trumpet Concerto and the Mozart Clarinet Concerto.

To honor Sarton's eightieth birthday, Susan Sherman solicited sixty-seven colleagues from the theatre, the visual arts, and literature to contribute to a Festschrift, Forward into the Past, *designed by John Kristensen in an edition of 150. (The title derives from the last line of "Letter from Chicago: For Virginia Woolf," 1953.) Sarton describes her amazement and delight on pages 252–54 of* Encore. *At her request, publisher William B. Ewert printed a thank-you card:*

> Dear
>   I can imagine no more adorable present
> than this garland of voices weaving eighty
> years of life into such a rich and moving whole.
> How blest I am!
>
>   May Sarton
>   York, Maine
>   May, 1992

The next three notes were written on this printed card.

TO IRENE SHARAFF   May [3] 1992
[York]   [Festschrift thank-you]
Dear Irene,
    What happy memories well up as I see your words in the festschrift, dear heart—gardenias in Florence and almond blossom, Café au lait at Foyots in your bed, dancing with LeG and Jo at Le Fétiche. Amazing! I who forget everything remember those days perfectly.

                              So much love,
                              May

Irene Sharaff: "Remembering those wonderful discovery days in Paris—Belgium and Italy and that exciting period in both our lives at the Civic," Sharaff (1910–93) had written in the Festschrift. When Sarton at 19 spent a year in Paris, the two women saw each other almost daily, and vacationed in Florence. In later life Sharaff became a notable set and costume designer; they had long been out of touch. See *At Eighty-Two,* p. 39.

TO BILL BROWN   May [3] 1992
[York]   [Festschrift thank-you]
Dear Bill,

I have read and re-read your life-giving image for me and my garden with tears of relief to hear your true voice again. Isn't it time, before we leave this earth, that we re-entered our friendship? We always did do better as correspondents than when we met, I think—Could we write a letter now and then? I have felt so deprived.

Ever your old
May

---

your life-giving image: Bill Brown had written: "I realized, when I first met May in June 1939 on a ship taking us to Europe that she had found the key to a secret garden, and indeed was already living in it. Of course May herself was the gardener planting and tending the flowers that grew in profusion in her yard, and more importantly to the rest of us, harvesting the poetry and prose she had cultivated in her imagination—that amalgam of thought, passion, and wit uniquely her own. As a friend of May's, I sometimes thought of myself as a plant in her garden encouraged to grow and nourished by her immense generosity. Happy Birthday, May!"

before we leave this earth: Sherman's request that Brown contribute to the Festschrift ended an eight-year silence between the two old friends, and their seminal correspondence resumed.

TO WILLIAM DRAKE   May [3] 1992
[York]   [Festschrift thank-you card]
Dear William Drake,

Yours is such rich, deep, encompassing praise, so much what my heart desired—I thought no one would ever recognize or see—I do not know how to thank you, blessed man! I have read it many times with grateful tears—good tears!

Ever your
May Sarton

Do I have permission to quote you in a final journal going to press Aug 1?

William Drake: 1922-99. Professor emeritus and former chair of the English Department, State University of New York at Oswego; wrote *Sara Teasdale: Woman and Poet* (Harper & Row; Univ. of Tennessee Press, 1979) and edited *Mirror of the Heart* (Macmillan, 1984), selected poems of Teasdale. As an independent critic, Drake became acquainted with Sarton in 1985 while working on *The First Wave: Women Poets in America 1915–1945* (Macmillan, 1987). "The book is amazing," she wrote him on 9 August 1987, "because it is written by a man with such extraordinary understanding of what it is to be a woman poet. It is interesting that it is far easier to be a woman novelist, isn't it? . . . H.D.[,] Millay[,] Wylie[,] Marianne Moore, Bogan make a goodly company. I feel honored that you included me in that final chapter ['The Passion of Friendship'] in such a supportive and perceptive way."

To *That Great Sanity: Critical Essays on May Sarton,* ed. Susan Swartzlander and Marilyn R. Mumford (Univ. of Michigan Press, 1992), Drake contributed "May Sarton's Lyric Strategy," exploring how "The genesis of a lyric poem, for May Sarton, lies in silence." He traces her spirituality, her conception of the poet's task, the influence upon her early poetic practice of Yeats and Valéry, and her affinities with not only her European roots but with Chinese and Japanese aesthetics as well.

encompassing praise: Drake had written: "May Sarton always seems to be speaking to each one of us personally, as if we were a friend. . . . We may not realize that what seems so personal is actually the presence of something far greater than any of us as individuals—a kind of grace, a visitation of the spirit. There are never more than a few in any generation who can share the world of the spirit. . . . But May Sarton is such a one, and we are grateful."

TO CATHY SANDER   Wed. May 13th, [1992]
[York]
Dear Cathy,

Your letter came this morning..I am so touched (I cried) that you could share your grief with me. We are surely bonded through dear Eleanor, you and I. As soon as I finished reading I thought of this by St. John Chrysostom

> She whom we love and lose,
> Is no longer where she was before
> She is now wherever we are.

I take comfort from knowing that to be true and when you say that whatever you do in your life, Eleanor will be with you in doing it, I know to be true. Now it is the cruel loss, I know, that is so hard to bear especially at a time of such pressure for you. No time to mourn, but that time will come.

I am in the same terribly pressured time because of my birthday, a big conference on my work at Westbrook College in June, several books coming out, and the endless devouring and exhausting correspondence and interviews. Today a woman to see the garden and write about me and gardens. Tomorrow Japanese flown in from Tokyo to interview me, bringing two photographers. Cathy, I am awfully sick. My heart is so tired I think I may just drop dead soon. I've had a wonderful life and am ready. But what is hard is to have to struggle like a drowning mouse to keep afloat. For me too Eleanor's death has come at a very bad time. Madeline wanted me to find some quote from the journals for the memorial service..I simply do not have the several hours it would take. I wonder whether my poem "The Great Transparencies" might be one to read at the memorial service? In memory of Eleanor. I enclose a copy. The other poem on that sheet was written for Eleanor after we had a fight. Years ago. You might like to have it.

Cathy, I have no home address for you—please be sure I have it before you leave Wellesley. Maybe you could come here and see me sometime this summer? Where do you live?

It is so human to wish you had done more and been there in the last days...but the very fact that it was such a struggle for Eleanor, must make us feel her death was <u>right</u>—no nursing home, Thank God. Cathy you brought Eleanor a last great friendship, so much joy and sharing and fun. You were a saving grace.

I am awfully sick today and that woman comes to see the garden so I must slip this in to a mailbox for now. We must keep in touch. With much love and much thanksgiving for all you did for E these last difficult years, bless you. And for trusting me with this grieving letter—

Your old
May

Bad typing but by hand would be even less legible.

Cathy Sander: As a student at Wellesley, Sander lived with and cared for Sarton's old friend, copy editor and photographer Eleanor Blair, until Blair's death in 1992 at 97; she had grown severely deaf and was legally blind. See *Encore,* pp. 68–69, 276–78. "My wonderful old friend," Sarton had written after a happy March 1983 visit (*At Seventy,* p. 303). "Eleanor is one of the few people I now see who knew Judy [Matlack] and remembered that Judy did not like her coffee too hot!" St. John Chrysostom ("golden-mouthed"), Syrian prelate, c. 347–407, wrote influential letters, commentaries, and homilies.

a woman to write . . . about me and gardens: Eleanor Dwight, Ph.D. in American literature and teacher at the New School for Social Research, wrote the lavish and thorough *Edith Wharton, an Extraordinary Life: An Illustrated Biography* (Abrams, 1994). Familiar with the work, she interviewed Sarton twice, but an article intended for *House & Garden* never appeared due to corporate shuffling. Dwight gives lectures using Sarton's collected remarks about gardening from throughout her life, accompanied by photographs of Wild Knoll.

Japanese flown in: A translator, an editor, a publishers' representative, and a critic—three women and a man, respectively. For their mutual "state of undisguised delight at meeting each other" and how Sarton got the male critic to kiss her, see *Encore,* pp. 279–83. For Naoko Takeda's renderings of Sarton in Japanese, see note to 31 July [1992].

written for Eleanor: "Friendship: The Storms." Both poems date from 1971.

TO MARI SCHATZ   June 6th [1992]
[York]
Dear Mari,

How grateful I am that you wrote..I called Charles that evening, three nights ago, and a young man, a care giver, answered said Charles was at the Dr.'s but very tired when he comes home. We had a good talk. I suggested that Charles call me collect any time he felt able. I had hoped we could have a talk as though meeting in a café every two or three days or every week. I thought he might feel able to complain to me as he may not feel he can to all the friends who come and help, that I might be a kind of safety valve.

I consider him the saint of AIDS and when I said so to his care giver the boy laughed and seemed to agree but I gather he is not an intellectual, does not read aloud except an occasional newspaper. I am sending Charles today a cassette (hoping he can play one??) an interview with me with music I love from a radio station called Castaways' Choice in L.A.. I am sending you with this, but by book post, my new journal [*Endgame*]. Maybe you could read it to Charles now and then. It is an easy read and would be like talking with me..

I'm better at last but still terribly frail, can walk only a few yards etc. But there is a lot going on around my 80th birthday..and the best news is that I am writing poems again and able to listen to music. After the stroke 6 years ago I could not because it touched the source where poetry lives and I simply cried with frustration. Now I can listen to Mozart again.

Thanks again. I remember you well dear Mari,
May Sarton

————

Mari Schatz: Charles Barber's friend, who wrote to say he had lost his sight; Sarton and Barber had continued to correspond regularly. For her seventy-eighth birthday "Letters and cards poured in all week but all I wanted to see was CAB on an envelope," she wrote 6 May 1990, after he had been in and out of the hospital. On 12 September 1991 he wrote about considering "some very experimental treatments" that were "risky, expensive, potentially damaging at a time when I'm doing relatively well. I'm also writing for a new lesbian and gay magazine called 'Q'. I hope it lasts longer than 'Outweek', where I wrote in '89 and '90 (it only lasted 2 years) . . . love and thanks from C.A.B."

"Did you see the review in Sunday's *Times* on a book on pain?" Sarton replied, 14 October [1991]. "It quotes Aristotle as saying 'pain upsets and destroys the nature of the person who feels it.' You are not immune to pain but seem angelically immune to letting the psyche be affected. . . . And how happy I am to think of you writing with such zest in spite of all the horrors you suffer and have suffered for so long."

Castaways' Choice: John McNally's program, *Castaway's Choice* (KCRW, Santa Monica), featured Sarton on 1 July 1988. Her ten choices ranged from Monteverdi to Mozart to the Fauré Requiem, from Duparc's setting of Baudelaire's "L'Invitation au Voyage" to Sinatra's "My Way" and the Beatles' "Let It Be." "I remember when they came on the Sullivan show the first time and he sort of shyly said, 'Here are some English boys,'" Sarton told McNally. "One was simply overwhelmed by the vitality, the charm, the wit of these boys." See the complete transcript in Ingersoll's *Conversations.*

TO BRAD DAZIEL   June 14, 1992
[York]
Dearest Brad—

When I was 16 or 17 maybe I dreamed that someday I would be famous and loved and someone would celebrate my 80th birthday by inviting scholars from all over the country to write essays about my poems and works—that this has happened 63 years later after a long struggle and much frustration and pain, although <u>also</u> the joys of creation malgré tout—that you have single-handedly brought this to pass for an 80-year-old, given her a kind of apotheosis <u>now</u>— Well, how can I ever tell you what it has meant? What I can do is give you this paper weight that belonged to my father—and is a medal struck for Le Nôtre, the great French landscape architect who designed the gardens at Versailles and elsewhere—to celebrate your avocation although your avocation lately at least has seemed to be celebrating Sarton!

Dear dear Brad, that you made it all such a life-giving festival for so many when you yourself are so ill, and exhausted, is little short of miraculous. I am dazzled, overwhelmed, and full of homage and love.

Your old
May

Brad Daziel: Bradford Dudley Daziel was the Dorothy M. Healy Professor of Literature at Westbrook College (see 5 May 1974), and Scholar-in-Residence at the Maine Women Writers Collection, which houses the May Sarton Room. In "May Sarton: 'As Does New Hampshire,' " he analyzed the state's role in her oeuvre (*New Hampshire Perspectives,* National Endowment for the Humanities, 1982); he edited *Sarton Selected: An Anthology of the Journals, Novels and Poetry of May Sarton* (W. W. Norton, 1991). His introduction concludes that "Her theme is always growth, rooted in love; and this is what the common reader finds so ennobling in her work."

Daziel had orchestrated, at Westbrook College (now the University of New England, Westbrook Campus), the national conference "May Sarton at 80: A Celebration of Her Life and Work," 11, 12, and 13 June 1992.

When I was 16 or 17: "Why wasn't I born ten years earlier so I could have known some of these people, Amy Lowell amongst others," young May demanded of her diary, 7 February 1928 (*At Fifteen*). "Well anyway I am making brazen strides towards meeting thrilling people that are alive." The dream had come full circle, "malgré tout"—in spite of everything.

Le Nôtre . . . your avocation: André Lenôtre (1613–1700) also designed in whole or part Kensington Gardens, London, and the gardens at the Vatican, among many others. Like Sarton, Daziel was a great gardener. Suffering from AIDS, he died in September 1994.

TO SIR JOHN SUMMERSON   June 17th, 1992
[York]

Oh my dear, what a surprise to find a poem, no less, from you in the festschrift! I think you can guess that when I sat and read it tears poured down my cheeks, tears of joy. What an extraordinary convocation of people. And there has just been a conference to celebrate my birthday in Portland Maine. There were 36 papers given on various aspects of this so far still critic-neglected oeuvre. But that is changing at last and I am coming into my own. It has been a long enduring battle to survive and not be quenched. I have always had lots of readers of all ages from nine to ninety and of both sexes but the critics have been malicious often and if not, simply indifferent. Being a lesbian woman poet gives one two strikes against one of course in the male dominated literary establishment. I was right to buy an 18th century farm in New Hampshire when I was forty-five after my father died..and to tell myself they would eventually come to me. That is happening at long last.

I am happier than I have ever been in spite of our appalling President. I am writing poems again... I am over the stroke I had four or six years ago [1986].

Oh John, give me a hug across the sea, as I do you! I hope you can imagine my face when I came to your poem, how deeply touched I was, and delighted.

Bless you

your old
May

This is my Himalayan cat, Pierrot ("mon ami, Pierrot") on the terrace here. The ocean is down at the end of the field.

––––––

Sir John Summerson: 1904–92, curator of the John Soane Museum (London) and considered the most distinguished and elegant British architectural historian of his generation. In January 1992 he contributed a witty sonnet to the Festschrift; upon reading of his death, Sarton wrote "Obit," *Coming into Eighty.*

an extraordinary convocation of people: For example, former president of the New York Public Library, Vartan Gregorian; he wrote: "You, an Enchantress of Our Times, have cast the most powerful spells because you yourself have been held in thrall by life."

our appalling President: George Bush, Sr. For the photo of "Pierrot on the stone wall," see *At Eighty-Two,* p. 105.

TO CHARLES BARBER   June 22, 1992
[York]
Dear Charles,

I was not wrong so many years ago to know you were a very good poet..how thrilling now to read your poems in Unending Dialogue. I feel so badly [sic] they got lost for so long in the chaos here because I was so ill..I hate disorder so coming up to my study is a kind of agony of guilt and misery...and I can write poems only because I discovered I never could at this desk so I do it at night in bed when I have to let Emperor Pierrot in and out, often at one or two A.M. He has the loudest Miaow of any cat who ever lived so I hear him even if I keep the window closed. Bramble was so clever she could climb up to my window but he is so stupid I think he would fall off if he managed to attain the roof.

Today "The Quick And The Dead" hit me very hard. The form is so elegant and strangely enough it is a very universal poem I think ([Glenn] Besco on the teddy bear is good but not as good as you). "What Was Said" is just about perfect. I know that Ding Darling Reservation well (have a friend [Adelaide Cherbonnier] with a house on Captiva, but isn't Florida really hell). With "Letterbook Poem and Fairy Book Lines" I sense that you have found your voice, the mixture of irony, humor and a fierce sense of reality, finding a very elegant way of using language in spite of everything.

I have a deadline on the new journal and lost 3 pages of it the other day..rather driven this A.M. but I wanted to get something off to you right away on the poems.

There are many reasons I am proud to know you, dearest Charles, but that you are a poet and such a good one makes me proudest of all.

Love and blessings

Your old
May

Wonderful to have a small talk on the phone—

———

Unending Dialogue: Voices From an AIDS Poetry Workshop by Rachel Hadas (Boston and London: Faber and Faber, 1991); Barber appeared with eight other poets. "Fairy Book Lines" and "Letter poem [Dear Future.]" are two separate pieces; "The Quick and the Dead" is a ghazal, a flexible classic Persian form that juxtaposes image and insight to convey intense spiritual experience. The others by Barber that Sarton does not name are "Lapel button," "Prose poem [But no, the palm trees had no reply. Clifford searched the beach . . .]," and "Thirteen things about a catheter."

Ding Darling Reservation: J. N. "Ding" Darling National Wildlife Refuge, Sanibel Island, Florida.

a poet and such a good one: On 14 October [1991] Sarton had written him, after reflecting on dark current events, "It is a glorious autumn day here anyway. Man may be vile but God remains. Am I a believer? I suppose in some secret way I am. Otherwise how go on? We must believe in something other than the heart of darkness."

On 7 August [1992] Sarton wrote Bill Brown about how she and Barber "connected at once" at Ohio Wesleyan, "and he has been a treasure for me." Having *Endgame* read aloud to him "was the only thing that gave him peace . . . But he was not fulfilled, never as far as I know had a truly happy love affair although he had to walk with his head down in N.Y. he was propositioned so often if he held it up. He was a poet. . . his death is hard, except that somehow he shines through the darkness." Charles Barber died 4 July 1992.

Sarton wrote two poems in memoriam, "After the Long Enduring, For Charles Barber" and "Elegy, Charles Barber 1956–1992," both included in *Coming into Eighty*. At the service, 24 July 1992, Mari Schatz read "After the Long Enduring." On 31 July his parents wrote

Sarton to "express our gratitude not only for the poems but for the rare and enduring friendship which bound you and Charlie together....You had a major impact on his life and on his writing.

"We have a picture of him with a radiant smile holding 'Grizzle', dated June 1987, possibly at your home in Maine. Could this be the little dog you wrote of in the 'Elegy'? . . .We miss him terribly but we are grateful that he isn't suffering any more. He suffered so much, and so bravely. . . .

"Kathy and Bob Barber

"P.S. Did you know that he willed your letters (to him) to the Berg Collection at the New York Public Library?"

[*Encore* ends 24 June 1992.]

TO EDA LESHAN   [July 7, 1992]
[York]
Dearest Eda,

So good to find your word in the mail—I have finished a stint of revising 50 pages (I do 50 pages a day because I have an Aug. 1st deadline and still have to choose photos) on the new and last journal which will be called Encore. Of course I wish I had sent you Endgame but I gave 50 copies away to friends for whom $23 is out of the question..isn't it awful what books cost? Anyway now you have it [*Endgame*] having ruined yourself which may be not what you hoped i.e. it is not really about old age; it is about pain.

I am much better, can work 6 hours a day..isn't that wonderful? My head is buzzing but alas I am horribly frail and physically hardly able to walk. Never mind, better have a head than able to run a race.

Everything here has been what is called "roll" I believe..I'm on a glory roll and it is pretty wonderful. Soon you will get your copies of the Festschrift, really the best birthday present anyone ever had..I sat there reading it with tears streaming down my cheeks.You will see John Summerson's darling poem .. I was in love with him and he wooed me by playing Bach on the harpsichord.We had rooms in the same house in Bloomsbury.The whole book has so much of my life in it and going so far back it is amazing. Susan (whom you will meet in Endgame) invented the whole thing and brought it to pass with the help of a former student of mine who put up vast sums to make it possible.

June 11, 12 and 13 was the three-day conference at Westbrook College in Portland; and to celebrate my birthday. People came, men and women, from 34 states including Alaska and also from Nova Scotia. I did not go to the first two days (in all 36 papers were read from scholars all over the country) but Susan went for me and told me all about it. The conference was quite unlike most academic gatherings because everyone was so happy to be with other Sarton lovers, it turned into a fest. On the last day I managed to read the new poems and a few others for 45 minutes. I then introduced my official biographer, Margot Peters. She is going to do a first rate job, not to be published till after I die. How awful if I live on and on! I do not intend or want to. I agree with you about the Times Review..why can't a woman reviewer for once say Bravo ..they are all so nit picking. And do I demand to be adored? If I did would I confess to a bad temper and in general be as honest as I am? Anaïs Nin wanted and demanded adoration. I do not.

But at the very end of the conference Sandra Gilbert gave the fourth keynote address that ended the conference and praised my poems to the skies..very good about the influences of Yeats and Rilke. This was what I have waited 50 years to hear..Carol Heilbrun kept saying at the lunch afterwards, "May, you know she is truly important. You have made it!"

The Portland papers (Sunday papers) had me headlined, "Sarton a success at 80"—this made me laugh but it was festive to see huge photos of me and very good interviews..precious to be someone locally.

You have now heard a good deal more than you ever wanted to know about penguins..how I wish we could talk. I noted your anniversary the other day and pined that we were not having a lobster together. Some time?

My book of the year is the new biog. of Eleanor Roosevelt..that great woman. It is painful because of Sara Delano Roosevelt who was worse than one had imagined even. You should have a chapter on how not to be a grandmother and one thing is not to bribe your grandchildren! She did. The book brings back the twenties and 30's so vividly...

Well, I must go down and make my supper.

Oh Eda, precious friend..how good to hear...grandmothers should be fun, no? Such a joy to be a mothering person without the awful responsibility.

So much love..take good care of thee

Your 80 year old

M

---

the best birthday present: In the festschrift, Eda LeShan wrote how encountering *Journal of a Solitude* at a Cape Cod library affected her life: "It has been hard to realize that so much beauty and wisdom and artistry has come from one human being." Lawrence LeShan wrote, "I remember clearly the almost overwhelming excitement of first reading her 'At Delphi' with that magnificent ending": "I tell you the gods are still alive / And they are not consoling."

a fest: For Sarton's fuller account of these days, see *Encore,* pp. 320–29.

the Times Review: Sue Halpern (21 June 1992) found that despite the focus on illness, "there are salutary passages" when Sarton's "passing thoughts bring insight and the shock of recognition that comes when one is in the presence of truth" and that she still writes—and gardens—"with the signal grace of defiance." Eda LeShan wrote in *Newsday* (5 September 1992) that now was the time for Sarton "to learn not just to endure old age but to use it for a creative fire. . . . If we are lucky and courageous, we can be tested and found to be triumphant as we move toward a final sunset."

Sandra Gilbert: b.1936; professor of English at the University of California, Davis; poet and critic. With Susan Gubar, co-wrote *The Madwoman in the Attic: The Woman Writer and the Nineteenth-Century Literary Imagination* (1979) and co-edited *The Norton Anthology of Literature by Women* (1985). In her address, Gilbert firmly situated Sarton amid the women poets who came to notice in the 1930s and to prominence in the 1950s and 1960s, pointing the way to their successors. See " 'That Great Sanity, That Sun, the Feminine Power': May Sarton and the (New) Female Poetic Tradition" in the book of essays from this conference, *A Celebration for May Sarton,* ed. Constance Hunting (Puckerbrush Press, 1994).

Carol Heilbrun kept saying: Heilbrun also gave a keynote speech, included in *A Celebration,* about "The May Sarton I Have Known": "an ornery, outspoken, virtuous, feisty, and too-long ignored woman of courage with a secret knowledge of what matters in life, which she has shared no matter what the price."

More recently, in *The Last Gift of Time: Life Beyond Sixty* (1997), Heilbrun devotes a chapter to "A Unique Person" who "was able to arouse affection so often, so deeply, and so widely because she offered affection with so lavish a hand, and with so much humor and attention and excitement" (p. 87). In the passage William Drake alludes to (see his "Appreciation" in this volume), Heilbrun stresses (p. 77), "However dubious of religion, [Sarton] always had a sense of hints, of guidance, of messages coming at exactly the right moment, and I recognized the experience. As Sartre brilliantly suggested, we moderns may not believe in the Father or the Son, but we understand the Holy Ghost."

new biog. of Eleanor Roosevelt: Blanche Wiesen Cook, *Eleanor Roosevelt* (1992).

take good care of thee: See *At Eighty-Two* for Sarton's October 1993 reunion with the LeShans. At the end of 2001, Eda was still writing regularly for the "Primetime" section of the *Cape Cod Times.* Born 1922, she died 2 March 2002, aged 79.

TO BILL BROWN   [July (12) 1992]
[York]
Dearest Bill,

It is wonderful to be in touch again..I am listening as I write to the two Mozart late quartets you sent me years ago, before the awful silence. But now I feel some missing part of my life has been given back. How I have missed you! And our letters..writing to you and your writing to me, equally important. Surely that is rare.

This cannot be a very good letter. I am working furiously to finish revising the new and last journal. Since the stroke I had to dictate and the result is far from Henry Jamesian. I am better at last so I can work about 6 hours a day. I have an Aug. 1st deadline and must also choose the photographs. Not good, but I sail into it so happily and know you will not expect a masterpiece.

I hope you like this strange ecstatic photo of me. I think it is one of the most beautiful I ever saw of an old face. I am trying to get copies but the photographer, a charming young man, is doing jury duty so I hear nothing. I really look terribly old and wrinkled because of the illness. I lost 50 pounds. An old turtle. Maybe that is why this photo gives me so much pleasure. Looking in the mirror I cringe these days. I was talking away when the photographer snapped it.

You sound awfully well, Bill, and like me coming into your own..three more shows in the next year or two! Oh how I wish I had seen the one in New York and Paul [Wonner]'s too. How good it is that you are both doing so well.

Of course I grieve over Lily, the death of pets is the worst death. I shall never get over Tamas and Bramble. It is hard to define why it is worse than the death of a person, but it is. Bruno too! I loved him so much. My Himalayan cat, Pierrot, is not a fur person but a luxurious work of art or nature, whole in himself. He is affectionate when I have my nap and the first day in this house when he was a terrified and exhausted kitten who had traveled with Carol Heilbrun from N.Y., I woke the next morning and found he was asleep on my head. So I guess he is my cat. He is partly responsible for my writing poems again at last—he miaows to be let in around 1:00 A.M. and to be let out at three or four. It means my going downstairs so I wake up and in the middle of the silent night away from my hellish desk, poems flow in. That is the great event of this magical year..I have not written poems except a very few for five [six] years, since the stroke jumbled my mind.

How marvelous that you went to New Zealand to see Janet Frame and that now she is alive not dying. We have the same publisher in England and they will bring out a book of her poems this spring, and also my last three books under one cover and title, Halfway to Silence. The poems have not been published in England since 1939— yes! So this is great news and I am so proud to be published with Janet so to speak.

One of the miracles of these last two years is, as you guessed, Susan. I realized after she came to take care of me how lonely I had been. Now it is like having a daughter, one as I was with my mother. I mean we are "best friends." She has edited what will be a remarkable book using all unpublished material of mine, including excerpts of letters to you, under the title, Among The Usual Days. It comes out in March. I think. Lots of books will come out next year, one The House of Gathering, by poets on my poetry .. at last!

We are having a horrible July, wet and cold. The garden is rotting and the deer eat whatever survives, all of 18 English old-fashioned roses I had planted this spring..they ate all the buds. I have a good gardener at last as I can't garden any more except lying down.

Oh Bill, I hate to stop, there is so much more to say. Too bad about Alan but I am glad for you that it is over. He did use you badly it seems to me. But more and more I see that the important thing is to be the lover not the beloved. The lover may suffer but he or she has all the deep feeling and that is what one wants, I guess.

The typing shows my fatigue so I must end this first letter but after Aug.1st there will be more.

Wasn't it wonderful that we met on that trip to Europe so long ago?..and I think our friendship was and is rare. It will be known surely after we both are dead.

What is the lovely quote "Arrêtons nous un peu, causons"?

Ever your old
May

---

far from Henry Jamesian: Finding it increasingly painful to write by hand as he grew older, James started dictating his work to secretaries, influencing the development of his "late style" (*The Ambassadors,* 1903, etc.). Sarton used a cassette recorder.

this strange ecstatic photo: On the fourteenth page of photographs in *Dear Juliette,* the shot was captioned "the bliss of old age"; see the insert of pictures in this volume. The "charming young" photographer has not yet been traced.

responsible for my writing poems: The special Ewert edition of *Coming into Eighty* (1993) was dedicated "To Susan Sherman, the guardian angel"; the Norton trade edition (1994) was dedicated "To Pierrot, The Muse Mews." Lily and Bruno were Brown's cats.

the same publisher in England: The Women's Press version of *Halfway to Silence* included poems selected from the American editions of that volume, *Letters from Maine,* and *The Silence Now.* W. W. Norton Ltd., of London, distributed in Great Britain a hardback of *A Grain of Mustard Seed* in 1971, the paperback in 1975, and *The Silence Now* in 1988; the distinction between "distributing" and "publishing" is a fine one.

Among the Usual Days: Publication was delayed until October 1993. (The title is taken from the poem "Humpty Dumpty," 1949.) On 16 October, Sarton had thanked Sherman for "this masterpiece of choices from all levels of my life with no false moves in it or a single lack of understanding the essences. I can't thank you. I just have to glow like a firefly on a June night and so I do..and keep going back and plunging into all it has brought about and now brings about for me as though I were living my life all over again."

The House of Gathering: See note to 8 February 1962. The title is that of a poem first published in *The Silence Now* (1988) and comes from Jung.

"Arrêtons nous un peu, causons": "Let us stop a moment, and chat."

"It is so good to have your letters—they are always so exactly <u>you</u>," Bill Brown wrote Sarton, 15 March 1993. "No wonder people are always clamoring for something from you, like a splinter from the true cross."

TO ANNE ROLLAND-POUSSIER   le 13 juillet [1992]
[York]
Dear Anne,

How moved I was to read your letter and know that you are the translator of As We Are Now and persuaded Mercure de France to publish. Bravo! Years ago a friend in Provence translated The Bridge of Years which is laid in Belgium, but could not find a publisher. You will be interested to know that other friends of mine who have a firm called Ishtar Films Inc. are hoping to make a film of As We Are Now and Joanne Woodward has agreed to play Caro if they can get funding. They did a superb video of me called World of Light twelve years ago. It is used a lot in the colleges where my work is now taught.

You know I suppose that I am 80, but how could you know without reading my last journal Endgame? that I have been dreadfully ill for two years? I can't write at length—I live in a nightmare of disorder because four or five letters a day come and I can manage at most two..there are piles and piles all around me whispering "answer me, answer me" and drive me mad. In fact I can only write poems now in bed at night away from this purgatory. Of course it is wonderful to be so loved.. people attach themselves to my work in an extraordinary way. I am not a best seller but my books have to be rebound every 6 months in the Boston Public Library and no doubt all over the country.

How I envy your living in Chartres! I always went to Chartres whenever I could get to Europe..and there are poems. If I had not begun this letter on an airletter page I would enclose one.

So we are friends! What an event for this old lady!

Thank you for writing and for all you have done for me. And let us keep in touch.

Bien cordialement à vous
May Sarton

———

Anne Rolland-Poussier: French translator of *As We Are Now* as *Nous, Les Vivants?* ("We, the living?"), 1993.

a friend in Provence: This would seem to have been Marianne Dubois; see *At Eighty-Two,* p. 193, and the letters to Camille Mayran, 13 May and 29 July 1967.

Joanne Woodward: The last tribute in the festschrift comes from this renowned and versatile actress (b. 1930), who wrote from Saugatuck, Connecticut, to wish a "Happy Birthday to Miss Sarton from one of your greatest admirers."

Chartres: "Return to Chartres" (1947), "At Chartres" (1960), and "Once More at Chartres" (1966).

Bien cordialement à vous: "Most cordially yours."

Taiwan also has its rendering of *As We Are Now.* Germany has seen *Mrs. Stevens* and *A Reckoning* thanks to the Frauenoffensive firm; the Netherlands also adds, in Dutch, *Journal of a Solitude.* In Japan, where the diary has a long history as a serious genre, *Solitude, As We Are Now,* and other titles have been best-sellers, thanks to the translations of Naoko Takeda (see *At Eighty-Two,* p. 270); her versions of twenty *Selected Poems* were published by Misuzo Shobo in October 2001. Three prominent Japanese reviewers named *Plant Dreaming Deep* one of the ten best books of 1996. In 1999 four of the journals were secured for publication in Beijing, and in 1994 *Kinds of Love* appeared in Moscow. More translations are on the way.

TO BETH BRIDGES   July 26th, 1992
[York]
Dear Beth Bridges,

When your letter, a whole lifetime in a letter, came in late October 1988, nearly four years ago I was ill as I have been off and on since, I was not able to respond. My last journal, Endgame, which came out for my 80th birthday in May, will tell you something of what I have been through. Anyway I am better at last though very shaky, frail, and in pain a lot of the time. And I have been trying to tame the chaos in my study, to answer at least some of the vast piles of letters that have accumulated.

I have just re-read yours, the story of your life..what an extraordinary person you are! How many gifts you have and what courage! I am so glad that Helen Riley came into your life. I realize that your friend Edward Fell Godwin enriched you in some ways but he also took a lot from you. Helen sounds like a true companion. You surely deserve that loving kindness. How brave you were to adopt the abused little girl, brave and patient and caring..only to see her go backwards in the end and resume her violent life. I write badly because there is too much really to take in and to respond to. But of course I envy your yearly escapes to Ireland—I have not been back since Elizabeth Bowen died and Bowen's Court (the house of A Shower of Summer Days) was torn down. I am glad you liked the book.

What is wonderful for me these days is that I have managed to live to 80 as everything is coming out, in the long game of solitaire I have played..at last my work is getting recognition. I have always had ardent readers, but been neglected by the critics for 50 years. That is changing at last, with books to come out about my work from 5 University Presses in the next few years.

I hope you are still at the address given and still working at Fungus Art..do let me know and try to forgive this very long silence! I'll enclose a card of my Himalayan cat, Pierrot on the terrace here and a poem.

With all warm wishes and thanks for sharing your life with me.

Maybe you and Helen could drive over and see me here some time. My phone number is [   ] should you be in the vicinity.

> Gratefully yours,
> May Sarton

P.S. I feel at home with your strong, sensitive face!

Beth Bridges: Friend of the work, living in Ireland.

Gratefully yours: Sarton always remained so: this letter is emblematic of her unquenchable outgoingness, and the time and intensity she put into connecting with absolute strangers who loved her work.

Her fans continued to range from every walk of life. There was the Right Reverend Sam B. Hulsey, D.D., bishop of the Episcopal Diocese of Northeast Texas. "I am <u>learning</u> a lot," she wrote him, 5 July [1990], "but it goes against the grain. Your letter was a Godsend." For as she had told Vincent Hepp, 17 April 1989, "I am learning old age, a new lesson, and not easy."

There was Claire Bolder, then 62, who wrote: "[Y]ou are still teaching me how to maintain one's spirit and joy while struggling with the aging ailing body. On almost every page I gasp in recognition—here, in 'simple,' strong, direct language are my deepest feelings and thoughts!" "[H]ow grateful I am for your understanding and ability to explain it to me," Sarton dictated, 21 June 1995. "This is rare."

Most simply, another reader wrote of the journals: "I shall miss them." "That is moving I must say," Sarton wrote Bill Brown, 3 January 1994, quoting a remark by Katherine Mansfield: "I must remember that as K.M. once said laughing, 'Not for nothing did the chicken sing.' "

TO BILL BROWN   September 3rd 92
[York]
Dearest Bill,

I hasten to plough through the thicket on my desk to say of course you are right to refuse to answer questions about me when Margot has our correspondence to read. She does some things that upset me a good deal. For instance she asked Susan if we were lovers! I am 80 after all, and she 53. I think of her as my daughter. It seemed an insensitive question. She also asked Susan (who refused to answer) who had refused to write in the Festschrift. In some ways I wish I had never agreed to the biography. On the other hand it does give me a chance to ask myself some crucial questions. Why were the love affairs such painful experiences on the whole? I do see that I have fallen in love with two kinds of people, those I called Les Mal-aimés, those who had never known tender giving love and needed it so much and I had it to give. Judy is the great example of this. The other kind were the furies, the glamorous kind such as Bowen, Huldah. Juliette I think has been so deep because she was both. It is wonderful that we see each other in a rapture of happiness for the last three years..such a strange and moving affair. 80 is rather a magical year for me.

I hope that dizzying ear infection has cleared up by now? Of course I can't get used to your being, I suppose, 70 or nearly 70 now. I think of you as you perhaps think of yourself deep down as a young man. Do you mind being old? Or do you in some ways rather enjoy it? I would enjoy it more if my body were not so frail and old and looking like a concentration camp victim. You I think are very trim.

You used a wonderful image in your letter, about my parents, "a tremendous field of force for creativity"—that is true. It is still a battle to love my father as himself outside of his relation to my mother which was selfish in the extreme (so unlike your father). But at last I am getting beyond dwelling on all mother suffered because of him and I think this poem is worthy of her and not spoiled by my grief and anger. My parents are with me nearly every day..hard to believe mother died forty years ago. They inform, each in his or her own way, many of my actions every day..answering letters (my father did conscientiously all his life), ordering bulbs which I did yesterday. Needing peaceful order where things show but never having the energy, unlike you and Paul, to see that drawers and cupboards are also neat and tidy. (That was my mother of course, I mean not having the energy).

My greatest luxury is having a gardener, and a good one. A couple of weeks ago I went down to the picking garden to pick some nasturtiums and fell twice and found it very hard to get up as I did not have my cane. There was no one here. So now Pat [Robinson], the gardener, a woman, picks flowers for me and I arrange them. What luxury! Unfortunately the deer are hungry and ate almost all the lily buds and even some English roses in bud..they are so beautiful one hates to scare them off. But it is rather hard. Luckily there are now apples and that keeps them munching something[,] better for me.

Pierrot was attacked in the night by some animal that huffed in the woods..Susan thought she saw a fox when she came back from N.Y. so I was terrified, put on lights and rushed out, calling him. There was still this curious huffing going on in the woods. I do not believe it was a fox but at first there was a bark. Finally I caught Pierrot and hauled him in like a sack of potatoes. I didn't sleep very well and am tired..so I'll send this off. Do send me a snap when you can and here is one of me on my 80th birthday.

Oh I am so happy to be in touch, Bill! All blessings and love

M

P.S. Do you have a catalogue of recent work? I so want to see it and could send it back.

Mal-aimés: The badly-loved, the mis-loved, the unloved.

frail and old: "Have had to buy all new clothes since I lost 50 pounds," Sarton had written Brown, 7 August [1992]. "Of course la ligne [her figure] is elegant now which is some comfort."

this poem is worthy of her: Written the same day as this letter: "For My Mother, August 3, 1992," *Coming into Eighty.*

TO SUSAN SHERMAN   Oct. 30th [1992]
[York]

Dearest Susan,

For your birthday because I love you and all your dear graces and loving kindnesses, for your deep discreet love, for the wonderful book (shall
we both become Stars? when it comes out) and for walking into the
hospital two years ago to bring me back to life —
     Let us celebrate this rarest of loves we share
                    forever!

                                                        Your old
                                                        May

the wonderful book: Sherman was working on *Among the Usual Days.* For the events of two
years prior to this letter, see *Endgame,* pp. 150–51: that retrospective entry, dated 26 August
1991, recounts what happened between 28 October and 10 November 1990 when Sarton's
cassette recorder malfunctioned and did not tape her remarks.

TO ROBERT A. SCHANKE   Saturday January 31st, 1993
[York]

Dear Robert Schanke,

What a tremendous job you had to do and in some ways how well you
have done it. The book finally came this week and I have devoured it.

What is very absorbing is your exact and full following of the career
itself, and to some extent what Le G's particular genius as an actress was.
But you have relied almost exclusively for this on the critics and on their
misconstruing her ability to play a feminine woman well. Yet you show
clearly that her Juliet was a triumph. Le Gallienne's reserve as an actress
did not stem from her life style off stage but from her temperament. She
was a very reserved human being and would have been had she chosen
to marry. So I come inevitably to the terrible way you have muddled the
waters as far as her private life is concerned. You have apparently
believed a lot of gossip. You have not checked a lot of actual facts. Just
one example when Jo talked to me in her dressing room at the Civic

about not having two love affairs at the same time she was referring I feel sure to a flirtation on Le G.'s part with an apprentice called Kim. Evensen was never a member of the Civic Rep. I think she came as a member of the company for L'Aiglon. The full story of Le G.'s relationship with Evensen remains to be told and will be told when Helen Sheehy's official biography appears a few years from now as she has had access to the journals.

What troubled me as I read was a sort of contempt on your part in the language used itself. Josephine Hutchinson was never called Josie by Le G. and by no one at the Civic. Possibly her third husband, Staats Cotsworth may have called her that, but as you use it it is so patronizing, as well as inaccurate.

You have over-used May Sarton with snippets of letters or conversation out of context. And you suggest that I was an intimate friend. I was not. I saw Le G. after the Civic days perhaps twice a year. I honored and loved her and treasured her friendship as I guess she did mine but it queers the picture to have made me so important. You are pitiless in the way you treat Le G. in her very old age. There is never a hint of compassion. It apparently does not occur to you that she was not always selfish and when it came to Anne Kaufman she was very old and losing her memory fast. She was not at all selfish in relation to the boy who went on after working with her in the garden to become a horticulturist.

You criticize Le G for not being more social.

Next Day

It is a hard time for me right now as I was ill with flu all through December and things have piled up. So this letter will not be as good as it ought to be for Miss Le Gallienne's sake.

Everywhere you show lack of taste in using nicknames for people who should have been treated with respect. Perhaps Eva would have worked when she was a child, but not after Liliom. Gun is simply rude and unworthy. Josie I have spoken of. Also these pet names make it sound as though you knew them all personally and called them so. You say that Le G. is arrogant. But you are unbelievably arrogant. It has not occurred to you that to handle not being used in the theatre in those last 20 years required an exceptionally brave and intelligent person to manage..she wrote books, made a magnificent garden, lectured, kept busy in life giving ways.

I cannot understand why you <u>blame</u> her for not being "social." She was a loner. So am I. I have contributed a great deal more to life with my 50 books than I would have by making up to the literary establishment.

There are too many errors of <u>fact</u>, unforgivable. There were no Tony awards being given the night Le G. died.. you just made that up for a corny end to your book. ~~When Jo Hutchinson talked to me in her dressing room about not ever having two love affairs at the same time, Le G did not even know Evenson who was never at the Civic. Hutchinson was referring to an apprentice called Kim with whom Le G. flirted You have muddied the waters where private life is concerned.~~ Sorry. I said this yesterday—

I never heard Le G. say anything that would suggest she was <u>ashamed</u> of being a lesbian. You say that lesbians think of themselves as men forced into a woman's body. Sappho? Ridiculous. Nonsense. You follow all the myths and avoid the truth. Le Gallienne was not sexy, but she was passionate..there is a difference. And it came through beautifully in Juliet.

Also you never really give her credit for her astonishing genius in all aspects of theatre..like her set for Romeo and Juliet; her wonderful expertise with lighting the shows. You always sound a little superior, a little patronizing. I deeply resent this.

Error of fact: I never had anything to do with the production of "Alice" as devised by Sharaff and Le G. If Irene sees what you said she will be livid. I was in Paris that winter and saw a great deal of Sharaff and also of Le G. and Jo. Incidentally Le G. did actually ride in the circus with the Fratellinis at least once for the fun of it. You do not seem aware of what courage it took for instance to learn to play the accordion to help get back her hands.

You actually say that she failed as a lover and as a theatre person! Would you say this of Richard Burton for instance? If she had been a man so much would have been acceptable. A relationship can be good for a number of years as Le G.'s was with Jo and then break apart. Is it 50% of marriages in the USA that end in divorce for one reason or another?

The Civic Repertory in its three years proved what Le Gallienne believed, that low prices and great plays would find an audience. We had one box office hit in every season and that hit supported the more experimental plays. Did the Theatre Guild? No.

Well, I am too old and tired to pursue this further. But I cannot consider you a friend, I can only thank God that my preface is in your book and the people who trust me—they are thousands—will perhaps not trust some of your mean-spirited, immature, tastelessly expressed judgements.

You seem never to have judged the people you talked to about Le G. in the cynical way you judged her. Some were clearly very neurotic.

Of course I cannot come to the Civic Reunion after reading your book. What illusions you have! I suspect that people like Buzz [Burgess]

Meredith who say they will come may change their minds after they read this libellous book. I hope they will.

Very sincerely yours

May Sarton

P.S. Of course I have copyright on all my own letters. And you should have gotten my permission—I shall not sue but I could—

Robert Schanke: b. 1940. Schanke is currently a professor of theatre at Central College, Pella, Iowa, and editor of the journal *Theatre History Studies.*

Sarton is responding to his biography *Shattered Applause: The Lives of Eva Le Gallienne* (hardback, Southern Illinois Univ. Press; paperback, Barricade Books; both 1992); the actress, born 1899, had died in 1991.

Sarton had written a brief foreword without having seen Schanke's text, a not uncommon publishing practice. He would have been recommended by his 1988 study *Ibsen in America* (The Scarecrow Press); the Norwegian playwright (1828–1906) had been crucial in developing young Sarton's passion for the theatre—see *At Fifteen.*

"At the highest level in all the arts genius communicates a vision of life. . . . Eva Le Gallienne was one of the very few actors I have seen who did" so, Sarton writes in her foreword, focusing on her years working with Le Gallienne and the actress's portrayal of Hilde Wangel in Ibsen's *The Master Builder* (1892). "I can imagine no actor who could approach a role with more acute sense of the writer's intention, nor with greater respect for the text, for the weight of each phrase, for 'tone,' for what is also between the lines."

Prof. Schanke willingly shared this letter for inclusion, despite its critical comments on his book.

Evensen: Actress Marion "Gun" Evensen; see note to 4 January 1964.

L'Aiglon, "The Eaglet," was French playwright Edmond de Rostand's 1900 verse drama about Napoleon's son.

official biography: Helen Sheehy, *Eva Le Gallienne: A Biography* (Knopf, 1996). In *The New York Times Book Review,* Margo Jefferson compared the two biographies, echoing some of Sarton's strictures. The interested reader should consult both, to gain the fullest view.

over-used May Sarton: As very few of Sarton's letters to LeGallienne are extant (see note to 4 January 1964), there is some uncertainty here. Perhaps the objection pertains to how Schanke made use of Le Gallienne's letters to Sarton; but that would not explain the postscript.

Le G. in her very old age: Sarton had never lost touch with Le Gallienne, who in later years suffered mental decline. Writing on 30 August 1986 to Margaret English, another lifelong friend from the Apprentice Theatre, Sarton rejoiced that "Le Gallienne did get that National arts medal—(Eudora Welty did too and I was pleased that she was in such good company)." But by that time Le Gallienne had to have an attendant and a housekeeper, though she was apparently "tranquil and happy and not aware how she has failed . . . She still feeds 8 or 9 raccoons every night after dark, hundreds of birds, and of course has a Yorkie as companion." She lived another five years.

not being used . . . those last 20 years: For Le Gallienne's performance, age 84, in the 1982–83 revival of *Alice,* see note to 8 June 1982 and *At Seventy,* pp. 227–28.

being a lesbian: In 1998, for the University of Michigan Press, Schanke would co-edit, with Kim Marra, *Passing Performances: Queer Readings of Leading Players in American Theatre History* up to 1969, when the Stonewall riots in New York City sparked the American gay rights movement.

never had anything to do with . . . "Alice": On the opening day of the Westbrook conference, 11 June 1992, recalling other comparable "peak experiences," Sarton remembered "hanging from a rope waiting for my entrance as the White Queen in Le Gallienne's production of *Alice in Wonderland,* music by Richard Addinsell. . . . There I was in Le Gallienne's costume, an exact replica of the Tenniel drawing. I had to glue on her semicircular wide chin as she did herself. . . . The New Amsterdam Theatre where we were playing both it and Chekhov's *Cherry Orchard,* in which I also played Le Gallienne's part of Varya for a week, was much larger than the Civic Repertory so the laughter was far louder than I had ever experienced. Thrilling!" (*Encore,* published September 1993, pp. 317–18). No date is given; perhaps, in this letter, Sarton is claiming she had no hand in "devising" the production?

TO PAM CONRAD   Feb. 25th [1993]
[York]
Dear Pam,

What fun that we are in the same anthology. I haven't seen it, but they may send me one. That is what usually happens with anthologies..Before I forget I thought "Waltzing in the Canal" was stunning! Unexpected, so real.

I do envy you your computers and loving them. My word processor is next door but I have about given up on it, I think partly because I never learned to type so have to look at the keys. My secretary uses it and files things in it which saves space. Thanks also for that poignant Akhmatova quote. It made me think of an occasion during World War II when I was reading poems of mine and said I felt apologetic not to be doing something more helpful toward getting rid of Hitler. A woman came up to me after the reading (she was Norwegian) and said, furious, "Never run your poetry down. I was in solitary confinement for 6 months and would have died without the poets I knew by heart..writing poems is the best thing you can do in the war."

I guess I wouldn't say that now because I get so many letters about what my work, some part of it, has done to keep someone alive. But I'm nearly 81 and so there is a lot back of me.

I got myself into an awkward place with that last sentence!

I am only now getting to answering the Xmas mail so have never thanked you for the adorable photo of you and your daughter on the Sarah Moon [a tall-sails ship].

I can see that 46 may be a kind of watershed, a time for radical change..except I don't think you should be afraid of repeating yourself..that one line is nothing! And as you say you are working with new forms..but I go along with a dream to be someone else myself. I once had a vivid dream of meeting Virginia Woolf in an obscure English town. She recognized me but somehow conveyed that she was there in hiding and I must not speak, that she had not committed suicide but gone underground to have peace. I bet the Lindberghs dreamed of doing that. I am reading a rather fascinating novel by their daughter Reeve Lindbergh called The Names of Mountains, really about what it was like to live with them as parents and now having to deal with Anne's (Alicia in the novel) Alzheimer's. She does have it, I know and I know how painful it is because I went through it with Judy with whom I lived for years..at the end she did not recognize me even.

I am very happy with the Clintons..at last I look forward to the News..and let us hope food for Bosnia can get there though it sounds a doubtful way to use such high flying planes which never hit the target— or didn't in France in World War II—

Much love,
May

Pam Conrad: 1948–96; prolific fiction writer who explored serious, often disturbing themes in such books for young readers as *What I Did for Roman* (1987), *My Daniel* (1989), *Pedro's Journal: A Voyage with Christopher Columbus* (1991), *Zoe Rising* (1996), and many others.

Akhmatova: Considered the greatest Russian woman poet, Anna Akhmatova (1889–1966) never stopped writing despite Soviet oppression.

Reeve Lindbergh: In October 2001 she published *No More Words: A Journal of My Mother, Anne Morrow Lindbergh,* chronicling the months before her death that February.

the Clintons: "Clinton has frightful problems handed to him," Sarton wrote Juliette Huxley, 23 January 1993, "but he is bound to be more effective than tired cynical old Bush so I feel hope, and that is a great relief. I could hardly bear to look at the news in the last weeks before the election." Clinton's public persona seemed "An odd combination of small town America and sophisticated Oxford," Sarton noted to Robbie Robertson, 2 February 1993, "and this is, I think, what made some people not understand him. More complex than he looks."

[At Eighty-Two begins 25 July 1993.]

TO LADY JULIETTE HUXLEY   September 1, '93
[York]
Dearest Juliette,

Yesterday we talked on the phone..at last I had the spirit to call. And you sounded absolutely your adorable self so after I put the receiver down I felt miserable to be cut off, and not able to come right over and see you and sit in the garden one more time…but time is an enemy now and I am disgustingly frail and tottery. Only, when I told Maggie, who has to be with me at the hotel and bear with a stroke if I fall on my face, so it is an awful responsibility for her, she said "We can go the day after tomorrow!" So maybe somehow I'll get over in the spring.

It sounded as though you are pleased with your housekeeper and that is very good news. I meant to ask about the cat whom you call "Not-my-cat" but who sits in the hall with his paws tucked in quite at home. Mon ami Pierrot, my cat, is the darling of my days because he is beautiful, a kind of sensationally luxurious being, as though he was an ermine coat when asleep..but he is blue gray and creamy white, not an ermine just a magnificent Himalayan cat. He is 7 now so perhaps he will accompany me to the end. It is astonishing that my parents both died at 72, so neither of them knew what old age is like. I spend hours looking for things, especially letters that get lost in the vast piles around me because I can never catch up with the accumulated mail of three or four months when I did not even open envelopes. I find extraordinary things, such as a letter written last year from a man who wants to write a biography of my father. He is coming this week-end to take a look at the files here for two days, a Canadian scholar [Lewis Pyenson]. But it is bad enough that Margot Peters is writing my autobiography [sic] and interviewing dozens of people who knew me when I was young..awful having to dig up the past when I only want to live in the present—or so I pretend.

We had a great full moon last night and a fine breeze from the sea, but now the sea is troubled and molten with a sinister look—there is a hurricane brewing farther South. My garden is a disaster area because the deer ate all the phlox, all the lilies in bud, all the roses and several bushes..they are so beautiful leaping off with their white tails up, one cannot complain. But also the gardener I have is rather clumsy and everything looks neglected.

When I can pack it I'll send you the American edition of Encore because the jacket is the best I have had. I know I asked Womens' Press to send their edition to you ages ago but maybe it never came. It was warmly reviewed in the TLS. I enclose an interview I had when I was in London last March. It came out in your paper, The Independent, and I liked it. I am sitting in Durrants Hotel with flowers beside me. I will also enclose a poem I sent out for my 81st birthday.

[closing not extant]

––––––––

Lady Juliette Huxley: At this time she was 96; Sarton, seeing her in London that April, found her fragile, and her ability to concentrate erratic.

sit in the garden: During 1994 and 1995 Sarton struggled with a novella she was unable to complete. *Lunch in the Garden,* also known as *Laure,* was inspired by a March 1992 visit to Huxley; see *Encore,* pp. 228–29. The thirty-one-page manuscript is divided into six chapters that alternate the viewpoints of Laure (Huxley), Vernon (Sarton), and Brent (Alan Best), Laure's former lover, now 87. This extract from Chapter 1 is narrated by Laure:

> I wake and it is like being born again. Who am I? For a few seconds I haven't the foggiest idea. Then Laure de Raynal Arnold comes to me, such a mixture of a name, French, rather grand, then English and Bloomsbury. It has amused me to try to fit the two together—and perhaps I never did quite succeed—Aujourd'hui je suis plutôt française. ["Today I am rather French."]
>
> One thing is certain, I am eighty-six, eighty-seven in three months, believe it or not. I don't, which is why I have to say it often.
>
> The cat who is Not-My-Cat is asleep on the end of my bed. Time he went home. "Not-My-Cat, go home!" I say to him but he pays no heed, curled up, a tight Tigger ball, one paw over his nose.
>
> Something is happening today. Someone is coming, but I can't remember who it is. It will come to me after breakfast. I shall lie here meanwhile being myself till Prudence comes.
>
> I see it is only six. Plenty of time to listen to the blackbird in peace.
>
> That is what Lady Arnold was thinking on that April morning in Highgate. She had accepted that memory is mercurial and there is not much to be done about that beyond accepting that "after all, eighty-five years of tumultuous living are gathered up in my mind."

Later on, this reflection occurs to Brent:

> Memory I suddenly think is an act of faith and requires if we are not actually on our knees, we be deeply open to meditation. The peak experience has to have time to come back to the surface. As I stand here waiting for my battered bag to turn up on the machine as it goes round and round, I am possessed by the sound of water dripping from a paddle somewhere . . .

Sarton had largely worked out the technical challenges of the narrative; lack of energy was the chief obstacle. But that she conceived of it, and managed to write this much during these sickest of months, says much for the passion she wished to memorialize, and eventually distilled into the poem for *Coming into Eighty,* "Lunch in the Garden": "Miracles do happen / When you are old."

warmly reviewed: In the 9 June 1993 *Times Literary Supplement,* Janette Turner Hospital pointed out that Sarton always has been "a transgressor of boundaries" and that in the journals "She can be a poet, novelist, political commentator and moral philosopher," in the art form where "her reputation will endure."

The interview has not yet been traced; it apparently had a photo of Sarton, taken at Durrants. *The Independent* was Huxley's paper in that Britain offers a variety of dailies, serious or light, to match one's political affiliations or lack thereof.

for my 81st birthday: "Bliss," another Ewert broadside, included in *Coming into Eighty.*

TO PENELOPE MORTIMER   Sept. 23rd, 1993
[York]
Dear Penelope Mortimer,

Lots of people write to me but very few writers do out of the blue, so your letter was a great event in the mail a few days ago. Before I answer let me explain that in April I had a mild stroke [her second] in London and since then have been rather ill and in hospital. I am much better at last but typing is difficult so forgive the typos I am sure to make.

First, Doris Grumbach has moved to Maine and her address is [ ]. She published last year a fascinating journal of her 70th year and another one is coming out in November, both from W. W. Norton. She was here sometime this summer and looks wonderfuly well, swims in the ocean and loves Maine. I'm amazed, as she always seemed like a city person partly because of her love of opera. No opera in Maine!

Rachel Mackenzie? I knew her long before she went to the New Yorker. For years she was very ill in Boston with some bug she had acquired in China. She was living on a shoestring. Then one day I had a letter from Mrs. White, my editor at the New Yorker, asking me whether I knew anyone I could recommend to succeed her as she was retiring. It felt like an act of God as I knew Rachel would make a superb editor. I wrote the strongest possible letter, she got the job, and it seemed miraculous. What an extraordinary, brave, humourous intelligence she was.

I am so pleased that you found Encore and have enjoyed it so much..do get hold of one or two of the others. Yes, I have started a new journal, mad though it seems. But two months ago my Dr. said, "May, you are 81, you will never be well, and I suggest that you pull in your horns." It sounded like a death sentence to me so I started a new journal the next day [*At Eighty-Two*] and feel a good deal better as a result.

I am thrilled that you wrote the script for Portrait of a Marriage. I do agree that Nicolson was badly miscast and that queered the balance of forces a good deal. But you must be pleased about it, surely a fascinating film which will become a classic. What did you think of Orlando? Marvelous visually but somehow not V. Woolf.

I must go down and cheer myself up on a dismal dark day with a drink and some food.

Very warm wishes and thanks
May Sarton

Penelope Mortimer: English writer (1918–99) of novels (*The Pumpkin Eater,* 1962; *The Home,* 1971; *The Handyman,* 1983), biography (*Queen Elizabeth: A Life of the Queen Mother,* 1986), and memoirs (*About Time Too, 1940–78,* 1993).

Rachel MacKenzie: See 27 July 1966 and, for a fuller reminiscence, *Endgame,* pp. 229–30. She had died in 1980. The timing of this recommendation suggests that White's request came soon after Sarton's letter to her, 7 September 1961.

Portrait of a Marriage: A film version of Nigel Nicolson's 1973 memoir about his parents, Vita Sackville-West and Harold Nicolson, British diplomat and author (1886–1968). Writing to Martha Wheelock, herself a director, on 20 October 1991, Sarton rated the film technically superb: "it made me so homesick for England." She praised the actors save that "Nicolson was badly treated by the writer, that witty, sophisticated man...and played [by David Haig] as a wimp as well, far from the truth." But the story itself was "disagreeable": "Vita was a very selfish woman who broke many hearts....[Her lover, Violet] Trefusis was simply a spoiled child monster, malicious, mean..besides which would you ever fall in love with someone who flattered you as she did Vita? I can't imagine falling in love with a toady." Virginia Woolf was the only woman Sackville-West treated with true tenderness, perhaps because with her Sackville-West's "conquering passionate side had to be controlled to some extent."

Sally Potter directed the 1992 film version of Woolf's historical fantasy *Orlando,* starring Tilda Swinton as the hero/heroine; Queen Elizabeth I was portrayed by Quentin Crisp.

TO ERIKA PFANDER   October 26th '93
[York]
Dear Erika,

There is something radically wrong with my life these too pressured days if I cannot after all this time write to you about your superb production of The Music Box Bird.

But I am not living my real life these days, nothing creative possible because there is too much on my desk and calendar—it is having 3 books out as well as the play. So I feel extremely depressed but I am determined to tell you something of what I felt as I watched the opening night with that superbly attentive audience. You are a great director..the pacing was perfect. It could have been too slow or too quick and was just right with time enough for a concept to sink in and yet the tempo felt quick except for a few meaningful silences. Superb, the moments when the music box bird first sings. I had a shiver down my spine. You had understood each of the characters so well that it all seemed as I had dreamed of it when I wrote it so long ago.

I admire the way you moved the characters about..so that one after another came to sit on the small sofa at the back and dominate the stage while she or he was there..All the movement was so natural and believable..and the not-easy use of the imaginary 4th wall worked very well I thought.

The typing is because of fatigue and the stroke. I am a cripple these days.

But now I am going out to have that wonderful drawing of the stage and signatures of all the players framed and pick up some typed copies of the play to send to various friends who might know a little theatre to show it to and get another production. My agent has sent it to Samuel French in N.Y. and we hope they will do it, they publish only plays as you know I am sure.

I hope the last performances are well attended..and maybe you can get a brief rest before Stevie..

It was about the best present I ever had to see The Music Box Bird staged so wonderfully well..bless you and thank you for all the hard work and the great imagination you showed in making my truth comprehensible.

Love and gratitude

Your

May

Please tell the cast how happy I was with their splendid imaginative performances—

Erika Pfander: Director of The Chamber Theatre of Maine, in Thomaston; on 8 October 1993 they presented the world premiere of Sarton's 1962 play.

The premise: After their mother's death, with their father incapacitated in a nursing home, three daughters and a son meet to settle the property, each with a different take on the truth about their family. Into this fray strides Ivy Richardson, a dynamic 78-year-old who had had relations with both parents. (This was the role Sarton wrote hoping Eva Le Gallienne would play.) Her presence galvanizes the siblings into fresh recognitions about power, money, and art, embodied in the contested ownership of the music box bird.

Pfander herself played one of the daughters; she repaired Sarton's own music box for use in the production. For the gratified author's account of this evening, see *At Eighty-Two,* pp. 75–77; *The Music Box Bird* has not yet been published.

On 28 October 1995, The Chamber Theatre presented the world premiere of Sarton's other play, *The Underground River* (1947); see note to 12 March 1968.

Stevie: British playwright Hugh Whitemore's play about mordant British poet Stevie Smith (1902–71); made into a movie starring Glenda Jackson.

In her 1981 blurb for *Me Again: Uncollected Writings of Stevie Smith* (ed. Jack Barbera and William McBrien), Sarton wrote: "*Me Again* is more than a compendium of essays, stories and reviews. I found it so witty, original and moving that I began to look at everything in a new light, and at Stevie Smith herself with enormous love and respect. Who else could pin G.B. Shaw down as she does? Or attack religious dogma with such piety? Or praise her dog and her tortoise with such delightful laughter?"

TO JOSEPH PARISI   [1 November 1993]

[York]

Dear Joe Parisi,

What a wonderful surprise! I have been depressed because the huge Collected Poems seems to have gone down the well, and the last thing I expected was a prize, such a prestigious one, for Poems written in my 79th year—

They will come out in a book of all new poems next year—

Will Poetry review the Collected Poems? I do hope so.

With delighted best wishes

May Sarton

P.S. Writing a note to Mrs. Scott today.

Joseph Parisi: The editor of *Poetry* magazine had written Sarton, 27 October 1993 that her poems in the December 1992 issue had won the Levinson Prize of one thousand dollars, the magazine's oldest award. All are included in *Coming into Eighty* (1994), which Norton editor Carol Houck Smith was seeing through the press, as she had done with the new *Collected Poems.* Sarton wrote and thanked the donor's widow, Elizabeth W. L. Scott, of Cape Elizabeth, Maine, "for your generosity and faith": "It is a great joy to be 81 and still writing poems."

I do hope so: Poetry does not seem to have reviewed *Collected Poems 1930–1993,* published in June; but Eda LeShan wrote a notice for *Newsday,* 18 September 1993, encapsulated in its title, "Turning Despair into Delight." Andrea Lockett, writing in the Spring 1994 *Belles Lettres* (9, no. 3), stressed that Sarton's poems display "the complex and compelling music and imagery that is characteristic of most poems that have stood the test of time," granting "a transparence and transcendence to her work that invite us into the poet's mind, where we are surprised to find not just a window into her soul but a mirror reflecting ours."

TO ERIC P. SWENSON   Nov. 20 [1993]
[York]
Dear Eric,

Your letter to Susan and me [found me?] yesterday—it does help me understand a lot about what the problems are in trying to promote a good writer who will just never "make it." I suppose that it is high time that I accepted that fact. And I will—But it leads me to hope that whoever arranges when people die will soon see that I am released—

I am so frail now I can hardly walk across the room.

I marvel at what Norton has done for me, especially publishing the poems, through all the years and am very grateful and feel very lucky, Eric, that we met at Breadloaf so long ago.

Thanks for taking the time to write us that good long letter—A great help.

Dear love always—

Your ancient turtle
May

I'm sick now but <u>hope</u> to try the little book about Pierrot when antibiotics do their work—

---

trying to promote a good writer: Swenson had worked with Sarton at Norton since *The Small Room,* 1961; "Eric is the only person I have ever known who appears to have no <u>angst</u>," she wrote in October 1979 (*Recovering,* p. 227). Born 1919, at this time he was semi-retired, though still a passionate sailor. They had been discussing the Catch-22 of publishers' not spending advertising dollars on a book that may not "move" in the market—and which will not "move" unless ads alert readers that it exists. See *At Eighty-Two,* p. 140, for further details, and pp. 302 and 334 for Sarton's astonishing sales figures with Norton over the years.

grateful and . . . lucky: Swenson expressed similar sentiments in the Festschrift. "I have been May Sarton's editor and publisher for thirty odd years. There is nothing in my career that has given me more pride than to have been involved in the publications of the work of this wonderfully productive human. . . . .

"Her love for people, nature, love itself, and for the political-social and emotional symbiosis between them have changed the lives of many thousands of her readers.

"What I speak for, however, is her courage. . . . [S]he has shown that, though 'form' is vital, convention is merely excuse.

"As she charges into her ninth decade, fighting illnesses that would fell a lesser spirit, she is as fiercely creative as ever. I salute May Sarton; she has made of her world a brighter, larger, more fertile space than it was before she entered it."

little book about Pierrot: At times, Sarton found the novella *Lunch in the Garden* too demanding, artistically and emotionally. On the day she wrote Joseph Parisi about the *Poetry* prize, Carol Houck Smith suggested she try a short book on Pierrot—though it would be very hard, Sarton told this editor, to do another cat book after *The Fur Person.*

Yet the twenty surviving pages are very different, a poignant portrait of their shared life. It opens: "We have been together now for seven years, Pierrot, a Himalayan cat, and I, an old writer. At times of the day our lives intersect but mostly each goes his own way, although always aware of where the significant other is. That is the magic of it, this happy and free dependency. . . .

"Grace is the word for him. He satisfies my hunger for the beautiful as going to a museum and looking at a painting used to. There are beautiful things to look at in this house where I am the prisoner of illness and old age, but they are not alive. . . . Like me, still somewhat childlike in my old age, Pierrot is still a kitten."

Some of it is narrative, recounting his misadventures; some like a painting, if a painting can be witty. "More often than not in the early morning he does not stay on the terrace but wanders out into the grassy path that goes through the field to the ocean. There he sits, his head bent, and concentrates sometimes for an hour on whatever may move or have life in the grass. A mouse catcher he aims to be."

It ends with a visit to the vet, and an effort to give him a bath—succeeded by a mutual understanding wherein he has "told me that he had been in Hell for a whole day, that I could have no idea how awful it had been."

As she had hoped, Pierrot did accompany her to the end. He died 27 December 2000, at fourteen years, eight months.

TO BILL BROWN   Feb. 16, 94
[York]
Dearest Bill,

In a minute I must stagger out into the freezing air and drive some distance over the dangerous icy road to get some fish for Pierrot who is very cross because he too hates the cold and is on a hunger strike. But before I do that I want at long last to answer your dear letter of Feb. 3rd. I have been in the deep freeze like a hibernating animal just managing to pay bills and write a few business letters.

I hope the beastly flu has withdrawn its fangs now but I'm afraid it is a very persistent and exhausting germ this year, maybe spring is in the air and in your garden and you will take a deep breath and feel a little better. Good news that Paul is healing...

I do understand that his painting is in such a different mode from yours, such a different world that you and he cannot exactly share painting ideas. But maybe that distance is just as well, less tension than if you were competitive in style. But I knew at once when I read the obit what a loss Diebenkorn's death is for you. Far more than what I felt when VW [Virginia Woolf] died because I knew her not well, as an acquaintance more than a friend. But I did hope to write something some day that she would like..there is certainly no writer whose work I wait for as I did hers, and there is no writer whose admiration would mean as much as hers would have..publishing these days is totally corrupt.

A book of the essays (some of the best) read at Westbrook College at a conference for my 80th birthday have been published. I'll send it if you would like me to..but even good criticism seems so boring to me these days it may not be worth your effort to read it. The best is an essay comparing me to Vermeer, the sacramentalization of the ordinary...as he does with light.

Margot would like to use a few of your letters to me or quote them in her biography and asked me whether you would be willing. I said I was fairly sure you would (yours are wonderful letters) but she had better ask you. She periodically enrages me and I sometimes wonder whether she understands anything about me. But that is partly because I feel sure she wants to stay very objective and aloof in order to do a good job. It's just as well that I shall be dead when it comes out. It is really time I got out but it is in God's hands so I just go on from day to day, unable to do real work and feeling at a loss in every way. But Pierrot is here and so all is mostly well. I have an envelope and a stamp so I thought why not send Bill the book with this letter? So here it is. I do not like the essay called "A Poetry of Absence" because it calls me sentimental—it did give me an insight thinking about it, that there is a similarity between sentimentality and violence and that is both are strong feeling without <u>thinking.</u> I have always thought a lot about feeling as you know..

Much love, dearest Bill, always your old Possum

M

Diebenkorn's: Richard Diebenkorn (1922-93) was noted for his vivid, almost totally abstract landscapes, especially the "Ocean Park" series with its whites, blues, and greens. Sarton is reiterating a point she made when writing Brown at the time of Diebenkorn's death, a year before; as well as a colleague, he was a close friend of the Diebenkorns.

essays . . . read at Westbrook: The 1994 Puckerbrush *Celebration,* ed. Hunting.

In "Sarton and Vermeer: A Diptych of Paper and Canvas," Darlene Davis finds both artists, with meticulous craft, taking as subject the solitary female in an enclosed space, seen the instant between thought and action, under a sensuous source of light. "If their lives had been reversed . . . [one could] imagine a woman, serene, self-possessed, standing by an open window, caressed by the light, reading a work written by May Sarton."

she had better ask you: "I did write her a detailed account of our meeting & why I began writing to you in the Army," Brown wrote Sarton, 20 September 1992. But he decided against an interview, having said he "couldn't possibly give opinions about an old friend who was so multi-faceted that it would be presumptuous of me to say anything. (I wrote something similar to a biographer of Stravinsky several years ago.) I like what Chopin wrote in a letter about an acquaintance—'She keeps rooting around in my rose-garden for truffles.' There's obviously a bit of this in all biographers."

Peters is currently at work on another biography, of Alfred Lunt and Lynn Fontanne.

calls me sentimental: In "A Poetry of Absence: May Sarton's Use of the Sentimental," Susan Alves revalues that term by redefining it to include an author-reader relationship mediated through the work of art; domestic imagery and concerns; and an idealistic, humanistic philosophy.

TO PAT CARROLL   March 18 '94
[York]
Dear Pat,

How relieved I am to know that you escaped the worst of the earthquake, but it must indeed have been terrifying. Three of my good friends were badly injured, I don't mean personally but houses wrecked etc. Meanwhile we are having the worst winter in memory, more than 90 inches of snow, hazardous icy roads and it is supposed to snow again tonight—unbelievable.

The great good news in your letter is that Teresa is really in the works . . . I am thrilled. It could be the greatest thing you've ever done and that is saying something. I can't wait..a reason to go on living. For I am in a serious depression and rather scared. The reason is that I am now deprived of my vocation as I cannot create—too frail, my head perhaps somehow damaged by the stroke I had in London in April. Here I am alone in this big house, imprisoned most of the winter, no family, no work..even getting dressed is difficult because I can't button my shirt. Still I am keeping a dictated journal to have something to do and to think about.

It is pretty measly that Harding get off when she obviously did engineer the attack on Kerrigan..she will now make millions skating in reviews and have full houses because of people's curiosity. Disgusting.

How dear of you to order the Puckerbrush book—it is excellent, the third book this year from a university press on my work, so things are beginning to happen. Next week my biographer comes again to ask questions and record my answers. The University of Chicago is sending a crew out to make a video sometime soon on creativity in old age. I did write poems again when I was 79 and 80 but now I have ideas but no energy with which to work them out on paper. At night in bed I am a genius but in the morning at my desk that proves to be an illusion!

Enough of all this wailing . . . who knows what may happen? I hope you do move to the Cape so I can see you now and then. What happy memories I keep of last time!

Dearest friend, bless you for being there
Have fun at the Helen Hayes awards!

Love from
May

P.S. No snow after all and Susan <u>will</u> get here at last—for the first time in <u>two months</u> because of the bad weather—

Pat Carroll: b. 1927, Emmy Award-winning actress. Since her 1947 debut in stock, Carroll has played more than two hundred roles, from Gertrude Stein to *H.M.S. Pinafore*'s Buttercup, Brecht's Mother Courage to Shakespeare's Falstaff. (See *At Seventy*, p. 219.) At this time she was preparing a play about St. Teresa of Avila (see note to 4 March 1970). In the Festschrift, Carroll saluted Sarton "with a prayer for your health, happiness, and most important, your hilarity."

Harding get off: Olympic figure-skating contender Tonya Harding hired a friend to injure rival Nancy Kerrigan; the plot was unmasked, Kerrigan recovered to compete successfully, and Harding was banned from competition skating.

the third book this year: With a title taken from "My Sisters, O My Sisters," *That Great Sanity*, ed. Swartzlander and Mumford, surveyed "Predecessors and contemporaries," "Art and artists," "Self and subtexts," and "Readers and response." The University of Chicago video project has not yet been identified.

happy memories: On 3 August 1993 Sarton lunched with Carroll, and the following day saw her perform in *Nunsense II* at the Ogunquit Playhouse; see *At Eighty-Two*, pp. 24–25.

TO TIMOTHY ANGLIN BURGARD   July 3rd [1994]
[York]

Dear Timothy Burgard,

I'm delighted to hear Polly Thayer's fine portrait of me has been accepted and will be hung. Thank you for your kind letter. I'm glad the Cross drawings have been useful—

Since a stroke at Easter [her third] I can't type, so will be brief—the hand is so illegible—

Sincerely yours
May Sarton

Timothy Anglin Burgard: Henry Luce Foundation Associate Curator of American Art at the Fogg Museum, Cambridge, Massachusetts.

Thayer's fine portrait: On 9 December 1993, Sarton had signed a statement about the picture that included this background: "In 1937 or 1938, Dr. Paul Sachs, curator of paintings at the Fogg Art Museum, bought a portrait of May Sarton from the painter Polly Thayer (Mrs. Donald Starr) and then kindly lent it to the Sartons with the proviso that it go to the Fogg Museum's permanent collection in due course."

The 1936 picture had been hanging in the front hall at Wild Knoll. See the dust jacket for *Encore,* the photo insert in *Dear Juliette,* and *Among the Usual Days,* p. 190 (where it appears with a contemporary etching of Sarton by Thayer), as well as *At Eighty-Two,* pp. 276–77.

After its transfer, and its formal acceptance on 10 May 1994 by the Fogg's curatorial committee, Burgard wrote on 26 June to thank Sarton, saying: "This work will diversify an American paintings collection that currently features few works by women artists and even fewer works that depict women renowned for their contributions to American culture. It will also enable scholars and students to examine the artistic practice of a woman who trained in the 'Boston School' style and will illuminate one of your earliest and most persistent themes—the role of women artists and writers in society." (For more about this portrait, see note to 24 October 1959.)

the Cross drawings: Jean Dominique (Marie Closset) bequeathed Sarton a notebook of sketches and studies by French artist Henri-Edmond Cross (1856–1910), who exhibited with Pointillistes such as Seurat and Signac. Sarton had donated it to the Fogg to make it available for researchers. She also gave the museum three very small oils on wood by Cross, stylistically akin to Pissarro and Monet: *Seascape, Women Harvesting Vegetables,* and *Three Swans.*

[*At Eighty-Two* ends 1 August 1994.]

TO BILL BROWN   Oct. 17 '94
[York]
Dearest Bill,

I haven't written for ages—too much has been happening—the heaviest to bear that Juliette died ten days ago after suffering a stroke that paralysed her left side—she was 98 or would be Dec. 6. It is a real blessing that she just stopped breathing after being in a coma for a week. The day she had the stroke I called to tell her Maggie Vaughan and I had our flight tickets for Nov. 3—Old as she was it has been a terrible shock. In the last ~~20~~ 15 years she has been extremely dear and loving—like a dream compared to Paris [1948]! The "Coming out" to what she really felt and it happened after Julian died (and so she had no guilt at last). My letters to her—the record of a long love (50 years since '36 when I met the Huxleys!). Norton wants to publish—but after she died I nearly decided <u>not to</u>—silence being the gift I could give her— then Carol Heilbrun who had read the letters said they must be published, that such a record did not exist, that she would have forgot her admonition when she read them—she also said no one could be offended—My agent was also very determined that I publish. But you can imagine all the self examination and panic this has caused—I must still talk it over with her son Francis—he is 70!

Meanwhile the journal I have dictated has to be revised and I am driven—exhausted.

But at last my illness has been diagnosed—the nerve ends in shoulder and down my arm <u>burned</u> by radiation after the mastectomy 9 years ago! It will never get better. Also I have been told what the last stroke did—(I'll never walk again, except out to the car, never type again—find it difficult to keep order, I'm told "Yes, you must settle for the life of an invalid")—Anyway here are new poems [*Coming into Eighty*]—Your last word said you were working well!

So much love
M

Juliette died: Born 6 December 1896, Juliette Huxley died 28 September 1994, at age 97.

they must be published: Dear Juliette: Letters of May Sarton to Juliette Huxley (1999) includes a foreword by Francis Huxley, drafts for an introduction Sarton did not complete, and some of Juliette Huxley's own letters.

my agent: Diarmuid Russell, who co-founded the literary agency Russell & Volkening in 1940, had been Sarton's agent all her professional life. He died in 1973; the year before, when Timothy Seldes became president of the firm, he started representing Sarton's interests, as he has done ever since.

nerve ends . . . <u>burned</u> by radiation: Sarton's mastectomy had been performed 18 June 1979; see note to 16 July [1979].

you were working well!: Brown continues to work daily in his studio, and exhibits in New York, Los Angeles, and San Francisco; a book about his work is due to be published in fall 2002.

TO LEWIS PYENSON   Dec. 19, '94
[York]
Dear Lewis—

What a treasure you sent me! I had never read Le Chain d'Or and had no copy of it. The one I do <u>not</u> have and if you ever see it advertised is Vie d'un Poète also printed privately—So he dreamed of being what I turned out to be!

I find Le Chain d'Or interesting because of the enormous self-projecting there is in Jean. GS often talked like this and never questioned <u>himself</u> about his own insincerities and often sentimental idealism. It is interesting also that he and Mabel actually were vegetarians—he often complained of the hardship of eating nuts! They were both Socialists and members of a group of intellectuals who tried at least to make friends of the working class. His descriptions of the girl are typical also of this sentimental idealism— Did he ever <u>see</u> Mabel? or imagine what it is like to work in a mine or as a farmer?

I doubt if you can decipher this—but I can't type because of the strokes— But au fond the book is touching as the sense of life of a very young man who found his destiny and served it with extraordinary persistence and courage. I am also struck, reading this in French, how amazing that he learned to write so beautifully in English—such a personal style!

Many thanks Lewis—I am greatly in your debt—

You must get the Guggenheim though I have been a jinx, recommending people every year who never get it!

Anyway happy fruitful New Year!

All the best to you and yours

Your devoted and admiring
May Sarton

Lewis Pyenson: Historian of science; at the time of this letter, teaching at the University of Montreal; biographer of George Sarton. More recently he was professor of history and mathematics at the University of Southwestern Louisiana, in Lafayette, where his late wife, Susan Sheets-Pyenson, was professor of history. He collaborated with her on her volume *The Norton History of Science in Society* (W. W. Norton, 1997); she in turn collaborated on his survey *Servants of Nature: A History of Scientific Institutions, Enterprises, and Sensibilities* (W. W. Norton, 1999). In 2001 he edited a collection of nine essays, *Elegance, Beauty, and Truth* (University of Louisiana at Lafayette Graduate School), including his own "Elegant Sartons: Platonic Scholarship, Platonic Letters," an examination of the relation between May and George Sarton, with many photographs.

Le Chain d'Or: An early, idealistic work by George Sarton propounding the idea that each human being is a link in "the golden chain," and that by doing our proper work, we each help one another.

In her comments, Sarton speaks alternately—and sometimes simultaneously—of her father George and her mother Mabel as real people, and of Jean (George) and Mabel as characters.

La Vie d'un Poète: A short, romantic autobiography, "the life of a poet," which George Sarton wrote in his twenties under the pseudonym Dominique DuBray.

TO LOUISE DUFAULT   March 6, 1995
[York]
Dear dear Lou,

It is hard to believe that Rene is no longer on earth—I miss her as you must, every day—and feel badly that I had not written or phoned after she told me how ill she was—I have been awfully ill myself—Everything is hard these days—

But the exquisite flowers on your card say "I am the Resurrection and the Life"—and so we must believe as she did and I know that you do.

I'll write better later—too frail today—

Immense love and gratitude for all you and Rene did for each other over the wonderful years—

Ever your old loving
May

Louise duFault: Companion of Rene Morgan, a dear friend Sarton often visited at her summer home, in Harwich, Massachusetts, on Cape Cod. See *Recovering,* pp. 184–85; *At Seventy,* 133–36; *Endgame,* pp. 64–73, for more about their long friendship. The quotation, often used in the funeral service, is from John 11:25, the words of Jesus.

TO BILL BROWN   May 4, '95
[York]
Dearest Bill,

I did not want my birthday—83 is too old, but it turned out a brilliant, heart-warming day. Crowned at about 5 by a host of red and white lilies, a tower of celebration—filling the house with their scent— It was <u>dear</u> to hear from you in such an elegant way! Susan helped with it, wonderful of course—and now I am recovering and looking out on a thousand daffodils and a rich blue sea breaking into white foam. And trying to believe I can get to the Juliette letters at last—

It was so great to <u>talk</u>, wasn't it?

Lots of love

M

[a heart]

---

so great to <u>talk</u>: Brown had phoned her well ahead of the birthday crush, the first time they had spoken since correspondence resumed in 1992. On 19 April he wrote: "[H]ow wonderful,—to hear your voice with its spirit very much intact," then thought "how different [all these] letters would be if read aloud (by you)." Foreseeing their eventual publication he asked, "But don't you find it curious both as writer & recipient of these letters for them to be transferred from a specific time & place & the <u>first</u> person, to the third person, and as if we were all suddenly butterflies in a display case, or possibly beetles!" Flowers that Brown sent to the hospital in July were the last Sarton saw.

TO ALAN EASTAUGH   May 26, 1995
[York]
Dear Alan,

What a lovely card for my birthday and a dear message! This is a very late answer to your birthday present which was a wonderful one. I am happy to tell you that I celebrated my birthday by playing the wonderfully vivacious Haydn quartet you sent and after that, alas, I fell ill and never did play the others, but I will. It's been discouraging, after our wonderful week, not to feel better, but now I'm back with one of my chorus of doctors and he really thinks he can solve the problem, so I'm on a rather strict regime, but not in pain, just terribly frail. I can hardly walk, but I have vivid happy memories of you and Maggie wheeling me in my wheelchair to Wigmore Hall and back to the hotel late at night but it didn't rain and was very glamorous as London is at night. Yes, it was a really splendid week that we had and one that will be long remembered. We make plans to come back even perhaps in the fall but everything is crowding up. My life is so frenetic which it should not be, but we keep a little bag of hope and who knows? We may yet emerge from the airport before the leaves fall.

Lots of love, dear Alan, and did you explain to the family why I was in London? I hope you did. A big hug from

May

Alan Eastaugh: Eastaugh's grandmother, Ann Cole Hayward, was the sister of Sarton's maternal grandmother, Eleanor Cole Elwes. Because of her frailty, time constraints and a few essential meetings with her publisher, the only member of her English family Sarton was able to see during this spring 1995 trip to London was Alan. He was fortunate in getting three front-row seats at Wigmore Hall to hear the young Petersen Quartet from Germany; they played a Haydn quartet, and one of the late quartets of Beethoven.

To close this selection we return to Europe, with a letter written to a distant cousin in the middle of June 1995. Solange Sarton, a lawyer, then 83, was the daughter of George Sarton's uncle Albert. Her parents were the last surviving members of their respective families, but through their offspring the European Sartons now flourish; in November 2000 she reported having "18 nephews and nieces plus their spouses," with their "44 children" and young descendants ranging from 18 years down "to 5 months and others yet to come!"

"My dear twin" refers to the striking resemblance between the two women at one point in their lives. After visiting her during 1982 in Lorient, France, May sent Solange a snapshot she at first thought May "had taken of me during her stay, but the photo was of May!" They habitually exchanged their political views, and even in extremis May's thoughts were on the world picture, as viewed from the private heart.

TO SOLANGE SARTON   16 June 1995
[York]   [In French]
My dear twin, dear Solange, it's ridiculous that I haven't managed to answer such dear letters as yours, dated March! But I am a genuine invalid these days—no energy at all, fallen into old age like a stone thrown into the water—I cannot type anymore, or walk except with difficulty—but I can still drive, and give thanks to God that I can do so—otherwise I would be terribly isolated here, alone in this huge house—Without Pierrot I would be dead.

The doctors cannot find anything but "getting old" to explain all this—but perhaps three strokes in recent years can explain it, I would think—I can still read—

The news from everywhere around the world is depressing—Where to look for a bit of comfort—our government seems to me completely mad, shredding all that's been done to preserve the social fabric since Roosevelt—It's an era of self-centeredness and disdain for the poor—the rich are getting richer than ever—I am disgusted—

But I think of you with great affection very glad to have this photo [of you] in the big handsome coat.

Tender kisses and tender thoughts from your twin—as always—

May

———

May Sarton died 16 July 1995, attended by her friend and editor of this volume, Susan Sherman.

APPENDIX

Text of Letters and Passages of Letters in French

Enfin nous avons eu le temps de nous connaître vraiment—le temps de parler du passé, de faire renaître la <u>présence</u> de Pierre Hepp. Je viens de ces quelques jours éblouié par la petite flamme en vous, si vraie et si pure aussi, qui jaillit encore toujours après tant d'angoisses, de pertes— comme vous êtes merveilleuse, mon amie! Et je vous vois seule la nuit sur la grande terrasse avec tout le pays à vos pieds, méditant les étoiles (ce qui m'accompagnait toute cette dernière nuit, et jusqu'à la descente de la lune, c'était le vers de Baudelaire—"Entends, ma chère, entends la douce nuit qui marche," car j'étais pleinement consciente de votre <u>présence</u> en bas, et la parfaite communion de nos coeurs à travers le silence complet)—et je vous vois le matin lisant Pascal à l'aube, et peut-être écrivant quelque chose de très profondément <u>pensée</u> après le thé matinal. Impossible de <u>dire</u> combien cela m'a fait du bien de vivre ainsi auprès de vous—de sentir lentement renaître la source de ma vie—la poésie—à force de me sentir pénêtrée par votre ambiance et celui ("du cher Mas"?).

Tout était richesse dans ces jours—je pense à la variété de vies humaines que vous m'avez donné à regarder comme des images bien-faisantes—les deux soeurs dans leur vielle maison, Marie Mauron, et le bourgeois planteur de vignes qui a trouvé sa vérité loin des usines, les Bellinos, et cette grande personne à la voix dure, au visage si <u>bon</u>, qui vient aider dans le jardin. Mais je pense surtout à nos deux promenades en haut vers les tours—le premier soir et le dernier, au thym sous nos pieds, aux lacs de ris reflétant le ciel en bas—aux ciels tirés comme de la soie, aux pierres où nous nous sommes étendues. Tout cela remue en moi—and <u>reverberates</u> comme de la musique. Et je pense à nos repas simples et parfaits aussi!

Ici je suis dans ma chambre de toujours—et je regarde le verger en bas où deux pigeons blancs se promenent sur un gazon de velours. Jamais je n'ai vu ce jardin (toujours un poème) si beau. Nous avons pris le thé hier sous les pommiers—accompagnés par Franz, l'oie et son épouse, par deux canards bruns, par un petit coq, une "guinea hen" grise, deux chiens, et la chatte persane—la grande amie de ma mère, qui a maintenant 79 ans et paraît en avoir 60, dirige ce petit monde comme une abbesse sage (je suis en train de lire Les Deux Mondiales—tres impressionant)—Je sens très profondément la prise de l'europe sur mon être.

Et voilà—comment vous remercier d'être <u>vous-même</u>? Car c'est cela la grande vérité de ces derniers jours pour moi. Merci, cher coeur éblouissant pour votre <u>lumière.</u>

C'est vraiment tout ce que je peux dire. Hélas, je suis arrivée ici avec une migraine atroce (effet du changement de climat dans l'avion, d'une chaleur immense, au vent froid, après le décalage je crois) pour être téléphoné <u>dans la première heure</u> de New York (!), un ami qui vient de perdre son ami et pleurait—d'Oxford, une amie aussi en détresse, et la Suisse (je ne sais pas qui, car on n'a plus re-téléphoné après avoir essayé de me joindre juste avant mon arrivée)—puis des tas de lettres auxquelles il fallait répondre—j'ai passé la journée à tâcher de mettre fin à toutes ces responsabilités humaines afin de rentrer dans le poème, demain.—

26 juin
    Et voilà le poème original j'ai tant travaillé, mais qui n'est pas encore tout à fait <u>là</u>. hélas!
    Très grande tendresse—

de ton
<u>May</u>

TO CAMILLE MAYRAN   le 10 fevrier [1963]
[Nelson]
Marianne si chère,
    Je crois qu'au fond c'est le nom qui te convient le mieux .. sais-tu que "R.F.D." sur l'addresse veut dire Rural Free Delivery et que la fermier qui est aussi "mailman" ici m'apporte avec les lettres des cigarettes ou du lait si j'en ai besoin. Comme cette campagne est humaine! Je suis ici, seule, depuis une semaine—semaine de temps très froid (20 degres dessous zero il y a quelques nuits) et la maison faisait des bruits extraordinaires comme du tonnerre à cause du froid. Il paraît que les clous sor-

tent des murs (tout est en bois ici) éclatant comme des coups de fusil.
J'ai eu peur! Je nourris des centaines d'oiseaux et un chat très sauvage
qui me regarde droit dans les yeux à travers la fenêtre, mais cours si j'ou-
vre la porte—mais il revient plus tard manger ce que je mets dehors
pour lui. Tout ce qui bouge dans ce monde de glace et de neige devient
cher; tout ce qui a du sang chaud on regarde avec tendresse effarée—
comment survivent-ils, les oiseaux, les écureuils, les chats?

le pain qu'elle peut donner ne va jamais nourrir cette affamée. Voilà la
vérité, pour moi. Au contraire, les miettes rendent encore plus affamée
cette pauvre demi-folle.

Next day
A soft snow falling, so it is like being in a cocoon. Pendant la nuit j'ai
beaucoup songé à ce que j'ai écrit au dessus, et je me suis demandée si
j'avais le droit, (et certainement que je n'avais pas la sagesse) de parler
avec une telle conviction. Car, il est vrai, n'est-ce pas, qu'un des miracles
de la vie (publié quelques fois par les psychoanalyses) c'est que chaque
relation entre deux êtres liés par l'émotion de la <u>communion</u> est dif-
férente d'aucune autre—il y n'a sans doute des desseins crus qui sont
clairs au medecin, mais il y a aussi des tas de variations dans le dessein et
c'est eux justement qui font le mystère de la vie.
    Je sais que cet enfant a parlé suicide—et c'est là le risque que Noémie
n'a pas osé prendre en mettant fin à la chose. Là aussi il me semble qu'il
faudrait parler avec une dure clarité—montrer qu'on comprend très
bien la <u>tentation</u> de suicide, que nous passons tous par là, <u>mais</u> qu'un suicide dans des circonstances pareilles est un attentat envers l'être aimé,
une punition. "Tout suicide est un muertre rentré"—
    Et si on disait à ce pauvre enfant, "Écoutes, prends six mois. Après six
mois nous verrons toutes les deux plus clairs. Je serais là alors comme
amie veritable, ce que je ne puis être maintenant."
    Au fond de ma pensée, et c'est difficile à dire, c'est que Noémie s'est
laissé entrainer par une compassion de toute bonne volonté, dans une
espèce de folie à deux. Toute la force d'une telle passion tend à nous
faire sentir une fausse culpabilité—nous ne donnons pas assez, nous
n'aimons pas assez bien, assez purement, (sans égoisme) etc.—mais la
vraie culpabilité c'est de ne pas avoir le courage de couper à vif <u>pour
guérir.</u>
    Chérie, pardonnes cette effusion qui vient (comme tu sais, je suis
sûre) de beaucoup de peine et de lente compréhension à travers la souf-
france de ma part. Dis à Noémie ce que tu veux où ce qui pourrait lui

venir en aide—et rien si cela te semble mieux. Je réponds seulement à ta question aussi bien que je le puis.

J'espère tant que maintenant tu retrouves le fil intérieur vers la méditation sur la mer et le ciel et le temps qui fut brisé par l'angoisse de ta soeur—ques les jours qui viennent avec leur aube de printemps m'apportent la joie de ce travail. J'ai lu avec la plus grande emotion ce que tu dis de moi—et de toi dans cette dernière lettre. Oui je crois que c'est la vérité que ce qui me sauve d'être vraiment une personne <u>impossible</u> (emotion immodérée, rage, passion etc) c'est l'intelligence et l'effort de <u>penser juste.</u>

Chérie, j'écrirai mieux la prochaine fois—

A bientôt, j'espere. Tes lettres m'inondent de lumière et j'en ai fort besoin en ce moment

Très tendrement à toi.

May

P.S. Je t'envoie un essai-portrait que j'ai ecrit sur mon père.

TO CAMILLE MAYRAN   le 10 mars [1964]
[Nelson]

J'écris un peu comme un caractère dans "<u>Hiver</u>" a la lumière d'une lampe à l'huile—au milieu d'une tempête (l'électricité est en panne c'est á dire aussi le chauffage centrale, mais j'ai un feu de bois, et ne sais pas pourquoi je suis en train de cuire des poires au poêle—cette vie de Crusoe me plaît enormement!) Il neige sans arrêt avec grand vent depuis hier soir, donc pendant 24 heures déjà—et c'est le jour du "yearly Village Meeting" d'où je reviens à pied—tout le monde de bonne humeur à cause de la tempête, des efforts surhumaine qu'ils ont fait pour venir, eux, de loin, en voiture etc—atmosphere très humaine ...

Comme ce grand morceau de ta vie, et de vues proches de la tienne m'a ému—J'étais tremblante quant j'ai laissé tomber la dernière de ces feuilles precieuses, de ces gouttes de sang .. tu as fais la grande chose, la seule chose possible c'est de me remettre au centre de la <u>vie</u>; tu as su briser le sens d'un isolement, d'une folie, et d'étrangeté, et de mystère qui m'était devenu un peu éffrayant, je dois avouer.

En plus tu me donnes l'autre manne—si necessaire—car un des tourments pour moi était que je n'ose pas montrer ces poèmes—sauf quelques-unes car le sujet est bien trop visible, ou l'<u>objet</u> je devrai dire—et me sentais emprisonnée deux fois, par la sentiment qui ne pouvait se livrer a l'être qui m'a tant ému, et par le fait que ce que j'en tire comme poète reste si secret.

L'histoire vraie (pas celle de mon imagination) continue à être trés déconcertante. Je suis déscendue vers les villes de ma tour d'ivorie il y a deux semaines—en partie pour assister à une conference au college donnée par un de nous écrivains-femmes les plus illustrés: Eudora Welty. Je ne m'attendais pas à voir le personnage de l'éclair, mais elle était là— et j'étais un instant à côté d'elle en sortant de la salle—sans me regarder elle a dit d'un ton simplement poli, très vite, "Nice to see you here, May"—et puis elle a disparu dans la nuit. J'ai passé cette nuit chez deux vieilles dames très charmantes, dont l'une vient de se retirer comme "Dean of Faculty"—elles m'avaient invitée d'un ton cherissant qui m'a tout à fait surprise et ému, je dois dire, et elles m'ont traité comme enfant de la maison. Le matin après je suis allée au "chapel"—les mercredi seulement, la Présidente parle aux étudiantes—je ne suis jamais été car je ne suis pas d'habitude au collège ce jour-là.

—te retromper dans ta vraie vie (une de tes vraies vies car il y a aussi le Mas)—Pour le grand poème de la mer, il faut chercher, passer outre— je ne puis croire qu'il n'y aurait quelqu'editeur qui comprendrait <u>Mercure de France</u> (publier d'abord dans un hebdomadaire—est-ce un mot français? Cela me fait toujours songer à un <u>animal</u> prehistorique)—

Do keep the poems—later tell me which ones seem to you to speak <u>as poems</u>—I am so in the dark!

Love and blessings, grande <u>toi</u>—

TO CAMILLE MAYRAN   le 13 mai [1967]
[Nelson]
Ma grande amie,

Comme tu sais, sans doute j'ai écrit tout de suite à Noémie pour lui dire ma joie de cette bonne nouvelle <u>enfin</u>—et je suis ravie de lire dans sa réponse qu'elle songe venir aux Etats-Unis—je suis moi-même tellement découragée au sujet de mon pays que cele m'a fait un grand bien de lire qu'elle aimerait y venir! (Je répondrai à sa lettre bientôt—comme cela serait beau si elle pouvait venir passer un week-end ici à Nelson en chemin!

Pour moi c'est un moment difficile. J'ai lu avec émotion ce que tu me dis de ta propre vieillese—J'écris le mot mais je ne l'associe pas du tout avec toi—seulement je <u>comprends</u>, car je vois avec étonnement dans moi-même comme tout deviant un peu plus lourd à porter, même à 55 ans. Peut-être que quelque chose est naturel à l'âge que tout dans notre civilization repousse—des heures de songerie, une vie peut-être spontanée dans le sens de laisser tomber le livre ou le travail quand l'esprit le veut—(Marie Closset) qui venait lui faire de petites visites—c'est cela surtout qui te mancue, mon âme, c'est cette solitude non chérie par des amitiés à racines profondes dans le passé...au fond tu es <u>dépaysée</u> et c'est un grand malheur il me semble.

TO CAMILLE MAYRAN   le 29 juillet [1967]
[Nelson]
Très chère Marianne,

Quelle joie cette lettre toute embaumée de la presence de Florence! Je la serre contre mon coeur avec contentement, et aussi de savoir que cette présence a dénoué pour un petit temps les soucis de Noémie envers son immense travail devant les nouveaux cours.

TO (MRS. E.) ANGÈLE OOSTERLINCK-BAELE
[York]   le 24 octobre [1973]
Chère Angèle,

Votre lettre du 14 est arrivée hier, avec sa triste nouvelle..triste d'un côte, mais en somme pas <u>trop</u> triste..que la pauvre Cécile est enfin en paix. Je suis touchée de savoir qu'elle portait la chemise de nuit que je lui avait offert pour son dernier voyage. Je suis moi-même surtout soulagée à la pensée que votre long et couteux dévouement a pris fin. Comme vous avez été bonne et compatissante..entreprenant un dur travail journalier pour entretenir cette pauvre malade! Que Dieu vous bénisse!

La photo m'a touché à fond.. le regard, tout a coup traversé comme par un sourire, de Cécile, me la rend vivante comme elle était quand j'é-tais moi-même un bébé. Grand merci.

J'ecris mal aujourd'hui car j'ai fait une chute il y a trois jours et j'ai félé trois côtes..cela fait mal jour et nuit et c'est une torture de me baisser pour mettre le plat du chat et de mon chien parterre. Ce n'est rien de grave mais j'étais déjà très fatiguée et maintenant je suis en morceaux..figurez-vous j'ai eu depuis le déménagement un hôteau moins tous les trois jours pendant 5 mois! Tous mes amis viennent pour voir la nouvelle maison qui est grande et belle avec une grande terrasse devant..puis une longue pelouse..puis la mer. Après un été très chaud et humide l'automne est merveilleux..la mer bleu foncé devant moi.

Mon dernièr livre va bien..il s'agit d'une pauvre vieille dans un "home" ..

Chère Angèle, je vous embrasse bien fort. Dites bien ma sympathie devant cette mort à toute la famille, et à vous ma reconnaissance émue devant tout ce que vous avez fait pour notre Cécile ..

Toujours votre
May

TO JACQUELINE LIMBOSCH   le 16 aôut dimanche [1981]
[York]

Coquine chérie,

Je ne sais pas pourquoi j'ai les larmes aux yeux en t'appellant par le petit nom de notre enfance (avec lequel tu as signé ta bonne lettre du 31 juillet) mais sans doute c'est que cela me fait penser à notre longue vie côte à côte..et maintenant nous sommes devenues je crois de vraies amies, qui partageons de longs souvenirs—quelle richesse dans le passé!

Au fond ton voyage a l'air d'avoir été nourrissant mais je comprend si bien ce cafard au début, la poignante absence à tes côtés! Toujours en Europe je suis comme toi assaillit par des souvenirs de mes voyages avec Judy, l'irremplacable amie.

J'espère que tu as trouvé Eugénie en bonne forme? certainement contente de partir chez Marianne. Je suis triste que, à cause de la pluie je n'ai pas pu faire la connaissance de ses trois poules, mais c'était si bon de la voir, elle, radieuse et sage comme toujours.

Ici ce n'est pas un tres beau été..le temps est humide, maussade, gris et presque jamais je me reveille à une mer bleue comme je l'aime. Les arbustes au jardin sont moisis et moi aussi je me sens un peu moisie, hélas. J'ai eu trop de personnes ici comme hôtes et en passant..et je dois lutter pour le temps de travail, mais j'espère qu'après le 1er septembre je retrouverai ma solitude et la paix. Heureusement que je ne donne pas de "poetry readings" jusqu'en avril.

Mais il y a de bons moments tout de même, surtout quand je peux écrire une page qui me semble bon..le livre commence à avoir une vie à lui..c'est bon signe quand j'écris des choses que je ne savais pas, pour ainsi dire, qui viennent tout simplement du sub-conscient et m'é-tonne! Comme tous mes livres ce roman est un grand hazard et comme toujours je souffre d'anxiété et de panique...au moins je ne suis pas comme le bélier de Marthe et Madeleine (tu te souviens?) "misérable de bien-être!"

Comme j'ai joui de cueillir des fleurs chez Nicole et j'ai beaucoup d'autres bon et tendres souvenirs de mon séjour, auxquelles je pense dans mon lit après la longue journée...

Je t'embrasse bien fort, ma chérie—écris-moi un mot quand tu en as envie—

Ta

M—

[York]

Chère Jumelle, chère Solange

C'est idiot que je n'arrive pas a répondre à des chères lettres comme la tienne, datée en mars! Mais je suis une vraie invalide ces jours-ci—tombée dans la vieillesse et sans énergie comme une pierre jetée a l'eau—Je ne puis plus écrire à la machine, ni marcher sauf avec difficultée—mais je conduis la voiture encore, et remercie Dieu que je puis le faire—Sinon je serais terriblement isolée ici, seule dans cette grande maison—Sans Pierrot je serais morte—

Les medicins ne trouvent rien sauf la Vieillesse pour exliquer tout cela—mais trois "choc" l'ans passés expliquent, je pense—Je sais lire—

Les nouvelles sont déprimantes partout dans le monde—Où regarde pour un peu du comfort—notre gouvernement me sent fou complètement brisant tout ce qui a été accomplit de preserver le vie sociale depuis Roosevelt—C'est l'ère de l'egoïsme, et le dédain des pauvres—les riches [Get?] sont plus riches que jamais—je suis révoltée—

Mais je pense à toi avec grand affection très contente d'avoir cette photo dans le grand et beau manteau—

Tendres baisers et tendres pensées de ta jumelle—comme toujours—

May

UNPUBLISHED POEMS

FOR ERNESTA
WHO TOOK HER OWN LIFE

Now it is quiet here on earth for it is snowing:
Now we remember your beauty who have left us living,
And we affirm your beauty in the great quiet space
Where snow falls from the pure cloud to this earthly place.

For you endured the rose of isolation and the pointed thorn
In perfect solitude; the wounds that you had borne
You chose to set beyond heart-beat to be untouched of men.
But by your action not your will you laid upon us then
The whole weight of that anguish and we could not move
Nor answer, nor through understanding come back into love.
Then you who had been solitary were attacked by thunder
Of many hearts startled to beating with an aching wonder.
You who were silent were covered then with words
And the slow painful tears that pierced our eyes like swords.
You were the living dead that we could not accept,
The aching questions of our lives for which we wept,
The sense of private failure and that harshest truth
That love can fail, can will and yet perform no ruth,
That love imprisoned is, so far from mortal pain
It is like tears upon a fire, upon a desert, rain.

For many days we tried to learn your death and could not.

Now it is snowing and after the long keeping you awake,

You shall sleep now, Ernesta, you shall never have to wake.
And we shall bury pain and in the stillness set you deep
Into the peace of earth, far from our dreams, to sleep.
Beyond heart-beat where you chose then to lay it, lay
Our pain with yours.
                            We shall not come again this way.

But in the spring wherever there is light, shall rise
Your pure unearthly face before our quiet eyes.
There in the very beat of heart your beauty is,
And you who found no comfort, still shall comfort us.
We shall remember you in our hour of solitude
And it shall be to each a fierce angelic good.
This is your present to us and your own achieving
Is that perfected and unearthly calm beyond all human grieving.
Some write their messages. You wrote upon yourself so well
You laid your beauty on us like a wilful spell
That we might never know the rose of your despair.
Now we shall try to bury it together and shall leave it there.

Farewell. The snow has ceased. We must go back to living.
                                            24 January 1940

Letter from the Country

It is raining. The ants fall down from the roof
Onto my paper; outside the greens are desolate.
The black-eyed susans wither. It is July's end.
And your letter falls into this day like fate—
Not the astrologer's dream of fate or the lover's
Delightful prefabricated house where happiness
Is sure to dwell, no not this kind of fate, the game
Of solitaire where the cards surely spell success
(For if you keep it up long enough, it will come out):
Your letter promises nothing, is no dream come true,
But, O better, it invokes the lost cold landscape,
The tranquil shore, the sea's pure splintering blue.
The hoarse screams of the gulls, the lonely flap of waves.
It opens all there is so see when the fog lifts
And the light is memory (that ringing of a thousand bells

In the mind when the sealed inner landscape shifts).
It has been too dreary here, too long and dreary,
Too empty, strange and dark like a wood in a fairy tale.
Now I remember it all. I remember the path and the house.
I can tell you how I got lost and break the witches' spell.
Opening your letter, opened the door into my life again.

There it is, just as I left it, serene and still,
And I am sure now it's a good life (like a face, plain
But endearing and, as they say, one that wears well).
Here is the desk, the typewriter, the empty page, the time
Half-past ten in the morning. I am writing to you
To say your letter fell like fate into July's end
And now I must stop because there's work to do.

                                                    July [1942]

After the War
for Elisabeth

This is security,
This island, this hour,
This high room where
In the summer-sounding air
You work and I sit,
Silent as the flower.

After the separate years,
The several wars
And their machines of horror,
When my image of you
Was broken by your danger
And made more intense
By your silence,
It seemed I would never see
You safe.
Fragments of time threw
Themselves down like broken glass.

No time is whole at last,
I here, you there

Where future meets the past,
Massed curtains in still air
And our face in repose:
Here I become myself.
The wounds of fear close.
As if I lived in this house,
As if I would stay here.

This, I think, is security,
The only sort we shall ever have
Between the tensions of work and love,
We who must choose to make
From some such hour as this
A human answer to the mysteries,
A small fertile silence in the middle of
A loud death.

Part of a sequence from
England/European Notebook
1947

Moment of Truth

It was recognition
That struck to the bone.
In that brilliant light
There was no not-seeing,
We were buckled to being.
We were locked in insight.

But the terrible blaze
Would not last many days.
As you looked, I was flying;
As I looked, you were going
In the long year's flowing;
As we looked, we were dying.

Now it's binding frost,
Harsh cruel frost
Bitter and lonely thing,
Makes one grind one's teeth,

And in it no saving truth
But the mortal sting.
                    for Evelyn Pember
                    December 1954

INSCRIPTION

—

Only your name wrote down,
I could not even spell;
Then, by an act of will,
Below inscribed my own,
The author of your book
Who would be early gone—
And not that my heart shook
With an uncertain blaze
And the too certain loss.

—

For in such circumstance
To recognize the muse,
Feel the long-buried blaze
Leap up and burn for once
Confuses middle age.
I hoped for more than chance;
Like actors on a stage
We play predestined parts,
Not this child's game of hearts.

—

What did desire serve?
That blaze is swiftly done,
The lightning come and gone.
I felt your profile curve,
Delicate as a leaf,
Itself into my nerve,
And was filled with such grief

Before Time's loss and mine.
There seemed no anodyne.

—

Then came into this thought,
And felt no more confused
Between what can be used
And what can be lived out:
Not this, though rich and strange.
A moment's vision brought
Our orbits into range,
Then, as they crossed unknown
The sacred fire was blown.

April 19th, 1958

IN A HIGH ROOM OF LEAVES

What was this holy country where we lay
In a high room of leaves and open sky,
Where the bird-throated voices sang all day
And we discoursed—through Mozart's other words.
And our tender caresses—what the birds
Made plain in ceaseless roundelay:
Now God be praised, since all is Mystery.

Intangible exchanges: Silence cast,
And overhead the leafy multitude
Spoke in a language understood at last,
We listened to the first beatitude:
Behold I make the air ring like a bell
With the amazing tidings, "All is well."
Here is eternity. There is no past.

It was an aviary or a simple nest
Woven of silence and of every grief
Where we, as secret as the birds and blest,
Folded our wings under a roof of leaf.

Angels and earthly creatures now are one.
We are the point of absolute communion,
Where love and God meet in the human breast.
What is this country where we came to rest?

July 15th, 1958
for Ellen Douglass Leyburn

[Note beside last three lines: "I can make this better—"
and in the margin: "<u>perfect</u> time—every single minute of it—"]

ELEGY FOR EVE

For one long week she fought for every breath,
The shadow of dark lashes on her cheek,
A delicate warmth about her like a gauze,
That touching beauty as it always was.
The essence burned so bright, it did not break;
She was borne whole and shining into death.

(But we live on with loss, with loss, with loss.)

Tender and merry, touched early by the tragic,
She made her peace with tension and with storm,
And, later, little children understood
Her healing power and trusted her. They could.
She learned with them a way of keeping warm:
Imagination flowered in her hands to magic.

(Even the children cannot bring her home.)

How to accept such radiance as past?
Life covers it over; winter streams
Over bright pebbles; life goes rushing on
Pitiless as the cold and brilliant moon.
Eurydice has come and gone in dream.
Not one of us could keep her safe at last.

(Not even the warm love she found in time.)

Who is not Orpheus, imploring empty air?

Stay, dear life, stay! You did not have to go!
You are not lost, O radiant one, to me.
Angels and demons, find Eurydice,
She whom cold death has rushed into the snow
As if some delicate wing had fallen there . . .

(But we know she is dead. They tell us so.)

January 1964

THE RUMINATIONS OF COLONEL FANCY

What can you do with such a joker?
I tell you the poor clown was barmy.
He couldn't play a hand of poker.
He never really joined the army.

The Captain chose not to salute.
The Captain called his patients "sir"—
And some were privates! This galoot
Had never learned to comb his hair.

Pockets unbuttoned, dusty shoes,
The captain was a living shame,
But what can you expect of Jews?
And Howard Levy was his name.

He spent his spare time helping out
The niggers in the dirty slums.
What can you do with such a lout?
An officer around with bums?

The pinko got his (was I glad!)
When he refused to train the medics.
What can you do with such a cad?
He had the nerve to talk of "ethics"!

A Doctor shouldn't teach his skill.
A Doctor shouldn't have a gun.
And never, never shoot to kill,
Just heal the bastards, one by one.

We all have gripes; we all complain,
Until we're "broken" as they say,
And can no longer feel the pain
Of the civilian still at bay.

The Captain was a bloody fool.
The Captain wouldn't break, you see.
He might as well have stayed in school
For all the good in his M.D.

[1967]

THE PRECIOUS SEED
FOR DONALD GATCH, BEAUFORT COUNTY, S.C.

It has become precious,
Precious this fertile seed
In a starving land.
Cherish it. Water it.
Keep it alive, O people,
For this seed is hope
And without it we perish.

In all the cold files,
Government buildings,
Sterile committee rooms
Where human faces blur,
We have seen the seed die,
Have said, "There is no hope,
There is nothing to be done."

But the Doctor says, "No."
He stays with his people,
Hardly eats or sleeps,
Keeping the seed alive,
Making the needs known.
The Doctor bears witness,
"Worms claim their bodies."

We are multitudes.
Each can move mountains.

(Impossible? He did it.
There is still time.)
We are given the seed.
Plant it. Bring it to harvest.
Teach us to hope again.

"Do you hear the lambs a–cryin'?"
Yes sir, Doctor, we hear them.
"Oh shepherd, feed-a thy sheep!"
The passive lift their hands.
The lonely join together,
Each of us a multitude,
Sowing hope and reaping it.
                                   —22 March 1969

THE BLESSING

Cecil Beaton
Placed her in a window
Sunlight touching her forehead,
One emaciated hand
Leaning on a pillow
The other holding
A "posy" on her knee.
The brilliant eyes
Are closed,
Everything is gathered
In her smile
Directed
To herself alone,
A smile of
Such acceptance
It has gone beyond words,
The story teller
Is silent.
Szherazade is alone
With her self.

Am I ready now
In the winter silence

And dazzle of the snow,
Have I arrived at last
In my seventieth year
At a place where I can speak of this?

For years it has stood
On my mother's desk
Where I passed it
More than once
Every day.
For years it has been there
Like a talisman
Like a magic box
Waiting for the key
That would open it
And let it bless me.

Perhaps I knew
What it would ask of me
But for years
I was not ready.

—1981

Requiem
for Judy

1.

The tree was decked when I heard the news
For it was close to Christmas when she died,
And the bright baubles that we chose
Hung there in festival while I cried.
There would be no service, I was told,
No last farewell that might provide a frame.
She had gone into her sleep, crazy and old.
The tears fell and scattered in her name.
But now, days later, I become aware
The true memorial was that lighted tree
And all our Christmases were gathered there
And all the years we lived in amity.
Under it I had placed one dark red rose.

There was the service here on Christmas day,
That flower a friend sent brought to a close
The grief, the love I cannot ever say.

2.

Secretive, shy, able to become
Fully herself and use her gifts only
As teacher. There she felt at home.
There she was great giver, never lonely.
The dark eyes, elegant pure profile,
Very white skin may have looked austere
Until she laughed or shone a tender smile.
Good Quaker, she gave time and care
In summers of work with the deprived.
Extremely modest, she never complained,
Loved deeply, all her long life tried
To conquer melancholy and attained
A hard-won strength. Now at the end
I see her whole, wise heart and noblest friend.

GUEST OF SILENCE
FOR THE CARMELITES, INDIANAPOLIS

Through the stone halls,
Behind thick oak doors,
In and out of the chapel
Multiple threads are woven
Continually.
So the still air gently vibrates
As meditations
Glide in and out,
Separate and joined
As an intricate invisible tapestry
Is being woven
Every hour.

No one comes here
Who is not made aware
Of this constant spiritual
Weaving in the air.

No one comes here
Who is not amazed
By the richness of the silence,
Who is not nourished
And amazed.

—May Sarton
December 1986

An Eightieth Birthday
for Dorothy Wallace

You can tell anyone
Close to Dorothy,
"Here comes the sun!"
They will know it is she
You are speaking of,
Shining identity
Whose other name is love.

A special way of caring
Informs the marvelous joys
Invented for her children
And friends, and always sharing
She lives through usual days
Clothed in a simple splendor.
Here comes the sun! What candor!

She has learned to rise
Through loss and tragedy
And we have seen
That shadow in her eyes
That never lost their sheen
Help her grow wise
Creating happiness.

Able to give herself
Also her own dreams
So now we see her
In a Palladian pool, high room

Where light even in winter
Comes to bloom,
And there she swims.

She has become the queen
Of an invented country.
I greet her, my incomparable friend,
And celebrate this Wallace land
Where she, ever renewed, does shine.
Here comes the sun!
Here comes the sun!

March 1, '93

In Belgium Now

My biographer
Is in Belgium now
And I wish
I could be there with her

But my travel days are over,
No more
Taking into myself
The turbulent air,
Trees permanently bent
In slanting lines
By the prevailing wind,
The tremendous skies.

Taking into myself
The treasured earth,
Even a small plot
Cultivated
And loved.

Taking into myself
The long-ago house
Covered with climbing roses,
The garden

Where I crawled
To devour strawberries
A gourmet
At eleven months old.

And some part of me
Always alive
Beside Jean Dominique
Who wrote,
"I work,
My soul occupied
With seeing."

There is
A passionate Belgian in me,
A survivor of battles,
One who goes on.
I find it now.
I recognize it
In my father's smile.

[1993]

ACKNOWLEDGMENTS

To May Sarton, for the beauty of her oeuvre, and the inexhaustible riches of her archive; for her belief and confidence in entrusting me to edit her letters; for the life-enhancing privilege of her companionship, and the enduring gift of her love.

To Polly Thayer Starr, whose percipience and tender regard for life make her heart and mind a haven for every dragonfly and field mouse, man and woman, poem and work of art that comes her way. For extending to me the grace of her friendship, for responding—like the most finely-tuned instrument—to every nuance and current around her, and for listening so well to this work.

To Bill Brown, who loved and understood May as well as anyone ever has, and who connects me to all the essences.

To Warren Keith Wright, scholar, poet, helpmeet *sui generis*—the *sine qua non* of this volume—for his advice, his research, his knowledge and taste, his uncommon understanding of May's heart and mind, and his tireless support of every aspect of this work. It was while translating the French in this volume, and copy-editing, that he asked what issues I meant to address in my Foreword. We talked over many themes, and quotations culled for that purpose, and at my request he cast our discussions into what I thought would be an outline from which to work. To my amazement and surprise he created, instead, a complete and fully realized work, encompassing my concerns, weaving in the quotations, and presenting all of it with a freshness, originality, and cogency I felt privileged to read. As part of my own foreword, I had planned to incorporate William Drake's letter, but seeing how eloquently Keith Wright's remarks complemented William Drake's, I resolved that each of these unusually discerning men should be allowed to speak for himself. How wonderful to have such friends to write on May's behalf.

To Jane Drake, for graciously and enthusiastically permitting me to turn her father's eloquent letter into this quintessential Appreciation by William Drake.

To Diana Der Hovanessian, Alan Eastaugh, Jennifer Evans of Shady Hill, Pat Ford, Connie Gordon, Beverly Hallam, the Reverend Richard Henry, Karen O. Hodges, Dee Dee Koval, Eileen Murphy, Kyoko Nishimura, Barnabas Quigley, Gay Sweet Scott, Mary-Leigh Smart, Henry Taylor, Michel Thiery, Polly Tompkins, Dan Wallace, and Timothy Matlack Warren, for their generous support and sleuthing.

To Stacey Grossman, diplomat and interlocutor extraordinaire, for making it all possible.

To Joan Palevsky, for her gallant and timely support, not only of this project, but of May's legacy, past and future.

To Solange Sarton, for the rich and moving material she openly and generously shared.

To Mary Morain *in memoriam,* for her ardent belief in this ongoing project and all she contributed to it, including the 1924 letter to Barbara Runkle Hawthorne which appears in the footnotes.

To J. Parker Huber, for being continually mindful of whatever might enrich this work.

To Lenora P. Blouin, for her abiding friendship and dedication. Her monumental and indispensable achievement, *May Sarton: A Bibliography,* 2d ed. (Scarecrow Press, 2000), has greatly enriched the accuracy of this volume. All Sarton scholars, and all who read their work, shall be henceforth in her debt.

To Beatrice Weingarten, for being steadfastly and lovingly and restoratively there, throughout.

To Shoji Masuzawa, for his alacrity and skill whenever necessary, in restoring "wonder" to the wonders of technology.

To Adelaide Cherbonnier, whose good-hearted interest in the progress of these projects has always been a welcome spur when it seemed most needed.

For their assistance and expertise in various disciplines, I would like to thank Janice Broder, Dolores M. Burdick, Richard Casement, Philip Clark, Sandra Costich, Jane Donahue Eberwein, James Gindin, Lauren Hahn, Patricia Hansen, Alexandra Hanson-Harding, Hermione Lee, Pamela Light, Gary K. Rendel, R. H. Super, Gertrude M. White, Sister Monica Kleffner of the Sisters of St. Joseph of Carondelet, and the Reverend Doctor Michael Piret, the Dean of Divinity, Magdalen College, Oxford.

To Nancy Jahn Hartley, May's longtime archivist—and my longtime friend—who, as with each of my previous volumes, has been unconditionally and indispensably *there*; her guidance, ingenuity, her unique knowledge of the Sarton canon and of library science—but most of all her wisdom, risibility and encouragement—have intensified the pleasures, assuaged the anxieties, and enriched the work.

And above all to May's innumerable correspondents whose continuous flood of letters over the decades sustained her with understanding, friendship and love. Although her unwavering commitment to respond inevitably proved burdensome, the sometimes equivocal joy of letter writing nevertheless remained a cornerstone of May's life, and an encouragement to her work. Such ongoing dialogues kept her mentally engaged and forced her to fight—intellectually speaking—and, in a singular paradox, drained her while nourishing her. As I go forward with a complete Life in Letters, I hope to draw on the countless correspondences unable to be represented in this volume.

To various special collections across the country for permission to use their Sarton holdings, grateful acknowledgment is hereby made: to Amherst College Special Collections for letters to Louise Bogan; to the Archives of American Art for letters to Beverly Hallam; to The Henry W. and Albert A. Berg Collection of English and American Literature for letters to Charles Barber, Bill Brown (prior to 1984), Katharine Davis, Basil de Sélincourt, John Holmes, Sir Julian Huxley, Judith Matlack, Muriel Rukeyser, George Sarton, and Lola Szladits; to Boston University, the Charles Angoff Collection, for the letter to the Poetry Society of America; to Coe College, Stewart Memorial Library, for letters to Signi Falk;

to Bryn Mawr College, Mariam Coffin Canaday Library for letters to Katharine White; to the College of St. Catherine, for letters to Sister Maris Stella (Sister Alice Gustava Smith); to Columbia University, Butler Library, for letters to Eleanor Belmont and Eric P. Swenson; to Dartmouth College, Baker Memorial Library, for letters to Robert Frost; to Harvard University, Houghton Library for letters to Ernest Hocking, Alice James, William James, Jr., and Dorothy Stimson; to Haverford College Library, the Quaker Collection, for letters to Elizabeth Gray Vining; to the New York Public Library, Rare Books, for the letter to Rachel MacKenzie and Katharine White; to the Rosenbach Museum and Library for letters to Marianne Moore;

to Radcliffe College, the Arthur and Elizabeth Schlesinger Library on the History of Women in America, for letters to Helen Howe, Ada Louise Comstock (Notestein), Katharine Taylor, and Rosalind Greene, although the letter to Greene in this volume came from Sarton's personal files; to Scripps College, the Ella Strong Denison Library for letters to Diane Divelbess; to Smith College, the Sophia Smith Collection, for letters to Nancy Hale; to Syracuse University, the George Arents Research Library, for letters to Jean Burden, Robb Sagendorph, and Granville Hicks;

to the University of California, Los Angeles, Special Collections, for letters to Alice and Haniel Long; to the University of New Hampshire, Special Collections, for letters to Lotte Jacobi;

to the University of Texas at Austin, Harry Ransom Humanities Center, for letters to Sybille Bedford, Elizabeth Bowen, and Anne Sexton; to the University of Virginia, Alderman Library, for letters to Doris Grumbach; to Washington University, John M. Olin Library, for the letters to William Jay Smith and Constance Urdang; to Westbrook College (now the University of New England), the Maine Women Writers Collection, for letters to Bradford Dudley Daziel, and Dorothy Healy; to Yale University, Beinecke Rare Book and Manuscript Library, for letters to Edmund Wilson.

Letters to the following correspondents came from May Sarton's personal files in York, Maine, all of which have now been transferred to the Henry W. and Albert A. Berg Collection of English and American Literature at the New York Public Library: Eleanor Blair, Helen Storm Corsa, Florence Day, Cora DuBois, Marynia F. Farnham, Robert Francis, Marion Hamilton, Carolyn G. Heilbrun, Lady Juliette Huxley, Joseph Parisi, Evelyn Pember, Margot Peters, Irene Sharaff, Lenore Straus, Sir John Summerson, the Reverend Mary Upton, and Dan Wallace.

To those individuals willing to share their Sarton letters for this volume my inordinate thanks: Ted Adams, Anne Alvord, Amyas Ames for letters to Evelyn Ames, Pamela Askew, Anthe Athas, the Reverend Thomas C. Barnes, Lenora P. Blouin, Beth Bridges, Bill Brown for letters after 1984, Timothy Anglin Burgard, Pat Carroll, Adelaide Cherbonnier, Shelley Armitage for letters to Peggy Pond Church, Pam Conrad, Christopher De Vinck, William Drake, Louise duFault, Alan Eastaugh, Connie Wallace Gordon for letters to her mother Dorothy Wallace, the Reverend Richard Henry, Vincent Hepp for his own letters and those to his mother Camille Mayran, Marcie Hershman, William Heyen, Jerri Hill, Karen O. Hodges, J. Parker Huber, Constance Hunting, Susan Kenney, Susan Kerestes, Madeleine L'Engle, Helen Sheehy for the letter to Eva Le Gallienne, Eda LeShan, Astrid Liljeblad, Jacqueline Limbosch, Ruth Limmer, Timothy Matlack Warren for letters to himself, his father Keith Faulkner Warren, and his aunt Constance

Revere Matlack Lloyd, Sister Jean Alice McGoff, Hugh McKinley, Ann McLaughlin, Nancy Mairs, Morgan Mead, Ashley Montagu, Penelope Mortimer, Kyoko Nishimura, Robert O'Leary, Angèle Oosterlink-Baele, Jean Pasche for the letters to her aunt Sylvie Pasche, Erika Pfander, Richard Pipe, Lewis Pyenson, Barnabas Quigley, Char Radintz (now Charlene Stellamaris), Paul Reed, Fred Rogers, Anne Rolland-Poussier, Cathy Sander, Solange Sarton, Edith Royce Schade, Robert A. Schanke, Mari Schatz, Huldah Sharpe, Marita Simpson, Mary-Leigh Smart, Polly Thayer Starr for her own letters and one to Susan Howe van Schlegall, Isobel Strickland, Michel Thiery, Peg Umberger, Ilse Vogel, Janine Wetter, and Martha Wheelock.

Acknowledgment and thanks are also due those whose letters to May or this editor are excerpted in the footnotes. They include: Charles Barber and his parents, Bob and Kathy; the Reverend Thomas C. Barnes, Timothy Anglin Burgard, Margaret Clapp (already printed in *Recovering*), Helen Storm Corsa, Katharine Davis, Cora DuBois, Signi Falk, Izette de Forest, Janet Frame, Rosalind Greene, Nancy Hale, Dorothy Healy, Helen Howe, Alice James, Sister Maris Stella (Sister Alice Gustava Smith), Kyoko Nishimura, Evelyn Pember, Florida Scott-Maxwell, and Dan Wallace.

Recipients

Ted ADAMS
Anne ALVORD
Evelyn AMES
Pamela ASKEW
Anthe ATHAS
Charles BARBER
Thomas C. BARNES
Sybille BEDFORD
Eleanor BELMONT
Eleanor BLAIR
Lenora P. BLOUIN
Louise BOGAN
Elizabeth BOWEN
Beth BRIDGES
Bill BROWN
Jean BURDEN
Timothy Anglin BURGARD
Pat CARROLL
Adelaide CHERBONNIER
Peggy Pond CHURCH
Pam CONRAD
Helen Storm CORSA
Katharine DAVIS
Bradford Dudley DAZIEL
Basil de SÉLINCOURT
Christopher De VINCK
Diane DIVELBESS
William DRAKE

Cora Du BOIS
Louise duFAULT
Alan EASTAUGH
Signi FALK
Marynia F. FARNHAM
Robert FRANCIS
Robert FROST
Rosalind GREENE
Doris GRUMBACH
Nancy HALE
Beverly HALLAM
Marion HAMILTON
Dorothy HEALY
Carolyn G. HEILBRUN
the Reverend Richard HENRY
Vincent HEPP
Marcie HERSHMAN
William HEYEN
Granville HICKS
Jerri HILL
Ernest HOCKING
Karen O. HODGES
John HOLMES
Helen HOWE
J. Parker HUBER
Constance HUNTING
Sir Julian HUXLEY
Lady Juliette HUXLEY

Lotte JACOBI
Alice JAMES
William JAMES Jr.
Susan KENNEY
Susan KERESTES
Madeleine L'ENGLE
Eva Le GALLIENNE
Eda LeSHAN
Astrid LILJEBLAD
Jacqueline LIMBOSCH
Ruth LIMMER
Constance Revere Matlack
   LLOYD
Alice and Haniel LONG
Sister Jean Alice McGOFF
Rachel MacKENZIE
Hugh McKINLEY
Ann McLAUGHLIN
Nancy MAIRS
Sister MARIS STELLA
(see also Sister Gustava SMITH)
Judith MATLACK
Camille MAYRAN
Morgan MEAD
Ashley MONTAGU
Marianne MOORE
Penelope MORTIMER
Kyoko NISHIMURA
Ada Louise Comstock
   NOTESTEIN
Robert O'LEARY
Angèle OOSTERLINK-BAELE
Joseph PARISI
Sylvie PASCHE
Evelyn PEMBER
Margot PETERS
Erika PFANDER
Richard PIPE
POETRY SOCIETY OF
   AMERICA
Lewis PYENSON
Barnabas QUIGLEY

Char RADINTZ
Paul REED
Fred ROGERS
Anne ROLLAND-POUSSIER
Muriel RUKEYSER
Robb SAGENDORPH
Cathy SANDER
George SARTON
Solange SARTON
Edith Royce SCHADE
Robert A. SCHANKE
Mari SCHATZ
Anne SEXTON
Irene SHARAFF
Huldah SHARPE
Gertrude SHERMAN
Susan SHERMAN
Marita SIMPSON
Mary-Leigh SMART
Sister Alice Gustava SMITH
(see also Sister MARIS STELLA)
William Jay SMITH
Polly Thayer STARR
Dorothy STIMSON
Lenore STRAUS
Isobel STRICKLAND
Sir John SUMMERSON
Eric P. SWENSON
Lola SZLADITS
Katharine TAYLOR
Michel THIERY
Peg UMBERGER
the Reverend Mary UPTON
Constance URDANG
Susan Howe van SCHLEGALL
Elizabeth Gray VINING
Ilse VOGEL
Dan WALLACE
Dorothy WALLACE
Keith Faulkner WARREN
Timothy Matlack WARREN
Janine WETTER

Martha WHEELOCK
Katharine WHITE
Edmund WILSON

Certain recipients are not represented in the text by complete
letters; extracts from Sarton's
correspondence with them are
utilized in the footnotes. They
include:

Doris BEATTY
Claire BOLDER
Dorothy BRYANT
Margaret CLAPP
Catherine CLAYTOR (Becker)
Jay de SÉLINCOURT

Eugene GARFIELD
Lillian Westcott HALE
Barbara Runkle HAWTHORNE
the Right Reverend Sam B.
    HULSEY
Jane LEONARD
Archibald MacLEISH
Robert MERTON
Theodore and Kathleen
    MORRISON
Phyllis PRICE
Mary Elsie ROBERTSON
Robbie ROBERTSON
Esther ROHR
Elizabeth W. L. SCOTT
Henry TAYLOR
Warren Keith WRIGHT

INDEX

Page numbers in *italics* refer to recipients of Sarton's letters.
Page numbers from 394 to 401 refer to letters in French.